CCH INCORPORATED
Federal and State Tax Group
4025 West Peterson Ave.
Chicago, IL 60646-6085

Order your copies TODAY!

Get the most complete resources available

BY PHONE:
Call 1 800 248 3248
Priority Code: GCY1708

BY FAX:
1 800 224 8299

ONLINE:
tax.cchgroup.com
(click on *Store*)

For the latest news on tax legislation developments, please visit the Tax.CCHGroup website at tax.cchgroup.com/specialreport

NO POSTAGE
NECESSARY
IF MAILED
IN THE
UNITED STATES

BUSINESS REPLY MAIL

FIRST-CLASS MAIL   PERMIT #57   CHICAGO, ILLINOIS

POSTAGE WILL BE PAID BY ADDRESSEE

CCH INCORPORATED
PO BOX 5490
CHICAGO IL   60680-9808

2002 Tax Legislation

Law, Explanation and Analysis

Job Creation and Worker Assistance Act of 2002

CCH INCORPORATED
Chicago

This publication is designed to provide accurate and authoritative information in regard to the subject matter covered. It is sold with the understanding that the publisher is not engaged in rendering legal, accounting, or other professional service. If legal advice or other expert assistance is required, the services of a competent professional person should be sought.

ISBN 0-8080-0791-2

Job Creation and Worker Assistance Act of 2002

Tax Relief for Businesses and Individuals Has Already Begun

Like a bolt out of the blue, a sudden burst of Congressional energy broke the political logjam that had blocked an economic stimulus package since Fall 2001. Several important business tax incentives and other critical tax law changes were quickly enacted with retroactive implications in the middle of tax compliance season.

The House and Senate unexpectedly came together to pass stimulus legislation to assist the economy following the terrorist attacks of September 11, 2001. The bipartisan Job Creation and Worker Assistance Act of 2002 (P.L. 107-147) sailed through Congress in less than 24 hours. Passed by the House on March 7, 2002, by a vote of 417 to 3, and the Senate on March 8 by a vote of 85 to 9, it was signed into law by President Bush the very next day.

The Act contains approximately $123 billion in tax breaks through 2004, including a number of general business incentives, special relief for New York City, individual incentives, extenders, as well as some necessary technical corrections. Tax professionals and business taxpayers alike will want to quickly understand these new benefits to determine whether they can take advantage of them immediately, and how. At first glance, the changes complicate the current tax season because of the many additional extensions and amended returns associated with the 2001 compliance season. The good news is that the additional effort will result in tax professionals being able to procure some immediate tax relief for their many business clients that have been adversely affected by the economic slowdown.

About This Work and CCH

CCH's *2002 Tax Legislation: Law, Explanation and Analysis* provides readers with a single integrated reference tool covering all aspects of the Job Creation and Worker Assistance Act of 2002. Along with the relevant Internal Revenue Code provisions, as amended by the Act, supporting committee reports and other related official materials, CCH editors, together with several leading tax practitioners and commentators, have put together the most timely and complete practical analysis of the new law. Tax professionals looking for the Joint Committee on Taxation's Technical Explanation of the Act, including the related bill text, can find it in a separate CCH publication. Other books and tax services relating to the new legislation can be found at our website http://tax.cchgroup.com.

As always, CCH remains dedicated to responding to the needs of the tax professional in helping them quickly understand and work with these new laws as they take effect.

Mark Hevrdejs

Executive Editor

Federal and State Tax Group

March 2002

OUTSIDE CONTRIBUTORS

Paul M. Bodner
Great Neck, New York

Michael J. Cohen
Levun, Goodman & Cohen
Northbrook, Illinois

Michael Kessel
OTS Tax Consulting, LLC
New York, New York

Charles R. Levun
Levun, Goodman & Cohen
Northbrook, Illinois

George A. Luscombe
Mayer, Brown, Rowe & Maw
Chicago, Illinois

Vincent J. O'Brien
Vincent J. O'Brien, CPA, P.C.
Lynbrook, New York

Michael Schlesinger
Schlesinger & Sussman
New York, New York

Sanford J. Schlesinger
Kaye Scholer LLP
New York, New York

CCH FEDERAL TAX GROUP
EDITORIAL STAFF

James de Gaspé Bonar
M.A., Ph.D.
Publisher

Mark Hevrdejs
J.D., LL.M., C.P.A.
Executive Editor

Charles F. Ter Bush
J.D., C.P.A.
Director of Marketing

Explanation and Analysis

Robert Ansani, J.D., LL.M.

Louis W. Baker, J.D., M.B.A.

Katherine Baransky, J.D.

Allison Batt, J.D.

David Becker, J.D.

Lisa Hughes Blanchard, J.D., LL.M.

Maureen Bornstein, J.D.
Managing Editor

Glenn L. Borst, J.D.

Anne E. Bowker, J.D.

Douglas Bretschneider
Managing Editor

Mildred Carter, J.D.

Tom Cody, J.D., LL.M., M.B.A.

Eileen Deane, J.D.

Kurt Diefenbach, J.D.
Managing Editor

Dragana Djordjevic-Laky, J.D., LL.M.

Karin R. Dunlap, J.D., LL.M.

Karen Elsner, C.P.A.

Jacqueline Fajardo, J.D.

Shannon Jett Fischer, J.D.

Daniel T. Fleischer, J.D., M.B.A.

Adrienne G. Gershon, J.D.

Laurel E. Gershon, J.D., LL.M.

Joseph S. Gornick
Executive Editor

Tony D. Graber, J.D., LL.M.

Bruno L. Graziano, J.D., M.S.A.

William L. Greene, J.D., M.B.A.

Kay L. Harris, J.D.

Karen Heslop, J.D.

Jane A. Hoffman, C.P.A.

Lawrence J. Holbrook, E.A.

Dem A. Hopkins, J.D.

David Jaffe, J.D.

George G. Jones, J.D., LL.M.
Managing Editor

Thomas Kabaker, J.D.

Alfredo Karam, J.D., LL.M.

Anastasia R. Karovic, J.D.

Mark E. Kissinger, M.B.A., J.D., M.S.T.

Lynn S. Kopon, J.D.

Mary W. Krackenberger, J.D.

Thomas K. Lauletta, J.D.

Jennifer M. Lowe, J.D.

Laura M. Lowe, J.D.
Managing Editor

Mark A. Luscombe, J.D., LL.M, C.P.A.
Principal Analyst

Michael A. Luster, J.D., LL.M.
Managing Editor

Sheila E. McFarland, J.D.

Nancy C. McGowan, J.D.

Jela Miladinovich, J.D.

Sheri Wattles Miller, J.D.

Sheila M. Milsap, J.D.

Ellen Mitchell

David Morris, J.D.

Tracy Gaspardo Mortenson, J.D., C.P.A.

John J. Mueller, J.D., LL.M.
Managing Editor

Anita Nagelis, J.D.

Jean T. Nakamoto, J.D.

Jerome Nestor, J.D., C.P.A., M.B.A.
Managing Editor

Larry Norris, M.S.
Managing Editor

Karen A. Notaro, J.D., LL.M.
Managing Editor

Linda J. O'Brien, J.D.

Marie O'Donnell, J.D., C.P.A.

Karin Old, J.D.

Stephen R. Paul, J.D.

Lawrence A. Perlman, C.P.A., J.D., LL.M.

Deborah M. Petro, J.D., LL.M.

Donna M. Poczatek, J.D.

Ricky E. Rems, J.D.

Neil A. Ringquist, J.D., C.P.A.

Warren L. Rosenbloom, A.S.A.

John W. Roth, J.D., LL.M.

Carolyn M. Schiess, J.D.

Karla A. Schreiber, J.D.

Michael G. Sem, J.D.

James Solheim, J.D., LL.M.

David M. Stitt, CLU, ChFC, CFP, RFC
Technical Principal Analyst

Marcia Richards Suelzer, J.D.
Managing Editor

Raymond G. Suelzer, J.D., LL.M.

Glenn Sulzer, J.D.

Kenneth L. Swanson, J.D., LL.M.

Irene E. Tatara, J.D.

Deanna Tenofsky, J.D., LL.M.

Laura A. Tierney, J.D.

David Trice, CFP

Dawn Wagner, J.D.

Richard Waldinger, J.D.

James C. Walschlager, M.A.

Kelley Wolf, J.D.

George L. Yaksick, Jr., J.D.

Nicholas J. Zafran III, J.D.

Washington News Staff

Jeff Carlson, M.A.
Paula L. Cruickshank
David A. Hansen, J.D.

Kathryn Hough
Catherine Hubbard, M.G.
Rosalyn Johns

Joyce Mutcherson-Ridley
William Pegler

Electronic and Print Production

Lilian Bajor
Ce'on Barnes
Brian A. Berens
Miranda Blunt
Stella Brown
William E. Buonincontro
Gina Carbone
Julia Careau
Angela D. Cashmore
Elizabeth A. Dudek
Tara K. Fenske
Christopher Freeman
Mary Ellen Guth
Ann Hartmann
Kathleen M. Higgins
Jenny Holland
Kristine J. Jacobs

Judith E. Jones
Kenneth R. Kuehl
Andrea M. Lacko
Faina Lerin
Rebecca Little
Chantal M. Mahler
Andrejs Makwitz
Jennifer McCarthy
Diane L. McComb
Helen Miller
Loretta Miller
Barbara Mittel
Molly Munson
Holly J. Porter
Diana Roozeboom
Christine Roth

Jennifer Schencker
David Schuster
Jennifer Seay
Diane Shultz
Sandy Silverman
Eileen Slivka
Monika Stefan
Jason Switt
Robyn Terrell
Emily Urban
James Waddick
Matthew Widmer
Jamie Wild
Lynn Wilson
Laura Zenner
Christopher Zwirek

How to Use

¶ 1

CCH's *2002 Tax Legislation: Law, Explanation and Analysis* provides you with CCH explanations and analysis of the Job Creation and Worker Assistance Act of 2002 (P.L. 107-147). In conjunction with CCH editors, practitioners have provided practical guidance and planning strategies and identified pitfalls to be avoided as a result of the law changes contained in the 2002 Act. Included in this text are the provisions of the Internal Revenue Code, as amended, added or repealed by the new law, and the relevant portions of the House Committee Report and Joint Committee on Taxation Explanation.

Here is a guide to the numerous features provided in this text:

HIGHLIGHTS

A summary of the Highlights of the 2002 Act provides references to the CCH Explanations to give you a quick overview of the major provisions of the 2002 Act. The Highlights are topically arranged by subject and provide a means of entry into the Explanations. *See ¶ 5.*

CCH EXPLANATIONS

CCH-prepared explanations of the Job Creation and Worker Assistance Act of 2002 are arranged according to subject matter for ease of use. Each explanation includes a discussion of background or prior law that helps to put the law changes into perspective.

Incorporated throughout the explanations is expert commentary provided by practitioners. This commentary highlights planning opportunities and strategies engendered by the new laws. Pitfalls to avoid are identified. Charts and examples illustrating the ramifications of specific law changes are incorporated throughout the explanations.

Each explanation chapter is preceded by a chapter table of contents. A detailed table of contents for the entire explanation portion of the Law, Explanation and Analysis text is also included for easy identification of subject matter.

Each individually numbered explanation paragraph ends with the applicable effective date of the provision discussed. The effective date is preceded by a star (★) symbol for easy reference.

The explanation paragraphs are followed by boldface amendment captions that (1) identify the Act Section and the Code Section added, amended or repealed and (2) provide cross references to the law and to the reproduced Committee Reports. *The CCH Explanations begin at ¶ 105.*

INDEX. Because the topical or subject matter approach to new legislation is usually the easiest to navigate, you may also access the material in the CCH Explanations through the extensive Index. The Index begins at *page 319.* The Index is also available on the electronic version of this publication.

AMENDED CODE PROVISIONS

CCH has reflected the changes to the Internal Revenue Code made by the Job Creation and Worker Assistance Act of 2002 in the "Law Added, Amended or Repealed" provisions. Deleted Code material or the text of the Code provision prior to amendment appears in the Amendment Notes following each reconstructed Code provision. *Any changed or added portion is set out in italics.*

The applicable effective date for each Amendment Note is set out in boldface type. Preceding each set of amendment notes, CCH provides references to (1) the corresponding relevant House Committee Report and Joint Committee on Taxation Explanation and (2) the CCH Explanation related to that added, amended or repealed Code provision. Subscribers to the electronic product can link to the related explanation or Committee Report material using these references. *The text of the Code begins at ¶ 5001.*

NON-CODE PROVISIONS

The sections of the Job Creation and Worker Assistance Act of 2002 that do *not* amend the Internal Revenue Code appear in full text in Act Section order following the "Law Added, Amended or Repealed" section of the text. Included is the text of Act Sections that amend prior tax acts, such as the Economic Growth and Tax Relief Reconciliation Act of 2001 (P.L. 107-16), the Taxpayer Relief Act of 1997 (P.L. 105-34), and the Employee Retirement Income Security Act of 1974 (ERISA) (P.L. 93-406). *The text of these provisions appears in Act Section order beginning at ¶ 7005.*

COMMITTEE REPORTS

Committee Reports explain the intent of Congress regarding the provisions in the 2002 Act. Included is the House Committee Report on H.R. 3090 as originally passed by the House on October 24, 2001, and the Joint Committee on Taxation's Technical Explanation of the 2002 Act. At the end of the Committee Report text, CCH provides a caption line that includes references to the corresponding explanation and Code provisions. Subscribers to the electronic version can link from these references to the corresponding material. *These Committee Reports appear in Act Section order beginning at ¶ 10,001.*

EFFECTIVE DATES

A table listing the major effective dates provides you with a reference bridge between Code Sections and Act Sections and indicates the retroactive or prospective nature of the laws explained. *This effective date table begins at ¶ 20,001.*

SPECIAL FINDING DEVICES

A table cross-referencing Code Sections to the CCH Explanations is included *(see ¶ 25,001)*. Other tables include Code Sections added, amended or repealed *(see ¶ 25,005)*, provisions of other acts that were amended *(see ¶ 25,010)*, Act Sections not amending Internal Revenue Code Sections *(see ¶ 25,015)*, Act Sections amending Code Sections *(see ¶ 25,020)* and a listing of clerical amendments to the Internal Revenue Code *(see ¶ 30,050)*, so that you can immediately determine whether a provision in which you are interested is affected.

A detailed table of contents for the entire Law, Explanation and Analysis text is also included for easy identification of subject matter.

¶ 1

Table of Contents

Detailed Table of Contents

CHAPTER 1. TAXPAYERS AFFECTED

CHAPTER 2. INDIVIDUALS

CHAPTER 3. BUSINESS AND INVESTMENT

CHAPTER 4. NEW YORK CITY TAX INCENTIVES

NYC Tax Incentives

Tax Benefits for New York Liberty Zone

CHAPTER 5. RETIREMENT AND BENEFIT PLANS

Contributions and Deductions

Rollovers and Distributions

Defined Benefit Plans

Special Plans

Credits

Extended Provisions

Highlights

¶ 5

INDIVIDUALS

Unemployment Assistance. All states may extend the maximum 26-week period for unemployment benefits by 13 weeks for workers who filed their initial claims on or after March 15, 2001. States with an insured unemployment rate of at least 4% may extend benefits for an additional 13 week period. .... ¶ 205

Foster Care Payments. The exclusion for qualified foster care payments is extended to payments made by certified placement agencies or other entities designated by state or local governments, and to payments made with respect to any person placed in foster care by a qualified agency, regardless of the person's age at the time of placement. .... ¶ 210

Deductions. In 2002 and 2003, primary and secondary school educators may claim an above-the-line deduction for up to $250 annually in unreimbursed expenses paid or incurred for books and supplies used in the classroom. .... ¶ 215

Standard deduction for married taxpayers. The standard deduction for married taxpayers filing separate returns after 2004 remains one half the standard deduction for married taxpayers filing joint returns. .... ¶ 220

Rate Reduction Credit. The rate reduction credit for 2001 is treated as a nonrefundable personal credit that is claimed before the taxpayer calculates refundable credits. .... ¶ 230

Adoption Credit. The pre-2002 limits on the credit for adoption expenses continue to apply with respect to expenses incurred before 2002, even if the credit is not claimed until after 2001. In tax years beginning after 2002, expenses taken into account for the credit are increased by the excess, if any, of $10,000 over the aggregate expenses paid or incurred for the adoption of a child with special needs. .... ¶ 236

Extensions. Individuals can continue to offset their personal nonrefundable credits against their alternative minimum tax liability in 2002 and 2003. .... ¶ 270

Archer MSAs. The Archer medical savings account (MSA) program is extended through 2003. .... ¶ 275

BUSINESS AND INVESTMENT

Depreciation Allowance. An additional 30% first-year depreciation allowance applies to qualified property that is depreciated for 20 years or less under the modified accelerated cost recovery system (MACRS); purchased, contracted for or produced by the taxpayer after September 10, 2001, and before September 11, 2004; and placed in service after September 10, 2001, and before 2005. The first-year depreciation deduction for luxury passenger automobiles is also increased by $4,600, to a total of $7,660. .... ¶ 305

NOL Carryback Periods. The carryback period for net operating losses (NOLs) arising in 2001 and 2002 is extended from two years to five years. The full amount of NOLs arising in or carried forward to 2001 and 2002 can be used to reduce the taxpayer's alternative minimum taxable income. .... ¶ 310

S Corporation Shareholders. Cancellation-of-debt income that is excluded from an S corporation's income can no longer be taken into account as income by the shareholders and, thus, cannot increase the basis of any shareholder's stock. .... ¶ 315

Accounting Methods. The nonaccrual experience method of accounting may be used for amounts owed for (1) the performance of qualified personal services and (2) nonqualified services performed by a corporation with average annual gross receipts of $5 million or less. .... ¶ 345

Information Returns. Information returns, including Forms 1099, may be furnished to recipients electronically. .... ¶ 350

Extensions. Taxpayers can continue to claim the full amount of the credit for qualified electric vehicles placed into service in 2002 and 2003. The credit begins to phase down in 2004. .... ¶ 370

Electricity credit. The credit for production of electricity from wind, closed loop biomass, and poultry waste is extended to facilities placed in service during 2002 and 2003. .... ¶ 372

Work opportunity credit. The employer's work opportunity credit is extended to workers hired from targeted groups in 2002 and 2003. .... ¶ 374

Welfare-to-work credit. The employer's welfare-to-work credit is extended to wages paid or incurred in 2002 and 2003. .... ¶ 376

Clean-fuel vehicles. The deduction for qualified costs of clean-fuel vehicle property and refueling property is extended to property placed in service in 2002 and 2003. The deduction begins to phase down in 2004. .... ¶ 378

Percentage depletion income limits. The 100%-of-income limit on percentage depletion deductions for marginal oil and gas wells is postponed until 2004. .... ¶ 380

Qualified zone academy bonds. State and local governments can continue to issue up to $400 million in qualified zone academy bonds annually in 2002 and 2003. .... ¶ 382

Mutual life insurance companies. For purposes of computing a mutual life insurance company's differential earnings amounts and recomputed differential earnings amount (true up), the differential earnings rate is zero in 2001, 2002 and 2003. .... ¶ 384

Investments on Indian reservations. The employer's credit for employing American Indians who live and work on Indian reservations, and the accelerated depreciation periods for property used in a trade or business on an Indian reservation are extended through 2004. .... ¶ 386

Subpart F exemption for active financing. Current exceptions from subpart F taxes for certain shareholders of controlled foreign corporations are extended for five years for foreign personal holding company income, base company services income, and insurance income derived from the active conduct of a banking, financing or insurance business. .... ¶ 388

Approved diesel and kerosene fuel facilities. The requirement that approved diesel and kerosene facilities must offer both dyed and undyed forms of the fuels is retroactively repealed. .... ¶ 392

¶ 5

NEW YORK CITY TAX INCENTIVES

Work Opportunity Credit. For wages paid or incurred in 2002 and 2003, the employer's work opportunity credit is expanded to new hires and existing employees who work in the New York Liberty Zone or who work for employers that relocated from the Zone to other locations in New York City because of physical damage caused by the terrorist attacks. .... ¶ 410

Bonus Depreciation. An additional 30% first-year depreciation allowance is available for qualified business property purchased and placed in service in the New York Liberty Zone after September 10, 2001. .... ¶ 415

Increased Expensing. The deduction that small businesses may claim in lieu of depreciation is increased for business property purchased and placed in service in the New York Liberty Zone after September 10, 2001, and before 2006. .... ¶ 420

Recovery Period for Leasehold Improvements. The depreciation period for qualified leasehold improvement property in the New York Liberty Zone is reduced to five years. .... ¶ 425

Extension of Replacement Period. The replacement period for property in the New York Liberty Zone that was involuntarily converted as a result of the terrorist attacks is extended to five years if substantially all of the use of the replacement property is in New York City. .... ¶ 430

Exempt Bonds. Before 2005, $8 billion in tax-exempt private activity bonds may be issued to finance construction and rehabilitation in New York City, and $9 billion in advance refund bonds may be issued with respect to New York City facility bonds for which advance refunding authority was exhausted. ..... ¶ 435

RETIREMENT AND BENEFIT PLANS

Additional Contribution Requirements. For purposes of determining additional contribution requirements, the interest rate range used in calculating a plan's current liability is increased. .... ¶ 505

Deduction Limits. Contribution deduction limits applicable to employers that maintain a combination of plans do not apply when only elective contributions are contributed to the employer's defined benefit plans. .... ¶ 510

Rollovers. Distributions from after-tax contributions may be directly rolled over to a qualified defined contribution plan that will separately account for the taxable and nontaxable portions of the distribution, and to traditional IRAs. .... ¶ 520

SEP Contribution Limits. The percentage of compensation used to determine allowable contributions to simplified employees pensions (SEPs) is increased to conform with the deduction limits. .... ¶ 565

Mental Health Parity Requirements. The excise tax on health plans that fail to comply with parity requirements for medical and mental health benefits is extended to 2002 and 2003. .... ¶ 615

¶ 5

Chapter 1

Taxpayers Affected

JOB CREATION AND WORKER ASSISTANCE ACT OF 2002

Overview

¶ 105

Something for Everyone.—The Job Creation and Worker Assistance Act of 2002 (P.L. 107-147) represents a bipartisan effort to reach compromise in an election year and to provide some stimulus for the economy while it still looks like the economy might be able to use some stimulus. The legislation has a projected 10-year budgeted cost of $42 billion, although its 5-year cost is projected at a much higher $94 billion due primarily to the nature of the depreciation and net operating loss carryback provisions. The title of the legislation reflects the differing priorities of the Republicans and Democrats. The Republicans in Congress, especially following their promise to the business community that last year's tax legislation, which focused on individual tax cuts, would be followed by legislation focused on business tax cuts, tended to emphasize business tax breaks to stimulate job creation and therefore stimulate the economy. The Democrats in Congress tended to favor provisions to directly benefit the workers most affected by the downturn in the economy and the events of September 11, 2001, both in the form of tax breaks and increased unemployment and health insurance assistance.

In order to reach a compromise, many of the proposed business tax breaks, such as corporate alternative minimum tax relief, reduced payroll taxes for small business, a general increase in the Code Sec. 179 expense limit, and acceleration of the 100-percent health insurance deduction for the self-employed, had to be put aside for later consideration. Republicans also were forced to hold off on efforts to accelerate or make permanent the individual tax breaks in the 2001 tax legislation. On the Democratic side, an expansion of tax rebates for low-income individuals who did not receive advance refund payments in 2001 and expanded health insurance coverage were put aside to get action on an expansion of unemployment benefits. These unemployment benefits were scheduled to start expiring for many workers who lost their jobs as a result of the events of last September 11 if this legislation was not enacted just before the six-month anniversary of September 11, 2001.

What has survived in this legislation are a couple of key business tax breaks, focused on bonus depreciation and an extension of the net operating loss carryback to five years; an extension on unemployment benefits; a package of tax breaks focused on New York City and particularly the area of lower Manhattan most adversely affected by the terrorist attacks on September 11, 2001; a package of provisions relating to Internal Revenue Code provisions that had expired or were scheduled to expire in the near future; a package of technical corrections to prior legislation; and some other miscellaneous provisions with enough political muscle to manage to get in or stay tacked on. The compromises have enabled almost everyone to get something out of this legislation, and incumbent Congressmen can now campaign on what was accomplished rather than just what the other side kept them from accomplishing.

IMPACT ON TAXPAYERS

Effect on Business and Investments

¶110

The key provisions impacting business are 30-percent bonus depreciation (¶ 305) and five-year net operating loss carryback (¶ 310). Both provisions could have an impact on tax returns for the 2001 calendar year. A package of tax incentives primarily directed at businesses associated with New York City and its recovery after September 11, 2001, will also be very significant to businesses in the recovery area (¶ 405, ¶ 410, ¶ 415, ¶ 420, ¶ 425, ¶ 430, ¶ 435). Also, generally applicable to businesses are extensions of the work opportunity tax credit (¶ 374), the welfare-to-work credit (¶ 376), the deduction for clean-fuel vehicles (¶ 378), the credit for electric vehicles (¶ 370), and a technical correction to the employer-provided child care credit (¶ 335). In addition, the new law enacts procedures for electronic filing of Form 1099s (¶ 350). There is also a technical correction to the small business credit for retirement plan start-up expenses (¶ 610).

Several provisions will have an impact on particular forms of business entities or particular business and investment activities:

Corporations. Corporations are affected by a technical correction concerning the basis of property received in an exchange by a corporation involving an assumption of liabilities (¶ 335).

S corporations. The new legislation overturns the result in the Supreme Court decision in *Gitlitz v. Commissioner* concerning the allocation of suspended losses in bankruptcy to S corporation shareholders but does not apply retroactively to reverse the *Gitlitz* decision itself (¶ 315).

Partnerships. The settlement procedures under the partnership audit rules are expanded to include not only settlements with the IRS but also settlements with the Attorney General (¶ 355). A change also clarifies the treatment of inventory items in a sale or exchange of a partnership interest whether or not the inventory items have substantially appreciated in value (¶ 363).

Service businesses. The availability of the nonaccrual experience method of accounting is more narrowly restricted to certain professional services (¶ 345).

International business. The subpart F exception for active financing income has been extended for five years (¶ 388). An extension is also provided for cover over payments to Puerto Rico and the Virgin Islands (¶ 390).

Real estate/REITs. A technical correction clarifies the calculation of the tax on improper allocations involving taxable REIT subsidiaries (¶ 360). Another technical correction involves clarification of the phaseout of the $25,000 amount for rental real estate under the passive loss rules (¶ 245).

Investments. In addition to the real estate provisions, there is a technical correction on the termination of securities futures contracts (¶ 325). There are also two clarifications to the deemed sale election for the 18-percent capital gain rate on

2001 returns, one concerning the sale of a principal residence and the other relating to the deduction of suspended passive activity losses (¶ 320). The new law also provides an extension of the authority to issue Qualified Zone Academy Bonds for which a credit is available to investors (¶ 382).

Securities dealers. The new law includes a technical correction that losses on Code Sec. 1256 contracts are not governed by the wash sale rules (¶ 330).

Insurance. Several provisions impact the insurance business including a technical correction concerning whether a life insurance contract is a modified endowment contract (¶ 365) and an extension of the suspension of the reduction of deductions for mutual life insurance companies (¶ 384). Also, included is a five-year extension of the exception to subpart F for active financing income and a change in the allowance of foreign statement reserves of foreign-based insurance companies (¶ 388).

Oil and gas. An extension is included in the new law for the taxable income limit on percentage depletion for marginal production (¶ 380). Also, the dyed-fuel requirement for diesel fuel and kerosene has been repealed (¶ 392).

Alternative energy producers. The credit for production of electricity from alternative sources has been extended (¶ 372).

Distilled spirits. An extension is provided in the new law for cover over payments to Puerto Rico and the Virgin Islands (¶ 390).

Indian reservations. An extension is included in the legislation for the Indian employment credit and the accelerated depreciation rules for reservation property (¶ 386).

Effect on Individual Taxpayers

¶ 115

Probably the key provision with respect to individual taxpayers is not a tax provision but the extension of unemployment benefits (¶ 205). Technical corrections are included for many of the individual tax credits, including the dependent care credit (¶ 240), the rate reduction credit (¶ 230), the child tax credit (¶ 232), the adoption credit (¶ 236, ¶ 238), the earned income credit (¶ 234), and the interaction of the Hope Credit with Coverdell education savings accounts (¶ 250). Also, credits that have been extended include the allowance of nonrefundable credits for alternative minimum tax purposes (¶ 270) and the credit for electric vehicles (¶ 370). The deduction for clean-fuel vehicles has also been extended (¶ 378). Included in the New York City tax relief provisions is a new five-year period for replacing involuntarily converted property (¶ 430). There is a technical correction affecting Medicare+Choice medical savings accounts (¶ 242) and an extension of Archer medical savings accounts (¶ 275). A technical correction is included with respect to the continuation of tax benefits related to missing children (¶ 225), for the adjustment in the standard deduction to eliminate the marriage penalty (¶ 220), and under the deemed sale provisions for 2001 returns related to the 18-percent capital gains rate and the deemed sale of a principal residence (¶ 320).

A couple of categories of individuals are particularly affected by this tax law:

Teachers. For the first time, teachers are allowed an above-the-line deduction for the purchase of classroom materials (¶ 215).

Foster-care providers. The exclusion in the Internal Revenue Code for foster-care payments has been expanded (¶ 210).

Effect on Pensions and Employee Benefits

¶ 120

The changes affecting pensions and employee benefits are all included in Chapter 5. More flexibility is provided in determining required contributions to defined benefit plans, and a higher rate is imposed for variable rate premiums to the Pension Benefit Guaranty Corporation (¶ 505). Technical corrections related to defined benefit plans relate to the anti-cutback rules (¶ 540), notification of reductions in plan benefits (¶ 545), the unfunded current liability limitation (¶ 550), and plan valuation dates (¶ 555). Technical corrections are also made to provisions affecting other types of plans: increased contribution limits (¶ 540, ¶ 575), limits on catch-up contributions (¶ 515), the definition of compensation (¶ 595), IRAs in employer plans (¶ 560), and Simplified Employee Pension plans (¶ 510, ¶ 565, ¶ 570). Two technical corrections are included in the new law related to the credit for elective deferrals and IRA contributions (¶ 605) and the credit for plan start-up expenses (¶ 610). Technical corrections are also included related to tax-sheltered annuity plans (¶ 585), church plans (¶ 590), and Employee Stock Ownership Plans (¶ 580). Further, technical corrections address the rollover rules (¶ 520, ¶ 525, ¶ 530), the top-heavy rules (¶ 535), and the rules on failure to comply with mental health parity requirements in group health plans (¶ 615).

Effect on Estate and Gift Tax Planning

¶ 125

Technical corrections are included relating to the gift tax treatment of transfers in trust (¶ 280), the state death tax credit (¶ 285), and the calculation of the estate tax on foreign nonresidents (¶ 282).

Effect on IRS Practices and Procedures

¶ 130

The new law includes procedures for the electronic filing of Form 1099s (¶ 350). Also, included are technical corrections related to disclosures by the Social Security Administration of information to federal child support agencies (¶ 255) and the extension of the limitations period for installment agreements (¶ 260).

Effect on Excise Taxes

¶ 135

Extensions are provided for cover over payments to Puerto Rico and the Virgin Islands (¶ 390) and the excise tax on the failure to comply with mental health parity requirements in group health plans (¶ 615). The dyed-fuel requirement for diesel fuel and kerosene has been repealed (¶ 392).

Effect on Governments and Exempt Organizations

¶ 140

The new law provides an extension of the authority to issue Qualified Zone Academy Bonds (¶ 382).

Chapter 2

Individuals

UNEMPLOYMENT ASSISTANCE

Temporary Extension of Benefits

¶ 205

Background

In most states, state governments provide up to 26 weeks of unemployment benefits to unemployed workers. These benefits are funded by state taxes levied on employers. Federal law provides that unemployment benefits may be extended for a period not exceeding 13 weeks, where a state is undergoing severe economic stress. Whether a state qualifies for the extra benefits depends on stringent formulas. The extended benefits are funded in part by the federal government.

Extended Unemployment Compensation Act Impact

Unemployment benefits extended.—The Temporary Extended Unemployment Compensation Act of 2002 (Title II of the Job Creation and Worker Assistance Act of 2002 (P.L. 107-147)) provides for up to an additional 13 weeks of unemployment benefits for workers in states suffering severe economic distress. The amount paid weekly to eligible individuals is the same amount as was paid under the regular unemployment compensation received under state law.

The 2002 Act also extends federal benefits to unemployed persons who have used up all of their available state unemployment compensation. Any state may enter into an agreement with the Secretary of Labor regarding the extension of federal unemployment benefits to workers who have exhausted their eligibility for state benefits. To be eligible, an individual must have exhausted all rights to regular unemployment compensation under state or federal law, and must not be receiving compensation under Canadian law. The individual must also have filed an initial claim for regular compensation on or after March 15, 2001.

An individual is considered to have exhausted all rights to unemployment compensation when no payments can be made to the individual because he or she has received all amounts available to him or her based on the individual's employment or wages. In addition, an individual has exhausted all benefits if the individual's rights to such compensation have been terminated based on the expiration of a benefit year as to which the rights existed.

Under the extension agreement, the state must establish an account for each individual who files an application for temporary extended unemployment compensation. The amount in the account is required to be, with reference to the individual's benefit year, the lesser of (1) 50 percent of the total regular compensation paid to the individual, or (2) 13 times the individual's average weekly benefit amount. When the account is exhausted, if the individual's state is in an "extended benefit period" (as defined in the Federal-State Extended Unemployment Compensation Act of 1970), the account must be augmented by the same amount as was initially deposited into it.

An individual who receives temporary extended unemployment compensation through fraud or nondisclosure is ineligible for further benefits and may be prosecuted under federal law.

The federal government will fully reimburse each state that has entered into an agreement for the amount paid by the state as temporary extended unemployment compensation (less other reimbursement to which the state is entitled under federal law).

The temporary extended unemployment compensation provisions apply to weeks of employment beginning after March 9, 2002, and ending prior to January 1, 2003 (Act Sec. 208 of the Job Creation and Worker Assistance Act of 2002 (P.L. 107-147)).

★ *Effective date.* No specific effective date is provided by the Job Creation and Worker Assistance Act of 2002 (P.L. 107-147). The provision is, therefore, considered effective on March 9, 2002, the date of enactment.

Act Secs. 201-208 of the Job Creation and Worker Assistance Act of 2002; Act Sec. 209, amending and repealing certain provisions of the Social Security Act (42 USC 1103); Act Sec. 209(d)(1), amending Code Sec. 3304(a)(4)(B) and Code Sec. 3306(f)(2). Law at ¶ 5320, ¶ 5325, ¶ 7010, ¶ 7015, ¶ 7020, ¶ 7025, ¶ 7030, ¶ 7035, ¶ 7040, ¶ 7045, ¶ 7050. Committee Report at ¶ 10,050 and ¶ 10,060.

¶ 205

EXCLUSIONS

Foster Care Payments Made by Placement Agencies

¶ 210

Background ⎯⎯⎯⎯⎯⎯⎯⎯⎯⎯⎯⎯⎯⎯⎯⎯⎯⎯⎯⎯⎯⎯⎯⎯⎯⎯⎯⎯⎯⎯⎯

"Qualified foster care payments" made to eligible foster care providers are excludable from gross income (Code Sec. 131(a)). These stipends consist of amounts paid for caring for a "qualified foster individual" in the foster care provider's home and "difficulty-of-care payments" (Code Sec. 131(b)(1)(B)). Qualified foster care payments, including difficulty-of-care payments, must be made (1) by state or local governmental agencies, regardless of the qualified foster individual's age at the time of the placement, or (2) by tax-exempt placement agencies licensed by state or local governments, but the qualified foster care individual must be under age 19 at the time of the placement (Code Sec. 131(b)(1)(A) and Code Sec. 131(b)(2), prior to amendment by the Job Creation and Worker Assistance Act of 2002 (P.L. 107-147)). While the exclusion applies to foster care payments for individuals over age 18, amounts paid for such persons are not excludable to the extent that they are made for more than five qualified foster individuals; no such limitation applies to foster care recipients under age 19 (Code Sec. 131(b)(4), as redesignated by the 2002 Act).

A difficulty-of-care payment is defined as a payment designated by the payor as compensation for providing the additional care of a qualified foster individual in the home of the foster care provider that is necessitated by the individual's physical, mental, or emotional handicap. A determination must be made by the state that there is a need for additional compensation (Code Sec. 131(c)).

Job Creation Act Impact

Expansion of exclusion from income of qualified foster care payments.—The definition of "qualified foster care payments" has been expanded to include payments made by either state or local governmental agencies or *any* "qualified foster care placement agency" that is licensed or certified by a state or local government, or an entity designated by a state or local government to make payments to foster care providers (Code Sec. 131(b)(3), as added by the Job Creation and Worker Assistance Act of 2002 (P.L. 107-147)). Thus, payments made by for-profit agencies contracting with state and local governments to provide foster home placements will now be excludable from gross income by foster care providers.

Comment. An identical provision was previously approved by the House of Representatives on May 15, 2001, as the Fairness for Foster Care Families Bill of 2001 (H.R. 586). According to a House of Representatives news release issued on May 15, 2001, the measure's sponsor, Rep. Ron Lewis (R-Tenn.), noted that the means by which states deliver foster care has changed, but the tax code does not reflect those changes. Although the role of private agencies in helping to provide foster services has expanded, foster care families that received placements from licensed, private providers were still precluded from obtaining the exclusion for foster care payments. The new definition of qualified foster care placement agency remedies that inequity.

Age restriction for foster children eliminated. The definition of a "qualified foster individual" has been expanded to include foster care individuals placed by qualified foster care placement agencies, regardless of their ages at the time of placement (Code Sec. 131(b)(2)(B), as amended by the 2002 Act).

Comment. Elimination of the age restriction allows foster care providers to exclude payments made by tax-exempt and for-profit placement agencies with respect to foster care individuals who are over age 18 at the time of placement.

★ *Effective date.* The provision applies to tax years beginning after December 31, 2001 (Act Sec. 404(d) of the Job Creation and Worker Assistance Act of 2002 (P.L. 107-147)).

Act Sec. 404(a) of the Job Creation and Worker Assistance Act of 2002, amending Code Sec. 131(b)(1); Act Sec. 404(b), amending Code Sec. 131(b)(2)(B); Act Sec. 404(c), redesignating Code Sec. 131(b)(3) as Code Sec. 131(b)(4) and adding new Code Sec. 131(b)(3); Act Sec. 404(d). Law at ¶ 5080. Committee Report at ¶ 10,230.

DEDUCTIONS

Above-the-Line Deduction for Teachers' Classroom Expenses

¶ 215

Background

In computing taxable income under Code Sec. 63, taxpayers are allowed to take certain deductions. Deductions for individuals fall into two basic categories: (1) those taken *from* adjusted gross income (AGI) (Code Sec. 62), if the taxpayer is eligible and elects to itemize deductions, and (2) those taken *in arriving at* AGI (i.e., from gross income) regardless of whether the taxpayer itemizes. Deductions from gross income ("above-the-line") are typically preferable to deductions from AGI ("below-the-line" or "itemized deductions") because itemized deductions are advantageous only if the total amount of itemized deductions exceeds the applicable standard deduction (Code Sec. 63(c)). Additionally, itemized deductions are subject to various floors based on a percentage of AGI and certain phaseouts applicable to high-income taxpayers.

For example, for tax years 2002 through 2005, taxpayers may take an above-the-line deduction for qualified education expenses under Code Sec. 222. However, unreimbursed employee business expenses are itemized deductions and are subject to the two-percent floor on miscellaneous deductions found in Code Sec. 67.

Teachers who incur unreimbursed, out-of-pocket expenses for supplies that they bring into their classrooms for the benefit of their students are entitled to deduct these expenses, if at all, as itemized deductions on their income tax returns, only to the extent that the individual's total miscellaneous deductions exceed two percent of their AGI (Code Sec. 67(a) and Code Sec. 67(b)).

Job Creation Act Impact

Above-the-line deduction for expenses of eligible educators.—For tax years 2002 and 2003, eligible educators are permitted an above-the-line deduction of up to $250 per year for unreimbursed expenses incurred in connection with books, supplies (other than nonathletic supplies for courses of instruction in health or physical education), computer equipment (including related software and services) and other equipment, and supplementary materials used in the classroom (Code Sec. 62(a)(2)(D), as added by the Job Creation and Worker Assistance Act of 2002 (P.L. 107-147)).

An eligible educator is an individual who, for at least 900 hours during a school year, is a kindergarten through grade 12 teacher, instructor, counselor, principal, or aide (Code Sec. 62(d)(1)(A), as added by the 2002 Act). The term school is defined as one that provides elementary or secondary education, as determined under state law (Code Sec. 62(d)(1)(B), as added by the 2002 Act).

Caution. To be deductible, the expenses must otherwise qualify under Code Sec. 162 as trade or business expenses (Code Sec. 62(a)(2)(D), as added by the 2002 Act). Thus, among other things, the taxpayer must be able to demonstrate that the expense was ordinary and necessary, and that it was not capital in nature (Code Sec. 162).

Caution. The $250 per year maximum above-the-line deduction is permitted only to the extent that the amount of the expenses exceeds the amount excludable for the year under Code Sec. 135 (relating to interest form United States Savings Bonds used to pay education expenses), Code Sec. 529(c)(1) (relating to distributions and earnings from qualified tuition programs), or Code Sec. 530(d)(2) (relating to distributions from education savings accounts) (Code Sec. 62(d)(2), as added by the 2002 Act).

Comment. A 1996 National Education Association (NEA) study found that the average kindergarten through grade 12 educator spent approximately $400 per year out of their personal funds for unreimbursed classroom supplies. The total benefit to educators across the nation from the deduction is expected to be $409 million over two years.

Comment. In supporting the idea of the deduction, President Bush stated that "teachers sometimes lead with their hearts and pay with their wallets." He asserted that if a business person could deduct a meal, "a teacher certainly ought to be able to deduct the cost of pencils or a Big Chief tablet."

★ *Effective date.* The provision is effective for tax years beginning after December 31, 2001 (Act Sec. 406(c) of the Job Creation and Worker Assistance Act of 2002 (P.L. 107-147)).

Act Sec. 406(a) of the Job Creation and Worker Assistance Act of 2002, adding Code Sec. 62(a)(2)(D); Act Sec. 406(b) adding Code Sec. 62(d); Act Sec. 406(c). Law at ¶ 5065. Committee Report at ¶ 10,250.

Standard Deduction for Married Filing Separately

¶ 220

Background————————————————————————

The Economic Growth and Tax Relief Reconciliation Act of 2001 (EGTRRA) (P.L. 107-16) sought to eliminate the so-called "marriage penalty" by, among other things, increasing the standard deduction for married couples filing jointly. Starting with tax years beginning after December 31, 2004, the standard deduction for joint filers begins to increase until it eventually reaches 200 percent of the deduction rate of singles in 2009 (Code Sec. 63(c)(7), as added by EGTRRA).

Additionally, EGTRRA changed the definition of the standard deduction amount for joint married filers from a set dollar amount to a percentage multiple. This multiple is used to calculate the married filing jointly standard deduction

Background

amount based on the inflation adjusted standard deduction amounts applicable to filers who were not filing joint returns or claiming head-of-household or surviving spouse status for the appropriate tax year (Code Sec. 63(c)(2), as amended by EGTRRA).

Comment. Starting in 2005, EGTRRA eliminated the separate standard deduction for married taxpayers filing separate returns (Code Sec. 63(c)(2)(D), prior to removal by EGTRRA). Instead, a married taxpayer who was not filing a joint return would claim the same standard deduction as a single person.

Technical Corrections Impact

Elimination of marriage penalty in standard deduction.—The separate standard deduction for married taxpayers filing separate returns is restored for post-2004 tax years (Code Sec. 63(c)(2)(C), as added by the Job Creation and Worker Assistance Act of 2002 (P.L. 107-147)). The category of married filing separately will not be eliminated in 2005, as originally provided by EGTRRA (P.L. 107-16). The basic standard deduction for these filers is one-half of the amount in effect for Code Sec. 63(c)(2)(A), as amended by EGTRRA (i.e., one-half of the basic deduction for joint filers).

Comment. Had this provision not been restored, then during the years 2005 through 2008, two married persons filing separate returns would have had a greater combined standard deduction (twice the standard deduction for singles) than a married couple filing a joint return (who will have a standard deduction that is between 174 percent to 190 percent of the standard deduction for singles during those years).

If, in determining the basic standard deduction for a joint return or a surviving spouse, the applicable percentage calculation results in an amount that is not a multiple of $50, then the amount is rounded down to the next lowest multiple of $50 (Code Sec. 62(c)(2)(A), as amended by the 2002 Act).

 Example. In 2005, the basic deduction for joint filers is 174 percent (the applicable percentage from Code Sec. 63(c)(7), as amended by EGTRRA) of $4750, assuming this is the 2005 inflation-adjusted standard deduction for unmarried filers under Code Sec. 63(c)(2)(D). Thus, the basic deduction would be $8,265, which is then rounded to $8,250 (the next lowest multiple of $50).

 ★ *Effective date.* The provision applies to tax years beginning after December 31, 2004 (Act Sec. 411(x) of the Job Creation and Worker Assistance Act of 2002 (P.L. 107-147); Act Sec. 301(d) of the Economic Growth and Tax Relief Reconciliation Act of 2001 (P.L. 107-16)).

Act Sec. 411(e)(1) of the Job Creation and Worker Assistance Act of 2002, amending Code Sec. 63(c)(2); Act Sec. 411(e)(2) amending Code Sec. 63(c)(4); Act Sec. 411(x). Law at ¶ 5070. Committee Report at ¶ 10,260.

PERSONAL EXEMPTIONS
Principal Residence for Missing Children
¶ 225

Background _____

Effective for tax years ending after December 21, 2000, a taxpayer's child who is presumed by law enforcement authorities to have been kidnapped by a nonrelative and who qualified as the taxpayer's dependent for the portion of the year prior to the kidnapping will be treated as the taxpayer's *dependent* for the following purposes:

(1) the dependency exemption under Code Sec. 151;

(2) the child tax credit under Code Sec. 24; and

(3) the determination of eligibility for surviving spouse or head of household filing status under Code Sec. 2 (Code Sec. 151(c)(6)(A)).

Relief is also provided for parents who would otherwise be eligible for the earned income credit had their child not been kidnapped. A child who is presumed by law enforcement authorities to have been kidnapped by a nonrelative and who shared the taxpayer's *principal place of abode* for more than one-half of the portion of the year prior to the date of the kidnapping will be treated as meeting the earned income credit residence requirement of Code Sec. 32(c)(3)(A)(ii) (Code Sec. 151(c)(6)(C)).

The definition of "surviving spouse" requires that the taxpayer maintain as his home a household that constitutes the principal place of abode of a son, stepson, daughter, or stepdaughter for whom the taxpayer is entitled to a dependency deduction under Code Sec. 151 (Code Sec. 2(a)(1)(B)). Similarly, part of the definition of "head of household" requires that the taxpayer maintain as his home a household that constitutes for more than one-half of the tax year the principal place of abode of a dependent for whom the taxpayer is entitled to a dependency deduction under Code Sec. 151 (Code Sec. 2(b)(1)(A)). Therefore, taxpayers intending to qualify for surviving spouse or head of household status must satisfy the principal place of abode requirement, in addition to having a dependent.

Although the earned income credit residence requirement is met by a taxpayer whose kidnapped child shared the taxpayer's principal place of abode prior to the kidnapping, the principal place of abode requirement for surviving spouse or head of household status (Code Sec. 2) is not addressed for taxpayers whose child was kidnapped (Code Sec. 151(c)(6)(C)).

Technical Corrections Impact

Surviving spouse and head of household status.—A technical correction clarifies that a taxpayer who met the *principal place of abode* requirement of Code Sec. 2 for surviving spouse or head of household filing status with respect to his or her dependent child immediately before the kidnapping of the child will continue to meet that requirement (Code Sec. 151(c)(6)(C), as amended by the Job Creation and Worker Assistance Act of 2002 (P.L. 107-147)). Furthermore, the taxpayer will be treated as meeting the principal place of abode requirement for all tax years ending during the period that the child is kidnapped (Code Sec. 151(c)(6)(C), as amended by the 2002 Act). This special treatment ends with the first tax year of the taxpayer that begins after the year in which the kidnapped child is determined to be deceased or in which the child would have reached age 18, whichever occurs earlier (Code Sec. 151(c)(6)(D)).

Planning Note. Filing an amended return may be appropriate for taxpayers who have already filed their 2000 or 2001 returns and failed to elect surviving spouse or head of household status on the basis of lack of continuing compliance with the principal place of abode requirement prior to the change. Taxpayers who have not yet filed their 2001 tax returns should reexamine their filing status in light of this change.

Caution. This provision does not apply to children who run away from home. Children presumed to have been kidnapped by relatives, e.g., during or after divorce proceedings, are also beyond the purview of this provision.

★ *Effective date.* This provision is effective for tax years ending after December 21, 2000 (Act Sec. 412(e) of the Job Creation and Worker Assistance Act of 2002 (P.L. 107-147); Act Sec. 306(b) of the Community Renewal Tax Relief Act of 2000 (P.L. 106-554)).

Act Sec. 412(b) of the Job Creation and Worker Assistance Act of 2002, amending Code Sec. 151(c)(6)(C); Act Sec. 412(e). Law at ¶ 5090. Committee Report at ¶ 10,280.

CREDITS

Rate Reduction Credit

¶ 230

Background ⎯⎯⎯⎯⎯⎯⎯⎯⎯⎯⎯⎯⎯⎯⎯⎯⎯⎯⎯⎯⎯⎯⎯⎯⎯⎯⎯⎯⎯⎯⎯⎯⎯⎯⎯⎯⎯

The Economic Growth and Tax Relief Reconciliation Act of 2001 (P.L. 107-16) (EGTRRA) imposed a new 10-percent income tax rate that is applicable to a portion of an individual's income that was previously taxed at 15 percent. For the 2001 tax year, taxpayers received the benefit of the new 10-percent rate through a rate reduction credit that applied in lieu of the 10-percent rate bracket.

The credit equaled 5 percent of the taxpayer's taxable income that did not exceed the initial bracket amount, or $300 for single taxpayers, $600 for married taxpayers filing jointly and surviving spouses, and $500 for heads of households. (Code Sec. 6428(a), as added by EGTRRA).

Comment. The refund check that most taxpayers received in 2001 was an advance payment of the rate reduction credit based on taxpayers' 2000 returns. Taxpayers who did not receive an advance refund check, or did not receive the full amount of the advance refund check, may be eligible for the rate reduction credit. The credit is claimed on line 47 of Form 1040, line 30 of Form 1040A or line 7 of Form 1040EZ.

Technical Corrections Impact

Rate reduction credit classified.⎯A technical correction clarifies that the rate reduction credit is treated as a nonrefundable personal credit (Code Sec. 6428(b), as amended by the Job Creation and Worker Assistance Act of 2002 (P.L. 107-147)).

Comment. Other nonrefundable personal credits include the credits for expenses related to household and dependent care services necessary for gainful employment (Code Sec. 21), the elderly and permanently disabled (Code Sec. 22), adoption expenses (Code Sec. 23, as amended by the 2002 Act), interest on certain home mortgages (Code Sec. 25), and higher education tuition and related expenses (Code Sec. 25A).

Comment. Although the child tax credit is also, generally, a nonrefundable personal credit, certain portions of the credit are refundable. For tax years beginning after December 31, 2000, up to 10 percent (15 percent for tax years beginning after December 31, 2004) of a taxpayer's earned income in excess of $10,000, up to the credit amount, is refundable (Code Sec. 24(d), as amended by the Economic Growth and Tax Relief Reconciliation Act of 2001 (P.L. 107-16) (EGTRRA) and the 2002 Act). An alternative calculation for the refundable portion of the child tax credit applies to families with three or more children.

Planning Note. As a nonrefundable personal credit, taxpayers can claim the rate reduction credit prior to determining refundable credits, such as the refundable portion of the child tax credit under Code Sec. 24(d)(1), as amended by EGTRRA and the 2002 Act (Joint Committee on Taxation, *Technical Explanation of the "Job Creation and Worker Assistance Act of 2002"* (JCX-12-02), March 6, 2002).

Example. Mary Jenkins is a single mother with two children under 17. In 2000, Jenkins and her two children lived with her parents. Jenkins had no income for the 2000 tax year and, therefore, did not receive an advance refund check. In 2001, Jenkins and her children moved into their own apartment and she began working. She has income in the amount of $30,000 for 2001 and can claim head of household status on her 2001 return. Because Jenkins did not receive an advance refund check, has taxable income for the 2001 tax year, and has a tax liability in excess of $500, she can claim a rate reduction credit for $500 on her 2001 tax return. Provided that Jenkins claims her children as dependents on her return, and otherwise meets the requirements, she may be able to claim the child tax credit.

★ *Effective date.* The amendments made by this provision apply for tax years beginning after December 31, 2000 (Act Sec. 411(x) of the Job Creation and Worker Assistance Act of 2002 (P.L. 107-147); Act Sec. 101(a)(1) of the Economic Growth and Tax Relief Reconciliation Act of 2001 (P.L. 107-16)). See ¶ 20,001 for a discussion of the impact of the sunset rule on this technical correction.

Act Sec. 411(a)(1) of the Job Creation and Worker Assistance Act of 2002, amending Code Sec. 6428(b); Act Sec. 411(a)(2)(A), amending Code Sec. 6428(d); Act Sec. 411(a)(2)(B), amending Code Sec. 6428(e)(2); Act Sec. 411(x). Law at ¶ 5385. Committee Report at ¶ 10,260.

Child Tax Credit

¶ 232

Background

The Economic Growth and Tax Relief Reconciliation Act of 2001 (P.L. 107-16) (EGTRRA) increased the child tax credit (CTC) to $600 per qualifying child for tax years 2001 through 2004 and added a refundable component effective for tax year 2001 and after (Code Sec. 24(a); Code Sec. 24(d)(1)). The threshold requirements for the refundable portion require that the taxpayer have: (1) a total tax liability (regular plus alternative minimum) of less than his or her allowable

CTC ($600 per qualifying child); and (2) earned income in excess of $10,000 in 2001. The CTC is refundable to the extent of 10 percent of the taxpayer's earned income in excess of $10,000, up to the per child credit amount (Code Sec. 24(d)(1)). In addition, the 10-percent-of-income refundable component applies in lieu of the refundable additional credit for families with three or more children if the resulting amount is larger under the 10-percent-of-income component (Code Sec. 24(d)(1)(B)).

A technical correction by the IRS Restructuring and Reform Act of 1998 (P.L. 105-206) clarified that the refundable additional credit for families with three or more children was to be treated in the same way as the other refundable credits (Code Sec. 24(d), as amended by the 1998 Act). Specifically, after all nonrefundable credits are applied according to the stacking rules, then the refundable credits are applied first to reduce the taxpayer's tax liability for the year, and then to provide a credit in excess of income tax liability for the year (Conference Committee Report to P.L. 105-206).

This continued to be the law as to the additional credit for families with three or more children until the 2001 Act (P.L. 107-16) added the 10-percent-of-income refundable component to the CTC and, in the process, changed the language of Code Sec. 24(d)(1)(B). The portion of the CTC that is refundable is equal to the *lesser* of:

> (1) the child credit that would be allowed if it were determined without regard to the refundable portion and the tax liability limitation, *or*

> (2) the amount that *the CTC*, determined without regard to the refundable portion, would increase if the tax liability limitation were increased by the *greater* of:

>> (a) 10 percent of the taxpayer's earned income that exceeds $10,000, *or*

>> (b) if the taxpayer has three or more qualifying children, the excess of the taxpayer's social security taxes over his or her earned income credit for the year (Code Sec. 24(d)(1), as amended by the 2001 Act).

Technical Corrections Impact

Refundable child tax credit (CTC).—For tax years beginning in 2001, the portion of the child tax credit that is refundable, either the additional credit for families with three or more children or the 10-percent-of-income refundable component, is determined by referring to the total nonrefundable credits allowed, *not* by referring to the CTC allowed (Code Sec. 24(d)(1)(B), as amended by the Job Creation and Worker Assistance Act of 2002 (P.L. 107-147)). This technical correction reinstates the language added by the IRS Restructuring and Reform Act of 1998 (P.L. 105-206) and clarifies that the refundable portions of the CTC are to be treated as all other refundable credits. After all nonrefundable credits are applied according to the stacking rules, then the refundable additional child credit for families with three or more children or the 10-percent-of-income refundable child credit is applied, first to reduce the taxpayer's tax liability for the year, and then to provide a credit in excess of income tax liability for the year.

★ *Effective date.* This provision applies to tax years beginning after December 31, 2000 (Act Sec. 411(x) of the Job Creation and Worker Assistance Act of

2002 (P.L. 107-147); Act Sec. 201(e)(1) of the Economic Growth and Tax Relief Reconciliation Act of 2001 (P.L. 107-16)). See ¶ 20,001 for a discussion of the impact of the sunset rule on this technical correction provision.

Act Sec. 411(b) of the Job Creation and Worker Assistance Act of 2002, amending Code Sec. 24(d)(1)(B); Act Sec. 411(x). Law at ¶ 5015. Committee Report at ¶ 10,260.

Advanced Payments of Earned Income Credit

¶ 234

Background ————————————————————————————————

The earned income credit (EIC) is a refundable credit and, as such, is recoverable even though there may be no tax liability against which it can be offset. Taxpayers who have a qualifying child for EIC purposes may elect to receive advance payment of the credit from their employer. The election is made by filing Form W-5, Earned Income Credit Advance Payment Certificate, with the employer. The advance payment of the EIC is handled through the withholding system. The appropriate advance payment amount is added to each paycheck during the tax year for which the advance payment election is in effect.

Taxpayers who receive advance EIC payments from their employer must file an income tax return regardless of their income level and report the amount of the advance EIC payment as an "other tax" due on Form 1040 or Form 1040A. The actual amount of the EIC for the tax year is shown on the tax return as a "payment." In essence, the advance EIC payments received are treated as an increase in tax in order to recapture any excess payments over the amount of the EIC on the income tax return. Any increase in tax resulting from such recapture is not considered a "tax" for purposes of computing other *refundable credits* (Code Sec. 32(g)(2)).

Technical Corrections Impact

Recapture of advance EIC payments.—A technical correction clarifies that any increase in tax resulting from the recapture of any excess advance EIC payments is not considered a "tax" for purposes of computing any other *credits*, refundable or nonrefundable (Code Sec. 32(g)(2), as amended by the Job Creation and Worker Assistance Act of 2002 (P.L. 107-147)). Therefore, the "tax" recaptured may not be used to offset any nonrefundable credit amounts.

The advance EIC payments must be reported as a tax on Form 1040 or Form 1040A strictly for purposes of recapturing any excess payments received over the amount of the EIC claimed on the tax return. These reportable advance EIC payments are not a tax for any other purpose. Specifically, the advance EIC payments are not a tax for purposes of offsetting nonrefundable credits.

★ *Effective date.* This amendment applies to tax years beginning after December 31, 1983, and to carrybacks from such years (Act Sec. 416(a)(2) of the Job Creation and Worker Assistance Act of 2002 (P.L. 107-147); Act Sec. 475(a) of the Tax Reform Act of 1984 (P.L. 98-369)).

Act Sec. 416(a)(1) of the Job Creation and Worker Assistance Act of 2002, amending Code Sec. 32(g)(2); Act Sec. 416(a)(2). Law at ¶ 5035. Committee Report at ¶ 10,320.

Adoption Tax Credit

¶ 236

Background

There are two related tax provisions to assist families who adopt children: a tax credit and an income exclusion for employer-paid or employer-reimbursed adoption expenses. For tax years beginning before January 1, 2002, the tax credit and the income exclusion apply to the first $5,000 of qualified expenses per adoption ($6,000 for adoption of special needs children). The credit and income exclusion dollar limitations increase to $10,000 for tax years beginning after December 31, 2001, including for special needs children (Code Sec. 23(b)(1) and Code Sec. 137(b)(1)). Both provisions may apply to the same adoption, but not for the same expenses (Code Sec. 23(b)(3)).

The dollar limitation for qualified expenses is cumulative for all years for the particular adoption. For credit purposes, expenses paid or incurred before the tax year in which the adoption becomes final must be taken into account in the tax year following the year they are paid or incurred. Expenses paid or incurred during or after the tax year in which the adoption is finalized are allowed as credits for the tax year in which they are paid or incurred (Code Sec. 23(a)(2)).

Beginning in 2002, in the case of a special needs adoption, the credit is only allowed in the tax year the adoption becomes final (Code Sec. 23(a)(2)). In the case of the adoption of a child with special needs in tax years beginning after December 31, 2002, $10,000 is allowed as an adoption credit regardless of whether the taxpayer has qualified adoption expenses (Code Sec. 23(a)(1)(B)).

The Economic Growth and Tax Relief Reconciliation Act of 2001 (P.L. 107-16) (EGTRRA) increased the dollar limitation for the adoption credit and income exclusion beginning in 2002, however, EGTRRA did not state a dollar limitation for amounts paid or incurred in tax years before 2002 for adoptions that do not become final in those years.

Technical Corrections Impact

Transition rule for pre-2002 expenses.—A technical correction clarifies that the $5,000 dollar limitation ($6,000 in the case of special needs adoptions) in effect prior to 2002 applies to qualified adoption expenses paid or incurred during tax years before 2002 that are taken into account in determining an adoption credit allowed in 2002 or thereafter (Act Sec. 411(c)(1)(F) of the Job Creation and Worker Assistance Act of 2002 (P.L. 107-147)). This change was necessitated by the rule that states that expenses paid or incurred before the tax year in which the adoption becomes final must be taken into account in the tax year following the year they are paid or incurred (Code Sec. 23(a)(2)).

Special needs adoption. For tax years beginning after December 31, 2002, for purposes of both the adoption credit and the income exclusion, the adoption expenses taken into account for a special needs adoption shall be increased by the excess, if any, of $10,000 over the aggregate adoption expenses for the tax year the adoption becomes final and all prior tax years (Code Sec. 23(a)(3), as added by the 2002 Act; Code Sec. 137(a), as amended by the 2002 Act). Further, in the case of a special needs adoption, the requirement that the adoption credit be taken in the tax year the adoption becomes final has been removed, effective for tax years beginning after December 31, 2001 (Code Sec. 23(a)(2), as amended by the 2002 Act).

¶ 236

★ *Effective date.* In general, these provisions apply to tax years beginning after December 31, 2002. However, removal of the special needs adoption requirement that the credit be taken in the tax year the adoption becomes final and the conforming amendments regarding the $10,000 dollar limitation of the credit and exclusion apply to tax years beginning after December 31, 2001 (Act Sec. 411(c)(3) of the Job Creation and Worker Assistance Act of 2002 (P.L. 107-147)). See ¶ 20,001 for a discussion of the impact of the sunset rule on this technical correction provision.

Act Sec. 411(c)(1)(A) of the Job Creation and Worker Assistance Act of 2002, amending Code Sec. 23(a)(1); Act Sec. 411(c)(1)(B), adding Code Sec. 23(a)(3); Act Sec. 411(c)(1)(C), amending Code Sec. 23(a)(2); Act Sec. 411(c)(1)(D), amending Code Sec. 23(b)(1); Act Sec. 411(c)(1)(E), amending Code Sec. 23(i); Act Sec. 411(c)(1)(F); Act Sec. 411(c)(2)(A), amending Code Sec. 137(a); Act Sec. 411(c)(2)(B), amending Code Sec. 137(b)(2); Act Sec. 411(c)(3). Law at ¶ 5010 and ¶ 5085. Committee Report at ¶ 10,260.

Rounding Rules for Adoption Credit and Exclusion

¶ 238

Background

An individual taxpayer may claim an adoption tax credit for 100 percent of the qualified adoption expenses incurred in connection with the adoption of an eligible child (Code Sec. 23). An exclusion is provided for amounts paid to an employee by his or her employer for qualified adoption expenses (Code Sec. 137). The applicable maximum credit and exclusion amounts depend on the tax year of the adoption, the taxpayer's adjusted gross income, and the status of the eligible child. These amounts are adjusted for inflation for years following 2001 (Code Sec. 23(h) and Code Sec. 137(f)). The rules for adoption expenses (Code Sec. 23) and adoption assistance programs (Code Sec. 137) were clarified by the Economic Growth and Tax Relief Reconciliation Act of 2001 (P.L. 107-16).

Technical Corrections Impact

Uniform rounding rules established.—A technical correction provides uniform rounding rules (to the nearest multiple of $10) for the inflation-adjusted dollar limits and income limitations in the adoption credit and the employer-provided adoption assistance exclusion (Joint Committee on Taxation, *Technical Explanation of the "Job Creation and Worker Assistance Act of 2002"* (JCX-12-02), March 6, 2002).

★ *Effective date.* The inflation adjustment provisions become effective for tax years beginning after December 31, 2001 (Act Sec. 418(c) of the Job Creation and Worker Assistance Act of 2002 (P.L. 107-147); Act. Sec. 202(g)(1) of the Economic Growth and Tax Relief Reconciliation Act of 2001 (P.L. 107-16)). See ¶ 20,001 for a discussion of the impact of the sunset rule on this technical correction.

Act Sec. 418(a)(1) of the Job Creation and Worker Assistance Act of 2002, amending Code Sec. 23(h); Act Sec. 418(a)(2), amending Code Sec. 137(f); Act Sec. 418(c). Law at ¶ 5010 and ¶ 5085. Committee Report at ¶ 10,320.

Dependent Care Credit

¶ 240

Background ——————————————————————————————

With married taxpayers, the expenses to be taken into account may not exceed the earned income of the spouse who earns the lesser amount. Thus, a married person with a nonworking spouse cannot take the credit unless the nonworking spouse is incapable of self-care or is a full-time student. If the nonworking spouse is incapable of self-care or is a student, that person is deemed to have earned income for each month of disability or school attendance of $200 if there is one qualifying child or dependent, or $400 if there are two or more (Code Sec. 21).

Technical Corrections Impact

Deemed earned income amounts increased.—A technical correction conforms the dollar limit on deemed earned income of a taxpayer's spouse who is either (1) a full-time student, or (2) physically or mentally incapable of caring for himself, to the dollar limit on employment-related expenses applicable in determining the maximum credit amount. The Economic Growth and Tax Reform Reconciliation Act of 2001 (P.L. 107-16) (EGTRRA) increased the dollar limit on employer-related expenses to $3,000 for one qualifying individual or $6,000 for two or more qualifying individuals annually but did not conform the dollar limit on deemed earned income of a spouse (Joint Committee on Taxation, *Technical Explanation of the "Job Creation and Worker Assistance Act of 2002"* (JCX-12-02), March 6, 2002). Thus, the $200 amount is increased to $250 and the $400 amount is increased to $500 (Code Sec. 21(d)(2), as amended by the Job Creation and Worker Assistance Act of 2002 (P.L. 107-147)).

Example. For the tax year ending December 31, 2003, the taxpayer, who has a four-year-old daughter and a two-year-old son, works full time while her husband is attending law school for 10 months during the year. She has adjusted gross income of $45,000 for the year and pays $5,800 for at-home child care expenses. Her husband has no earned income for the year. The student-husband is deemed to be gainfully employed while in law school and to have earned $500 for each of the 10 months of schooling, or a total of $5,000 earned income for the year. The couple's employment-related child care expenses may not exceed $5000 and their credit would be limited to $1,000 (20% × $5,000) for the year. The 20 percent credit rate is based upon an adjusted gross income of $45,000.

★ *Effective date.* The provision is effective for tax years beginning after December 31, 2002 (Act Sec. 418(c) of the Job Creation and Worker Assistance Act of 2002 (P.L. 107-147); Act. Sec. 204(c) of the Economic Growth and Tax Relief Reconciliation Act of 2001 (P.L. 107-16)). See ¶ 20,001 for a discussion of the impact of the sunset rule on this technical correction.

Act Sec. 418(b) of the Job Creation and Worker Assistance Act of 2002, amending Code Sec. 21(d)(2); Act Sec. 418(c). Law at ¶ 5005. Committee Report at ¶ 10,320.

Effect of Medicare+Choice MSA Distribution Penalty

¶ 242

Background —————————————————————————————————

The Balanced Budget Act of 1997 (BBA 97) added the Medicare+Choice Medical Savings Account as an option for Medicare participants (Code Sec. 138, as added by the Balanced Budget Act of 1997 (P.L. 105-33); Act Sec. 4006(a)). Under this option, the government contributes funds to a medical savings account, and distributions are not included in the taxable income of the account holder as long as they are used exclusively for the qualified medical expenses of the account holder.

Withdrawals for nonqualified purposes are includible in income, and are subject to a penalty (Code Sec. 138(c)(2) and Code Sec. 220(f)(2)). The penalty equals 50 percent of the amount of the withdrawal minus an amount that equals the value of the assets in the account at the end of the previous year minus 60 percent of the deductible under the plan covering the account holder as of January 1 of the tax year (Code Sec. 138(c)(2)).

Under these provisions as originally enacted, imposition of the Medicare+Choice withdrawal penalty could potentially help a taxpayer by increasing the limit on the aggregate amount of nonrefundable personal credits the taxpayer could claim. The credit limit is calculated by subtracting the taxpayer's tentative minimum tax from his or her regular tax liability for the tax year (Code Sec. 26(a)). All things being equal, the larger the regular tax liability, the more generous the limit. Unlike many other tax provisions designed to discourage certain behaviors, this penalty was not excluded from the definition of regular tax liability (Code Sec. 26(b)(2), prior to amendment by the Job Creation and Worker Assistance Act of 2002 (P.L. 107-147)). Accordingly, imposition of the withdrawal penalty could increase the maximum amount of aggregate nonrefundable personal credits the taxpayer could claim.

Technical Corrections Impact

Medicare+Choice MSA penalties not included in regular tax liability.—The Medicare+Choice MSA distribution penalty is added to the list of taxes that are excluded from the definition of regular tax liability (Code Sec. 26(b)(2), as amended by the Job Creation and Worker Assistance Act of 2002 (P.L. 107-147)).

Comment. Since the Medicare+Choice MSA distribution penalty will not increase the amount of regular tax liability, a taxpayer can no longer benefit from the imposition of this penalty for purposes of increasing his or her aggregate nonrefundable personal credits.

★ *Effective date.* The addition of the Medicare+Choice MSA distribution penalty to the list of taxes excluded from the definition of regular tax liability is effective for tax years beginning after December 31, 1998 (Act Sec. 415(b) of the Job Creation and Worker Assistance Act of 2002 (P.L. 107-147); Act Sec. 4006(c) of the Balanced Budget Act of 1997 (P.L. 105-33)).

Act Sec. 415(a) of the Job Creation and Worker Assistance Act of 2002, amending Code Sec. 26(b)(2); Act Sec. 415(b). Law at ¶ 5025. Committee Report at ¶ 10,310.

PASSIVE ACTIVITY LOSSES

Phaseout of $25,000 Amount for Rental Real Estate

¶ 245

Background _____

Under the passive activity loss rules, rental activities constitute passive activities and the losses cannot be used to offset nonpassive income. However, a taxpayer is allowed to treat a rental real estate business as a nonpassive activity, provided the taxpayer materially participated in the business. If a taxpayer did not materially participate in the business, the taxpayer is still allowed to deduct up to $25,000 of passive losses and the deduction equivalent of the passive tax credits attributable to rental real estate from nonpassive sources such as salary and compensation for personal services (Code Sec. 469(i)).

In order to qualify for the $25,000 offset, the taxpayer must be an individual (or the taxpayer's estate for the tax years ending less than two years after the date of the taxpayer's death), and the taxpayer must actively participate in the rental real estate activity. The $25,000 amount is an aggregate for both losses and tax credits. Low-income housing and rehabilitation investment tax credits can be used as part of the overall $25,000 whether or not the individual actively participates in the rental real estate activity to which the credit relates. The $25,000 allowance is applied by first netting income and loss from all of the taxpayer's rental real estate activities in which the taxpayer actively participates. If there is a net loss for the year from such activities, net passive income, if any, from other activities is then applied against it in determining the amount eligible for the $25,000 allowance.

The $25,000 maximum offset amount is reduced, but not below zero, by 50 percent of the amount by which the taxpayer's adjusted gross income exceeds $100,000. The $25,000 offset is completely phased out when the taxpayer's adjusted gross income reaches $150,000 (Code Sec. 469(i)(3)(a)). The phaseout rule does not apply, or applies separately, in the case of the rehabilitation credit (Code Sec. 469(i)(3)(B), the commercial revitalization deduction (Code Sec. 469(i)(3)(C)), and the low-income housing credit (Code Sec. 469 (i)(3)(D)).

For the rehabilitation credit, the phaseout range for offsetting tax on up to $25,000 of nonpassive income is between $200,000 and $250,000 of adjusted gross income (phaseout is 50 percent of the adjusted gross income in excess of $200,000). The phaseout rules do not apply to any portion of the passive activity loss or credit for the tax year that is attributable of the low-income housing credit or the revitalization deduction.

The Community Renewal Tax Relief Act of 2000 (P.L. 106-554) provided that if the special phaseout rules for the commercial revitalization deduction, low-income housing credit, or rehabilitation credit apply, then the remaining portion of the $25,000 amount is applied in the following order:

(1) to the portion of the passive activity loss to which the exception for the commercial revitalization deduction does not apply;

(2) to the portion of the passive activity credit to which the special phaseout rule for the rehabilitation credit or exception for the low-income housing credit does not apply;

(3) to the portion of such credit to which the special phaseout rule for the rehabilitation credit applies;

(4) to the portion of such loss to which the exception for the commercial revitalization deduction applies; and

(5) to the portion of such credit to which the exception for the low-income housing credit applies (Code Sec. 469(i)(3), as amended by P.L. 106-554).

The rehabilitation credit, low-income housing credit, and the commercial revitalization deduction are allowed under the $25,000 rule regardless of whether the taxpayer actively participates in the rental real estate activity that generates the credit or deduction (Code Sec. 469(i)(6)(B)).

Technical Corrections Impact

Clarification of the phaseout of the $25,000 amount.—The operation of the ordering rules is clarified under the new law. In applying the phaseout of the $25,000 amount for rental real estate activities and the applicable exceptions and separate phaseouts for the commercial revitalization deduction, low-income housing credit, or rehabilitation credit, the phaseout rule is applied:

(1) to the portion of the passive activity loss to which the exception for the commercial revitalization deduction does not apply;

(2) to the portion of such loss to which the exception for the commercial revitalization deduction applies;

(3) to the portion of the passive activity credit to which the special phaseout rule for the rehabilitation credit or the exception for the low-income housing credit does not apply;

(4) to the portion of such credit to which the special phaseout rule for the rehabilitation credit applies, and;

(5) to the portion of such credit to which the exception for the low-income housing credit applies (Code Sec. 469(i)(3)(E), as amended by the Job Creation and Worker Assistance Act of 2002 (P.L. 107-147)).

Comment. The technical correction does not change the ordering rules in (1) or (5), above. The substantive changes are in (2), (3), and (4). The change in (2) results in the same meaning as under the old law. However, where under the old law the rule for the phaseout of the $25,000 amount was applied third to the portion of the passive activity credit to which the special phaseout rule for the rehabilitation credit applied, under the 2002 Act the phaseout rule applies third to the portion of the credit to which the special phaseout of the rehabilitation credit or the exception for the low-income housing credit does not apply. Also under the old law, the rule for the phaseout of the $25,000 amount applied fourth to the portion of the loss to which the exception for the commercial revitalization deduction applied, while under the 2002 Act the phaseout rule applies fourth to the portion of the passive activity credit to which the special phaseout rule for the rehabilitation credit applies.

Comment. The American Bar Association Section on Taxation, the American Institute of Certified Public Accountants, and the Tax Executives Institute released identical tax simplification proposals on February 25, 2000. The proposals noted that the numerous limitations and qualifications of the loss limitation rules under Code Sec. 469 were extremely complicated and difficult to comprehend. These groups stated that "substantial simplification could be achieved by combining, rationalizing and harmonizing the loss limitation provisions. (Statement of Richard M. Lipton, American Bar Association Section on Taxation, Address to United States Senate Committee on Finance, April 26, 2001).

★ *Effective date.* The amendments made by this section are effective on December 21, 2000 (Act Sec. 412(e) of the Job Creation and Worker Assistance Act of 2002 (P.L. 107-147)).

Act Sec. 412(a) of the Job Creation and Worker Assistance Act of 2002, amending Code Sec. 469(i)(3)(E); Act Sec. 412(e). Law at ¶ 5200. Committee Report at ¶ 10,280.

EDUCATION SAVINGS ACCOUNTS

Nonapplication of Additional 10-percent Tax

¶ 250

Background

The Economic Growth and Tax Relief Reconciliation Act of 2001 (P.L. 107-16) (EGTRRA) made substantial modifications to what was then referred to as education IRAs. To better reflect the true nature of the accounts, education IRAs were subsequently renamed Coverdell education savings accounts by P.L. 107-22. Prior to EGTRRA, a taxpayer could not claim an exclusion for the earnings portion of a distribution from an education IRA and the education credits under Code Sec. 25A (Hope and Lifetime Learning credits) in the same tax year. In order to claim the education credits under Code Sec. 25A, a taxpayer was required to waive tax-free treatment for distributions from the education IRA. A special exception relieved taxpayers electing the waiver from the additional 10-percent tax that normally applied to taxable education IRA distributions (Code Sec. 530(d)(4)(B)(iv)). The waiver requirement was eliminated by EGTRRA because coordination rules were added that allowed a taxpayer to take advantage of both the Coverdell education savings account, the education credits, and the qualified tuition program under Code Sec. 529 in the same tax year (Code Sec. 530(d)(2)(C)). However, the language relating to the exception from the 10-percent additional tax was not modified accordingly.

Technical Corrections Impact

Exception from 10-percent additional tax.—An exception from the 10-percent additional tax continues to apply to taxpayers who receive taxable distributions from a Coverdell education savings account solely because they claim the education credits under Code Sec. 25A. The exception is modified to reflect a taxpayer's ability to claim both the education credits and exclude gross income from a Coverdell education savings account in the same tax year, as long as the credit is not allowed for the same expenses. The 10-percent additional tax will not apply if, after application of the coordination rule, the distribution from the Coverdell education savings account is taxable. Under the coordination rule, expenses used to claim the education credits are deducted from qualified educational expenses when determining whether aggregate distributions from a Coverdell education savings account exceed qualified education expenses. The 10-percent additional tax will not apply to the portion of the distribution that is used to pay qualified higher education expenses, but for which the taxpayer elects to claim the education credits under Code Sec. 25A (Code Sec. 530(d)(4)(B)(iv), as amended by the Job Creation and Worker Assistance Act of 2002 (P.L. 107-147)). Distributions from qualified tuition programs are protected from the additional 10-percent tax in the same manner (Code Sec. 529(c)(6)).

Example. Joe Bradford establishes a Coverdell education savings account for his son, Jim. A $2,000 distribution is made from the account in 2002. Qualified education expenses for the tax year are $2,000, $500 of which are used to claim the Hope credit. Qualified education expenses of $2,000 are reduced by $500. Thus, aggregate distributions of $2,000 exceed qualified education expenses of $1,500 by $500. Although a portion of the distribution will be included in income, the 10-percent additional tax will not be imposed.

★ *Effective date.* The provision applies to tax years beginning after December 31, 2001 (Act Sec. 411(x) of the Job Creation and Worker Assistance Act of 2002 (P.L. 107-147); Act Sec. 401(h) of the Economic Growth and Tax Relief Reconciliation Act of 2001 (P.L. 107-16)). See ¶ 20,001 for a discussion of the impact of the sunset rule on this technical correction.

Act Sec. 411(f) of the Job Creation and Worker Assistance Act of 2002, amending Code Sec. 530(d)(4)(B)(iv); Act Sec. 411(x). Law at ¶ 5215. Committee Report at ¶ 10,260.

PROCEDURE AND ADMINISTRATION

Disclosure of Information to Federal Child Support Enforcement Agencies

¶ 255

*Background*_____

The Social Security Administration (SSA) may directly disclose certain tax information in its possession to state and local child support enforcement agencies (Code Sec. 6103(l)(8)). Child support at the federal level is overseen by the Office of Child Support Enforcement (OCSE), which acts as a coordinator for a variety of programs involved with support enforcement. OCSE serves as a conduit for disclosing tax information from the IRS to many state and local child support enforcement agencies (Joint Committee on Taxation, *Technical Explanation of the "Job Creation and Worker Assistance Act of 2002"* (JCX-12-02), March 6, 2002). Under current law, the SSA can not disclose tax information directly to a federal agency such as OCSE (Code Sec. 6103(l)(8)).

Technical Corrections Impact

SSA authorized to make disclosures directly to OCSE.—The SSA is allowed to make disclosures directly to a federal child support agency such as the OCSE (Code Sec. 6103(l)(8), as amended by the Job Creation and Worker Assistance Act of 2002 (P.L. 107-147)). The OCSE may, in turn, make disclosures to appropriate state and local child support enforcement agencies. (Joint Committee on Taxation, *Technical Explanation of the "Job Creation and Worker Assistance Act of 2002"* (JCX-12-02), March 6, 2002).

★ *Effective date.* This provision is effective on March 9, 2002 (Act Sec. 416(c)(2) of the Job Creation and Worker Assistance Act of 2002 (P.L. 107-147)).

Act Sec. 416(c)(1) of the Job Creation and Worker Assistance Act of 2002, amending Code Sec. 6103(l)(8); Act Sec. 416(c)(2). Law at ¶ 5340. Committee Report at ¶ 10,320.

Limitations Period for Installment Agreements

¶ 260

Background

Prior to the enactment of the Community Renewal Tax Relief Act of 2000 (P.L. 106-554), uncertainty existed as to whether the extension of the period of limitations on collection in the context of installment agreements was governed by reference to an agreement of the parties pursuant to Code Sec. 6502 or by reference to the period of time during which the installment agreement is in effect and levy is blocked, pursuant to Code Sec. 6331(k)(3) and Code Sec. 6331(i)(5) (Conference Committee Report to the Community Renewal Tax Relief Act of 2000 (H.R. Conf. Rep. No. 106-1033)). A technical correction to Code Sec. 6331(k)(3) attempted to clarify that the collections limitations period in the context of installment agreements is governed by the pertinent provisions of Code Sec. 6502 and, thus, the agreement of the parties (Code Sec. 6331(k)(3), as amended by the Community Renewal Tax Relief Act of 2000 (P.L. 106-554), Act Sec. 313(b)(3); Conference Committee Report to the Community Renewal Tax Relief Act of 2000 (H.R. Conf. Rep. No. 106-1033)).

Despite the technical correction to Code Sec. 6331(k)(3), uncertainty still remained regarding the permissible extension of the limitations period. In fact, the Joint Committee on Taxation indicated that a further technical correction was necessary to clarify that the elimination of the application of the Code Sec. 6331(i)(5) statutory suspension of the statute of limitation on collection applies only to Code Sec. 6331(k)(2)(C), which describes installment agreements that are in effect, as opposed to those that are pending, rejected, or terminated (Joint Committee on Taxation, General Explanation of Tax Legislation Enacted in the 106th Congress (JCS-2-01), footnote 185a).

Technical Corrections Impact

Clarification of collections limitations period for installment agreements.—A technical correction clarifies that the suspension of the collections limitation period under Code Sec. 6331(i)(5) does not apply with respect to an installment agreement for payment of unpaid tax that is in effect, as described in Code Sec. 6331(k)(2)(C) (Code Sec. 6331(k)(3), as amended by the Job Creation and Worker Assistance Act of 2002 (P.L. 107-147)).

Comment. The statutory suspension of the collections limitation statute will apply during the period in which the IRS is prohibited from making a levy because an installment agreement is pending with the IRS. The statutory suspension will also apply for the period of time that the IRS is prohibited from making a levy after an installment agreement is rejected or terminated by the IRS. While an installment agreement is in effect, the collection limitation period is governed solely by the installment agreement.

★ *Effective date.* This provision is effective on March 9, 2002 (Act Sec. 416(e)(2) of the Job Creation and Worker Assistance Act of 2002 (P.L. 107-147)).

Act Sec. 416(e)(1) of the Job Creation and Worker Assistance Act of 2002, amending Code Sec. 6331(k)(3); Act Sec. 416(e)(2). Law at ¶ 5380. Committee Report at ¶ 10,320.

EXTENDED PROVISIONS

Treatment of Nonrefundable Personal Credits

¶ 270

Background————————————————————————————

Generally, individuals may claim certain nonrefundable personal tax credits only to the extent that their regular income tax liability, without reduction for credits, exceeds their tentative minimum tax liability (as determined without regard to the alternative minimum tax (AMT) foreign tax credit). The nonrefundable personal credits include the dependent care credit (Code Sec. 21), the credit for the elderly and disabled (Code Sec. 22), the adoption credit (Code Sec. 23), a portion of the child tax credit (Code Sec. 24), the credit for interest on certain home mortgages (Code Sec. 25), the Hope Scholarship and Lifetime Learning Credits (Code Sec. 25A), the IRA credit (Code Sec. 25B), and the District of Columbia homebuyer's credit (Code Sec. 1400C).

The Tax Relief Extension Act of 1999 (P.L. 106-170) provided that, for tax years beginning in 2000 and 2001, all of the nonrefundable personal credits were allowed to the full extent of the taxpayer's regular tax and AMT.

However, pursuant to the Economic Growth and Tax Relief Reconciliation Act of 2001 (P.L. 107-16) (EGTRRA), the general tax limitation rule took effect again for tax years beginning after 2001 and before 2011, except that it does not apply to certain nonrefundable credits. Specifically, under Code Sec. 26(a)(1), as amended by EGTRRA, the nonrefundable personal credits, other than the adoption, child, and IRA credits, are allowed only to the extent that a taxpayer's regular income tax liability exceeds tentative minimum tax, determined without regard to the AMT foreign tax credit. On the other hand, the adoption, child, and IRA credits are allowed to the full extent of the taxpayer's regular tax and AMT.

Alternative minimum tax overview. The AMT is the amount by which the tentative minimum tax exceeds the regular income tax. An individual's tentative minimum tax is an amount equal to (1) 26 percent of the first $175,000 ($87,500 for married individuals filing separately) of alternative minimum taxable income (AMTI) in excess of a phased-out exemption amount, and (2) 28 percent of the remaining AMTI (Code Sec. 55(b)(1)(A)). The maximum tax rates on net capital gain used in computing the tentative minimum tax are the same as under the regular tax (Code Sec. 55(b)(3)). AMTI is the individual's taxable income adjusted to take account of specified preferences and adjustments (Code Sec. 55(b)(2)).

The AMT exemption amounts are as follows: (1) $45,000 ($49,000 in tax years beginning before 2005) for married individuals filing jointly and surviving spouses; (2) $33,750 ($35,750 in tax years beginning before 2005) for other unmarried individuals; (3) $22,500 ($24,500 in tax years beginning before 2005) for married individuals filing separately; and (4) $22,500 for an estate or trust. The exemption amounts are phased out by an amount equal to 25 percent of the amount by which an individual's AMTI exceeds (1) $150,000 for married individuals filing jointly and surviving spouses, (2) $112,500 for unmarried individuals other than surviving spouses, and (3) $75,000 for married individuals filing separately or for estates or trusts. Those amounts are not indexed for inflation (Code Sec. 55(d)).

Job Creation Act Impact

Offset for both regular tax and AMT allowed in 2002 and 2003.—For tax years beginning in 2002 and 2003, individuals may offset their entire regular tax liability and AMT liability by their personal nonrefundable credits. This is accomplished by limiting the amount of nonrefundable credits by the sum of (1) the taxpayer's regular tax liability, less any allowable Code Sec. 27(a) foreign tax credit, plus (2) the amount of AMT liability (Code Sec. 26(a)(2), as amended by the Job Creation and Worker Assistance Act of 2002 (P.L. 107-147)).

PRACTICAL ANALYSIS. Vincent O'Brien, President of Vincent J. O'Brien, CPA, P.C., Lynbrook, New York, observes that year after year, more and more taxpayers are affected by the alternative minimum tax (AMT). The AMT recalculates a taxpayer's liability using alternative rules and tax rates. The AMT provisions that most commonly affect taxpayers are those that disallow the personal and dependent exemptions and that disallow the itemized deductions for taxes (real estate and state and local income taxes) and for miscellaneous deductions. The recalculated tax under the alternative rules is referred to as the tentative minimum tax. If this tentative minimum tax exceeds the regular tax, then the taxpayer pays the difference (which is referred to as the AMT) in addition to the regular tax.

The reason that the AMT snares an increasing number of taxpayers each year is the lack of inflation indexing in the amounts, thresholds, and rates used to calculate it. While the regular tax system sees cost-of-living adjustments in most of its components (e.g., exemptions, brackets for each tax rate, etc.), the AMT amounts remain static. In fact, the Treasury Department recently indicated that approximately one-third of all taxpayers are expected be subject to the AMT by 2010.

The Tax Relief Extension Act of 1999 (P.L. 106-170) extended and expanded the AMT relief that was originally enacted in 1998. Effective for the 2000 tax year, the 1999 Act made all personal nonrefundable credits deductible against the AMT.

Prior to 2000, these credits were only deductible against the regular tax liability. Beginning with the 2000 version of Form 1040, the AMT line was moved, so that it immediately followed the line for regular tax. This reflected the deductibility of the nonrefundable personal credits from both the regular and alternative minimum tax liabilities. This line is, again, in the same place on the 2001 version of the form.

The nonrefundable personal credits include the child credit, the education credits (Hope and Lifetime Learning), the dependent care credit, the credit for the elderly and disabled, the adoption credit and the DC homebuyer's credit and home mortgage interest credit. Effective for 2002, the new savers' credit for retirement account contributions has been added to the list.

The provision enacted in 1999 was effective for only the 2000 and 2001 tax years. The recently enacted Economic Growth and Tax Relief Reconciliation Act of 2001 (P.L. 107-16) addressed the child,

adoption and savers' credits, allowing taxpayers to deduct them from both regular and AMT tax liabilities until December 31, 2010 (except for the savers' credit, which expires after 2006). However, it did not address the other commonly used nonrefundable credits. The 2002 Act addresses these other credits, allowing taxpayers to deduct them from regular and AMT tax liabilities for 2002 and 2003.

Example (1). John and Mary are married and have two children, both of whom are attending college. Their regular tax liability, before credits, is $4,300 and their tentative minimum tax liability before credits is $3,000. In 2002, they are eligible for education credits totaling $2,500.

Without the new provision, the education credits would have been deducted from the regular tax and the net result would have been compared to the tentative minimum tax. Thus, the $4,300 would be reduced by $2,500 of credits, resulting in a net regular tax of $1,800. This would have then been compared to the $3,000 tentative minimum tax. Since the tentative minimum tax would have been higher, this would have triggered an AMT for the $1,200 difference. The AMT would have made the couple's total tax liability $3,000, thereby reducing the benefit of the education credits.

Under the provision of the new law, in 2002, the couple will compare the $4,300 regular tax liability before credits to the tentative minimum tax of $3,000. Since the regular tax is higher than the tentative minimum tax, no AMT will apply. Then the couple will reduce the regular tax liability by the full $2,500 of education credits, resulting in a net tax of $1,800. Since the comparison to the tentative minimum tax was done before applying the credits, the AMT will not be triggered by the credits.

Example (2). Use the same facts as in Example (1), except assume that John and Mary have a regular tax liability, before credits, of $0. Without the new provision, the couple's net liability would have been $3,000, since the education credits would not have been deductible from their AMT liability. However, with the new provision, they will be able to reduce their $3,000 AMT liability by the $2,500 of credits, resulting in a net liability of $500.

★ *Effective date.* The provision applies to tax years beginning after December 31, 2001 (Act Sec. 601(c) of the Job Creation and Worker Assistance Act of 2002 (P.L. 107-147)).

Act Sec. 601(a) of the Job Creation and Worker Assistance Act of 2002, amending Code Sec. 26(a)(2); Act Sec. 601(b)(1), amending Code Sec. 904(h); Act Sec. 601(b)(2). Law at ¶ 5025, ¶ 5240, and ¶ 7090. Committee Report at ¶ 10,400.

Archer Medical Savings Accounts

¶ 275

*Background*_____

The Health Insurance Portability and Accountability Act of 1996 (P.L. 104-191) added Code Sec. 220, which permitted eligible individuals to establish medical savings accounts (Archer MSAs) under a pilot project effective for tax years beginning after December 31, 1996. Code Sec. 220 allows employees of small businesses and self-employed individuals to establish Archer MSAs to pay for medical expenses, a concept similar to establishing an individual retirement account for retirement purposes. An Archer MSA is a tax-exempt trust or custodial account established to pay medical expenses in conjunction with a high deductible health plan. The number of taxpayers who may benefit from an Archer MSA contribution is limited to a threshold level (generally 750,000 participants each year).

An advantage of using an Archer MSA is that premiums on high deductible health insurance should be lower than premiums on lower deductible plans. Eligible individuals (or their employers) may use the difference to fund their Archer MSAs. Tax incentives are provided for using Archer MSAs instead of traditional coverage. Within limits, contributions to an Archer MSA are deductible in determining adjusted gross income if made by an eligible individual and excludable from gross income and wages for employment tax purposes if made by a participating small employer (50 employees or less) of an eligible individual. This exclusion does not apply to contributions made through a cafeteria plan. Earnings on amounts in an Archer MSA are not currently taxable. Distributions from an Archer MSA for medical expenses are not taxable. However, distributions not used for medical expenses are included in the account holder's gross income. In addition, distributions not used for medical expenses are subject to an additional 15-percent tax unless the distribution is made after age 65, or upon death or disability.

For 2002, a high deductible plan was defined as a health plan with an annual deductible of at least $1650 and no more than $2500 for an individual and at least $3300 and no more than $4950 for family coverage. The maximum out-of-pocket expenses, including the deductible, must be no more than $3300 for an individual and no more than $6050 in the case of family coverage. In the case of a self-insured plan, the plan must be insurance and not merely a reimbursement arrangement.

To date, the number of Archer MSAs established has not exceeded the 750,000 threshold level. The IRS reported that as of August 1, 2001, 36,250 MSA returns counted toward the applicable statutory limitation of 750,000. (IRS Announcement 2001-99, I.R.B. 2001-42 (September 28, 2001)).

After 2002, no new contributions may be made to Archer MSAs except by or on behalf of individuals who already have made Archer MSA contributions and employees who are employed by a participating employer. An employer is a participating employer if (1) the employer made any contributions for any year to an Archer MSA on behalf of employees or (2) at least 20 percent of the employees covered under a high deductible health plan made Archer MSA contributions of at least $100 in the tax year ending with or within the cut-off year. Self-employed individuals who made contributions to an Archer MSA during the period 1997-2002 may also continue to make contributions after 2002.

Job Creation Act Impact

Availability of medical savings accounts extended.—This amendment extends the Archer MSA program for another year, through December 31, 2003 (Code Sec. 220(i)(2) and Code Sec. 220(i)(3)(B), as amended by the Job Creation and Worker Assistance Act of 2002 (P.L. 107-147)).

★ *Effective date.* The amendments made by this section are effective on January 1, 2002 (Act Sec. 612(c) of the Job Creation and Worker Assistance Act of 2002 (P.L. 107-147)).

Act Sec. 612(a) of the Job Creation and Worker Assistance Act of 2002, amending Code Sec. 220(i)(2) and Code Sec. 220(i)(3)(B); Act Sec. 612(b), amending Code Sec. 220(j)(2) and Code Sec. 220(j)(4)(A); Act Sec. 612(c). Law at ¶ 5115. Committee Report at ¶ 10,530.

ESTATE AND GIFT TAXES

Treatment of Certain Transfers in Trust

¶ 280

Background

A federal gift tax is imposed on gratuitous lifetime transfers of property (Code Sec. 2501). Although the Economic Growth and Tax Relief Reconciliation Act of 2001 (P.L. 107-16) (EGTRRA) repealed the estate and generation-skipping transfer taxes effective in 2010, the gift tax was retained, with some modifications (incremental decrease in the gift tax top marginal rate to 35 percent in 2010 and increase of applicable exclusion amount to $1 million in 2002 and beyond). These provisions are set to sunset in 2011, at which time all Code provisions will be applied as if EGTRRA had not been enacted, unless further legislative action is taken.

Comment. The gift tax was apparently retained, according to some commentators, because complete repeal of the transfer tax system would have resulted in taxpayers reducing or avoiding income taxes by transfers of assets to family members or others in lower income tax brackets.

The gift tax applies to direct or indirect transfers of real or personal property, in trust or otherwise, for less than adequate and full consideration (Code Sec. 2511(a)). The transfer must place the property beyond the donor's dominion and control and the donor must make a complete transfer of legal title and control. Thus, if a donor retains any use or benefit from the property, the transfer would not constitute a completed gift (Reg. § 25.2511-2).

Code Sec. 2503 allows a donor an annual gift tax exclusion for the first $11,000 (as adjusted for inflation) in gifts of present interests made to any one person during each calendar year. If the transfer of property is to a trust, the donor may elect the annual exclusion for each beneficiary that has a present interest in the trust. An unrestricted right to the immediate use, possession or enjoyment of the income of trust property qualifies as a present interest (Reg. § 25.2503-3(b)).

Transfers in trust made after December 31, 2009, will be treated as taxable gifts under Code Sec. 2503, except if the trust is treated as wholly owned by the grantor or the grantor's spouse for income tax purposes under Code Sec. 671 through Code Sec. 679 (Code Sec. 2511(c) as added by EGTRRA).

Comment. After enactment of new Code Sec. 2511(c), several commentators raised questions regarding the extent to which the provision would apply, such as whether all transfers to a trust, particularly transfers now considered incomplete for gift tax purposes, are to be treated as taxable gifts and the extent to which any existing exclusions or deductions would apply.

Technical Corrections Impact

Treatment of transfers in trust clarified.—Transfers in trust after December 31, 2009 will be treated as *transfers of property by gifts,* unless the trust is wholly owned by the grantor or the grantor's spouse for purposes of the income tax grantor trust rules (Code Sec. 2511(c) as amended by the Job Creation and Worker Assistance Act of 2002 (P.L. 107-147)). This clarification allows the gift tax annual exclusion and the gift tax marital and charitable deduction, to apply to transfers in trust that are taxable gifts thereunder. Transfers of property that prior to 2010 would be treated as incomplete for gift tax purposes are to be treated as transfers of property by gift if made after December 31, 2009.

> **Example.** In 2010, Ed Baxter transfers property to a trust under which the income is payable to his daughter, Mary, for her life. Ed retains the power to determine the remainder beneficiaries and the amount each is to receive. Under Code Sec. 2511(c), as amended, the transfer is deemed a completed, taxable gift, whereas, before 2010 it would not be (Reg. § 25.2511-2(c)).

PRACTICAL ANALYSIS. Sanford J. Schlesinger, chair, Wills and Estates Dept., of Kaye Scholer LLP, New York, New York, notes that this technical correction does clarify some of the issues that arose following enactment of the Economic Growth and Tax Relief Reconciliation Act of 2001. While it was not clear under prior law, the correction clarifies that a transfer in trust that is not a grantor trust that would have been viewed as an incomplete gift under prior law will, however, be treated as a completed gift under Code Sec. 2511(c). It also clarifies that Code Sec. 2511(c) was not an attempt to abolish the use of Crummey trusts. It further clarifies that the marital and charitable deductions and the annual exclusions normally applicable to completed gifts will apply to transfers in trust treated as gifts under this provision.

★ *Effective date.* The provision applies to gifts made after December 31, 2009 (Act Sec. 411(x) of the Job Creation and Worker Assistance Act of 2002 (P.L. 107-147); Act Sec. 511(f)(3) of the Economic Growth and Tax Relief Reconciliation Act of 2001 (P.L. 107-16)). See ¶ 20,001 for a discussion of the impact of the sunset rule on this technical correction.

Act Sec. 411(g)(1) of the Job Creation and Worker Assistance Act of 2002, amending Code Sec. 2511(c); Act Sec. 411(x). Law at ¶ 5315. Committee Report at ¶ 10,260.

Adjustment for Surtax Eliminated for Nonresidents

¶ 282

Background ——————————————————————————————

Nonresident decedents who are not U.S. citizens are generally subject to the same unified rate schedule that applies to U.S. citizens, with the tentative tax on a nonresident decedent's taxable estate computed under Code Sec. 2001(c) (Code Sec. 2101). However, a nonresident, non-U.S. citizen is not generally entitled to the same applicable (unified) credit amount that a resident enjoys under Code Sec. 2010, unless permitted by treaty (Code Sec. 2102).

Prior to the enactment of the Economic Growth and Tax Relief Reconciliation Act of 2001 (P.L. 107-16) (EGTRRA), a five-percent surtax was imposed on cumulative taxable transfers between $10 million and $17,184,000 (Code Sec. 2001(c)(2), prior to amendment by EGTRRA). The surtax had the effect of phasing out the benefit of the graduated rates for taxable transfers falling between those amounts. For purposes of computing a nonresident decedent's tentative tax, an "appropriate adjustment" was required to be made in the application of the surtax in order to reflect the difference between the amount of the unified credit allowed under Code Sec. 2102(c) (nonresidents) and the amount of the unified credit allowed under Code Sec. 2010 (residents) (Code Sec. 2101(b)). This adjustment was designed to ensure that the benefit of the graduated rates was phased out in accordance with the actual credit amount that was available to the nonresident, non-U.S. citizen decedent.

EGTRRA eliminated the five-percent surtax, effective for the estates of decedents dying after December 31, 2001 (Code Sec. 2001(c)(2), as amended by EGTRRA).

Technical Corrections Impact

Reference to five-percent surtax eliminated.—The Job Creation and Worker Assistance Act of 2002 (P.L. 107-147) amends Code Sec. 2101(b) by eliminating the language that directs that an adjustment be made in applying the five-percent surtax that existed prior to the enactment of the Economic Growth and Tax Relief Reconciliation Act of 2001 (P.L. 107-16) (EGTRRA). Because the surtax was eliminated for the estates of decedents dying after December 31, 2001, the cross-reference to that provision in Code Sec. 2101 has no effect for years after 2001, making it superfluous and therefore appropriate for deletion.

Comment. The amendment to Code Sec. 2101(b) "shall take effect as if included in the provisions of [EGTRRA] to which [it] relate[s]" (Act Sec. 411(x) of the 2002 Act.) The repeal of the Code Sec. 2001(c)(2) five-percent surtax was contained in Act Sec. 511 of EGTRRA. Code Sec. 2101(b) was not, however, amended by EGTRRA as originally enacted, thereby raising a potential question as to the amendment's exact effective date under a technical reading of the 2002 Act. But the general effective date language quoted above, coupled with the clear intent of the amendment and logical consistency, strongly appear to indicate that the amendment applies to the estates of decedents dying after December 31, 2001.

★ *Effective date.* The provision is effective for the estates of decedents dying after December 31, 2001 (Act. Sec. 411(x) of the Job Creation and Worker Assistance Act of 2002 (P.L. 107-147); Act Sec. 511(f)(1) of the Economic Growth and Tax Relief Reconciliation Act of 2001 (P.L. 107-16)). See ¶ 20,001 for a discussion of the impact of the sunset rule on this technical correction.

Act Sec. 411(g)(2) of the Job Creation and Worker Assistance Act of 2002, amending Code Sec. 2101(b); Act Sec. 411(x). Law at ¶ 5310. Committee Report at ¶ 10,260.

Elimination of Reference to State Death Tax Credit

¶ 285

Background———————————————————————————

A decedent's estate is entitled, under Code Sec. 2011, to claim a federal credit for state death taxes paid to a state or the District of Columbia. The amount of the credit is based on the decedent's "adjusted taxable estate," which is the taxable estate less $60,000 (Code Sec. 2011(b)(3)). For decedents dying in 2002, the maximum state death tax credit allowable is reduced by 25 percent of the amount in effect for decedents dying in 2001, and will be further reduced by 50 percent and 75 percent of the 2001 amount for estates of decedents dying in 2003 and 2004, respectively. The state death tax credit is scheduled to be repealed for estates of decedents dying after 2004 and will be replaced by a deduction until the phaseout of the federal estate tax is complete in 2010 (Economic Growth and Tax Relief Reconciliation Act of 2001 (P.L. 107-16) (EGTRRA). Beginning in 2005, a decedent's taxable estate will be determined by deducting from the gross estate the amount of any estate, inheritance, legacy, or succession taxes paid to any state or the District of Columbia with respect to property included in the decedent's gross estate.

In the event a decedent's estate receives a refund of any state death taxes claimed as a credit against the decedent's federal estate taxes, Code Sec. 2016 requires the IRS to be notified within 30 days after receipt of the refund. The notice must include the name of decedent, the date of the decedent's death, and the name and address of the person receiving the refund. In addition, the notice must specify the property with respect to which the refund was made, and the amount and date of the refund.

In order to comply with the Congressional Budget Act of 1974, a sunset provision was added to EGTRRA that requires in 2011 that all provisions of, and amendments made by, EGTRRA be applied as if EGTRRA had not been enacted, unless further legislative action is taken.

Technical Corrections Impact

Reference to state death tax credit eliminated.—In order to remove from the Code any superfluous language, the reference to any estate, inheritance, legacy, or succession taxes paid to any state or the District of Columbia in Code Sec. 2016 is eliminated upon the repeal of the state death tax credit in 2005. Thereafter, Code Sec. 2016 will apply only to refunds of any foreign death taxes claimed as a credit against the decedent's federal estate taxes (Code Sec. 2016, as amended by the Job Creation and Worker Assistance Act of 2002 (P.L. 107-147)).

★ *Effective date.* The provision is effective for the estates of decedents dying after December 31, 2004 (Act Sec. 411(x) of the Job Creation and Worker Assistance Act of 2002 (P.L. 107-147); Act Sec. 532(d) of the Economic Growth and Tax Relief Reconciliation Act of 2001 (P.L. 107-16)). See ¶ 20,001 for a discussion of the impact of the sunset rule on this technical correction.

Act Sec. 411(h) of the Job Creation and Worker Assistance Act of 2002, amending Code Sec. 2016; Act Sec. 411(x). Law at ¶ 5305. Committee Report at ¶ 10,260.

Chapter 3

Business and Investment

DEPRECIATION

Thirty-Percent Additional First-Year Depreciation Allowance

¶ 305

Background

The cost of depreciable property placed in service after 1986 is generally recovered using the Modified Accelerated Cost Recovery System (MACRS). Each type of property is assigned to a property class in accordance with the property class table issued by the IRS in Rev. Proc. 87-56 (1987-2 CB 674). The property classes for personal property are: 3-year property, 5-year property, 7-year property, 10-year property, 15-year property, and 20-year property. The depreciation periods are three years for 3-year property, five years for 5-year property, seven years for 7-year property, 10 years for 10-year property, etc. Water utility property is depreciated over 25 years. Real property is generally classified as either residential rental property (a 27.5-year depreciation period applies) or nonresidential real property (a 39-year depreciation period applies). Structural components, including leasehold improvements, are depreciated as real property. Longer recovery periods apply if the MACRS alternative depreciation system (ADS) is used.

In the case of 3-, 5-, 7-, and 10-year property, the applicable depreciation method is the 200-percent declining balance method. The 150-percent declining balance method applies to 10- and 15-year property. The straight-line method and mid-month convention apply to residential rental and nonresidential real property. Under this convention, an asset is considered placed in service or disposed of on the midpoint of the month in which it is placed in service or disposed of. The half-year or mid-quarter convention applies to personal property.

Subject to certain limitations, a taxpayer may claim a current deduction under Code Sec. 179 for the cost of tangible personal property acquired for use in the active conduct of a trade or business. For 2001 and 2002, the maximum deduction is $24,000. It increases to $25,000 thereafter. The cost of any property expensed under Code Sec. 179 is reduced for purposes of computing depreciation.

Depreciation caps on passenger automobiles. The amount of depreciation that may be claimed on a passenger automobile is limited under Code Sec. 280F. For a passenger car placed in service during the 2001 or 2002 calendar year and used 100 percent for business, the annual depreciation deductions are capped at $3,060 in the first year, $4,900 in the second year, $2,950 in the third year, and $1,775 in each subsequent year. Even though these limitations are popularly referred to as the "luxury car rules," they affect cars costing as little as $15,300 ($15,300 × 20% (first-year depreciation percentage) = $3,060).

Computer software. Computer software which is separately purchased is generally amortized over three years using the straight-line method beginning on the first day of the month in which it is placed in service (Code Sec. 167(f)(1)(A)). Computer software acquired in connection with the acquisition of a business is amortized over 15 years under Code Sec. 197 unless it is available to the general public and is not substantially modified. Software with a useful life of less than one year is currently deducted.

Job Creation Act Impact

Special 30-percent depreciation allowance for property acquired after September 10, 2001, and before September 11, 2004.—The provision permits a taxpayer to claim an additional first-year depreciation allowance (the "Code Sec. 168(k) allowance") on new MACRS property for which the recovery period is 20 years or less, MACRS water utility property, computer software which is depreciable under Code Sec. 167, and qualified leasehold improvement property. The additional allowance is equal to 30 percent of the adjusted basis of the property after reduction by any Code Sec. 179 expense allowance. The regular MACRS deduction is computed after reducing the adjusted basis of the property by any Code Sec. 179 expense allowance and the additional first-year allowance. Property which must be depreciated under the MACRS alternative depreciation system (ADS) does not qualify. The additional allowance may be claimed for alternative minimum tax purposes and no depreciation adjustment is required. The additional allowance is subject to the general rules regarding whether an item is deductible under Code Sec. 162 or subject to capitalization under Code Sec. 263 or Code Sec. 263A (Code Sec. 168(k), as added by the Job Creation and Worker Assistance Act of 2002 (P.L. 107-147)).

As explained more fully below, the Code Sec. 168(k) allowance generally applies to property acquired after September 10, 2001, and before September 11, 2004, and placed in service before January 1, 2005. A taxpayer may also make an election not to claim the allowance with respect to any class of property.

Comment. A qualifying taxpayer who has already filed a 2001 return will need to file an amended return to claim the additional allowance. Undoubtedly, the IRS will issue guidance explaining how the additional allowance should be reported. The IRS could reissue Form 4562 (Depreciation and Amortization) and/or provide a procedure for claiming the allowance on the existing version of the form.

Comment. With the limited exception of software which is depreciable under Code Sec. 167, the 30-percent additional allowance only applies to property which is depreciated under Code Sec. 168 (that is, MACRS property) (Code Sec. 168(k)(2)(A)(i)(I)). Therefore, intangibles amortized over 15 years under Code Sec. 197 do not qualify for the allowance.

Example (1). Joseph Long purchases $100,000 of new machinery on January 17, 2002. Assume that the machinery is MACRS 5-year property, that the half-year convention applies, and that no amount is expensed under Code Sec. 179. Long is entitled to deduct a $30,000 ($100,000 × 30%) special depreciation allowance. The depreciable basis of the property is reduced to $70,000 ($100,000 − $30,000). Regular MACRS depreciation (using the table percentages for 5-year property) is computed as follows:

Recovery Year		Deduction
2002	bonus depreciation	$ 30,000
2002	$70,000 × 20% =	$ 14,000
2003	$70,000 × 32% =	$ 22,400
2004	$70,000 × 19.20% =	$ 13,440
2005	$70,000 × 11.52% =	$ 8,064
2006	$70,000 × 11.52% =	$ 8,064
2007	$70,000 × 5.76% =	$ 4,032
Total		$ 100,000

Example (2). The following chart compares depreciation when the special allowance is not claimed with depreciation when the special allowance is claimed, assuming the same facts as in Example (1), above.

Recovery Year		No bonus claimed	Bonus claimed
2002	$100,000 × 20% =	$ 20,000	$ 44,000 ($14,000 + $30,000)
2003	$100,000 × 32% =	$ 32,000	$ 22,400
2004	$100,000 × 19.20% =	$ 19,200	$ 13,440
2005	$100,000 × 11.52% =	$ 11,520	$ 8,064
2006	$100,000 × 11.52% =	$ 11,520	$ 8,064
2007	$100,000 × 5.76% =	$ 5,760	$ 4,032
Total		$100,000	$100,000

Comment. As can be seen by the above example, the additional depreciation allowance reduces the amount of regular depreciation that would otherwise be claimed during the regular depreciation period because the basis on which depreciation is claimed is reduced by the bonus depreciation allowance.

Comment. Since bonus depreciation is treated as a depreciation deduction, it should be subject to recapture as ordinary income under Code Sec. 1245 when property is sold at a gain.

Coordination with Code Sec. 179. The Joint Committee on Taxation indicates that the Code Sec. 179 expense allowance is claimed prior to the additional depreciation allowance (Joint Committee on Taxation, *Technical Explanation of the "Job Creation and Worker Assistance Act of 2002"* (JCX-12-02), March 6, 2002).

> **Example (3).** An item of 5-year property placed in service in 2002 costs $100,000. The taxpayer expenses $20,000 of the cost under Code Sec. 179. The taxpayer's bonus depreciation is $24,000 ($80,000 × 30%). The depreciable basis after reduction by the Code Sec. 179 expense allowance and bonus depreciation is $56,000 ($100,000 − $20,000 − $24,000).

This required order of allocation will reduce the size of the bonus depreciation claimed on an asset with respect to which a Code Sec. 179 expense allowance is claimed. If bonus depreciation could be calculated prior to reduction by any amount expensed under Code Sec. 179, the bonus depreciation would have been $30,000 ($100,000 × 30%) rather than $24,000.

Planning Note. Taxpayers should continue to expense assets with the longest recovery (depreciation) period in order to accelerate the recovery of their costs. For example, given the choice of expensing the cost of 20-year property or 3-year property, the Code Sec. 179 expense allowance should be allocated to the 20-year property since the full cost of the 3-year property will be recovered in three years.

Acquisition and placed-in-service dates. Property cannot qualify for the special allowance unless each of the following three requirements is met (Code Sec. 168(k)(2)(A)):

(1) The original use of the property must commence with the taxpayer after September 10, 2001.

Comment. The original use requirement prevents used property from qualifying. The Joint Committee on Taxation indicates that the factors used in determining whether property qualified as "new section 38 property" for purposes of the investment tax credit apply in determining whether the property is original use property. These factors are contained in Reg. § 1.48-2. Under these guidelines additional capital expenditures incurred to recondition or rebuild property satisfy the original use requirement. However, the cost of reconditioned or rebuilt property acquired by the taxpayer does not satisfy the requirement.

> **Example (4).** Al Stevens, a taxpayer, purchases a used machine after September 10, 2001, for $50,000. Stevens then pays $20,000 to recondition the machine. No part of the $50,000 cost qualifies for additional depreciation. However, the $20,000 expenditure (assuming that it is capitalized) will qualify.

A limited exception to the original use requirement applies to sale-leasebacks. The rule applies to property that is originally placed in service after September 10, 2001, by a person who sells it to the taxpayer and then leases it from the taxpayer

¶ 305

within three months after the date that the property was originally placed in service. In this situation, the property is treated as originally placed in service by the taxpayer and the placed-in-service date is deemed to occur no earlier than the date that the property is used under the leaseback (Code Sec. 168(k)(2)(D)(ii), as added by the 2002 Act).

(2) The taxpayer must either acquire the property after September 10, 2001, and before September 11, 2004, or acquire the property pursuant to a written binding contract that was entered into after September 10, 2001, and before September 11, 2004 (Code Sec. 168(k)(2)(A)(iii), as added by the 2002 Act).

Comment. Property which is acquired after September 10, 2001, and before September 11, 2004, does *not* qualify if it was acquired pursuant to a written binding contract that was in effect before September 11, 2001.

Property which is manufactured, constructed, or produced by a taxpayer for the taxpayer's own use is considered to meet requirement 2, above, if the taxpayer begins manufacturing, constructing, or producing the property after September 10, 2001, and before September 11, 2004 (Code Sec. 168(k)(2)(D)(i), as added by the 2002 Act). The Joint Committee on Taxation Explanation states that property that is manufactured, constructed, or produced for a taxpayer by another person under a contract that is entered into prior to the manufacture, construction, or production of the property is considered to be manufactured, constructed, or produced by the taxpayer.

(3) The taxpayer must place the property in service before January 1, 2005 (Code Sec. 168(k)(2)(A)(iv), as added by the 2002 Act). However, certain property considered to have a "longer production period" must be placed in service before January 1, 2006 (Code Sec. 168(k)(2)(B), as added by the 2002 Act).

Comment. The date of acquisition of property is not necessarily the date it is placed in service. A property is considered placed in service for depreciation purposes when it is ready and available for use.

Property with longer production periods. The January 1, 2006, placed-in-service date applies to property which:

(1) has a recovery period of at least 10 years or is transportation property;

(2) is subject to the uniform capitalization rules (Code Sec. 263A) because it is considered produced by the taxpayer; and

(3) has a production period exceeding two years, or a production period exceeding one year and a cost exceeding $1 million (Code Sec. 168(k)(2)(B), as added by the 2002 Act).

Transportation property is defined as tangible personal property used in the trade or business of transporting persons for hire, for example, a passenger aircraft (Code Sec. 168(k)(2)(B)(iii), as added by the 2002 Act).

Although a January 1, 2006, placed-in-service date applies to property with longer production periods, the 30-percent additional depreciation allowance applies only to the adjusted basis of the property attributable to manufacture, construction, or production before September 11, 2004 (Code Sec. 168(k)(2)(B)(ii), as added by the 2002 Act). The Joint Committee on Taxation Explanation refers to these amounts as "progress expenditures." According to the JCT, it is intended that rules similar to Code Sec. 46(d)(3) (relating to the former investment tax credit) as in effect prior to the Tax Reform Act of 1986 will apply for purposes of determining the amount of progress expenditures.

Mandatory ADS property does not qualify. Property which must be depreciated using the MACRS alternative depreciation system (ADS) does not qualify for bonus depreciation. However, property that a taxpayer elects to depreciate using ADS is not disqualified (Code Sec. 168(k)(2)(C), as added by the 2002 Act).

Comment. Subject to an exception for qualifying leasehold improvements and water utility property, the 30-percent allowance is only allowed for MACRS property with a "recovery period" of 20 years or less (Code Sec. 168(k)(2)(A)(i)(I)). It was probably the intent of Congress that the 20-year period would only be tested against the MACRS general depreciation system (GDS) recovery period (i.e., the regular recovery period). A technical correction may be necessary to clarify that if a taxpayer elects ADS then the election will not disqualify a property even though the ADS recovery period for the property is greater than 20 years so long as the GDS recovery period for the property is 20 years or less. Note that any property with a GDS recovery period of 20 years will have an ADS recovery period greater than 20 years. A few types of property with a 15-year recovery period have an ADS recovery period of 20 years or greater.

The following property must be depreciated using ADS and, therefore, does not qualify for bonus depreciation:

(1) tangible property used predominantly outside of the United States during the tax year;

(2) tax-exempt use property;

(3) tax-exempt bond-financed property; and

(4) property imported from a foreign country for which an Executive Order is in effect because the country maintains trade restrictions or engages in other discriminatory acts (Code Sec. 168(g)(1)).

If "listed property," such as a car, must be depreciated using ADS in the first year that it is placed in service because it is not predominantly used in a qualified business use, then bonus depreciation may not be claimed (Code Sec. 168(k)(2)(C)(i)(II), as added by the 2002 Act). Because the additional depreciation allowance is treated as depreciation, it would be subject to recapture under the listed property rules if business use fell to 50 percent or lower in a tax year after it was placed in service (Code Sec. 168(k)(2)(E)(ii), as added by the 2002 Act).

Comment. As defined in Code Sec. 280F(d)(4), listed property includes any passenger automobile, any other property used as a means of transportation, any property of a type generally used for purposes of entertainment, recreation, or amusement, any computer or peripheral equipment, any cellular telephone (or similar telecommunications equipment), and certain other property specified in regulations.

Qualified leasehold improvement property. The additional depreciation allowance may be claimed on "qualified leasehold improvement property." Qualified leasehold improvement property is any improvement to an interior portion of nonresidential real property made under or pursuant to a lease by the lessee, sublessee, or lessor. The improvement must be placed in service more than three years after the date the building was first placed in service. In addition, the interior of the building must be occupied exclusively by the lessee or sublessee (Code Sec. 168(k)(3), as added by the 2002 Act).

¶ 305

Comment. The law does not say that three years must pass after the building was first placed in service "*by the taxpayer.*" The requirement appears aimed at newly constructed buildings.

Expenditures for (1) the enlargement of a building, (2) any elevator or escalator, (3) any structural component that benefits a common area, or (4) the internal structural framework of a building are not considered qualified leasehold improvement property.

A commitment to enter into a lease is treated as a lease, with the parties to the commitment treated as the lessor and lessee.

The lease may not be between related persons. Members of an affiliated group (as defined in Code Sec. 1504) are related persons. Persons with a relationship described in Code Sec. 267(b) are related persons. However, the phrase "80 percent or more" is substituted in each place that the phrase "more than 50 percent" appears.

Qualified New York Liberty Zone leasehold improvement property does not qualify for the 30-percent additional depreciation allowance. However, this property does qualify for a reduced recovery period of five years (Code Sec. 168(k)(2)(C)(ii) and Code Sec. 1400L, as added by the 2002 Act). See ¶ 425.

Election out of bonus depreciation. Bonus depreciation must be claimed unless a taxpayer makes an election out. The election out is made at the property class level. The election out applies to all property in the class or classes for which the election out is made that is placed in service for the tax year of the election (Code Sec. 168(k)(2)(C)(iii), as added by the 2002 Act). The new law provides no other details regarding the election out.

Comment. Property class refers to the 3-, 5-, 7-, 10-, 15-, and 20-year asset classifications. For example, a taxpayer may make the election out for all 3-year property placed in service in the tax year. The election out cannot be made for some, but not all, 3-year property placed in service during the tax year. Similarly, the election out may be made for all qualifying software placed in service during a tax year and all water utility property placed in service during a tax year.

Computer software. The special depreciation allowance applies to computer software as defined in Code Sec. 167(f)(1)(B) for which a deduction is allowable under Code Sec. 167(a) without regard to the bonus depreciation allowance allowed under Code Sec. 168(k) (Code Sec. 168(k)(2)(A)(i)(II), as added by the 2002 Act). Software amortized over 15 years under Code Sec. 197 does not qualify for additional depreciation.

Increase in first-year luxury car depreciation caps. The new law increases the first-year Code Sec. 280F depreciation cap by $4,600 for passenger automobiles that qualify for bonus depreciation (Code Sec. 168(k)(2)(E)(i), as added by the 2002 Act). The first-year cap without regard to the increase is $3,060 for cars placed in service in 2001 and 2002. The Joint Committee on Taxation indicates that the $4,600 figure is not adjusted for inflation. Thus, as increased, the first-year cap is $7,660 ($3,060 + $4,600).

Comment. Since the increased cap applies only to a passenger automobile which is "qualified property," a vehicle must be acquired after September 10, 2001, and placed in service before January 1, 2005, in order to obtain the benefit of the $4,600 increase. Also, bonus depreciation must be claimed on the vehicle—the increase is not available if the election out is made. See definition of qualified property, above.

Planning Note. Prior to the increase, a car needed to cost only $15,300 before the $3,060 first-year cap was triggered ($15,300 × 20% = $3,060), assuming that the half-year convention applies. A car that is eligible for the increased $7,660 cap may now cost as much as $17,409 before that cap is triggered.

Example (5). A car (MACRS 5-year property) costing $17,409 is placed in service in December 2001. Assume that the half-year convention applies, that the vehicle is used 100% for business, and no amount is expensed under Code Sec. 179. Bonus depreciation is $5,223 ($17,409 × 30%). Regular depreciation is $2,437 (($17,409 − $5,223) × 20% (first-year table percentage)). The sum of bonus and regular depreciation is $7,660 ($5,223 + $2,437 = $7,660), the same as the first-year cap.

Example (6). A car costing $35,000 is placed in service in December 2001 and used 100% for business purposes. No amount is expensed under Code Sec. 179. Assume that the half-year convention applies. Bonus depreciation for 2001 is $10,500 ($35,000 × 30%). Regular first-year depreciation is $4,900 (($35,000 − $10,500) × 20%). Since the sum of the first-year regular and bonus depreciation deductions ($15,400) exceeds the first-year cap, depreciation is limited to the first-year cap of $7,660. The $7,740 excess ($15,400 − $7,660) may only be recovered after the regular recovery period ends at the rate of $1,775 per year. See Background section, above.

Comment. Under present law, the depreciation caps are tripled for electric vehicles. It is not entirely clear from the legislative language whether the $4,600 figure is tripled for electric vehicles, but this approach would probably be consistent with legislative intent.

Alternative minimum tax. The additional depreciation allowance may be claimed for alternative minimum tax purposes in the year that qualifying property is placed in service. No AMT adjustment is required. (Code Sec. 168(k)(2)(F), as added by the 2002 Act; Joint Committee on Taxation, *Technical Explanation of the "Job Creation and Worker Assistance Act of 2002"* (JCX-12-02), March 6, 2002).

Planning Note. The full amount of the additional depreciation allowance is claimed whether or not the mid-quarter convention applies. Also, in determining whether more than 40 percent of the property's basis is placed in service in the last three months of a tax year so as to make the mid-quarter convention applicable, it does not appear that the basis of any property is reduced by the additional depreciation allowance.

PRACTICAL ANALYSIS. George A. Luscombe of Mayer, Brown, Rowe & Maw, Chicago, Illinois, notes that the additional first year depreciation allowance reduces the after-tax cost of investing in new equipment by increasing the present value of capital recovery allowances. Taxpayers subject to the alternative minimum tax (AMT) can obtain the benefit of the increased allowance against alternative minimum taxable income, although at the lower AMT rate.

For taxpayers who cannot use the increased allowance or who are subject to the AMT, the benefits of leasing are increased. The increased allowance can be used by lessors in leasing transactions. The increased capital recovery allowances make a leasing transaction more profitable since there are more rapid depreciation allowances that can be priced into the transaction for the benefit of the lessee. A sale and leaseback can be accomplished with respect to property already placed in service by the lessee if the sale and leaseback is consummated within the three-month window. Otherwise, a sale and leaseback cannot result in the lessor being eligible for the increased allowance, since used property does not qualify. Lessees and lessors can now accomplish sales and leasebacks on assets placed in service before the enactment of the provisions provided there is compliance with the three-month rule, since the allowance applies to property placed in service after September 10, 2001.

Even though the increased allowance applies to certain nonstructural leasehold improvements, it is still better for a lessee to negotiate to have the build-out constructed by the lessor, or to structure a build-out allowance to qualify for the exclusion contained in Code Sec. 110.

While the new allowance provides an increased incentive to invest in new equipment and other qualified property, the incentive probably will only affect decisions at the margin. The added benefit may cause a taxpayer to buy new property when the economics of the decision are close to the margin. However, there will be an incentive in 2004 to accelerate purchases of new equipment before the new allowance terminates for equipment that would have been purchased anyway. This may result in an acceleration of equipment orders in early 2004, followed by a drop-off in orders in late 2004 and in 2005.

★ *Effective date.* The provision applies to property placed in service after September 10, 2001, in tax years ending after such date (Act Sec. 101(b) of the Job Creation and Worker Assistance Act of 2002 (P.L. 107-147)).

Act Sec. 101(a) of the Job Creation and Worker Assistance Act of 2002, adding Code Sec. 168(k); Act Sec. 101(b). Law at ¶ 5095. Committee Report at ¶ 10,010.

NET OPERATING LOSSES

Carryback Period Extended to Five Years

¶ 310

Background ————————————————————————————————

A taxpayer has a net operating loss (NOL) if certain deductions exceed gross income in a particular tax year (Code Sec. 172(c)). The taxpayer may be able to carry back or carry over this amount to the extent the loss was incurred in a trade or business, from a casualty loss, or from a loss on the sale of depreciable property or real estate used in a trade or business (Code Sec. 172).

An NOL can be carried back to the two years immediately preceding the loss year (three years for certain casualty and theft losses, and NOLs of small business taxpayers and farmers attributable to presidentially declared disasters). An NOL can be carried over for up to 20 years (Code Sec. 172(b)(1) and (i)). The entire NOL is carried to the earliest year and, if not completely used to offset income in

Background

that year, is applied to succeeding years until it is used up or expires (Code Sec. 172(b)(2)). Taxpayers can elect to forgo the applicable carryback period and only deduct the NOL in future years during the 20-year carryover period (Code Sec. 172(b)(3)).

Special NOL computations are required for taxpayers subject to the alternative minimum tax (AMT). When applying an NOL to a particular tax year, the taxpayer must calculate the AMT by taking an adjusted NOL amount against AMT income (AMTI). NOL deductions against AMTI are limited to no more than 90 percent of AMTI calculated without reference to the NOL (Code Sec. 56(d)).

Job Creation Act Impact

Five-year NOL carryback allowed.—For net operating losses (NOLs) arising in tax years ending in 2001 and 2002, the two- and three-year carryback periods are extended to five years (Code Sec. 172(b)(1)(H), as added by the Job Creation and Worker Assistance Act of 2002 (P.L. 107-147)). For each applicable tax year, a taxpayer can make an irrevocable election to waive the five-year period and adhere to the existing carryback periods (Code Sec. 172(j), as added by the 2002 Act). With respect to the alternative minimum tax (AMT), the limit on NOL deductions from AMT income is increased from 90 percent of AMT income to 100 percent for NOLs generated or taken as carryforwards in tax years ending in 2001 and 2002 (see below).

Under the new law, taxpayers now must determine which one of the three carryback and carryover rules applies to their NOLs, as illustrated in the following chart.

NOLs arising in tax years	*General carryback*	*General carryover*
beginning before 8/6/97 (and certain casualty, theft and disaster-related losses)	3 years	15 years
beginning after 8/5/97 and ending before 12/31/00	2 years	20 years
ending after 12/31/00 and before 1/1/03	5 years	20 years

Election. The taxpayer must make the election to waive the extended five-year carryback period by the due date, including extensions, for filing the taxpayer's return for the tax year of the NOL. The procedures for making the election will be set forth by the IRS (Code Sec. 172(j), as added by the 2002 Act).

Planning Note. Although the election not to take advantage of the extended carryback rule could mean postponement of the NOL deduction, electing to waive the benefit of the new rule can make sense for some taxpayers. Here are some considerations.

(1) Taxpayers may want to avoid carrying back NOLs to years in which their tax rates were relatively low since the NOLs may be more valuable in future years if the taxpayer anticipates being in a higher tax bracket in the future.

(2) Taxpayers need to consider the adverse effects of carryback NOLs on deductions, exemptions, and credits that are limited by taxable or adjusted gross income. The reduction of income in a tax year caused by a carryback NOL deduction could result in reduced deductions for IRA contributions

(Code Sec. 219) or for passive activity losses from real estate activities (Code Sec. 469(i)). The additional deduction might trigger the overall itemized deductions limits (Code Sec. 68). Any reduction in taxable income caused by the NOL might result in a lower business tax credit (Code Sec. 38(c)).

(3) Taxpayers should also consider the positive effects that the reduction of income might have on other income-sensitive tax attributes. For example, a reduction of income could reduce taxable social security and tier 1 railroad retirement benefits (Code Sec. 86). It could also reduce the phaseout of tax savings on excludable savings bond interest (Code Sec. 135), employer-provided adoption benefits (Code Sec. 137), and student loan interest (Code Sec. 221). An NOL carryback could increase deductions for medical expenses (Code Sec. 213), casualty losses (Code Sec. 165(h)), and certain miscellaneous itemized deductions (Code Sec. 68). An earned income tax credit might become available or increase due to lower income (Code Sec. 32).

(4) Taxpayers may need to weigh the benefits of carrybacks against the benefits of carryovers for some deductions. Certain deductions limited by income do not take into account NOL carrybacks in calculating the income limit and, hence, treat carrybacks favorably compared to carryovers. For example, charitable deductions are limited to a percentage of adjusted gross income for individuals, and calculation of income for purposes of the deduction limit is done without reference to a carryback NOL (Code Sec. 170(b) and (d)), making the carryback potentially more valuable than a carryover. Depletion allowances are treated similarly (Code Sec. 613A).

Example (1). Sam Johnson has a $100,000 NOL in 2001. In 1996 through 2000, he had $40,000, $35,000, $25,000, $35,000, and $40,000 in adjusted gross income each year, respectively. Under the two-year carryback rule, he could apply $75,000 (subject to AMT) of his NOL to his income in 1999 and 2000 and carry over the rest. Under the new law, he can apply $100,000 (subject to AMT) against his income in 1996 through 1998. Sam decides not to elect to waive the five-year carryback since the new rule allows him to file immediately for a refund based on the full $100,000 of NOL, and it leaves plenty of room to claim subsequent NOLs for 1999 and 2000.

PRACTICAL ANALYSIS. Vincent O'Brien, President of Vincent J. O'Brien, CPA, P.C., Lynbrook, New York, observes that the new provision does not permanently alter the existing NOL rules that generally permit a carryback of two years and a carryforward of 20 years; rather, it provides only a temporary reprieve from it. NOLs that occur in tax years *ending* in 2001 and 2002 can be carried back for five years, instead of the standard two years. For calendar year taxpayers, the rules will affect their 2001 and 2002 returns.

This provision may be useful for taxpayers that have experienced economic difficulties due to the economic downturn. However, it will only be useful if a taxpayer had taxable income during the five-year period occurring before the year in which the NOL occurs. For taxpayers that did not conduct business in these earlier years or that had no taxable income for five or more of the past tax years, the temporary NOL provisions will not be helpful. Nevertheless, these taxpayers can still carry the NOLs forward for up to 20 years.

¶ **310**

The new provision does not change the ability to elect out of carrying back an NOL. As in the past, taxpayers can irrevocably elect to forego the carryback of an NOL and choose instead to carry the entire NOL forward. In addition, the new provision adds an additional election: Taxpayers can forego the five-year carryback and instead use the standard two-year carryback. This election is also irrevocable.

It is important to note that the new provision does not affect NOLs that were created in tax years that ended prior to January 1, 2001. Thus, for example, if a taxpayer had an NOL in 2000 that exceeded its 1998 and 1999 taxable income, the excess NOL cannot be carried back to any earlier year. Only a new NOL occurring in 2001 or 2002 can be carried back for the five-year period.

It is unlikely that this new provision will result in any procedural changes to obtain refunds resulting from an NOL carryback. Generally, taxpayers can obtain refunds by filing amended returns for the year(s) to which the carryback will be made or by filing an application for a tentative carryback adjustment. In the near future, the IRS may issue guidance to review and clarify these procedures.

Alternative minimum tax. An alternative tax net operating loss (ATNOL) is based on the Code Sec. 172 NOL, with certain adjustments (Code Sec. 56(d)). Under the new law, the ATNOL deduction based on NOLs generated or taken as carryforwards in tax years ending in 2001 and 2002 is limited to 100 percent of AMT income instead of 90 percent (Code Sec. 56(b)(1)(A), as amended by the 2002 Act). More specifically, the new law provides that the ATNOL deduction is limited to the sum of (1) the lesser of (a) the amount of the NOL deduction attributable to NOLs other than NOLs generated or taken as carryforwards in tax years ending in 2001 and 2002 (ordinary NOLs), or (b) 90 percent of the alternative minimum tax income (AMTI) determined without regard to the ATNOL, plus (2) the lesser of (a) NOLs attributable to tax years ending in 2001 and 2002 (special NOLs), and (b) the AMTI determined without regard to the ATNOL deduction reduced by the amount determined in (1) above (Code Sec. 56(b)(1)(a), as amended by the 2002 Act). In short, the ATNOL deduction is the sum of ordinary (non-2001 or 2002) NOLs subject to a limit of 90 percent of AMTI, plus the special (2001 and 2002) NOLs subject to a limit of 100 percent of AMTI.

> **Example (2).** In 1996, Rogers, Inc. had $100,000 in AMTI, against which it had taken $89,000 in ATNOLs. In 2001, Rogers generated an NOL of $50,000, which it wanted to carry back to 1996 under Code Sec. 172. Under the old ATNOL rules, Rogers' total ATNOL deduction would have been limited to 90 percent of its AMTI (90 percent of $100,000, or $90,000), so its 2001 NOL for AMT purposes would be limited to $1,000 ($90,000 − $89,000). However, under the new ATNOL rules providing special treatment for NOLs generated in tax years ending in 2001 and 2002, Rogers can carry back $11,000. The ATNOL deduction limit would be the lower of (i) the ordinary NOLs in 1996 ($89,000) or (ii) 90 percent of AMTI ($90,000), which is $89,000, plus the lower of (i) the special NOLs ($50,000) or (ii) AMTI minus the first figure ($100,000 − $89,000), which is $11,000. $89,000 plus $11,000 equals $100,000, so that is the ATNOL deduction limit for 1996. Under the new AMT rule, Rogers can, therefore, carry back $11,000 ($100,000 − $89,000) of its 2001 NOL to 1996.

PRACTICAL ANALYSIS. George A. Luscombe of Mayer, Brown, Rowe & Maw, Chicago, Illinois, observes that extending the net operating loss carryback from two to five years will enable taxpayers to obtain increased refunds due to NOL carrybacks. The flexibility of electing not to carryback five years, but to carryback two years, will allow taxpayers added flexibility to obtain some carryback benefit without losing the benefit of tax credits that were used in prior years. Some tax credits (for example, Code Sec. 29 tax credits) cannot be carried forward if the taxpayer does not have sufficient regular tax liability to use the credits in the year produced. Careful planning is essential in deciding whether to make the decision not to carryback the NOL.

★ *Effective date.* The amendments made by the new law apply to NOLs for tax years ending after December 31, 2000, except for the amendments to Code Sec. 56(d)(1)(A) regarding AMT which are effective for tax years ending before January 1, 2003 (Act Sec. 102(d) of the Job Creation and Worker Assistance Act of 2002 (P.L. 107-147)).

Act Sec. 102(a) of the Job Creation and Worker Assistance Act 2002, adding Code Sec. 172(b)(1)(H); Act Sec. 102(b), redesignating Code Sec. 172(j) as Code Sec. 172(k) and adding new Code Sec. 172(j); Act Sec. 102(c), amending Code Sec. 56(d)(1)(A); Act Sec. 102(d). Law at ¶ 5060 and ¶ 5105. Committee Report at ¶ 10,020.

S CORPORATION SHAREHOLDERS

Discharge of Indebtedness of an S Corporation

¶ 315

Background

On January 9, 2001, in an eight-to-one decision, the United States Supreme Court held that cancellation of indebtedness (COD) income is an "item of income" that passes through to S corporation shareholders to increase their basis in their S corporation stock (*Gitlitz v. Commissioner*, 2001-1 USTC ¶ 50,147, 121 SCt 701 (2001)). Although COD is usually included in gross income, Code Sec. 108(a) provides an exception. Under the plain language of Code Sec. 108(a), COD is not included in gross income when an S corporation is insolvent. However, the COD income remains an item of income.

The Supreme Court concluded that COD income is passed through to S corporation shareholders before it is used to reduce the S corporation's tax attributes. As a result, shareholders are able to deduct losses up to the amount of their stock basis that has been increased by the COD income. Any suspended loss that remains is treated as corporate net operating loss and reduced by the discharged debt amount. The Court emphasized this point by stating "Section 108(b)(4)(A) expressly addresses the sequencing question, directing that the attribute reductions shall be made after the determination of the tax imposed . . . for the taxable year of the discharge."

Background

The *Gitlitz* case originated when, in 1991, an insolvent S corporation, in which petitioners David Gitlitz and Philip Winn were shareholders, excluded its entire cancellation of indebtedness amount from gross income. In filing their tax returns, Gitlitz and Winn used their pro rata shares of the discharged amount to increase their basis in the corporation's stock on the theory that it was an "item of income," under Code Secs. 1366 and 1367, subject to passthrough. With their increased basis they were able to deduct their pro rata shares of corporate losses and deductions, including suspended losses and deductions from previous years. The IRS determined that they could not use the corporation's COD income to increase their stock basis and denied their loss deductions. The Tax Court ultimately agreed. In affirming the Tax Court, the Tenth Circuit assumed that excluded COD income is an income item subject to passthrough, but held that the discharge amount must first be used to reduce certain tax attributes of the S corporation under Code Sec. 108(b). Only the leftover amount could be used to increase shareholder basis. Because the tax attribute to be reduced (the corporation's net operating loss) equaled the debt amount that was cancelled, that entire amount was absorbed by the reduction at the corporate level. Nothing remained to be passed through to the shareholders. The Supreme Court reversed the Tenth Circuit, stating that COD income does increase S corporation shareholder basis and this increased basis can be used by shareholders to deduct suspended losses and deductions.

Justice Breyer, in the Supreme Court's single dissenting opinion, interpreted Code Sec. 108(d)(7)(A) to limit both the COD exclusion and the tax attribute reduction to the corporate level, concluding that COD income does not flow through to S corporation shareholders, nor does it increase shareholder basis in S corporation stock to help shareholders take "otherwise unavailable deductions for suspended losses." The dissent pointed out that the majority's interpretation ignored the policy consequences and stated that arguments from the plain text on both sides produce ambiguity, not certainty. He noted that "other things being equal, we should read ambiguous statutes as closing, not maintaining tax loopholes."

Job Creation Act Impact

COD income of an S corporation and stock basis.—The provision reverses the Supreme Court's decision in *Gitlitz*. Income from the discharge of indebtedness of an S corporation that is excluded from the corporation's income under Code Sec. 108(a) is not taken into account as an item of income that flows through to any shareholder under Code Sec. 1366(a) (Code Sec. 108(d)(7)(A), as amended by the Job Creation and Worker Assistance Act of 2002 (P.L. 107-147)). Thus, a shareholder's basis in S corporation stock does not increase and the corporation's suspended loss does not pass through to the shareholder. The tax consequences now reflect the economics of the situation and an S corporation shareholder will no longer be allowed to deduct a loss that it did not economically incur.

Comment. The report of the Joint Committee on Taxation (*Technical Explanation of the "Job Creation and Worker Assistance Act of 2002"* (JCX-12-02), March 6, 2002) indicates that this provision closes a perceived loophole that allowed shareholders a deduction for an amount of loss that was not economically borne by the shareholders. The Committee's reasoning reflected the language from the dissent in *Gitlitz.*

¶ 315

PRACTICAL ANALYSIS. Michael Schlesinger of Schlesinger & Sussman, New York, New York, points out that Congress' amendment to Code Sec. 108 accomplishes two things: (1) it will raise $1 billion and (2) it establishes an economic reality in Code Sec. 108. To illustrate the economic reality aspect, the Joint Committee on Taxation Explanation sets forth the following example:

"[A]ssume that a sole shareholder of an S corporation has zero basis in its stock of the corporation. The S corporation borrows $100 from a third party and loses the entire $100. Because the shareholder has no basis in its stock, the $100 is 'suspended' at the corporate level. If the $100 debt is forgiven when the corporation is in bankruptcy or is insolvent, the $100 income from the discharge of indebtedness is excluded from income, and the $100 'suspended' loss should be eliminated in order to achieve a tax result that is consistent with the economics of the transactions in that the shareholder has no economic gain or loss from these transactions."

Accordingly, Code Sec. 108's amendment now places S corporations on a par with partnerships. In a partnership, a partner's basis is increased by the partner's share of discharge of indebtedness income; then, simultaneously, the partner's basis is decreased by the same amount pursuant to Code Sec. 752.

Congress has decided not to make the amendment to Code Sec. 108 retroactive to the date *D.A. Gitlitz*, 531 US 206 (2001), was decided. Consequently, shareholders relying on *Gitlitz* who have placed funds in an S corporation before Congress considered reversing *Gitlitz*, or creditors involved in re-structurings who provided funds in contemplation of the tax result set forth in *Gitlitz*, are not prejudiced. However, not allowing S corporation shareholders the *Gitlitz* break for future insolvency situations probably will cause the early demise of S corporations that are having, or can expect, credit problems.

As for pending cases prior to Code Sec. 108's amendment's effective date, most probably, the IRS's position will be to honor *Gitlitz*. When *Gitlitz* was first decided, the IRS, in LTR 200208016, allowed a taxpayer to reverse course because of the recently decided *Gitlitz*. There is no reason to believe that the IRS would make a taxpayer take a different course for cases pending before the effective date of Code Sec. 108's amendment.

★ *Effective date.* In general, the provision applies to discharges of indebtedness after October 11, 2001, in tax years ending after such date. The amendment made by this section shall not apply to any discharge of indebtedness before March 1, 2002, pursuant to a plan of reorganization filed with a bankruptcy court on or before October 11, 2001 (Act Sec. 402(b) of the Job Creation and Worker Assistance Act of 2002 (P.L. 107-147)).

Act Sec. 402(a) of the Job Creation and Worker Assistance Act of 2002, amending Code Sec. 108(d)(7)(A); Act Sec. 402(b). Law at ¶ 5075. Committee Report at ¶ 10,210.

SALES AND EXCHANGES

Election to Recognize Gain on Assets Held on January 1, 2001

¶ 320

Background _____

A noncorporate taxpayer holding a capital asset on January 1, 2001, may elect to treat that asset as having been both sold and reacquired on that date for an amount equal to its fair market value (Act Sec. 311(e) of the Taxpayer Relief Act of 1997 (P.L. 105-34)). The benefit to the taxpayer from such an election is that the holding period for the asset begins after December 31, 2000, making the asset eligible for the lower 18-percent capital gain rate under Code Sec. 1(h) for assets held for more than five years and acquired after December 31, 2000. The basis is also stepped up. The negative aspect of the election for the taxpayer is that any gain from the election must be "recognized" notwithstanding any other provision of the Code as of the date the asset is treated as sold.

An election to mark to market under Act Sec. 311(e) arguably can trigger Code Sec. 121 or Code Sec. 469(g)(1)(A), both of which provide taxpayers with significant benefits from a disposition of certain assets.

Code Sec. 121 allows a taxpayer to exclude from gross income up to $250,000 ($500,000 for certain jointly filed returns) of gain realized on the sale or exchange of property owned and used as the taxpayer's principal residence. The question arose as to whether a taxpayer making an Act Sec. 311(e) election for his or her residence can use Code Sec. 121 to shelter the gain from the January 1, 2001 deemed sale.

Code Sec. 469(g)(1)(A) provides favorable tax treatment for taxpayers in the year they dispose of a passive activity. Passive activities include any rental activity and any activity that involves the conduct of a trade or business in which the taxpayer does not materially participate. Normally, passive activity losses can be offset only against passive activity gains, and unused losses from a passive activity are suspended until a tax year in which there is income from a passive activity (Code Sec. 469(b)). An exception is made under Code Sec. 469(g)(1)(A) for the tax year in which the taxpayer disposes of his or her entire interest in a passive activity or a former passive activity in a taxable disposition. Under this provision, a taxpayer can take all of his or her suspended losses against passive or nonpassive income. These provisions raise the question whether a deemed sale under the Act Sec. 311(e) election is a disposition triggering Code Sec. 469(g)(1)(A) so that the taxpayer can take suspended losses in 2001 even though the taxpayer will continue the passive activity.

Technical Corrections Impact

Treatment of gain from residence and disposition of interest in passive activity.—The Job Creation and Worker Assistance Act of 2002 (P.L. 107-147) clarifies the application of the January 1, 2001, mark-to-market election for purposes of the capital gain rules by substituting "included in gross income" for "recognized" (Act Sec. 311(e)(2)(A) of the Taxpayer Relief Act of 1997 (P.L. 105-34), as amended by the 2002 Act). It is now clear that gain resulting from an Act Sec. 311(e) election with respect to a taxpayer's residence is included in gross income notwithstanding any other Code provision. This means that the exclusion of gain on a sale of a principal residence under Code Sec. 121 does not apply in the case of an Act Sec. 311(e) election. This clarification is consistent with the IRS' interpretation of the mark-to-market election as expressed in Rev. Rul. 2001-57, I.R.B. 2001-46, 488, October 30, 2001.

Suspended passive activity losses. The 2002 Act provides that the suspended loss rules of Code Sec. 469(g)(1)(A) shall not apply by reason of an Act Sec. 311(e) election (Act Sec. 311(e)(5) of P.L. 105-34, as added by the 2002 Act). Accordingly, a taxpayer making an Act Sec. 311(e), January 1, 2001, mark-to-market election for an interest in a passive activity cannot take suspended losses by reason of the deemed disposition of the passive activity interest.

Comment. Taxpayers still deciding whether to make the Act Sec. 311(e) election for a particular asset have to weigh the future savings resulting from lower capital gains rates against the cost of paying tax on the built-in gain as of January 1, 2001. The corrections imposed by the 2002 Act shift the balance away from making the election for a taxpayer's residence or passive activity interest and may require the filing of an amended 2001 return.

The availability of the Code Sec. 121 exclusion for gain from the sale of a residence made the Act Sec. 311(e) mark-to-market election very attractive for a taxpayer's home, not only because it would have reduced or eliminated capital gains tax on the gain in 2001 from the deemed sale, but also because the taxpayer could use the Code Sec. 121 exclusion again in a future tax year when the taxpayer actually sold the house.

Although, in Rev. Rul. 2001-57, the IRS adopted the position that Code Sec. 121 does not apply to such deemed sale gain, that ruling was sure to be challenged and taxpayers had reason to hope Code Sec. 121 would be available despite the ruling. Now, however, with the correction to Act Sec. 311(e) of P.L. 105-34, it is clear that taxpayers should not make an Act Sec. 311(e) election with the idea that the built-in gain will be sheltered by Code Sec. 121.

Example (1). Martha and Joseph Jefferson buy a principal residence in 1998 worth $1 million. As of January 1, 2001, the home is worth $1.5 million. They make the Act Sec. 311(e) election, recognize $500,000 in gain, and step up their basis to $1.5 million. Although Code Sec. 121 can shelter up to $500,000 from the sale of a principal residence, Code Sec. 121 is unavailable to shelter gain resulting from an Act Sec. 311(e) election. Accordingly, the Jeffersons will have to pay capital gains tax on the $500,000 they recognize from the deemed sale in 2001.

Comment. Another situation in which taxpayers seemed able to have their cake and eat it too applied to taxpayers with suspended passive activity losses. Under Code Sec. 469(g)(1)(A), a taxpayer who makes a complete disposition of the passive activity can take suspended passive activity losses first against that year's passive income, next against nonpassive activity income. If an Act Sec. 311(e) election triggered Code Sec. 469(g)(1)(A), the taxpayer could have taken the suspended losses in 2001, even though the taxpayer was deemed to have immediately reacquired the passive activity interest.

Example (2). Janine Wellington owns a partnership interest in an oil well, which is classified as a passive activity. On January 1, 2001, her interest had a fair market value of $10,000, a basis of $5,000, and suspended losses of $8,000. In 2001, she had $1,000 in passive income from another passive activity. If Wellington makes an Act Sec. 311(e) election, she would recognize a $5,000 gain. However, if Code Sec. 469(g)(1)(A) would have been triggered by this deemed sale, Wellington could have applied her $8,000 in suspended passive losses in 2001 as follows: the first $5,000 against her $5,000 gain from the sale of her oil well interest, the next $1,000 against her other income from her other passive activity, and the next $2,000 against her wage income. Since it is now clear that the Act Sec. 311(e) election does not trigger Code Sec. 469(g)(1)(A), Wellington must simply pay tax on her $5,000 gain from the deemed sale and hold her suspended losses for a future year.

PRACTICAL ANALYSIS. Mark Luscombe, Principal Analyst for the Federal and State Tax Group at CCH INCORPORATED, Riverwoods, Illinois, observes that the changes in the law with respect to the availability of the deemed sale election, coming in the middle of the filing season for the 2001 calendar year, create a problem for taxpayers who may have already filed their returns contemplating the use of either Code Sec. 121 or Code Sec. 469(g)(1)(A) to avoid taxation as a result of the deemed sale election. Such taxpayers may now want to amend their return to eliminate the deemed sale election since the premise upon which the election was made is no longer valid due to a change in the tax law. However, once the deemed sale election is made, it is irrevocable. Taxpayers who have already filed returns making the election would not appear to be allowed to back out of that election due to the change in the tax law. This is likely to leave taxpayers trapped in paying a capital gain tax that they had at least some expectation of avoiding.

The IRS is probably not likely to be too sympathetic since it probably views the law changes as clarifications of existing law, not unforeseeable changes in the law. On the Code Sec. 121 issue, the IRS can point to the position taken in Rev. Rul. 2001-57. Taxpayers generally had been well advised, if filing returns early, to file the returns without the election since they could be amended until October 15, 2002, to add the election, and even without the law change, waiting provided the advantage of flexibility and hindsight at a cost of only some additional filing expense. Hopefully, therefore, few taxpayers will find themselves facing this predicament.

★ *Effective date.* These changes are effective for tax years ending after May 6, 1997 (Act Sec. 414(b) of the Job Creation and Worker Assistance Act of 2002 (P.L. 107-147); Act Sec. 311(d) of the Taxpayer Relief Act of 1997 (P.L. 105-34)).

Act Sec. 414(a) of the Job Creation and Worker Assistance Act of 2002, amending Act Sec. 311(e) of the Taxpayer Relief Act of 1997; Act Sec. 414(b). Law at ¶ 7070. Committee Report at ¶ 10,300.

Securities Futures Contracts

¶ 325

Background ————————————————————————————

A securities futures contract is defined as a contract of sale for future delivery of a single security or a narrow-based security index (Code Sec. 1234B(c); section 3(a)(55)(A) of the Securities and Exchange Act of 1934, as in effect on December

Background

21, 2000). These contracts are sometimes referred to as single stock futures. Although not yet available, it is expected that securities futures contracts will be traded on the Chicago Board Options Exchange and the Chicago Mercantile Exchange in the near future after the rules for trading have been finalized.

Gain or loss on the sale or exchange of a securities futures contract generally would be treated in the same manner and would have the same character as gain or loss from the sale or exchange of the underlying security (Code Sec. 1234B(a)(1); IRS Publication 550, Investment Income and Expenses (Including Capital Gains and Losses) (2001)). Thus, if the underlying security was a capital asset, gain or loss on the sale or exchange of the securities futures contract would be treated as capital gain or loss. Any capital gain or loss on a sale or exchange of a securities futures contract to sell property would be considered short term, regardless of how long the contract was held (Code Sec. 1234B(b)). Special rules apply to *dealer* securities futures contracts (Code Sec. 1256).

In the case of the termination of a securities futures contract, however, any gain or loss attributable to the termination would be treated by reference to the status of the contract, rather than the underlying security, in the hands of the taxpayer. Thus, gain or loss from the termination of a securities futures contract would be treated as capital gain or loss if the contract was a capital asset in the hands of the taxpayer (Code Sec. 1234A).

Under the short sale rules, gain or loss is not realized until property is delivered to close the short sale. If the property used to close the short sale is a capital asset, then the gain or loss is treated as capital gain or loss. In general, whether the gain or loss on the short sale is treated as short term or long term depends on the length of time that the property used to close the short sale was held, unless that taxpayer also holds substantially identical property (Code Sec. 1233; IRS Publication 550, Investment Income and Expenses (Including Capital Gains and Losses) (2001)).

Certain short sales are also covered by the wash sale rules. Under these rules, no deduction is allowed for losses realized from the closing of a short sale of stock or securities in a wash sale unless the loss was incurred by a dealer in the ordinary course of business. In general, a wash sale has occurred if, within 30 days before and 30 days after the closing of the short sale, substantially identical stock or securities are sold or another short sale of substantially identical stock or securities is entered into by the taxpayer (Code Sec. 1091; IRS Publication 550, Investment Income and Expenses (Including Capital Gains and Losses) (2001)).

Technical Corrections Impact

Treatment of securities futures contracts clarified.—The tax treatment of securities futures contracts has been clarified in order to treat terminations of contracts and sales and exchanges of contracts in the same manner, to apply the wash sale rules to short sales of securities futures contracts to sell, and to apply the holding period rules for short sales to securities futures contracts to sell. The corrections and clarifications are effective on December 21, 2000 (Act Sec. 412(e) of the Job Creation and Worker Assistance Act of 2002 (P.L. 107-147); Act Sec. 401(j) of the Community Renewal Tax Relief Act of 2000 (P.L. 106-554)).

¶ **325**

Comment. Although the technical corrections and clarifications dealing with securities futures contracts are effective on December 21, 2000, securities futures contracts are not expected to be available for trading until late spring 2002.

Terminations of securities futures contracts. Terminations of securities futures contracts will be treated in the same manner as sales or exchanges of securities futures contracts for purposes of determining the character of any gain or loss. Thus, gain or loss from the termination of a securities futures contract would have the same character that the gain or loss from the sale or exchange of the underlying property would have in the hands of the taxpayer (Code Sec. 1234B(a)(1), as amended by the 2002 Act; Joint Committee on Taxation, *Technical Explanation of the "Job Creation and Worker Assistance Act of 2002"* (JCX-12-02), March 6, 2002).

Where the gain or loss from the termination of a securities futures contract to sell property is considered capital gain or loss, it would be treated as short term (Code Sec. 1234B(b), as amended by the 2002 Act). However, the straddle rules (Code Sec. 1092) and the special holding period rules that apply to short sales, see below, may override short-term treatment.

Wash sale rules. The wash sale rules that apply to the closing of short sales of stock and securities will also be applied to securities futures contracts to *sell* (Code Sec. 1091(e), as amended by the 2002 Act). Thus, loss realized on the sale, exchange or termination of a securities futures contract to sell stock or securities will generally be disallowed if, within 30 days before and 30 days after the date of the sale, exchange or termination:

(1) substantially identical stock or securities were sold;

(2) a short sale of substantially identical stock or securities was entered into; or

(3) another securities futures contract to sell was entered into by the taxpayer (Code Sec. 1091(e), as amended by the 2002 Act; Joint Committee on Taxation, *Technical Explanation of the "Job Creation and Worker Assistance Act of 2002"* (JCX-12-02), March 6, 2002).

Holding period rules for short sales. The 2002 Act clarifies that the entering into of a securities futures contract to *sell* will be treated as a short sale for purposes of the special holding period rules for short sales. The settlement date of the contract will be treated as the closing of the short sale (Code Sec. 1233(e)(2)(E), as added by the 2002 Act). Although the short sale rules generally treat gain or loss on the short sale as short term or long term depending on the length of time that the property actually used to close the short sale was held, special rules apply where the taxpayer also holds substantially identical property. Under the current rules, a securities futures contract to *acquire* substantially identical property will be treated as substantially identical property (Code Sec. 1233(e)(2)(D), as amended by the 2002 Act).

Where substantially identical property was held for more than one year on the date the securities futures contract to sell was entered into, losses realized on the settlement date of the contract will be treated as long-term capital loss, even if the property actually used to settle the contract was held for one year or less (Code Sec. 1233(d) and Code Sec. 1233(e)(2)(D), as amended by the 2002 Act). The short sale rules will also characterize certain capital gains from securities futures contracts to sell as short-term capital gain and will be used to determine the holding period of the substantially identical property. Thus, if substantially identical property was

¶ 325

held for one year or less on the date the securities futures contract to sell was entered into, or if substantially identical property was acquired after the contract was entered into but on or before the settlement date of the contract, then gain from the settlement of the contract is treated as short-term capital gain (Code Sec. 1233(b) and Code Sec. 1233(e)(2)(D), as amended by the 2002 Act). In that case, the holding period of the substantially identical property would begin on the earlier of the contract's settlement date or the date of the sale or disposition of the substantially identical property (Code Sec. 1233(b) and Code Sec. 1233(e)(2)(D), as amended by the 2002 Act).

★ *Effective date.* The provision is effective on December 21, 2000 (Act Sec. 412(e) of the Job Creation and Worker Assistance Act of 2002 (P.L. 107-147); Act Sec. 401(j) of the Community Renewal Tax Relief Act of 2000 (P.L. 106-554)).

Act Sec. 412(d)(1)(A) of the Job Creation and Worker Assistance Act of 2002, amending Code Sec. 1234A(1) and Code Sec. 1234A(2) and striking Code Sec. 1234A(3); Act Sec. 412(d)(1)(B), amending Code Sec. 1234B(a)(1) and Code Sec. 1234B(b) and adding Code Sec. 1234B(f); Act Sec. 412(d)(2), amending Code Sec. 1091(e); Act Sec. 412(d)(3)(A), amending Code Sec. 1233(e)(2)(C) and Code Sec. 1233(e)(2)(D) and adding Code Sec. 1233(e)(2)(E); Act Sec. 412(d)(3)(B), amending Code Sec. 1234B(b); Act Sec. 412(e). Law at ¶ 5265, ¶ 5275, ¶ 5280, and ¶ 5282. Committee Report at ¶ 10,280.

Wash Sale Losses

¶ 330

Background

Gains and losses from "section 1256 contracts" must be reported on an annual basis under a mark-to-market rule that corresponds to the daily cash settlement, mark-to-market system employed by commodity futures exchanges in the United States for determining margin requirements. A "section 1256 contract" is a contract that meets the following conditions:

(1) it is marked-to-market under a daily cash flow system of the type used by United States futures exchanges to determine the amount which must be deposited, in the case of losses, or the amount which may be withdrawn, in the case of gains, as a result of price changes on the contract during the business day; and

(2) it is traded on or subject to the rules of a domestic board of trade that is designated as a contract market by the Commodity Futures Trading Commission, or any other board of trade or exchange that the IRS determines to operate under a mark-to-market system.

Section 1256 contracts also include any foreign currency contract, nonequity options, dealer equity options and, for tax years beginning after December 20, 2000, dealer securities futures contracts (Code Sec. 1256(b), as amended by the Community Renewal Tax Relief Act of 2000 (P.L. 106-554)).

Generally, section 1256 contracts must be marked-to-market at the end of each year. Each section 1256 contract held by a taxpayer is treated as if it were sold for fair market value on the last business day of the year. Any gain or loss on the contract is taken into account for the tax year, together with the gain or loss on other contracts which were held during the year, but closed out before the last business day. As a result, taxpayers' net gains or losses are approximately equal to

Background

the aggregate net amounts which are credited to their margin accounts, or which they have had to pay into their accounts during the tax year (Code Sec. 1256(a)).

Loss deductions are disallowed, however, where they result from wash sales of stock or securities. A wash sale occurs if stock or securities are sold at a loss and the seller acquires substantially identical stock or securities 30 days before or after the sale (Code Sec. 1091(a), as amended by the Job Creation and Worker Assistance Act of 2002 (P.L. 107-147); Reg. § 1.1091-1(a)). Stock or securities for this purpose include contracts or options to acquire or sell stock or securities unless regulations provide otherwise (Code Sec. 1091(a)).

Comment. The disallowed loss is reflected in the basis of the newly acquired stock or securities.

Technical Corrections Impact

Coordination of wash sale rules and Code Sec. 1256 contracts.—A technical correction clarifies that the Code Sec. 1091 wash sale rules do not apply to any loss attributable to a Code Sec. 1256 contract (Code Sec. 1256(f)(5), as added by the Job Creation and Worker Assistance Act of 2002 (P.L. 107-147)).

Comment. According to the Joint Committee on Taxation, this correction is similar to Code Sec. 475(d)(1), which states that the wash sale rules do not apply to any loss recognized using the mark-to-market accounting method for securities (Joint Committee on Taxation, *Technical Explanation of the "Job Creation and Worker Assistance Act of 2002"* (JCX-12-02), March 6, 2002).

★ *Effective date.* The amendments made by this provision apply to sales in tax years beginning after November 10, 1988 (Act Sec. 416(b)(2) of the Job Creation and Worker Assistance Act of 2002 (P.L. 107-147); Act Sec. 5075 of the Technical and Miscellaneous Revenue Act of 1988 (P.L. 100-647)).

Act Sec. 416(b)(1) of the Job Creation and Worker Assistance Act of 2002, adding Code Sec. 1256(f)(5); Act Sec. 416(b)(2). Law at ¶ 5285. Committee Report at ¶ 10,320.

CORPORATIONS

Basis Reduction Rule Where Liabilities Assumed

¶ 335

Background

Generally, no gain or loss is recognized when one or more persons transfer property to a corporation in exchange for its stock if, immediately after the transfer, those persons are in control of the corporation (Code Sec. 351(a)). The assumption of liabilities is not usually treated as boot received by the transferor; however, the transferor recognizes gain to the extent that the liabilities assumed exceed the total adjusted basis of the property transferred to the controlled corporation (Code Sec. 357(c)).

Under the general rule, the assumption of liabilities by the controlled corporation will reduce the transferor's basis in the stock received. However, assumed liabilities that would give rise to a deduction do not reduce the basis of the stock received by the transferor provided that the liabilities did not result in the creation or increase of basis of any property when incurred. This rule, however, is subject to the limitation described in Code Sec. 358(h).

Code Sec. 358(h) was enacted by the Community Renewal Tax Relief Act of 2000 (P.L. 106-554) in an effort to prevent the acceleration or duplication of losses through the assumption of liabilities giving rise to a deduction. The section provides that, if the basis of the stock received by the transferor as part of a tax-free exchange with a controlled corporation exceeds the fair market value of the stock, then the basis of the stock received is reduced, but not below fair market value, by any liability that is assumed in exchange for the stock and which did not otherwise reduce the company's basis by reason of the assumption.

> **Example.** A taxpayer transfers assets with an adjusted basis and a fair market value of $100 to its wholly-owned corporation and the corporation assumes $40 of liabilities (the payment of which would give rise to a deduction). The value of the stock received is $60. Pursuant to Code Sec. 358(h), the basis of the stock ($100 without regard to Code Sec. 358(h)) is reduced by $40 to $60.

Under an exception to Code Sec. 358(h), no basis reduction would be required in the preceding example if the transferred assets consisted of the trade or business, or substantially all of the assets, with which the liability was associated.

Technical Corrections Impact

Clarification of basis reduction for assumption of liability.—The amendment to Code Sec. 358(h)(1)(A) clarifies that the basis reduction rule of Code Sec. 358(h) only applies to the amount of any liability that is assumed by *another person* (i.e., a party other than the person transferring the property in exchange for stock), assuming that the other requirements of Code Sec. 358(h) apply (Code Sec. 358(h)(1)(A), as amended by the Job Creation and Worker Assistance Act of 2002 (P.L. 107-147)).

Comment. Without the clarification, an assumption of liabilities by the party transferring the property to the corporation in exchange for its stock would permit such transferor to reduce the basis of the stock received in the exchange by the amount of the liability.

> **Example.** An individual transfers assets with a basis of $200 and a fair market value of $100 for stock in a controlled corporation. The individual receiving the stock assumes a $25 liability. Since the liability was not assumed by another person (i.e., a person other than the transferor), the basis of the individual's stock is not reduced by the amount of the liability.

★ *Effective date.* This provision applies to assumptions of liability after October 18, 1999 (Act Sec. 412(e) of the Job Creation and Worker Assistance Act of 2002 (P.L. 107-147); Act Sec. 309(d) of the Community Renewal Tax Relief Act of 2000 (P.L. 106-554)).

Act Sec. 412(c) of the Job Creation and Worker Assistance Act of 2002, amending Code Sec. 358(h)(1)(A); Act Sec. 412(e). Law at ¶ 5130. Committee Report at ¶ 10,280.

CREDITS

Employer-Provided Child Care Credit

¶ 340

Background _____

As an incentive for providing child care to employees, businesses are entitled to claim a tax credit equal to the sum of 25 percent of qualified child care expenses and 10 percent of qualified child care resources and referral expenses, up to an annual limit of $150,000, for tax years beginning after December 31, 2001 (Code Sec. 45F, as added by the Economic Growth and Tax Relief Reconciliation Act of 2001 (P.L. 107-16) (EGTRRA)). The credit is made a part of, and subject to, the limitation and carryover provisions of the general business credit (Code Sec. 38(b)(15), as amended by EGTRRA).

If an employer terminates its interest in providing child care, or triggers a recapture event, all or part of the credit claimed must be recaptured as an increase in tax (Code Sec. 45F(d)(1), as added by EGTRRA). However, any increase in tax resulting from the recapture event is not to be treated as a tax imposed for purposes of determining the amount of any nonrefundable personal credits under Chapter 1, Subchapter A, Part IV, Subpart A of the Internal Revenue Code, other credits under Subpart B, or business-related credits under Subpart D (Code Sec. 45F(d)(4)(B), as added by EGTRRA).

Technical Corrections Impact

Treatment of recapture tax with respect to employer-provided child care credit.—A technical correction clarifies that recapture tax with respect to the credit for employer-provided child care expenses is treated in the same manner as recapture taxes with respect to any credits under Chapter 1 of the Code. Thus, it would not be treated as a tax for purposes of determining the amounts of any credits or of alternative minimum tax (Code Sec. 45F(d)(4)(B), as amended by the Job Creation and Worker Assistance Act of 2002 (P.L. 107-147)).

Further, a reference in Code Sec. 38(b)(15), dealing with the computation of the current year general business credit, clarifies that it is referring to the employer-provided child care credit determined under "Code Sec. 45F(a)." The current reference is to "Code Sec. 45F" (Code Sec. 38(b)(15), as amended by the 2002 Act).

★ *Effective date.* These provisions apply to tax years beginning after December 31, 2001 (Act Sec. 411(x) of the Job Creation and Worker Assistance Act of 2002 (P.L. 107-147); Act Sec. 205(c) of the Economic Growth and Tax Relief Reconciliation Act of 2001 (P.L. 107-16)). See ¶ 20,001 for a discussion of the impact of the sunset rule on this technical correction.

Act Sec. 411(d)(1) of the Job Creation and Worker Assistance Act of 2002, amending Code Sec. 45F(d)(4)(B); Act Sec. 411(d)(2), amending Code Sec. 38(b)(15); Act Sec. 411(x). Law at ¶ 5040 and 5053. Committee Report at ¶ 10,260.

ACCOUNTING METHODS

Limit of Use of Nonaccrual Experience Method of Accounting

¶ 345

Background

Under the "nonaccrual experience method of accounting," a person who uses an accrual method to account for amounts received for the performance of services is not required to accrue any portion of such amounts which, on the basis of experience, will not be collected. This rule applies regardless of the types of services performed or the amount of gross receipts received by the service provider. However, this rule does not apply to any amount for which interest is required to be paid or for which there is any penalty for failure to timely pay (Code Sec. 448(d)(5)).

Job Creation Act Impact

Nonaccrual experience method limited to qualified services or businesses.—The nonaccrual experience method of accounting is only available to an accrual method service provider for amounts received for the performance of services in certain fields of endeavor or if the service provider meets a $5,000,000 gross receipts test (Code Sec. 448(d)(5), as amended by the Job Creation and Worker Assistance Act of 2002 (P.L. 107-147)). As is currently the case, the nonaccrual experience method does not apply to any amount for which interest is required to be paid or for which there is any penalty for failure to timely pay (Code Sec. 448(d)(5)(B), as amended by the 2002 Act).

The nonaccrual experience method is available for amounts received for the performance of services in the fields of:

(1) health,

(2) law,

(3) engineering,

(4) architecture,

(5) accounting,

(6) actuarial science,

(7) performing arts, or

(8) consulting (Code Sec. 448(d)(5)(A)(i), as amended by the 2002 Act).

The nonaccrual experience method is also available for amounts received for the performance of services by a person who meets the $5,000,000 gross receipts test of Code Sec. 448(c) for *all* prior tax years (Code Sec. 448(d)(5)(A)(ii), as amended by the 2002 Act). In general, an entity meets the $5,000,000 gross receipts test for any prior tax year if the average annual gross receipts of such entity, for the three-year tax period ending with such prior tax year, does not exceed $5,000,000 (Code Sec. 448(c)).

Comment. The myriad rules of Code Sec. 448(c) regarding the aggregation of related taxpayers, the treatment of taxpayers who are not in existence for the entire three-year tax period, the computations for short tax years, the definition of gross receipts, and the treatment of predecessors apply in determining the average annual gross receipts test for a taxpayer who wants to use the nonaccrual experience method.

The IRS is required to issue regulations to permit taxpayers to determine amounts which, on the basis of experience, will not be collected. The amounts will be determined using computations or formulas which, based on experience, accurately reflect the amount of year-end receivables that will not be collected. It is anticipated that the IRS will consider providing safe harbors in such regulations. A taxpayer may adopt, or request the consent of the IRS to change to, a computation or formula that clearly reflects the taxpayer's experience. Such a request will be approved if the computation or formula clearly reflects the taxpayer's experience (Code Sec. 448(d)(5)(C), as amended by the 2002 Act).

★ *Effective date.* The limitation on the use of the nonaccrual experience method of accounting applies in tax years ending after March 9, 2002 (Act Sec. 403(b)(1) of the Job Creation and Worker Assistance Act of 2002 (P.L. 107-147)). In the case of a taxpayer required to change its method of accounting for its first tax year ending after March 9, 2002, the change is treated as initiated by the taxpayer, made with the consent of the IRS, and the net amount of the required Code Sec. 481 adjustments is to be taken into account over a period of four tax years (or, if less, the number of tax years that the taxpayer has used the nonaccrual experience method) (Act Sec. 403(b)(2) of the 2002 Act).

Act Sec. 403(a) of the Job Creation and Worker Assistance Act of 2002, amending Code Sec. 448(d)(5); Act Sec. 403(b). Law at ¶ 5190. Committee Report at ¶ 10,220.

INFORMATION REPORTING

Allowance of Electronic 1099s

¶ 350

Background ───

The Internal Revenue Code requires certain persons and entities to file information returns with the IRS and to provide copies to taxpayers. Generally, the information returns are provided to taxpayers on paper and are delivered via the U.S. mail. Under Reg. § 31.6051-1T(j), the IRS allowed providers of certain information statements required by Code Sec. 6051 to furnish a Form W-2 electronically, rather than on paper.

Timeliness requirements. Statements are treated as timely furnished within the meaning of the regulation if (1) the recipient electronically consents or agrees to receive the statement electronically; (2) the furnisher discloses certain information at or before the time consent to receive the statement electronically is given; (3) the furnisher posts the statement on a website on or before January 31 and maintains access through October 15 of the year following the year to which the statement relates; and (4) the furnisher notifies the recipient on or before January 31 of the year following the year to which the statement relates that the statement is available on the website.

Affirmative consent. Pursuant to the regulation, the recipient must have affirmatively consented to receive the Form W-2 in an electronic format and must not have withdrawn that consent before the Form W-2 is furnished. The consent must be made electronically in a manner that reasonably demonstrates that the

*Background*_____

recipient can access the Form W-2 in the electronic format in which it will be furnished to the recipient. The consent may also be made in a different manner (for example in an e-mail or in a paper document) if it is confirmed electronically in the manner described in the preceding sentence.

Comment. According to IRS Commissioner Charles O. Rosotti, "The rules were implemented in response to requests from lenders, educational institutions, employers and other furnishers of information statements who wanted the option to deliver the statements electronically." The option also permitted providers to save on the cost of processing, printing and mailing paper statements, while recipients received the information faster and more efficiently.

Similar rules could not be implemented with respect to certain information returns because the Internal Revenue Code requires that the copies furnished to individuals must be furnished either in person or in a statement sent by first-class mail in a specified format.

Job Creation Act Impact

Allowance of electronic Forms 1099.—The Job Creation and Worker Assistance Act of 2002 (P.L. 107-147) removes the statutory impediment to providing copies of specified information returns (the Form 1099 series) to taxpayers electronically (Act Sec. 401 of the 2002 Act). Accordingly, without regard to any Internal Revenue Code first-class mailing requirement, providers of information returns under any section of subpart B of Part III of subchapter A of chapter 61 of the Internal Revenue Code (Code Secs. 6041 through 6050S) may electronically furnish such statements to any recipient who has consented to receiving copies of the returns electronically in a manner similar to the one permitted under regulations issued under Code Sec. 6051 or in any manner provided by the IRS.

Form 1099s and any other statement filed under the following Code sections are covered:

(1) Code Sec. 6041(a) or (b) (Information at source) (Generally reported on Form 1099-INT, Interest Income, and Form 1099-MISC, Miscellaneous Income),

(2) Code Sec. 6041A (Returns regarding payments of remuneration for services and direct sales) (Form 1099-MISC, Miscellaneous Income),

(3) Code Sec. 6042(a)(1) (Returns regarding payment of dividends and corporate earnings and profits) (Generally reported on Form 1099-DIV, Dividends and Distributions),

(4) Code Sec. 6043(a)(2) (Returns regarding distributions in liquidation) (Form 1099-DIV, Dividends and Distributions),

(5) Code Sec. 6044(a)(1) (Returns regarding patronage dividends) (Form 1099-PATR, Taxable Distributions Received from Cooperatives),

(6) Code Sec. 6045(a) or (d) (Relating to returns of brokers) (Generally reported on Form 1099-B, Proceeds from Broker and Barter Exchange Transactions) and Code Sec. 6045(e) (Form 1099-S, Proceeds from Real Estate Transactions; and Form 1099-MISC, for certain substitute payments, compen-

sation such as fees, commissions and awards, and golden parachute payments, paid to a nonemployee for certain services),

(7) Code Sec. 6046 (Returns regarding organization or reorganization of foreign corporations and as to acquisitions of their stock) (Generally reported on Form 5471, Information Return of U.S. Persons with Respect to Certain Foreign Corporations, and accompanying schedules),

(8) Code Sec. 6046A (Returns as to interests in foreign partnerships) (Form 8865, Return of U.S. Persons with Respect to Certain Foreign Partnerships),

(9) Code Sec. 6047 (Information relating to trusts and annuity plans) (Form 5498, IRA Contribution Information; Form 1099-R, Distributions From Pensions, Annuities, Retirement or Profit-Sharing Plans, IRAs, Insurance Contracts, etc.,),

(10) Code Sec. 6048 (Returns relating to foreign trusts) (Generally reported on Form 3520, Annual Return To Report Transactions With Foreign Trusts and Receipt of Certain Foreign Gifts),

(11) Code Sec. 6049(a) (Returns regarding interest) (Form 1099-INT, Interest Income) and Code Sec. 6049(d)(6) (Relating to issuers of bonds or certificates of deposit to report original issue discount of $10 or more) (Generally reported on Form 1099-OID, Original Issue Discount),

(12) Code Sec. 6050A(a) (Relating to reporting requirements of certain fishing boat operators) (Generally reported on Form 1099-MISC, Miscellaneous Income),

(13) Code Sec. 6050B (Returns relating to unemployment compensation) (Form 1099-G, Certain Government and Qualified State Tuition Program Payments),

(14) Code Sec. 6050D (Returns relating to energy grants and financing) (Form 1099-G, Certain Government and Qualified State Tuition Program Payments),

(15) Code Sec. 6050E (Returns regarding state and local income tax refunds) (Form 1099-G, Certain Government and Qualified State Tuition Program Payments),

(16) Code Sec. 6050F (Returns regarding social security benefits),

(17) Code Sec. 6050G (Returns regarding railroad retirement benefits),

(18) Code Sec. 6050H (Returns regarding mortgage interest received in trade or business from individuals) (Form 1098, Mortgage Interest Statement),

(19) Code Sec. 6050I (Returns regarding cash received in trade or business) (Form 8300, Report of Cash Payments Over $10,000 Received in a Trade or Business),

(20) Code Sec. 6050J(a) (Relating to foreclosures and abandonments of security) (Generally reported on Form 1099-A, Acquisition or Abandonment of Secured Property),

(21) Code Sec. 6050K (Returns relating to exchanges of certain partnership interests) (Form 8308, Report of a Sale or Exchange of Certain Partnership Interests),

(22) Code Sec. 6050L (Returns relating to dispositions of donated property) (Form 8282, Donee Information Return),

(23) Code Sec. 6050M (Returns relating to persons receiving contracts from federal executive agencies) (Form 8596, Information Return for Federal Contracts),

(24) Code Sec. 6050N(a) (Returns regarding royalties) (Generally reported on Form 1099-MISC, Miscellaneous Income),

(25) Code Sec. 6050P(a) or (b) (Returns regarding cancellation of indebtedness) (Generally reported on Form 1099-C, Cancellation of Debt),

(26) Code Sec. 6050Q (Returns relating to certain long-term care and accelerated death benefits) (Generally reported on Form 1099-LTC, Long-Term Care and Accelerated Death Benefits),

(27) Code Sec. 6050R (Returns relating to certain purchases of fish) (Form 1099-MISC, Miscellaneous Income), and

(28) Code Sec. 6050S (Returns relating to higher education expenses) (Generally reported on Form 1098-E, Student Loan Interest Statement, and Form 1098-T, Tuition Payments Statement).

Also affected are the following forms:

(1) Form 1099-MSA, Distributions from an MSA or Medicare+Choice MSA,

(2) Form 5498-MSA, MSA or Medicare+Choice MSA Information (Code Sec. 138 and Code Sec. 220), and

(3) Form 1099-R, Distributions from Pensions, Annuities, Retirement or Profit-Sharing Plans, IRAs, Insurance Contracts, etc. (Code Sec. 408).

★ *Effective date.* No specific effective date is provided by the Job Creation and Worker Assistance Act of 2002 (P.L. 107-147). The provision is, therefore, considered effective on March 9, 2002, the date of enactment.

Act Sec. 401 of the Job Creation and Worker Assistance Act of 2002. Law at ¶ 7055. Committee Report at ¶ 10,200.

PARTNERSHIPS AND REITS

Settlements Under Partnership Audit Rules

¶ 355

Background————————————————————————————

The unified partnership audit procedures provide consistent treatment of partners and partnerships (Code Secs. 6221 through 6231). The determination of the tax treatment of partnership items is made at the partnership level in a single unified administrative partnership proceeding, rather than in separate proceedings with each partner. Special rules apply to proceedings that are conducted at the partnership level for the assessment and collection of tax deficiencies or for tax refunds arising out of the partners' distributive shares of income, deductions, credits, etc. Under these rules a partner may enter into a settlement agreement with the IRS. If the IRS enters into a settlement agreement with a partner with respect to a partnership item, that item converts to a nonpartnership item and the other partners have a right to request consistent settlement terms. The conversion of the settling partner's partnership items to nonpartnership items serves to remove the settling partner from the ongoing partnership proceedings.

The IRS issued final regulations relating to unified partnership audit procedures in 2001 (T.D. 8965, October 4, 2001 amending Reg. § 301.6224(c)-1T, Reg. § 301.6224(c)-2T and Reg. § 301.6229(f)-1T as well as other sections).

These regulations specify that partnership-level determinations of a penalty may be resolved in a settlement agreement between the IRS and a partner in a partnership. With regard to partnership-level determinations of penalties, the final regulations clarify that a settlement agreement between the tax matters partner and the IRS with respect to partnership items, binds partners other than the notice partner and members of a notice group (Reg. § 301.6224(c)-1). Under the final regulations, a settlement agreement between a passthrough partner and the IRS with respect to penalties binds indirect partners (Reg. § 301.6224(c)-2) and the rules applicable to partial settlements of partnership items also apply to partnership-level determinations of penalties (Reg. § 301.6229(f)-1).

If a settlement is reached between the IRS and a partner, the IRS must offer consistent settlement terms with respect to those partnership-level determinations of the penalty to the other partners in the partnership, subject to the limitations of Code Sec. 6224(c)(2) (Reg. § 301.6225(c)-3). There were no provisions addressing settlement agreements entered into between the Attorney General and a partner in the Code or regulations.

Technical Corrections Impact

Settlement agreements entered into with the Attorney General.—The Act clarifies that partnership audit procedures that apply to settlement agreements entered into by the IRS also apply to settlement agreements entered into by the Attorney General (or his delegate). The provisions amended relating to settlement agreements include the general rule that a settlement agreement between the IRS and the Attorney General (or his delegate) binds all parties to the agreement and other partners have a right to enter into consistent agreements (Code Sec. 6224(c)(1) and (2), as amended by the Job Creation and Worker Assistance Act of 2002 (P.L. 107-147)). If a partner enters into a settlement agreement with the IRS or the Attorney General (or his delegate) with respect to only part of the disputed items, then the period of limitations is determined as if such settlement agreement had not been entered (Code Sec. 6229(f)(2), as amended by the 2002 Act). A partner's partnership items become nonpartnership items as of the date that the IRS or the Attorney General (or his delegate) enters into a settlement with the partner as to such items (Code Sec. 6231(b)(1)(C), as amended by the 2002 Act). For purposes of Code Sec. 6234(g), partnership items are treated as finally determined if the IRS or the Attorney General (or his delegate) enters into a settlement agreement with the taxpayer regarding such items (Code Sec. 6234(g)(4)(A), as amended by the 2002 Act).

Comment. Without this technical correction, it is possible that a settling partner would be inadvertently bound by the outcome of the partnership proceeding instead of the settlement agreement entered into with the Attorney General. (Joint Committee on Taxation, *Technical Explanation of the "Job Creation and Worker Assistance Act of 2002"* (JCX-12-02), March 6, 2002).

★ *Effective date.* The amendments apply with respect to settlement agreements entered into after March 9, 2002 (Act Sec. 416(d)(2) of the Job Creation and Worker Assistance Act of 2002 (P.L. 107-147)).

Act Sec. 416(d)(1)(A) of the Job Creation and Worker Assistance Act of 2002, amending Code Sec. 6224(c)(1) and (2); Act. Sec. 416(d)(1)(B), amending Code Sec. 6229(f)(2); Act. Sec. 416(d)(1)(C), amending Code Sec. 6231(b)(1)(C); Act. Sec. 416(d)(1)(D), amending Code Sec. 6234(g)(4)(A); Act Sec. 416(d)(2). Law at ¶ 5350, ¶ 5365, ¶ 5370 and ¶ 5375. Committee Report at ¶ 10,320.

Taxable REIT Subsidiaries

¶ 360

Background

Congress made substantial changes to the taxation of Real Estate Investment Trusts (REITs) and their beneficiaries in the Tax Relief Extension Act of 1999 (P.L. 106-170). One of the changes was the establishment of a 100-percent excise tax in connection with improperly allocated rents, deductions and interest between a REIT and its taxable REIT subsidiaries (Code Sec. 857(b)(7), as added by the Tax Relief Extension Act of 1999 (P.L. 106-170)). The 100-percent excise tax is imposed on redetermined rents, redetermined deductions and excess interest (Code Sec. 857(b)(7)) and is imposed in lieu of reallocation by the IRS.

In general, "redetermined rents" means rents from real property, the amount of which would be reduced on distribution, apportionment or allocation under the "reallocation rules" of Code Sec. 482 in order to clearly reflect income as a result of services furnished or rendered by a taxable REIT subsidiary of the REIT to a tenant of such trust (Code Sec. 857(b)(7)(B)). The Code Sec. 482 reallocation rules will not actually apply in this situation; this 100-percent excise tax is in lieu of the application of Code Sec. 482 (Code Sec. 857(b)(7)(E)).

"Redetermined deductions" generally means deductions (other than redetermined rents) of a taxable REIT subsidiary of a real estate investment trust if the amount of such deductions would be decreased on distribution, apportionment, or allocation under the "reallocation rules" of Code Sec. 482 to clearly reflect income as between that subsidiary and that trust (Code Sec. 857(b)(7)(C)). As is the case in computing "redetermined rents," the Code Sec. 482 reallocation rules will not actually apply; this 100-percent excise tax is in lieu of the application of Code Sec. 482 (Code Sec. 857(b)(7)(E)).

Technical Corrections Impact

100-percent tax on improperly allocated amounts clarified.—The definitions of "redetermined rents," and "redetermined deductions" have been clarified (Code Sec. 857(b)(7), as amended by the Job Creation and Worker Assistance Act of 2002 (P.L. 107-147)). The terms "redetermined rents" and "redetermined deductions" are key concepts in the application of the 100-percent excise tax on rents, deductions and interest improperly allocated between a REIT and its taxable REIT subsidiaries (Code Sec. 857(b)(7)).

"Redetermined rents" are the excess of the amount treated by a REIT as rents from real property over the amount that would be so treated after reduction under the "reallocation rules" of Code Sec. 482 to clearly reflect income as the result of services furnished or rendered by a taxable REIT subsidiary of the REIT to a tenant of the REIT (Code Sec. 857(b)(7)(B)(i), as amended by the 2002 Act). Similarly, "redetermined deductions" are the excess of the amount treated by the taxable REIT subsidiary as other deductions over the amount that would be so treated after reduction under Code Sec. 482 (Code Sec. 857(b)(7)(C), as amended by the 2002 Act).

Comment. The changes make it clear that the 100-percent excise tax applies only to the extent that rent or deductions would be reallocated were the IRS to apply Code Sec. 482. It does not apply to the entire amount of rent or deductions simply because portions would be reallocated under Code Sec. 482.

★ *Effective date.* These clarifications are effective for tax years beginning after December 31, 2000 (Act Sec. 413(b) of the Job Creation and Worker Assistance Act of 2002 (P.L. 107-147); Act Sec. 546(a) of the Tax Relief Extension Act of 1999 (P.L. 106-170)).

Act Sec. 413(a) of the Job Creation and Worker Assistance Act of 2002, amending Code Sec. 857(b)(7); Act Sec. 413(b). Law at ¶ 5235. Committee Report at ¶ 10,290.

Sales of Partnership Interest with Appreciated Inventory

¶ 363

Background

Prior to amendment by the Taxpayer Relief Act of 1997 (P.L. 105-34), Code Sec. 751(a) provided that upon the sale or exchange of a partnership interest, the amount of any money or fair market value of property received by a transferor partner that was attributable to unrealized receivables, or to inventory that had "substantially appreciated," was treated as an amount realized from the sale or exchange of property that was not a capital asset (that is, the amount received was treated as ordinary income rather than capital gain). The inventory of a partnership was treated as substantially appreciated if the fair market value of the inventory exceeded 120 percent of the adjusted basis of the inventory to the partnership. The 1997 Act amended Code Sec. 751(a) by removing the substantial appreciation requirement for inventory. Thus, any amount realized that was attributable to inventory was ordinary income whether or not the inventory was "substantially appreciated."

The 1997 Act did not amend Code Sec. 741 to remove the "substantially appreciated" reference. Code Sec. 741 provides that gain or loss recognized by a transferor partner is treated as gain or loss from the sale of a capital asset, "except as otherwise provided in section 751 (relating to unrealized receivables and inventory items which have *substantially appreciated* in value)" (emphasis added).

Job Creation Act Impact

Ordinary gain or loss recognized on inventory.—The Job Creation and Worker Assistance Act of 2002 (P.L. 107-147) amends Code Sec. 741 by deleting the words "substantially appreciated." This change clarifies that a transferor partner recognizes ordinary gain or loss with respect to inventory whether or not the inventory is substantially appreciated (Code Sec. 741, as amended by the 2002 Act).

Comment. This provision is in the "Clerical Amendments" section of the 2002 Act. There is no Joint Committee on Taxation Explanation for the amendment.

PRACTICAL ANALYSIS. Charles R. Levun and Michael J. Cohen of Levun, Goodman & Cohen, Northbrook, Illinois, observe that the 1997 Tax Act changed the operation of the "hot asset" rules of Code Sec. 751 by providing that inventory items were hot assets in the case of a sale or exchange of a partnership interest, whether or not the inventory items were substantially appreciated (*i.e.*, fair market value in excess of 120 percent of basis). The substantial appreciation test remains for inventory in the case of a redemption of a partnership interest. As a result of the 1997 Tax Act change, it was generally believed that a sale of a partnership interest in a partnership holding inventory items with a value less than basis could generate an ordinary loss with respect to the portion of the sale proceeds attributable to the inventory items. The only hesitation was Code Sec. 741, which remained unchanged by the 1997 Tax Act and which provided that a sale of a partnership interest generated capital gain or loss "except as otherwise provided in section 751 (relating to unrealized receivables and inventory items which have appreciated substantially in value)." Act Sec. 417 of the 2002 Tax Act eliminates any uncertainty regarding ordinary loss treatment for depreciated inventory items in a sale or exchange of a partnership interest by removing from Code Sec. 741 the words "which have appreciated substantially in value."

★ *Effective date.* No effective date is provided by the Job Creation and Worker Assistance Act of 2002 (P.L. 107-147). The provision is, therefore, considered effective on March 9, 2002, the date of enactment.

Act Sec. 417(12) of the Job Creation and Worker Assistance Act of 2002, amending Code Sec. 741. Law at ¶ 5225.

INSURANCE COMPANIES

Modified Endowment Contracts

¶ 365

Background

Under Code Sec. 7702A, if a life insurance contract that is not a modified endowment contract is actually or deemed exchanged for a new life insurance contract, then the 7-pay limit under the new contract would first be computed without reference to the premium paid using the cash surrender value of the old contract, and then would be reduced by 1/7 of the premium paid, taking into account the cash surrender value of the old contract. For example, if the old contract had a cash surrender value of $14,000 and the 7-pay premium on the new contract would equal $10,000 per year but for the fact that there was an exchange, the 7-pay premium on the new contract would equal $8,000 ($10,000 − ($14,000 ÷ 7)).

Background————————————————————————————————————

Prior to the enactment of the Community Renewal Tax Relief Act of 2000 (P.L. 106-554), it was thought that Code Sec. 7702A(c)(3)(A) arguably might be read to suggest that if the cash surrender value on the new contract was $0 in the first two years (due to surrender charges), then the 7-pay premium might be $10,000 in the above example, unintentionally permitting policyholders to engage in a series of "material changes" to circumvent the premium limitations in Code Sec. 7702A.

The Community Renewal Tax Relief Act of 2000 (P.L. 106-554, Act Sec. 318(a)(2)) clarified Code Sec. 7702A(c)(3)(A) to refer to the cash surrender value of the *old* contract, effective as if enacted with the Technical and Miscellaneous Revenue Act of 1988 (generally, for contracts entered into on or after June 21, 1988).

———————————————————————————————————————

Technical Corrections Impact

Modified endowment contract definition clarified.—The Community Renewal Tax Relief Act of 2000 (P.L. 106-554) clarifying reference to the cash surrender value of the "old" contract under Code Sec. 7702A(c)(3)(A)(ii), has been retroactively repealed (Code Sec. 7702A(c)(3)(A)(ii), as amended by the Job Creation and Worker Assistance Act of 2002 (P.L. 107-147)). Code Sec. 7702A(c)(3)(A)(ii) is to be read and applied as if the word "old" had not ever appeared (Act Sec. 416(f) of the 2002 Act).

No reference is needed to the cash surrender under the old contract because prior and present law provide a definition of cash surrender value for this purpose, by cross reference to Code Sec. 7702(f)(2)(A) (Joint Committee on Taxation, *Technical Explanation of the "Job Creation and Worker Assistance Act of 2002"* (JCX-12-02), March 6, 2002). If there is a material change to the contract, appropriate adjustments are made in determining whether the contract meets the 7-pay test to take into account the cash surrender value under the contract.

Comment. Code Sec. 7702A(c)(3)(A)(ii) is not intended to permit a policyholder to engage in a series of "material changes" to circumvent the premium limitations in Code Sec. 7702A (Joint Committee on Taxation, *Technical Explanation of the "Job Creation and Worker Assistance Act of 2002"* (JCX-12-02), March 6, 2002).

If there is a material change to a life insurance contract, it is intended that the fair market value of the contract be used as the cash surrender value in instances where the amount of the putative cash surrender value of the contract is artificially depressed. For example, if there is a material change because of an increase in the face amount of the contract, any artificial or temporary reduction in the cash surrender value of the contract is not to be taken into account. Rather, it is intended that the fair market value of the contract be used as cash surrender value, so that the substance rather than the form of the transaction is reflected (Joint Committee on Taxation, *Technical Explanation of the "Job Creation and Worker Assistance Act of 2002"* (JCX-12-02), March 6, 2002).

In applying the 7-pay test to any premiums paid under a contract that has been materially changed, the 7-pay premium for each of the first 7 contract years after the change is to be reduced by the product of:

(1) the cash surrender value of the contract as of the date that the material change takes effect (determined without regard to any increase in the cash surrender value that is attributable to the amount of the premium payment that is not necessary), and

(2) a fraction, the numerator of which equals the 7-pay premium for the future benefits under the contract, and the denominator of which equals the net single premium for such benefits computed using the same assumptions used in determining the 7-pay premium (Joint Committee on Taxation, *Technical Explanation of the "Job Creation and Worker Assistance Act of 2002"* (JCX-12-02), March 6, 2002).

★ *Effective date.* This technical correction to the definition of modified endowment contracts is effective March 9, 2002 (Act Sec. 416(f) of the Job Creation and Worker Assistance Act of 2002 (P.L. 107-147); Act Sec. 318(a) of the Community Renewal Tax Relief Act of 2000 (P.L. 106-554)).

Act Sec. 416(f) of the Job Creation and Worker Assistance Act of 2002, amending Code Sec. 7702A(c)(3)(A)(ii) and repealing Act Sec. 318(a)(2) of the Community Renewal Tax Relief Act of 2000 (P.L. 106-554). Law at ¶ 5395. Committee Report at ¶ 10,320.

EXTENDED PROVISIONS

Qualified Electric Vehicle Credit

¶ 370

Background

Taxpayers are entitled to a tax credit of 10 percent of the cost of a qualified electric vehicle (Code Sec. 30(a)). The credit is available in the year that the vehicle is placed into service for tax years beginning after June 30, 1993, and before January 1, 2005, irrespective of whether the vehicle is used in a trade or business. A qualified electric vehicle is a motor vehicle that is powered primarily by an electric motor drawing current from rechargeable batteries, fuel cells or other portable sources of electrical current, the original use of which commences with the taxpayer, and is acquired for use by the taxpayer and not held for sale (Code Sec. 30(c)). The credit is available only with respect to qualified electric vehicles used in the United States.

The maximum amount that may be claimed as a credit against the cost of a qualified electric vehicle is $4,000. The amount allowable as a credit, however, is reduced by a percentage depending upon the year that the vehicle is placed into service. The amount allowable as a credit is reduced by 25 percent for vehicles placed into service in 2002, by 50 percent for vehicles placed into service in 2003, and by 75 percent for vehicles placed into service in 2004 (Code Sec. 30(b)(1)). The credit is not available for tax years beginning after December 31, 2004 (Code Sec. 30(e)).

The amount that a taxpayer can claim as a depreciation deduction for any passenger vehicle is limited (Code Sec. 280F(a)(1)(A)). These limits are based on the year that the passenger vehicle is placed into service and are adjusted annually for inflation (Code Sec. 280F(d)(7)).

The Taxpayer Relief Act of 1997 (P.L. 105-34) created several exceptions to the depreciation deduction limits.

Background

Comment. These exceptions apply to both electric and other clean-fuel passenger vehicles.

For electric, or other clean-fuel, passenger vehicles built by an original equipment manufacturer, the depreciation deduction limits are tripled (Code Sec. 280F(a)(1)(C)(ii)). For passenger vehicles modified to allow them to be propelled by electricity, or other clean-burning fuel, the depreciation deduction limits do not apply to the cost of the installed device that equips the car to use clean-burning fuel (Code Sec. 280F(a)(1)(C)(i)). The exceptions to the depreciation deduction limits apply to electric or other clean-fuel passenger vehicles and property placed into service on or after August 5, 1997, and before January 1, 2005.

Job Creation Act Impact

Extension of credit for purchase of electric vehicles.—The phase-down of the credit for the cost of a qualified electric vehicle is deferred for two years (Code Sec. 30(b)(2), as amended by the Job Creation and Worker Assistance Act of 2002 (P.L. 107-147)). For qualified electric vehicles placed into service in 2002 or 2003, taxpayers are entitled to a credit for 10 percent of the vehicles' cost up to the maximum credit amount, or $4,000 (Code Sec. 30(a) and Code Sec. 30(b)(1)). The credit amount is reduced by 25 percent for qualified electric vehicles placed into service in 2004, 50 percent for qualified electric vehicles placed into service in 2005, and 75 percent for qualified electric vehicles placed into service in 2006 (Code Sec. 30(b)(2), as amended by the 2002 Act). The credit is not available for qualified electric vehicles placed into service after December 31, 2006 (Code Sec. 30(e), as amended by the 2002 Act).

> **Example.** Steve Henderson purchases a qualified electric vehicle in 2002 for his personal use for $50,000. Prior to amendment of Code Sec. 30(b)(2) by the 2002 Act, Henderson would have been able to claim a $3,000 credit against tax for the cost of the vehicle (ten percent of $50,000 ($5,000) or $4,000 limitation, whichever is lower, less 25 percent of that amount). However, following enactment of the 2002 Act, Henderson is entitled to the full $4,000 maximum credit amount.

Comment. A conforming amendment in the 2002 Act also extends the time period during which the exceptions to the depreciation deduction limits apply, to electric or clean-fuel passenger vehicles placed into service after August 5, 1997, and before January 1, 2007 (Code Sec. 280F(a)(1)(C)(iii), as added by the 2002 Act). See ¶ 305 regarding a temporary increase in the depreciation deduction limits.

★ *Effective date.* The amendments made by this provision apply to qualified electric vehicles placed into service after December 31, 2001 (Act Sec. 602(c) of the Job Creation and Worker Assistance Act of 2002 (P.L. 107-147)).

Act Sec. 602(a)(1) of the Job Creation and Worker Assistance Act of 2002, amending Code Sec. 30(b)(2); Act Sec. 602(a)(2), amending Code Sec. 30(e); Act Sec. 602(b)(1), adding Code Sec. 280F(a)(1)(C)(iii); Act Sec. 602(b)(2), amending Act Sec. 971(b) of the Taxpayer Relief Act of 1997 (P.L. 105-34); Act Sec. 602(c). Law at ¶ 5030, ¶ 5120 and ¶ 7095. Committee Report at ¶ 10,410.

¶ 370

Credit for Electricity from Renewable Resources

¶ 372

Background ――――――――――――――――――――――――――――――――――

An income tax credit is allowed for the production of electricity from either qualified wind energy, qualified "closed-loop" biomass, or qualified poultry waste facilities (Code Sec. 45(c)(3)).

The credit is generally 1.5 cents (adjusted for inflation) per kilowatt hour of electricity produced. It applies (1) to electricity produced by a wind energy facility placed in service after December 31, 1993, and before January 1, 2002; (2) to electricity produced by a closed-loop biomass facility placed in service after December 31, 1992, and before January 1, 2002; and (3) to a poultry waste facility placed in service after December 31, 1999 and before January 1, 2002. The credit is allowable for production during the 10-year period after a facility is originally placed in service.

Job Creation Act Impact

Two-year extension of credit for electricity produced from renewable resources.—The provision extends the placed-in-service date for qualified facilities by two years to include those facilities placed in service prior to January 1, 2004 (Code Sec. 45(c)(3), as amended by the Job Creation and Worker Assistance Act of 2002 (P.L. 107-147)).

Comment. The House Ways and Means Committee believes that continued economic incentive is warranted to increase the presence of these more environmentally friendly generation sources in the nation's electricity grid (House Committee Report to H.R. 3090, H.R. Rep. No. 107-251, October 17, 2001).

★ *Effective date.* The provision is effective for facilities placed in service after December 31, 2001 (Act Sec. 603(b) of the Job Creation and Worker Assistance Act of 2002 (P.L. 107-147)).

Act Sec. 603(a) of the Job Creation and Worker Assistance Act of 2002, amending Code Sec. 45(c)(3); Act Sec. 603(b). Law at ¶ 5050. Committee Report at ¶ 10,420.

Work Opportunity Credit

¶ 374

Background ――――――――――――――――――――――――――――――――――

The work opportunity tax credit provides employers with an incentive to hire individuals from eight targeted groups having a particularly high unemployment rate or other special employment needs (Code Sec. 51). The credit was designed to help such employers offset the costs of hiring, training, and supervising workers who have little, if any, work experience and few prospects for employment.

Employers hiring members of the following groups are eligible for the credit: (1) families eligible to receive benefits under the Temporary Assistance for Needy Families (TANF) program (Code Sec. 51(d)(2)); (2) high-risk youth (Code Sec. 51(d)(5)); (3) qualified ex-felons (Code Sec. 51(d)(4)); (4) vocational rehabilitation referrals (Code Sec. 51(d)(6)); (5) qualified summer youth employees (Code Sec. 51(d)(7)); (6) qualified veterans (Code Sec. 51(d)(3)); (7) families receiving food

Background ───────────────────────────────────

stamps (Code Sec. 51(d)(8)); and (8) persons receiving certain Supplemental Security Income benefits (Code Sec. 51(d)(9)). An employer must obtain certification from a state employment security agency that an individual is a member of a targeted group (Code Sec. 51(d)(12)).

The credit is equal to 40 percent of up to $6,000 of the targeted employee's qualified first-year wages ($3,000 for qualified summer youth employees), provided the employee completes a minimum of 400 hours of service (Code Sec. 51(a)-(c)). Thus, the maximum credit per targeted employee is $2,400 ($1,200 for qualified summer youth employees). The credit is reduced to 25 percent for employees who complete less than 400 hours of service, and no credit is allowed for employees who complete less than 120 hours of service (Code Sec. 51(i)(3)). An employer's business expense deduction for wages is reduced by the amount of the work opportunity tax credit (Code Sec. 280C(a)).

The current version of the work opportunity tax credit was enacted by the Small Business Job Protection Act of 1996 (P.L. 104-188), and amended by the Taxpayer Relief Act of 1997 (P.L. 105-34). The credit has been extended, most recently by the Tax Relief Extension Act of 1999 (P.L. 106-170), to cover wages earned by workers who begin work no later than December 31, 2001.

───────────────────────────────────

Job Creation Act Impact

Two-year extension of work opportunity credit.—The work opportunity tax credit has been extended for 24 months and is now scheduled to expire for individuals who begin work for an employer after December 31, 2003 (Code Sec. 51(c)(4)(B), as amended by the Job Creation and Worker Assistance Act of 2002 (P.L. 107-147)).

★ *Effective date.* The provision is effective for an individual who begins work for an employer after December 31, 2001 (Act Sec. 604(b) of the Job Creation and Worker Assistance Act of 2002 (P.L. 107-147)).

Act Sec. 604(a) of the Job Creation and Worker Assistance Act of 2002, amending Code Sec. 51(c)(4)(B); Act Sec. 604(b). Law at ¶ 5055. Committee Report at ¶ 10,430.

Welfare-to-Work Credit

¶ 376

Background ───────────────────────────────────

A tax credit of up to $8,500 per individual is allowed to employers for eligible first- and second-year wages paid to qualified long-term family assistance recipients (Code Sec. 51A). The purpose of the credit is to provide employers with an incentive to hire long-term welfare recipients, to promote the transition from welfare to work by increasing access to employment, and to encourage employers to provide these individuals with training, health coverage, dependent care and better job attachment.

The credit is equal to 35 percent of the first $10,000 of eligible wages paid in the first year of employment, plus 50 percent of the first $10,000 of the eligible wages paid in the second year of employment (Code Sec. 51A(a)). If a welfare-to-work tax credit is allowed to an employer for an individual for any tax year, that

Background

individual is not deemed to be a member of a targeted group for that tax year for purposes of the Code Sec. 51 work opportunity tax credit (Code Sec. 51A(e)).

Introduced in the Taxpayer Relief Act of 1997 (P.L. 105-34), the credit was extended by the Tax Relief Extension Act of 1999 (P.L. 106-170), to cover wages paid to employees who start work no later than December 31, 2001.

Job Creation Act Impact

Two-year extension of welfare-to-work credit.—The new law extends the welfare-to-work tax credit for 24 months to cover wages paid to employees who start work no later than December 31, 2003 (Code Sec 51A(f), as amended by the Job Creation and Worker Assistance Act of 2002 (P.L. 107-147)).

★ *Effective date.* This provision is effective for individuals who begin work for an employer after December 31, 2001 (Act Sec. 605(b) of the Job Creation and Worker Assistance Act of 2002 (P.L. 107-147)).

Act Sec. 605(a) of the Job Creation and Worker Assistance Act of 2002, amending Code Sec. 51A(f); Act Sec. 605(b). Law at ¶ 5057. Committee Report at ¶ 10,440.

Qualified Clean-Fuel Vehicle and Refueling Property Deduction

¶ 378

Background

Taxpayers are entitled to a deduction for the cost of qualified clean-fuel vehicle property (Code Sec. 179A(a)(1)). The deduction is available for property placed in service after June 30, 1993, and before January 1, 2005, irrespective of whether the property is used in a trade or business. Qualified clean-fuel vehicle property includes motor vehicles produced by an original equipment manufacturer that can be propelled by a clean-burning fuel. Clean-burning fuel includes natural gas, liquefied natural gas, liquefied petroleum gas, hydrogen, electricity and any other fuel when at least 85 percent of the fuel is methanol, ethanol, any other alcohol, ether or any combination of these. Qualified clean-fuel vehicle property also includes retrofit parts and components (Code Sec. 179A(c)(1)). It does not include any qualified electric vehicle (Code Sec. 179A(c)(3)).

The amount of the deduction is generally the cost of the qualified clean-fuel vehicle property. However, certain limitations apply to the maximum amount allowable as a deduction, based on the type of vehicle. The limitation is $50,000 for any truck or van with a gross vehicle weight rating greater than 26,000 pounds or a bus with a seating capacity of at least 20 adults, not including the driver. The limitation is $5,000 for a truck or van with a gross vehicle weight rating greater than 10,000 pounds, but not greater than 26,000 pounds. For any other motor vehicle, the limitation is $2,000 (Code Sec. 179A(b)(1)(A)).

The amount allowable as a deduction is reduced by a percentage depending upon the year that the vehicle is placed into service. The reduction is 25 percent for qualified clean-fuel vehicle property placed into service in 2002, 50 percent for vehicles placed into service in 2003, and 75 percent for vehicles placed into service in 2004 (Code Sec. 179A(b)(1)(B)). The deduction is not available for property placed into service after December 31, 2004 (Code Sec. 179A(f)).

Background ——————————————————————————————

The amount that a taxpayer can claim as a depreciation deduction for any passenger vehicle is limited (Code Sec. 280F(a)(1)(A)). For clean-fuel passenger vehicles built by an original equipment manufacturer, the depreciation deduction limits are tripled (Code Sec. 280F(a)(1)(C)(ii)). For passenger vehicles modified to allow them to be propelled by electricity, or other clean-burning fuel, the depreciation deduction limits do not apply to the cost of the installed device that equips the car to use clean-burning fuel (Code Sec. 280F(a)(1)(C)(i)). The exceptions to the depreciation deduction limits apply to property placed into service on or after August 5, 1997, and before January 1, 2005.

———————————————————————————————————————

Job Creation Act Impact

Extension of deduction for qualified clean-fuel vehicle property.—The phase-down of the deduction for clean-fuel vehicle property is deferred for two years (Code Sec. 179A(b)(1)(B), as amended by the Job Creation and Worker Assistance Act of 2002 (P.L. 107-147)). Taxpayers who place clean fuel vehicle property into service in 2002 or 2003 can claim the full amount of the deduction, i.e., $50,000 for any truck or van with a gross vehicle weight rating greater than 26,000 pounds or a bus with a seating capacity of at least 20 adults, not including the driver, $5,000 for a truck or van with a gross vehicle weight rating greater than 10,000 pounds, but not greater than 26,000 pounds, or $2,000 for any other motor vehicle (Code Sec. 179A(b)(1)(A)).

The deduction amount is reduced by 25 percent for clean-fuel property placed into service in 2004, 50 percent for clean-fuel vehicle property placed into service in 2005, and 75 percent for clean-fuel vehicle property placed into service in 2006. No deduction is available for clean-fuel vehicle property placed into service after December 31, 2006 (Code Sec. 179A(f), as amended by the 2002 Act).

> **Example.** Steve Wilson, a calendar-year taxpayer, purchases for $40,000 and places into service for personal use on January 1, 2002, a clean-fuel passenger automobile, a portion of which is qualified clean-fuel vehicle property. The qualified clean-fuel vehicle property costs $20,000. Prior to amendment of Code Sec. 179A(b)(1)(B) by the 2002 Act, Wilson would have been able to claim a deduction of only $1,500 on his 2002 tax return ($2,000 less 25 percent of that amount). However, following enactment of the 2002 Act, Wilson can claim the full amount of the deduction, $2,000, on his 2002 tax return.

A conforming amendment in the 2002 Act also extends the time period during which the exceptions to the depreciation deduction limits for electric vehicles and retrofit clean-fuel vehicle property apply by two years. The exceptions now apply to property placed into service after August 5, 1997, and before January 1, 2007 (Code Sec. 280F(a)(1)(C)(iii), as added by the 2002 Act).

★ *Effective date.* The amendments made by this provision apply to property placed into service after December 31, 2001 (Act Sec. 606(b) of the Job Creation and Worker Assistance Act of 2002 (P.L. 107-147)).

Act Sec. 606(a)(1) of the Job Creation and Worker Assistance Act of 2002, amending Code Sec. 179A(b)(1)(B); Act Sec. 606(a)(2), amending Code Sec. 179A(f); Act Sec. 606(b). Law at ¶ 5110. Committee Report at ¶ 10,450.

¶ **378**

Taxable Income Limit on Percentage Depletion

¶ 380

Background _____

Taxpayers are permitted to recover their investments in oil and gas wells through depletion deductions. In the case of certain properties, the deductions may be determined using the percentage depletion method. Among the limitations that apply in calculating percentage depletion deductions is a restriction that, for oil and gas properties, the amount deducted may not exceed 100 percent of the net income from that property in any year (Code Sec. 613(a)). Special percentage depletion rules apply to oil and gas production from marginal properties (Code Sec. 613A(c)(6)). Under one such special rule, the 100-percent-of-net-income limitation does not apply to domestic oil and gas production from marginal properties during tax years beginning after December 31, 1997, and before January 1, 2002 (Code Sec. 613A(c)(6)(H)).

Job Creation Act Impact

Suspension of income limitation on marginal properties extended.— The temporary suspension of the taxable income limit on the percentage depletion for marginal production has been extended to include tax years beginning in 2002 and 2003. Thus, the limitation on the amount of a percentage depletion deduction to 100 percent of the net income from an oil or gas producing property does not apply to domestic oil and gas production from marginal properties during tax years beginning after December 31, 1997, and before January 1, 2004 (Code Sec. 613A(c)(6)(H), as amended by the Job Creation and Worker Assistance Act of 2002 (P.L. 107-147)).

★ *Effective date.* The extension of the period during which the 100-percent-of-net-income limit is suspended is effective for tax years beginning after December 31, 2001 (Act Sec. 607(b) of the Job Creation and Worker Assistance Act of 2002 (P.L. 107-147)).

Act Sec. 607(a) of the Job Creation and Worker Assistance Act of 2002, amending Code Sec. 613A(c)(6)(H); Act Sec. 607(b). Law at ¶ 5220. Committee Report at ¶ 10,470.

Qualified Zone Academy Bond Credit

¶ 382

Background _____

Traditionally, bonds are issued by states and local school districts to fund school renovation and expansion projects. Under Code Sec. 103(a), the interest earned on these bonds is exempt from federal taxes. The tax-exempt nature of these bonds make them attractive to many investors and, therefore, the issuing authorities can sell them at a lower interest rate than the rate attached to standard corporate bonds. Generally, interest payments can equal up to 50 percent of the economic cost of a bond. The lower rate saves the issuing authorities about 20 percent of the interest costs in the current market.

The Taxpayer Relief Act of 1997 (P.L. 105-34) created a new financial tool known as a qualified zone academy bond that can be used by state education agencies to encourage the formation of partnerships between public schools and local businesses. The federal government provides bond holders with a tax credit in lieu of cash interest payments and the school district or other issuer is then only responsible for repaying the amount borrowed. The economic theory involves the term of the indebtedness being set so that the state or local government's obligation to repay in present value terms will be 50 percent of the borrowed amount. In effect, school districts save the cost of the interest on the bonds.

Qualified zone academy bonds are bonds issued by a state or local government where at least 95 percent of the funds raised are used to renovate, provide equipment to, develop course materials for use at, or train teachers and others at certain public schools (qualified zone academies) that provide education or training below the postsecondary level. These public schools must be located in empowerment zones or enterprise communities *or* have a reasonable expectation that at least 35 percent of the students will be eligible for free or reduced-cost lunches under the National School Lunch Act. In addition, private entities must promise to contribute equipment, technical assistance or training, employee services, or other property or services with a value equal to at least 10 percent of the value of the bond proceeds (Code Sec. 1397E(d); Conference Committee Report, Taxpayer Relief Act of 1997 (P.L. 105-34)).

Banks, insurance companies, and certain corporate lenders may hold these taxable qualified zone academy bonds and are entitled to a nonrefundable credit (Code Sec. 1397E(a) and Code Sec. 1397E(d)(6)). The credit is allowed to eligible taxpayers holding a qualified zone academy bond on the credit allowance date (the anniversary of the issuance of the bond) for each year in which the bond is held (Code Sec. 1397E(f)(1)). The amount of the credit is equal to a credit rate set monthly by the Treasury Department multiplied by the face amount of the bond (Code Sec. 1397E(b); Reg. § 1.1397E-1(b)). The credit is includible in income as if it were an interest payment on the bond and may be claimed against regular income tax and alternative minimum tax (AMT) liability (Code Sec. 1397E(g); Reg. § 1.1397E-1(a)).

Up to $400 million in qualified zone academy bonds may be issued nationally in each calendar year beginning in 1998 and ending in 2001 (Code Sec. 1397E(e)(1)). The annual $400 million amount is allocated among the states based upon their population below the poverty level. Each state's educational agency is responsible for apportionment of the allocation within its boundaries. A state is permitted a three-year carryforward of unused allocations from 1998 and 1999. The carryforward is only two years for 2000 and 2001 unused allocations.

Job Creation Act Impact

Extension of authority to issue additional qualified zone academy bonds.—The $400 million national zone academy bond limitation for each calendar year has been extended to calendar years 2002 and 2003. The limitation is zero for calendar years after 2003 (Code Sec. 1397E(e)(1), as amended by the Job Creation and Worker Assistance Act of 2002 (P.L. 107-147)). Any unused limitation amount for any state from calendar years 2002 and 2003 may be carried forward only to the first two years following the year in which the allocation arises. The unused allocation or limitation amounts are treated as used on a first-in, first-out basis (Code Sec. 1397E(e)(4)). Each issuer is deemed to use the oldest qualified zone academy bond authority that has been allocated to it first, when new bonds are issued (Conference Committee Report, Tax Relief Extension Act of 1999 (P.L. 106-170)).

¶ 382

Comment. The National Education Association (NEA) has stressed the dire need for the type of funds that the qualified zone academy bonds are intended to raise. According to the NEA's School Modernization Needs Assessments published in early 2001, over the next five to ten years, $268.2 billion is needed for repairs to aging school structures in the United States. An additional $53.7 billion is needed in the next three to five years for educational technologies. The study revealed that 46 percent of current school buildings lack adequate wiring to support the use of technology, thus requiring major renovation before technological equipment can be added. Federal leadership is required, according to the study, since in fiscal year 1999 all of the states' surpluses totaled only $31 billion. Assuming that the full amount could be invested in modernization, that does not begin to meet the projected needs.

★ *Effective date.* The extension of the authority to issue qualified zone academy bonds applies to obligations issued after March 9, 2002 (Act Sec. 608(b) of the Job Creation and Worker Assistance Act of 2002 (P.L. 107-147)).

Act Sec. 608(a) of the Job Creation and Worker Assistance Act of 2002, amending Code Sec. 1397E(e)(1); Act Sec. 608(b). Law at ¶ 5295. Committee Report at ¶ 10,480.

Temporary Rules for Taxation of Life Insurance Companies

¶ 384

Background

Ordinarily, a life insurance company can deduct policyholder dividends distributed to policyholders in their capacity as such (Code Sec. 808(a)). In the case of mutual life insurance companies, however, the deduction for policyholder dividends must be reduced, but not below zero, by the "differential earnings amount" (Code Sec. 808(c)(2) and Code Sec. 809(a)(1)).

The "differential earnings amount" is computed by multiplying a life insurance company's "average equity base" for the tax year by the "differential earnings rate" for the tax year (Code Sec. 809(a)(3)). A recomputation or "true-up" in the succeeding tax year is required if the "differential earnings amount" for the company's prior tax year either exceeds, or is less than, the "recomputed differential earnings amount" (Code Sec. 809(f)). For any tax year, the "recomputed differential earnings amount" is the amount which would be the company's "differential earnings amount" for the tax year if the "average mutual earnings rate" taken into account were the "average mutual earnings rate" for the calendar year in which the tax year began (Code Sec. 809(f)(3)). The amount of the "true-up" for any tax year is added to, or deducted from, the mutual company's income for the succeeding tax year (Code Sec. 809(f)(1) and (2)).

Job Creation Act Impact

Zero differential earnings rate applies.—The differential earnings rate is treated as zero for purposes of computing both the "differential earnings amount" and the "recomputed differential earnings amount" ("true-up") for mutual life insurance companies' tax years beginning in 2001, 2002 or 2003, notwithstanding any provisions in Code Sec. 809(c) and (f) to the contrary (Code Sec. 809(j), as added by the Job Creation and Worker Assistance Act of 2002 (P.L. 107-147)).

Comment. Since the differential earnings rate will be treated as zero for the 2001 through 2003 tax years, the differential earnings amount of Code Sec. 809(a) and the recomputed differential earnings amount of Code Sec. 809(f)(3), which are products of computations involving the differential earnings rate, will also be treated as zero during that time period. Thus, any reduction in a mutual life insurance company's policyholder dividends deduction otherwise required by Code Sec. 809 will be suspended during the applicable time period.

★ *Effective date.* This provision is effective for tax years beginning after December 31, 2000 (Act Sec. 611(b) of the Job Creation and Worker Assistance Act of 2002 (P.L. 107-147)).

Act Sec. 611(a) of the Job Creation and Worker Assistance Act of 2002, adding Code Sec. 809(j); Act Sec. 611(b). Law at ¶ 5230. Committee Report at ¶ 10,520.

Tax Incentives for Indian Reservations

¶ 386

Background

The Omnibus Budget Reconciliation Act of 1993 (P.L. 103-66), enacted August 10, 1993, provided two tax incentives to stimulate economic development and to encourage investment on Indian reservations. The tax incentives included (1) a tax credit under Code Sec. 45A for employers of qualified employees that work on an Indian reservation that allowed businesses to use a portion of the wages paid and health insurance benefits provided to Indian employees to directly reduce their tax liability, and, thus, increase after-tax income, and (2) accelerated recovery periods for qualified property on Indian reservations that allowed businesses to depreciate their capital expenses more rapidly than other properties (Code Sec. 168(j)).

Indian employment credit. The credit is a nonrefundable tax credit equal to 20 percent of the difference between a qualified employee's wages and health insurance costs during the current year and the same employee's wages and benefits paid in the 1993 tax year, and it is available for 10 years (January 1, 1994 through December 31, 2003) up to a maximum of $20,000 of a qualified employee's income. Thus, the maximum annual credit per employee is $4,000. Employees generally are qualified employees if they (or their spouses) are enrolled in an Indian tribe and work on an Indian reservation or live on or near an Indian reservation and whose wages are less than $30,000 (adjusted for inflation after 1994) per year.

Accelerated depreciation of property on Indian reservations. Accelerated depreciation under Code Sec. 168 provides a special recovery period for qualified Indian reservation property that is placed in service after 1993 and before 2004. Special modified accelerated cost recovery periods (MACRS) are provided that permit faster writeoffs than those allowed to other businesses. Qualified Indian reservation property is generally property that is (1) used in the active conduct of a trade or business within an Indian reservation; (2) not used or located outside an Indian reservation on a regular basis; (3) not acquired (directly or indirectly) from a related person as defined in Code Sec. 465(b)(3)(C); and (4) not used for certain gaming purposes.

Job Creation Act Impact

Extension of accelerated depreciation rules and Indian employee credit.—The Job Creation and Worker Assistance Act of 2002 (P.L. 107-147) extends the Code Sec. 45A Indian employment tax credit through December 31, 2004. Code Sec. 168(j) is amended to extend the accelerated depreciation rules for qualified property on Indian reservations through December 31, 2004 (Code Sec. 45A(f) and Code Sec. 168(j)(8), as amended by the 2002 Act).

★ *Effective date.* No specific effective date is provided by the Job Creation and Worker Assistance Act of 2002 (P.L. 107-147). The provision is, therefore, considered effective on March 9, 2002, the date of enactment.

Act Sec. 613(a) of the Job Creation and Worker Assistance Act of 2002, amending Code Sec. 45A(f); Act Sec. 613(b), amending Code Sec. 168(j)(8). Law at ¶ 5051 and ¶ 5095. Committee Report at ¶ 10,540.

Subpart F Exemption for Active Financing

¶ 388

Background

Subpart F, which was added to the Internal Revenue Code in 1962, limits the deferral of U.S. tax on foreign income by certain U.S. owners of controlled foreign corporations (CFCs) (Code Secs. 951 through 964). Specifically, U.S. shareholders who own 10 percent or more of a CFC are subject to U.S. tax currently on their portion of the corporation's foreign personal holding company income, foreign base company services income and insurance income regardless of whether the income has been distributed (Code Sec. 951 and Code Sec. 952).

Congress enacted the subpart F rules largely to prevent tax avoidance and tax haven abuse, to promote greater tax equity and economic efficiency, and to avoid hindering the international competitiveness of U.S.-based multinational corporations. Certain modifications to the provisions have been introduced over the years, ostensibly preserving the broad objectives of the subpart F regime while adjusting to changes in international commerce, political priorities, and business practices, generally. However, Congressional concerns about competitiveness have led to a number of complex exceptions and special rules under subpart F, including the recent temporary provisions for active financing income ("*The Deferral of Income Earned Through U.S. Controlled Foreign Corporations*," Office of Tax Policy, Department of the Treasury, December 2000).

Temporary exceptions from subpart F income for active financing income were part of tax legislation enacted in 1997, 1998 and 1999. The Taxpayer Relief Act of 1997 (P.L. 105-34) provided temporary one-year exceptions from foreign personal holding company income and foreign base company services income, for tax years beginning in 1998, with respect to income derived from the active conduct of a banking, finance, or similar business, or in the conduct of an insurance business. The Tax and Trade Extension Act of 1998 (P.L. 105-277) modified these exceptions to treat various kinds of businesses with active financing income in a

Background _____

more comparable manner and extended the exceptions for one year, to tax years beginning in 1999. In addition, the 1998 Act broadened both the subpart F insurance income exception and the active financing income exception for investments of insurance income. In general, these exceptions, which had applied to income derived from risks within the CFC's country of organization or creation, were temporarily extended to include certain income derived from risks outside the CFC's country of organization or creation, provided nexus requirements were met.

The Tax Relief Extension Act of 1999 (P.L. 106-170) extended the active financing exceptions for two years, making the exceptions applicable to tax years of a CFC beginning in 1999, 2000, or 2001, and to tax years of a U.S. shareholder with or within which any such tax year of such corporation ends. The 1999 Act clarified that the more limited "same country" exception for insurance income that had been in effect prior to amendment by the 1998 Act applies with respect to a tax year of a CFC beginning after 2001. These temporary exceptions from subpart F income for active financing income were scheduled to expire on December 31, 2001.

_____

Job Creation Act Impact

Active financing income exceptions extended for five years.—The active financing income exceptions under subpart F are modified and extended for five years. Accordingly, the temporary exceptions from subpart F foreign personal holding company income, foreign base company services income and insurance income for certain income derived from the active conduct of a banking, finance, or similar business, or in the conduct of an insurance business apply to tax years of a CFC that begin in 2002, 2003, 2004, 2005, and 2006, and to tax years of U.S. shareholders with or within which any such tax year of such corporation ends (Code Sec. 953(e)(10) and Code Sec. 954(h)(9), as amended by the Job Creation and Worker Assistance Act of 2002 (P.L. 107-147)).

While the 2002 Act generally retains the current law regarding the determination of an insurance company's reserve for life insurance and annuity contracts under these exceptions, it allows for the use of the foreign statement reserve in some circumstances (Code Sec. 954(i)(4)(B), as amended by the 2002 Act). Specifically, under certain circumstances and subject to IRS approval through the ruling process or as provided in published guidance, a taxpayer may establish that the reserve for the contract is the amount considered in determining the foreign statement reserve for the contract (minus catastrophe, deficiency, equalization, or similar reserves). In granting its approval, the IRS will evaluate whether the method, interest rate, mortality and morbidity tables, and any other factors considered when determining foreign statement reserves (separately or as a whole) provide an "appropriate means" of measuring income for federal income tax purposes (Joint Committee on Taxation, *Technical Explanation of the "Job Creation and Worker Assistance Act of 2002"* (JCX-12-02), March 6, 2002).

In seeking IRS approval, the taxpayer must provide necessary and appropriate information regarding these factors so that the IRS can make a comparison to the reserve amount determined under the tax reserve method that would apply if the qualifying insurance company were subject to tax under Subchapter L of the Code. As noted in the JCT Explanation, the IRS may issue published guidance indicating its approval. In cases where the IRS has not approved the use of the foreign statement reserve, current law continues to apply with respect to reserves for life insurance or annuity contracts (Joint Committee on Taxation, *Technical Explanation of the "Job Creation and Worker Assistance Act of 2002"* (JCX-12-02), March 6, 2002).

Comment. The revenue effect of the extension of the active financing income exceptions under subpart F for fiscal years 2002–2007 is estimated to cost over $9 billion (Joint Committee on Taxation, *Estimated Revenue Effects of the Job Creation and Worker Assistance Act of 2002* (JCX-13-02), March 6, 2002).

PRACTICAL ANALYSIS. Paul Bodner, Esq., Great Neck, New York, comments that, in general, subpart F foreign personal holding company income does not include active business income. However, Congress carved out an exception for banks, insurance companies and other similar financial institutions. This was done when Congress needed revenue raisers and commercial banks did some politically foolish things that antagonized both the public and Congress. Since then, financial institutions have engaged in extensive lobbying efforts to correct this situation. Congress granted temporary relief for certain active financing income, necessitating continual lobbying. This five-year extension will provide some rest for the lobbyists; however, a permanent exception remains the goal.

In the insurance area, the IRS has had difficulty in determining what is insurance and what is an appropriate insurance reserve. Domestically, the Courts, and, perhaps somewhat reluctantly the IRS, have relied on State insurance regulators. Offshore insurance regulators, particularly those located on islands primarily noted for their beaches and sunshine, have not provided the same comfort. Thus, as a practical matter, in my experience, Revenue Agents have required offshore captive insurance companies to have reserves commensurate with the requirements of the New York State Insurance Commissioner. For life insurance and annuities, a competent actuary can make a determination more easily than in the casualty insurance area. The new legislation gives taxpayers the opportunity to have the computation blessed by way of a private revenue ruling. Presumably, if the IRS receives enough ruling requests providing enough necessary and appropriate information, it will publish a public ruling, eliminating the need for individual private rulings.

★ *Effective date.* This provision applies to tax years beginning after December 31, 2001 (Act Sec. 614(c) of the Job Creation and Worker Assistance Act of 2002 (P.L. 107-147)).

Act Sec. 614(a)(1) of the Job Creation and Worker Assistance Act of 2002, amending Code Sec. 953(e)(10); Act Sec. 614(a)(2), amending Code Sec. 954(h)(9); Act Sec. 614(b)(1), amending Code Sec. 954(i)(4)(B); Act Sec. 614(c). Law at ¶ 5250 and ¶ 5255. Committee Report at ¶ 10,550.

Cover Over of Tax on Distilled Spirits

¶ 390

Background ───────────────────────────────────────

Puerto Rico and the Virgin Islands receive a payment ("cover over") in the amount of $13.25 per proof gallon of the excise tax imposed on rum imported into the United States, regardless of the country of origin (Code Sec. 7652(f)). Amounts covered over to Puerto Rico and the Virgin Islands are deposited into the treasuries of the two possessions for use as those possessions determine. The excise tax does not apply to distilled spirits that are exported from the United States or consumed in U.S. possessions.

Prior to the enactment of the Tax Relief Extension Act of 1999 (P.L. 106-170), the rate of tax was $10.50 per proof gallon. The 1999 legislation increased the payment rate by $2.75 per proof gallon for the period July 1, 1999, through December 31, 2001. Beginning on January 1, 2002, the cover over rate was scheduled to return to its permanent level of $10.50 per proof gallon.

Job Creation Act Impact

Increased cover over rate extended.—The Job Creation and Worker Assistance Act of 2002 (P.L. 107-147) extends the $2.75 per proof gallon increase in the cover over rate for two additional years, through December 31, 2003 (Code Sec. 7652(f)(1), as amended by the 2002 Act). Thus, during 2002 and 2003, the cover over rate will continue to be $13.25 per proof gallon.

Comment. This extension is being granted because Congress believes that maintaining the increased rate of tax will contribute to economic stability in the two U.S. possessions (House Committee Report to H.R. 3090, H.R. Rep. No. 107-251, October 17, 2001). Furthermore, the House Committee Report notes that the Ways and Means Committee believes it is appropriate that Puerto Rico continue to allocate a portion of the cover over rate it receives to the Puerto Rico Conservation Trust.

★ *Effective date.* The provision applies to articles brought into the United States after December 31, 2001 (Act Sec. 609(b) of the Job Creation and Worker Assistance Act of 2002 (P.L. 107-147)).

Act Sec. 609(a) of the Job Creation and Worker Assistance Act of 2002, amending Code Sec. 7652(f)(1); Act Sec. 609(b). Law at ¶ 5390. Committee Report at ¶ 10,490.

Repeal of Requirement for Approved Diesel or Kerosene Terminals

¶ 392

Background ───────────────────────────────────────

Excise taxes are imposed on gasoline, diesel fuel and kerosene at various rates (Code Sec. 4081(a)). The tax is imposed at the time of the fuel's removal from a refinery or upon its importation unless the fuel is transferred by pipeline or barge to a terminal facility registered with the IRS. In such cases, the fuel is taxed upon its removal from the terminal rack (Reg. § 48.4081-2(b)).

However, diesel fuel and kerosene removed or sold for certain uses are exempt from the Code Sec. 4081 excise tax. To qualify for the exemption, the diesel fuel or

Background

kerosene must be used or sold for a nontaxable purpose (e.g., as heating oil) and it must be indelibly dyed for identification purposes (Code Sec. 4082(a)).

In order for a terminal facility to be eligible to handle non-tax-paid diesel fuel and kerosene, it must be registered with the IRS. If a terminal offers diesel fuel or kerosene for sale, it must offer both dyed and undyed forms of the fuel in order to be registered with the IRS (Code Sec. 4101(e)). This dyed-fuel mandate was enacted by the Taxpayer Relief Act of 1997 (P.L. 105-34) to be effective on July 1, 1998. The Surface Transportation Revenue Act of 1998 (P.L. 105-178) delayed this date until July 1, 2000. The Tax Relief Extension Act of 1999 (P.L. 106-170) further delayed this date until January 1, 2002, in order to give Congress time to evaluate whether the provision should be retained or repealed.

Job Creation Act Impact

Diesel fuel and kerosene mandate repealed.—The Job Creation and Worker Assistance Act of 2002 (P.L. 107-147) repeals the diesel fuel and kerosene dyeing mandate, effective January 1, 2002.

Comment. Since the repeal of Code Sec. 4101(e) is retroactive to January 1, 2002, the mandate technically never took effect.

Had the mandate not been repealed, terminals that sold diesel fuel would have been required to offer both dyed and undyed diesel fuel for sale in order to be registered with the IRS (Code Sec. 4101(e), prior to repeal by the 2002 Act). Similarly, as a prerequisite to registration, if a terminal offered kerosene for sale, it would have had to offer the fuel in both dyed and undyed forms.

The mandate was originally enacted to ensure availability of untaxed, dyed fuels in those markets where those fuels were commonly used. Since then, markets have provided dyed diesel fuel and dyed kerosene for nontaxable uses where there is a demand for them, even when there was no statutory requirement in effect to do so (House Committee Report to H.R. 3090, H.R. Rep. No. 107-251, October 17, 2001).

★ *Effective date.* The provision is effective on January 1, 2002 (Act Sec. 615(b) of the Job Creation and Worker Assistance Act of 2002 (P.L. 107-147)).

Act Sec. 615(a) of the Job Creation and Worker Assistance Act of 2002, repealing Code Sec. 4101(e); Act Sec. 615(b). Law at ¶ 5330. Committee Report at ¶ 10,560.

Chapter 4

New York City Tax Incentives

NYC TAX INCENTIVES

Tax Benefits for Area of NYC Damaged in Terrorist Attacks

¶ 405

Background

The area of New York City south of Canal Street was substantially damaged in the September 11, 2001, terrorist attacks. Many businesses operating in the area of the World Trade Center have experienced economic hardships since the attack. In response, New York Governor George E. Pataki lobbied Congress for a meaningful response to the economic needs of the area. A proposal was put forth in November 2001 to create a new "Liberty Zone" with an accompanying series of tax breaks. Rep. Amo Houghton (R-NY) introduced the original bill, H.R. 3373, as the New York Liberty Zone Tax Relief Act of 2001. The package of provisions was subsequently attached to an early version of the Victims of Terrorism Tax Relief Act (H.R. 2884), passed by the House on December 13, 2001, and in the Economic Security and Worker Assistance Act, but was not adopted as law. The provisions, packaged as new Code Sec. 1400L, ultimately were enacted as part of the Job Creation and Worker Assistance Act of 2002 (P.L. 107-147) on March 9, 2002.

Job Creation Act Impact

Tax benefits for New York Liberty Zone and New York City.—The Job Creation and Worker Assistance Act of 2002 (P.L. 107-147) includes a $5.5 billion economic rebuilding package specifically designed to reward investments in the area of lower Manhattan damaged by the terrorist attack on September 11, 2001. The area damaged in the attack is specifically defined and designated as the New York Liberty Zone. The new law includes a number of tax incentives for business activity in the Liberty Zone, including tax credits for hiring workers in the Liberty Zone, a 30-percent additional depreciation deduction for new property investments in the Liberty Zone, a five-year recovery period for leasehold improvements, a larger immediate write-off allowance for depreciable property, plus an authorization for $8 billion in new private activity bonds for reconstruction efforts in New York City.

¶ 405

The New York Liberty Zone is defined as the area on or south of Canal Street, East Broadway (east of its intersection with Canal Street), or Grand Street (east of its intersection with East Broadway) in the Borough of Manhattan in New York City.

The Liberty Zone tax benefits created by the 2002 Act are:

- a tax credit of up to $2,400 per employee to be available to Liberty Zone employers with 200 or fewer employees on average, in the form of work opportunity tax credits (¶ 410);

- a 30-percent additional first-year depreciation deduction for certain property investments in the Liberty Zone (¶ 415);

- a $35,000 increase in the amount of depreciable property that can be immediately expensed under Code Sec. 179 (¶ 420);

- a special five-year recovery period for leasehold improvements made to Liberty Zone property (¶ 425);

- an extension of the amount of time allowed to purchase replacements for involuntarily converted property to five years (¶ 430); and

- authorization of $8 billion in tax-exempt bonds over 2002-2004 to finance construction and renovation of real estate and infrastructure in the Liberty Zone, plus a waiver of certain bond refinancing rules giving New York City temporary access to additional funds (¶ 435).

PRACTICAL ANALYSIS. Michael Kessel, Esq., of OTS Tax Consulting, LLC, New York, New York, observes that the New York Liberty Zone provisions of the 2002 Act provide for rebuilding and growth of businesses in southern New York City and also may provide some strategic business planning opportunities for those businesses in the future.

The provisions establishing an additional 30-percent first-year depreciation deduction and the increase in expensing under Code Sec. 179 afford businesses a low-cost method of rebuilding and growing their businesses. Additionally, business taxpayers, in order to take advantage of the increased deductions, may wish to match the purchase of qualifying depreciable property and property that can be expensed with their more profitable years to offset any potential taxable income in those years.

Additionally, the extension of the work opportunity tax credit to new hires as well as existing employees affords Liberty Zone businesses and businesses relocated from the Liberty Zone a method of maintaining and even expanding their workforces to their pre-September 11, 2001, levels through 2003 while maintaining advantageous reduced salary expenses.

¶ 405

★ *Effective date.* No specific effective date is provided by the Job Creation and Worker Assistance Act of 2002 (P.L. 107-147). The provision is, therefore, considered effective on March 9, 2002, the date of enactment.

Act Sec. 301 of the Job Creation and Worker Assistance Act of 2002, adding Code Sec. 1400L. Law at ¶ 5300. Committee Reports at ¶ 10,100, ¶ 10,110, ¶ 10,120, ¶ 10,130, ¶ 10,140, ¶ 10,150 and ¶ 10,160.

TAX BENEFITS FOR NEW YORK LIBERTY ZONE

Work Opportunity Credit for Liberty Zone Employees

¶ 410

Background ———————————————————————

The work opportunity credit provides employers with an incentive to hire persons from targeted groups. Members of the targeted groups ordinarily have particularly high unemployment rates or other special employment needs. Currently, targeted groups of employees include recipients of Temporary Assistance for Needy Families, food stamp and Supplemental Security Income recipients, veterans, ex-felons, high-risk youth, vocational rehabilitation referrals, and summer youth employees. Employers wishing to claim the credit are required to obtain certification from a state employment security agency that a worker is a member of a targeted group.

The amount of the credit is 40 percent of qualified wages paid during the employee's first year of employment, provided the employee works at least 400 hours for the employer (Code Sec. 51(a)). The credit is 25 percent for employees working more than 120 but less than 400 hours during their first year. The credit is limited to the first $6,000 of wages paid to each targeted group individual, making the maximum credit $2,400 per employee (40 percent of $6,000). Wages taken into account for the work opportunity credit may not also be counted toward claiming the empowerment zone employment credit (under Code Sec. 1396(c)(3)) or the renewal community employment credit (under Code Sec. 1400H(a)).

The work opportunity credit is part of the general business credit under Code Sec. 38. The amount of the general business credit that can be claimed by a taxpayer is generally subject to a limit based on the tax liability of the taxpayer (Code Sec. 38(c)(1)). The formula used to calculate the limit has the effect of preventing a taxpayer from using the general business credit to offset alternative minimum tax liability. The general business credit can be used to offset 75 percent of a taxpayer's net regular tax liability (not AMT) in excess of $25,000. Net regular tax liability is the taxpayer's tax reduced by certain other credits.

The empowerment zone employment credit is excluded from the general limitation formula and limitations for it are computed separately (Code Sec. 38(c)(2)). The renewal community employment credit is included as part of the empowerment zone employment credit for this purpose (Code Sec. 1400H). The empowerment zone employment credit may generally be used to offset up to 25 percent of alternative minimum tax liability. The empowerment zone employment credit may also be used to offset 75 percent of a taxpayer's net regular tax liability in excess of $25,000, after being reduced by any other general business credits allowed for the tax year.

The amount of business credits that cannot be used because of these limitations (unused business credit) can generally be carried back one year and carried

¶ 410

forward for 20 years. Separate carryover records are required to be maintained for the portion of the general business credit attributable to the empowerment zone employment credit (Code Sec. 38(c)(2)).

Job Creation Act Impact

Work opportunity credit available for all NY Liberty Zone employee wages.—Employees of New York Liberty Zone businesses will be treated as members of a targeted group under a new work opportunity credit rule (Code Sec. 1400L(a)(1), as added by the Job Creation and Worker Assistance Act of 2002 (P.L. 107-147)). Wages paid to Liberty Zone business employees during 2002 and 2003 will thus be eligible for a work opportunity credit of up to 40 percent for the first $6,000 paid each year ($2,400 per employee). The credit is 25 percent for employment of less than 400 hours. Businesses that relocated outside of the Liberty Zone due to destruction or damage of their place of business may generally claim the credit for the number of employees in the Liberty Zone as of September 11, 2001. Large businesses averaging over 200 employees are ineligible for the credit.

Comment. The Liberty Zone work opportunity credit is available for both new hires and longstanding employees. For businesses located in the Liberty Zone, there is no limit on the number of employees for which the credit can be claimed—provided that the business averages no more than 200 employees on business days during the tax year.

New York Liberty Zone businesses eligible for the credit. Wages eligible for the Liberty Zone work opportunity credit must be paid to employees of a New York Liberty Zone business. A New York Liberty Zone business is any trade or business located in the New York Liberty Zone or located elsewhere in New York City as a result of the physical destruction or damage of its place of business by the terrorist attack on September 11, 2001 (Code Sec. 1400L(a)(2)(C)(i), as added by the 2002 Act). A large business with an average of more than 200 employees on business days during the tax year does not qualify as a New York Liberty Zone business (Code Sec. 1400L(a)(2)(C)(ii), as added by the 2002 Act).

Planning Note. A business currently operating elsewhere can qualify for the new credit by relocating in the New York Liberty Zone and having its employees perform services there.

New York Liberty Zone. The New York Liberty Zone is the area located on or south of Canal Street, East Broadway (east of its intersection with Canal Street), or Grand Street (east of its intersection with East Broadway) in the Borough of Manhattan in New York City (Code Sec. 1400L(h), as added by the 2002 Act).

Services must generally be performed in the Liberty Zone. Wages eligible for the Liberty Zone work opportunity credit must generally be paid to employees who perform substantially all of their services in the New York Liberty Zone (Code Sec. 1400L(a)(2)(A), as added by the 2002 Act). An exception applies for businesses that were forced to relocate as a result of the physical damage of their place of business as a result of the attack on September 11, 2001. For those businesses forced to relocate, the employee is eligible if substantially all services are performed in New York City (Code Sec. 1400L(a)(2)(B)(i), as added by the 2002 Act).

¶410

Comment. A Liberty Zone business that employs members of other targeted groups may continue to claim credits for those employees in addition to claiming credits for Liberty Zone business employees.

Businesses that relocated due to terrorist attack. Businesses that previously operated in the Liberty Zone but that relocated elsewhere due to the physical destruction or damage of their place of business on September 11, 2001, as a result of the terrorist attack, are considered Liberty Zone businesses. Wages paid to relocated Liberty Zone businesses' employees qualify for the credit if substantially all the employees' services are performed somewhere in New York City (Code Sec. 1400L(a)(2)(B), as added by the 2002 Act). A business relocated outside New York City, such as to New Jersey, does not qualify.

Comment. The definition of a qualifying relocated business states that the business must be located outside of the Liberty Zone as a result of the physical destruction or damage of the place of business by the September 11, 2001 terrorist attack. This definition does not include businesses that relocated for other reasons, such as diminished services in the Liberty Zone, perceived continuing danger, or other reasons other than physical damage.

Comment. The accommodation for relocated Liberty Zone businesses means that the Liberty Zone work opportunity credit is not limited to wages paid to employees currently working in the Liberty Zone.

Limit on credits for workers outside Liberty Zone. Relocated Liberty Zone businesses are limited in the number of employees working outside the Liberty Zone for whom they can claim the Liberty Zone work opportunity credit. The limit is the excess of the number of employees who were employed by the taxpayer in the Liberty Zone on September 11, 2001, over the number of employees who are currently employed by the taxpayer in the Liberty Zone (Code Sec. 1400L(a)(2)(B)(ii), as added by the 2002 Act). The IRS reserves the right to verify the number of a business's employees as of September 11, 2001, with the New York State Department of Labor. Current employees who are considered Liberty Zone business employees because they perform substantially all of their services in the Liberty Zone are subtracted from this limit (Code Sec. 1400L(a)(2)(B)(ii)(II), as added by the 2002 Act). However, workers who qualify because they continue to perform substantially all of their services in the Liberty Zone may be claimed without regard to any limit (i.e., they are added back to the limit) (Code Sec. 1400L(a)(2)(A), as added by the 2002 Act).

Planning Note. A relocated Liberty Zone employer that employs members of other target groups can claim the credit for more employees than it employed in the Liberty Zone on September 11, 2001—additional credits may be claimed for the workers who are members of other targeted groups as well as for workers in excess of the 9/11 number continuing to perform services in the Liberty Zone.

Example (1). SignCo's lower Manhattan place of business is sufficiently damaged in the September 11 attacks that it is forced to relocate its business elsewhere in New York City. On September 11 SignCo had 100 employees in the Liberty Zone. In 2002, SignCo has 90 employees, 10 of whom work in the Liberty Zone installing signs, and 80 of whom work elsewhere in New York City preparing the signs. SignCo may claim the credit for all 80 employees working outside the Liberty Zone in addition to the 10 employees working in the Zone. The limit on the number of non-Zone employees SignCo can claim is 90: the 100 Liberty Zone employees on September 11 minus the 10 employees

¶ 410

currently working in the Liberty Zone (Code Sec. 1400L(a)(2)(B), as added by the 2002 Act).

Example (2). Assume that SignCo has relocated out of the damaged part of Manhattan and now has 150 employees, 30 of whom are working in the Liberty Zone installing signs and 120 of whom work elsewhere in New York City. In this case only 70 of SignCo's 120 non-Zone employees may be claimed for the credit. The limit on the number of non-Zone employees for whom SignCo can claim the credit is 70: the 100 Liberty Zone employees on September 11 minus the 30 employees currently working in the Zone. The 30 Zone employees may also be claimed, for a total of 100 employees. The 50 employees added since September 11, 2001, do not qualify for the credit since they work outside of the Liberty Zone.

Example (3). Assume that SignCo has relocated and now has 150 employees, 120 of whom work in the Zone and 30 of whom work elsewhere in New York City. SignCo may claim the credit for none of its non-Zone employees (the limit is the excess of the number of employees working in the Zone on 9/11 (100) over the number of employees currently working in the Zone (120)), but may claim credits for all of its 120 Zone employees.

Maximum number of employees eligible for credit. A Liberty Zone business still operating in the Liberty Zone may claim the credit for all employees, without limit, provided that the business does not have an average of more than 200 employees on business days during the tax year. A business that relocated from the Liberty Zone due to damage to its place of business may claim the credit for up to the number of employees employed in the Liberty Zone on September 11, 2001 (Code Sec. 1400L(a)(2)(B)(ii), as added by the 2002 Act). Relocated businesses are also subject to the 200-average-number-of-employees limit.

Example (4). After an extended interruption in business, CopyCo resumes its business operations in the Liberty Zone in March 2002. CopyCo's employees perform substantially all of their services in the Liberty Zone. There are 250 business days for CopyCo during 2002. For the first 125 business days in 2002 CopyCo has only 50 employees. For the remaining 125 days in 2002 CopyCo increases its payroll to 300 employees. The average number of employees for business days during 2002 is 175: $(50 \times 125) + (300 \times 125) / 250 = 175$. Assuming all employees performed more than 120 hours of work during 2002, CopyCo may claim the Liberty Zone business employee credit for each of its 300 employees at the end of 2002.

Rules for counting the number of employees. The number of employees at a Liberty Zone business is determined by combining related businesses. The rules for determining the number of employees are identical to those applied to work opportunity credits for other targeted groups under Code Sec. 52 (Code Sec. 1400L(a)(2)(D), as added by the 2002 Act). All employees of all corporations that are members of the same controlled group are treated as employees of a single employer (Code Sec. 52(a)). Control for this purpose means ownership of more than 50 percent. Similarly, all employees of businesses that are under common control (as partnerships, sole proprietorships, etc.) are treated as employed by a single employer (Code Sec. 52(b)).

Planning Note. A business operating in the NY Liberty Zone with an average of 200 employees on business days in 2002 can claim the work opportunity credit for every one of its employees. Claiming the credit for each of 200 employees at $2,400 each means a potential $480,000 payroll savings in the form of tax

¶410

credits. A Liberty Zone business with an average of more than 200 employees on business days in 2002, on the other hand, is completely ineligible for the credit—there is no phaseout range as a business becomes larger. A Liberty Zone business hovering near the 200-employee mark can achieve a large tax savings by keeping its employee count average under 200 during the test period.

Ineligible employees. Certain types of workers cannot be included in calculating wages eligible for the work opportunity credit. Employees who are relatives or dependents of the employer are ineligible, as are individuals who own half or more of the employer's business (Code Sec. 51(i)).

Comment. The ban on claiming the credit for related employees means that family businesses that employ large numbers of related persons may be limited in the amount of credits for which they are eligible.

An ineligible employee is a person who bears one of the following relationships to the taxpayer:

(1) a child, grandchild, brother, sister, parent, aunt, uncle, niece or nephew;

(2) a step-child, step-sibling or step-parent;

(3) a son- or daughter-in-law, father- or mother-in-law, or brother- or sister-in-law;

(4) a person who owns, directly or indirectly, more than 50 percent of a taxpayer that is a corporation;

(5) a person who owns, directly or indirectly, more than 50 percent of the capital and profits of the business, if it is an entity other than a corporation;

(6) if the taxpayer is an estate or trust, a grantor, beneficiary, or fiduciary of the estate or trust, or any of the relatives listed in (1) through (3) of the grantor, beneficiary, or fiduciary; or

(7) a dependent living with the taxpayer.

Comment. Rehires do qualify for the Liberty Zone business employee credit (Code Sec. 1400L(a)(2)(D)(iii), as added by the 2002 Act, and Code Sec. 51(i)(2)). This is contrary to the eligibility rules applicable to work opportunity tax credits claimed for members of other targeted groups.

Qualified wages not limited to first-year wages. Wages eligible for the credit include any wages paid to a Liberty Zone business employee for work performed during calendar years 2002 and 2003 (Code Sec. 1400L(a)(2)(D)(iv), as added by the 2002 Act). Unlike other targeted groups, wages paid to Liberty Zone business employees do not need to be first-year wages in order to qualify for the credit (Code Sec. 1400L(a)(2)(D)(i), as added by the 2002 Act).

Comment. Qualifying wages must be paid or incurred for work performed in 2002 or 2003, but there is no requirement that all eligible wages must be paid during those years.

Part-time or temporary employees. Wages eligible for the credit must be paid to employees who worked at least 120 hours for the employer (Code Sec. 51(i)(3)). The amount of the credit is reduced to 25 percent of the first $6,000 in wages for employees who worked fewer than 400 hours (but more than 120 hours). Wages paid to employees working 400 or more hours are eligible for the full 40-percent credit.

¶410

Dates the credit will apply. The credit is available for wages paid or incurred for work performed in 2002 and 2003, whether or not those years were the first year of employment for the eligible employee. The credit for Liberty Zone business employees is not limited by the credit sunset provision in Code Sec. 51(c)(4), under which the credit is currently scheduled to expire at the end of 2003 (Code Sec. 1400L(a)(2)(D)(iii), as added by the 2002 Act, and Code Sec. 51(c)(4)(B), as amended by the 2002 Act (see ¶ 374)). The Code Sec. 51 sunset provision limits the credit to wages paid to or incurred by an individual who begins work on or before December 31, 2003.

Comment. Both the Liberty Zone work opportunity credit and the regular work opportunity credit under Code Sec. 51 now extend to eligible wages paid or incurred for work during 2002 and 2003. Technically, however, the regular work opportunity credit can also be claimed for work done in 2004. The employee must *begin work* for the employer before the end of 2003; however, assuming this condition is met, the employee's first-year wages will be eligible for the credit regardless of whether part of the work for which the eligible wages are paid is performed in 2004 (Code Sec. 51(c)(4)). The exemption of the Liberty Zone work opportunity credit from the Code Sec. 51 sunset thus puts employers claiming Liberty Zone business employee credits in a slightly disadvantageous position.

Certification of employees not required. The definition of the Liberty Zone targeted group of employees does *not* include a certification requirement (Code Sec. 1400L(a)(1) and Code Sec. 1400L(a)(2), as added by the 2002 Act). Most targeted groups under the work opportunity credit are defined as employees who are certified by a designated local agency as being members of a specific group. Certification is ordinarily required to be obtained prior to the employment start date, or within 21 days of starting work (Code Sec. 51(d)(12)). Liberty Zone businesses will not be required to obtain certification in order to treat employees as qualified Liberty Zone business employees.

Credit applies for both regular and AMT purposes. The Liberty Zone work opportunity credit is allowed to offset *all of* a taxpayer's alternative minimum tax liability as well as 75 percent of the taxpayer's regular net tax liability in excess of $25,000, as reduced by any allowable general business credit (Code Sec. 38(c)(3), as added by the 2002 Act).

The general formula used to place limits on the allowable general business credit states that the allowable credit may not exceed the net income tax minus the greater of (1) the tentative minimum tax, or (2) 25 percent of net regular tax liability above $25,000 (Code Sec. 38(c)(1)). For purposes of computing the limit on the Liberty Zone business employee credit, the formula is revised to assume that the tentative minimum tax is zero (Code Sec. 38(c)(3)(A)(ii), as amended by the 2002 Act). The limitation on the Liberty Zone business employee credit is thus the taxpayer's "net income tax" minus 25 percent of the taxpayer's regular income tax in excess of $25,000, reduced by any other business credits allowed for the tax year (including the empowerment zone employment credit).

Net income tax for purposes of the formula is the regular tax liability plus alternative minimum tax liability, reduced by certain credits (personal credits, foreign tax credits, and credits for production of nonconventional fuels) (Code Sec. 38(c)). A taxpayer who has no regular income tax and claims no other business credits would be allowed to offset the full alternative minimum tax liability with Liberty Zone business employee credits. A similar taxpayer with only a regular tax liability would be able to offset 75 percent of the tax liability exceeding $25,000.

¶ 410

Ordering rule. A taxpayer's net income tax is first reduced by the general business credit (as combined on Form 3800, General Business Credit, or reported separately if only one component of the credit is claimed), and is subsequently reduced by any allowable empowerment zone employment credit (Code Sec. 38(c)(2)(A)(ii), as amended by the 2002 Act; see Form 8844, Empowerment Zone Employment Credit). Any remaining net income tax will be reduced by the New York Liberty Zone business employee credit (Code Sec. 38(c)(3)(A)(ii), as amended by the 2002 Act). The order of claiming credits means that the greatest component of credit carryovers will consist of Liberty Zone business employee credits, since these are the last to be used to reduce tax liability. This order is advantageous to the taxpayer since, unlike the general business credit, Liberty Zone business employee credits may be used to offset alternative minimum tax liability.

Comment. Presumably, a form similar to Form 8844 will be developed to calculate allowable Liberty Zone business employee credits and carryovers, if any.

Separate carryover and carryback records. The Liberty Zone business employee credit must be separately calculated from other business credits and is subject to different limitations (Code Sec. 38(c)(3)(A)(i), as added by the 2002 Act). The credit particularly differs in that it may be used to offset all of a taxpayer's alternative minimum tax liability. For this reason, separate records are necessary to track permissible carryback and carryforward periods. The carryback period for the credit is the same as other business credits, namely, unused portions of the credit may be carried back for one tax year and forward for 20 tax years.

Planning Note. The carryback allowance means that a taxpayer who anticipates having unusable credits for the 2002 tax year, for example, because the taxpayer's 2002 tax liability was eliminated by this and other Liberty Zone tax incentives, can plan to carry back the unused credits to offset 2001 tax liability.

Comment. The work opportunity credit must be separately calculated for employees who qualify as New York Liberty Zone business employees and employees who qualify as members of other targeted groups under Code Sec. 51. The general work opportunity credit is combined with other general business credits and subject to the general business credit limitations.

★ *Effective date.* For the New York Liberty Zone work opportunity credit under Code Sec. 1400L(a), no specific effective date is provided by the Job Creation and Worker Assistance Act of 2002 (P.L. 107-147). The provision is, therefore, considered effective on March 9, 2002, the date of enactment. The special rule for determining the limitation based on tax liability for the New York Liberty Zone business employee credit is effective for tax years ending after December 31, 2001 (Act Sec. 301(b)(3) of the Job Creation and Worker Assistance Act of 2002 (P.L. 107-147)).

Act Sec. 301(a) of the Job Creation and Worker Assistance Act of 2002, adding Code Sec. 1400L(a) and Code Sec. 1400L(h); Act Sec. 301(b)(1), redesignating Code Sec. 38(c)(3) as Code Sec. 38(c)(4) and adding new Code Sec. 38(c)(3); Act Sec. 301(b)(2), amending Code Sec. 38(c)(2)(A)(ii)(II); Act Sec. 301(b)(3). Law at ¶ 5300 and ¶ 5040. Committee Report at ¶ 10,100.

Bonus Depreciation for Liberty Zone Property

¶ 415

Background ————————————————————————————————

The cost of depreciable property placed in service after 1986 is generally recovered using the Modified Accelerated Cost Recovery System (MACRS). Each type of property is assigned to a property class in accordance with the property class table issued by the IRS in Rev. Proc. 87-56 (1987-2 CB 674). The property classes for personal property are: 3-year property, 5-year property, 7-year property, 10-year property, 15-year property, and 20-year property. The depreciation periods are three years for 3-year property, five years for 5-year property, etc. Longer recovery periods apply if the MACRS alternative depreciation system (ADS) is used. Real property is generally classified as either residential rental property (a 27.5-year depreciation period applies) or nonresidential real property (a 39-year depreciation period applies). Water utility property is depreciated over 25 years.

In the case of 3-, 5-, 7-, and 10-year property, the applicable depreciation method is the 200-percent declining balance method. The 150- percent declining balance method applies to 10- and 15-year property. A half-year convention applies to personal property unless the mid-quarter convention applies. Under the half-year convention, one-half year's depreciation is claimed in the year that an asset is placed in service or disposed of. The mid-quarter convention applies if more than 40 percent of the total basis of all personal property placed in service in the tax year is placed in service in the last three months of the tax year. When the mid-quarter convention applies, an asset is considered placed in service or disposed of on the mid-point of the quarter in which it is placed in service or disposed of.

The straight-line method and mid-month convention apply to residential rental and nonresidential real property. Under this convention, an asset is considered placed in service or disposed of on the midpoint of the month it is placed in service or disposed of.

Subject to certain limitations, a taxpayer may claim a current deduction under Code Sec. 179 for the cost of tangible personal property acquired for use in the active conduct of a trade or business. The maximum deduction is $24,000 for 2001 and 2002 and $25,000 for 2003 and thereafter. The cost of any property expensed under Code Sec. 179 is reduced for purposes of computing depreciation.

Job Creation Act Impact

Thirty-percent additional depreciation allowance for qualified Liberty Zone property acquired on or after September 11, 2001.—Qualified New York Liberty Zone property is eligible for an additional 30-percent first-year depreciation allowance (Code Sec. 1400L(b)(1)(A), as added by the Job Creation and Worker Assistance Act of 2002 (P.L. 107-147)). This 30-percent allowance (the "Code Sec. 1400L(b) allowance") is computed on the adjusted basis of qualified property and reduces the adjusted basis of the property before any other allowable depreciation deduction is computed on the property (Code Sec. 1400L(b)(1)(B), as added by the 2002 Act). In addition, it may not be claimed on property that also otherwise qualifies for the 30-percent depreciation allowance that is provided by new Code Sec. 168(k) (the "Code Sec. 168(k) allowance) and described at ¶ 305 (Code Sec. 1400L(b)(2)(C)(i), as added by the 2002 Act).

New York Liberty Zone. The New York Liberty Zone is the area located on or south of Canal Street, East Broadway (east of its intersection with Canal Street), or Grand Street (east of its intersection with East Broadway) in the Borough of Manhattan in New York City (Code Sec. 1400L(h), as added by the 2002 Act).

Comment. Although the definition of "property" for purposes of computing the additional depreciation allowance under new Code Sec. 168(k) is specifically included in the definition of "property" under new Code Sec. 1400L(b) (Code Sec. 1400L(b)(2)(A)(i)(I)), there are a number of important differences between the definitions that should be noted. The most significant of these are that: (1) certain destroyed or condemned real property qualifies under Code Sec. 1400L(b) (Code Sec. 1400L(b)(2)(A)(i)(II)), (2) used property can qualify (Code Sec. 1400L(b)(2)(A)(iii)), and (3) more time is given for placing qualifying property in service (Code Sec. 1400L(b)(2)(A)(v)).

Basis for computing Liberty Zone additional depreciation. The adjusted basis of qualified Liberty Zone property is first reduced by any Code Sec. 179 deduction claimed (see ¶ 420). The 30-percent additional depreciation allowance is computed on the adjusted basis as reduced by the Code Sec. 179 expense allowance. The MACRS depreciation deductions are then computed on the adjusted basis as reduced by the Code Sec. 179 allowance and the 30-percent additional depreciation allowance (Code Sec. 1400L(b)(1)(B)), as added by the 2002 Act). These are the same ordering rules that apply to the Code Sec. 168(k) allowance. See ¶ 305 for computation examples.

Comment. As explained at ¶ 420, the otherwise allowable Code Sec. 179 deduction has been increased by an additional $35,000 for qualifying property used in the Liberty Zone. Thus, in 2001 (for property acquired after September 10, 2001) and 2002, the maximum deduction is $59,000 ($24,000 + $35,000) and $60,000 thereafter ($25,000 + $35,000).

Qualified New York Liberty Zone property. The following types of property can qualify for the additional Liberty Zone depreciation allowance under Code Sec. 1400L(b)(2)(A)(i)(I):

(1) Property that is depreciable under MACRS and has a recovery period of 20 years or less;

(2) Computer software which is depreciable under Code Sec. 167(f)(1)(B) using the straight-line method over 36 months;

(3) Water utility property;

(4) Qualified leasehold improvement property; or

(5) Certain real property to the extent it constitutes a rehabilitation or replacement of property destroyed or condemned as a result of the September 11, 2001, terrorist attack (Code Sec. 1400L(b)(2)(A)(i)(II)).

Comment. The first four types of property are the only types of property that are eligible for the Code Sec. 168(k) allowance. These categories are described as property to which Code Sec. 168 applies. Intangibles depreciable under Code Sec. 197 thus do not qualify for the additional allowance (Code Sec. 1400L(b)(2)(A)(i)(I), as added by the 2002 Act, and Code Sec. 168(k)(2)(A)(i)(I), as added by the 2002 Act.

The following additional requirements must also be met in order for property to qualify for the Code Sec. 1400L(b) allowance:

(1) substantially all of the use of the property must be in the New York Liberty Zone (Code Sec. 1400L(b)(2)(A)(ii));

(2) the property must be used in the active conduct of a trade or business by the taxpayer in the Liberty Zone (Code Sec. 1400L(b)(2)(A)(ii));

(3) the original use of the property in the Liberty Zone must commence with the taxpayer after September 10, 2001 (Code Sec. 1400L(b)(2)(A)(iii));

(4) the property must be acquired by purchase (as defined in Code Sec. 179(d), see below) after September 10, 2001 (but see below if a binding contract applies) (Code Sec. 1400L(b)(2)(A)(iv)); and

(5) the property must be placed in service by the taxpayer on or before the "termination date", which is December 31, 2006 (December 31, 2009, in the case of nonresidential real property and residential rental property) (See below for further qualifications on eligible real property) (Code Sec. 1400L(b)(2)(A)(v)).

Comment. Property can qualify under the Code Sec. 168(k) allowance only if it is placed in service on or before December 31, 2004 (December 31, 2005, for certain property with a longer production period). See ¶ 305.

Comment. The active conduct of a trade or business use requirement does not apply to the Code Sec. 168(k) allowance. Depreciable investment property thus qualifies for bonus depreciation under Code Sec. 168(k), but does not qualify for the Liberty Zone additional depreciation.

Property acquired by purchase after September 10, 2001. Property will not qualify if a binding written contract for the acquisition of the property was in effect before September 11, 2001 (Code Sec. 1400L(b)(2)(A)(iv)). Property is considered acquired by purchase if it meets the requirements under Code Sec. 179(d)(2). This section defines "purchase" as any acquisition of property *except* property: (1) acquired from a person whose relationship to the taxpayer would bar recognition of a loss in any transaction between them under Code Sec. 267 or Code Sec. 707(b); (2) acquired from a another member of a controlled group (substituting a more-than-50-percent ownership test for the at-least-80-percent ownership test in Code Sec. 1563(a)(1)); (3) with a substituted basis (in whole or in part); or (4) acquired from a decedent with a fair-market value basis (Code Sec. 1400L(b)(2)(A)(iv), as added by the 2002 Act).

Comment. The Code Sec. 168(k) allowance does not have an acquisition by purchase requirement. See ¶ 305.

Used property. The Joint Committee Explanation indicates that used property may qualify as long as it was not previously used in the Liberty Zone. The Explanation further states that additional capital expenditures incurred to recondition or rebuild property for which the original use in the Liberty Zone began with the taxpayer will also satisfy the original use requirement (Joint Committee on Taxation, *Technical Explanation of the "Job Creation and Worker Assistance Act of 2002"* (JCX-12-02), March 6, 2002).

Comment. Used property does not qualify for the Code Sec. 168(k) allowance.

Sale-leasebacks. A limited exception to the original use requirement applies to sale-leasebacks. The rule applies to property that is originally placed in service after September 10, 2001, by a person who sells it to the taxpayer and then leases it from the taxpayer within three months after the date that the property was originally placed in service. In this situation, the property is treated as originally placed in serviced by the taxpayer and the placed in service date is deemed to occur no earlier than the date that the property is used under the leaseback (Code Sec. 1400L(b)(2)(D)(ii), as added by the 2002 Act).

Self-constructed property for use by the taxpayer. Property manufactured, constructed, or produced by a taxpayer for the taxpayer's own use is treated as acquired after September 10, 2001, if the taxpayer began manufacturing, constructing, or producing the property after September 10, 2001 (Code Sec. 1400L(b)(2)(D)(i), as added by the 2002 Act). The Joint Committee Explanation states that property that is manufactured, constructed, or produced for the taxpayer by another person under a contract that is entered into prior to the manufacture, construction, or production of the property is considered manufactured, constructed, or produced by the taxpayer (Joint Committee on Taxation, *Technical Explanation of the "Job Creation and Worker Assistance Act of 2002"* (JCX-12-02), March 6, 2002).

Eligible real property. Eligible real property is defined as nonresidential real property or residential rental property that rehabilitates real property damaged, or replaces real property destroyed or condemned, as a result of the September 11, 2001, terrorist attack.

Property is treated as replacing real property destroyed or condemned if, as part of an integrated plan, the property replaces real property which is included in a continuous area which includes real property destroyed or condemned (Code Sec. 1400L(b)(2)(B), as added by the 2002 Act).

Comment. The Joint Committee Explanation states that real property destroyed or condemned only includes circumstances in which an entire building or structure was destroyed or condemned as a result of the terrorist attacks. Otherwise, the property is considered damaged real property. If structural components of a building (for example, walls, floors, or plumbing fixtures) are damaged or destroyed and the building is not destroyed or condemned, then only costs related to replacing the damaged or destroyed components qualify for the additional allowance.

Mandatory ADS property is disqualified. Property which must be depreciated under the MACRS alternative depreciation system (ADS) (Code Sec. 168(k)(2)(C)(i)) does not qualify for the Code Sec. 1400L(b) allowance or the Code Sec. 168(k) allowance (Code Sec. 1400L(b)(2)(C)(ii)). Property for which ADS is elected does qualify, assuming all other requirements are satisfied. See ¶ 305.

Certain leasehold improvement property is disqualified. "Qualified New York Liberty Zone leasehold improvement property" does not qualify for the Code Sec. 1400L(b) allowance or the Code Sec. 168(k) allowance (Code Sec. 1400L(b)(2)(C)(iii), as added by the 2002 Act). This property, however, may be depreciated using the straight-line method over five years. See ¶ 425.

Comment. The five-year depreciation period is a significant tax break. Leasehold improvements are generally depreciable using the straight-line method over 27.5 years if made to residential rental property and over 39 years if made to nonresidential real property.

Election. A taxpayer may elect out of the provision. Rules similar to those that apply under Code Sec. 168(k) are to apply under Code Sec. 1400L(b) (Code Sec. 1400L(b)(2)(C)(iv), as added by the 2002 Act). Thus, the election out is made at the property class level. Code Sec. 168(k)(2)(C)(iii) provides that the election applies to all property in the class or classes for which the election out is made that is placed in service for the tax year of the election.

Alternative minimum tax. The Code Sec. 1400L(b) allowance may be claimed against alternative minimum tax in the tax year that the qualifying property is placed in service. No AMT adjustment is made (Code Sec. 1400L(b)(2)(E), as added by the 2002 Act; Joint Committee on Taxation, *Technical Explanation of the "Job Creation and Worker Assistance Act of 2002"* (JCX-12-02), March 6, 2002). The same rule applies to property for which the Code Sec. 168(k) allowance is claimed (Code Sec. 168(k)(2)(F), as added by the 2002 Act).

★ *Effective date.* No specific effective date is provided by the Job Creation and Worker Assistance Act of 2002 (P.L. 107-147). The provision is, therefore, considered effective on March 9, 2002, the date of enactment.

Act Sec. 301(a) of the Job Creation and Worker Assistance Act of 2002, adding Code Sec. 1400L(b). Law at ¶ 5300. Committee Report at ¶ 10,110.

Increase in Expensing for Liberty Zone Property

¶ 420

Background

A taxpayer with a sufficiently small amount of annual investment in qualifying property may elect to deduct up to $24,000 of the cost of qualifying property in lieu of depreciation for the year the property is placed in service (Code Sec. 179). This amount is increased to $25,000 of the cost of qualified property placed in service for tax years beginning in 2003 and thereafter. Property that qualifies for expensing under Code Sec. 179 is generally depreciable tangible personal property that is purchased for use in the active conduct of a trade or business. No general business credit under Code Sec. 38 is allowed with respect to any amount for which a deduction is allowed under Code Sec. 179.

Investment limitation. Taxpayers with very large annual investments of qualifying property may not be eligible for expensing. The $24,000 amount eligible for expensing is reduced (but not below zero) by the amount by which the total cost of qualifying property placed in service during the tax year exceeds $200,000 (Code Sec. 179(b)(2)). Thus, the Code Sec. 179 deduction is completely phased out once a taxpayer's annual investment reaches $224,000 ($225,000 for 2003 and thereafter).

Property used in an empowerment zone. A business that uses qualified property in an empowerment zone (within the meaning of Code Sec. 1397A) may elect to expense an additional $35,000 for tax years beginning in 2002 and thereafter, for a total expensing limit of $59,000 in 2002 ($35,000 plus $24,000) and $60,000 in 2003 ($35,000 plus $25,000) (Code Sec. 1397A(a)(1)). This maximum is reduced to the cost of qualified empowerment zone property placed in service during the year if that amount is lower than $35,000.

In addition, the Code Sec. 179 deduction is subject to a modified investment limitation for enterprise zone businesses. Only 50 percent of the cost of qualified empowerment zone property that is Code Sec. 179 property is taken into account in determining whether the taxpayer has reached the phaseout range. Thus, an enterprise zone business investing in property in an empowerment zone would be able to invest up to $400,000 annually before the deduction is reduced due to this limitation.

Background

Taxable income limitation. The amount eligible to be expensed for a tax year may not exceed the amount of taxable income derived from the active conduct of a trade or business for that year. Any amount that is not allowed as a deduction because of the taxable income limitation may be carried forward to succeeding tax years.

Job Creation Act Impact

Increase in expensing limitation for property used in New York Liberty Zone.—The maximum annual amount of depreciable property that may be expensed under Code Sec. 179 will be increased by $35,000 for qualifying property used in the New York Liberty Zone (Code Sec. 1400L(f)(1)(A), as added by the Job Creation and Worker Assistance Act of 2002). The $35,000 additional expensing allowance is limited to the cost of Code Sec. 179 property that is qualified New York Liberty Zone property placed in service during the tax year, if this amount is less than $35,000 (Code Sec. 1400L(f)(1)(A)(ii), as added by the 2002 Act). The maximum total amount eligible for expensing under Code Sec. 179 for this type of property is thus $59,000 for 2001 and 2002 and $60,000 for 2003 through 2006 ($35,000 plus the otherwise available limit of $24,000 for 2002 and $25,000 for 2003 and thereafter). The additional deduction ends for property placed in service after December 31, 2006.

In addition to the increased expensing allowance, the deduction phaseout rule based on a taxpayer's total investments for the tax year is modified to take into account only 50 percent of the taxpayer's investments in Code Sec. 179 property that qualify as New York Liberty Zone property (Code Sec. 1400L(f)(1)(B)). The revised formula in effect increases the beginning of the phaseout range to $400,000, assuming all the invested property is Liberty Zone property.

Comment. The provision treats taxpayers in the New York Liberty Zone similar to enterprise zone businesses under Code Sec. 1397A.

Qualified New York Liberty Zone property. The additional expensing allowance is limited to the cost of qualified New York Liberty Zone property placed in service during the tax year (as defined in Code Sec. 1400L(b)(2), as added by the 2002 Act). The requirements for claiming the additional Liberty Zone expensing allowance are:

- the property must otherwise qualify as Code Sec. 179 property

- the property must be purchased (within the meaning of Code Sec. 179(d)) and placed in service after September 10, 2001, and before January 1, 2007

- the original use of the property in the Liberty Zone must commence with the taxpayer after September 10, 2001

- substantially all of the use of the property must be in the New York Liberty Zone in the active conduct of a trade or business by the taxpayer in the Zone (Code Sec. 1400L(f)(2) and Code Sec. 1400L(b)(2), as added by the 2002 Act).

Property for which the MACRS alternative depreciation system (ADS) is mandatory does not qualify for the increased Code Sec. 179 allowance.

Property can qualify for both the Liberty Zone 50-percent bonus depreciation (see ¶ 415) and the additional Code Sec. 179 allowance.

Comment. The increased allowance means that more small businesses in the Liberty Zone will be released from the need to make depreciation computations or, at least, will need to make fewer computations. The increase in the investment limitation (described below) for investments in the Liberty Zone also means that many larger businesses that would otherwise be ineligible to claim the Code Sec. 179 deduction will be able to claim it.

New York Liberty Zone. The New York Liberty Zone is the area located on or south of Canal Street, East Broadway (east of its intersection with Canal Street), or Grand Street (east of its intersection with East Broadway) in the Borough of Manhattan in New York City (Code Sec. 1400L(h), as added by the 2002 Act).

Property purchased after September 10, 2001. Property is not considered purchased by the taxpayer if it is acquired from a related party or by a member of a controlled group, has a substituted basis or is acquired from a decedent with a fair market value basis (Code Sec. 1400L(b)(2)(A)(iv), as added by the 2002 Act, and Code Sec. 179(d)(2)). Property will not qualify if a binding written contract for the acquisition of the property was in effect before September 11, 2001.

Property manufactured, constructed, or produced by a taxpayer for the taxpayer's own use is treated as acquired after September 10, 2001, if the taxpayer began manufacturing, constructing, or producing the property after September 10, 2001 (Code Sec. 1400L(b)(2)(D), as added by the 2002 Act). The Joint Committee Explanation states that property that is manufactured, constructed, or produced for the taxpayer by another person under a contract that is entered into prior to the manufacture, construction, or production of the property is considered manufactured, constructed, or produced by the taxpayer (Joint Committee on Taxation, *Technical Explanation of the "Job Creation and Worker Assistance Act of 2002"* (JCX-12-02), March 6, 2002).

Original use of property in Liberty Zone commences with taxpayer after September 10, 2001. The Joint Committee Explanation indicates that used property may qualify as long as it was not previously used in the Liberty Zone. The Explanation further states that additional capital expenditures incurred to recondition or rebuild property for which the original use in the Liberty Zone began with the taxpayer will also satisfy the original use requirement (Joint Committee on Taxation, *Technical Explanation of the "Job Creation and Worker Assistance Act of 2002"* (JCX-12-02), March 6, 2002).

Increased investment limitation for Liberty Zone property. The Code Sec. 179 allowance is generally reduced for taxpayers with investments above $200,000 during the year. For qualifying Liberty Zone property, the expensing limitation is reduced by the excess of (1) 50 percent of the cost of Code Sec. 179 property that is qualified Liberty Zone property placed in service during the tax year plus the total amount of any other Code Sec. 179 property placed in service during the tax year, over (2) $200,000. The practical implication of this formula is to double the amount that can be invested in Liberty Zone property before the deduction begins to phase out (phaseouts begin at $400,000, rather than $200,000). For Liberty Zone property placed in service in 2002, the deduction will be completely phased out once the amount invested equals or exceeds $518,000 (the deduction limit is $59,000). In 2003, the deduction will be completely phased out at $520,000 (the deduction limit is $60,000).

¶ 420

Example. NYCorp places a new machine in service in the New York Liberty Zone in 2002. The machine is Code Sec. 179 property that is qualified NY Liberty Zone property and has a cost of $64,000. Under the dollar limitation alone, $59,000 of this cost is deductible in 2002. If NYCorp also has placed other Code Sec. 179 Liberty Zone property in service in 2002 with a cost of $450,000, then only $2,000 of the cost of the machine would be deductible under Code Sec. 179. One-half of the total cost of all Code Sec. 179 property that is Liberty Zone property, or $257,000, is used in computing the reduction amount. $200,000 is subtracted from this amount ($64,000 + $450,000) × ½ = $257,000 minus $200,000 is $57,000). The expensing limitation of $59,000 has to be reduced by $57,000, leaving a maximum deduction of $2,000.

Planning Note. Taxpayers may time the placing of property in service in such a way as to avoid the investment limitation. The amount by which the Code Sec. 179 expense deduction is reduced under the investment limitation rule is lost and may not be carried forward and deducted in later tax years. While this might ordinarily mean that a taxpayer should consider delaying the purchase of qualifying property, the $400,000 plus limit allows extra room for placing property in service for tax years 2002 and 2003. It encourages smaller businesses to purchase more assets for use in the Liberty Zone since they do not need to worry as much about losing the Code Sec. 179 allowance.

Other Code Sec. 179 provisions apply. Other than the increased dollar amount limitation and increased phaseout range, the provisions of Code Sec. 179 are applied to Liberty Zone property in the same manner as they are applied to other businesses. Thus, all members of a controlled group are treated as a single taxpayer for purposes of applying the dollar limitations. The limitations apply at both the partnership and partner level and at the S corporation and shareholder level.

Planning Note. Generally, it is beneficial to a taxpayer to allocate the deduction to assets with the longest depreciation period to enhance value of the deduction. For example, if the cost of an item of 10-year property or three-year property may be expensed, the taxpayer will recover his or her entire costs within three years if he or she expenses the 10-year property immediately.

Recapture of amounts expensed. A Code Sec. 179 deduction attributable to investments in Liberty Zone property must be recaptured if the property ceases to be used predominantly in the active conduct of a trade or business in the New York Liberty Zone (Code Sec. 1400L(f)(3), as added by the 2002 Act). Recapture means that the taxpayer must include as ordinary income the tax benefit derived from the Code Sec. 179 deduction from the time the property was placed in service to the time the property is no longer used in the Liberty Zone (Code Sec. 179(d)(10) and Reg. § 1.179-1(e)(2)). The recaptured amount is the difference between the depreciation deduction that would have been permitted under MACRS for the time the property was in use in the Liberty Zone and the amount that was actually deducted using the Code Sec. 179 election (Reg. § 1.179-1(e)(1)).

Comment. Presumably, removal of the property from the Liberty Zone for continued business use outside of the Zone would result in recapture with respect to the $35,000 additional Code Sec. 179 allowance provided for property used in the Liberty Zone but not the $24,000 or $25,000 standard Code Sec. 179 allowance. The sum of both components of the allowance ($59,000/$60,000) should be subject to recapture in the year that the property is not used predominantly for business purposes even if the property remains in the Zone (e.g., if personal use falls to 50 percent or less).

Planning Note. Many taxpayers time the acquisition and placing in service of property within a tax year to avoid application of the mid-quarter depreciation convention because the mid-quarter convention usually results in less overall depreciation than the half-year convention in the first year of the recovery period. The mid-quarter depreciation convention applies when more than 40 percent of the depreciable basis of personal property is placed in service during the fourth quarter of the tax year. Amounts expensed under Code Sec. 179, however, are not taken into account in determining whether the mid-quarter convention applies. Thus, if the mid-quarter depreciation convention would otherwise apply, the expense allowance may be allocated to fourth quarter purchases to avoid its application. Note that this type of mid-quarter convention tax planning is not necessary for a tax year that includes September 11, 2001, in either the third or fourth quarter of a taxpayer's tax year. The IRS is allowing taxpayers with tax years that include September 11, 2001, in the third or fourth quarter of their tax year to elect out of the mid-quarter convention (Notice 2001-70, I.R.B. 2001-45; Notice 2001-74, I.R.B. 2001-49).

Caution. For property placed in service beginning in 2007 and thereafter, the special treatment for Liberty Zone property will expire, and the dollar limitation under Code Sec. 179 will decrease from $60,000 to $25,000. The full cost of the property, rather than 50 percent, will be taken into account in applying the phaseout.

Comment. There is no alternative minimum tax adjustment required for property expensed under the Code Sec. 179 provision. Thus, the deduction is available for both regular and AMT purposes.

★ *Effective date.* No specific effective date is provided by the Job Creation and Worker Assistance Act of 2002 (P.L. 107-147). The provision is, therefore, considered effective on March 9, 2002, the date of enactment.

Act Sec. 301(a) of the Job Creation and Worker Assistance Act of 2002, adding Code Sec. 1400L(b)(2), Code Sec. 1400L(f) and Code Sec. 1400L(h). Law at ¶ 5300. Committee Report at ¶ 10,140.

Five-Year Recovery Period for Leasehold Improvements

¶ 425

Background _____

Leasehold improvements made by a lessor or lessee are depreciated under the Modified Accelerated Cost Recovery System (MACRS). The person who owns the improvement claims the deduction. Most leasehold improvements are considered structural components. Structural components are depreciated in the same manner that the building would be depreciated if the building were placed in service when the structural component was placed in service.

> **Example.** A lessee leases a commercial building for 20 years and constructs a wall to divide an open area into two offices in January of 2002. The wall is a structural component of the building. Since the building would be 39-year nonresidential real property if placed in service in January 2002, the wall is depreciated as nonresidential real property placed in service in January 2002 using the straight-line method and a 39-year recovery period. The fact that the lease term is only 20 years is irrelevant.

Certain types of improvements, such as removable partitions, flooring, or carpeting, may be considered personal property rather than structural components. Generally, the principles of the former investment tax credit rules apply for

Background ————————————————————————————————

purposes of determining whether an improvement is personal property or a structural component (real property) (Reg. § 1.48-1(e)(1)). Improvements that are classified as personal property are depreciated under MACRS using accelerated depreciation methods and shortened recovery periods which depend on the property class that the personal property is assigned to under MACRS.

Comment. Taxpayers engaged in new building construction will often hire "cost segregation" specialists to identify costs that are attributable to personal property in order to maximize their depreciation deductions.

A lessor who disposes of a leasehold improvement (made by the lessor for the lessee) may take the adjusted basis of the improvement into account for purposes of determining gain or loss if the improvement is irrevocably disposed of or abandoned by the lessor at the termination of the lease. For example, if the leasehold improvement is destroyed or abandoned, the lessor may claim an ordinary loss in the amount of the improvement's remaining adjusted basis (Code Sec. 168(i)(8)(B)). However, if the entire building is demolished, the undepreciated cost of the improvements is included in the basis of the land (Code Sec. 280B). A similar rule applies to lessees who abandon their improvements at the end of the lease.

Under MACRS, property with a class life of more than four but less than ten years is generally classified as 5-year property (Code Sec. 168(e)(1)). Certain other property is also classified as 5-year property even though its class life does not fall within this class life range. Five-year property generally includes property used in a retail or wholesale trade or business (Asset Class 7.0 of Rev. Proc. 87-56).

———

Job Creation Act Impact

Qualified New York Liberty Zone leasehold improvements treated as MACRS 5-year property.—Qualified New York Liberty Zone leasehold improvements placed in service after September 10, 2001, and before January 1, 2007, are depreciable over five years instead of the usual 39 years. The new law classifies qualified New York Liberty Zone leasehold improvement property as 5-year property for purposes of the Modified Accelerated Cost Recovery System (MACRS) (Code Sec. 1400L(c)(1), as added by the Job Creation and Worker Assistance Act of 2002 (P.L. 107-147)).

Comment. Liberty Zone leasehold improvements that are eligible for a five-year recovery period are *not* also eligible for the 30-percent first-year bonus depreciation under Code Sec. 168(k) or Code Sec. 1400L(b) (Code Sec. 168(k)(2)(C)(ii), as added by the 2002 Act, and Code Sec. 1400L(b)(2)(C)(iii)). See ¶ 305 and ¶ 415 for discussion of bonus depreciation.

Qualified New York Liberty Zone leasehold improvement property. The term "qualified New York Liberty Zone leasehold improvement property" means qualified leasehold improvement property as defined under new Code Sec. 168(k)(3) (see ¶ 305) if:

● the building is located in the New York Liberty Zone;

● the improvement is placed in service after September 10, 2001, and before January 1, 2007; and

● no binding written contract for such improvement was in effect before September 11, 2001 (Code Sec. 1400L(c)(2), as added by the 2002 Act).

New York Liberty Zone. The New York Liberty Zone is the area located on or south of Canal Street, East Broadway (east of its intersection with Canal Street), or Grand Street (east of its intersection with East Broadway) in the Borough of Manhattan in New York City (Code Sec. 1400L(h), as added by the 2002 Act).

Qualified leasehold improvement property. Qualified leasehold improvement property generally consists of interior improvements to nonresidential real estate. The term is defined in Code Sec. 168(k)(3), as added by the 2002 Act (see ¶ 305). In general, qualified leasehold improvement property must satisfy the following requirements:

(1) the improvement must be to the interior portion of a building that is nonresidential real property;

(2) the improvement must be made under or pursuant to a lease by a lessee, sublessee, or lessor, or pursuant to a commitment to enter into a lease;

(3) the lessor and lessee may not be related persons;

(4) the portion of the building that is improved must be exclusively tenant-occupied (by a lessee or sublessee); and

(5) the improvement must be placed in service more than three years after the date that the building was first placed in service (Code Sec. 168(k)(3), as added by the 2002 Act).

Structural components. The definition of qualified leasehold property under Code Sec. 168(k)(3) (see ¶ 305) describes the property as any improvement to an interior portion of a building that is nonresidential real property. Although the term leasehold improvement is not defined for purposes of this provision, presumably the term includes only structural components. Leasehold improvements that qualify as personal property under the investment tax rules could presumably continue to be depreciated over the appropriate MACRS recovery period (generally five or seven years using the 200-percent declining balance method) pursuant to the principles discussed by the Tax Court in *Hospital Corp. of America*, 109 TC 21, CCH Dec. 52,163.

Residential property does not qualify. Leasehold improvements to residential rental property, such as apartment buildings, are not considered qualified leasehold improvements. Exterior leasehold improvements to nonresidential real property, such as the addition of a roof, are also excluded from the definition.

Comment. Improvements that do not qualify as New York Liberty Zone leasehold improvements may still be eligible for the 30-percent first year "bonus depreciation" allowance under Code Sec. 168(k) and Code Sec. 1400L(b), according to the Joint Committee Explanation. See ¶ 305 and ¶ 415. For qualified leasehold improvements made during 2002 through 2004, the taxpayer can thus use either the five-year recovery period under Code Sec. 1400L(b) by picking a property location within the New York Liberty Zone or choose to use the 30-percent additional allowance under Code Sec. 168(k) by leasing property located outside the New York Liberty Zone. For 2005 and 2006, the 30-percent additional allowance under Code Sec. 168(k) will be unavailable.

Excluded improvements. The following improvements are not considered qualified leasehold improvement property:

(1) improvements that enlarge the building;

(2) elevators and escalators;

(3) any structural component benefiting a common area; and

(4) improvements to the internal structural framework of the building (Code Sec. 168(k)(3)(B), as added by the 2002 Act).

Straight-line method applies. The straight-line method must be used to depreciate qualified Liberty Zone leasehold improvement property (Code Sec. 1400L(c)(3), as added by the 2002 Act). Ordinarily, 5-year property is depreciated using a 200-percent declining balance method switching to straight line.

ADS recovery period. A 9-year recovery period is assigned to qualified leasehold improvement property for purposes of the MACRS alternative depreciation system (ADS) under Code Sec. 168(g) (Code Sec. 1400L(c)(4), as added by the 2002 Act).

Comment. Generally, the 200-percent declining balance method is used to depreciate 5-year property under the MACRS general depreciation system. The new law, however, requires use of the straight-line method for New York Liberty Zone leasehold improvement, presumably to cut the costs associated with reducing the otherwise applicable 39-year recovery period to 5 years.

Date property deemed placed in service. The half-year or mid-quarter convention will apply to qualified Liberty Zone leasehold improvements since they are categorized as 5-year property under MACRS. Note that taxpayers are currently allowed to elect not to apply the mid-quarter convention to property placed in service during 2001, to accommodate disruptions caused by the September 11 events (Notice 2001-70, I.R.B. 2001-45, 437). Ordinarily, leasehold improvements to nonresidential real property are classified as 39-year MACRS nonresidential real property and, therefore, are subject to the mid-month convention.

Comment. No depreciation adjustment is required on qualified Liberty Zone leasehold improvements for alternative minimum tax (AMT) purposes. AMT depreciation will be computed in the same manner as regular tax depreciation (i.e., 5-year recovery period and straight-line method). See Code Sec. 56(a)(1)(A)). Ordinarily, property on a 5-year recovery period would be required to move from 200-percent declining balance to 150-percent declining balance, unless the property is already on a straight-line schedule. In that case, the property remains on a straight-line schedule and no AMT adjustment is required.

★ *Effective date.* No specific effective date is provided by the Job Creation and Worker Assistance Act of 2002 (P.L. 107-147). The provision is, therefore, considered effective on March 9, 2002, the date of enactment.

Act Sec. 301(a) of the Job Creation and Worker Assistance Act of 2002, adding Code Sec. 1400L(c) and Code Sec. 1400L(h). Law at ¶ 5300. Committee Report at ¶ 10,160.

Extension of Property Replacement Period

¶ 430

Background ————————————————————————

An involuntary conversion occurs when property is destroyed, stolen, condemned, or disposed of under the threat of condemnation and the taxpayer receives other property or money as compensation (e.g., insurance proceeds or a condemnation award). Gain from an involuntary conversion is generally not recognized for tax purposes if (1) the property is involuntarily converted into other property that is similar or related in service or use (Code Sec. 1033(a)(1)), or (2) when property is involuntarily converted into money (e.g., property is destroyed by fire and an insurance award is recovered), and the owner elects to postpone gain recognition by buying qualified property within a specified replacement period (Code Sec. 1033(a)(2)). If only part of the property is replaced, the owner can elect to defer recognition of gain only to the extent that cost of the replacement property exceeds the amount realized from the converted property.

Replacement property must generally be similar or related in service or use to the property converted. A taxpayer can also replace property with an 80-percent control interest of a corporation owning similar property. An actual purchase must take place (e.g., title must have passed) in order for acquisition to occur; an enforceable contract to purchase is not sufficient.

Business or investment property converted as a result of a Presidentially declared disaster can be replaced with *any* tangible property of a type held for productive use in a trade or business, whether or not the property is related in service or use (Code Sec. 1033(h)(2)).

Replacement period. The general replacement period is two years from the end of the year in which money in excess of basis is received for the conversion (the year that gain is realized). The replacement period begins with the actual date of destruction and ends two years after the close of the first tax year in which any part of the gain on the conversion is realized (in the year insurance proceeds are collected, etc.). Condemnations of real estate are entitled to a replacement period of three years (Code Sec. 1033(g)(4)), and homeowners whose principal residence is destroyed in a Presidentially declared disaster have four years to replace the property (Code Sec. 1033(h)(1)(B)). The IRS is allowed to extend the replacement period on application of the taxpayer. Reasons for extension might include unfavorable financing and market conditions or similar barriers.

Job Creation Act Impact

Extension of replacement period for property converted in Liberty Zone increased to five years.—The replacement period for property that was involuntarily converted in the New York Liberty Zone as a result of the terrorist attacks on September 11, 2001, is increased from two to five years. This new rule applies only if substantially all of the use of the replacement property is in New York City (Code Sec. 1400L(g), as added by the Job Creation and Worker Assistance Act of 2002 (P.L. 107-147)). The five-year replacement period applies regardless of any other extensions that might apply under Code Sec. 1033(g), relating to condemnation of property held for use in a trade or business, or Code Sec. 1033(h), which provides special rules for property damaged by Presidentially declared disasters.

Comment. The New York Liberty Zone is also part of a Presidentially declared disaster area. Property converted as a result of a Presidentially declared disaster is subject to special rules in addition to the new replacement period for Liberty Zone conversions (Code Sec. 1033(h)).

¶ **430**

New York Liberty Zone. The New York Liberty Zone is the area located on or south of Canal Street, East Broadway (east of its intersection with Canal Street), or Grand Street (east of its intersection with East Broadway) in the Borough of Manhattan in New York City (Code Sec. 1400L(h), as added by the 2002 Act).

Comment. The replacement property does not need to be used in the Liberty Zone for the extended period to apply, but substantially all of the use must be in New York City.

Measurement of replacement period. The replacement period is not counted from the actual date of the destruction of the converted property. It is counted from the end of the year gain is realized. The replacement period for property involuntarily converted in the Liberty Zone as a result of the terrorist attacks on September 11, 2001, will end five years after the close of the first tax year in which any part of the gain on the conversion is realized (Code Sec. 1400L(g), as added by the 2002 Act, and Code Sec. 1033(a)(2)(B)). For a calendar year taxpayer whose property was destroyed on September 11, 2001, and who realized some gain on the conversion during 2002, the extended replacement period would end five years from the end of 2002, on December 31, 2007. If insurance proceeds resulting in gain were received in 2001, the extended replacement period would end on December 31, 2006 (five years from December 31, 2001).

If insurance proceeds are received in more than one tax year, the five-year period is measured from the end of the first tax year in which the total proceeds received result in realized gain. This would occur when the total amount received first exceeds the taxpayer's basis in the property.

Comment. The replacement property needs to cost at least as much as the reimbursement received in order to postpone all of the gain. If it costs less, some gain may need to be recognized.

Example. Laura Silverman has a basis in a commercial building, excluding the underlying land, of $10,000,000. The building is located in the New York Liberty Zone and is destroyed as a result of the attacks on September 11, 2001. Silverman receives a $5,000,000 settlement from her insurance company in 2001 and another $10,000,000 settlement on November 30, 2002, thus realizing a gain of $5,000,000 in 2002. If she acquires a new building for $15,000,000 (or more) by December 31, 2007, five years from the end of the year in which her gain was realized, she may elect not to recognize any gain on the involuntary conversion. If the replacement building costs only $14,000,000, Silverman must recognize $1,000,000 of gain, but she may elect nonrecognition treatment for the remainder. Since the property was also located in a Presidentially declared disaster area, Silverman may elect to purchase *any* tangible property for use in a trade or business with her $15,000,000 proceeds, if she does not wish to replace the building. If Silverman purchases computer equipment for $15,000,000 by December 31, 2007, and begins operating an internet business in New York City, her gain will still qualify for nonrecognition treatment.

Planning Note. If a contractor is paid to construct new replacement property, the property is not considered replaced until the work is finished. It is thus important to plan for all construction work to be completed before the end of the replacement period.

Comment. A taxpayer with no insurance proceeds from destroyed property is unlikely to realize a gain as a result of the conversion. In this situation, the taxpayer has a loss and need not be concerned with nonrecognition. The loss will be deductible if the loss related to business or income-producing property, or it may be deductible under the casualty loss rules.

Destruction of taxpayer's main home. The New York Liberty Zone is included in a Presidentially declared disaster area. If a taxpayer's principal residence in this area is involuntarily converted as a result of the attacks on September 11, 2001, the taxpayer will have up to five years from the end of the tax year in which gain is realized from the conversion to replace any *scheduled* property on a tax-free basis. Note that the taxpayer may also exclude any realized gain up to the $250,000/$500,000 maximum as if the home had been sold (Code Sec. 121(d)(5)). If the total realized gain is more than the maximum allowable exclusion, the excess can be postponed under Code Sec. 1033 by purchasing replacement property.

If the homeowner does not replace the residence with property located in New York City, the usual rule for Presidentially declared disaster areas will apply (instead of Code Sec. 1400L(g)). In this situation the replacement period would be four years from the end of the tax year in which the gain is realized, under Code Sec. 1033(h), instead of five years.

Comment. Insurance proceeds for *unscheduled* personal property that was contained in a home destroyed in a Presidentially declared disaster area, including the Liberty Zone, are excluded from income altogether and do not need to be rolled over to similar personal property in order to obtain nonrecognition (Code Sec. 1033(h)(1)(A)). This would include most household goods covered by a homeowner's or renter's policy.

Election. Nonrecognition treatment for involuntary conversions is an election. Form 4684, Casualties and Thefts, is used to report involuntary conversions from casualties and thefts, including destruction of business property. Schedule D, Capital Gains and Losses, is used to report gains from involuntary conversions (other than from casualty or theft) of capital assets not held for business or profit.

★ *Effective date.* No specific effective date is provided by the Job Creation and Worker Assistance Act of 2002 (P.L. 107-147). The provision is, therefore, considered effective on March 9, 2002, the date of enactment.

Act Sec. 301(a) of the Job Creation and Worker Assistance Act of 2002, adding Code Sec. 1400L(g) and 1400L(h). Law at ¶ 5300. Committee Report at ¶ 10,150.

Tax-Exempt Bonds for Rebuilding New York City

¶ 435

Background _____

Interest on bonds issued by states or political subdivisions is not includable in gross income if the bonds are used to finance governmental functions or repaid with government funds (Code Sec. 103(a)). Interest on governmental bonds used to finance private activities is taxable unless the bonds meet certain narrow restrictions. Tax-exempt qualified private activity bonds include exempt facility bonds to finance certain types of property, mortgage revenue bonds and qualified 501(c)(3) bonds (Code Sec. 141(e)). All tax-exempt bonds must be registered and are restricted against arbitrage investments (Code Sec. 103(b)(2)).

The aggregate volume of tax-exempt private activity bonds that may be issued by a state is restricted by annual volume limits. The annual volume limits are based on state population. The amount is $75 per resident for 2002, or $225 million, if greater. The amount is adjusted annually for inflation (Code Sec. 146(d)).

Background

Private activity bonds. Private activity bonds are state or local bonds issued for nongovernmental use in trade or business and secured by payments from property used or issued for private loans. These bonds are not tax exempt unless the type and amount of the private use of the proceeds are limited. Strict limitations apply to bonds used to finance the purchase of output facilities used by or purchased from private persons (electric and gas generation and transmission facilities). The specific types of allowable qualified private activity bonds are (Code Sec. 141(e)):

- exempt facility bonds
- qualified mortgage bonds
- qualified veterans mortgage bonds
- qualified small issue bonds
- qualified 501(c)(3) bonds
- qualified student loan bonds
- qualified redevelopment bonds

Exempt facility bonds. Exempt facility bonds are used to fund one of 13 types of qualifying facilities. At least 95 percent of the bond proceeds must be used for the facility, including functionally related and subordinate uses. The facility must be actually and practically available for use by the general public. Qualifying facilities include transportation facilities, such as airports and facilities for mass commuting, waste disposal utilities, hydroelectric generating facilities, enterprise zone facility bonds, and qualified public educational facilities (Code Sec. 142).

Bond arbitrage. If any part of the proceeds of a state or local bond are reasonably expected to be used to acquire, or are intentionally used to acquire, investments that are higher yielding than the bonds, the bonds are non-tax-exempt arbitrage bonds. Arbitrage is the difference in yield between the tax-exempt bonds and the higher yield earned on investment of the bond proceeds. Investment of a minor portion of the bond proceeds, investment for a temporary period before the proceeds are needed for the governmental purpose, and investment in a reasonably required reserve or replacement fund are excepted from the arbitrage yield restrictions (Code Sec. 148).

Advance refunding of bonds. Tax-exempt bonds can be refunded currently an indefinite number of times, meaning that the refunded debt is redeemed within 90 days of the new bond issue. Bonds issued to advance refund private activity bonds are generally not tax-exempt. A bond is issued to advance refund another bond if it is issued more than 90 days before the redemption of the refunded bond. Advance refunding bonds must be called at the earliest redemption date, and abusive transactions using advance refundings are prohibited (Code Sec. 149(d)).

Bonds used for governmental purposes and qualified 501(c)(3) bonds used to provide working capital for Code Sec. 501(c)(3) charitable organizations may be advance refunded once, if issued after 1985, or twice, if issued before 1986 (Code Sec. 149(d)(3)(A)).

Job Creation Act Impact

Tax exempt bond financing and advance refunding for New York City.—An aggregate of $8 billion in additional tax-exempt private activity bonds, called New York Liberty Bonds, are authorized during 2002, 2003, and 2004 for the purpose of financing the construction and repair of real estate and infrastructure in New York City (Code Sec. 1400L(d), as added by the Job Creation and Worker Assistance Act of 2002 (P.L. 107-147)). In addition, advance refundings may be available with respect to certain tax-exempt bonds under criteria discussed below (Code Sec. 1400L(e)(1), as added by the 2002 Act). The additional bond issues are in addition to the amount of private activity bonds otherwise authorized under the state's volume cap. Repairs and construction of both residential and nonresidential real property are authorized, as well as public utility projects.

Comment. The 2002 private activity bond volume cap for the state of New York is $1.4 billion, not counting the new New York Liberty Bonds.

New York Liberty Zone. The New York Liberty Zone is the area located on or south of Canal Street, East Broadway (east of its intersection with Canal Street), or Grand Street (east of its intersection with East Broadway) in the Borough of Manhattan in New York City (Code Sec. 1400L(h), as added by the 2002 Act).

Qualified New York Liberty Bonds. The special exempt facility bonds for rebuilding the Liberty Zone are referred to as "Qualified New York Liberty Bonds" (Code Sec. 1400L(d)(2), as added by the 2002 Act). A Qualified New York Liberty Bond is a bond that is part of an issue if:

(1) 95 percent or more of the net proceeds (Code Sec. 150(a)(3)) of the issue are to be used for qualified project costs (see discussion below on qualified project costs);

(2) the bond is issued by the State of New York or a political subdivision thereof;

(3) the Governor of New York or the Mayor of New York City designates the bond as a New York Liberty Bond; and

(4) the bond is issued after March 9, 2002, and before January 1, 2005 (Code Sec. 1400L(d)(2), as added by the 2002 Act).

Special exemption of interest from alternative minimum tax. Interest on New York Liberty Bonds is not a preference item (Code Sec. 57(a)(5)) for purposes of the alternative minimum tax (AMT) (Code Sec. 1400L(d)(5)(E), as added by the 2002 Act). This means that investors in the bonds may earn tax-exempt interest regardless of whether they are otherwise subject to the alternative minimum tax.

Comment. Interest on private activity bonds is ordinarily included in alternative minimum taxable income. The current trend is that an increasing number of individuals are being subject to AMT liability. This means that for most private activity bonds, the desirability and thus the interest rates commanded by the bonds may be affected since the federal tax benefits of owning them are unavailable for an increasing number of investors.

Project costs eligible for financing. Types of property eligible for financing under the special bond issues include buildings and their structural components, including both nonresidential and residential real property, fixed tenant improvements, and public utilities such as gas, water, electric and telecommunication lines. Projects both within and outside of the Liberty Zone are authorized, provided all are within New York City. Specifically, approved projects must relate to the acquisition, construction, reconstruction, and renovation of:

(1) nonresidential real property located in the Liberty Zone;

(2) residential rental property located in the Liberty Zone, including fixed tenant improvements;

(3) public utility property located in the Liberty Zone; or

(4) nonresidential real property located in the City of New York outside of the Liberty Zone, if the property is part of a project having at least 100,000 square feet of usable office or other commercial space located in a single building or multiple adjacent buildings (Code Sec. 1400L(d)(4), as added by the 2002 Act).

No movable property. New York Liberty Bonds may not be issued for costs relating to movable fixtures and equipment (Code Sec. 1400L(d)(3)(C), as added by the 2002 Act).

Gubernatorial or Mayoral approval. Projects that will qualify under the provision must be approved by the Mayor of New York City or the Governor of New York State, each of whom may designate up to $4 billion of the authorized Liberty Zone bonds over the eligible time period (through December 31, 2004) (Code Sec. 1400L(d)(3)(A) and Code Sec. 1400L(i), as added by the 2002 Act). The amount that may be approved is limited by specific projects as follows:

● No more than $2 billion may be issued for use by projects located outside of the New York Liberty Zone—i.e., for commercial property elsewhere in New York City with 100,000 square feet of usable space (Code Sec. 1400L(d)(3)(B)(i), as added by the 2002 Act)

● No more than $1.6 billion may be issued for costs relating to residential rental property (Code Sec. 1400L(d)(3)(B)(ii), as added by the 2002 Act)

● No more than $800 million shall be issued for costs related to property used for retail sales of tangible property and functionally related and subordinate property (Code Sec. 1400L(d)(3)(B)(iii), as added by the 2002 Act)

For each of the specific project limits, the amounts are to be allocated proportionately to bonds designated by the Governor and bonds designated by the Mayor.

Comment. The Act does not address the limitations to apply in the case of mixed-use property.

Note that if the Mayor or the Governor decides that it is not feasible to use all of the authorized bond proceeds he is authorized to designate for use in the Liberty Zone, up to $1 billion of the bonds may be designated by each for the acquisition, construction or rehabilitation of property outside of the Liberty Zone, but within New York City. This amount is an aggregate amount to be spread over the three years during which Liberty Bonds are authorized.

Property outside the Liberty Zone. Property located outside the Liberty Zone must be located in the City of New York and have at least 100,000 square feet of usable office or other commercial space in a single building or multiple adjacent buildings in order to qualify for funding with New York Liberty Bonds.

Comment. The Act does not define commercial space. It is unclear whether all nonresidential property is commercial.

Exemption from annual state bond volume limits. The New York Liberty Bonds are not subject to the ordinarily applicable annual limits on the aggregate amount of bonds that may be issued by a particular state (Code Sec. 1400L(d)(5)(A), as added by the 2002 Act).

Acquisition of existing property. If existing property is to be acquired with Liberty Zone bond proceeds, rehabilitation expenditures with respect to the property must equal or exceed 50 percent of the cost of the building (Code Sec. 1400L(d)(5)(B), as added by the 2002 Act). This percentage is an increase from the 15 percent required for other exempt facility bond issues (Code Sec. 147(d)).

Construction arbitrage rules. The existing arbitrage rules apply to construction proceeds of New York Liberty Zone Bonds (Code Sec. 1400L(d)(5)(C), as added by the 2002 Act). Under this exception, bonds used to finance construction that meet spending and other requirements are given a 24- month exception from the arbitrage rebating requirements (Code Sec. 148(f)(4)(C)). Seventy-five percent of the proceeds of the bond issue must be used for construction costs. Under the arbitrage rebating requirements, an issuer is ordinarily required to pay to the United States the excess of the earnings on nonpurpose investments over the amount the investments would have earned if they carried the same interest as the associated government bonds, along with the income attributable to the excess (rebate payments) (Code Sec. 148(f)(2)).

Repayments. Repayments of loans financed with New York Liberty Bonds may not be used to make additional loans, but must be used to retire outstanding bonds (Code Sec. 1400L(d)(5)(D), as added by the 2002 Act). The first retirement must occur by the end of 10 years after issuance of the bonds.

Separate issue treatment of portions of an issue. The issuer may elect not to apply these new rules to the portion of an issue which (if issued as a separate issue) would be treated as a qualified bond or as a bond that is not a private activity bond (Code Sec. 1400L(d)(6), as added by the 2002 Act).

One additional advance refunding authorized for bonds used for NY facilities. Certain types of bonds used to fund facilities located in New York City are permitted one additional advanced refunding after March 9, 2002 (the effective date of the enactment of this section), and before January 1, 2005 (Code Sec. 1400L(e)(1), as added by the 2002 Act). Advance refunding occurs when the refunded debt is not redeemed within 90 days after the refunding bonds are issued, and is normally prohibited by the Code with the exception of certain government and Code Sec. 501(c)(3) issues.

Bonds that are allowed the additional advance refunding under the new rule are limited to issues for which all permissible refundings under current law were exhausted before September 12, 2001, and with respect to which the advance refunding bonds will be the only other outstanding issue with respect to the refunded bond (Code Sec. 1400L(e)(4), as added by the 2002 Act). At least 90 percent of the net bond proceeds must have been used to finance facilities located in New York City (95 percent for 501(c)(3) bonds). Facilities functionally related to New York City facilities for the furnishing of water also qualify. In addition, the bond must be:

　　(1) a state or local bond that is a general obligation of the City of New York;

(2) a state or local bond issued by the New York Municipal Water Finance Authority or the Metropolitan Transportation Authority of the City of New York (other that a private activity bond); or

(3) a qualified Code Sec. 501(c)(3) bond which is a qualified hospital bond issued by or on behalf of the State of New York or the City of New York (Code Sec. 1400L(e)(2), as added by the 2002 Act).

The maximum amount of advance refunding bonds that may be issued under the special waiver is $9 billion, half of which may be designated by the Governor of New York and half of which may be designated by the Mayor of New York City (Code Sec. 1400L(e)(3), as added by the 2002 Act). In addition, advance refunding bonds issued under Code Sec. 1400L must satisfy the requirements of Code Sec. 148 (relating to arbitrage bonds) and Code Sec. 149(d) (other than the limit on advance refundings) (Code Sec. 1400L(e)(4)(C), as added by the 2002 Act).

★ *Effective date.* No specific effective date is provided by the Job Creation and Worker Assistance Act of 2002 (P.L. 107-147). The provision is, therefore, considered effective on March 9, 2002, the date of enactment.

Act Sec. 301(a) of the Job Creation and Worker Assistance Act of 2002, adding Code Sec. 1400L(d), Code Sec. 1400L(e), Code Sec. 1400L(h), and Code Sec. 1400L(i). Law at ¶ 5300. Committee Reports at ¶ 10,120 and ¶ 10,130.

Chapter 5

Retirement and Benefit Plans

CONTRIBUTIONS AND DEDUCTIONS

Interest Rate Range for Additional Funding Requirements

¶ 505

Background ─────────────────────────────────

The Internal Revenue Code and ERISA (Employee Retirement Income Security Act of 1974) (P.L. 93-406) impose minimum and maximum funding requirements for defined benefit plans. The minimum funding requirements are designed to provide a certain level of benefit security by requiring the employer to make at least minimum contributions to the plan.

A single-employer defined benefit plan is, generally, underfunded if it has a funded current liability percentage of less than 90 percent for a plan year. Additional contributions are required to be made to single-employer defined benefit plans that are underfunded (Code Sec. 412(l)(1)). However, a plan with a funded liability percentage of at least 80 percent is not subject to the special rules on underfunded plans as long as its funded current liability percentage for each of the two immediately preceding plan years, or each of the second and third immediately preceding plan years, is at least 90 percent (Code Sec. 412(l)(9)). A plan's funded current liability percentage for a plan year represents the value of the plan's assets as a percentage of the plan's current liability (Code Sec. 412(l)(8)(B)).

Background ⎯⎯⎯⎯⎯⎯⎯⎯⎯⎯⎯⎯⎯⎯⎯⎯⎯⎯⎯⎯⎯⎯⎯⎯⎯⎯⎯⎯⎯

A plan's current liability means all liabilities to employees and their benefi-ciaries under the plan. A plan may use the same interest rate to determine current liability that it uses to calculate costs under the plan. However, if this rate is not within the prescribed permissible range, the plan must establish a new rate of interest to calculate current liability that is within the permissible range. In order to be within the permissible range to be used in determining the current liability component of the full-funding limitation, the interest rate must be not less than 90 percent or greater than 105 percent of the weighted average of 30-year Treasury securities during the four year period prior to the beginning of the plan year (Code Sec. 412(b)(5); ERISA Sec. 302(b)(5); IRS Notice 90-11, 1990-1 CB 319).

In light of the Treasury Department's decision to suspend issuance of the 30-year Treasury bond and to no longer hold auctions for either the 30-year nominal or inflation adjusted bonds (Treasury Department News Release, October 21, 2001), the yield on 30-year bonds has been declining, producing lower interest rate assumptions. This has resulted in increased employer contributions to plans, higher insurance premium payments to the Pension Benefit Guaranty Corporation (PBGC), and larger lump-sum benefit payments to employees who terminate employment.

PBGC variable rate premiums. Benefits under a defined benefit pension plan may be funded over a period of years. As a result, plan assets may not be sufficient to provide the benefits owed under the plan to employees and their beneficiaries if the plan terminates before all benefits are paid. In order to protect employees and their beneficiaries, the PBGC insures the benefits owed under defined benefit pension plans. Employers pay premiums to the PBGC for this coverage.

For underfunded plans, additional PBGC premiums must be paid. The amount is based on the amount of unfunded vested benefits. These premiums are referred to as variable rate premiums. The interest rate used to determine the amount of unfunded vested benefits is 85 percent of the 30-year Treasury rate for the month preceding the month in which the plan year begins.

Job Creation Act Impact

Permissible interest rate range.—The provision expands the permissible range of the statutory interest rate used in calculating a plan's current liability for purposes of applying the additional contribution requirements for plan years beginning after December 31, 2001, and before January 1, 2004. Under the provision, the permissible range is from 90 percent to 120 percent for these years. Use of a higher interest rate under the expanded range will affect the plan's current liability which may, in turn, affect the need to make additional contribu-tions and, also, the amount of any additional contributions (Code Sec. 412(l)(7)(C), as amended by the Job Creation and Worker Assistance Act of 2002 (P.L. 107-147)).

Because the quarterly contributions requirements are based on current liabil-ity for the preceding plan year, the provision also provides special rules for applying these requirements for plan years beginning in 2002, when the expanded range first applies, and 2004, when the expanded range no longer applies. In each of those years, current liability for the preceding year is redetermined using the permissible range applicable to the present year. This redetermined current liabil-ity will be used for purposes of the plan's funded current liability percentage for the preceding year. This may affect the need to make quarterly contributions. It will also be used for purposes of determining the amount of any quarterly contributions in the present year which is based, in part, on the preceding year (Code Sec. 412(m), as amended by the 2002 Act).

In addition to amending the Internal Revenue Code, the 2002 Act makes conforming amendments to the corresponding provisions of ERISA (ERISA Secs. 302(d)(7)(C) and 302(e), as amended by the 2002 Act).

Comment. As indicated in a letter dated March 4, 2002, from Mark A. Weinberger, Assistant Secretary (Tax Policy), Department of the Treasury, to Mr. Robert N. Burt, Chairman and CEO of FMC Corp, the staff of the Department of the Treasury's Office of Tax Policy actively advised congressional staff in the development of the portion of the House bill addressing relief for plan sponsors from the current interest rate used in calculating pension plan liabilities. Their recommendation was to increase the interest rate used in the calculation from the yield on 30-year Treasury securities to 120 percent of the 30-year Treasury securities rate.

PBGC variable rate premiums. The interest rate used in determining the amount of unfunded vested benefits for variable rate premium purposes is increased, effective for plan years beginning after December 31, 2001, and before January 1, 2004, to 100 percent of the interest rate on 30-year Treasury securities for the month preceding the month in which the plan year begins (Act Sec. 4006(a)(3)(E) of ERISA, as amended by the 2002 Act).

★ *Effective date.* The provision is effective on March 9, 2002, the date of enactment of the Job Creation and Worker Assistance Act of 2002 (P.L. 107-147).

Act Sec. 405(a)(1) of the Job Creation and Worker Assistance Act of 2002, adding Code Sec. 412(l)(7)(C)(i)(III); Act Sec. 405(a)(2), adding Code Sec. 412(m)(7); Act Sec. 405(b), adding ERISA Secs. 302(d)(7)(C)(i)(III) and 302(e)(7); Act Sec. 405(c), adding ERISA Sec. 4006(a)(3)(E)(iii)(IV). Law at ¶ 5165 and ¶ 7060. Committee Report at ¶ 10,240.

Combination of Plans

¶ 510

Background ——————————————————————————————

As a general rule, when an employer sponsors a defined contribution plan (e.g., a profit-sharing plan) and a defined benefit plan (e.g., a pension plan), a limitation is imposed on the overall deduction that may be claimed for contributions to the plans.

The basic limitation is 25 percent of compensation paid to the participants in the various plans. However, the deduction limit can never be less than the contributions to the defined benefit plan (or, if there is more than one defined benefit plan, the sum of the contributions to the plans) that are necessary to satisfy the minimum funding standard of Code Sec. 412 for the plan year ending with or within the employer's tax year.

It is important to note that the 25 percent limitation does *not* come into play when an employer offers a defined contribution plan and a defined benefit plan, and no employee participates in both types of plans.

Example (1). Apex Corporation maintains both a defined benefit pension plan and a money-purchase pension plan. The corporation's tax year is a calendar year, as are the accounting years of both plans. At least one employee of Apex is a participant in both plans. In 2001, aggregate compensation of all of the participants in both plans is $2 million. Under the plan's contribution formula, the required contribution to the money-purchase plan for 2002 is $200,000. The contribution to the defined benefit plan for 2002 that is necessary to satisfy the minimum funding standard of Code Sec. 412 is $600,000. The allowable deduction for 2002 is $600,000 (the *greater* of $500,000 (25% of $2 million) or the $600,000 necessary to satisfy the minimum funding standard).

Technical Corrections Impact

New exception to deduction limit for combination of plans.—The deduction limit on plan contributions that generally applies when an employer maintains a combination of plans will not be imposed when only "elective contributions" are contributed to any of the defined contribution plans during the tax year (Code Sec. 404(a)(7(C), as amended by the Job Creation and Worker Assistance Act of 2002 (P.L. 107-147)). The term "elective contributions" includes contributions made to 401(k) plans, SIMPLE 401(k) plans, 403(b) plans and simplified employee pensions (SEPs), provided such contributions are not currently included in the employee's income.

Example (2). Assume the same facts as in Example (1) above in "Background," except that Apex Corporation sponsors a pension plan and a 401(k) plan. During 2002, the only contributions made to the 401(k) plan were elective contributions. In this situation, the general limit on the employer's deduction for contributions made to the plan need not be considered, because the new exception for "elective contributions" made to a defined contribution plan would prevent its application.

★ *Effective date.* This provision applies to years beginning after December 31, 2001 (Act Sec. 411(x) of the Job Creation and Worker Assistance Act of 2002 (P.L. 107-147); Act Secs. 614(b) and 616(c) of the Economic Growth and Tax Relief Reconciliation Act of 2001 (P.L. 107-16)). See ¶ 20,001 for a discussion of the sunset rule on this technical correction.

Act Sec. 411(l)(4) of the Job Creation and Worker Assistance Act of 2002, amending Code Sec. 404(a)(7)(C); Act Sec. 411(x). Law at ¶ 5150. Committee Report at ¶ 10,270.

Catch-Up Contributions

¶ 515

Individuals who have reached at least age 50 are permitted to contribute extra amounts to their tax-sheltered retirement plans (e.g., IRAs and 401(k) plans). For example, for 2002, an individual over age 49 who participates in a 401(k) plan, is able to contribute $11,000 to the plan under the limits that are generally imposed on contributions and, if financially able, an additional $1,000 as a "catch-up contribution." Catch-up contributions are permitted in tax years beginning after December 31, 2001.

Background————————————————————————————————————

Congress decided to allow catch-up contributions based upon the theory that older, and presumably more financially secure individuals, should be able to contribute more to their retirement plans in order to catch-up, or make-up, for prior years when they could not fully fund their retirement plans or such plans were not available.

Technical Corrections Impact

Catch-up rules clarified.—The new provisions clarify the tax treatment of catch-up contributions. In addition, the new provisions establish rules concerning the interrelationship and impact of catch-up contributions upon amounts that may be generally contributed to various types of retirement plans (e.g., 401(k) plans and 457 plans).

Eligible individual. An individual who will attain age 50 by the end of the tax year is entitled to make catch-up contributions for that tax year (Code Sec. 414(v)(5), as amended by the Job Creation and Worker Assistance Act of 2002 (P.L. 107-147)). Under the original rule, an individual would have to actually attain age 50 before the individual was entitled to make catch-up contributions.

Example (1). Patricia Aubrey will reach age 50 on December 28, 2002. For 2002, she may make catch-up contributions to her retirement plans (e.g., IRAs and 401(k) plans) before December 28, due to the fact that she will reach age 50 *by the end of the tax year.*

Impact of catch-up contributions on elective deferrals. Catch-up contributions made to "elective deferral plans" do not have to be included in the individual's gross income, provided the amount of the catch-up contribution does not exceed the maximum allowable for the tax year (Code Sec. 402(g)(1)(C), as added by the 2002 Act; Code Sec. 401(a)(30), as amended by the 2002 Act).

Example (2). Steve Matrin, who participates in his employer's 401(k) plan, will reach age 50 on October 1, 2002. The maximum amount that Matrin may contribute to the 401(k) plan under the general rules is $11,000. His maximum catch-up contribution to the plan for 2002 is $1,000. The 2002 Act clarifies that Matrin, by making the $1,000 catch-up contribution, in addition to his elective deferral of $11,000, does not exceed his maximum contribution (i.e., $12,000) for 2002.

Aggregation of plans is required. When determining the maximum amount of catch-up contributions that an individual may make during a tax year, certain retirement plans maintained by one employer are treated as *one plan* (Code Sec. 414(v)(2)(D), as added by the 2002 Act). The plans that will be treated as one plan are all qualified retirement plans, 403(b) plans, SEPs and SIMPLEs (Code Sec. 414(v)(6)(A)(i), (ii) and (iv)). The determination if the plans are maintained by the "same employer," and thus subject to the aggregation rule, is made under the rules that apply to employees of controlled groups of corporations, partnerships and proprietorships under common control, affiliated service groups, and as determined by IRS regulation (Code Sec. 414(b), (c), (m) and (o)). Aggregation is also required of 457 plans (i.e., plans maintained by state and local governments) maintained by the same employer (Code Sec. 414(v)(2)(D), as added by the 2002 Act).

Nondiscrimination regarding catch-up provisions. Plans must allow all eligible individuals to make the same election with regard to catch-up contributions (Code

Sec. 414(v)(4)(A)). In determining if an employer's plans discriminate, all plans of a single employer are considered to be one plan. As a result, if one plan of a single employer discriminates concerning catch-up contributions, all the plans will be treated as though they discriminate (Code Sec. 414(v)(4)(B), as amended by the 2002 Act). However, this aggregation requirement is waived for a limited period during certain dispositions or acquisitions. Under this rule, a plan need not be aggregated with other plans until the expiration of a transition period that:

(1) begins on the date of the change in members of a group, and

(2) ends on the last day of the first plan year beginning after the date of such change (Code Sec. 410(b)(6)(C)(i)).

Comment. The main purpose of this temporary waiver of the aggregation rules is to allow time for the retirement plans of recently acquired businesses to be brought into conformity with the provisions of other retirement plans maintained by the same employer.

Nondiscrimination requirements. As a general rule, catch-up contributions, or the mere right to make such contributions, will not cause a plan to fail the nondiscrimination requirements that are universally imposed on qualified retirement plans (Code Sec. 414(v)(3)(B), as amended by the 2002 Act.) However, the requirement that all plans of a single employer have to be aggregated (see "Nondiscrimination regarding catch-up provisions") has to be considered when applying this general rule.

Treatment of catch-up contributions. The catch-up contributions made by an eligible individual to specific types of retirement plans will not be subject to the usual limit imposed on such plans (Code Sec. 414(v)(3)(A)(i), as amended by the 2002 Act). The specific types of plans are those that accept elective deferrals (e.g., 401(k) plans), SEPs, 403(b) plans, SIMPLE IRAs, defined contribution plans (i.e., 415(c) plans), and 457 plans. With regard to 457 plans, a special rule controls the interrelationship of the catch-up contributions and the additional amount that employees may contribute to such plans in the last three years before reaching normal retirement age (Code Sec. 457(b)(3)). See "Relationship to 457 plan "catch-up" contributions," below, for the explanation of this special rule.

Relationship to 457 plan "catch-up" contributions. Employees covered by 457 plans offered by state governments may make "catch-up" contributions under a special rule (Code Sec. 457(e)(18), as added by the 2002 Act). This special rule was added because these state employees, during their last three years of employment before retirement, may not make the catch-up contributions that may generally be made by individuals age 50 or over (Code Sec. 414(v)(6)(C), as amended by the Economic Growth and Tax Relief Reconciliation Act of 2001 (P.L. 107-16) (EGTRRA)). Specifically, normal catch-up contributions may not be made by employees covered by a 457 plan offered by a state, political subdivision of a state, and any agency or instrumentality of a state or one of its subdivisions (Code 457(e)(1)(A)). Traditionally, however, these state employees have been able to avail themselves of increased contribution limits for one or more years during the last three tax years before attaining normal retirement age (Code Sec. 457(b)(3)). For 2002, this increased contribution limit is the *lesser* of: (1) $22,000 (two times the $11,000 dollar limit applicable in 2002), or (2) the sum of $11,000 plus the amount by which the limit applicable in preceding years of participation exceeded deferrals for that year (Code Sec. 457(b)(3)(A), as amended by EGTRRA).

The new catch-up contribution rule applies to state employees covered by a 457 plan and who are age 50 or over. If these qualifications are met, then for one or more years during the last three tax years that end before the employee attains normal retirement age, the maximum contribution that may be made is the *greater* of (1) the total of (a) the ceiling established for plan contributions under Code Sec. 457(b)(2) (i.e., for 2002, this amount is the *lesser* of $11,000 or 100% of compensation) and (b) the catch-up amount that generally applies to other employees (i.e., for 2002, $1,000), or (2) the amount determined under the rule that generally applies during the last three years before normal retirement age (Code Sec. 457(e)(18), as added by the 2002 Act).

> **Example (3).** During 2002, Brad Smith reached age 50. He is a state employee covered by his employer's 457 plan. Further, Smith will reach normal retirement age within the next three tax years. Based upon these facts he will be able to make catch-up contributions to the 457 plan under the special rule for state employees. Assume his salary for 2002 is $50,000 and he has always made the maximum allowable contributions to the plan. In this situation, his maximum allowable catch-up contribution for 2002 would be the *greater* of (1) $12,000 (i.e., the sum of $11,000 (normal maximum contribution) and $1,000 (normal catch-up contribution), or (2) $11,000 (i.e., the *lesser* of $22,000 or $11,000 plus $0 (unused deferrals). Thus, the maximum contribution that Smith may make to the 457 plan for 2002 is $12,000.

★ *Effective date.* These provisions apply to years beginning after December 31, 2001 (Act Sec. 411(x) of the Job Creation and Worker Assistance Act of 2002 (P.L. 107-147); Act Sec. 611(i) and Act Sec. 631(b) of the Economic Growth and Tax Relief Reconciliation Act of 2001 (P.L. 107-16)). See ¶ 20,001 for a discussion of the impact of the sunset rule on this technical correction.

Act Sec. 411(o)(1) of the Job Creation and Worker Assistance Act of 2002, adding Code Sec. 402(g)(1)(C); Act Sec. 411(o)(2), amending Code Sec. 401(a)(30); Act Sec. 411(o)(3), adding Code Sec. 414(v)(2)(D); Act Sec. 411(o)(4), amending Code Sec. 414(v)(3)(A)(i); Act Sec. 411(o)(5), amending Code Sec. 414(v)(3)(B); Act Sec. 411(o)(6), amending Code Sec. 414(v)(4)(B); Act Sec. 411(o)(7), amending Code Sec. 414(v)(5); Act Sec. 411(o)(8), amending Code Sec. 414(v)(6)(C); Act Sec. 411(o)(9), adding Code Sec. 457(e)(18); Act Sec. 411(p)(6), amending Code Sec. 402(g)(7)(B); Act Sec. 411(x). Law at ¶ 5135, ¶ 5140, ¶ 5170, and ¶ 5195. Committee Report at ¶ 10,270.

ROLLOVERS AND DISTRIBUTIONS

Direct Rollovers of After-Tax Contributions

¶ 520

Background _____

A qualified plan must allow for the direct rollover (trustee-to-trustee transfer) of certain distributions into an eligible retirement plan (Code Sec. 401(a)(31)). Specifically, the plan must allow a participant to elect to have a distribution paid directly to a qualified trust, a qualified annuity plan under Code Sec. 403(a), a Code Sec. 403(b) tax-sheltered annuity plan, a Code Sec. 457 governmental deferred compensation plan or a traditional individual retirement arrangement (IRA).

The Economic Growth and Tax Relief Reconciliation Act of 2001 (P.L. 107-16) (EGTRRA) liberalized the rollover rules to allow for the rollover of after-tax contributions from a qualified plan (Code Sec. 402(c)). Specifically, plan participants are permitted to roll over after-tax contributions to either a qualified defined contribution plan that agrees to separately account for the after-tax contributions or to an IRA.

The direct rollover requirements for qualified plans were also amended by EGTRRA to provide that a qualified plan must permit direct trustee-to-trustee transfers of after-tax contributions to an eligible plan. As amended, the provision allows transfers of after-tax contributions to a qualified plan that agrees to separately account for the after-tax amounts or to an IRA (Code Sec. 401(a)(31)(C)). The provision does not limit rollovers of after-tax contributions to defined contribution plans.

Technical Corrections Impact

Distributions of after-tax contributions.—The rules that require a plan to provide for direct rollovers from qualified plans are clarified with respect to distributions of after-tax contributions. While a plan is required to permit direct transfers of after-tax contributions only to a qualified plan or traditional IRA, the qualified plan must be a *qualified defined contribution plan* that agrees to separately account for the taxable and nontaxable portions of the distribution (Code Sec. 401(a)(31)(C)(i), as amended by the Job Creation and Worker Assistance Act of 2002 (P.L. 107-147)). An IRA may accept these after-tax contributions without having to separately account for them (Code Sec. 401(a)(31)(C)(ii)).

Comment. The change conforms the direct rollover rules for plan administrators under Code Sec. 401(a)(31) with the participant rules covering direct trustee-to-trustee transfers under Code Sec. 402(c)(2)(A), under which after-tax contributions may only be transferred to a qualified defined contribution plan.

★ *Effective date.* The provision applies to distributions made after December 31, 2001 (Act Sec. 411(x) of the Job Creation and Worker Assistance Act of 2002 (P.L. 107-147); Act Sec. 643(d) of the Economic Growth and Tax Relief Reconciliation Act of 2001 (P.L. 107-16)). See ¶ 20,001 for a discussion of the impact of the sunset rule on this technical correction.

Act Sec. 411(q)(1) of the Job Creation and Worker Assistance Act of 2002, amending Code Sec. 401(a)(31)(C)(i); Act Sec. 411(x). Law at ¶ 5135. Committee Report at ¶ 10,270.

Rollover Characterization

¶ 525

The Economic Growth and Tax Relief Reconciliation Act of 2001 (P.L. 107-16) allowed for the rollover of after-tax contributions from a qualified plan to a qualified defined contribution plan or individual retirement arrangement. The direct rollover of after-tax contributions from a qualified plan to another qualified plan can be accomplished, however, only through a direct trustee-to-trustee transfer. Further, to accept a rollover of after-tax contributions, a qualified plan is required to separately track the contributions and any related earnings. After-tax contributions from a qualified plan can be rolled over into an individual retirement arrangement with fewer restrictions. Neither the direct trustee-to-trustee transfer

Background _____

or the separate accounting requirements apply to rollovers of after-tax contributions to an IRA (Code Sec. 402(c)(2)).

Code Sec. 72(e) provides a pro rata basis recovery rule for distributions from plan accounts with both pre-tax amounts and after-tax contributions. For any distribution from a qualified plan consisting of both pre-tax amounts and after-tax contributions, a portion of the distribution will be treated as taxable to the employee and a portion will be treated as a tax-free recovery of the participant's basis (attributable to after-tax contributions).

With respect to after-tax rollovers allowed by EGTRRA, the law was unclear as to whether the ordering rules for basis recovery under Code Sec. 72(e) would apply and some practitioners contended that a participant should have the option to designate rollovers as deriving from either pre-tax or after-tax amounts.

_____

Technical Corrections Impact

Characterization of rollover distribution.—A rollover to a qualified defined contribution plan or IRA that includes both pre-tax amounts and after-tax contributions will be characterized as coming first from pre-tax amounts (contributions and earnings that would be includible in income if no rollover occurred) (Code Sec. 402(c)(2), as amended by the Job Creation and Worker Assistance Act of 2002 (P.L. 107-147)). The ordering rules under Code Sec. 72(e) under which distributions are attributable to pre-tax amounts on a pro-rata basis are disregarded for the limited purpose of characterizing rollovers of after-tax contributions to a defined contribution plan or IRA.

A distribution of a participant's entire interest in a plan which is rolled over in its entirety to a single new plan does not need to be allocated between pre-tax and after-tax amounts. Thus, the new ordering rule is needed only for situations in which a portion of the participant's interest is not rolled over to the new plan.

Example. Joe Smith is a participant in his employer's 401(k) plan. His account holds $12,000, $3,000 of which represents after-tax contributions. Joe wants to direct a rollover of $10,000 into another defined contribution plan. Under the new rule, $9,000 would be from pre-tax amounts and $1,000 would be from after-tax amounts.

Comment. The new ordering rule conforms to the ordering rule for distributions from a traditional IRA that are rolled over to a qualified plan. In that situation, the distribution is deemed to derive first from amounts other than after-tax contributions (Code Sec. 408(d)(3)(H)). The ordering rule for IRA rollovers to plans has the effect of maximizing the amount that will qualify for the rollover, since after-tax contributions to an IRA may not be rolled over to a qualified plan.

Comment. Since EGTRRA allows both pre- and after-tax amounts to be rolled over to a new qualified defined contribution plan or IRA, the amendment does not affect an employee's ability under the law to roll over amounts to a new plan. As a practical consideration, however, plans are permitted to decline to accept rollovers of after-tax contributions and an employee may have difficulty in achieving an after-tax rollover. The new ordering rule maximizes the amount of a distribution deemed to derive from pre-tax contributions which are more likely to be accepted by the new plan.

¶ 525

Since pre-tax amounts will be deemed to be the first amounts rolled over to the new plan or IRA, this allows an employee taking a partial cash distribution from a plan to avoid the penalty under Code Sec. 72 on amounts attributable to after-tax contributions.

★ *Effective date.* The provision applies to distributions made after December 31, 2001 (Act Sec. 411(x) of the Job Creation and Worker Assistance Act of 2002 (P.L. 107-147); Act Sec. 643(d) of the Economic Growth and Tax Relief Reconciliation Act of 2001 (P.L. 107-16)). See ¶ 20,001 for a discussion of the impact of the sunset rule on this technical correction.

Act Sec. 411(q)(2) of the Job Creation and Worker Assistance Act of 2002, amending Code Sec. 402(c)(2); Act Sec. 411(x). Law at ¶ 5140. Committee Report at ¶ 10,270.

Cash-Outs

¶ 530

Background———————————————————————————

A qualified retirement plan may involuntarily "cash out" a participant whose employment by the plan sponsor has terminated, if the present value of the participant's plan benefits does not exceed $5,000 (Code Sec. 411(a)(11)(A)). An involuntary cash out generally means that the plan may pay the value of the participant's benefit without the participant's consent or that of his or her spouse, if applicable. For purposes of determining the present value of a participant's benefits, any forfeitable benefits may be ignored.

The Economic Growth and Tax Relief Reconciliation Act of 2001 (P.L. 107-16) (EGTRRA) amended the rules governing the valuation of a plan participant's nonforfeitable plan benefit for purposes of determining whether the participant may be involuntarily cashed out. EGTRRA provided that after December 31, 2001, the present value of the plan benefit could be calculated without including any portion attributable to rollover contributions, or the earnings allocable to such rollover contributions (Code Sec. 411(a)(11)(D), as added by EGTRRA). A "rollover" for purposes of Code Sec. 411(a)(11)(D) means a rollover from qualified plans under Code Sec. 402(c), annuity plans under Code Sec. 403(a)(4) and Code Sec. 403(b)(8), individual retirement accounts (IRAs) under Code Sec. 408(d)(3)(A)(ii), or governmental Code Sec. 457 plans under Code Sec. 457(e)(16) (Code Sec. 411(a)(11)(D), as added by EGTRRA).

Comment. A similar provision was added to the Employee Retirement Income Security Act of 1974 (ERISA) (29 U.S.C. § 1053(c)) (ERISA Sec. 203(e)(4), as added by EGTRRA).

Automatic rollover of certain mandatory cash-out distributions. EGTRRA also required that an involuntary cash out of an amount in excess of $1,000 be in the form a direct transfer to a designated IRA, unless the participant consents to a cash payment or a transfer to a different IRA or qualified plan (Act Sec. 657(a) of EGTRRA). A related amendment was made to ERISA so that if an automatic direct rollover occurs in accordance with regulations provided by the Secretary of Labor, the participant is treated as exercising control over the assets in the individual retirement account or annuity upon the earlier of (1) the rollover of any portion of the assets to another individual retirement account or annuity, or (2) one year after the automatic rollover (ERISA Sec. 404(c)(3), as added by EGTRRA).

Technical Corrections Impact

Disregarding rollovers in determining the involuntary cash-out threshold.—A technical correction clarifies that a qualified joint and survivor annuity (QJSA) or qualified preretirement survivor annuity can also permit exclusion of a participant's rollover contributions (and the earnings thereon) from the present value of the participant's benefit for purposes of determining whether the participant, or the participant's spouse, must consent to the cash-out of the benefit (Code Sec. 417(e)(1) and Code Sec. 417(e)(2), as amended by the Job Creation and Worker Assistance Act of 2002 (P.L. 107-147)).

A similar correction amends the Employee Retirement Security Act of 1974 (ERISA) (29 U.S.C. § 1053(c)) (ERISA Sec. 205(g)(1) and ERISA Sec. 205(g)(2)(A)).

Example. Charlie Anderson is a participant in the qualified plan of ACME Inc. Under the plan, 65 is considered normal retirement age. Anderson takes early retirement at age 57, at which time he is entitled to receive a QJSA. Anderson would prefer to wait until normal retirement age to commence the QJSA. The present value of Anderson's accrued benefit in the plan immediately before commencement of the benefit is $6,000 (however, $2,000 of the total amount is attributable to a rollover contribution, and the earnings therefrom). In determining the amount of Anderson's accrued benefit, any amounts attributable to a rollover contribution (and any income allocable to it) are not taken into account. Accordingly, the plan may pay out the $4,000 amount in a lump sum without Anderson's or his spouse's consent. However, because the present value of Anderson's accrued benefit exceeds $1,000, the involuntary cash out must be in the form of a direct rollover to a designated IRA, unless Anderson elects to receive the distribution in cash or to have it transferred to a different IRA or qualified plan.

Automatic rollover of certain mandatory cash-out distributions. Certain language errors that occurred when section 404(c)(3) was added to ERISA are also addressed. In section 404(c)(3)(A), the phrase "the earlier of" appears twice. The second occurrence is now removed. Additionally, in section 404(c)(3)(B), the phrase "if the transfer" is replaced with the phrase "a transfer that."

★ *Effective date.* The technical corrections to Code Sec. 417(e) and section 205(g) of ERISA are effective for distributions after December 31, 2001 (Act Sec. 411(x) of the Job Creation and Worker Assistance Act of 2002 (P.L. 107-147); Act Sec. 648(c) of the Economic Growth and Tax Relief Reconciliation Act of 2001 (P.L. 107-16)). The technical corrections to section 404(c) of ERISA apply to distributions made after the Secretary of Labor issues final regulations implementing the safe harbor provisions as prescribed in EGTRRA (Act Sec. 411(x) of the 2002 Act; Act Sec. 657(d) of EGTRRA). See ¶ 20,001 for a discussion of the impact of the sunset rule on these technical corrections.

Act Sec. 411(r)(1)(A) of the Job Creation and Worker Assistance Act of 2002, amending Code Sec. 417(e)(1); Act Sec. 411(r)(1)(B), amending Code Sec. 417(e)(2)(A); Act Sec. 411(r)(2)(A), amending ERISA Sec. 205(g)(1); Act Sec. 411(r)(2)(B), amending ERISA Sec. 205(g)(2)(A); Act Sec. 411(t), amending ERISA Sec. 404(c)(3)(A) and (B); Act Sec. 411(x). Law at ¶ 5185 and ¶ 7065. Committee Report at ¶ 10,270.

Top-Heavy Rules

¶ 535

Background _____

Defined benefit plans or defined contribution plans that provide a disproportionate portion of benefits or contributions to key employees are called "top-heavy plans"(Code Sec. 416). Any defined benefit plan is a top-heavy plan for a plan year if, as of the determination date, the present value of the accumulated accrued benefits for participants who are key employees for the plan year exceeds 60 percent of the present value of the accumulated accrued benefits for all employees under the plan (Code Sec. 416(g)(1)(A)(i)). A defined contribution plan is top-heavy if, as of the determination date, the sum of the account balances of key employees exceeds 60 percent of the account balances of all employees under the plan.

When calculating a participant's accrued benefit or account balance for purposes of determining whether a plan is top heavy, the accrued benefit or account balance is increased for distributions made to the participant during the year ending on the determination date (Code Sec. 416(g)(3), as amended by the Economic Growth and Tax Relief Reconciliation Act of 2001 (P.L. 107-16) (EGTRRA)). However, if a distribution is made for a reason other than (1) separation from service, (2) death, or (3) disability, a five-year look-back period is employed, rather than the one-year period (Code Sec. 416(g)(3)(B), as added by EGTRRA).

Comment. Prior to the passage of EGTRRA, use of the phrase "separation from service" resulted in a great deal of confusion in certain situations, for example, where an employee continued on the same job for a different employer when companies merged, liquidated, or consolidated. As a result of what was often called the "same desk rule," an employee who continued to perform his or her job for the new or modified employer was deemed not to have separated from service. Thus, even after a merger or acquisition, an employer was often forced to retain the terminated employees in their plans even though the employees were working for the purchasing employer. In acknowledging this confusion, the House Committee Report to EGTRRA noted that a separation from service occurred only upon a participant's death, retirement, resignation or discharge, and not when the employee continued on the same job for a different employer as a result of the liquidation, merger, consolidation, or other similar corporate transaction. However, a "severance from employment" occurs when a participant ceases to be employed by the employer that maintains the plan. Thus, under the same desk rule, a participant's severance from employment would not necessarily result in a separation from service.

With respect to retirement plans generally, changes made by EGTRRA were intended to improve the portability of retirement benefits. Among these changes was the elimination of the same desk rule.

In addition, a plan will not constitute a qualified plan under Code Sec. 401(a) for any plan year in which it is a part of a top-heavy plan for the plan year unless it meets specified vesting requirements and minimum benefit requirements (Code Sec. 416(a)). In determining whether a plan meets the minimum benefit requirements, any year in which the plan is frozen is not considered a year of service for purposes of determining an employee's years of service. A plan is frozen for a year when no key employee or former key employee benefits under the plan (Code Sec. 416(c)(1)(C)(iii), as added by EGTRRA).

Technical Corrections Impact

Clarification of top-heavy determination.—The Job Creation and Worker Assistance Act of 2002 (P.L. 107-147) replaces the phrase "separation from service" in Code Sec. 416(g)(3)(B) with "severance from employment" to conform with the changes made by the Economic Growth and Tax Relief Reconciliation Act of 2001 (P.L. 107-16) (EGTRRA) with respect to plans covered under Code Sec. 401(k), Code Sec. 403(b), and Code Sec. 457, which allowed for distributions from these plans when an employee continued on the same job for a different employer following a corporate transaction. Accordingly, in determining top-heavy status, distributions made after a severance from employment are taken into account for only one year.

Change in title. The 2002 Act also corrects the title to Code Sec. 416(c)(1)(C)(iii), as added by EGTRRA. The new title more clearly reflects that the exception applies to plans for which no key employee or former key employee benefited.

★ *Effective date.* The provision applies to years beginning after December 31, 2001 (Act Sec. 411(x) of the Job Creation and Worker Assistance Act of 2002 (P.L. 107-147); Act Sec. 613(f) of the Economic Growth and Tax Relief Reconciliation Act of 2001 (P.L. 107-16)). See ¶ 20,001 for a discussion of the impact of the sunset rule on this technical correction.

Act Sec. 411(k)(1) of the Job Creation and Worker Assistance Act of 2002, amending Code Sec. 416(c)(1)(C)(iii); Act Sec. 411(k)(2), amending Code Sec. 416(g)(3)(B); Act Sec. 411(x). Law at ¶ 5180. Committee Report at ¶ 10,270.

DEFINED BENEFIT PLANS

Anti-Cutback Rules

¶ 540

Background

For plan years ending before January 1, 2002, the maximum dollar limit on employee benefits under a defined benefit plan was the *lesser* of (1) an inflation adjusted dollar amount (e.g., $140,000 for 2001), or (2) 100 percent of the employee's average compensation for the three highest consecutive years during which the employee was an active participant in the plan (Code Sec. 415(b)(1), before amendment by the Economic Growth and Tax Relief Reconciliation Act of 2001 (P.L. 107-16) (EGTRRA)). For plan years beginning after December 31, 2001, EGTRRA, among other changes to defined benefit plans, increased the base amount used for future inflation adjustments to $160,000 (Code Sec. 415(b)(1)(A), as amended by EGTRRA).

Under what are commonly termed the "anti-cutback rules," an otherwise qualified retirement plan will lose its qualified status if the plan is amended in a manner that will decrease the accrued benefits of employees (Code Sec. 411(d)(6)). A similar anti-cutback rule is also imposed by Section 204(g)(1) of the Employee Retirement Income Security Act of 1974 (ERISA).

Technical Corrections Impact

Exception to anti-cutback rule.—A special provision states that if very specific requirements are satisfied, a qualified defined benefit plan will not violate the anti-cutback rules of Code Sec. 411(d)(6) and ERISA Section 204(g)(1), if it is amended to reduce the amount of benefits that it would otherwise be required to pay (Act Sec. 611(i) of the Economic Growth and Tax Relief Reconciliation Act of 2001 (P.L. 107-16) (EGTRRA), as amended by Act Sec. 411(j)(3) of the Job Creation and Worker Assistance Act of 2002 (P.L. 107-147)). In short, if the requirements are satisfied, a defined benefit plan may be amended to reduce benefits to the level that would have applied without regard to the increase in benefits mandated by EGTRRA.

Comment. This exception to the anti-cutback rules is not as dramatic as it may appear. The intent of this exception is to provide relief to defined benefit plans that operate on a fiscal year. Without this special provision, these fiscal-year plans would generally be required to pay increased retirement benefits before the year that Congress intended the increase to take effect.

Specific requirements. In order to take advantage of this exception to the anti-cutback rules, the plan on June 7, 2001 (date that EGTRRA was enacted into law), must have incorporated by reference the dollar limit imposed by Code Sec. 415(b)(1)(A) (i.e., $140,000 before enactment of EGTRRA and $160,000 after enactment), and:

(1) the plan amendment reducing the benefits that would otherwise be payable is adopted on or before June 30, 2002,

(2) the plan amendment reduces benefits to the level that existed prior to the increase otherwise required by EGTRRA, and

(3) the plan amendment is not effective earlier than years ending after December 31, 2001 (Act Sec. 611(i)(3) of EGTRRA, as added by the 2002 Act).

Example (1). Megacorp has sponsored a defined benefit plan for its employees for a number of years. The plan, which operates on a fiscal year that runs from July 1 through June 30, provides that the maximum benefit payable under the plan will be the amount calculated by using the provisions of Internal Revenue Code Sec. 415(b)(1). Under EGTRRA, an increase in the amount of benefits payable under Code Sec. 415(b)(1) went into effect for years ending after December 31, 2001. As a result of EGTRRA, and given the fact that Megacorp's defined benefit plan runs from July 1, 2001 through June 30, 2002, the plan would have to start applying the increased benefit formula as of July 1, 2001.

Example (2). Under the special provision in the 2002 Act, Megacorp may amend its defined benefit plan no later than June 30, 2002, in order to reduce the plan benefits that it would otherwise be required to pay to their pre-EGTRRA level. The amendment may not be effective earlier than years ending after December 31, 2001 (Act Sec. 611(i)(3)(C) of EGTRRA, as added by the 2002 Act). The amendment will not violate the anti-cutback requirements.

★ *Effective date.* This provision is effective on June 7, 2001 (Act Sec. 411(x) of the Job Creation and Worker Assistance Act of 2002 (P.L. 107-147)). See ¶ 20,001 for a discussion of the impact of the sunset rule on this technical correction.

¶ 540

Act Sec. 411(j)(3) of the Job Creation and Worker Assistance Act of 2002, adding Act Sec. 611(i)(3) to the Economic Growth and Tax Relief Act of 2001; Act Sec. 411(x). Law at ¶ 7065. Committee Report at ¶ 10,270.

Notification of Reduction in Plan Benefits

¶ 545

Background

The rules for notification of reduction in plan benefits were clarified by the Economic Growth and Tax Relief Reconciliation Act of 2001 (P.L. 107-16) (EGT-RRA). EGTRRA added a provision to the Internal Revenue Code whereby defined benefit pension plans must notify affected participants, alternate payees, and employee organizations before a plan amendment that significantly reduces future benefit accruals goes into effect (Code Sec. 4980F).

Comment. One of the reasons for the change was the awareness of significant publicity concerning conversions of traditional defined benefit plans to "cash balance" plans, with particular focus on the impact such conversions have on affected workers. The Committee believed that employees are entitled to meaningful disclosure concerning plan amendments that may result in reductions of future benefit accruals, and determined that the law at that time did not require employers to provide such disclosure (House Committee Report to H.R. 1836, H.R. Rep. No. 107-51, pt. 1, May 1, 2001).

Technical Corrections Impact

Clarification of notice requirements.—A technical correction clarifies that if an applicable pension plan is amended to provide for a significant reduction in the rate of future benefit accrual, including any elimination or reduction of an early retirement benefit or retirement-type subsidy, the written notice that shall be provided by the plan administrator to each applicable individual (and to each employee organization representing applicable individuals) shall be written in a manner calculated to be understood by the average plan participant and shall provide sufficient information (as defined in Treasury regulations) to allow applicable individuals to understand the effect of the plan amendment. The IRS may provide a simplified form of notice for, or exempt from any notice requirement, a plan that has fewer than 100 participants who have accrued a benefit under the plan or a plan that offers participants the option to choose between the new benefit formula and the old benefit formula (Code Sec. 4980F(e)(1), as amended by the Job Creation and Worker Assistance Act of 2002 (P.L. 107-147), and Code Sec. 4980F(e)(2)).

Further technical corrections clarify that the notice requirement applies to a defined benefit plan only if the plan is qualified (Code Sec. 4980F(f)(2)(A), as amended by the 2002 Act) and in the case of an amendment that eliminates an early retirement benefit or retirement-type subsidy, notice is required only if the early retirement benefit or retirement-type subsidy is significant (Code Sec. 4980F(f)(3), as amended by the 2002 Act; Joint Committee on Taxation, *Technical Explanation of the "Job Creation and Worker Assistance Act of 2002"* (JCX-12-02), March 6, 2002).

★ *Effective date.* The provisions generally apply to plan amendments taking effect on or after June 7, 2001 (Act Sec. 411(x) of the Job Creation and Worker Assistance Act of 2002 (P.L. 107-147); Act Sec. 659(c) of the Economic Growth and Tax Relief Reconciliation Act of 2001 (P.L. 107-16)). See ¶ 20,001 for a discussion of the impact of the sunset rule on this technical correction.

Act Sec. 411(u)(1)(A) of the Job Creation and Worker Assistance Act of 2002, amending Code Sec. 4980F(e)(1); Act Sec. 411(u)(1)(B), amending Code Sec. 4980F(f)(2)(A); Act Sec. 411(u)(1)(C), amending Code Sec. 4980F(f)(3); Act Sec. 411(u)(2), amending ERISA Sec. 204(h)(9); Act Sec. 411(u)(3), amending Act Sec. 659(c)(3)(B) of EGTRRA; Act Sec. 411(x). Law at ¶ 5338 and ¶ 7065. Committee Report at ¶ 10,270.

Unfunded Current Liability Limitation

¶ 550

Background ——

The special rule allowing a deduction for amounts contributed of up to 100 percent of a plan's unfunded current liability was extended by the Economic Growth and Tax Relief Reconciliation Act of 2001 (P.L. 107-16) (EGTRRA) to all defined benefit pension plans for plan years beginning after 2001 (Code Sec. 404(a)(1)(D)(i)).

For most plans, the deductible contribution amount is increased for the year in which the plan terminates. If a plan to which the Employee Retirement Income Security Act of 1974 (P.L. 93-406) (ERISA) applies terminates during a plan year, the deduction limit becomes the amount required to make the plan sufficient for benefit liabilities within the meaning of ERISA Sec. 4041(d) (Code Sec. 404(a)(1)(D)(iv), prior to amendment by the Job Creation and Worker Assistance Act of 2002).

Technical Corrections Impact

Terminating plans.—A technical correction changes the heading of Code Sec. 404(a)(1)(D)(iv) from "PLANS MAINTAINED BY PROFESSIONAL SERVICE EMPLOYERS" to "SPECIAL RULE FOR TERMINATING PLANS". The text of the provision expressly applies to plans subject to ERISA Sec. 4041. Pursuant to ERISA Sec. 4021(b)(13), the title does not apply to plans maintained by professional service employers that do not have more than 25 participants. Based on the text and legislative history of Code Sec. 404(a)(1)(D)(iv), the increase in deductible contributions in the year of a plan's termination is not limited to professional service employers. Thus, the change in the provision's heading was necessary.

Comment. The Committee Reports (Joint Committee on Taxation, *Technical Explanation of the "Job Creation and Worker Assistance Act of 2002"* (JCX-12-02), March 6, 2002) for technical corrections involving pension issues can be found at ¶ 10,270. However, it does not appear that a Committee Report explanation was provided for Act Sec. 411(s) of the 2002 Act.

★ *Effective date.* This provision is effective for plan years beginning after December 31, 2001 (Act Sec. 411(x) of the Job Creation and Worker Assistance Act of 2002 (P.L. 107-147); Act Sec. 652(c) of the Economic Growth and Tax Relief Reconciliation Act of 2001 (P.L. 107-16)). See ¶ 20,001 for a discussion of the impact of the sunset rule on this technical correction.

Act Sec. 411(s) of the Job Creation and Worker Assistance Act of 2002, amending Code Sec. 404(a)(1)(D)(iv); Act Sec. 411(x). Law at ¶ 5150. Committee Report at ¶ 10,270.

Plan Valuation Dates

¶ 555

*Background*_____

As a general rule, the determination of a defined benefit plan's experience gains and losses and its liability must be made annually. The Economic Growth and Tax Relief Reconciliation Act of 2001 (P.L. 107-16) liberalized the valuation timing rules and provided for an exception to this annual valuation rule. Under the exception, the valuation date can be in the prior plan year. The exception applies only where the plan is well funded. Specifically, the value of the plan assets must not be less than 125 percent of the plan's current liability, on the prior plan year valuation date (Code Sec. 412(c)(9)(B)(ii)).

_____

Technical Corrections Impact

Prior year valuation thresholds revised.—The 125-percent threshold required to value defined benefit plan assets using a prior plan year valuation date is decreased to 100 percent. Thus, the value of the plan assets cannot be less than 100 percent of the plan's current liability on the prior plan year valuation date (Code Sec. 412(c)(9)(B)(ii), as amended by the Job Creation and Worker Assistance Act of 2002 (P.L. 107-147)).

The 100-percent threshold is increased to 125 percent in the case of a change in funding method that is made to take advantage of prior plan year valuation (Code Sec. 412(c)(9)(B)(iv), as added by 2002 Act).

The rules under both the Internal Revenue Code and the Employee Retirement Income Security Act of 1974 (ERISA) (P.L. 93-406) have been amended to reach the same result (ERISA Sec. 302(c)(9)(B), as amended by 2002 Act).

Comment. The change is made to clear up discrepancies that existed between Code Sec. 412, as amended by P.L. 107-16, and the Conference Committee Report for P.L. 107-16 (H.R. Conf. Rep. No. 107-84). In explaining the rationale for the change, the Joint Committee on Taxation states that the Conference Committee Report, which provided for the 100-percent and 125-percent thresholds, was a better expression of Congressional intent (Joint Committee on Taxation *Technical Explanation of the "Job Creation and Worker Assistance Act of 2002"* (JCX-12-02), March 6, 2002).

★ *Effective date.* The provision applies to plan years beginning after December 31, 2001 (Act Sec. 411(x) of the Job Creation and Worker Assistance Act of 2002 (P.L. 107-147); Act Sec. 661(c) of the Economic Growth and Tax Relief Reconciliation Act of 2001 (P.L. 107-16)). See ¶ 20,001 for a discussion of the impact of the sunset rule on this technical correction.

Act Sec. 411(v)(1) of the Job Creation and Worker Assistance Act of 2002, amending Code Sec. 412(c)(9)(B)(ii) and adding Code Sec. 412(c)(9)(B)(iv); Act Sec. 411(v)(2), amending ERISA Sec. 302(c)(9)(B); Act Sec. 411(x). Law at ¶ 5165 and ¶ 7065. Committee Report at ¶ 10,270.

SPECIAL PLANS

Deemed IRAs

¶ 560

Background ———————————————————————————

For plan years beginning after December 31, 2002, an employer maintaining a qualified plan, a qualified annuity under Code Sec. 403(a), a Code Sec. 403(b) tax-sheltered annuity plan or a Code Sec. 457 governmental deferred compensation plan will be able to allow employees to make voluntary employee contributions to a separate individual retirement account (IRA) or annuity established under the plan. If the account or annuity meets the Code Sec. 408 requirements for traditional IRAs or the Code Sec. 408A requirements for Roth IRAs under the terms of the plan, the account or annuity will be deemed an individual retirement plan, and not a qualified plan, for all Code purposes (Code Sec. 408(q)(1)). A qualified plan will not lose its qualified status solely as a result of establishing and maintaining a deemed IRA program (Code Sec. 408(q)(2)).

Employer plans that are eligible to establish deemed IRA programs include plans meeting the requirements of Code Sec. 401(a), qualified annuities under Code Sec. 403(a), Code Sec. 403(b) tax-sheltered annuities, and Code Sec. 457 governmental deferred compensation plans (Code Sec. 408(q)(3)(A) and Code Sec. 72(p)(4)).

Deemed IRAs, and contributions made to deemed IRAs, are not subject to the usual rules governing retirement plans. Instead, the accounts are subject to the rules governing IRAs.

The deemed IRA, and contributions to it, are subject to ERISA's exclusive benefit and fiduciary rules, to the extent otherwise applicable to the plan. They are not subject to the ERISA reporting and disclosure, participation, vesting, funding, and enforcement requirements applicable to eligible retirement plans (ERISA Sec. 4(c)).

———————————————————————————————————————

Technical Corrections Impact

"Qualified employer plan" definition clarified.—This provision clarifies that for purposes of deemed IRAs, the term "qualified employer plan" includes the following types of plans maintained by a governmental employer: (1) a qualified retirement plan under Code Sec. 401(a); (2) a qualified annuity plan under Code Sec. 403(a); (3) a tax-sheltered annuity plan under Code Sec. 403(b); and (4) an eligible deferred compensation plan under Code Sec. 457(b) (Code Sec. 408(q)(3)(A), as amended by the Job Creation and Worker Assistance Act of 2002 (P.L. 107-147)).

This provision also clarifies that the deemed IRA, and contributions to it, are subject to ERISA's administration and enforcement rules. It is further clarified that ERISA is intended to apply to a deemed IRA in a manner similar to a simplified employee pension (SEP) (ERISA Sec. 4(c), as amended by the 2002 Act).

★ *Effective date.* The amendments made by this provision are effective for plan years beginning after December 31, 2002 (Act Sec. 411(x) of the Job Creation and Worker Assistance Act of 2002 (P.L. 107-147); Act Sec. 602(c) of the Economic Growth and Tax Relief Reconciliation Act of 2001 (P.L. 107-16)). See ¶ 20,001 for a discussion of the impact of the sunset rule on this technical correction.

Act Sec. 411(i)(1) of the Job Creation and Worker Assistance Act of 2002, amending Code Sec. 408(q)(3)(A); Act Sec. 411(i)(2), amending ERISA Sec. 4(c); Act. Sec. 411(x). Law at ¶ 5155 and ¶ 7065. Committee Report at ¶ 10,270.

SEP Deduction Limits

¶ 565

Background

Generally, for years prior to 2002, an employer may contribute to each participating employee's SEP (simplified employee pension), and take a deduction for, the *lesser* of 15 percent of the employee's compensation or $35,000 (for 2001). In applying this formula for 2001, the maximum employee compensation that can be taken into consideration is $170,000.

> **Example.** For 2001, Sue Smith's compensation, prior to her employer's contribution to her SEP, is $180,000. Sue's employer may contribute and deduct up to $25,500 (i.e., the lesser of 15% × $170,000, or $35,000), with respect to her SEP for 2001.

The Economic Growth and Tax Relief Reconciliation Act of 2001 (P.L. 107-16) (EGTRRA) amended Code Sec. 404(h)(1)(C) in order to increase the maximum SEP *deduction* to 25 percent of the employee's compensation. The increase in the deduction limit is effective for years beginning after December 31, 2001. EGTRRA also increased the maximum amount of compensation that may be taken into consideration when determining SEP contributions to $200,000 and the maximum SEP contribution to $40,000. However, EGTRRA did not amend Code Sec. 402(h)(2)(A) to provide for a corresponding increase in the percentage limit for *contributions* made to a SEP after 2001. In short, EGTRRA created the conundrum of approving an increase in the percentage used to compute SEP *deductions*, while not approving an increase in the percentage used to compute SEP *contributions*.

Technical Corrections Impact

Deduction percentage increased.—The formula used to determine the maximum *contribution* to an employee's SEP now provides that the allowable contribution is the *lesser* of 25 percent of the employee's compensation ($200,000 maximum compensation that may be considered) or $40,000 (for 2002) (Code Sec. 402(h)(2)(A), as amended by the Job Creation and Worker Assistance Act of 2002 (P.L. 107-147)). This increase in the percentage used to compute the contribution limit from 15 percent to 25 percent brings it into conformance with the percentage used to compute the deduction limit for SEP contributions.

> **Example.** For 2002, Sue Smith's compensation, prior to her employer's contribution to her SEP, is $170,000. Sue's employer may contribute and deduct up to $40,000 (i.e., the lesser of 25% × $170,000, or $40,000), with respect to her SEP for 2002.

Planning Note. Fortunately Congress has corrected the EGTRRA error early enough in 2002 to avoid any serious problems that might have otherwise arisen when employers, and their tax advisors, attempt to determine the maximum allowable SEP contributions and deductions for 2002. This correction also helps bring to mind that the contribution limits for most types of qualified retirement plans (e.g., 401(k)s and IRAs) have been dramatically increased starting in 2002. Effective tax planning for 2002, and future tax years, must take these increases into consideration.

★ *Effective date.* This provision applies to years beginning after December 31, 2001 (Act Sec. 411(x) of the Job Creation and Worker Assistance Act of 2002 (P.L. 107-147); Act Sec. 616(c) of the Economic Growth and Tax Relief Reconciliation Act of 2001 (P.L. 107-16)). See ¶ 20,001 for a discussion of the sunset rule on this technical correction.

Act Sec. 411(l)(3) of the Job Creation and Worker Assistance Act of 2002, amending Code Sec. 402(h)(2)(A); Act Sec. 411(x). Law at ¶ 5140. Committee Report at ¶ 10,270.

SEP Compensation Defined

¶ 570

Background ——————————————————————————————

Prior to the Economic Growth and Tax Relief Reconciliation Act of 2001 (EGTRRA), the term "compensation" was defined differently for purposes of computing the allowable *contribution* to a qualified plan and when computing the allowable *deduction* for the same plan. When computing the allowable contribution, the amount of an employee's compensation that could be taken into consideration included elective deferrals to such plans as 401(k) plans or 403(b) annuities. Thus, for purposes of determining the allowable contribution, an employee's compensation would be greater than the taxable compensation shown on the employee's Form W-2. However, when computing the allowable deduction, an employee's compensation only included taxable compensation. That is, elective deferrals (e.g., 401(k) contributions) were not taken into consideration. The result of this disparity in the definitions of "compensation" is illustrated in the following example.

> **Example.** For 2001, Jay's Trucking paid $1,000,000 in compensation to the employees benefiting under its 401(k) plan in 2001, and they sponsor no other retirement plan. All employees contributed 10% under salary reduction agreements and Jay's contributes 10% in matching contributions. Jay's *total contribution* to the 401(k) plan will be $200,000 (the employees' elective deferrals of $100,000 and the company matching contribution of $100,000). However, the *deduction limit* for Jay's Trucking is $135,000 (15% of total compensation paid after reduction by the elective deferral amount of $100,000). The total contributed by Jay's Trucking ($200,000) is more than the deduction limit ($135,000) applicable to a 401(k) plan; therefore, only $135,000 of the $200,000 contributed is deductible by Jay's Trucking. (This example only considers the employer's deduction limitation. Other limitations and consequences are ignored.)

In addressing this conflict between the definitions of "compensation," EGTRRA amended the Code to provide that, for purposes of determining the amount of an employer's deduction for contributions to certain types of qualified plans, specific types of "elective deferrals" will not be subject to any limitation that applies to stock bonus and profit sharing plans, combinations of defined benefit and defined contributions plans, and ESOPs. In addition, these "elective deferrals" will not be taken into account in applying any such limits to any other contributions (Code Sec. 404(n)). The "elective deferrals" referred to are contributions under 401(k), SARSEP, 403(b) and 401(k) SIMPLE plans (Code Sec. 402(g)(3)).

In addition, EGTRRA stipulated that when applying the employer deduction limits to contributions made (1) to stock bonus and profit sharing plans, (2) to ESOPs, and (3) in situations when there is a combination of defined benefit and defined contribution plans, the definition of "compensation" will include "elective deferrals" (e.g., an employee's 401(k) contributions) (Code Sec. 404(a)(12)).

Technical Corrections Impact

Treatment of SEP elective deferrals clarified.—The new law makes clear that deductions for elective deferrals (e.g., 401(k) contributions) are not subject to any limit imposed on deductions to SEP plans, as well as stock bonus and profit sharing plans, combinations of defined benefit and defined contributions plans, and ESOPs (Code Sec. 404(n), as amended by the Job Creation and Worker Assistance Act of 2002 (P.L. 107-147)).

In addition, when determining "compensation" for purposes of computing the allowable deduction to SEP plans, as well as to stock bonus and profit sharing plans, ESOPs, and in situations when there is a combination of defined benefit and defined contribution plans, the definition of "compensation" will include "elective deferrals" (e.g., an employee's 401(k) contributions) (Code Sec. 404(a)(12), as amended by the 2002 Act).

Comment. The primary result of the changes made to the definition of "compensation" by EGTRRA and the 2002 Act is that a more uniform definition may be applied when applying the contribution and deduction rules. In addition, by including elective contributions in compensation when computing the allowable deduction to SEPs and other types of qualified plans, the deduction may be increased.

★ *Effective date.* These provisions apply to years beginning after December 31, 2001 (Act Sec. 411(x) of the Job Creation and Worker Assistance Act of 2002 (P.L. 107-147); Act Secs. 614(b) and 616(c) of the Economic Growth and Tax Relief Reconciliation Act of 2001 (P.L. 107-16)). See ¶ 20,001 for a discussion of the impact of the sunset rule on this technical correction.

Act Sec. 411(l)(1) of the Job Creation and Worker Assistance Act of 2002, amending Code Sec. 404(a)(12); Act Sec. 411(l)(2), amending Code Sec. 404(n); Act Sec. 411(x). Law at ¶ 5150. Committee Report at ¶ 10,270.

SEP Participation

¶ 575

Background

In order to be recognized as a valid plan, a simplified employee pension (SEP) must satisfy minimum participation requirements. These requirements stipulate that an employer must contribute to the SEP of each employee who has (1) attained the age of 21, (2) performed services for the employer during at least three out of the immediately preceding five calendar years, and (3) received a specified minimum dollar amount of compensation from the employer for the tax year in question. This minimum dollar amount of compensation is subject to an annual inflation adjustment. Originally, the minimum compensation established by the Code was $300. However, the inflation adjusted amount is $450 for the year 2002.

Technical Corrections Impact

Compensation base increased.—The minimum amount of compensation used to determine participation in the SEP has been increased to $450 (Code Sec. 408(k)(2)(C) and Code Sec. 408(k)(8), as amended by the Job Creation and Worker Assistance Act of 2002 (P.L. 107-147)). The $450 amount will also be used as the base for future inflation adjustments to the minimum compensation amount.

Comment. This change in the Code's definition of minimum compensation needed for participation in a SEP has no immediate impact because the annual inflation adjustment had already established $450 as the minimum wage amount for 2002. The change was needed, however, in order to bring the amount used for inflation into compliance with the new base period used for future cost-of-living adjustments.

★ *Effective date.* This provision applies to years beginning after December 31, 2001 (Act Sec. 411(x) of the Job Creation and Worker Assistance Act of 2002 (P.L. 107-147); Act Sec. 611 of the Economic Growth and Tax Relief Reconciliation Act of 2001 (P.L. 107-16)). See ¶ 20,001 for a discussion of the impact of the sunset rule on this technical correction.

Act Sec. 411(j)(1) of the Job Creation and Worker Assistance Act of 2002, amending Code Sec. 408(k)(2)(C) and Code Sec. 408(k)(8); Act Sec. 411(x). Law at ¶ 5155. Committee Report at ¶ 10,270.

ESOP Dividend Reinvestment and Indexing

¶ 580

C corporations are entitled to deduct dividends paid with respect to employer stock held by an employee stock ownership plan (ESOP) described in Code Sec. 4975(e)(7) that, in accordance with plan provisions, are:

(1) paid in cash directly to the plan participants or their beneficiaries,

(2) paid to the plan and subsequently distributed to the participants or beneficiaries in cash no later than 90 days after the close of the plan year in which the dividends are paid to the plan, or

(3) applied to a leveraged ESOP's loan payment (Code Sec. 404(k)(2)(A)).

The deduction may be claimed for the corporation's tax year in which the dividends are paid or distributed to the participants or beneficiaries (Code Sec. 404(k)(1)).

The Economic Growth and Tax Relief Reconciliation Act of 2001 (P.L. 107-16) (EGTRRA) expanded the allowable deduction available to employers for ESOP dividends to include dividends that an employee would voluntarily reinvest back into the ESOP for more of the employer's stock (Code Sec. 404(k)(2)(A)).

Background

ESOP distribution and payment requirements. Unless an ESOP provides that a participant may elect a longer distribution period, the plan must provide distributions of the participant's account balance in substantially equal periodic payments, at least annually, over a period not longer than five years. However, if the participant's account balance exceeds $500,000, the distribution period is extended by one year (up to an additional five years) for each $100,000 (or fraction thereof) by which the account exceeds $500,000 (Code Sec. 409(o)(1)(C)). These dollar amounts are to be indexed for cost-of-living adjustments at the same time and in the same manner as are the dollar limits under Code Sec. 415(d). Although EGTRRA reset many of the statutory dollar amounts previously adjusted on an annual basis under Code Sec. 415 and added other new limitation amounts, it did not reset the dollar amounts for determining the maximum account balance in an ESOP subject to a five-year distribution period.

Comment. Effective January 1, 2001, the dollar amounts were increased to $155,000 and $780,000, respectively, by Notice 2000-66, I.R.B. 2000-52, 600, and effective January 1, 2002, the amounts were increased to $160,000 and $800,000, respectively, by Notice 2001-84, I.R.B. 2001-53, 642.

Technical Corrections Impact

Reinvestment of ESOP dividends.—A technical correction clarifies that the deduction for dividends paid, at the election of the plan participants or their beneficiaries, to an ESOP and reinvested in qualified employer securities is allowed for the tax year of the corporation in which the later of the following occurs:

(1) the dividends are reinvested in qualified employer securities, or

(2) the election is made by the plan participant to have the dividend paid to the plan and reinvested in qualifying employer securities (Code Sec. 404(k)(4)(B), as added by the Job Creation and Worker Assistance Act of 2002 (P.L. 107-147)).

Example. Widget Corp. is a calendar year C corporation that maintains an ESOP that accumulates dividends during the year for distribution within 90 days from the end of the plan year. Following the 2001 legislation, Widget Corp. amended its ESOP to provide participants with an election to receive a distribution in cash of the 2001 dividends within the first 90 days of 2002 or to reinvest the dividends in employer securities within the first 90 days of 2002. All the 2001 dividends accumulated and paid by the ESOP that the plan participants elect to reinvest are reinvested in January 2002. Widget Corp. can deduct the amount of the 2001 dividends reinvested in employer securities on its 2002 returns. Similarly, any 2001 dividends distributed in cash during 2002 pursuant to an election are deducted on the corporation's 2002 return (Example (1), IRS Notice 2002-2, I.R.B. 2002-2, 285).

Comment. Notice 2002-2, I.R.B. 2002-2, 285, which provides guidance with respect to the timing of the deduction for dividends reinvested into qualified employer securities, was issued by the IRS on December 17, 2001, prior to enactment of the 2002 Act. It states that the deduction is claimed in the later of the tax year in which (a) the dividends are reinvested into the qualified employer securities at the participant's election or (b) at the time the election by the plan participant is made irrevocable. Although Notice 2002-2 is more narrow than Code

Sec. 404(k)(4), as amended by the 2002 Act, in that it defines an election as being made on the date that it become irrevocable, it is not inconsistent with the 2002 Act amendments.

Nonforfeitable contributions. The technical correction further clarifies that applicable dividends paid to the plan and reinvested in qualifying employer securities at the participant's election must be nonforfeitable in order to satisfy the minimum vesting standards of Code Sec. 411(a) (Code Sec. 404(k)(7), as added by the 2002 Act).

ESOP distributions. In conjunction with EGTRRA's increases in benefit and contribution limits, a new base period applies in indexing the 2002 dollar amounts for future cost-of-living adjustments. The same indexing method applies to the dollar amounts used to determine the proper period for distributions from an ESOP. The dollar amounts in Code Sec. 409(o)(C)(ii) have been changed to the 2002 indexed amounts specified in Notice 2001-84, I.R.B. 2001-53, 642, in order to ensure that future indexing will operate properly. Thus, if the participant's account balance exceeds $800,000, the distribution period is extended by one year, up to an additional five years, for each $160,000 (or fraction thereof) by which the account exceeds $800,000 (Code Sec. 409(o)(1)(C)(ii), as amended by the 2002 Act).

★ *Effective date.* The provisions are effective for tax years beginning after December 31, 2001 (Act Sec. 411(x) of the Job Creation and Worker Assistance Act of 2002 (P.L. 107-147); Act Secs. 611(i) and 662(c) of the Economic Growth and Tax Relief Reconciliation Act of 2001). See ¶ 20,001 for a discussion of the impact of the sunset rule on this technical correction.

Act Sec. 411(j)(2) of the Job Creation and Worker Assistance Act of 2002, amending Code Sec. 409(o)(1)(C)(ii); Act Sec. 411(w)(1)(A), amending Code Sec. 404(k)(1); Act Sec. 411(w)(1)(B), amending Code Sec. 404(k)(2)(B); Act Sec. 411(w)(1)(C), amending Code Sec. 404(k)(4)(B); Act Sec. 411(w)(1)(D), redesignating Code Sec. 404(k)(4)(B) as Code Sec. 404(k)(4)(C) and adding new Code Sec. 404(k)(4)(B); Act Sec. 411(w)(2), adding Code Sec. 404(k)(7); Act Sec. 411(x). Law at ¶ 5150 and ¶ 5160. Committee Report at ¶ 10,270.

Tax-Sheltered Annuity Plans

¶ 585

Background ⎯⎯⎯⎯⎯⎯⎯⎯⎯⎯⎯⎯⎯⎯⎯⎯⎯⎯⎯⎯⎯⎯⎯⎯⎯⎯⎯⎯⎯⎯⎯⎯⎯⎯⎯⎯⎯

An employee's basis in a retirement plan includes contributions made by the employer to a plan, other than a tax-sheltered annuity or simplified employee pension (SEP), that fails to qualify under Code Sec. 401, provided that the right of the employee to those contributions is substantially vested at the time the contributions are made (Code Sec. 72(f), Code Sec. 83, Code Sec. 402(b)(1), Code Sec. 403(c); Reg. § 1.72-8(a)(1)).

Contributions to a nonqualified plan are not included in an employee's gross income if they are not substantially vested when made (Code Sec. 83, Code Sec. 402(b)(1), and Code Sec. 403(c)). However, if part or all of an employee's interest in a plan later becomes substantially vested, its value must be included in the employee's gross income to the extent attributed to contributions made by the employer after August 1, 1969. (Code Sec. 402(b)(1), Code Sec. 403(c); Reg. § 1.402(b)-1(b)(1), Reg. § 1.402(b)-1(b)(3), Reg. § 1.403(c)-1(b)(3)). When substantial vesting occurs, the employee's basis in the plan is increased by the amount included in gross income (Reg. § 1.402(b)-1(b)(5)).

Tax-sheltered annuities are subject to the same contribution limitations as tax-qualified plans. The limits on contributions to a tax-sheltered annuity plan apply at the time the contributions become vested.

The maximum amount that may be deferred under a Code Sec. 403(b) annuity plan is the lesser of $11,000 in 2002 or 100 percent of the participant's includible compensation and is increased in $1,000 annual increments until the limit reaches $15,000 in 2006. After 2006, the limit is adjusted for inflation in increments of $500 (Code Sec. 402(g)(1), as amended by the Economic Growth and Tax Relief Reconciliation Act of 2001 (P.L. 107-16)). These limits are subject to a sunset provision (see ¶ 20,001).

Technical Corrections Impact

Limits apply to contributions in year made.—The provision clarifies that the limits apply to contributions to a tax-sheltered annuity plan in the year the contributions are made without regard to when the contributions become vested (Code Sec. 403(b)(1), as amended by the Job Creation and Worker Assistance Act of 2002 (P.L. 107-147); Code Sec. 403(b)(6), stricken by the 2002 Act).

The provision also clarifies that contributions may be made for an employee for up to five years after retirement, based on includible compensation for the last year of service before retirement (Code Sec. 403(b)(3), as amended by the 2002 Act).

★ *Effective date.* The amendments made by this provision are effective for plan years beginning after December 31, 2001 (Act Sec. 411(x) of the Job Creation and Worker Assistance Act of 2002 (P.L. 107-147); Act Sec. 632(a)(4) of the Economic Growth and Tax Relief Reconciliation Act of 2001 (P.L. 107-16)). See ¶ 20,001 for a discussion of the impact of the sunset rule on this technical correction.

Act Sec. 411(p)(1) of the Job Creation and Worker Assistance Act of 2002, amending Code Sec. 403(b)(1); Act Sec. 411(p)(2), striking Code Sec. 403(b)(6); Act Sec. 411(p)(3), amending Code Sec. 403(b)(3); Act Sec. 411(x). Law at ¶ 5145. Committee Report at ¶ 10,270.

Church Plan Provision Reinstated

¶ 590

For tax years beginning after December 31, 2001, the alternative exclusion allowance that applied to church employees was repealed. As a result, the tax-sheltered annuities contribution limitation for church employees was generally the same as that for tax-qualified plans (Code Sec. 403(b)(2)(d), before being stricken by the Economic Growth and Tax Relief Reconciliation Act of 2001 (P.L. 107-16) (EGTRRA)). Code 403(b) plans are treated as defined contribution plans and any contributions made by the employer are to be treated as employer contributions to a defined contribution plan (Code Sec. 415(k)(4), as added by EGTRRA).

*Background*_____

Even though the alternative exclusion allowance was eliminated, there is still a special contribution limit for church employees. Church employees may make an election to increase the general contribution limit by up to $10,000 for any year, subject to a $40,000 lifetime cap (Code Sec. 415(c)(7), as amended by EGTRRA).

Technical Corrections Impact

Alternative contribution limit.—The provision restores special rules for ministers and lay employees of churches and for foreign missionaries, that were inadvertently eliminated by EGTRRA. Therefore, in determining years of service with related church organizations, all years of service are treated as years of service with a single employer. Thus, although a minister or lay employee may, during his career with a church, transfer from one organization to another within the particular denomination, or from a church to an associated organization, all service is treated as service with a single employer (Code Sec. 415(c)(7)(B)(i), as amended by the Job Creation and Worker Assistance Act of 2002 (P.L. 107-147)). Similarly, all tax-sheltered annuity contributions for an employee by related church organizations are treated as made by a single employer (Code Sec. 415(c)(7)(B)(ii), as amended by the 2002 Act).

In the case of foreign missionaries performing services outside the United States, contributions and other additions to a Code 403(b) annuity contract or retirement account for such an individual will not be treated as exceeding the limit if they are not in excess of the greater of $3,000 or the individual's includible compensation as determined under Code Sec. 403(b)(2) (Code Sec. 415(c)(7)(C), as amended by the 2002 Act).

In addition, the new provision conforms the definition of the terms "church" and "convention or association of churches" to have the same meaning as they do in Code Sec. 414(e) (Code Sec. 415(c)(7)(E), as amended by the 2002 Act).

★ *Effective date.* The amendments made by this provision are effective for plan years beginning after December 31, 2001 (Act Sec. 411(x) of the Job Creation and Worker Assistance Act of 2002 (P.L. 107-147); Act Sec. 632(a)(4) of the Economic Growth and Tax Relief Reconciliation Act of 2001 (P.L. 107-16)). See ¶ 20,001 for a discussion of the impact of the sunset rule on this technical correction.

Act Sec. 411(p)(4) of the Job Creation and Worker Assistance Act of 2002, amending Code Sec. 415(c)(7); Act Sec. 411(x). Law at ¶ 5175. Committee Report at ¶ 10,270.

Eligible Deferred Compensation Plans—Definition of Compensation

¶ 595

*Background*_____

Includible compensation means compensation for service performed for the employer that is currently includible in gross income. The maximum amount of compensation that may be deferred by a Code Sec. 457 eligible deferred compensation plan participant is limited. The maximum amount that may be deferred under a Code Sec. 457 plan is the lesser of $11,000 in 2002 or 100 percent of the

Background

participant's includible compensation and is increased in $1,000 annual increments until the limit reaches $15,000 in 2006. After 2006, the limit is adjusted for inflation in increments of $500 (Code Sec. 457(b)(2) and Code Sec. 457(e)(15)(B)). These limits are subject to a sunset provision (see ¶ 20,001).

Technical Corrections Impact

Includible compensation defined.—Amounts deferred under an eligible deferred compensation plan are generally subject to the same contribution limits as qualified defined contribution plans. The technical correction provision conforms the definition of compensation used in applying the limits to an eligible Code Sec. 457 (state and local government or tax-exempt organization) deferred compensation plan to the definition used for defined contribution plans. For purposes of Code Sec. 457 deferred compensation plans, includible compensation has the meaning given to the term "participant's compensation" as provided in Code Sec. 415(c)(3) (Code Sec. 457(e)(5), as amended by the Job Creation and Worker Assistance Act of 2002 (P.L. 107-147)). Participant's compensation means the compensation for the participant from the employer for the plan year (Code Sec. 415(c)(3)).

★ *Effective date.* The amendments made by this provision are effective for tax years beginning after December 31, 2001 (Act Sec. 411(x) of the Job Creation and Worker Assistance Act of 2002 (P.L. 107-147); Act Sec. 632(c) of the Economic Growth and Tax Relief Reconciliation Act of 2001 (P.L. 107-16)). See ¶ 20,001 for a discussion of the impact of the sunset rule on this technical correction.

Act Sec. 411(p)(5) of the Job Creation and Worker Assistance Act of 2002, amending Code Sec. 457(e)(5); Act Sec. 411(x). Law at ¶ 5195. Committee Report at ¶ 10,270.

CREDITS

Elective Deferrals and IRA Contributions

¶ 605

Background

In order to encourage low- and middle-income taxpayers to establish or maintain private savings accounts to ensure adequate savings for retirement, the Economic Growth and Tax Relief Reconciliation Act of 2001 (P.L. 107-16) added Code Sec. 25B, which provided for a temporary, nonrefundable credit for contributions or deferrals to retirement savings plans. The credit applies to tax years beginning after 2001, and is scheduled to terminate in tax years beginning after 2006 (Code Sec. 25B(h), as redesignated by Act Sec. 417(1) of the Job Creation and Worker Assistance Act of 2002; see ¶ 5020).

The credit, which is in addition to any deduction or exclusion that would otherwise apply with respect to the contribution, offsets both alternative minimum tax and regular tax liability. The amount of the credit is equal to the applicable percentage times the amount of qualified retirement savings contributions, not to exceed $2,000, made by an eligible individual in the tax year to certain specified retirement plans. The applicable percentage is determined by the taxpayer's filing status and adjusted gross income (Code Sec. 25B(b)).

*Background*_____

The contribution amount is to be reduced by any distributions received from specified qualified retirement plans during the testing period. The testing period for a tax year is (1) the current tax year, (2) the two preceding tax years, and (3) the period after such tax year and before the due date, including extensions, for filing the return for the tax year (Code Sec. 25B(d)(2)(B)).

The qualified retirement savings contribution amount for any tax year equals the sum of the following contributions or deferrals made during the tax year by eligible individuals to qualified retirement plans, including Roth IRAs:

(1) qualified retirement contributions under Code Sec. 219(e), relating to retirement savings;

(2) elective deferrals defined under Code Sec. 402(g)(3), relating to deferrals to Code Sec. 401(k) plans, to SARSEP plans, to Code Sec. 403(b) tax-sheltered annuity plans, and to SIMPLE plans under Code Sec. 408(p);

(3) elective deferrals of compensation of eligible Code Sec. 457(b) state and local government and tax-exempt organization deferred compensation arrangements; and

(4) voluntary employee contributions to any qualified retirement plan defined at Code Sec. 4974(c), relating to the excise tax on certain accumulations in qualified retirement plans (Code Sec. 25B(d)(1)).

Reduction of total contribution amount. The total contribution amount is reduced by the following:

(1) any distributions from a qualified retirement plan (as defined in Code Sec. 4974(c)) or an eligible compensation plan (as defined in Code Sec. 457(b)) received by the individual during the testing period that is includible in gross income, and

(2) any distributions from a Roth IRA or Roth account received by the individual during the testing period that are not qualified rollover contributions (as defined in Code Sec. 408A(e)) to a Roth IRA or rollovers under Code Sec. 402(c)(8)(B) to a Roth account (Code Sec. 25B(d)(2)(A), prior to amendment by the 2002 Act).

Technical Corrections Impact

Reduction of total contribution amount by certain distributions.—A technical correction clarifies the amount by which contributions taken into account in determining the credit for elective deferrals and IRA contributions are reduced by the amount of plan distributions. The list of sources from which distributions will reduce contributions has been replaced with a simplified provision that mirrors the list of entities set forth in Code Sec. 25B(d)(1) to which qualified retirement savings contributions may be made (Code Sec. 25B(d)(2)(A), as amended by the Job Creation and Worker Assistance Act of 2002 (P.L. 107-147)). It is still the case that contributions are to be reduced by distributions from qualified retirement plans, eligible deferred compensation plans, or traditional IRAs that are includible in income or that consist of after-tax contributions. Qualified retirement savings contributions determined under Code Sec. 25B(d)(1) are to be reduced, but not below zero, by the aggregate distributions that a taxpayer receives from such plans.

¶ **605**

The rule that distributions that are rolled over to another retirement plan do not affect the credit has been retained. This applies to any distribution that is not includible in gross income due to a trustee-to-trustee transfer or a rollover distribution (Code Sec. 25B(d)(2)(A), as amended by the 2002 Act).

★ *Effective date.* The credit applies to tax years beginning after December 31, 2001, and is scheduled to terminate in tax years beginning after December 31, 2006 (Act Sec. 411(x) of the Job Creation and Worker Assistance Act of 2002 (P.L. 107-147); Act Sec. 618(d) of the Economic Growth and Tax Relief Reconciliation Act of 2001 (P.L. 107-16)).

Act Sec. 411(m) of the Job Creation and Worker Assistance Act of 2002, amending Code Sec. 25B(d)(2)(A); Act Sec. 411(x). Law at ¶ 5020. Committee Report at ¶ 10,270.

Plan Start-Up Costs

¶ 610

Background ───

Effective for tax years beginning after December 31, 2001, certain small employers are entitled to a nonrefundable income tax credit for 50 percent of the qualified start-up costs incurred relating to the establishment and maintenance of new employee retirement plans. The credit is available for the first $1,000 in administrative and retirement-education expenses for each of the first three years of the plan.

───

Technical Corrections Impact

Small employer pension plan start-up costs.—For purposes of the aggregation rules, a technical correction clarifies that all employees of the members of an affiliated service group shall be treated as being employed by a single employer pursuant to Code Sec. 414(m). All eligible employer plans shall be treated as one eligible employer plan (Code Sec. 45E(e)(1), as amended by the Job Creation and Worker Assistance Act of 2002 (P.L. 107-147)).

Comment. As originally enacted, for purposes of being a single employer, Code Sec. 45E(e)(1) inadvertently referred to Code Sec. 414(n), which relates to leased employees. That reference has now been changed to a reference to Code Sec. 414(m), relating to employees of affiliated service groups.

Qualified employer plans. A technical correction to the effective date clarifies that the credit applies to costs paid or incurred in tax years beginning after December 31, 2001, with respect to qualified employer plans that are "first effective" after December 31, 2001 (Act Sec. 619(d) of the Economic Growth and Tax Relief Reconciliation Act of 2001, as amended by the 2002 Act).

Comment. Prior to this amendment, the effective date provided that the provision was effective with respect to plans "established" after December 31, 2001. Thus, the amendment clarifies that the provision can apply to plans adopted before December 31, 2001, so long as they are first effective after that date (Joint Committee on Taxation, *Technical Explanation of the "Job Creation and Worker Assistance Act of 2002"* (JCX-12-02), March 6, 2002).

★ *Effective date.* The provision applies to costs paid or incurred in tax years beginning after December 31, 2001, with respect to qualified employer plans established after such date (Act. Sec. 411(x) of the Job Creation and Worker Assistance Act of 2002 (P.L. 107-147); Act Sec. 619(d) of the Economic Growth and Tax Relief Reconciliation Act of 2001 (P.L. 107-16)). See ¶ 20,001 for a discussion of the impact of the sunset rule on this technical correction.

Act Sec. 411(n)(1) of the Job Creation and Worker Assistance Act of 2002, amending Code Sec. 45E(e)(1); Act Sec. 411(n)(2), amending Act Sec. 619(d) of the Economic Growth and Tax Relief Reconciliation Act of 2001; Act Sec. 411(x). Law at ¶ 5052 and ¶ 7065. Committee Report at ¶ 10,270.

EXTENDED PROVISIONS

Mental Health Parity Requirements

¶ 615

Background

As a result of the Health Insurance Portability and Accountability Act of 1996 (HIPAA) (P.L. 104-191), group health plans (including HMO plans) are required to expand the availability of coverage for plan years beginning after June 30, 1997. Code Sec. 4980D imposes an excise tax on plans that fail to comply with the expanded requirements. In 1997, the Mental Health Parity Act of 1996 (Title VII, P.L. 104-204) was incorporated into the Internal Revenue Code (Code Sec. 9812, as added by Act Sec. 1531 of the Taxpayer Relief Act of 1997 (P.L. 105-34)). Code Sec. 9812 imposes parity requirements between medical/surgical benefits and mental health benefits in group health plans. Failure to comply with the mental health benefits parity requirements for group health plans triggered the Code Sec. 4980D excise tax. The mental health benefits parity requirements were applicable with respect to plan years beginning on or after January 1, 1998, and expired with respect to benefits for services provided on or after September 30, 2001.

Section 701 of P.L. 107-116 (providing appropriations for the Departments of Labor, Health and Human Services, and Education for fiscal year 2002), enacted on January 10, 2002, restored the excise tax retroactively to September 30, 2001. The excise tax was scheduled to expire with respect to benefits for services furnished on or after December 31, 2002.

The Mental Health Parity Act provides that group health plans that offer both medical and surgical benefits and mental health benefits cannot impose aggregate lifetime or annual dollar limits on mental health benefits if the limits are not also imposed on substantially all medical and surgical benefits.

The basic penalty is $100 for each affected individual for every day in the noncompliance period and is imposed on the employer sponsoring the plan. The noncompliance period begins on the day the failure first occurs and ends on the date of correction. No tax is imposed where the failure would not have been discovered in the exercise of reasonable diligence or if the failure is due to reasonable cause and not willful neglect and the failure is corrected within 30 days after it is discovered or should have been discovered. An additional rule imposes a minimum penalty tax if a correction of the failure occurs after the taxpayer is notified of an income tax examination covering the year of the failure. The minimum tax for *de minimis* failure is the lesser of $2500 or the basic penalty tax. Where the failure is not *de minimis*, the $2500 penalty is increased to $15,000. A maximum penalty applies for unintentional failures.

Background ——————————————————————————————

The IRS may waive part or all of the penalty computed under the rules if the penalty is excessive in relation to the failure and if the failure is due to reasonable cause and not willful neglect.

Job Creation Act Impact

Mental health parity requirements extended.—The application of the excise tax on the failure to comply with mental health parity requirements is clarified (Code Sec. 9812(f), as amended by the Job Creation and Worker Assistance Act of 2002 (P.L. 107-147)). The excise tax does not apply to benefits for services furnished on or after September 30, 2001, and before January 10, 2002, and sunsets after December 31, 2003. Thus, it applies to benefits or services furnished on or after January 10, 2002, and before January 1, 2004.

★ *Effective date.* The amendment applies to plan years beginning after December 31, 2000 (Act Sec. 610(b) of the Job Creation and Worker Assistance Act of 2002 (P.L. 107-147)).

Act Sec. 610 of the Job Creation and Worker Assistance Act of 2002, amending Code Sec. 9812(f); Act Sec. 610(b). Law at ¶ 5400. Committee Report at ¶ 10,500.

———————————————

CODE SECTIONS ADDED, AMENDED OR REPEALED

[¶ 5001] INTRODUCTION.

The Internal Revenue Code provisions amended by the Job Creation and Worker Assistance Act of 2002 (P.L. 107-147) are shown in the following paragraphs. Deleted Code material or the text of the Code Section prior to amendment appears in the amendment notes following each amended Code provision. *Any changed or added material is set out in italics.*

[¶ 5005] CODE SEC. 21. EXPENSES FOR HOUSEHOLD AND DEPENDENT CARE SERVICES NECESSARY FOR GAINFUL EMPLOYMENT.

* * *

(d) EARNED INCOME LIMITATION.—

* * *

[Caution: Code Sec. 21(d)(2), below, as amended by Act Sec. 418(b)(1)-(2), applies to tax years beginning after December 31, 2002.—CCH.]

(2) SPECIAL RULE FOR SPOUSE WHO IS A STUDENT OR INCAPABLE OF CARING FOR HIMSELF.—In the case of a spouse who is a student or a qualified individual described in subsection (b)(1)(C), for purposes of paragraph (1), such spouse shall be deemed for each month during which such spouse is a full-time student at an educational institution, or is such a qualifying individual, to be gainfully employed and to have earned income of not less than—

(A) *$250* if subsection (c)(1) applies for the taxable year, or

(B) *$500* if subsection (c)(2) applies for the taxable year.

In the case of any husband and wife, this paragraph shall apply with respect to only one spouse for any one month.

* * *

[CCH Explanation at ¶ 240. Committee Reports at ¶ 10,320.]

<table>
<tr><td>

Amendment Notes

Act Sec. 418(b)(1)-(2) amended Code Sec. 21(d)(2) by striking "$200" and inserting "$250" in subparagraph (A), and by striking "$400" and inserting "$500" in subparagraph (B).
</td><td>

The above amendment is effective as if included in the provision of the Economic Growth and Tax Relief Reconciliation Act of 2001 (P.L.107-16) to which it relates [applicable to tax years beginning after December 31, 2002.—CCH].
</td></tr>
</table>

[¶ 5010] CODE SEC. 23. ADOPTION EXPENSES.

(a) ALLOWANCE OF CREDIT.—

[Caution: Code Sec. 23(a)(1), below, as amended by Act Sec. 411(c)(1)(A), applies to tax years beginning after December 31, 2002.—CCH.]

(1) IN GENERAL.—In the case of an individual, there shall be allowed as a credit against the tax imposed by this chapter the amount of the qualified adoption expenses paid or incurred by the taxpayer.

(2) YEAR CREDIT ALLOWED.—The credit under paragraph (1) with respect to any expense shall be allowed—

(A) in the case of any expense paid or incurred before the taxable year in which such adoption becomes final, for the taxable year following the taxable year during which such expense is paid or incurred, and

(B) in the case of an expense paid or incurred during or after the taxable year in which such adoption becomes final, for the taxable year in which such expense is paid or incurred.

Code Sec. 23(a)   ¶ 5010

[Caution: Code Sec. 23(a)(3), below, as added by Act Sec. 411(c)(1)(B), applies to tax years beginning after December 31, 2002.—CCH.]

(3) $10,000 CREDIT FOR ADOPTION OF CHILD WITH SPECIAL NEEDS REGARDLESS OF EXPENSES.—*In the case of an adoption of a child with special needs which becomes final during a taxable year, the taxpayer shall be treated as having paid during such year qualified adoption expenses with respect to such adoption in an amount equal to the excess (if any) of $10,000 over the aggregate qualified adoption expenses actually paid or incurred by the taxpayer with respect to such adoption during such taxable year and all prior taxable years.*

[CCH Explanation at ¶ 236. Committee Reports at ¶ 10,260.]

Amendment Notes

Act Sec. 411(c)(1)(A) amended Code Sec. 23(a)(1) to read as above. Prior to amendment, Code Sec. 23(a)(1) read as follows:

(1) IN GENERAL.—In the case of an individual, there shall be allowed as a credit against the tax imposed by this chapter—

(A) in the case of an adoption of a child other than a child with special needs, the amount of the qualified adoption expenses paid or incurred by the taxpayer, and

(B) in the case of an adoption of a child with special needs, $10,000.

Act Sec. 411(c)(1)(B) amended Code Sec. 23(a) by adding at the end a new paragraph (3) to read as above.

The above amendments apply to tax years beginning after December 31, 2002.

Act Sec. 411(c)(1)(C) amended Code Sec. 23(a)(2) by striking the last sentence. Prior to being stricken, the last sentence of Code Sec. 23(a)(2) read as follows:

In the case of the adoption of a child with special needs, the credit allowed under paragraph (1) shall be allowed for the taxable year in which the adoption becomes final.

The above amendment applies to tax years beginning after December 31, 2001.

(b) LIMITATIONS.—

(1) DOLLAR LIMITATION.—The aggregate amount of qualified adoption expenses which may be taken into account under *subsection (a)* for all taxable years with respect to the adoption of a child by the taxpayer shall not exceed $10,000.

* * *

[CCH Explanation at ¶ 236. Committee Reports at ¶ 10,260.]

Amendment Notes

Act Sec. 411(c)(1)(D) amended Code Sec. 23(b)(1) by striking "subsection (a)(1)(A)" and inserting "subsection (a)".

The above amendment applies to tax years beginning after December 31, 2001. For a special rule, see Act Sec. 411(c)(1)(F), below.

Act Sec. 411(c)(1)(F) provides:

(F) Expenses paid or incurred during any taxable year beginning before January 1, 2002, may be taken into account in determining the credit under section 23 of the Internal Revenue Code of 1986 only to the extent the aggregate of such expenses does not exceed the applicable limitation under section 23(b)(1) of such Code as in effect on the day before the date of the enactment of the Economic Growth and Tax Relief Reconciliation Act of 2001.

(h) ADJUSTMENTS FOR INFLATION.—In the case of a taxable year beginning after December 31, 2002, each of the dollar amounts in *subsection (a)(3)* and paragraphs (1) and (2)(A)(i) of subsection (b) shall be increased by an amount equal to—

(1) such dollar amount, multiplied by

(2) the cost-of-living adjustment determined under section 1(f)(3) for the calendar year in which the taxable year begins, determined by substituting "calendar year 2001" for "calendar year 1992" in subparagraph (B) thereof.

If any amount as increased under the preceding sentence is not a multiple of $10, such amount shall be rounded to the nearest multiple of $10.

[CCH Explanation at ¶ 238. Committee Reports at ¶ 10,320.]

Amendment Notes

Act Sec. 418(a)(1)(A)-(B) amended Code Sec. 23(h) by striking "subsection (a)(1)(B)" and inserting "subsection (a)(3)", and by adding at the end a new flush sentence to read as above.

The above amendment is effective as if included in the provision of the Economic Growth and Tax Relief Reconciliation Act of 2001 (P.L. 107-16) to which it relates [effective for tax years beginning after December 31, 2001.—CCH].

[Caution: Code Sec. 23(i), below, as amended by Act Sec. 411(c)(1)(E), applies to tax years beginning after December 31, 2002.—CCH.]

(i) REGULATIONS.—The Secretary shall prescribe such regulations as may be appropriate to carry out this section and section 137, including regulations which treat unmarried individuals who pay or incur qualified adoption expenses with respect to the same child as 1 taxpayer for purposes of applying *the dollar amounts in subsections (a)(3) and (b)(1)* of this section and in section 137(b)(1).

[CCH Explanation at ¶ 236. Committee Reports at ¶ 10,260.]

Amendment Notes

Act Sec. 411(c)(1)(E) amended Code Sec. 23(i) by striking "the dollar limitation in subsection (b)(1)" and inserting "the dollar amounts in subsections (a)(3) and (b)(1)".

The above amendment applies to tax years beginning after December 31, 2002.

[¶ 5015] CODE SEC. 24. CHILD TAX CREDIT.

* * *

(d) PORTION OF CREDIT REFUNDABLE.—

(1) IN GENERAL.—The aggregate credits allowed to a taxpayer under subpart C shall be increased by the lesser of—

(A) the credit which would be allowed under this section without regard to this subsection and the limitation under subsection (b)(3), or

(B) the amount by which the *aggregate amount of credits allowed by this subpart* (determined without regard to this subsection) would increase if the limitation imposed by subsection (b)(3) were increased by the greater of—

(i) 15 percent (10 percent in the case of taxable years beginning before January 1, 2005) of so much of the taxpayer's earned income (within the meaning of section 32) which is taken into account in computing taxable income for the taxable year as exceeds $10,000, or

(ii) in the case of a taxpayer with 3 or more qualifying children, the excess (if any) of—

(I) the taxpayer's social security taxes for the taxable year, over

(II) the credit allowed under section 32 for the taxable year.

The amount of the credit allowed under this subsection shall not be treated as a credit allowed under this subpart and shall reduce the amount of credit otherwise allowable under subsection (a) without regard to subsection (b)(3).

* * *

[CCH Explanation at ¶ 232. Committee Reports at ¶ 10,260.]

Amendment Notes

Act Sec. 411(b) amended Code Sec. 24(d)(1)(B) by striking "amount of credit allowed by this section" and inserting "aggregate amount of credits allowed by this subpart".

The above amendment is effective as if included in the provision of the Economic Growth and Tax Relief Reconciliation Act of 2001 (P.L. 107-16) to which it relates

[effective for tax years beginning after December 31, 2000.—CCH].

Act Sec. 601(b)(2) provides:

(2) The amendments made by sections 201(b), 202(f), and 618(b) of the Economic Growth and Tax Relief Reconciliation Act of 2001 shall not apply to taxable years beginning during 2002 and 2003.

[¶ 5020] CODE SEC. 25B. ELECTIVE DEFERRALS AND IRA CONTRIBUTIONS BY CERTAIN INDIVIDUALS.

* * *

(d) QUALIFIED RETIREMENT SAVINGS CONTRIBUTIONS.—For purposes of this section—

* * *

(2) REDUCTION FOR CERTAIN DISTRIBUTIONS.—

(A) IN GENERAL.—The qualified retirement savings contributions determined under paragraph (1) shall be reduced (but not below zero) by the aggregate distributions received by the individual during the testing period from any entity of a type to which contributions under paragraph (1) may be made. The preceding sentence shall not apply to the portion of any distribution which is not includible in gross income by reason of a trustee-to-trustee transfer or a rollover distribution.

* * *

[CCH Explanation at ¶ 605. Committee Reports at ¶ 10,270.]

Amendment Notes

Act Sec. 411(m) amended Code Sec. 25B(d)(2)(A) to read as above. Prior to amendment, Code Sec. 25B(d)(2)(A) read as follows:

(A) IN GENERAL.—The qualified retirement savings contributions determined under paragraph (1) shall be reduced (but not below zero) by the sum of—

(i) any distribution from a qualified retirement plan (as defined in section 4974(c)), or from an eligible deferred compensation plan (as defined in section 457(b)), received by the individual during the testing period which is includible in gross income, and

(ii) any distribution from a Roth IRA or a Roth account received by the individual during the testing period which is

not a qualified rollover contribution (as defined in section 408A(e)) to a Roth IRA or a rollover under section 402(c)(8)(B) to a Roth account.

The above amendment is effective as if included in the provision of the Economic Growth and Tax Relief Reconciliation Act of 2001 (P.L. 107-16) to which it relates [effective for tax years beginning after December 31, 2001.—CCH].

Act Sec. 601(b)(2) provides:

(2) The amendments made by sections 201(b), 202(f), and 618(b) of the Economic Growth and Tax Relief Reconciliation Act of 2001 shall not apply to taxable years beginning during 2002 and 2003.

(h) TERMINATION.—This section shall not apply to taxable years beginning after December 31, 2006.

[CCH Explanation at ¶ 30,050. Committee Reports at ¶ 10,320.]

Amendment Notes

Act Sec. 417(1) amended Code Sec. 25B by redesignating subsection (g) as subsection (h).

The above amendment is effective on March 9, 2002.

[¶ 5025] CODE SEC. 26. LIMITATION BASED ON TAX LIABILITY; DEFINITION OF TAX LIABILITY.

(a) LIMITATION BASED ON AMOUNT OF TAX.—

* * *

(2) SPECIAL *RULE FOR 2000, 2001, 2002, AND 2003.*—For purposes of any taxable year beginning *during 2000, 2001, 2002, or 2003,* the aggregate amount of credits allowed by this subpart for the taxable year shall not exceed the sum of—

(A) the taxpayer's regular tax liability for the taxable year reduced by the foreign tax credit allowable under section 27(a), and

(B) the tax imposed by section 55(a) for the taxable year.

[CCH Explanation at ¶ 270. Committee Reports at ¶ 10,400.]

Amendment Notes

Act Sec. 601(a)(1)-(2) amended Code Sec. 26(a)(2) by striking "RULE FOR 2000 AND 2001.—" and inserting "RULE FOR 2000, 2001, 2002, AND 2003.—", and by striking "during

2000 or 2001," and inserting "during 2000, 2001, 2002, or 2003,".

The above amendment applies to tax years beginning after December 31, 2001.

(b) REGULAR TAX LIABILITY.—For purposes of this part—

(1) IN GENERAL.—The term "regular tax liability" means the tax imposed by this chapter for the taxable year.

(2) EXCEPTION FOR CERTAIN TAXES.—For purposes of paragraph (1), any tax imposed by any of the following provisions shall not be treated as tax imposed by this chapter:

(A) section 55 (relating to minimum tax),

(B) section 59A (relating to environmental tax),

(C) subsection (m)(5)(B), (q), (t), or (v) of section 72 (relating to additional taxes on certain distributions),

(D) section 143(m) (relating to recapture of proration of Federal subsidy from use of mortgage bonds and mortgage credit certificates),

(E) section 530(d)(3) (relating to additional tax on certain distributions from Coverdell education savings accounts),

(F) section 531 (relating to accumulated earnings tax),

(G) section 541 (relating to personal holding company tax),

(H) section 1351(d)(1) (relating to recoveries of foreign expropriation losses),

(I) section 1374 (relating to tax on certain certain built-in gains of S corporations),

(J) section 1375 (relating to tax imposed when passive investment income of corporation having subchapter C earnings and profits exceeds 25 percent of gross receipts),

(K) subparagraph (A) of section 7518(g)(6) (relating to nonqualified withdrawals from capital construction funds taxed at highest marginal rate),

(L) sections 871(a) and 881 (relating to certain income of nonresident aliens and foreign corporations),

(M) section 860E(e) (relating to taxes with respect to certain residual interests),

(N) section 884 (relating to branch profits tax),

(O) sections 453(l)(3) and 453A(c) (relating to interest on certain deferred tax liabilities),

(P) section 860K (relating to treatment of transfers of high-yield interests to disqualified holders),

(Q) section 220(f)(4) (relating to additional tax on Archer MSA distributions not used for qualified medical expenses), *and*

(R) section 138(c)(2) (relating to penalty for distributions from Medicare+Choice MSA not used for qualified medical expenses if minimum balance not maintained).

* * *

[CCH Explanation at ¶ 242. Committee Reports at ¶ 10,310.]

Amendment Notes

Act Sec. 415(a) amended Code Sec. 26(b)(2) by striking "and" at the end of subparagraph (P), by striking the period and inserting ", and" at the end of subparagraph (Q), and by adding at the end a new subparagraph (R) to read as above.

The above amendment is effective as if included in section 4006 of the Balanced Budget Act of 1997 (P.L. 105-33) [effective for tax years beginning after December 31, 1998.—CCH].

[¶ 5030] CODE SEC. 30. CREDIT FOR QUALIFIED ELECTRIC VEHICLES.

* * *

(b) LIMITATIONS.—

* * *

(2) PHASEOUT.—In the case of any qualified electric vehicle placed in service after *December 31, 2003,* the credit otherwise allowable under subsection (a) (determined after the application of paragraph (1)) shall be reduced by—

(A) 25 percent in the case of property placed in service in calendar year *2004,*

(B) 50 percent in the case of property placed in service in calendar year *2005,* and

(C) 75 percent in the case of property placed in service in calendar year *2006.*

* * *

[CCH Explanation at ¶ 370. Committee Reports at ¶ 10,410.]

Amendment Notes

Act Sec. 602(a)(1)(A)-(B) amended Code Sec. 30(b)(2) by striking "December 31, 2001," and inserting "December 31, 2003,", and in subparagraphs (A), (B), and (C), by striking "2002", "2003", and "2004", respectively, and inserting "2004", "2005", and "2006", respectively.

The above amendment applies to property placed in service after December 31, 2001.

(e) TERMINATION.—This section shall not apply to any property placed in service after *December 31, 2006.*

[CCH Explanation at ¶ 370. Committee Reports at ¶ 10,410.]

Amendment Notes

Act Sec. 602(a)(2) amended Code Sec. 30(e) by striking "December 31, 2004" and inserting "December 31, 2006".

The above amendment applies to property placed in service after December 31, 2001.

[¶ 5035] CODE SEC. 32. EARNED INCOME.

* * *

(g) COORDINATION WITH ADVANCE PAYMENTS OF EARNED INCOME CREDIT.—

* * *

(2) RECONCILIATION OF PAYMENTS ADVANCED AND CREDIT ALLOWED.—Any increase in tax under paragraph (1) shall not be treated as tax imposed by this chapter for purposes of determining the amount of any credit (other than the credit allowed by subsection (a)) allowable under this *part.*

* * *

[CCH Explanation at ¶ 234. Committee Reports at ¶ 10,320.]

Amendment Notes

Act Sec. 416(a)(1) amended Code Sec. 32(g)(2) by striking "subpart" and inserting "part".

The above amendment is effective as if included in section 474 of the Tax Reform Act of 1984 (P.L. 98-369)

[generally effective for tax years beginning after December 31, 1983.—CCH].

[¶ 5040] CODE SEC. 38. GENERAL BUSINESS CREDIT.

* * *

(b) CURRENT YEAR BUSINESS CREDIT.—For purposes of this subpart, the amount of the current year business credit is the sum of the following credits determined for the taxable year:

(1) the investment credit determined under section 46,

(2) the work opportunity credit determined under section 51(a),

(3) the alcohol fuels credit determined under section 40(a),

(4) the research credit determined under section 41(a),

(5) the low-income housing credit determined under section 42(a),

(6) the enhanced oil recovery credit under section 43(a),

(7) in the case of an eligible small business (as defined in section 44(b)), the disabled access credit determined under section 44(a),

(8) the renewable electricity production credit under section 45(a),

(9) the empowerment zone employment credit determined under section 1396(a),

(10) the Indian employment credit as determined under section 45A(a),

(11) the employer social security credit determined under section 45B(a),

(12) the orphan drug credit determined under section 45C(a),

(13) the new markets tax credit determined under section 45D(a),

(14) in the case of an eligible employer (as defined in section 45E(c)), the small employer pension plan startup cost credit determined under section 45E(a), plus

(15) the employer-provided child care credit determined under section *45F(a)*.

[CCH Explanation at ¶ 340. Committee Reports at ¶ 10,260.]

Amendment Notes

Act Sec. 411(d)(2) amended Code Sec. 38(b)(15) by striking "45F" and inserting "45F(a)".

The above amendment is effective as if included in the provision of the Economic Growth and Tax Relief Rec-

onciliation Act of 2001 (P.L.107-16) to which it relates [effective for tax years beginning after December 31, 2001.—CCH].

(c) LIMITATION BASED ON AMOUNT OF TAX.—

* * *

(2) EMPOWERMENT ZONE EMPLOYMENT CREDIT MAY OFFSET 25 PERCENT OF MINIMUM TAX.—

(A) IN GENERAL.—In the case of the empowerment zone employment credit credit—

(i) this section and section 39 shall be applied separately with respect to such credit, and

(ii) for purposes of applying paragraph (1) to such credit—

(I) 75 percent of the tentative minimum tax shall be substituted for the tentative minimum tax under subparagraph (A) thereof, and

(II) the limitation under paragraph (1) (as modified by subclause (I)) shall be reduced by the credit allowed under subsection (a) for the taxable year (other than the empowerment zone employment credit *or the New York Liberty Zone business employee credit*).

* * *

(3) SPECIAL RULES FOR NEW YORK LIBERTY ZONE BUSINESS EMPLOYEE CREDIT.—

(A) IN GENERAL.—In the case of the New York Liberty Zone business employee credit—

(i) this section and section 39 shall be applied separately with respect to such credit, and

(ii) in applying paragraph (1) to such credit—

(I) the tentative minimum tax shall be treated as being zero, and

(II) the limitation under paragraph *(1)* (as modified by subclause *(I))* shall be reduced by the credit allowed under subsection *(a)* for the taxable year (other than the New York Liberty Zone business employee credit).

(B) NEW YORK LIBERTY ZONE BUSINESS EMPLOYEE CREDIT.—For purposes of this subsection, the term "New York Liberty Zone business employee credit" means the portion of work opportunity credit under section 51 determined under section 1400L(a).

(4) SPECIAL RULES.—

(A) MARRIED INDIVIDUALS.—In the case of a husband or wife who files a separate return, the amount specified under subparagraph (B) of paragraph (1) shall be $12,500 in lieu of $25,000. This subparagraph shall not apply if the spouse of the taxpayer has no business credit carryforward or carryback to, and has no current year business credit for, the taxable year of such spouse which ends within or with the taxpayer's taxable year.

(B) CONTROLLED GROUPS.—In the case of a controlled group, the $25,000 amount specified under subparagraph (B) of paragraph (1) shall be reduced for each component member of such group by apportioning $25,000 among the component members of such group in such manner as the Secretary shall by regulations prescribe. For purposes of the preceding sentence, the term "controlled group" has the meaning given to such term by section 1563(a).

(C) LIMITATIONS WITH RESPECT TO CERTAIN PERSONS.—In the case of a person described in subparagraph (A) or (B) of section 46(e)(1) (as in effect on the day before the date of the enactment of the Revenue Reconciliation Act of 1990), the $25,000 amount specified under subparagraph (B) of paragraph (1) shall equal such person's ratable share (as determined under section 46(e)(2) (as so in effect)) of such amount.

(D) ESTATES AND TRUSTS.—In the case of an estate or trust, the $25,000 amount specified under subparagraph (B) of paragraph (1) shall be reduced to an amount which bears the same ratio to $25,000 as the portion of the income of the estate or trust which is not allocated to beneficiaries bears to the total income of the estate or trust.

* * *

[CCH Explanation at ¶ 410. Committee Reports at ¶ 10,100.]

Amendment Notes

Act Sec. 301(b)(1) amended Code Sec. 38(c) by redesignating paragraph (3) as paragraph (4) and by inserting after paragraph (2) a new paragraph (3) to read as above.

Act Sec. 301(b)(2) amended Code Sec. 38(c)(2)(A)(ii)(II) by inserting "or the New York Liberty Zone business employee credit" after "employment credit".

The above amendments apply to tax years ending after December 31, 2001.

[¶ 5045] CODE SEC. 42. LOW-INCOME HOUSING CREDIT.

* * *

(h) LIMITATION ON AGGREGATE CREDIT ALLOWABLE WITH RESPECT TO PROJECTS LOCATED IN A STATE.—

* * *

(3) HOUSING CREDIT DOLLAR AMOUNT FOR AGENCIES.—

* * *

(C) STATE HOUSING CREDIT CEILING.—The State housing credit ceiling applicable to any State for any calendar year shall be an amount equal to the sum of—

(i) the unused State housing credit ceiling (if any) of such State for the preceding calendar year,

(ii) the greater of—

(I) $1.75 ($1.50 for 2001) multiplied by the State population, or

(II) $2,000,000,

(iii) the amount of State housing credit ceiling returned in the calendar year, plus

(iv) the amount (if any) allocated under subparagraph (D) to such State by the Secretary.

For purposes of clause (i), the unused State housing credit ceiling for any calendar year is the excess (if any) of the sum of *the amounts described in clauses (ii) through (iv) over the aggregate housing credit dollar amount allocated for such year.* For purposes of clause (iii), the amount of State housing credit ceiling returned in the calendar year equals the housing credit dollar amount previously allocated within the State to any project which fails to meet the 10 percent test under paragraph (1)(E)(ii) on a date after the close of the calendar year in which the allocation was made or which does not become a qualified low-income housing project within the period required by this section or the terms of the allocation or to any project with respect to which an allocation is cancelled by mutual consent of the housing credit agency and the allocation recipient.

* * *

[CCH Explanation at ¶ 30,050. Committee Reports at ¶ 10,320.]

Amendment Notes

Act Sec. 417(2) amended the second sentence of Code Sec. 42(h)(3)(C) by striking "the amounts described in" and all that follows through the period and inserting "the amounts described in clauses (ii) through (iv) over the aggregate housing credit dollar amount allocated for such year." Prior to amendment, the second sentence of Code Sec. 42(h)(3)(C) read as follows:

For purposes of clause (i), the unused State housing credit ceiling for any calendar year is the excess (if any) of the sum of the amounts described in clauses (i)[(ii)] through (iv) over the aggregate housing credit dollar amount allocated for such year.

The above amendment is effective on March 9, 2002.

(m) RESPONSIBILITIES OF HOUSING CREDIT AGENCIES.—

(1) PLANS FOR ALLOCATION OF CREDIT AMONG PROJECTS.—

* * *

(B) QUALIFIED ALLOCATION PLAN.—For purposes of this paragraph, the term "qualified allocation plan" means any plan—

(i) which sets forth selection criteria to be used to determine housing priorities of the housing credit agency which are appropriate to local conditions,

(ii) which also gives preference in allocating housing credit dollar amounts among selected projects to—

(I) projects serving the lowest income tenants,

(II) projects obligated to serve qualified tenants for the longest periods,

(III) projects which are located in qualified census tracts (as defined in subsection (d)(5)(C)) and the development of which contributes to a concerted community revitalization plan, *and*

(iii) which provides a procedure that the agency (or an agent or other private contractor of such agency) will follow in monitoring for noncompliance with the provisions of this section and in notifying the Internal Revenue Service of such noncompliance which such agency becomes aware of and in monitoring for noncompliance with habitability standards through regular site visits.

* * *

[CCH Explanation at ¶ 30,050. Committee Reports at ¶ 10,320.]

Amendment Notes

Act Sec. 417(3) amended Code Sec. 42(m)(1)(B)(ii) by striking the second [first] "and" at the end of subclause (II) and by inserting "and" at the end of subclause (III).

The above amendment is effective on March 9, 2002.

[¶ 5050] CODE SEC. 45. ELECTRICITY PRODUCED FROM CERTAIN RENEWABLE RESOURCES.

* * *

(c) DEFINITIONS.—For purposes of this section—

* * *

(3) QUALIFIED FACILITY.—

(A) WIND FACILITY.—In the case of a facility using wind to produce electricity, the term "qualified facility" means any facility owned by the taxpayer which is originally placed in service after December 31, 1993, and before January 1, *2004.*

(B) CLOSED-LOOP BIOMASS FACILITY.—In the case of a facility using closed-loop biomass to produce electricity, the term "qualified facility" means any facility owned by the taxpayer which is originally placed in service after December 31, 1992, and before January 1, *2004.*

(C) POULTRY WASTE FACILITY.—In the case of a facility using poultry waste to produce electricity, the term "qualified facility" means any facility of the taxpayer which is originally placed in service after December 31, 1999, and before January 1, *2004.*

* * *

[CCH Explanation at ¶ 372. Committee Reports at ¶ 10,420.]

Amendment Notes

Act Sec. 603(a) amended Code Sec. 45(c)(3)(A)-(C) by striking "2002" and inserting "2004".

The above amendment applies to facilities placed in service after December 31, 2001.

[¶ 5051] CODE SEC. 45A. INDIAN EMPLOYMENT CREDIT.

* * *

(f) TERMINATION.—This section shall not apply to taxable years beginning after *December 31, 2004.*

[CCH Explanation at ¶ 386. Committee Reports at ¶ 10,540.]

Amendment Notes

Act Sec. 613(a) amended Code Sec. 45A(f) by striking "December 31, 2003" and inserting "December 31, 2004".

The above amendment is effective on March 9, 2002.

[¶ 5052] CODE SEC. 45E. SMALL EMPLOYER PENSION PLAN STARTUP COSTS.

* * *

(e) SPECIAL RULES.—For purposes of this section—

(1) AGGREGATION RULES.—All persons treated as a single employer under subsection (a) or (b) of section 52, or subsection *(m)* or (o) of section 414, shall be treated as one person. All eligible employer plans shall be treated as 1 eligible employer plan.

* * *

[CCH Explanation at ¶ 610. Committee Reports at ¶ 10,270.]

Amendment Notes

Act Sec. 411(n)(1) amended Code Sec. 45E(e)(1) by striking "(n)" and inserting "(m)".

The above amendment is effective as if included in the provision of the Economic Growth and Tax Relief Rec-

onciliation Act of 2001 (P.L.107-16) to which it relates [effective for costs paid or incurred in tax years beginning after December 31, 2001, with respect to qualified employer plans first effective after such date.—CCH].

[¶ 5053] CODE SEC. 45F. EMPLOYER-PROVIDED CHILD CARE CREDIT.

* * *

(d) RECAPTURE OF ACQUISITION AND CONSTRUCTION CREDIT.—

* * *

(4) SPECIAL RULES.—

* * *

(B) NO CREDITS AGAINST TAX.—Any increase in tax under this subsection shall not be treated as a tax imposed by this chapter for purposes of determining the amount of any credit under *this chapter or for purposes of section 55.*

* * *

[CCH Explanation at ¶ 340. Committee Reports at ¶ 10,260.]

Amendment Notes

Act Sec. 411(d)(1) amended Code Sec. 45F(d)(4)(B) by striking "subpart A, B, or D of this part" and inserting "this chapter or for purposes of section 55".

The above amendment is effective as if included in the provision of the Economic Growth and Tax Relief Rec-

onciliation Act of 2001 (P.L.107-16) to which it relates [effective for tax years beginning after December 31, 2001.—CCH].

[¶ 5055] CODE SEC. 51. AMOUNT OF CREDIT.

* * *

(c) WAGES DEFINED.—For purposes of this subpart—

* * *

(4) TERMINATION.—The term "wages" shall not include any amount paid or incurred to an individual who begins work for the employer—

(A) after December 31, 1994, and before October 1, 1996, or

(B) after December 31, *2003*.

* * *

[CCH Explanation at ¶ 374. Committee Reports at ¶ 10,430.]

Amendment Notes

Act Sec. 604(a) amended Code Sec. 51(c)(4)(B) by striking "2001" and inserting "2003".

The above amendment applies to individuals who began work for the employer after December 31, 2001.

[¶ 5057] CODE SEC. 51A. TEMPORARY INCENTIVES FOR EMPLOYING LONG-TERM FAMILY ASSISTANCE RECIPIENTS.

* * *

(c) LONG-TERM FAMILY ASSISTANCE RECIPIENTS.—For purposes of this section—

(1) IN GENERAL.—The term "long-term family assistance recipient" means any individual who is certified by the designated local agency (as defined in section *51(d)(11)*)—

(A) as being a member of a family receiving assistance under a IV-A program (as defined in section 51(d)(2)(B)) for at least the 18-month period ending on the hiring date,

(B)(i) as being a member of a family receiving such assistance for 18 months beginning after the date of the enactment of this section, and

(ii) as having a hiring date which is not more than 2 years after the end of the earliest such 18-month period, or

(C)(i) as being a member of a family which ceased to be eligible after the date of the enactment of this section for such assistance by reason of any limitation imposed by Federal or State law on the maximum period such assistance is payable to a family, and

(ii) as having a hiring date which is not more than 2 years after the date of such cessation.

* * *

[CCH Explanation at ¶ 30,050. Committee Reports at ¶ 10,320.]

Amendment Notes

Act Sec. 417(4) amended Code Sec. 51A(c)(1) by striking "51(d)(10)" and inserting "51(d)(11)".

The above amendment is effective on March 9, 2002.

(f) TERMINATION.—This section shall not apply to individuals who begin work for the employer after December 31, *2003*.

[CCH Explanation at ¶ 376. Committee Reports at ¶ 10,440.]

Amendment Notes

Act Sec. 605(a) amended Code Sec. 51A(f) by striking "2001" and inserting "2003".

The above amendment applies to individuals who began work for the employer after December 31, 2001.

[¶ 5060] CODE SEC. 56. ADJUSTMENTS IN COMPUTING ALTERNATIVE MINIMUM TAXABLE INCOME.

(a) ADJUSTMENTS APPLICABLE TO ALL TAXPAYERS.—In determining the amount of the alternative minimum taxable income for any taxable year the following treatment shall apply (in lieu of the treatment applicable for purposes of computing the regular tax):

(1) DEPRECIATION.—

(A) IN GENERAL.—

* * *

(ii) 150-PERCENT DECLINING BALANCE METHOD FOR CERTAIN PROPERTY.—The method of depreciation used shall be—

(I) the 150 percent declining balance method,

(II) switching to the straight line method for the 1st taxable year for which using the straight line method with respect to the adjusted basis as of the beginning of the year will yield a higher allowance.

The preceding sentence shall not apply to any section 1250 property (as defined in section 1250(c)) (and the straight line method shall be used for *such section 1250* property) or to any other property if the depreciation deduction determined under section 168 with respect to such other property for purposes of the regular tax is determined by using the straight line method.

* * *

[CCH Explanation at ¶ 30,050. Committee Reports at ¶ 10,320.]

Amendment Notes

Act Sec. 417(5) amended the flush sentence at the end of Code Sec. 56(a)(1)(A)(ii) by striking "such 1250" and inserting "such section 1250".

The above amendment is effective on March 9, 2002.

(d) ALTERNATIVE TAX NET OPERATING LOSS DEDUCTION DEFINED.—

(1) IN GENERAL.—For purposes of subsection (a)(4), the term "alternative tax net operating loss deduction" means the net operating loss deduction allowable for the taxable year under section 172, except that—

(A) the amount of such deduction shall not exceed the sum of—

(i) the lesser of—

(I) the amount of such deduction attributable to net operating losses (other than the deduction attributable to carryovers described in clause (ii)(I)), or

(II) 90 percent of alternative minimum taxable income determined without regard to such deduction, plus

(ii) the lesser of—

(I) the amount of such deduction attributable to the sum of carrybacks of net operating losses for taxable years ending during 2001 or 2002 and carryforwards of net operating losses to taxable years ending during 2001 and 2002, or

(II) alternative minimum taxable income determined without regard to such deduction reduced by the amount determined under clause (i), and

* * *

[CCH Explanation at ¶ 310. Committee Reports at ¶ 10,020.]

Amendment Notes

Act Sec. 102(c)(1) amended Code Sec. 56(d)(1)(A) to read as above. Prior to amendment, Code Sec. 56(d)(1)(A) read as follows.

(A) the amount of such deduction shall not exceed 90 percent of alternate minimum taxable income determined without regard to such deduction, and

The above amendment applies to tax years ending before January 1, 2003.

[¶ 5065] CODE SEC. 62. ADJUSTED GROSS INCOME DEFINED.

(a) GENERAL RULE.—For purposes of this subtitle, the term "adjusted gross income" means, in the case of an individual, gross income minus the following deductions:

* * *

(2) CERTAIN TRADE AND BUSINESS DEDUCTIONS OF EMPLOYEES.—

* * *

(D) CERTAIN EXPENSES OF ELEMENTARY AND SECONDARY SCHOOL TEACHERS.—In the case of taxable years beginning during 2002 or 2003, the deductions allowed by section 162 which consist of expenses, not in excess of $250, paid or incurred by an eligible educator in connection with books, supplies (other than nonathletic supplies for courses of instruction in health or physical education), computer equipment (including related software and services) and other equipment, and supplementary materials used by the eligible educator in the classroom.

* * *

[CCH Explanation at ¶ 215. Committee Reports at ¶ 10,250.]

Amendment Notes

Act Sec. 406(a) amended Code Sec. 62(a)(2) by adding at the end a new subparagraph (D) to read as above.

The above amendment applies to tax years beginning after December 31, 2001.

(d) DEFINITION; SPECIAL RULES.—

(1) ELIGIBLE EDUCATOR.—

(A) IN GENERAL.—For purposes of subsection (a)(2)(D), the term "eligible educator" means, with respect to any taxable year, an individual who is a kindergarten through grade 12 teacher, instructor, counselor, principal, or aide in a school for at least 900 hours during a school year.

(B) SCHOOL.—The term "school" means any school which provides elementary education or secondary education (kindergarten through grade 12), as determined under State law.

(2) COORDINATION WITH EXCLUSIONS.—A deduction shall be allowed under subsection (a)(2)(D) for expenses only to the extent the amount of such expenses exceeds the amount excludable under section 135, 529(c)(1), or 530(d)(2) for the taxable year.

[CCH Explanation at ¶ 215. Committee Reports at ¶ 10,250.]

<table>
<tr><td>Amendment Notes</td><td>The above amendment applies to tax years beginning</td></tr>
<tr><td>Act Sec. 406(b) amended Code Sec. 62 by adding at the end a new subsection (d) to read as above.</td><td>after December 31, 2001.</td></tr>
</table>

[¶ 5070] CODE SEC. 63. TAXABLE INCOME DEFINED.

* * *

(c) STANDARD DEDUCTION.—For purposes of this subtitle—

* * *

> *[Caution: Code Sec. 63(c)(2), below, as amended by P.L. 107-16 and Act Sec. 411(e)(1)(A)-(E), applies to tax years beginning after December 31, 2004.—CCH.]*

(2) BASIC STANDARD DEDUCTION.—For purposes of paragraph (1), the basic standard deduction is—

(A) the applicable percentage of the dollar amount in effect under *subparagraph (D)* for the taxable year in the case of—

(i) a joint return, or

(ii) a surviving spouse (as defined in section 2(a)),

(B) $4,400 in the case of a head of household (as defined in section 2(b)),

(C) one-half of the amount in effect under subparagraph (A) in the case of a married individual filing a separate return, or

(D) $3,000 in any other case.

If any amount determined under subparagraph (A) is not a multiple of $50, such amount shall be rounded to the next lowest multiple of $50.

* * *

> *[Caution: Code Sec. 63(c)(4), below, as amended by P.L. 107-16 and Act Sec. 411(e)(2)(A)-(C), applies to tax years beginning after December 31, 2004.—CCH.]*

(4) ADJUSTMENTS FOR INFLATION.—In the case of any taxable year beginning in a calendar year after 1988, each dollar amount contained in *paragraph (2)(B), (2)(D), or (5)* or subsection (f) shall be increased by an amount equal to—

(A) such dollar amount, multiplied by

(B) the cost-of-living adjustment determined under section 1(f)(3) for the calendar year in which the taxable year begins, by substituting for "calendar year 1992" in subparagraph (B) thereof—

(i) "calendar year 1987" in the case of the dollar amounts contained in *paragraph (2)(B), (2)(D), or (5)(A)* or subsection (f), and

(ii) "calendar year 1997" in the case of the dollar amount contained in paragraph (5)(B).

* * *

[CCH Explanation at ¶ 220. Committee Reports at ¶ 10,260.]

<table>
<tr><td colspan="2" align="center">Amendment Notes</td></tr>
<tr><td>Act Sec. 411(e)(1)(A)-(E) amended Code Sec. 63(c)(2) by striking "subparagraph (C)" and inserting "subparagraph (D)" in subparagraph (A), by striking "or" at the end of</td><td>subparagraph (B), by redesignating subparagraph (C) as subparagraph (D), by inserting after subparagraph (B) a new subparagraph (C), and by inserting a new flush sentence at the end to read as above.</td></tr>
</table>

Act Sec. 411(e)(2)(A) amended Code Sec. 63(c)(4) by striking "paragraph (2) or (5)" and inserting "paragraph (2)(B), (2)(D), or (5)".

Act Sec. 411(e)(2)(B) amended Code Sec. 63(c)(4)(B)(i) by striking "paragraph (2)" and inserting "paragraph (2)(B), (2)(D),".

Act Sec. 411(e)(2)(C) amended Code Sec. 63(c)(4) by striking the flush sentence at the end. Prior to being stricken, the flush sentence at the end of Code Sec. 63(c)(4) read as follows:

The preceding sentence shall not apply to the amount referred to in paragraph (2)(A).

The above amendments are effective as if included in the provisions of the Economic Growth and Tax Relief Reconciliation Act of 2001 (P.L. 107-16) to which they relate [applicable to tax years beginning after December 31, 2004.—CCH].

[¶ 5075] CODE SEC. 108. INCOME FROM DISCHARGE OF INDEBTEDNESS.

* * *

(d) MEANING OF TERMS; SPECIAL RULES RELATING TO CERTAIN PROVISIONS.—

* * *

(7) SPECIAL RULES FOR S CORPORATION.—

(A) CERTAIN PROVISIONS TO BE APPLIED AT CORPORATE LEVEL.—In the case of an S corporation, subsections (a), (b), (c), and (g) shall be applied at the corporate level, *including by not taking into account under section 1366(a) any amount excluded under subsection (a) of this section.*

* * *

[CCH Explanation at ¶ 315. Committee Reports at ¶ 10,210.]

Amendment Notes

Act Sec. 402(a) amended Code Sec. 108(d)(7)(A) by inserting before the period ", including by not taking into account under section 1366(a) any amount excluded under subsection (a) of this section".

The above amendment generally applies to discharges of indebtedness after October 11, 2001, in tax years ending after such date. For an exception, see Act Sec. 402(b)(2), below.

Act Sec. 402(b)(2) provides:

(2) EXCEPTION.—The amendment made by this section shall not apply to any discharge of indebtedness before March 1, 2002, pursuant to a plan of reorganization filed with a bankruptcy court on or before October 11, 2001.

[¶ 5080] CODE SEC. 131. CERTAIN FOSTER CARE PAYMENTS.

* * *

(b) QUALIFIED FOSTER CARE PAYMENT DEFINED.—For purposes of this section—

(1) IN GENERAL.—The term "qualified foster care payment" means any payment made pursuant to a foster care program of a State or political subdivision thereof—

(A) which is paid by—

(i) a State or political subdivision thereof, or

(ii) a qualified foster care placement agency, and

(B) which is—

(i) paid to the foster care provider for caring for a qualified foster individual in the foster care provider's home, or

(ii) a difficulty of care payment.

(2) QUALIFIED FOSTER INDIVIDUAL.—The term "qualified foster individual" means any individual who is living in a foster family home in which such individual was placed by—

(A) an agency of a State or a political subdivision thereof, or

(B) a qualified foster care placement agency.

(3) QUALIFIED FOSTER CARE PLACEMENT AGENCY DEFINED.—The term "qualified foster care placement agency" means any placement agency which is licensed or certified by—

(A) a State or political subdivision thereof, or

(B) an entity designated by a State or political subdivision thereof,

for the foster care program of such State or political subdivision to make foster care payments to providers of foster care.

(4) LIMITATION BASED ON NUMBER OF INDIVIDUALS OVER THE AGE OF 18.—In the case of any foster home in which there is a qualified foster care individual who has attained age 19, foster care

payments (other than difficulty of care payments) for any period to which such payments relate shall not be excludable from gross income under subsection (a) to the extent such payments are made for more than 5 such qualified foster individuals.

* * *

[CCH Explanation at ¶ 210. Committee Reports at ¶ 10,230.]

Amendment Notes

Act Sec. 404(a) amended the matter preceding Code Sec. 131(b)(1)(B) to read as above. Prior to amendment, the matter preceding Code Sec. 131(b)(1)(B) read as follows:

(1) IN GENERAL.—The term "qualified foster care payment" means any amount—

(A) which is paid by a State or political subdivision thereof or by a placement agency which is described in section 501(c)(3) and exempt from tax under section 501(a), and

Act Sec. 404(b) amended Code Sec. 131(b)(2)(B) to read as above. Prior to amendment, Code Sec. 131(b)(2)(B) read as follows:

(B) in the case of an individual who has not attained age 19, an organization which is licensed by a State (or political subdivision thereof) as a placement agency and which is described in section 501(c)(3) and exempt from tax under section 501(a).

Act Sec. 404(c) amended Code Sec. 131(b) by redesignating paragraph (3) as paragraph (4) and by inserting after paragraph (2) a new paragraph (3) to read as above.

The above amendments apply to tax years beginning after December 31, 2001.

[¶ 5085] CODE SEC. 137. ADOPTION ASSISTANCE PROGRAMS.

[Caution: Code Sec. 137(a), below, as amended by Act Sec. 411(c)(2)(A), applies to tax years beginning after December 31, 2002.—CCH.]

(a) EXCLUSION.—

(1) IN GENERAL.—Gross income of an employee does not include amounts paid or expenses incurred by the employer for qualified adoption expenses in connection with the adoption of a child by an employee if such amounts are furnished pursuant to an adoption assistance program.

(2) $10,000 EXCLUSION FOR ADOPTION OF CHILD WITH SPECIAL NEEDS REGARDLESS OF EXPENSES.—In the case of an adoption of a child with special needs which becomes final during a taxable year, the qualified adoption expenses with respect to such adoption for such year shall be increased by an amount equal to the excess (if any) of $10,000 over the actual aggregate qualified adoption expenses with respect to such adoption during such taxable year and all prior taxable years.

[CCH Explanation at ¶ 236. Committee Reports at ¶ 10,260.]

Amendment Notes

Act Sec. 411(c)(2)(A) amended Code Sec. 137(a) to read as above. Prior to amendment, Code Sec. 137(a) read as follows:

(a) IN GENERAL.—Gross income of an employee does not include amounts paid or expenses incurred by the employer for adoption expenses in connection with the adoption of a child by an employee if such amounts are furnished pursuant to an adoption assistance program. The amount of the exclusion shall be—

(1) in the case of an adoption of a child other than a child with special needs, the amount of the qualified adoption expenses paid or incurred by the taxpayer, and

(2) in the case of an adoption of a child with special needs, $10,000.

The above amendment applies to tax years beginning after December 31, 2002.

(b) LIMITATIONS.—

* * *

(2) INCOME LIMITATION.—The amount excludable from gross income under *subsection (a)* for any taxable year shall be reduced (but not below zero) by an amount which bears the same ratio to the amount so excludable (determined without regard to this paragraph but with regard to paragraph (1)) as—

(A) the amount (if any) by which the taxpayer's adjusted gross income exceeds $150,000, bears to

(B) $40,000.

* * *

[CCH Explanation at ¶ 236. Committee Reports at ¶ 10,260.]

Amendment Notes

Act Sec. 411(c)(2)(B) amended Code Sec. 137(b)(2) by striking "subsection (a)(1)" and inserting "subsection (a)"

[Note: this amendment was superfluous as Code Sec. 137(b)(2) already read "subsection (a)".—CCH].

The above amendment applies to tax years beginning after December 31, 2001.

(f) ADJUSTMENTS FOR INFLATION.—In the case of a taxable year beginning after December 31, 2002, each of the dollar amounts in subsection (a)(2) and paragraphs (1) and (2)(A) of subsection (b) shall be increased by an amount equal to—

(1) such dollar amount, multiplied by

(2) the cost-of-living adjustment determined under section 1(f)(3) for the calendar year in which the taxable year begins, determined by substituting "calendar year 2001" for "calendar year 1992" in subparagraph (B) thereof.

If any amount as increased under the preceding sentence is not a multiple of $10, such amount shall be rounded to the nearest multiple of $10.

[CCH Explanation at ¶ 238. Committee Reports at ¶ 10,320.]

Amendment Notes

Act Sec. 418(a)(2) amended Code Sec. 137(f) by adding at the end a new flush sentence to read as above.

The above amendment is effective as if included in the provision of the Economic Growth and Tax Relief Rec-onciliation Act of 2001 (P.L. 107-16) to which it relates [effective for tax years beginning after December 31, 2001.—CCH].

[¶ 5090] CODE SEC. 151. ALLOWANCE OF DEDUCTIONS FOR PERSONAL EXEMPTIONS.

* * *

(c) ADDITIONAL EXEMPTION FOR DEPENDENTS.—

* * *

(6) TREATMENT OF MISSING CHILDREN.—

* * *

(B) PURPOSES.—Subparagraph (A) shall apply solely for purposes of determining—

(i) the deduction under this section,

(ii) the credit under section 24 (relating to child tax credit), and

(iii) whether an individual is a surviving spouse or a head of a household (*as* such terms are defined in section 2).

(C) COMPARABLE TREATMENT *FOR PRINCIPAL PLACE OF ABODE REQUIREMENTS.—An* individual—

(i) who is presumed by law enforcement authorities to have been kidnapped by someone who is not a member of the family of such individual or the taxpayer, and

(ii) who had, for the taxable year in which the kidnapping occurred, the same principal place of abode as the taxpayer for more than one-half of the portion of such year before the date of the kidnapping,

shall be treated as meeting the *principal place of abode requirements of section 2(a)(1)(B), section 2(b)(1)(A), and section 32(c)(3)(A)(ii)* with respect to a taxpayer for all taxable years ending during the period that the individual is kidnapped.

* * *

[CCH Explanation at ¶ 225 and ¶ 30,050. Committee Reports at ¶ 10,280 and ¶ 10,320.]

Amendment Notes

Act Sec. 412(b)(1)-(2) amended Code Sec. 151(c)(6)(C) by striking "FOR EARNED INCOME CREDIT.—For purposes of section 32, an" and inserting "FOR PRINCIPAL PLACE OF ABODE REQUIREMENTS.—An", and by striking "requirement of section 32(c)(3)(A)(ii)" and inserting "principal place of abode requirements of section 2(a)(1)(B), section 2(b)(1)(A), and section 32(c)(3)(A)(ii)".

The above amendment is effective as if included in the provision of the Community Renewal Tax Relief Act of 2000 (P.L. 106-554) to which it relates [effective for tax years ending after December 31, 2000.—CCH].

Act Sec. 417(6) amended Code Sec. 151(c)(6)(B)(iii) by inserting "as" before "such terms".

The above amendment is effective on March 9, 2002.

[¶ 5095] CODE SEC. 168. ACCELERATED COST RECOVERY SYSTEM.

* * *

(j) PROPERTY ON INDIAN RESERVATIONS.—

* * *

(8) TERMINATION.—This subsection shall not apply to property placed in service after *December 31, 2004.*

[CCH Explanation at ¶ 386. Committee Reports at ¶ 10,540.]

Amendment Notes

Act Sec. 613(b) amended Code Sec. 168(j)(8) by striking "December 31, 2003" and inserting "December 31, 2004".

The above amendment is effective on March 9, 2002.

(k) SPECIAL ALLOWANCE FOR CERTAIN PROPERTY ACQUIRED AFTER SEPTEMBER 10, 2001, AND BEFORE SEPTEMBER 11, 2004.—

(1) ADDITIONAL ALLOWANCE.—In the case of any qualified property—

(A) the depreciation deduction provided by section 167(a) for the taxable year in which such property is placed in service shall include an allowance equal to 30 percent of the adjusted basis of the qualified property, and

(B) the adjusted basis of the qualified property shall be reduced by the amount of such deduction before computing the amount otherwise allowable as a depreciation deduction under this chapter for such taxable year and any subsequent taxable year.

(2) QUALIFIED PROPERTY.—For purposes of this subsection—

(A) IN GENERAL.—The term "qualified property" means property—

(i)(I) to which this section applies which has a recovery period of 20 years or less,

(II) which is computer software (as defined in section 167(f)(1)(B)) for which a deduction is allowable under section 167(a) without regard to this subsection,

(III) which is water utility property, or

(IV) which is qualified leasehold improvement property,

(ii) the original use of which commences with the taxpayer after September 10, 2001,

(iii) which is—

(I) acquired by the taxpayer after September 10, 2001, and before September 11, 2004, but only if no written binding contract for the acquisition was in effect before September 11, 2001, or

(II) acquired by the taxpayer pursuant to a written binding contract which was entered into after September 10, 2001, and before September 11, 2004, and

(iv) which is placed in service by the taxpayer before January 1, 2005, or, in the case of property described in subparagraph (B), before January 1, 2006.

(B) CERTAIN PROPERTY HAVING LONGER PRODUCTION PERIODS TREATED AS QUALIFIED PROPERTY.—

(i) IN GENERAL.—The term "qualified property" includes property—

(I) which meets the requirements of clauses (i), (ii), and (iii) of subparagraph (A),

(II) which has a recovery period of at least 10 years or is transportation property, and

(III) which is subject to section 263A by reason of clause (ii) or (iii) of subsection (f)(1)(B) thereof.

(ii) ONLY PRE-SEPTEMBER 11, 2004, BASIS ELIGIBLE FOR ADDITIONAL ALLOWANCE.—In the case of property which is qualified property solely by reason of clause (i), paragraph (1) shall apply only to the extent of the adjusted basis thereof attributable to manufacture, construction, or production before September 11, 2004.

(iii) TRANSPORTATION PROPERTY.—For purposes of this subparagraph, the term "transportation property" means tangible personal property used in the trade or business of transporting persons or property.

(C) EXCEPTIONS.—

(i) ALTERNATIVE DEPRECIATION PROPERTY.—The term "qualified property" shall not include any property to which the alternative depreciation system under subsection (g) applies, determined—

(I) without regard to paragraph (7) of subsection (g) (relating to election to have system apply), and

(II) after application of section 280F(b) (relating to listed property with limited business use).

(ii) QUALIFIED NEW YORK LIBERTY ZONE LEASEHOLD IMPROVEMENT PROPERTY.—The term "qualified *property" shall not include any qualified New York Liberty Zone leasehold improvement property (as defined in section 1400L(c)(2)).*

(iii) ELECTION OUT.—If a taxpayer makes an election under this clause with respect to any class of property for any taxable year, this subsection shall not apply to all property in such class placed in service during such taxable year.

(D) SPECIAL RULES.—

(i) SELF-CONSTRUCTED PROPERTY.—In the case of a taxpayer manufacturing, constructing, or producing property for the taxpayer's own use, the requirements of clause (iii) of subparagraph (A) shall be treated as met if the taxpayer begins manufacturing, constructing, or producing the property after September 10, 2001, and before September 11, 2004.

(ii) SALE-LEASEBACKS.—For purposes of subparagraph (A)(ii), if property—

(I) is originally placed in service after September 10, 2001, by a person, and

(II) sold and leased back by such person within 3 months after the date such property was originally placed in service,

such property shall be treated as originally placed in service not earlier than the date on which such property is used under the leaseback referred to in subclause (II).

(E) COORDINATION WITH SECTION 280F.—For purposes of section 280F—

(i) AUTOMOBILES.—In the case of a passenger automobile (as defined in section 280F(d)(5)) which is qualified property, the Secretary shall increase the limitation under section 280F(a)(1)(A)(i) by $4,600.

(ii) LISTED PROPERTY.—The deduction allowable under paragraph (1) shall be taken into account in computing any recapture amount under section 280F(b)(2).

(F) DEDUCTION ALLOWED IN COMPUTING MINIMUM [MINIMUM] TAX.—For purposes of determining alternative minimum taxable income under section 55, the deduction under subsection (a) for qualified property shall be determined under this section without regard to any adjustment under section 56.

(3) QUALIFIED LEASEHOLD IMPROVEMENT PROPERTY.—For purposes of this subsection—

(A) IN GENERAL.—The term "qualified leasehold improvement property" means any improvement to an interior portion of a building which is nonresidential real property if—

(i) such improvement is made under or pursuant to a lease (as defined in subsection (h)(7))—

(I) by the lessee (or any sublessee) of such portion, or

(II) by the lessor of such portion,

(ii) such portion is to be occupied exclusively by the lessee (or any sublessee) of such portion, and

(iii) such improvement is placed in service more than 3 years after the date the building was first placed in service.

(B) CERTAIN IMPROVEMENTS NOT INCLUDED.—Such term shall not include any improvement for which the expenditure is attributable to—

(i) the enlargement of the building,

(ii) any elevator or escalator,

(iii) any structural component benefiting a common area, and

(iv) the internal structural framework of the building.

(C) DEFINITIONS AND SPECIAL RULES.—For purposes of this paragraph—

(i) COMMITMENT TO LEASE TREATED AS LEASE.—A commitment to enter into a lease shall be treated as a lease, and the parties to such commitment shall be treated as lessor and lessee, respectively.

(ii) RELATED PERSONS.—A lease between related persons shall not be considered a lease. For purposes of the preceding sentence, the term "related persons" means—

Code Sec. 168(k)   ¶ 5095

(I) *members of an affiliated group (as defined in section 1504), and*

(II) *persons having a relationship described in subsection (b) of section 267; except that, for purposes of this clause, the phrase "80 percent or more" shall be substituted for the phrase "more than 50 percent" each place it appears in such subsection.*

[CCH Explanation at ¶ 305. Committee Reports at ¶ 10,010.]

Amendment Notes

Act Sec. 101(a) amended Code Sec. 168 by adding at the end a new subsection (k) to read as above.

The above amendment applies to property placed in service after September 10, 2001, in tax years ending after such date.

[¶ 5100] CODE SEC. 170. CHARITABLE, ETC., CONTRIBUTIONS AND GIFTS.

* * *

(e) CERTAIN CONTRIBUTIONS OF ORDINARY INCOME AND CAPITAL GAIN PROPERTY.—

* * *

(6) SPECIAL RULE FOR CONTRIBUTIONS OF COMPUTER TECHNOLOGY AND EQUIPMENT FOR EDUCATIONAL PURPOSES.—

* * *

(B) QUALIFIED COMPUTER CONTRIBUTION.—For purposes of this paragraph, the term "qualified computer contribution" means a charitable contribution by a corporation of any computer technology or equipment, but only if—

(i) the contribution is to—

(I) an educational organization described in subsection (b)(1)(A)(ii),

(II) an entity described in section 501(c)(3) and exempt from tax under section 501(a) (other than an entity described in subclause (I)) that is organized primarily for purposes of supporting elementary and secondary education, or

(III) a public library (within the meaning of section 213(2)(A) of the Library Services and Technology Act (20 U.S.C. 9122(2)(A)), as in effect on the date of the enactment of the Community Renewal Tax Relief Act of *2000)*, established and maintained by an entity described in subsection (c)(1),

(ii) the contribution is made not later than 3 years after the date the taxpayer acquired the property (or in the case of property constructed by the taxpayer, the date the construction of the property is substantially completed),

(iii) the original use of the property is by the donor or the donee,

(iv) substantially all of the use of the property by the donee is for use within the United States for educational purposes that are related to the purpose or function of the donee,

(v) the property is not transferred by the donee in exchange for money, other property, or services, except for shipping, installation and transfer costs,

(vi) the property will fit productively into the donee's education plan,

(vii) the donee's use and disposition of the property will be in accordance with the provisions of clauses (iv) and (v), and

(viii) the property meets such standards, if any, as the Secretary may prescribe by regulation to assure that the property meets minimum functionality and suitability standards for educational purposes.

* * *

[CCH Explanation at ¶ 30,050. Committee Reports at ¶ 10,320.]

Amendment Notes

Act Sec. 417(7) amended Code Sec. 170(e)(6)(B)(i)(III) by striking "2000," and inserting "2000),".

The above amendment is effective on March 9, 2002.

[¶ 5105] CODE SEC. 172. NET OPERATING LOSS DEDUCTION.

* * *

(b) NET OPERATING LOSS CARRYBACKS AND CARRYOVERS.—

(1) YEARS TO WHICH LOSS MAY BE CARRIED.—

* * *

(F) Retention of 3-Year Carryback in Certain Cases.—

(i) In general.—Subparagraph (A)(i) shall be applied by substituting "*3 taxable years*" for "*2 taxable years*" with respect to the portion of the net operating loss for the taxable year which is an eligible loss with respect to the taxpayer.

* * *

(H) In the case of a taxpayer which has a net operating loss for any taxable year ending during 2001 or 2002, subparagraph (A)(i) shall be applied by substituting "5" for "2" and subparagraph (F) shall not apply.

* * *

[CCH Explanation at ¶ 310 and ¶ 30,050. Committee Reports at ¶ 10,020 and ¶ 10,320.]

Amendment Notes

Act Sec. 102(a) amended Code Sec. 172(b)(1) by adding at the end a new subparagraph (H) to read as above.

The above amendment applies to net operating losses for tax years ending after December 31, 2000.

Act Sec. 417(8)(A)-(B) amended Code Sec. 172(b)(1)(F)(i) by striking "3 years" and inserting "3 taxable years", and by striking "2 years" and inserting "2 taxable years".

The above amendment is effective on March 9, 2002.

(j) Election to Disregard 5-Year Carryback for Certain Net Operating Losses.—Any taxpayer entitled to a 5-year carryback under subsection (b)(1)(H) from any loss year may elect to have the carryback period with respect to such loss year determined without regard to subsection (b)(1)(H). Such election shall be made in such manner as may be prescribed by the Secretary and shall be made by the due date (including extensions of time) for filing the taxpayer's return for the taxable year of the net operating loss. Such election, once made for any taxable year, shall be irrevocable for such taxable year.

[CCH Explanation at ¶ 310. Committee Reports at ¶ 10,020.]

Amendment Notes

Act Sec. 102(a) amended Code Sec. 172 by redesignating subsection (j) as subsection (k) and by inserting after subsection (i) a new subsection (j) to read as above.

The above amendment applies to net operating losses for tax years ending after December 31, 2000.

(k) Cross References.—

(1) For treatment of net operating loss carryovers in certain corporate acquisitions, see section 381.

(2) For special limitation on net operating loss carryovers in case of a corporate change of ownership, see section 382.

[CCH Explanation at ¶ 310. Committee Reports at ¶ 10,020.]

Amendment Notes

Act Sec. 102(b) amended Code Sec. 172 by redesignating subsection (j) as subsection (k).

The above amendment applies to net operating losses for tax years ending after December 31, 2000.

[¶ 5110] CODE SEC. 179A. DEDUCTION FOR CLEAN-FUEL VEHICLES AND CERTAIN REFUELING PROPERTY.

* * *

(b) Limitations.—

(1) Qualified clean-fuel vehicle property.—

* * *

(B) Phaseout.—In the case of any qualified clean-fuel vehicle property placed in service after *December 31, 2003*, the limit otherwise applicable under subparagraph (A) shall be reduced by—

(i) 25 percent in the case of property placed in service in calendar year *2004*,

(ii) 50 percent in the case of property placed in sevice in calendar year *2005*, and

(iii) 75 percent in the case of property placed in service in calendar year *2006*.

* * *

[CCH Explanation at ¶ 378. Committee Reports at ¶ 10,450.]

Amendment Notes

Act Sec. 606(a)(1)(A)-(B) amended Code Sec. 179A(b)(1)(B) by striking "December 31, 2001," and inserting "December 31, 2003,", and in clauses (i), (ii), and

(iii), by striking "2002", "2003", and "2004", respectively, and inserting "2004", "2005", and "2006", respectively.

The above amendment applies to property placed in service after December 31, 2001.

(f) TERMINATION.—This section shall not apply to any property placed in service after *December 31, 2006.*

[CCH Explanation at ¶ 378. Committee Reports at ¶ 10,450.]

Amendment Notes

Act Sec. 606(a)(2) amended Code Sec. 179A(f) by striking "December 31, 2004" and inserting "December 31, 2006".

The above amendment applies to property placed in service after December 31, 2001.

[¶ 5115] CODE SEC. 220. ARCHER MSAs.

* * *

(i) LIMITATION ON NUMBER OF TAXPAYERS HAVING ARCHER MSAs.—

* * *

(2) CUT-OFF YEAR.—For purposes of paragraph (1), the term "cut-off year" means the earlier of—

(A) calendar year *2003*, or

(B) the first calendar year before *2003* for which the Secretary determines under subsection (j) that the numerical limitation for such year has been exceeded.

(3) ACTIVE MSA PARTICIPANT.—For purposes of this subsection—

* * *

(B) SPECIAL RULE FOR CUT-OFF YEARS BEFORE *2003.*—In the case of a cut-off year before *2003*—

(i) an individual shall not be treated as an eligible individual for any month of such year or an active MSA participant under paragraph (1)(A) unless such individual is, on or before the cut-off date, covered under a high deductible health plan, and

(ii) an employer shall not be treated as an MSA-participating employer unless the employer, on or before the cut-off date, offered coverage under a high deductible health plan to any employee.

* * *

[CCH Explanation at ¶ 275. Committee Reports at ¶ 10,530.]

Amendment Notes

Act Sec. 612(a) amended Code Sec. 220(i)(2) and (3)(B) by striking "2002" each place it appears and inserting "2003".

The above amendment is effective on January 1, 2002.

(j) DETERMINATION OF WHETHER NUMERICAL LIMITS ARE EXCEEDED.—

* * *

(2) DETERMINATION OF WHETHER LIMIT EXCEEDED FOR *1998, 1999, 2001, OR 2002.*—

(A) IN GENERAL.—The numerical limitation for *1998, 1999, 2001, or 2002* is exceeded if the sum of—

(i) the number of MSA returns filed on or before April 15 of such calendar year for taxable years ending with or within the preceding calendar year, plus

(ii) the Secretary's estimate (determined on the basis of the returns described in clause (i)) of the number of MSA returns for such taxable years which will be filed after such date, exceeds 750,000 (600,000 in the case of 1998). For purposes of the preceding sentence, the term "MSA return" means any return on which any exclusion is claimed under section 106(b) or any deduction is claimed under this section.

(B) ALTERNATIVE COMPUTATION OF LIMITATION.—The numerical limitation for *1998, 1999, 2001, or 2002* is also exceeded if the sum of—

(i) 90 percent of the sum determined under subparagraph (A) for such calendar year, plus

(ii) the product of 2.5 and the number of Archer MSAs established during the portion of such year preceding July 1 (based on the reports required under paragraph (4)) for taxable years beginning in such year,

exceeds 750,000.

* * *

(4) REPORTING BY MSA TRUSTEES.—

(A) IN GENERAL.—Not later than August 1 of 1997, 1998, 1999, *2001, and 2002* each person who is the trustee of an Archer MSA established before July 1 of such calendar year shall make a report to the Secretary (in such form and manner as the Secretary shall specify) which specifies—

(i) the number of Archer MSAs established before such July 1 (for taxable years beginning in such calendar year) of which such person is the trustee,

(ii) the name and TIN of the account holder of each such account, and

(iii) the number of such accounts which are accounts of previously uninsured individuals.

* * *

[CCH Explanation at ¶ 275. Committee Reports at ¶ 10,530.]

Amendment Notes

Act Sec. 612(b)(1) amended Code Sec. 220(j)(2) by striking "1998, 1999, or 2001" each place it appears and inserting "1998, 1999, 2001, or 2002".

Act Sec. 612(b)(2) amended Code Sec. 220(j)(4)(A) by striking "and 2001" and inserting "2001, and 2002".

The above amendments are effective on January 1, 2002.

[¶ 5120] CODE SEC. 280F. LIMITATION ON DEPRECIATION FOR LUXURY AUTOMOBILES; LIMITATION WHERE CERTAIN PROPERTY USED FOR PERSONAL PURPOSES.

(a) LIMITATION ON AMOUNT OF DEPRECIATION FOR LUXURY AUTOMOBILES.—

(1) DEPRECIATION.—

* * *

(C) SPECIAL RULE FOR CERTAIN CLEAN-FUEL PASSENGER AUTOMOBILES.—

* * *

(iii) APPLICATION OF SUBPARAGRAPH.—This subparagraph shall apply to property placed in service after August 5, 1997, and before January 1, 2007.

* * *

[CCH Explanation at ¶ 370. Committee Reports at ¶ 10,410.]

Amendment Notes

Act Sec. 602(b)(1) amended Code Sec. 280F(a)(1)(C) by adding at the end a new clause (iii) to read as above.

The above amendment applies to property placed in service after December 31, 2001.

[¶ 5125] CODE SEC. 351. TRANSFER TO CORPORATION CONTROLLED BY TRANSFEROR.

* * *

(h) CROSS REFERENCES.—

(1) For special rule where another party to the exchange assumes a liability, see section 357.

* * *

[CCH Explanation at ¶ 30,050. Committee Reports at ¶ 10,320.]

Amendment Notes

Act Sec. 417(9) amended Code Sec. 351(h)(1) by inserting a comma after "liability".

The above amendment is effective on March 9, 2002.

[¶ 5130] CODE SEC. 358. BASIS TO DISTRIBUTEES.

* * *

(h) SPECIAL RULES FOR ASSUMPTION OF LIABILITIES TO WHICH SUBSECTION (D) DOES NOT APPLY.—

(1) IN GENERAL.—If, after application of the other provisions of this section to an exchange or series of exchanges, the basis of property to which subsection (a)(1) applies exceeds the fair market value of such property, then such basis shall be reduced (but not below such fair market value) by the amount (determined as of the date of the exchange) of any liability—

(A) which is assumed by another person as part of the exchange, and

(B) with respect to which subsection (d)(1) does not apply to the assumption.

* * *

[CCH Explanation at ¶ 335. Committee Reports at ¶ 10,280.]

Amendment Notes

Act Sec. 412(c) amended Code Sec. 358(h)(1)(A) to read as above. Prior to amendment, Code Sec. 358(h)(1)(A) read as follows:

(A) which is assumed in exchange for such property, and

The above amendment is effective as if included in the provision of the Community Renewal Tax Relief Act of 2000 (P.L. 106-554) to which it relates [effective for assumptions of liabilities after October 18, 1999.— CCH].

[¶ 5135] CODE SEC. 401. QUALIFIED PENSION, PROFIT-SHARING, AND STOCK BONUS PLANS.

(a) REQUIREMENTS FOR QUALIFICATION.—A trust created or organized in the United States and forming part of a stock bonus, pension, or profit-sharing plan of an employer for the exclusive benefit of his employees or their beneficiaries shall constitute a qualified trust under this section—

* * *

(30) LIMITATIONS ON ELECTIVE DEFERRALS.—In the case of a trust which is part of a plan under which elective deferrals (within the meaning of section 402(g)(3)) may be made with respect to any individual during a calendar year, such trust shall not constitute a qualified trust under this subsection unless the plan provides that the amount of such deferrals under such plan and all other plans, contracts, or arrangements of an employer maintaining such plan may not exceed the amount of the limitation in effect under section *402(g)(1)(A)* for taxable years beginning in such calendar year.

(31) DIRECT TRANSFER OF ELIGIBLE ROLLOVER DISTRIBUTIONS.—

* * *

(C) LIMITATION.—Subparagraphs (A) and (B) shall apply only to the extent that the eligible rollover distribution would be includible in gross income if not transferred as provided in subparagraph (A) (determined without regard to sections 402(c), 403(a)(4), 403(b)(8), and 457(e)(16)). The preceding sentence shall not apply to such distribution if the plan to which such distribution is transferred—

(i) *is a qualified trust which is part of a plan which is a defined contribution plan and* agrees to separately account for amounts so transferred, including separately accounting for the portion of such distribution which is includible in gross income and the portion of such distribution which is not so includible, or

(ii) is an eligible retirement plan described in clause (i) or (ii) of section 402(c)(8)(B).

* * *

[CCH Explanation at ¶ 515 and ¶ 520. Committee Reports at ¶ 10,270.]

Amendment Notes

Act Sec. 411(o)(2) amended Code Sec. 401(a)(30) by striking "402(g)(1)" and inserting "402(g)(1)(A)".

The above amendment is effective as if included in the provision of the Economic Growth and Tax Relief Reconciliation Act of 2001 (P.L. 107-16) to which it relates [effective for tax years beginning after December 31, 2001.—CCH].

Act Sec. 411(q)(1) amended Code Sec. 401(a)(31)(C)(i) by inserting "is a qualified trust which is part of a plan which is a defined contribution plan and" before "agrees".

The above amendment is effective as if included in the provision of the Economic Growth and Tax Relief Reconciliation Act of 2001 (P.L. 107-16) to which it relates [effective for distributions made after December 31, 2001.—CCH].

[¶ 5140] CODE SEC. 402. TAXABILITY OF BENEFICIARY OF EMPLOYEES' TRUST.

* * *

(c) RULES APPLICABLE TO ROLLOVERS FROM EXEMPT TRUSTS.—

* * *

(2) MAXIMUM AMOUNT WHICH MAY BE ROLLED OVER.—In the case of any eligible rollover distribution, the maximum amount transferred to which paragraph (1) applies shall not exceed the portion of such distribution which is includible in gross income (determined without regard to paragraph (1)). The preceding sentence shall not apply to such distribution to the extent—

(A) such portion is transferred in a direct trustee-to-trustee transfer to a qualified trust which is part of a plan which is a defined contribution plan and which agrees to separately account for amounts so transferred, including separately accounting for the portion of such distribution which is includible in gross income and the portion of such distribution which is not so includible, or

(B) such portion is transferred to an eligible retirement plan described in clause (i) or (ii) of paragraph (8)(B).

In the case of a transfer described in subparagraph (A) or (B), the amount transferred shall be treated as consisting first of the portion of such distribution that is includible in gross income (determined without regard to paragraph (1)).

* * *

[CCH Explanation at ¶ 525. Committee Reports at ¶ 10,270.]

Amendment Notes

Act Sec. 411(q)(2) amended Code Sec. 402(c)(2) by adding at the end a new flush sentence to read as above.

The above amendment is effective as if included in the provision of the Economic Growth and Tax Relief Rec-

onciliation Act of 2001 (P.L. 107-16) to which it relates [effective for distributions made after December 31, 2001.—CCH].

(g) LIMITATION ON EXCLUSION FOR ELECTIVE DEFERRALS.—

(1) IN GENERAL.—

* * *

(C) CATCH-UP CONTRIBUTIONS.—In addition to subparagraph (A), in the case of an eligible participant (as defined in section 414(v)), gross income shall not include elective deferrals in excess of the applicable dollar amount under subparagraph (B) to the extent that the amount of such elective deferrals does not exceed the applicable dollar amount under section 414(v)(2)(B)(i) for the taxable year (without regard to the treatment of the elective deferrals by an applicable employer plan under section 414(v)).

* * *

(7) SPECIAL RULE FOR CERTAIN ORGANIZATIONS.—

* * *

(B) QUALIFIED ORGANIZATION.—For purposes of this paragraph, the term "qualified organization" means any educational organization, hospital, home health service agency, health and welfare service agency, church, or convention or association of churches. Such term includes any organization described in section 414(e)(3)(B)(ii). Terms used in this subparagraph shall have the same meaning as when used in section 415(c)(4) (as in effect before the enactment of the Economic Growth and Tax Relief Reconciliation Act of *2001*).

* * *

[CCH Explanation at ¶ 515. Committee Reports at ¶ 10,270.]

Amendment Notes

Act Sec. 411(o)(1) amended Code Sec. 402(g)(1) by adding at the end a new subparagraph (C) to read as above.

Act Sec. 411(p)(6) amended Code Sec. 402(g)(7)(B) by striking "2001." and inserting "2001).".

The above amendments are effective as if included in the provisions of the Economic Growth and Tax Relief Reconciliation Act of 2001 (P.L. 107-16) to which they relate [effective for tax years beginning after December 31, 2001.—CCH].

(h) SPECIAL RULES FOR SIMPLIFIED EMPLOYEE PENSIONS.—For purposes of this chapter—

* * *

(2) LIMITATIONS ON EMPLOYER CONTRIBUTIONS.—Contributions made by an employer to a simplified employee pension with respect to an employee for any year shall be treated as distributed or made available to such employee and as contributions made by the employee to the extent such contributions exceed the lesser of—

(A) *25 percent* of the compensation (within the meaning of section 414(s)) from such employer includible in the employee's gross income for the year (determined without regard to the employer contributions to the simplified employee pension), or

(B) the limitation in effect under section 415(c)(1)(A), reduced in the case of any highly compensated employee (within the meaning of section 414(q)) by the amount taken into account with respect to such employee under section 408(k)(3)(D).

* * *

[CCH Explanation at ¶ 565. Committee Reports at ¶ 10,270.]

Amendment Notes

Act Sec. 411(l)(3) amended Code Sec. 402(h)(2)(A) by striking "15 percent" and inserting "25 percent".

The above amendment is effective as if included in the provision of the Economic Growth and Tax Relief Rec-

onciliation Act of 2001 (P.L. 107-16) to which it relates [effective for years beginning after December 31, 2001.— CCH].

[¶ 5145] CODE SEC. 403. TAXATION OF EMPLOYEE ANNUITIES.

* * *

(b) TAXABILITY OF BENEFICIARY UNDER ANNUITY PURCHASED BY SECTION 501(c)(3) ORGANIZATION OR PUBLIC SCHOOL.—

(1) GENERAL RULE.—If—

(A) an annuity contract is purchased—

(i) for an employee by an employer described in section 501(c)(3) which is exempt from tax under section 501(a),

(ii) for an employee (other than an employee described in clause (i)), who performs services for an educational organization described in section 170(b)(1)(A)(ii), by an employer which is a State, a political subdivision of a State, or an agency or instrumentality of any one or more of the foregoing, or

(iii) for the minister described in section 414(e)(5)(A) by the minister or by an employer,

(B) such annuity contract is not subject to subsection (a),

(C) the employee's rights under the contract are nonforfeitable, except for failure to pay future premiums,

(D) except in the case of a contract purchased by a church, such contract is purchased under a plan which meets the nondiscrimination requirements of paragraph 12, and

(E) in the case of a contract purchased under a salary reduction agreement, the contract meets the requirements of section 401(a)(30),

then contributions and other additions by such employer for such annuity contract shall be excluded from the gross income of the employee for the taxable year to the extent that the aggregate of such contributions and additions (when expressed as an annual addition (within the meaning of section 415(c)(2))) does not exceed the applicable limit under section 415. The amount actually distributed to any distributee under such contract shall be taxable to the distributee (in the year in which so distributed) under section 72 (relating to annuities). For purposes of applying the rules of this subsection to contributions and other additions by an employer for a taxable year, amounts transferred to a contract described in this paragraph by reason of a rollover contribution described in paragraph (8) of this subsection or section 408(d)(3)(A)(ii) shall not be considered contributed by such employer.

* * *

(3) INCLUDIBLE COMPENSATION.—For purposes of this subsection, the term "includible compensation" means, in the case of any employee, the amount of compensation which is received from the employer described in paragraph (1)(A), and which is includible in gross income (computed without regard to section 911) for the most recent period (ending not later than the close of the taxable year) which under paragraph (4) may be counted as one year of service, *and which precedes the taxable year by no more than five years.* Such term does not include any amount contributed by the employer for any annuity contract to which this subsection applies. Such term includes—

(A) any elective deferral (as defined in section 402(g)(3)), and

(B) any amount which is contributed or deferred by the employer at the election of the employee and which is not includible in the gross income of the employee by reason of section 125, 132(f)(4), or 457.

* * *

(6) *[Stricken.]*

* * *

[CCH Explanation at ¶ 585. Committee Reports at ¶ 10,270.]

Amendment Notes

Act Sec. 411(p)(1) amended Code Sec. 403(b)(1) by striking, in the matter that follows subparagraph (E), "then amounts contributed" and all that follows and inserting new text to read as above. Prior to amendment, the matter that followed Code Sec. 403(b)(1)(E) read as follows:

then amounts contributed by such employer for such annuity contract on or after such rights become nonforfeitable shall be excluded from the gross income of the employee for the taxable year to the extent that the aggregate of such amounts does not exceed the applicable limit under section 415. The amount actually distributed to any distributee under such contract shall be taxable to the distributee (in the year in which so distributed) under section 72 (relating to annuities). For purposes of applying the rules of this subsection to amounts contributed by an employer for a taxable year, amounts transferred to a contract described in this paragraph by reason of a rollover contribution described in paragraph (8) of this subsection or section 408(d)(3)(A)(ii) shall not be considered contributed by such employer.

Act Sec. 411(p)(2) amended Code Sec. 403(b) by striking paragraph (6). Prior to amendment, Code Sec. 403(b)(6) read as follows:

(6) FORFEITABLE RIGHTS WHICH BECOME NONFORFEITABLE.—For purposes of this subsection and section 72(f) (relating to special rules for computing employees' contributions to annuity contracts), if rights of the employee under an annuity contract described in subparagraphs (A) and (B) of paragraph (1) change from forfeitable to nonforfeitable rights, then the amount (determined without regard to this subsection) includible in gross income by reason of such change shall be treated as an amount contributed by the employer for such annuity contract as of the time such rights become nonforfeitable.

Act Sec. 411(p)(3)(A)-(B) amended Code Sec. 403(b)(3) by inserting ", and which precedes the taxable year by no more than five years" before the period at the end of the first sentence, and by striking "or any amount received by a former employee after the fifth taxable year following the taxable year in which such employee was terminated" in the second sentence following "this subsection applies".

The above amendments are effective as if included in the provisions of the Economic Growth and Tax Relief Reconciliation Act of 2001 (P.L. 107-16) to which they relate [generally applicable to years beginning after December 31, 2001.—CCH].

[¶ 5150] CODE SEC. 404. DEDUCTION FOR CONTRIBUTIONS OF AN EMPLOYER TO AN EMPLOYEES' TRUST OR ANNUITY PLAN AND COMPENSATION UNDER A DEFERRED-PAYMENT PLAN.

(a) GENERAL RULE.—If contributions are paid by an employer to or under a stock bonus, pension, profit-sharing, or annuity plan, or if compensation is paid or accrued on account of any employee under a plan deferring the receipt of such compensation, such contributions or compensation shall not be deductible under this chapter; but if they would otherwise be deductible, they shall be deductible under this section, subject, however, to the following limitations as to the amounts deductible in any year:

(1) PENSION TRUSTS.—

* * *

(D) SPECIAL RULE IN CASE OF CERTAIN PLANS.—

* * *

(iv) *SPECIAL RULE FOR TERMINATING PLANS.*—In the case of a plan which, subject to section 4041 of the Employee Retirement Income Security Act of 1974, terminates during the plan year, clause (i) shall be applied by substituting for unfunded current liability the amount required to make the plan sufficient for benefit liabilities (within the meaning of section 4041(d) of such Act).

* * *

(7) LIMITATION ON DEDUCTIONS WHERE COMBINATION OF DEFINED CONTRIBUTION PLAN AND DEFINED BENEFIT PLAN.—

* * *

(C) *PARAGRAPH NOT TO APPLY IN CERTAIN CASES.*—

(i) *BENEFICIARY TEST.*—This paragraph shall not have the effect of reducing the amount otherwise deductible under paragraphs (1), (2), and (3), if no employee is a beneficiary under more than 1 trust or under a trust and an annuity plan.

(ii) *ELECTIVE DEFERRALS.*—If, in connection with 1 or more defined contribution plans and 1 or more defined benefit plans, no amounts (other than elective deferrals (as defined in section 402(g)(3))) are contributed to any of the defined contribution plans for the taxable year, then subparagraph (A) shall not apply with respect to any of such defined contribution plans and defined benefit plans.

* * *

(12) DEFINITION OF COMPENSATION.—For purposes of paragraphs (3), (7), (8), and *(9) and subsection (h)(1)(C),* the term "compensation" shall include amounts treated as "participant's compensation" under subparagraph (C) or (D) of section 415(c)(3).

* * *

[CCH Explanation at ¶ 510, ¶ 550 and ¶ 570. Committee Reports at ¶ 10,270.]

Amendment Notes

Act Sec. 411(l)(1) amended Code Sec. 404(a)(12) by striking "(9)," and inserting "(9) and subsection (h)(1)(C),".

Act Sec. 411(l)(4) amended Code Sec. 404(a)(7)(C) to read as above. Prior to amendment, Code Sec. 404(a)(7)(C) read as follows:

(C) PARAGRAPH NOT TO APPLY IN CERTAIN CASES.—This paragraph shall not have the effect of reducing the amount otherwise deductible under paragraphs (1), (2), and (3), if no employee is a beneficiary under more than 1 trust or under a trust and an annuity plan.

The above amendments are effective as if included in the provisions of the Economic Growth and Tax Relief Reconciliation Act of 2001 (P.L. 107-16) to which they relate [effective for years beginning after December 31, 2001.—CCH].

Act Sec. 411(s) amended Code Sec. 404(a)(1)(D)(iv) by striking "PLANS MAINTAINED BY PROFESSIONAL SERVICE EMPLOYERS" and inserting "SPECIAL RULE FOR TERMINATING PLANS".

The above amendment is effective as if included in the provision of the Economic Growth and Tax Relief Reconciliation Act of 2001 (P.L. 107-16) to which it relates [effective for plan years beginning after December 31, 2001.—CCH].

(k) DEDUCTION FOR DIVIDENDS PAID ON CERTAIN EMPLOYER SECURITIES.—

(1) GENERAL RULE.—In the case of a C corporation, there shall be allowed as a deduction for a taxable year the amount of any applicable dividend paid in cash by such corporation with respect to applicable employer securities. Such deduction shall be in addition to the deductions allowed under subsection (a).

(2) APPLICABLE DIVIDEND.—For purposes of this subsection—

* * *

(B) LIMITATION ON CERTAIN DIVIDENDS.—A dividend described in subparagraph *(A)(iv)* which is paid with respect to any employer security which is allocated to a participant shall not be treated as an applicable dividend unless the plan provides that employer securities with a fair market value of not less than the amount of such dividend are allocated to such participant for the year which (but for subparagraph (A)) such dividend would have been allocated to such participant.

* * *

(4) TIME FOR DEDUCTION.—

* * *

(B) REINVESTMENT DIVIDENDS.—For purposes of subparagraph (A), an applicable dividend reinvested pursuant to clause (iii)(II) of paragraph (2)(A) shall be treated as paid in the taxable year of the corporation in which such dividend is reinvested in qualifying employer securities or in which the election under clause (iii) of paragraph (2)(A) is made, whichever is later.

(C) REPAYMENT OF LOANS.—In the case of an applicable dividend described in clause *(iv)* of paragraph (2)(A), the deduction under paragraph (1) shall be allowable in the taxable year of the corporation in which such dividend is used to repay the loan described in such clause.

* * *

(7) FULL VESTING.—In accordance with section 411, an applicable dividend described in clause (iii)(II) of paragraph (2)(A) shall be subject to the requirements of section 411(a)(1).

* * *

[CCH Explanation at ¶ 580. Committee Reports at ¶ 10,270.]

Amendment Notes

Act Sec. 411(w)(1)(A)-(D) amended Code Sec. 404(k) by striking "during the taxable year" before "with respect to" in paragraph (1), by striking "(A)(iii)" and inserting "(A)(iv)" in paragraph (2)(B), by striking "(iii)" and inserting "(iv)" in paragraph (4)(B), by redesignating subparagraph (B) of paragraph (4) (as amended) as subparagraph (C) of paragraph (4), and by inserting after subparagraph (A) a new subparagraph (B) to read as above.

Act Sec. 411(w)(2) amended Code Sec. 404(k) by adding at the end a new paragraph (7) to read as above.

The above amendments are effective as if included in the provisions of the Economic Growth and Tax Relief Reconciliation Act of 2001 (P.L. 107-16) to which they relate [effective for tax years beginning after December 31, 2001.—CCH].

(n) ELECTIVE DEFERRALS NOT TAKEN INTO ACCOUNT FOR PURPOSES OF DEDUCTION LIMITS.—Elective deferrals (as defined in section 402(g)(3)) shall not be subject to any limitation contained in paragraph (3), (7), or (9) of *subsection (a) or paragraph (1)(C) of subsection (h)*, and such elective deferrals shall not be taken into account in applying any such limitation to any other contributions.

[CCH Explanation at ¶ 570. Committee Reports at ¶ 10,270.]

¶ 5150   Code Sec. 404(k)

Amendment Notes

Act Sec. 411(l)(2) amended Code Sec. 404(n) by striking "subsection (a)," and inserting "subsection (a) or paragraph (1)(C) of subsection (h)".

The above amendment is effective as if included in the provision of the Economic Growth and Tax Relief Rec-

onciliation Act of 2001 (P.L. 107-16) to which it relates [effective for years beginning after December 31, 2001.—CCH].

[¶ 5155] CODE SEC. 408. INDIVIDUAL RETIREMENT ACCOUNTS.

* * *

(k) SIMPLIFIED EMPLOYEE PENSION DEFINED.—

* * *

(2) PARTICIPATION REQUIREMENTS.—This paragraph is satisfied with respect to a simplified employee pension for a year only if for such year the employer contributes to the simplified employee pension of each employee who—

(A) has attained age 21,

(B) has performed service for the employer during at least 3 of the immediately preceding 5 years, and

(C) received at least *$450* in compensation (within the meaning of section 414(q)(4)) from the employer for the year.

* * *

(8) COST-OF-LIVING ADJUSTMENT.—The Secretary shall adjust the *$450* amount in paragraph (2)(C) at the same time and in the same manner as under section 415(d) and shall adjust the $200,000 amount in paragraphs (3)(C) and (6)(D)(ii) at the same time, and by the same amount, as any adjustment under section 401(a)(17)(B); except that any increase in the *$450* amount which is not a multiple of $50 shall be rounded to the next lowest multiple of $50.

* * *

[CCH Explanation at ¶ 575. Committee Reports at ¶ 10,270.]

Amendment Notes

Act Sec. 411(j)(1)(A)-(B) amended Code Sec. 408(k) by striking "$300" and inserting "$450" in paragraph (2)(C), and by striking "$300" both places it appears and inserting "$450" in paragraph (8).

The above amendment is effective as if included in the provision of the Economic Growth and Tax Relief Reconciliation Act of 2001 (P.L. 107-16) to which it relates [effective for years beginning after December 31, 2001.—CCH].

(q) DEEMED IRAs UNDER QUALIFIED EMPLOYER PLANS.—

* * *

(3) DEFINITIONS.—For purposes of this subsection—

[Caution: Code Sec. 408(q)(3)(A), below, as amended by Act Sec. 411(i)(1), applies to plan years beginning after December 31, 2002.—CCH.]

(A) QUALIFIED EMPLOYER PLAN.—The term "qualified employer plan" has the meaning given such term by section 72(p)(4)(A)(i); except that such term shall also include an eligible deferred compensation plan (as defined in section 457(b)) of an eligible employer described in section 457(e)(1)(A).

* * *

[CCH Explanation at ¶ 560. Committee Reports at ¶ 10,270.]

Amendment Notes

Act Sec. 411(i)(1) amended Code Sec. 408(q)(3)(A) to read as above. Prior to amendment, Code Sec. 408(q)(3)(A) read as follows:

(A) QUALIFIED EMPLOYER PLAN.—The term "qualified employer plan" has the meaning given such term by section 72(p)(4); except such term shall not include a government plan which is not a qualified plan unless the plan is an

eligible deferred compensation plan (as defined in section 457(b)).

The above amendment is effective as if included in the provision of the Economic Growth and Tax Relief Reconciliation Act of 2001 (P.L. 107-16) to which it relates [applicable to plan years beginning after December 31, 2002.—CCH].

[¶ 5160] CODE SEC. 409. QUALIFICATIONS FOR TAX CREDIT EMPLOYEE STOCK OWNERSHIP PLANS.

* * *

(o) DISTRIBUTION AND PAYMENT REQUIREMENTS.—A plan meets the requirements of this subsection if—

(1) DISTRIBUTION REQUIREMENT.—

* * *

(C) LIMITED DISTRIBUTION PERIOD.—The plan provides that, unless the participant elects otherwise, the distribution of the participant's account balance will be in substantially equal periodic payments (not less frequently than annually) over a period not longer than the greater of—

(i) 5 years, or

(ii) in the case of a participant with an account balance in excess of *$800,000,* 5 years plus 1 additional year (but not more than 5 additional years) for each *$160,000* or fraction thereof by which such balance exceeds *$800,000.*

* * *

[CCH Explanation at ¶ 580. Committee Reports at ¶ 10,270.]

Amendment Notes

Act Sec. 411(j)(2)(A)-(B) amended Code Sec. 409(o)(1)(C)(ii) by striking "$500,000" both places it appears and inserting "$800,000" and by striking "$100,000" and inserting "$160,000".

The above amendment is effective as if included in the provision of the Economic Growth and Tax Relief Reconciliation Act of 2001 (P.L. 107-16) to which it relates [applies generally to years beginning after December 31, 2001.—CCH].

[¶ 5165] CODE SEC. 412. MINIMUM FUNDING STANDARDS.

* * *

(c) SPECIAL RULES.—

* * *

(9) ANNUAL VALUATION.—

* * *

(B) VALUATION DATE.—

* * *

(ii) USE OF PRIOR YEAR VALUATION.—The valuation referred to in subparagraph (A) may be made as of a date within the plan year prior to the year to which the valuation refers if, as of such date, the value of the assets of the plan are not less than *100 percent* of the plan's current liability (as defined in paragraph (7)(B)).

(iii) ADJUSTMENTS.—Information under clause (ii) shall, in accordance with regulations, be actuarially adjusted to reflect significant differences in participants.

(iv) LIMITATION.—A change in funding method to use a prior year valuation, as provided in clause (ii), may not be made unless as of the valuation date within the prior plan year, the value of the assets of the plan are not less than 125 percent of the plan's current liability (as defined in paragraph (7)(B)).

* * *

[CCH Explanation at ¶ 555. Committee Reports at ¶ 10,270.]

Amendment Notes

Act Sec. 411(v)(1)(A)-(B) amended Code Sec. 412(c)(9)(B) by striking "125 percent" and inserting "100 percent" in clause (ii), and by adding at the end a new clause (iv) to read as above.

The above amendment is effective as if included in the provision of the Economic Growth and Tax Relief Reconciliation Act of 2001 (P.L. 107-16) to which it relates [effective for plan years beginning after December 31, 2001.—CCH].

(l) ADDITIONAL FUNDING REQUIREMENTS FOR PLANS WHICH ARE NOT MULTIEMPLOYER PLANS.—

* * *

(7) CURRENT LIABILITY.—For purposes of this subsection—

* * *

(C) INTEREST RATE AND MORTALITY ASSUMPTIONS USED.—Effective for plan years beginning after December 31, 1994—

(i) INTEREST RATE.—

* * *

(III) SPECIAL RULE FOR 2002 AND 2003.—For a plan year beginning in 2002 or 2003, notwithstanding subclause (I), in the case that the rate of interest used under

subsection (b)(5) exceeds the highest rate permitted under subclause (I), the rate of interest used to determine current liability under this subsection may exceed the rate of interest otherwise permitted under subclause (I); except that such rate of interest shall not exceed 120 percent of the weighted average referred to in subsection (b)(5)(B)(ii).

* * *

[CCH Explanation at ¶ 505. Committee Reports at ¶ 10,240.]

Amendment Notes
Act Sec. 405(a)(1) amended Code Sec. 412(l)(7)(C)(i) by adding at the end a new subclause (III) to read as above.

The above amendment is effective on March 9, 2002.

(m) QUARTERLY CONTRIBUTIONS REQUIRED.—

* * *

(7) SPECIAL RULES FOR 2002 AND 2004.—In any case in which the interest rate used to determine current liability is determined under subsection (l)(7)(C)(i)(III)—

(A) 2002.—For purposes of applying paragraphs (1) and (4)(B)(ii) for plan years beginning in 2002, the current liability for the preceding plan year shall be redetermined using 120 percent as the specified percentage determined under subsection (l)(7)(C)(i)(II).

(B) 2004.—For purposes of applying paragraphs (1) and (4)(B)(ii) for plan years beginning in 2004, the current liability for the preceding plan year shall be redetermined using 105 percent as the specified percentage determined under subsection (l)(7)(C)(i)(II).

* * *

[CCH Explanation at ¶ 505. Committee Reports at ¶ 10,240.]

Amendment Notes
Act Sec. 405(a)(2) amended Code Sec. 412(m) by adding at the end a new paragraph (7) to read as above.

The above amendment is effective on March 9, 2002.

[¶ 5170] CODE SEC. 414. DEFINITIONS AND SPECIAL RULES.

* * *

(v) CATCH-UP CONTRIBUTIONS FOR INDIVIDUALS AGE 50 OR OVER.—

* * *

(2) LIMITATION ON AMOUNT OF ADDITIONAL DEFERRALS.—

* * *

(D) AGGREGATION OF PLANS.—For purposes of this paragraph, plans described in clauses (i), (ii), and (iv) of paragraph (6)(A) that are maintained by the same employer (as determined under subsection (b), (c), (m) or (o)) shall be treated as a single plan, and plans described in clause (iii) of paragraph (6)(A) that are maintained by the same employer shall be treated as a single plan.

(3) TREATMENT OF CONTRIBUTIONS.—In the case of any contribution to a plan under paragraph (1)—

(A) such contribution shall not, with respect to the year in which the contribution is made—

(i) be subject to any otherwise applicable limitation contained in *section 401(a)(30), 402(h), 403(b), 408, 415(c), and 457(b)(2) (determined without regard to section 457(b)(3))*, or

(ii) be taken into account in applying such limitations to other contributions or benefits under such plan or any other such plan, and

(B) except as provided in paragraph (4), such plan shall not be treated as failing to meet the requirements of *section 401(a)(4), 401(k)(3), 401(k)(11), 403(b)(12), 408(k), 410(b), or 416* by reason of the making of (or the right to make) such contribution.

(4) APPLICATION OF NONDISCRIMINATION RULES.—

* * *

(B) AGGREGATION.—For purposes of subparagraph (A), all plans maintained by employers who are treated as a single employer under subsection (b), (c), (m), or (o) of section 414 shall be treated as 1 plan, *except that a plan described in clause (i) of section 410(b)(6)(C) shall not be treated as a plan of the employer until the expiration of the transition period with respect to such plan (as determined under clause (ii) of such section).*

(5) ELIGIBLE PARTICIPANT.—For purposes of this subsection, the term "eligible participant" means a participant in a plan—

(A) who would attain age 50 by the end of the taxable year,

(B) with respect to whom no other elective deferrals may (without regard to this subsection) be made to the plan for the *plan (or other applicable) year* by reason of the application of any limitation or other restriction described in paragraph (3) or comparable limitation or restriction contained in the terms of the plan.

(6) OTHER DEFINITIONS AND RULES.—For purposes of this subsection—

* * *

(C) EXCEPTION FOR SECTION 457 PLANS.—This subsection shall not apply to a participant for any year for which a higher limitation applies to the participant under section 457(b)(3).

[CCH Explanation at ¶ 515. Committee Reports at ¶ 10,270.]

Amendment Notes

Act Sec. 411(o)(3) amended Code Sec. 414(v)(2) by adding at the end a new subparagraph (D) to read as above.

Act Sec. 411(o)(4) amended Code Sec. 414(v)(3)(A)(i) by striking "section 402(g), 402(h), 403(b), 404(a), 404(h), 408(k), 408(p), 415, or 457" and inserting "section 401(a)(30), 402(h), 403(b), 408, 415(c), and 457(b)(2) (determined without regard to section 457(b)(3))".

Act Sec. 411(o)(5) amended Code Sec. 414(v)(3)(B) by striking "section 401(a)(4), 401(a)(26), 401(k)(3), 401(k)(11), 401(k)(12), 403(b)(12), 408(k), 408(p), 408B, 410(b), or 416" and inserting "section 401(a)(4), 401(k)(3), 401(k)(11), 403(b)(12), 408(k), 410(b), or 416".

Act Sec. 411(o)(6) amended Code Sec. 414(v)(4)(B) by inserting before the period at the end ", except that a plan described in clause (i) of section 410(b)(6)(C) shall not be treated as a plan of the employer until the expiration of the transition period with respect to such plan (as determined under clause (ii) of such section)".

Act Sec. 411(o)(7)(A)-(C) amended Code Sec. 414(v)(5) by striking ", with respect to any plan year," after "means," in

the matter preceding subparagraph (A), by amending subparagraph (A) to read as above, and by striking "plan year" and inserting "plan (or other applicable) year" in subparagraph (B). Prior to amendment, Code Sec. 414(v)(5)(A) read as follows:

(A) who has attained the age of 50 before the close of the plan year, and

Act Sec. 411(o)(8) amended Code Sec. 414(v)(6)(C) to read as above. Prior to amendment, Code Sec. 414(v)(6)(C) read as follows:

(C) EXCEPTION FOR SECTION 457 PLANS.—This subsection shall not apply to an applicable employer plan described in subparagraph (A)(iii) for any year to which section 457(b)(3) applies.

The above amendments are effective as if included in the provisions of the Economic Growth and Tax Relief Reconciliation Act of 2001 (P.L. 107-16) to which they relate [effective for tax years beginning after December 31, 2001.—CCH].

[¶ 5175] CODE SEC. 415. LIMITATIONS ON BENEFITS AND CONTRIBUTION UNDER QUALIFIED PLANS.

* * *

(c) LIMITATION FOR DEFINED CONTRIBUTION PLANS.—

* * *

(7) SPECIAL RULES RELATING TO CHURCH PLANS.—

(A) ALTERNATIVE CONTRIBUTION LIMITATION.—

(i) IN GENERAL.—Notwithstanding any other provision of this subsection, at the election of a participant who is an employee of a church or a convention or association of churches, including an organization described in section 414(e)(3)(B)(ii), contributions and other additions for an annuity contract or retirement income account described in section 403(b) with respect to such participant, when expressed as an annual addition to such participant's account, shall be treated as not exceeding the limitation of paragraph (1) if such annual addition is not in excess of $10,000.

(ii) $40,000 AGGREGATE LIMITATION.—The total amount of additions with respect to any participant which may be taken into account for purposes of this subparagraph for all years may not exceed $40,000.

(B) NUMBER OF YEARS OF SERVICE FOR DULY ORDAINED, COMMISSIONED, OR LICENSED MINISTERS OR LAY EMPLOYEES.—For purposes of this paragraph—

(i) all years of service by—

(I) a duly ordained, commissioned, or licensed minister of a church, or

(II) *a lay person,*

as an employee of a church, a convention or association of churches, including an organization described in section 414(e)(3)(B)(ii), shall be considered as years of service for 1 employer, and

(ii) *all amounts contributed for annuity contracts by each such church (or convention or association of churches) or such organization during such years for such minister or lay person shall be considered to have been contributed by 1 employer.*

(C) FOREIGN MISSIONARIES.—*In the case of any individual described in subparagraph (D) performing services outside the United States, contributions and other additions for an annuity contract or retirement income account described in section 403(b) with respect to such employee, when expressed as an annual addition to such employee's account, shall not be treated as exceeding the limitation of paragraph (1) if such annual addition is not in excess of the greater of $3,000 or the employee's includible compensation determined under section 403(b)(3).*

(D) ANNUAL ADDITION.—*For purposes of this paragraph, the term "annual addition" has the meaning given such term by paragraph (2).*

(E) CHURCH, CONVENTION OR ASSOCIATION OF CHURCHES.—*For purposes of this paragraph, the terms "church" and "convention or association of churches" have the same meaning as when used in section 414(e).*

* * *

[CCH Explanation at ¶ 590. Committee Reports at ¶ 10,270.]

Amendment Notes

Act Sec. 411(p)(4) amended Code Sec. 415(c)(7) to read as above. Prior to amendment, Code Sec. 415(c)(7) read as follows:

(7) CERTAIN CONTRIBUTIONS BY CHURCH PLANS NOT TREATED AS EXCEEDING LIMIT.—

(A) IN GENERAL.—Notwithstanding any other provision of this subsection, at the election of a participant who is an employee of a church or a convention or association of churches, including an organization described in section 414(e)(3)(B)(ii), contributions and other additions for an annuity contract or retirement income account described in section 403(b) with respect to such participant, when expressed as an annual addition to such participant's account,

shall be treated as not exceeding the limitation of paragraph (1) if such annual addition is not in excess of $10,000.

(B) $40,000 AGGREGATE LIMITATION.—The total amount of additions with respect to any participant which may be taken into account for purposes of this subparagraph for all years may not exceed $40,000.

(C) ANNUAL ADDITION.—For purposes of this paragraph, the term "annual addition" has the meaning given such term by paragraph (2).

The above amendment is effective as if included in the provision of the Economic Growth and Tax Relief Reconciliation Act of 2001 (P.L. 107-16) to which it relates [effective generally for years beginning after December 31, 2001.—CCH].

[¶ 5180] CODE SEC. 416. SPECIAL RULES FOR TOP-HEAVY PLANS.

* * *

(c) PLAN MUST PROVIDE MINIMUM BENEFITS.—

(1) DEFINED BENEFIT PLANS.—

* * *

(C) YEARS OF SERVICE.—For purposes of this paragraph—

* * *

(iii) *EXCEPTION FOR PLAN UNDER WHICH NO KEY EMPLOYEE (OR FORMER KEY EMPLOYEE) BENEFITS FOR PLAN YEAR.*— For purposes of determining an employee's years of service with the employer, any service with the employer shall be disregarded to the extent that such service occurs during a plan year when the plan benefits (within the meaning of section 410(b)) no key employee or former key employee.

* * *

[CCH Explanation at ¶ 535. Committee Reports at ¶ 10,270.]

Amendment Notes

Act Sec. 411(k)(1) amended Code Sec. 416(c)(1)(C)(iii) by striking "EXCEPTION FOR FROZEN PLAN" and inserting "EXCEPTION FOR PLAN UNDER WHICH NO KEY EMPLOYEE (OR FORMER KEY EMPLOYEE) BENEFITS FOR PLAN YEAR".

The above amendment is effective as if included in the provision of the Economic Growth and Tax Relief Reconciliation Act of 2001 (P.L. 107-16) to which it relates [effective for years beginning after December 31, 2001.—CCH].

(g) TOP-HEAVY PLAN DEFINED.—For purposes of this section—

* * *

(3) DISTRIBUTIONS DURING LAST YEAR BEFORE DETERMINATION DATE TAKEN INTO ACCOUNT.—

* * *

(B) 5-YEAR PERIOD IN CASE OF IN-SERVICE DISTRIBUTION.—In the case of any distribution made for a reason other than *severance from employment*, death, or disability, subparagraph (A) shall be applied by substituting "5-year period" for "1-year period".

* * *

[CCH Explanation at ¶ 535. Committee Reports at ¶ 10,270.]

Amendment Notes

Act Sec. 411(k)(2) amended Code Sec. 416(g)(3)(B) by striking "separation from service" and inserting "severance from employment".

The above amendment is effective as if included in the provision of the Economic Growth and Tax Relief Rec-

onciliation Act of 2001 (P.L. 107-16) to which it relates [effective for years beginning after December 31, 2001.— CCH].

[¶ 5185] CODE SEC. 417. DEFINITIONS AND SPECIAL RULES FOR PURPOSES OF MINIMUM SURVIVOR ANNUITY REQUIREMENTS.

* * *

(e) RESTRICTIONS ON CASH-OUTS.—

(1) PLAN MAY REQUIRE DISTRIBUTION IF PRESENT VALUE NOT IN EXCESS OF DOLLAR LIMIT.—A plan may provide that the present value of a qualified joint and survivor annuity or a qualified preretirement survivor annuity will be immediately distributed if such value does not *exceed the amount that can be distributed without the participant's consent under section 411(a)(11)*. No distribution may be made under the preceding sentence after the annuity starting date unless the participant and the spouse of the participant (or where the participant has died, the surviving spouse) consents in writing to such distribution.

(2) PLAN MAY DISTRIBUTE BENEFIT IN EXCESS OF DOLLAR LIMIT ONLY WITH CONSENT.—If—

(A) the present value of the qualified joint and survivor annuity or the qualified preretirement survivor annuity *exceeds the amount that can be distributed without the participant's consent under section 411(a)(11)*, and

(B) the participant and the spouse of the participant (or where the participant has died, the surviving spouse) consent in writing to the distribution,

the plan may immediately distribute the present value of such annuity.

* * *

[CCH Explanation at ¶ 530. Committee Reports at ¶ 10,270.]

Amendment Notes

Act Sec. 411(r)(1)(A)-(B) amended Code Sec. 417(e) by striking "exceed the dollar limit under section 411(a)(11)(A)" and inserting "exceed the amount that can be distributed without the participant's consent under section 411(a)(11)" in paragraph (1), and by striking "exceeds the dollar limit under section 411(a)(11)(A)" and inserting "exceeds the amount that can be distributed without the partici-

pant's consent under section 411(a)(11)" in paragraph (2)(A).

The above amendment is effective as if included in the provision of the Economic Growth and Tax Relief Reconciliation Act of 2001 (P.L. 107-16) to which it relates [effective for distributions after December 31, 2001.— CCH].

[¶ 5190] CODE SEC. 448. LIMITATION ON USE OF CASH METHOD OF ACCOUNTING.

* * *

(d) DEFINITIONS AND SPECIAL RULES.—For purposes of this section—

* * *

(5) SPECIAL RULE FOR CERTAIN SERVICES.—

(A) IN GENERAL.—In the case of any person using an accrual method of accounting with respect to amounts to be received for the performance of services by such person, such person shall not be required to accrue any portion of such amounts which (on the basis of such person's experience) will not be collected if—

(i) such services are in fields referred to in paragraph (2)(A), or

(ii) such person meets the gross receipts test of subsection (c) for all prior taxable years.

(B) Exception.—This paragraph shall not apply to any amount if interest is required to be paid on such amount or there is any penalty for failure to timely pay such amount.

(C) Regulations.—The Secretary shall prescribe regulations to permit taxpayers to determine amounts referred to in subparagraph (A) using computations or formulas which, based on experience, accurately reflect the amount of income that will not be collected by such person. A taxpayer may adopt, or request consent of the Secretary to change to, a computation or formula that clearly reflects the taxpayer's experience. A request under the preceding sentence shall be approved if such computation or formula clearly reflects the taxpayer's experience.

* * *

[CCH Explanation at ¶ 345. Committee Reports at ¶ 10,220.]

Amendment Notes

Act Sec. 403(a) amended Code Sec. 448(d)(5) to read as above. Prior to amendment, Code Sec. 448(d)(5) read as follows:

(5) Special rule for services.—In the case of any person using an accrual method of accounting with respect to amounts to be received for the performance of services by such person, such person shall not be required to accrue any portion of such amounts which (on the basis of experience) will not be collected. This paragraph shall not apply to any amount if interest is required to be paid on such amount or there is any penalty for failure to timely pay such amount.

The above amendment generally applies to tax years ending after March 9, 2002. For a special rule, see Act Sec. 403(b)(2), below.

Act Sec. 403(b)(2) provides:

(2) Change in Method of Accounting.—In the case of any taxpayer required by the amendments made by this section to change its method of accounting for its first taxable year ending after the date of the enactment of this Act—

(A) such change shall be treated as initiated by the taxpayer,

(B) such change shall be treated as made with the consent of the Secretary of the Treasury, and

(C) the net amount of the adjustments required to be taken into account by the taxpayer under section 481 of the Internal Revenue Code of 1986 shall be taken into account over a period of 4 years (or if less, the number of taxable years that the taxpayer used the method permitted under section 448(d)(5) of such Code as in effect before the date of the enactment of this Act) beginning with such first taxable year.

[¶ 5195] CODE SEC. 457. DEFERRED COMPENSATION PLANS OF STATE AND LOCAL GOVERNMENTS AND TAX-EXEMPT ORGANIZATIONS.

* * *

(e) Other Definitions and Special Rules.—For purposes of this section—

* * *

(5) Includible compensation.—The term "includible compensation" has the meaning given to the term "participant's compensation" by section 415(c)(3).

* * *

(18) Coordination with catch-up contributions for individuals age 50 or older.—In the case of an individual who is an eligible participant (as defined by section 414(v)) and who is a participant in an eligible deferred compensation plan of an employer described in paragraph (1)(A), subsections (b)(3) and (c) shall be applied by substituting for the amount otherwise determined under the applicable subsection the greater of—

(A) the sum of—

(i) the plan ceiling established for purposes of subsection (b)(2) (without regard to subsection (b)(3)), plus

(ii) the applicable dollar amount for the taxable year determined under section 414(v)(2)(B)(i), or

(B) the amount determined under the applicable subsection (without regard to this paragraph).

* * *

[CCH Explanation at ¶ 515 and ¶ 595. Committee Reports at ¶ 10,270.]

Amendment Notes

Act Sec. 411(o)(9) amended Code Sec. 457(e) by adding at the end a new paragraph (18) to read as above.

The above amendment is effective as if included in the provision of the Economic Growth and Tax Relief Reconciliation Act of 2001 (P.L. 107-16) to which it relates [effective for tax years beginning after December 31, 2001.—CCH].

Act Sec. 411(p)(5) amended Code Sec. 457(e)(5) to read as above. Prior to amendment, Code Sec. 457(e)(5) read as follows:

(5) Includible compensation.—The term "includible compensation" means compensation for service performed for the employer which (taking into account the provisions of this section and other provisions of this chapter) is currently includible in gross income.

The above amendment is effective as if included in the provision of the Economic Growth and Tax Relief Reconciliation Act of 2001 (P.L. 107-16) to which it relates [effective generally for years beginning after December 31, 2001.—CCH].

[¶ 5200] CODE SEC. 469. PASSIVE ACTIVITY LOSSES AND CREDITS LIMITED.

* * *

(i) $25,000 OFFSET FOR RENTAL REAL ESTATE ACTIVITIES.—

* * *

(3) PHASE-OUT OF EXEMPTION.—

* * *

(E) ORDERING RULES TO REFLECT EXCEPTIONS AND SEPARATE PHASE-OUTS.—If subparagraph (B), (C), or (D) applies for a taxable year, paragraph (1) shall be applied—

(i) first to the portion of the passive activity loss to which subparagraph (C) does not apply,

(ii) second to the portion of such loss to which subparagraph (C) applies,

(iii) third to the portion of the passive activity credit to which subparagraph (B) or (D) does not apply,

(iv) fourth to the portion of such credit to which subparagraph (B) applies, and

(v) then to the portion of such credit to which subparagraph (D) applies.

* * *

[CCH Explanation at ¶ 245. Committee Reports at ¶ 10,280.]

Amendment Notes

Act Sec. 412(a) amended Code Sec. 469(i)(3)(E) by striking clauses (ii)-(iv) and inserting new clauses (ii)-(iv) to read as above. Prior to amendment, Code Sec. 469(i)(3)(E)(ii)-(iv) read as follows:

(ii) second to the portion of the passive activity credit to which subparagraph (B) or (D) does not apply,

(iii) third to the portion of such credit to which subparagraph (B) applies,

(iv) fourth to the portion of such loss to which subparagraph (C) applies, and

The above amendment is effective as if included in the provision of the Community Renewal Tax Relief Act of 2000 (P.L. 106-554) to which it relates [effective on December 21, 2000.—CCH].

[¶ 5205] CODE SEC. 475. MARK TO MARKET ACCOUNTING METHOD FOR DEALERS IN SECURITIES.

* * *

(g) REGULATORY AUTHORITY.—The Secretary shall prescribe such regulations as may be necessary or appropriate to carry out the purposes of this section, including rules—

(1) to prevent the use of year-end transfers, related parties, or other arrangements to avoid the provisions of this section,

(2) to provide for the application of this section to any security which is a hedge which cannot be identified with a specific security, position, right to income, or liability, and

(3) to prevent the use by taxpayers of subsection (c)(4) to avoid the application of this section to a receivable that is inventory in the hands of the taxpayer (or a person who bears a relationship to the taxpayer described in *section 267(b)* or *707(b)*).

[CCH Explanation at ¶ 30,050. Committee Reports at ¶ 10,320.]

Amendment Notes

Act Sec. 417(10) amended Code Sec. 475(g)(3) by striking "sections" and inserting "section".

The above amendment is effective on March 9, 2002.

[¶ 5210] CODE SEC. 529. QUALIFIED TUITION PROGRAMS.

* * *

(e) OTHER DEFINITIONS AND SPECIAL RULES.—For purposes of this section—

* * *

(3) QUALIFIED HIGHER EDUCATION EXPENSES.—

* * *

(B) ROOM AND BOARD INCLUDED FOR STUDENTS WHO ARE AT LEAST HALF-TIME.—

(i) IN GENERAL.—In the case of an individual who is an eligible student (as defined in section 25A(b)(3)) for any academic period, such term shall also include reasonable costs for such period (as determined under the qualified tuition program) incurred by the designated beneficiary for room and board while attending such institution. For purposes of *subsection (b)(6)*, a designated beneficiary shall be treated as meeting the requirements of this clause.

* * *

[CCH Explanation at ¶ 30,050. Committee Reports at ¶ 10,320.]

<table>
<tr><td>Amendment Notes</td><td>The above amendment is effective on March 9, 2002.</td></tr>
</table>

Act Sec. 417(11) amended Code Sec. 529(e)(3)(B)(i) by striking "subsection (b)(7)" and inserting "subsection (b)(6)".

[¶ 5215] CODE SEC. 530. COVERDELL EDUCATION SAVINGS ACCOUNTS.

* * *

(d) TAX TREATMENT OF DISTRIBUTIONS.—

* * *

(4) ADDITIONAL TAX FOR DISTRIBUTIONS NOT USED FOR EDUCATIONAL EXPENSES.—

* * *

(B) EXCEPTIONS.—Subparagraph (A) shall not apply if the payment or distribution is—

(i) made to a beneficiary (or to the estate of the designated beneficiary) on or after the death of the designated beneficiary,

(ii) attributable to the designated beneficiary's being disabled (within the meaning of section 72(m)(7)),

(iii) made on account of a scholarship, allowance, or payment described in section 25A(g)(2) received by the account holder to the extent the amount of the payment or distribution does not exceed the amount of the scholarship, allowance, or payment, or

(iv) an amount which is includible in gross income solely *by application of paragraph (2)(C)(i)(II)* for the taxable year.

* * *

[CCH Explanation at ¶ 250. Committee Reports at ¶ 10,260.]

Amendment Notes

Act Sec. 411(f) amended Code Sec. 530(d)(4)(B)(iv) by striking "because the taxpayer elected under paragraph (2)(C) to waive the application of paragraph (2)" and inserting "by application of paragraph (2)(C)(i)(II)".

The above amendment is effective as if included in the provision of the Economic Growth and Tax Relief Reconciliation Act of 2001 (P.L. 107-16) to which it relates [effective for tax years beginning after December 31, 2001.—CCH].

[¶ 5220] CODE SEC. 613A. LIMITATIONS ON PERCENTAGE DEPLETION IN CASE OF OIL AND GAS WELLS.

* * *

(c) EXEMPTION FOR INDEPENDENT PRODUCERS AND ROYALTY OWNERS.—

* * *

(6) OIL AND NATURAL GAS PRODUCED FROM MARGINAL PROPERTIES.—

* * *

(H) TEMPORARY SUSPENSION OF TAXABLE INCOME LIMIT WITH RESPECT TO MARGINAL PRODUCTION.—The second sentence of subsection (a) of section 613 shall not apply to so much of the allowance for depletion as is determined under subparagraph (A) for any taxable year beginning after December 31, 1997, and before January 1, *2004*.

* * *

[CCH Explanation at ¶ 380. Committee Reports at ¶ 10,470.]

Amendment Notes

Act Sec. 607(a) amended Code Sec. 613A(c)(6)(H) by striking "2002" and inserting "2004".

The above amendment applies to tax years beginning after December 31, 2001.

[¶ 5225] CODE SEC. 741. RECOGNITION AND CHARACTER OF GAIN OR LOSS ON SALE OR EXCHANGE.

In the case of a sale or exchange of an interest in a partnership, gain or loss shall be recognized to the transferor partner. Such gain or loss shall be considered as gain or loss from the sale or exchange of a capital asset, except as otherwise provided in section 751 (relating to unrealized receivables and inventory items).

[CCH Explanation at ¶ 363. Committee Reports at ¶ 10,320.]

Amendment Notes	
Act Sec. 417(12) amended Code Sec. 741 by striking "which have appreciated substantially in value" following "inventory items".	The above amendment is effective on March 9, 2002.

[¶ 5230] CODE SEC. 809. REDUCTION IN CERTAIN DEDUCTIONS OF MUTUAL LIFE INSURANCE COMPANIES.

* * *

(j) DIFFERENTIAL EARNINGS RATE TREATED AS ZERO FOR CERTAIN YEARS.—*Notwithstanding subsection (c) or (f), the differential earnings rate shall be treated as zero for purposes of computing both the differential earnings amount and the recomputed differential earnings amount for a mutual life insurance company's taxable years beginning in 2001, 2002, or 2003.*

[CCH Explanation at ¶ 384. Committee Reports at ¶ 10,520.]

Amendment Notes	
Act Sec. 611(a) amended Code Sec. 809 by adding at the end a new subsection (j) to read as above.	The above amendment applies to tax years beginning after December 31, 2000.

[¶ 5235] CODE SEC. 857. TAXATION OF REAL ESTATE INVESTMENT TRUSTS AND THEIR BENEFICIARIES.

* * *

(b) METHOD OF TAXATION OF REAL ESTATE INVESTMENT TRUSTS AND HOLDERS OF SHARES OR CERTIFICATES OF BENEFICIAL INTEREST.—

* * *

(7) INCOME FROM REDETERMINED RENTS, REDETERMINED DEDUCTIONS, AND EXCESS INTEREST.—

* * *

(B) REDETERMINED RENTS.—

(i) IN GENERAL.—The term "redetermined rents" means rents from real property (as defined in *section 856(d)*) *to the extent the amount of the rents* would (but for subparagraph (E)) be reduced on distribution, apportionment, or allocation under section 482 to clearly reflect income as a result of services furnished or rendered by a taxable REIT subsidiary of the real estate investment trust to a tenant of such trust.

* * *

(C) REDETERMINED DEDUCTIONS.—The term "redetermined deductions" means deductions (other than redetermined rents) of a taxable REIT subsidiary of a real estate investment trust *to the extent the amount* of such deductions would (but for subparagraph (E)) be decreased on distribution, apportionment, or allocation under section 482 to clearly reflect income as between such subsidiary and such trust.

* * *

[CCH Explanation at ¶ 360 and ¶ 30,050. Committee Reports at ¶ 10,290 and ¶ 10,320.]

Amendment Notes	
Act Sec. 413(a)(1)-(2) amended Code Sec. 857(b)(7) by striking "the amount of which" and inserting "to the extent the amount of the rents" in clause (i) of subparagraph (B), and by striking "if the amount" and inserting "to the extent the amount" in subparagraph (C).	The above amendment is effective as if included in section 545 of the Tax Relief Extension Act of 1999 (P.L. 106-170) [effective for tax years beginning after December 31, 2000.—CCH].
	Act Sec. 417(13) amended Code Sec. 857(b)(7)(B)(i) by striking "subsection 856(d)" and inserting "section 856(d)".
	The above amendment is effective on March 9, 2002.

[¶ 5240] CODE SEC. 904. LIMITATION ON CREDIT.

* * *

(h) COORDINATION WITH NONREFUNDABLE PERSONAL CREDITS.—In the case of an individual, for purposes of subsection (a), the tax against which the credit is taken is such tax reduced by the sum of the credits allowable under subpart A of part IV of subchapter A of this chapter (other than sections 23, 24, and 25B). This subsection shall not apply to taxable years beginning *during 2000, 2001, 2002 or 2003.*

* * *

[CCH Explanation at ¶ 270. Committee Reports at ¶ 10,400.]

Amendment Notes

Act Sec. 601(b)(1) amended Code Sec. 904(h) by striking "during 2000 or 2001" and inserting "during 2000, 2001, 2002, or 2003".

The above amendment applies to tax years beginning after December 31, 2001.

Act Sec. 601(b)(2) provides:

(2) The amendments made by sections 201(b), 202(f), and 618(b) of the Economic Growth and Tax Relief Reconciliation Act of 2001 shall not apply to taxable years beginning during 2002 and 2003.

[¶ 5245] CODE SEC. 943. OTHER DEFINITIONS AND SPECIAL RULES.

* * *

(e) ELECTION TO BE TREATED AS DOMESTIC CORPORATION.—

* * *

(4) SPECIAL RULES.—

* * *

(B) EFFECT OF ELECTION, REVOCATION, AND TERMINATION.—

(i) ELECTION.—For purposes of section 367, a foreign corporation making an election under this subsection shall be treated as transferring (as of the first day of the first taxable year to which the election applies) all of its assets to a domestic corporation in connection with an exchange to which section 354 applies.

(ii) REVOCATION AND TERMINATION.—For purposes of section 367, if—

(I) an election is made by a corporation under paragraph (1) for any taxable year, and

(II) such election ceases to apply for any subsequent taxable year,

such corporation shall be treated as a domestic corporation transferring (as of the 1st day of the first such subsequent taxable year to which such election ceases to apply) all of its property to a foreign corporation in connection with an exchange to which section 354 applies.

* * *

[CCH Explanation at ¶ 30,050. Committee Reports at ¶ 10,320.]

Amendment Notes

Act Sec. 417(14) amended Code Sec. 943(e)(4)(B) by aligning the left margin of the flush language with subparagraph (A).

The above amendment is effective on March 9, 2002.

[¶ 5250] CODE SEC. 953. INSURANCE INCOME.

* * *

(e) EXEMPT INSURANCE INCOME.—For purposes of this section—

* * *

(10) APPLICATION.—This subsection and section 954(i) shall apply only to taxable years of a foreign corporation beginning after December 31, 1998, and before *January 1, 2007,* and to taxable years of United States shareholders with or within which any such taxable year of such foreign corporation ends. If this subsection does not apply to a taxable year of a foreign corporation beginning after *December 31, 2006* (and taxable years of United States shareholders ending with or within such taxable year), then, notwithstanding the preceding sentence, subsection (a) shall be applied to such taxable years in the same manner as it would if the taxable year of the foreign corporation began in 1998.

* * *

[CCH Explanation at ¶ 388. Committee Reports at ¶ 10,550.]

Amendment Notes

Act Sec. 614(a)(1)(A)-(B) amended Code Sec. 953(e)(10) by striking "January 1, 2002" and inserting "January 1, 2007", and by striking "December 31, 2001" and inserting "December 31, 2006".

The above amendment applies to tax years beginning after December 31, 2001.

[¶ 5255] CODE SEC. 954. FOREIGN BASE COMPANY INCOME.

* * *

(h) SPECIAL RULE FOR INCOME DERIVED IN THE ACTIVE CONDUCT OF BANKING, FINANCING, OR SIMILAR BUSINESSES.—

* * *

(9) APPLICATION.—This subsection, subsection (c)(2)(C)(ii), and the last sentence of subsection (e)(2) shall apply only to taxable years of a foreign corporation beginning after December 31, 1998, and before *January 1, 2007*, and to taxable years of United States shareholders with or within which any such taxable year of such foreign corporation ends.

[CCH Explanation at ¶ 388. Committee Reports at ¶ 10,550.]

Amendment Notes

Act Sec. 614(a)(2) amended Code Sec. 954(h)(9) by striking "January 1, 2002" and inserting "January 1, 2007".

The above amendment applies to tax years beginning after December 31, 2001.

(i) SPECIAL RULE FOR INCOME DERIVED IN THE ACTIVE CONDUCT OF INSURANCE BUSINESS.—

* * *

(4) METHODS FOR DETERMINING UNEARNED PREMIUMS AND RESERVES.—For purposes of paragraph (2)(A)—

* * *

(B) *LIFE INSURANCE AND ANNUITY CONTRACTS.—*

(i) *IN GENERAL.—Except as provided in clause (ii), the amount of the reserve of a qualifying insurance company or qualifying insurance company branch for any life insurance or annuity contract shall be equal to the greater of—*

(I) *the net surrender value of such contract (as defined in section 807(e)(1)(A)), or*

(II) *the reserve determined under paragraph (5).*

(ii) *RULING REQUEST, ETC.—The amount of the reserve under clause (i) shall be the foreign statement reserve for the contract (less any catastrophe, deficiency, equalization, or similar reserves), if, pursuant to a ruling request submitted by the taxpayer or as provided in published guidance, the Secretary determines that the factors taken into account in determining the foreign statement reserve provide an appropriate means of measuring income.*

[CCH Explanation at ¶ 388. Committee Reports at ¶ 10,550.]

Amendment Notes

Act Sec. 614(b)(1) amended Code Sec. 954(i)(4)(B) to read as above. Prior to amendment, Code Sec. 954(i)(4)(B) read as follows:

(B) LIFE INSURANCE AND ANNUITY CONTRACTS.—The amount of the reserve of a qualifying insurance company or qualifying insurance company branch for any life insurance or annuity contract shall be equal to the greater of—

(i) the net surrender value of such contract (as defined in section 807(e)(1)(A)), or

(ii) the reserve determined under paragraph (5).

The above amendment applies to tax years beginning after December 31, 2001.

[¶ 5260] CODE SEC. 995. TAXATION OF DISC INCOME TO SHAREHOLDERS.

* * *

(b) DEEMED DISTRIBUTIONS.—

* * *

(3) TAXABLE INCOME ATTRIBUTABLE TO MILITARY PROPERTY.—

* * *

(B) MILITARY PROPERTY.—For purposes of subparagraph (A), the term "military property" means any property which is an arm, ammunition, or implement of war designated in the munitions list published pursuant to section 38 of the *Arms Export Control Act* (22 U.S.C. 2778).

* * *

[CCH Explanation at ¶ 30,050. Committee Reports at ¶ 10,320.]

Amendment Notes
Act Sec. 417(15) amended Code Sec. 995(b)(3)(B) by striking "International Security Assistance and Arms Export Control Act of 1976" and inserting "Arms Export Control Act".

The above amendment is effective on March 9, 2002.

[¶ 5265] CODE SEC. 1091. LOSS FROM WASH SALES OF STOCK OR SECURITIES.

* * *

(e) CERTAIN SHORT SALES OF STOCK OR *SECURITIES AND SECURITIES FUTURES CONTRACTS TO SELL*.—Rules similar to the rules of subsection (a) shall apply to any loss realized on the closing of a short sale of *(or the sale, exchange, or termination of a securities futures contract to sell)* stock or securities if, within a period beginning 30 days before the date of such closing and ending 30 days after such date—

(1) substantially identical stock or securities were sold, or

(2) another short sale of *(or securities futures contracts to sell)* substantially identical stock or securities was entered into.

For purposes of this subsection, the term "securities futures contract" has the meaning provided by section 1234B(c).

* * *

[CCH Explanation at ¶ 325. Committee Reports at ¶ 10,280.]

Amendment Notes
Act Sec. 412(d)(2)(A)-(D) amended Code Sec. 1091(e) by striking "SECURITIES.—" and inserting "SECURITIES AND SECURITIES FUTURES CONTRACTS TO SELL.—", by inserting "(or the sale, exchange, or termination of a securities futures contract to sell)" following "closing of a short sale of", by inserting in paragraph (2) "(or securities futures contracts to sell)" following "short sale of", and by adding at the end a new sentence to read as above.

The above amendment is effective as if included in the provision of the Community Renewal Tax Relief Act of 2000 (P.L. 106-554) to which it relates [effective on December 21, 2000.—CCH].

[¶ 5270] CODE SEC. 1221. CAPITAL ASSET DEFINED.

* * *

(b) DEFINITIONS AND SPECIAL RULES.—

(1) COMMODITIES DERIVATIVE FINANCIAL INSTRUMENTS.—For purposes of subsection (a)(6)—

* * *

(B) COMMODITIES DERIVATIVE FINANCIAL INSTRUMENT.—

(i) IN GENERAL.—The term "commodities derivative financial instrument" means any contract or financial instrument with respect to commodities (other than a share of stock in a corporation, a beneficial interest in a partnership or trust, a note, bond, debenture, or other evidence of indebtedness, or a section 1256 contract (as defined in section *1256(b)))*, the value or settlement price of which is calculated by or determined by reference to a specified index.

* * *

[CCH Explanation at ¶ 30,050. Committee Reports at ¶ 10,320.]

Amendment Notes
Act Sec. 417(20) amended Code Sec. 1221(b)(1)(B)(i) by striking "1256(b))" and inserting "1256(b)))".

The above amendment is effective on March 9, 2002.

[¶ 5275] CODE SEC. 1233. GAINS AND LOSSES FROM SHORT SALES.

* * *

(e) RULES FOR APPLICATION OF SECTION.—

* * *

(2) For purposes of subsections (b) and (d)—

(A) the term "property" includes only stocks and securities (including stocks and securities dealt with on a "when issued" basis), and commodity futures, which are capital assets in the hands of the taxpayer, but does not include any position to which section 1092(b) applies;

(B) in the case of futures transactions in any commodity on or subject to the rules of a board of trade or commodity exchange, a commodity future requiring delivery in 1 calendar month shall not be considered as property substantially identical to another commodity future requiring delivery in a different calendar month;

(C) in the case of a short sale of property by an individual, the term "taxpayer", in the application of this subsection and subsections (b) and (d), shall be read as "taxpayer or his spouse"; but an individual who is legally separated from the taxpayer under a decree of divorce or of separate maintenance shall not be considered as the spouse of the taxpayer;

(D) a securities futures contract (as defined in section 1234B) to acquire substantially identical property shall be treated as substantially identical property; and

(E) entering into a securities futures contract (as so defined) to sell shall be considered to be a short sale, and the settlement of such contract shall be considered to be the closing of such short sale.

* * *

[CCH Explanation at ¶ 325. Committee Reports at ¶ 10,280.]

Amendment Notes

Act Sec. 412(d)(3)(A) amended Code Sec. 1233(e)(2) by striking "and" at the end of subparagraph (C), by striking the period and inserting "; and" at the end of subparagraph (D), and inserting after subparagraph (D) a new subparagraph (E) to read as above.

The above amendment is effective as if included in the provision of the Community Renewal Tax Relief Act of 2000 (P.L. 106-554) to which it relates [effective on December 21, 2000.—CCH].

[¶ 5280] CODE SEC. 1234A. GAINS OR LOSSES FROM CERTAIN TERMINATIONS.

Gain or loss attributable to the cancellation, lapse, expiration, or other termination of—

(1) a right or obligation (other than a securities futures contract, as defined in section 1234B) with respect to property which is (or on acquisition would be) a capital asset in the hands of the taxpayer, or

(2) a section 1256 contract (as defined in section 1256) not described in paragraph (1) which is a capital asset in the hands of the taxpayer,

shall be treated as gain or loss from the sale of a capital asset. The preceding sentence shall not apply to the retirement of any debt instrument (whether or not through a trust or other participation arrangement).

[CCH Explanation at ¶ 325. Committee Reports at ¶ 10,280.]

Amendment Notes

Act Sec. 412(d)(1)(A) amended Code Sec. 1234A by inserting "or" after the comma at the end of paragraph (1), by striking "or" at the end of paragraph (2), and by striking paragraph (3). Prior to being stricken, Code Sec. 1234A (3) read as follows:

(3) a securities futures contract (as so defined) which is a capital asset in the hands of the taxpayer,

The above amendment is effective as if included in the provision of the Community Renewal Tax Relief Act of 2000 (P.L. 106-554) to which it relates [effective on December 21, 2000.—CCH].

[¶ 5282] CODE SEC. 1234B. GAINS OR LOSSES FROM SECURITIES FUTURES CONTRACTS.

(a) TREATMENT OF GAIN OR LOSS.—

(1) IN GENERAL.—Gain or loss attributable to the *sale, exchange, or termination* of a securities futures contract shall be considered gain or loss from the sale or exchange of property which has the same character as the property to which the contract relates has in the hands of the taxpayer (or would have in the hands of the taxpayer if acquired by the taxpayer).

* * *

[CCH Explanation at ¶ 325. Committee Reports at ¶ 10,280.]

Amendment Notes

Act Sec. 412(d)(1)(B)(i) amended Code Sec. 1234B(a)(1) by striking "sale or exchange" the first place it appears and inserting "sale, exchange, or termination".

The above amendment is effective as if included in the provision of the Community Renewal Tax Relief Act of 2000 (P.L. 106-554) to which it relates [effective on December 21, 2000.—CCH].

(b) SHORT-TERM GAINS AND LOSSES.—Except as provided in the regulations under section 1092(b) or this section, *or in section 1233*, if gain or loss on the *sale, exchange, or termination* of a securities futures contract to sell property is considered as gain or loss from the sale or exchange of a capital asset, such gain or loss shall be treated as short-term capital gain or loss.

* * *

[CCH Explanation at ¶ 325. Committee Reports at ¶ 10,280.]

Amendment Notes

Act Sec. 412(d)(1)(B)(i) amended Code Sec. 1234B(b) by striking "sale or exchange" the first place it appears and inserting "sale, exchange, or termination".

Act Sec. 412(d)(3)(B) amended Code Sec. 1234B(b) by inserting "or in section 1233," following "or this section,".

The above amendments are effective as if included in the provisions of the Community Renewal Tax Relief Act of 2000 (P.L. 106-554) to which they relate [effective on December 21, 2000.—CCH].

(f) CROSS REFERENCE.—

For special rules relating to dealer securities futures contracts, see section 1256.

[CCH Explanation at ¶ 325. Committee Reports at ¶ 10,280.]

Amendment Notes

Act Sec. 412(d)(1)(B)(ii) amended Code Sec. 1234B by adding at the end a new subsection (f) to read as above.

The above amendment is effective as if included in the provision of the Community Renewal Tax Relief Act of 2000 (P.L. 106-554) to which it relates [effective on December 21, 2000.—CCH].

[¶ 5285] CODE SEC. 1256. SECTION 1256 CONTRACTS MARKED TO MARKET.

* * *

(f) SPECIAL RULES.—

* * *

(5) *SPECIAL RULE RELATED TO LOSSES.—Section 1091 (relating to loss from wash sales of stock or securities) shall not apply to any loss taken into account by reason of paragraph (1) of subsection (a).*

* * *

[CCH Explanation at ¶ 330. Committee Reports at ¶ 10,320.]

Amendment Notes

Act Sec. 416(b)(1) amended Code Sec. 1256(f) by adding at the end a new paragraph (5) to read as above.

The above amendment is effective as if included in section 5075 of the Technical and Miscellaneous Reve-nue Act of 1988 (P.L. 100-647) [effective for sales made after November 10, 1988, in tax years ending after such date.—CCH].

[¶ 5290] CODE SEC. 1394. TAX-EXEMPT ENTERPRISE ZONE FACILITY BONDS.

* * *

(c) LIMITATION ON AMOUNT OF BONDS.—

* * *

(2) AGGREGATE ENTERPRISE ZONE FACILITY BOND BENEFIT.—For purposes of *paragraph (1)*, the aggregate amount of outstanding enterprise zone facility bonds allocable to any person shall be determined under rules similar to the rules of section 144(a)(10), taking into account only bonds to which subsection (a) applies.

* * *

[CCH Explanation at ¶ 30,050. Committee Reports at ¶ 10,320.]

Amendment Notes

Act Sec. 417(16) amended Code Sec. 1394(c)(2) by striking "subparagraph (A)" and inserting "paragraph (1)".

The above amendment is effective on March 9, 2002.

[¶ 5295] CODE SEC. 1397E. CREDIT TO HOLDERS OF QUALIFIED ZONE ACADEMY BONDS.

* * *

(e) LIMITATION ON AMOUNT OF BONDS DESIGNATED.—

(1) NATIONAL LIMITATION.—There is a national zone academy bond limitation for each calendar year. Such limitation is $400,000,000 for 1998, 1999, *2000, 2001, 2002, and 2003*, and, except as provided in paragraph (4), zero thereafter.

* * *

[CCH Explanation at ¶ 382. Committee Reports at ¶ 10,480.]

Amendment Notes

Act Sec. 608(a) amended Code Sec. 1397E(e)(1) by striking "2000, and 2001" and inserting "2000, 2001, 2002, and 2003".

The above amendment applies to obligations issued after March 9, 2002.

[¶ 5300] *CODE SEC. 1400L. TAX BENEFITS FOR NEW YORK LIBERTY ZONE.*

(a) EXPANSION OF WORK OPPORTUNITY TAX CREDIT.—

(1) IN GENERAL.—For purposes of section 51, a New York Liberty Zone business employee shall be treated as a member of a targeted group.

(2) NEW YORK LIBERTY ZONE BUSINESS EMPLOYEE.—For purposes of this subsection—

(A) IN GENERAL.—The term "New York Liberty Zone business employee" means, with respect to any period, any employee of a New York Liberty Zone business if substantially all the services performed during such period by such employee for such business are performed in the New York Liberty Zone.

(B) INCLUSION OF CERTAIN EMPLOYEES OUTSIDE THE NEW YORK LIBERTY ZONE.—

(i) IN GENERAL.—In the case of a New York Liberty Zone business described in subclause (II) of subparagraph (C)(i), the term "New York Liberty Zone business employee" includes any employee of such business (not described in subparagraph (A)) if substantially all the services performed during such period by such employee for such business are performed in the City of New York, New York.

(ii) LIMITATION.—The number of employees of such a business that are treated as New York Liberty Zone business employees on any day by reason of clause (i) shall not exceed the excess of—

(I) the number of employees of such business on September 11, 2001, in the New York Liberty Zone, over

(II) the number of New York Liberty Zone business employees (determined without regard to this subparagraph) of such business on the day to which the limitation is being applied.

The Secretary may require any trade or business to have the number determined under subclause (I) verified by the New York State Department of Labor.

(C) NEW YORK LIBERTY ZONE BUSINESS.—

(i) IN GENERAL.—The term "New York Liberty Zone business" means any trade or business which is—

(I) located in the New York Liberty Zone, or

(II) located in the City of New York, New York, outside the New York Liberty Zone, as a result of the physical destruction or damage of such place of business by the September 11, 2001, terrorist attack.

(ii) CREDIT NOT ALLOWED FOR LARGE BUSINESSES.—The term "New York Liberty Zone business" shall not include any trade or business for any taxable year if such trade or business employed an average of more than 200 employees on business days during the taxable year.

(D) SPECIAL RULES FOR DETERMINING AMOUNT OF CREDIT.—For purposes of applying subpart F of part IV of subchapter B of this chapter to wages paid or incurred to any New York Liberty Zone business employee—

(i) section 51(a) shall be applied by substituting "qualified wages" for "qualified first-year wages",

(ii) the rules of section 52 shall apply for purposes of determining the number of employees under subparagraph (B),

(iii) subsections (c)(4) and (i)(2) of section 51 shall not apply, and

(iv) in determining qualified wages, the following shall apply in lieu of section 51(b):

(I) QUALIFIED WAGES.—The term "qualified wages" means wages paid or incurred by the employer to individuals who are New York Liberty Zone business employees of such employer for work performed during calendar year 2002 or 2003.

(II) ONLY FIRST $6,000 OF WAGES PER CALENDAR YEAR TAKEN INTO ACCOUNT.—The amount of the qualified wages which may be taken into account with respect to any individual shall not exceed $6,000 per calendar year.

(b) SPECIAL ALLOWANCE FOR CERTAIN PROPERTY ACQUIRED AFTER SEPTEMBER 10, 2001.—

(1) ADDITIONAL ALLOWANCE.—In the case of any qualified New York Liberty Zone property—

(A) the depreciation deduction provided by section 167(a) for the taxable year in which such property is placed in service shall include an allowance equal to 30 percent of the adjusted basis of such property, and

(B) the adjusted basis of the qualified New York Liberty Zone property shall be reduced by the amount of such deduction before computing the amount otherwise allowable as a depreciation deduction under this chapter for such taxable year and any subsequent taxable year.

(2) QUALIFIED NEW YORK LIBERTY ZONE PROPERTY.—For purposes of this subsection—

(A) IN GENERAL.—The term "qualified New York Liberty Zone property" means property—

(i)(I) which is described in section 168(k)(2)(A)(i), or

(II) which is nonresidential real property, or residential rental property, which is described in subparagraph (B),

(ii) substantially all of the use of which is in the New York Liberty Zone and is in the active conduct of a trade or business by the taxpayer in such Zone,

(iii) the original use of which in the New York Liberty Zone commences with the taxpayer after September 10, 2001,

(iv) which is acquired by the taxpayer by purchase (as defined in section 179(d)) after September 10, 2001, but only if no written binding contract for the acquisition was in effect before September 11, 2001, and

(v) which is placed in service by the taxpayer on or before the termination date.

The term "termination date" means December 31, 2006 (December 31, 2009, in the case of nonresidential real property and residential rental property).

(B) ELIGIBLE REAL PROPERTY.—Nonresidential real property or residential rental property is described in this subparagraph only to the extent it rehabilitates real property damaged, or replaces real property destroyed or condemned, as a result of the September 11, 2001, terrorist attack. For purposes of the preceding sentence, property shall be treated as replacing real property destroyed or condemned if, as part of an integrated plan, such property replaces real property which is included in a continuous area which includes real property destroyed or condemned.

(C) EXCEPTIONS.—

(i) 30 PERCENT ADDITIONAL ALLOWANCE PROPERTY.—Such term shall not include property to which section 168(k) applies.

(ii) ALTERNATIVE DEPRECIATION PROPERTY.—The term "qualified New York Liberty Zone property" shall not include any property described in section 168(k)(2)(C)(i).

(iii) QUALIFIED NEW YORK LIBERTY ZONE LEASEHOLD IMPROVEMENT PROPERTY.—Such term shall not include any qualified New York Liberty Zone leasehold improvement property.

(iv) ELECTION OUT.—For purposes of this subsection, rules similar to the rules of section 168(k)(2)(C)(iii) shall apply.

(D) SPECIAL RULES.—For purposes of this subsection, rules similar to the rules of section 168(k)(2)(D) shall apply, except that clause (i) thereof shall be applied without regard to "and before September 11, 2004".

(E) ALLOWANCE AGAINST ALTERNATIVE MINIMUM TAX.—For purposes of this subsection, rules similar to the rules of section 168(k)(2)(F) shall apply.

(c) 5-YEAR RECOVERY PERIOD FOR DEPRECIATION OF CERTAIN LEASEHOLD IMPROVEMENTS.—

(1) IN GENERAL.—For purposes of section 168, the term "5-year property" includes any qualified New York Liberty Zone leasehold improvement property.

(2) QUALIFIED NEW YORK LIBERTY ZONE LEASEHOLD IMPROVEMENT PROPERTY.—For purposes of this section, the term "qualified New York Liberty Zone leasehold improvement property" means qualified leasehold improvement property (as defined in section 168(k)(3)) if—

(A) such building is located in the New York Liberty Zone,

Code Sec. 1400L(c) ¶ 5300

(B) such improvement is placed in service after September 10, 2001, and before January 1, 2007, and

(C) no written binding contract for such improvement was in effect before September 11, 2001.

(3) REQUIREMENT TO USE STRAIGHT LINE METHOD.—The applicable depreciation method under section 168 shall be the straight line method in the case of qualified New York Liberty Zone leasehold improvement property.

(4) 9-YEAR RECOVERY PERIOD UNDER ALTERNATIVE SYSTEM.—For purposes of section 168(g), the class life of qualified New York Liberty Zone leasehold improvement property shall be 9 years.

(d) TAX-EXEMPT BOND FINANCING.—

(1) IN GENERAL.—For purposes of this title, any qualified New York Liberty Bond shall be treated as an exempt facility bond.

(2) QUALIFIED NEW YORK LIBERTY BOND.—For purposes of this subsection, the term "qualified New York Liberty Bond" means any bond issued as part of an issue if—

(A) 95 percent or more of the net proceeds (as defined in section 150(a)(3)) of such issue are to be used for qualified project costs,

(B) such bond is issued by the State of New York or any political subdivision thereof,

(C) the Governor or the Mayor designates such bond for purposes of this section, and

(D) such bond is issued after the the date of the enactment of this section and before January 1, 2005.

(3) LIMITATIONS ON AMOUNT OF BONDS.—

(A) AGGREGATE AMOUNT DESIGNATED.—The maximum aggregate face amount of bonds which may be designated under this subsection shall not exceed $8,000,000,000, of which not to exceed $4,000,000,000 may be designated by the Governor and not to exceed $4,000,000,000 may be designated by the Mayor.

(B) SPECIFIC LIMITATIONS.—The aggregate face amount of bonds issued which are to be used for—

(i) costs for property located outside the New York Liberty Zone shall not exceed $2,000,000,000,

(ii) residential rental property shall not exceed $1,600,000,000, and

(iii) costs with respect to property used for retail sales of tangible property and functionally related and subordinate property shall not exceed $800,000,000.

The limitations under clauses (i), (ii), and (iii) shall be allocated proportionately between the bonds designated by the Governor and the bonds designated by the Mayor in proportion to the respective amounts of bonds designated by each.

(C) MOVABLE PROPERTY.—No bonds shall be issued which are to be used for movable fixtures and equipment.

(4) QUALIFIED PROJECT COSTS.—For purposes of this subsection—

(A) IN GENERAL.—The term "qualified project costs" means the cost of acquisition, construction, reconstruction, and renovation of—

(i) nonresidential real property and residential rental property (including fixed tenant improvements associated with such property) located in the New York Liberty Zone, and

(ii) public utility property (as defined in section 168(i)(10)) located in the New York Liberty Zone.

(B) COSTS FOR CERTAIN PROPERTY OUTSIDE ZONE INCLUDED.—Such term includes the cost of acquisition, construction, reconstruction, and renovation of nonresidential real property (including fixed tenant improvements associated with such property) located outside the New York Liberty Zone but within the City of New York, New York, if such property is part of a project which consists of at least 100,000 square feet of usable office or other commercial space located in a single building or multiple adjacent buildings.

(5) SPECIAL RULES.—In applying this title to any qualified New York Liberty Bond, the following modifications shall apply:

(A) Section 146 (relating to volume cap) shall not apply.

(B) Section 147(d) (relating to acquisition of existing property not permitted) shall be applied by substituting "50 percent" for "15 percent" each place it appears.

(C) Section 148(f)(4)(C) (relating to exception from rebate for certain proceeds to be used to finance construction expenditures) shall apply to the available construction proceeds of bonds issued under this section.

(D) Repayments of principal on financing provided by the issue—

(i) may not be used to provide financing, and

(ii) must be used not later than the close of the 1st semiannual period beginning after the date of the repayment to redeem bonds which are part of such issue.

The requirement of clause (ii) shall be treated as met with respect to amounts received within 10 years after the date of issuance of the issue (or, in the case of a refunding bond, the date of issuance of the original bond) if such amounts are used by the close of such 10 years to redeem bonds which are part of such issue.

(E) Section 57(a)(5) shall not apply.

(6) Separate Issue Treatment of Portions of an Issue.—This subsection shall not apply to the portion of an issue which (if issued as a separate issue) would be treated as a qualified bond or as a bond that is not a private activity bond (determined without regard to paragraph (1)), if the issuer elects to so treat such portion.

(e) Advance Refundings of Certain Tax-Exempt Bonds.—

(1) In General.—With respect to a bond described in paragraph (2) issued as part of an issue 90 percent (95 percent in the case of a bond described in paragraph (2)(C)) or more of the net proceeds (as defined in section 150(a)(3)) of which were used to finance facilities located within the City of New York, New York (or property which is functionally related and subordinate to facilities located within the City of New York for the furnishing of water), one additional advanced refunding after the date of the enactment of this section and before January 1, 2005, shall be allowed under the applicable rules of section 149(d) if—

(A) the Governor or the Mayor designates the advance refunding bond for purposes of this subsection, and

(B) the requirements of paragraph (4) are met.

(2) Bonds Described.—A bond is described in this paragraph if such bond was outstanding on September 11, 2001, and is—

(A) a State or local bond (as defined in section 103(c)(1)) which is a general obligation of the City of New York, New York,

(B) a State or local bond (as so defined) other than a private activity bond (as defined in section 141(a)) issued by the New York Municipal Water Finance Authority or the Metropolitan Transportation Authority of the State of New York, or

(C) a qualified 501(c)(3) bond (as defined in section 145(a)) which is a qualified hospital bond (as defined in section 145(c)) issued by or on behalf of the State of New York or the City of New York, New York.

(3) Aggregate Limit.—For purposes of paragraph (1), the maximum aggregate face amount of bonds which may be designated under this subsection by the Governor shall not exceed $4,500,000,000 and the maximum aggregate face amount of bonds which may be designated under this subsection by the Mayor shall not exceed $4,500,000,000.

(4) Additional Requirements.—The requirements of this paragraph are met with respect to any advance refunding of a bond described in paragraph (2) if—

(A) no advance refundings of such bond would be allowed under any provision of law after September 11, 2001,

(B) the advance refunding bond is the only other outstanding bond with respect to the refunded bond, and

(C) the requirements of section 148 are met with respect to all bonds issued under this subsection.

(f) Increase in Expensing Under Section 179.—

(1) *In General.*—For purposes of section 179—

(A) the limitation under section 179(b)(1) shall be increased by the lesser of—

(i) $35,000, or

(ii) the cost of section 179 property which is qualified New York Liberty Zone property placed in service during the taxable year, and

(B) the amount taken into account under section 179(b)(2) with respect to any section 179 property which is qualified New York Liberty Zone property shall be 50 percent of the cost thereof.

(2) *Qualified New York Liberty Zone Property.*—For purposes of this subsection, the term "qualified New York Liberty Zone property" has the meaning given such term by subsection (b)(2).

(3) *Recapture.*—Rules similar to the rules under section 179(d)(10) shall apply with respect to any qualified New York Liberty Zone property which ceases to be used in the New York Liberty Zone.

(g) *Extension of Replacement Period for Nonrecognition of Gain.*—Notwithstanding subsections (g) and (h) of section 1033, clause (i) of section 1033(a)(2)(B) shall be applied by substituting "5 years" for "2 years" with respect to property which is compulsorily or involuntarily converted as a result of the terrorist attacks on September 11, 2001, in the New York Liberty Zone but only if substantially all of the use of the replacement property is in the City of New York, New York.

(h) *New York Liberty Zone.*—For purposes of this section, the term "New York Liberty Zone" means the area located on or south of Canal Street, East Broadway (east of its intersection with Canal Street), or Grand Street (east of its intersection with East Broadway) in the Borough of Manhattan in the City of New York, New York.

(i) *References to Governor and Mayor.*—For purposes of this section, the terms "Governor" and "Mayor" mean the Governor of the State of New York and the Mayor of the City of New York, New York, respectively.

[CCH Explanation at ¶ 405, ¶ 410, ¶ 415, ¶ 420, ¶ 425, ¶ 430 and ¶ 435. Committee Reports at ¶ 10,100, ¶ 10,110, ¶ 10,120, ¶ 10,130, ¶ 10,140, ¶ 10,150 and ¶ 10,160.]

Amendment Notes

The above amendment is effective on March 9, 2002.

Act Sec. 301(a) amended chapter 1 by adding at the end a new subchapter Y (Code Sec. 1400L) to read as above.

[¶ 5305] CODE SEC. 2016. RECOVERY OF TAXES CLAIMED AS CREDIT.

[Caution: Code Sec. 2016, below, as amended by P.L. 107-16 and Act Sec. 411(h), applies to estates of decedents dying, and generation-skipping transfers, after December 31, 2004.—CCH.]

If any tax claimed as a credit under section 2014 is recovered from any foreign country, the executor, or any other person or persons recovering such amount, shall give notice of such recovery to the Secretary at such time and in such manner as may be required by regulations prescribed by him, and the Secretary shall (despite the provisions of section 6501) redetermine the amount of the tax under this chapter and the amount, if any, of the tax due on such redetermination, shall be paid by the executor or such person or persons, as the case may be, on notice and demand. No interest shall be assessed or collected on any amount of tax due on any redetermination by the Secretary resulting from a refund to the executor of tax claimed as a credit under section 2014, for any period before the receipt of such refund, except to the extent interest was paid by the foreign country on such refund.

[CCH Explanation at ¶ 285. Committee Reports at ¶ 10,260.]

Amendment Notes

Act Sec. 411(h) amended Code Sec. 2016 by striking "any State, any possession of the United States, or the District of Columbia," following "any foreign country,".

The above amendment is effective as if included in the provision of the Economic Growth and Tax Relief Reconciliation Act of 2001 (P.L. 107-16) to which it relates [applicable to estates of decedents dying, and generation-skipping transfers, after December 31, 2004.—CCH].

[¶ 5310] CODE SEC. 2101. TAX IMPOSED.

* * *

(b) COMPUTATION OF TAX.—The tax imposed by this section shall be the amount equal to the excess (if any) of—

(1) a tentative tax computed under section 2001(c) on the sum of—

(A) the amount of the taxable estate, and

(B) the amount of the adjusted taxable gifts, over

(2) a tentative tax computed under section 2001(c) on the amount of the adjusted taxable gifts.

* * *

[CCH Explanation at ¶ 282. Committee Reports at ¶ 10,260.]

Amendment Notes

Act Sec. 411(g)(2) amended Code Sec. 2101(b) by striking the last sentence. Prior to being stricken, the last sentence of Code Sec. 2101(b) read as follows:

For purposes of the preceding sentence, there shall be appropriate adjustments in the application of section 2001(c)(2) to reflect the difference between the amount of the credit provided under section 2102(c) and the amount of the credit provided under section 2010.

The above amendment is effective as if included in the provision of the Economic Growth and Tax Relief Reconciliation Act of 2001 (P.L. 107-16) to which it relates [applicable to estates of decedents dying and gifts made after December 31, 2001.—CCH].

[¶ 5315] CODE SEC. 2511. TRANSFERS IN GENERAL.

* * *

[Caution: Code Sec. 2511(c), below, as added by P.L. 107-16 and amended by Act Sec. 411(g)(1), applies to gifts made after December 31, 2009.—CCH.]

(c) TREATMENT OF CERTAIN TRANSFERS IN TRUST.—Notwithstanding any other provision of this section and except as provided in regulations, a transfer in trust shall be treated as a *transfer of property by gift*, unless the trust is treated as wholly owned by the donor or the donor's spouse under subpart E of part I of subchapter J of chapter 1.

[CCH Explanation at ¶ 280. Committee Reports at ¶ 10,260.]

Amendment Notes

Act Sec. 411(g)(1) amended Code Sec. 2511(c) by striking "taxable gift under section 2503," and inserting "transfer of property by gift,".

The above amendment is effective as if included in the provision of the Economic Growth and Tax Relief Reconciliation Act of 2001 (P.L. 107-16) to which it relates [applicable to gifts made after December 31, 2009.—CCH].

[¶ 5320] CODE SEC. 3304. APPROVAL OF STATE LAWS.

(a) REQUIREMENTS.—The Secretary of Labor shall approve any State law submitted to him, within 30 days of such submission, which he finds provides that—

* * *

(4) all money withdrawn from the unemployment fund of the State shall be used solely in the payment of unemployment compensation, exclusive of expenses of administration, and for refunds of sums erroneously paid into such fund and refunds paid in accordance with the provisions of section 3305(b); except that—

(A) an amount equal to the amount of employee payments into the unemployment fund of a State may be used in the payment of cash benefits to individuals with respect to their disability, exclusive of expenses of administration;

(B) the amounts specified by section 903(c)(2) *or 903(d)(4)* of the Social Security Act may, subject to the conditions prescribed in such section, be used for expenses incurred by the State for administration of its unemployment compensation law and public employment offices;

(C) nothing in this paragraph shall be construed to prohibit deducting an amount from unemployment compensation otherwise payable to an individual and using the amount so deducted to pay for health insurance, or the withholding of Federal, State, or local individual income tax, if the individual elected to have such deduction made and such deduction was made under a program approved by the Secretary of Labor;

(D) amounts may be deducted from unemployment benefits and used to repay overpayments as provided in section 303(g) of the Social Security Act;

(E) amounts may be withdrawn for the payment of short-time compensation under a plan approved by the Secretary of Labor; and

(F) amounts may be withdrawn for the payment of allowances under a self-employed assistance program (as defined in section 3306(t));

* * *

[CCH Explanation at ¶ 205. Committee Reports at ¶ 10,060.]

Amendment Notes

Act Sec. 209(d)(1) amended Code Sec. 3304(a)(4)(B) by inserting "or 903(d)(4)" before "of the Social Security Act".

The above amendment is effective on March 9, 2002. For a special rule, see Act Sec. 209(e), below.

Act Sec. 209(e) provides:

(e) REGULATIONS.—The Secretary of Labor may prescribe any operating instructions or regulations necessary to carry out this section and the amendments made by this section.

[¶ 5325] CODE SEC. 3306. DEFINITIONS.

* * *

(f) UNEMPLOYMENT FUND.—For purposes of this chapter, the term "unemployment fund" means a special fund, established under a State law and administered by a State agency, for the payment of compensation. Any sums standing to the account of the State agency in the Unemployment Trust Fund established by section 904 of the Social Security Act, as amended (42 U. S. C. 1104), shall be deemed to be a part of the unemployment fund of the State, and no sums paid out of the Unemployment Trust Fund to such State agency shall cease to be a part of the unemployment fund of the State until expended by such State agency. An unemployment fund shall be deemed to be maintained during a taxable year only if throughout such year, or such portion of the year as the unemployment fund was in existence, no part of the moneys of such fund was expended for any purpose other than the payment of compensation (exclusive of expenses of administration) and for refunds of sums erroneously paid into such fund and refunds paid in accordance with the provisions of section 3305(b); except that—

* * *

(2) the amounts specified by section 903(c)(2) *or 903(d)(4)* of the Social Security Act may, subject to the conditions prescribed in such section, be used for expenses incurred by the State for administration of its unemployment compensation law and public employment offices;

* * *

[CCH Explanation at ¶ 205. Committee Reports at ¶ 10,060.]

Amendment Notes

Act Sec. 209(d)(1) amended Code Sec. 3306(f)(2) by inserting "or 903(d)(4)" before "of the Social Security Act".

The above amendment is effective on March 9, 2002. For a special rule, see Act Sec. 209(e), below.

Act Sec. 209(e) provides:

(e) REGULATIONS.—The Secretary of Labor may prescribe any operating instructions or regulations necessary to carry out this section and the amendments made by this section.

[¶ 5330] CODE SEC. 4101. REGISTRATION AND BOND.

* * *

(e) *[Repealed.]*

[CCH Explanation at ¶ 392. Committee Reports at ¶ 10,560.]

Amendment Notes

Act Sec. 615(a) repealed Code Sec. 4101(e). Prior to repeal, Code Sec. 4101(e) read as follows:

(e) CERTAIN APPROVED TERMINALS OF REGISTERED PERSONS REQUIRED TO OFFER DYED DIESEL FUEL AND KEROSENE FOR NONTAXABLE PURPOSES.—

(1) IN GENERAL.—A terminal for kerosene or diesel fuel may not be an approved facility for storage of non-tax-paid

diesel fuel or kerosene under this section unless the operator of such terminal offers such fuel in a dyed form for removal for nontaxable use in accordance with section 4082(a).

(2) EXCEPTION.—Paragraph (1) shall not apply to any terminal exclusively providing aviation-grade kerosene by pipeline to an airport.

The above amendment is effective on January 1, 2002.

[¶ 5335] *CODE SEC. 4980E. FAILURE OF EMPLOYER TO MAKE COMPARABLE ARCHER MSA CONTRIBUTIONS.*

* * *

[CCH Explanation at ¶ 30,050. Committee Reports at ¶ 10,320.]

Amendment Notes

Act Sec. 417(17)(A) amended the section heading for Code Sec. 4980E to read as above. Prior to amendment, the section heading for Code Sec. 4980E read as follows:

SEC. 4980E. FAILURE OF EMPLOYER TO MAKE COMPARABLE MEDICAL SAVINGS ACCOUNT CONTRIBUTIONS.

The above amendment is effective on March 9, 2002.

[¶ 5338] CODE SEC. 4980F. FAILURE OF APPLICABLE PLANS REDUCING BENEFIT ACCRUALS TO SATISFY NOTICE REQUIREMENTS.

* * *

(e) NOTICE REQUIREMENTS FOR PLANS SIGNIFICANTLY REDUCING BENEFIT ACCRUALS.—

(1) IN GENERAL.—If an applicable pension plan is amended to provide for a significant reduction in the rate of future benefit accrual, the plan administrator shall provide *the notice described in paragraph (2)* to each applicable individual (and to each employee organization representing applicable individuals).

* * *

[CCH Explanation at ¶ 545. Committee Reports at ¶ 10,270.]

Amendment Notes

Act Sec. 411(u)(1)(A) amended Code Sec. 4980F(e)(1) by striking "written notice" and inserting "the notice described in paragraph (2)".

The above amendment is effective as if included in the provision of the Economic Growth and Tax Relief Rec-

onciliation Act of 2001 (P.L. 107-16) to which it relates [generally applicable to plan amendments taking effect on or after June 7, 2001.—CCH].

(f) DEFINITIONS AND SPECIAL RULES.—For purposes of this section—

* * *

(2) APPLICABLE PENSION PLAN.—The term "applicable pension plan" means—

(A) *any defined benefit plan described in section 401(a) which includes a trust exempt from tax under section 501(a),* or

(B) an individual account plan which is subject to the funding standards of section 412.

Such term shall not include a governmental plan (within the meaning of section 414(d)) or a church plan (within the meaning of section 414(e)) with respect to which the election provided by section 410(d) has not been made.

(3) EARLY RETIREMENT.—A plan amendment which eliminates or reduces any early retirement benefit or retirement-type subsidy (within the meaning of section 411(d)(6)(B)(i)) shall be treated as having the effect of reducing the rate of future benefit accrual.

* * *

[CCH Explanation at ¶ 545. Committee Reports at ¶ 10,270.]

Amendment Notes

Act Sec. 411(u)(1)(B) amended Code Sec. 4980F(f)(2)(A) to read as above. Prior to amendment, Code Sec. 4980F(f)(2)(A) read as follows:

(A) any defined benefit plan, or

Act Sec. 411(u)(1)(C) amended Code Sec. 4980F(f)(3) by striking "significantly" preceding "reduces" and "reducing", respectively, both places it appears.

The above amendments are effective as if included in the provisions of the Economic Growth and Tax Relief Reconciliation Act of 2001 (P.L. 107-16) to which they relate [generally applicable to plan amendments taking effect on or after June 7, 2001.—CCH].

[¶ 5340] CODE SEC. 6103. CONFIDENTIALITY AND DISCLOSURE OF RETURNS AND RETURN INFORMATION.

* * *

(l) DISCLOSURE OF RETURNS AND RETURN INFORMATION FOR PURPOSES OTHER THAN TAX ADMINISTRATION.—

* * *

(8) DISCLOSURE OF CERTAIN RETURN INFORMATION BY SOCIAL SECURITY ADMINISTRATION TO *FEDERAL, STATE, AND LOCAL* CHILD SUPPORT ENFORCEMENT AGENCIES.—

(A) IN GENERAL.—Upon written request, the Commissioner of Social Security shall disclose directly to officers and employees of a *Federal or* State or local child support enforcement agency return information from returns with respect to social security account numbers[,] net earnings from self-employment (as defined in section 1402), wages (as defined in section 3121(a) or 3401(a)), and payments of retirement income which have been disclosed to the Social Security Administration as provided by paragraph (1) or (5) of this subsection.

* * *

[CCH Explanation at ¶ 255. Committee Reports at ¶ 10,320.]

Code Sec. 6103(l)   ¶ 5340

Amendment Notes

Act Sec. 416(c)(1)(A)-(B) amended the heading for Code Sec. 6103(l)(8) by striking "STATE AND LOCAL" and inserting "FEDERAL, STATE, AND LOCAL", and in subparagraph (A), by inserting "Federal or" before "State or local".

The above amendment is effective on March 9, 2002.

[¶ 5345] CODE SEC. 6105. CONFIDENTIALITY OF INFORMATION ARISING UNDER TREATY OBLIGATIONS.

* * *

(c) DEFINITIONS.—For purposes of this section—

(1) TAX CONVENTION INFORMATION.—The term "tax convention information" means any—

(A) agreement entered into with the competent authority of one or more foreign governments pursuant to a tax convention,

(B) application for relief under a tax convention,

(C) background information related to such agreement or application,

(D) document implementing such agreement, and

(E) other information exchanged pursuant to a tax convention which is treated as confidential or secret under the tax convention.

* * *

[CCH Explanation at ¶ 30,050. Committee Reports at ¶ 10,320.]

Amendment Notes

Act Sec. 417(18) amended Code Sec. 6105(c)(1) by striking "any" preceding "background" in subparagraph (C) and by striking "any" preceding "other information" in subparagraph (E).

The above amendment is effective on March 9, 2002.

[¶ 5350] CODE SEC. 6224. PARTICIPATION IN ADMINISTRATIVE PROCEEDINGS; WAIVERS; AGREEMENTS.

* * *

(c) SETTLEMENT AGREEMENT.—In the absence of a showing of fraud, malfeasance, or misrepresentation of fact—

(1) BINDS ALL PARTIES.—A settlement agreement between the Secretary *or the Attorney General (or his delegate)* and 1 or more partners in a partnership with respect to the determination of partnership items for any partnership taxable year shall (except as otherwise provided in such agreement) be binding on all parties to such agreement with respect to the determination of partnership items for such partnership taxable year. An indirect partner is bound by any such agreement entered into by the pass-thru partner unless the indirect partner has been identified as provided in section 6223(c)(3).

(2) OTHER PARTNERS HAVE RIGHT TO ENTER INTO CONSISTENT AGREEMENTS.—If the Secretary *or the Attorney General (or his delegate)* enters into a settlement agreement with any partner with respect to partnership items for any partnership taxable year, the Secretary *or the Attorney General (or his delegate)* shall offer to any other partner who so requests settlement terms for the partnership taxable year which are consistent with those contained in such settlement agreement. Except in the case of an election under paragraph (2) or (3) of section 6223(e) to have a settlement agreement described in this paragraph apply, this paragraph shall apply with respect to a settlement agreement entered into with a partner before notice of a final partnership administrative adjustment is mailed to the tax matters partner only if such other partner makes the request before the expiration of 150 days after the day on which such notice is mailed to the tax matters partner.

* * *

[CCH Explanation at ¶ 355. Committee Reports at ¶ 10,320.]

Amendment Notes

Act Sec. 416(d)(1)(A) amended Code Sec. 6224(c)(1)-(2) by inserting "or the Attorney General (or his delegate)" after "Secretary" each place it appears.

The above amendment applies with respect to settlement agreements entered into after March 9, 2002.

[¶ 5355] CODE SEC. 6227. ADMINISTRATIVE ADJUSTMENT REQUESTS.

* * *

(d) OTHER REQUESTS.—If any partner files a request for an administrative adjustment (other than a request described in *subsection (c)*), the Secretary may—

(1) process the request in the same manner as a claim for credit or refund with respect to items which are not partnership items,

(2) assess any additional tax that would result from the requested adjustments,

(3) mail to the partner, under subparagraph (A) of section 6231(b)(1) (relating to items becoming nonpartnership items), a notice that all partnership items of the partner for the partnership taxable year to which such request relates shall be treated as nonpartnership items, or

(4) conduct a partnership proceeding.

* * *

[CCH Explanation at ¶ 30,050. Committee Reports at ¶ 10,320.]

Amendment Notes

Act Sec. 417(19)(A) amended Code Sec. 6227(d) by striking "subsection (b)" and inserting "subsection (c)".

The above amendment is effective on March 9, 2002.

[¶ 5360] CODE SEC. 6228. JUDICIAL REVIEW WHERE ADMINISTRATIVE ADJUSTMENT REQUEST IS NOT ALLOWED IN FULL.

(a) REQUEST ON BEHALF OF PARTNERSHIP.—

(1) IN GENERAL.—If any part of an administrative adjustment request filed by the tax matters partner under *subsection (c) of section 6227* is not allowed by the Secretary, the tax matters partner may file a petition for an adjustment with respect to the partnership items to which such part of the request relates with—

* * *

(3) COORDINATION WITH ADMINISTRATIVE ADJUSTMENT.—

(A) ADMINISTRATIVE ADJUSTMENT BEFORE FILING OF PETITION.—No petition may be filed under this subsection after the Secretary mails to the tax matters partner a notice of final partnership administrative adjustment for the partnership taxable year to which the request under section 6227 relates.

* * *

[CCH Explanation at ¶ 30,050. Committee Reports at ¶ 10,320.]

Amendment Notes

Act Sec. 417(19)(B)(i) amended Code Sec. 6228(a)(1) by striking "subsection (b) of section 6227" and inserting "subsection (c) of section 6227".

Act Sec. 417(19)(B)(ii) amended Code Sec. 6228(a)(3)(A) by striking "subsection (b) of" preceding "section 6227".

The above amendments are effective on March 9, 2002.

(b) OTHER REQUESTS.—

(1) NOTICE PROVIDING THAT ITEMS BECOME NONPARTNERSHIP ITEMS.—If the Secretary mails to a partner, under subparagraph (A) of section 6231(b)(1) (relating to items ceasing to be partnership items), a notice that all partnership items of the partner for the partnership taxable year to which a timely request for administrative adjustment under *subsection (d) of section 6227* relates shall be treated as nonpartnership items—

(A) such request shall be treated as a claim for credit or refund of an overpayment attributable to nonpartnership items, and

(B) the partner may bring an action under section 7422 with respect to such claim at any time within 2 years of the mailing of such notice.

(2) OTHER CASES.—

(A) IN GENERAL.—If the Secretary fails to allow any part of an administrative adjustment request filed under *subsection (d) of section 6227* by a partner and paragraph (1) does not apply—

(i) such partner may, pursuant to section 7422, begin a civil action for refund of any amount due by reason of the adjustments described in such part of the request, and

Code Sec. 6228(b)   ¶ 5360

(ii) on the beginning of such civil action, the partnership items of such partner for the partnership taxable year to which such part of such request relates shall be treated as nonpartnership items for purposes of this subchapter.

* * *

[CCH Explanation at ¶ 30,050. Committee Reports at ¶ 10,320.]

Amendment Notes	
Act Sec. 417(19)(B)(iii) amended Code Sec. 6228(b)(1) and Code Sec. 6228(b)(2)(A) by striking "subsection (c) of section 6227" and inserting "subsection (d) of section 6227".	The above amendment is effective on March 9, 2002.

[¶ 5365] CODE SEC. 6229. PERIOD OF LIMITATIONS FOR MAKING ASSESSMENTS.

* * *

(f) SPECIAL RULES.—

* * *

(2) SPECIAL RULE FOR PARTIAL SETTLEMENT AGREEMENTS.—If a partner enters into a settlement agreement with the Secretary *or the Attorney General (or his delegate)* with respect to the treatment of some of the partnership items in dispute for a partnership taxable year but other partnership items for such year remain in dispute, the period of limitations for assessing any tax attributable to the settled items shall be determined as if such agreement had not been entered into.

* * *

[CCH Explanation at ¶ 355. Committee Reports at ¶ 10,320.]

Amendment Notes	
Act Sec. 416(d)(1)(B) amended Code Sec. 6229(f)(2) by inserting "or the Attorney General (or his delegate)" after "Secretary".	The above amendment applies with respect to settlement agreements entered into after March 9, 2002.

[¶ 5370] CODE SEC. 6231. DEFINITIONS AND SPECIAL RULES.

* * *

(b) ITEMS CEASE TO BE PARTNERSHIP ITEMS IN CERTAIN CASES.—

(1) IN GENERAL.—For purposes of this subchapter, the partnership items of a partner for a partnership taxable year shall become nonpartnership items as of the date—

(A) the Secretary mails to such partner a notice that such items shall be treated as nonpartnership items,

(B) the partner files suit under section 6228(b) after the Secretary fails to allow an administrative adjustment request with respect to any of such items,

(C) the Secretary *or the Attorney General (or his delegate)* enters into a settlement agreement with the partner with respect to such items, or

(D) such change occurs under subsection (e) of section 6223 (relating to effect of Secretary's failure to provide notice) or under subsection (c) of this section.

(2) CIRCUMSTANCES IN WHICH NOTICE IS PERMITTED.—The Secretary may mail the notice referred to in subparagraph (A) of paragraph (1) to a partner with respect to partnership items for a partnership taxable year only if—

(A) such partner—

(i) has complied with subparagraph (B) of section 6222(b)(1) (relating to notification of inconsistent treatment) with respect to one or more of such items, and

(ii) has not, as of the date on which the Secretary mails the notice, filed a request for administrative adjustments which would make the partner's treatment of the item or items with respect to which the partner complied with subparagraph (B) of section 6222(b)(1) consistent with the treatment of such item or items on the partnership return, or

(B)(i) such partner has filed a request under *section 6227(d)* for administrative adjustment of one or more of such items, and

(ii) the adjustments requested would not make such partner's treatment of such items consistent with the treatment of such items on the partnership return.

* * *

[CCH Explanation at ¶ 355 and ¶ 30,050. Committee Reports at ¶ 10,320.]

Amendment Notes

Act Sec. 416(d)(1)(C) amended Code Sec. 6231(b)(1)(C) by inserting "or the Attorney General (or his delegate)" after "Secretary".

The above amendment applies with respect to settlement agreements entered into after March 9, 2002.

Act Sec. 417(19)(C) amended Code Sec. 6231(b)(2)(B)(i) by striking "section 6227(c)" and inserting "section 6227(d)".

The above amendment is effective on March 9, 2002.

[¶ 5375] CODE SEC. 6234. DECLARATORY JUDGMENT RELATING TO TREATMENT OF ITEMS OTHER THAN PARTNERSHIP ITEMS WITH RESPECT TO AN OVERSHELTERED RETURN.

* * *

(g) COORDINATION WITH OTHER PROCEEDINGS UNDER THIS SUBCHAPTER.—

* * *

(4) FINALLY DETERMINED.—For purposes of this subsection, the treatment of partnership items shall be treated as finally determined if—

(A) the Secretary *or the Attorney General (or his delegate)* enters into a settlement agreement (within the meaning of section 6224) with the taxpayer regarding such items,

(B) a notice of final partnership administrative adjustment has been issued and—

(i) no petition has been filed under section 6226 and the time for doing so has expired, or

(ii) a petition has been filed under section 6226 and the decision of the court has become final, or

(C) the period within which any tax attributable to such items may be assessed against the taxpayer has expired.

* * *

[CCH Explanation at ¶ 355. Committee Reports at ¶ 10,320.]

Amendment Notes

Act Sec. 416(d)(1)(D) amended Code Sec. 6234(g)(4)(A) by inserting "or the Attorney General (or his delegate)" after "Secretary".

The above amendment applies with respect to settlement agreements entered into after March 9, 2002.

[¶ 5380] CODE SEC. 6331. LEVY AND DISTRAINT.

* * *

(k) NO LEVY WHILE CERTAIN OFFERS PENDING OR INSTALLMENT AGREEMENT PENDING OR IN EFFECT.—

* * *

(3) CERTAIN RULES TO APPLY.—*Rules similar to the rules of—*

(A) paragraphs (3) and (4) of subsection (i), and

(B) except in the case of paragraph (2)(C), paragraph (5) of subsection (i),

shall apply for purposes of this subsection.

* * *

[CCH Explanation at ¶ 260. Committee Reports at ¶ 10,320.]

Amendment Notes

Act Sec. 416(e)(1) amended Code Sec. 6331(k)(3) to read as above. Prior to amendment, Code Sec. 6331(k)(3) read as follows:

(3) CERTAIN RULES TO APPLY.—Rules similar to the rules of paragraphs (3) and (4) of subsection (i) shall apply for purposes of this subsection.

The above amendment is effective on March 9, 2002.

[¶ 5385] CODE SEC. 6428. ACCELERATION OF 10 PERCENT INCOME TAX RATE BRACKET BENEFIT FOR 2001.

* * *

(b) CREDIT TREATED AS NONREFUNDABLE PERSONAL CREDIT.—*For purposes of this title, the credit allowed under this section shall be treated as a credit allowable under subpart A of part IV of subchapter A of chapter 1.*

* * *

[CCH Explanation at ¶ 230. Committee Reports at ¶ 10,260.]

Amendment Notes

Act Sec. 411(a)(1) amended Code Sec. 6428(b) to read as above. Prior to amendment, Code Sec. 6428(b) read as follows:

(b) LIMITATION BASED ON AMOUNT OF TAX.—The credit allowed by subsection (a) shall not exceed the excess (if any) of—

(1) the sum of the regular tax liability (as defined in section 26(b)) plus the tax imposed by section 55, over

(2) the sum of the credits allowable under part IV of subchapter A of chapter 1 (other than the credits allowable under subpart C thereof, relating to refundable credits).

The above amendment is effective as if included in the provision of the Economic Growth and Tax Relief Reconciliation Act of 2001 (P.L. 107-16) to which it relates [applicable to tax years beginning after December 31, 2000.—CCH].

(d) *COORDINATION WITH ADVANCE REFUNDS OF CREDIT.*—

(1) *IN GENERAL.*—*The amount of credit which would (but for this paragraph) be allowable under this section shall be reduced (but not below zero) by the aggregate refunds and credits made or allowed to the taxpayer under subsection (e). Any failure to so reduce the credit shall be treated as arising out of a mathematical or clerical error and assessed according to section 6213(b)(1).*

(2) *JOINT RETURNS.*—*In the case of a refund or credit made or allowed under subsection (e) with respect to a joint return, half of such refund or credit shall be treated as having been made or allowed to each individual filing such return.*

[CCH Explanation at ¶ 230. Committee Reports at ¶ 10,260.]

Amendment Notes

Act Sec. 411(a)(2)(A) amended Code Sec. 6428(d) to read as above. Prior to amendment, Code Sec. 6428(d) read as follows:

(d) SPECIAL RULES.—

(1) COORDINATION WITH ADVANCE REFUNDS OF CREDIT.—

(A) IN GENERAL.—The amount of credit which would (but for this paragraph) be allowable under this section shall be reduced (but not below zero) by the aggregate refunds and credits made or allowed to the taxpayer under subsection (e). Any failure to so reduce the credit shall be treated as arising out of a mathematical or clerical error and assessed according to section 6213(b)(1).

(B) JOINT RETURNS.—In the case of a refund or credit made or allowed under subsection (e) with respect to a joint return, half of such refund or credit shall be treated as having been made or allowed to each individual filing such return.

(2) COORDINATION WITH ESTIMATED TAX.—The credit under this section shall be treated for purposes of section 6654(f) in the same manner as a credit under subpart A of part IV of subchapter A of chapter 1.

The above amendment is effective as if included in the provision of the Economic Growth and Tax Relief Reconciliation Act of 2001 (P.L. 107-16) to which it relates [applicable to tax years beginning after December 31, 2000.—CCH].

(e) ADVANCE REFUNDS OF CREDIT BASED ON PRIOR YEAR DATA.—

* * *

(2) *ADVANCE REFUND AMOUNT.*—*For purposes of paragraph (1), the advance refund amount is the amount that would have been allowed as a credit under this section for such first taxable year if—*

(A) *this section (other than subsections (b) and (d) and this subsection) had applied to such taxable year, and*

(B) *the credit for such taxable year were not allowed to exceed the excess (if any) of—*

(i) *the sum of the regular tax liability (as defined in section 26(b)) plus the tax imposed by section 55, over*

(ii) *the sum of the credits allowable under part IV of subchapter A of chapter 1 (other than the credits allowable under subpart C thereof, relating to refundable credits).*

* * *

[CCH Explanation at ¶ 230. Committee Reports at ¶ 10,260.]

Amendment Notes

Act Sec. 411(a)(2)(B) amended Code Sec. 6428(e)(2) to read as above. Prior to amendment, Code Sec. 6428(e)(2) read as follows:

(2) ADVANCE REFUND AMOUNT.—For purposes of paragraph (1), the advance refund amount is the amount that would have been allowed as a credit under this section for such first

taxable year if this section (other than subsection (d) and this subsection) had applied to such taxable year.

The above amendment is effective as if included in the provision of the Economic Growth and Tax Relief Reconciliation Act of 2001 (P.L. 107-16) to which it relates [applicable to tax years beginning after December 31, 2000.—CCH].

[¶ 5390] CODE SEC. 7652. SHIPMENTS TO THE UNITED STATES.

* * *

(f) LIMITATION ON COVER OVER OF TAX ON DISTILLED SPIRITS.—For purposes of this section, with respect to taxes imposed under section 5001 or this section on distilled spirits, the amount covered into the treasuries of Puerto Rico and the Virgin Islands shall not exceed the lesser of the rate of—

(1) $10.50 ($13.25 in the case of distilled spirits brought into the United States after June 30, 1999, and before *January 1, 2004*), or

(2) the tax imposed under section 5001(a)(1), on each proof gallon.

* * *

[CCH Explanation at ¶ 390. Committee Reports at ¶ 10,490.]

Amendment Notes

Act Sec. 609(a) amended Code Sec. 7652(f)(1) by striking "January 1, 2002" and inserting "January 1, 2004".

The above amendment applies to articles brought into the United States after December 31, 2001.

[¶ 5395] CODE SEC. 7702A. MODIFIED ENDOWMENT CONTRACT DEFINED.

* * *

(c) COMPUTATIONAL RULES.—

* * *

(3) TREATMENT OF MATERIAL CHANGES.—

(A) IN GENERAL.—If there is a material change in the benefits under (or in other terms of) the contract which was not reflected in any previous determination under this section, for purposes of this section—

(i) such contract shall be treated as a new contract entered into on the day on which such material change takes effect, and

(ii) appropriate adjustments shall be made in determining whether such contract meets the 7-pay test of subsection (b) to take into account the cash surrender value *under the contract.*

* * *

[CCH Explanation at ¶ 365. Committee Reports at ¶ 10,320.]

Amendment Notes

Act Sec. 416(f) provides that section 318(a)(2) of the Community Renewal Tax Relief Act of 2000 (P.L. 106-554) is repealed, and Code Sec. 7702A(c)(3)(A)(ii) shall read and be applied as if this amendment had not been enacted. P.L.

106-554, § 318(a)(2), amended Code Sec. 7702A(c)(3)(A)(ii) by striking "under the contract" and inserting "under the old contract".

The above amendment is effective on March 9, 2002.

[¶ 5400] CODE SEC. 9812. PARITY IN THE APPLICATION OF CERTAIN LIMITS TO MENTAL HEALTH BENEFITS.

* * *

(f) APPLICATION OF SECTION.—This section shall not apply to benefits for services furnished—

(1) on or after September 30, 2001, and before January 10, 2002, and

(2) after December 31, 2003.

[CCH Explanation at ¶ 615. Committee Reports at ¶ 10,500.]

Amendment Notes

Act Sec. 610(a) amended Code Sec. 9812(f) to read as above. Prior to amendment, Code Sec. 9812(f) read as follows:

(f) SUNSET.—This section shall not apply to benefits for services furnished on or after December 31, 2002.

The above amendment applies to plan years beginning after December 31, 2000.

ACT SECTIONS NOT AMENDING CODE SECTIONS

JOB CREATION AND WORKER ASSISTANCE ACT OF 2002

[¶ 7005] ACT SEC. 1. SHORT TITLE; ETC.

(a) SHORT TITLE.—This Act may be cited as the "Job Creation and Worker Assistance Act of 2002".

(b) REFERENCES TO INTERNAL REVENUE CODE OF 1986.—Except as otherwise expressly provided, whenever in this Act an amendment or repeal is expressed in terms of an amendment to, or repeal of, a section or other provision, the reference shall be considered to be made to a section or other provision of the Internal Revenue Code of 1986.

* * *

TITLE II—UNEMPLOYMENT ASSISTANCE

[¶ 7010] ACT SEC. 201. SHORT TITLE.

This title may be cited as the "Temporary Extended Unemployment Compensation Act of 2002".

[CCH Explanation at ¶ 205. Committee Reports at ¶ 10,050.]

[¶ 7015] ACT SEC. 202. FEDERAL-STATE AGREEMENTS.

(a) IN GENERAL.—Any State which desires to do so may enter into and participate in an agreement under this title with the Secretary of Labor (in this title referred to as the "Secretary"). Any State which is a party to an agreement under this title may, upon providing 30 days' written notice to the Secretary, terminate such agreement.

(b) PROVISIONS OF AGREEMENT.—Any agreement under subsection (a) shall provide that the State agency of the State will make payments of temporary extended unemployment compensation to individuals who—

(1) have exhausted all rights to regular compensation under the State law or under Federal law with respect to a benefit year (excluding any benefit year that ended before March 15, 2001);

(2) have no rights to regular compensation or extended compensation with respect to a week under such law or any other State unemployment compensation law or to compensation under any other Federal law;

(3) are not receiving compensation with respect to such week under the unemployment compensation law of Canada; and

(4) filed an initial claim for regular compensation on or after March 15, 2001.

(c) EXHAUSTION OF BENEFITS.—For purposes of subsection (b)(1), an individual shall be deemed to have exhausted such individual's rights to regular compensation under a State law when—

(1) no payments of regular compensation can be made under such law because such individual has received all regular compensation available to such individual based on employment or wages during such individual's base period; or

(2) such individual's rights to such compensation have been terminated by reason of the expiration of the benefit year with respect to which such rights existed.

(d) WEEKLY BENEFIT AMOUNT, ETC.—For purposes of any agreement under this title—

(1) the amount of temporary extended unemployment compensation which shall be payable to any individual for any week of total unemployment shall be equal to the amount of the regular compensation (including dependents' allowances) payable to such individual during such individual's benefit year under the State law for a week of total unemployment;

(2) the terms and conditions of the State law which apply to claims for regular compensation and to the payment thereof shall apply to claims for temporary extended unemployment compensation and the payment thereof, except—

(A) that an individual shall not be eligible for temporary extended unemployment compensation under this title unless, in the base period with respect to which the individual exhausted all rights to regular compensation under the State law, the individual had 20 weeks of full-time insured employment or the equivalent in insured wages, as determined under the

Act Sec. 202(d)   ¶ 7015

provisions of the State law implementing section 202(a)(5) of the Federal-State Extended Unemployment Compensation Act of 1970 (26 U.S.C. 3304 note); and

(B) where otherwise inconsistent with the provisions of this title or with the regulations or operating instructions of the Secretary promulgated to carry out this title; and

(3) the maximum amount of temporary extended unemployment compensation payable to any individual for whom a temporary extended unemployment compensation account is established under section 203 shall not exceed the amount established in such account for such individual.

(e) ELECTION BY STATES.—Notwithstanding any other provision of Federal law (and if State law permits), the Governor of a State that is in an extended benefit period may provide for the payment of temporary extended unemployment compensation in lieu of extended compensation to individuals who otherwise meet the requirements of this section. Such an election shall not require a State to trigger off an extended benefit period.

[CCH Explanation at ¶ 205. Committee Reports at ¶ 10,050.]

[¶ 7020] ACT SEC. 203. TEMPORARY EXTENDED UNEMPLOYMENT COMPENSATION ACCOUNT.

(a) IN GENERAL.—Any agreement under this title shall provide that the State will establish, for each eligible individual who files an application for temporary extended unemployment compensation, a temporary extended unemployment compensation account with respect to such individual's benefit year.

(b) AMOUNT IN ACCOUNT.—

(1) IN GENERAL.—The amount established in an account under subsection (a) shall be equal to the lesser of—

(A) 50 percent of the total amount of regular compensation (including dependents' allowances) payable to the individual during the individual's benefit year under such law, or

(B) 13 times the individual's average weekly benefit amount for the benefit year.

(2) WEEKLY BENEFIT AMOUNT.—For purposes of this subsection, an individual's weekly benefit amount for any week is the amount of regular compensation (including dependents' allowances) under the State law payable to such individual for such week for total unemployment.

(c) SPECIAL RULE.—

(1) IN GENERAL.—Notwithstanding any other provision of this section, if, at the time that the individual's account is exhausted, such individual's State is in an extended benefit period (as determined under paragraph (2)), then, such account shall be augmented by an amount equal to the amount originally established in such account (as determined under subsection (b)(1)).

(2) EXTENDED BENEFIT PERIOD.—For purposes of paragraph (1), a State shall be considered to be in an extended benefit period if, at the time of exhaustion (as described in paragraph (1))—

(A) such a period is then in effect for such State under the Federal-State Extended Unemployment Compensation Act of 1970; or

(B) such a period would then be in effect for such State under such Act if section 203(d) of such Act were applied as if it had been amended by striking "5" each place it appears and inserting "4".

[CCH Explanation at ¶ 205. Committee Reports at ¶ 10,050.]

[¶ 7025] ACT SEC. 204. PAYMENTS TO STATES HAVING AGREEMENTS FOR THE PAYMENT OF TEMPORARY EXTENDED UNEMPLOYMENT COMPENSATION.

(a) IN GENERAL.—There shall be paid to each State that has entered into an agreement under this title an amount equal to 100 percent of the temporary extended unemployment compensation paid to individuals by the State pursuant to such agreement.

(b) TREATMENT OF REIMBURSABLE COMPENSATION.—No payment shall be made to any State under this section in respect of any compensation to the extent the State is entitled to reimbursement in respect of such compensation under the provisions of any Federal law other than this title or chapter 85 of title 5, United States Code. A State shall not be entitled to any reimbursement under such chapter 85 in respect of any compensation to the extent the State is entitled to reimbursement under this title in respect of such compensation.

¶ 7020   Act Sec. 203(a)

(c) DETERMINATION OF AMOUNT.—Sums payable to any State by reason of such State having an agreement under this title shall be payable, either in advance or by way of reimbursement (as may be determined by the Secretary), in such amounts as the Secretary estimates the State will be entitled to receive under this title for each calendar month, reduced or increased, as the case may be, by any amount by which the Secretary finds that the Secretary's estimates for any prior calendar month were greater or less than the amounts which should have been paid to the State. Such estimates may be made on the basis of such statistical, sampling, or other method as may be agreed upon by the Secretary and the State agency of the State involved.

[CCH Explanation at ¶ 205. Committee Reports at ¶ 10,050.]

[¶ 7030] ACT SEC. 205. FINANCING PROVISIONS.

(a) IN GENERAL.—Funds in the extended unemployment compensation account (as established by section 905(a) of the Social Security Act (42 U.S.C. 1105(a)) of the Unemployment Trust Fund (as established by section 904(a) of such Act (42 U.S.C. 1104(a)) shall be used for the making of payments to States having agreements entered into under this title.

(b) CERTIFICATION.—The Secretary shall from time to time certify to the Secretary of the Treasury for payment to each State the sums payable to such State under this title. The Secretary of the Treasury, prior to audit or settlement by the General Accounting Office, shall make payments to the State in accordance with such certification, by transfers from the extended unemployment compensation account (as so established) to the account of such State in the Unemployment Trust Fund (as so established).

(c) ASSISTANCE TO STATES.—There are appropriated out of the employment security administration account (as established by section 901(a) of the Social Security Act (42 U.S.C. 1101(a)) of the Unemployment Trust Fund, without fiscal year limitation, such funds as may be necessary for purposes of assisting States (as provided in title III of the Social Security Act (42 U.S.C. 501 et seq.)) in meeting the costs of administration of agreements under this title.

(d) APPROPRIATIONS FOR CERTAIN PAYMENTS.—There are appropriated from the general fund of the Treasury, without fiscal year limitation, to the extended unemployment compensation account (as so established) of the Unemployment Trust Fund (as so established) such sums as the Secretary estimates to be necessary to make the payments under this section in respect of—

(1) compensation payable under chapter 85 of title 5, United States Code; and

(2) compensation payable on the basis of services to which section 3309(a)(1) of the Internal Revenue Code of 1986 applies.

Amounts appropriated pursuant to the preceding sentence shall not be required to be repaid.

[CCH Explanation at ¶ 205. Committee Reports at ¶ 10,050.]

[¶ 7035] ACT SEC. 206. FRAUD AND OVERPAYMENTS.

(a) IN GENERAL.—If an individual knowingly has made, or caused to be made by another, a false statement or representation of a material fact, or knowingly has failed, or caused another to fail, to disclose a material fact, and as a result of such false statement or representation or of such nondisclosure such individual has received an amount of temporary extended unemployment compensation under this title to which he was not entitled, such individual—

(1) shall be ineligible for further temporary extended unemployment compensation under this title in accordance with the provisions of the applicable State unemployment compensation law relating to fraud in connection with a claim for unemployment compensation; and

(2) shall be subject to prosecution under section 1001 of title 18, United States Code.

(b) REPAYMENT.—In the case of individuals who have received amounts of temporary extended unemployment compensation under this title to which they were not entitled, the State shall require such individuals to repay the amounts of such temporary extended unemployment compensation to the State agency, except that the State agency may waive such repayment if it determines that—

(1) the payment of such temporary extended unemployment compensation was without fault on the part of any such individual; and

(2) such repayment would be contrary to equity and good conscience.

(c) RECOVERY BY STATE AGENCY.—

(1) IN GENERAL.—The State agency may recover the amount to be repaid, or any part thereof, by deductions from any temporary extended unemployment compensation payable to such

individual under this title or from any unemployment compensation payable to such individual under any Federal unemployment compensation law administered by the State agency or under any other Federal law administered by the State agency which provides for the payment of any assistance or allowance with respect to any week of unemployment, during the 3-year period after the date such individuals received the payment of the temporary extended unemployment compensation to which they were not entitled, except that no single deduction may exceed 50 percent of the weekly benefit amount from which such deduction is made.

(2) OPPORTUNITY FOR HEARING.—No repayment shall be required, and no deduction shall be made, until a determination has been made, notice thereof and an opportunity for a fair hearing has been given to the individual, and the determination has become final.

(d) REVIEW.—Any determination by a State agency under this section shall be subject to review in the same manner and to the same extent as determinations under the State unemployment compensation law, and only in that manner and to that extent.

[CCH Explanation at ¶ 205. Committee Reports at ¶ 10,050.]

[¶ 7040] ACT SEC. 207. DEFINITIONS.

In this title, the terms "compensation", "regular compensation", "extended compensation", "additional compensation", "benefit year", "base period", "State", "State agency", "State law", and "week" have the respective meanings given such terms under section 205 of the Federal-State Extended Unemployment Compensation Act of 1970 (26 U.S.C. 3304 note).

[CCH Explanation at ¶ 205. Committee Reports at ¶ 10,050.]

[¶ 7045] ACT SEC. 208. APPLICABILITY.

An agreement entered into under this title shall apply to weeks of unemployment—

(1) beginning after the date on which such agreement is entered into; and

(2) ending before January 1, 2003.

[CCH Explanation at ¶ 205. Committee Reports at ¶ 10,050.]

[¶ 7050] ACT SEC. 209. SPECIAL REED ACT TRANSFER IN FISCAL YEAR 2002.

(a) REPEAL OF CERTAIN PROVISIONS ADDED BY THE BALANCED BUDGET ACT OF 1997.—

(1) IN GENERAL.—The following provisions of section 903 of the Social Security Act (42 U.S.C. 1103) are repealed:

(A) Paragraph (3) of subsection (a).

(B) The last sentence of subsection (c)(2).

(2) SAVINGS PROVISION.—Any amounts transferred before the date of enactment of this Act under the provision repealed by paragraph (1)(A) shall remain subject to section 903 of the Social Security Act, as last in effect before such date of enactment.

(b) SPECIAL TRANSFER IN FISCAL YEAR 2002.—Section 903 of the Social Security Act is amended by adding at the end the following:

"Special Transfer in Fiscal Year 2002

"(d)(1) The Secretary of the Treasury shall transfer (as of the date determined under paragraph (5)) from the Federal unemployment account to the account of each State in the Unemployment Trust Fund the amount determined with respect to such State under paragraph (2).

"(2)(A) The amount to be transferred under this subsection to a State account shall (as determined by the Secretary of Labor and certified by such Secretary to the Secretary of the Treasury) be equal to—

"(i) the amount which would have been required to have been transferred under this section to such account at the beginning of fiscal year 2002 if—

"(I) section 209(a)(1) of the Temporary Extended Unemployment Compensation Act of 2002 had been enacted before the close of fiscal year 2001, and

"(II) section 5402 of Public Law 105-33 (relating to increase in Federal unemployment account ceiling) had not been enacted,

"minus

"(ii) the amount which was in fact transferred under this section to such account at the beginning of fiscal year 2002.

"(B) Notwithstanding the provisions of subparagraph (A)—

"(i) the aggregate amount transferred to the States under this subsection may not exceed a total of $8,000,000,000; and

"(ii) all amounts determined under subparagraph (A) shall be reduced ratably, if and to the extent necessary in order to comply with the limitation under clause (i).

"(3)(A) Except as provided in paragraph (4), amounts transferred to a State account pursuant to this subsection may be used only in the payment of cash benefits—

"(i) to individuals with respect to their unemployment, and

"(ii) which are allowable under subparagraph (B) or (C).

"(B)(i) At the option of the State, cash benefits under this paragraph may include amounts which shall be payable as—

"(I) regular compensation, or

"(II) additional compensation, upon the exhaustion of any temporary extended unemployment compensation (if such State has entered into an agreement under the Temporary Extended Unemployment Compensation Act of 2002), for individuals eligible for regular compensation under the unemployment compensation law of such State.

"(ii) Any additional compensation under clause (i) may not be taken into account for purposes of any determination relating to the amount of any extended compensation for which an individual might be eligible.

"(C)(i) At the option of the State, cash benefits under this paragraph may include amounts which shall be payable to 1 or more categories of individuals not otherwise eligible for regular compensation under the unemployment compensation law of such State, including those described in clause (iii).

"(ii) The benefits paid under this subparagraph to any individual may not, for any period of unemployment, exceed the maximum amount of regular compensation authorized under the unemployment compensation law of such State for that same period, plus any additional compensation (described in subparagraph (B)(i)) which could have been paid with respect to that amount.

"(iii) The categories of individuals described in this clause include the following:

"(I) Individuals who are seeking, or available for, only part-time (and not full-time) work.

"(II) Individuals who would be eligible for regular compensation under the unemployment compensation law of such State under an alternative base period.

"(D) Amounts transferred to a State account under this subsection may be used in the payment of cash benefits to individuals only for weeks of unemployment beginning after the date of enactment of this subsection.

"(4) Amounts transferred to a State account under this subsection may be used for the administration of its unemployment compensation law and public employment offices (including in connection with benefits described in paragraph (3) and any recipients thereof), subject to the same conditions as set forth in subsection (c)(2) (excluding subparagraph (B) thereof, and deeming the reference to 'subsections (a) and (b)' in subparagraph (D) thereof to include this subsection).

"(5) Transfers under this subsection shall be made within 10 days after the date of enactment of this paragraph.".

(c) LIMITATIONS ON TRANSFERS.—Section 903(b) of the Social Security Act shall apply to transfers under section 903(d) of such Act (as amended by this section). For purposes of the preceding sentence, such section 903(b) shall be deemed to be amended as follows:

(1) By substituting "the transfer date described in subsection (d)(5)" for "October 1 of any fiscal year".

(2) By substituting "remain in the Federal unemployment account" for "be transferred to the Federal unemployment account as of the beginning of such October 1".

Act Sec. 209(c) ¶ **7050**

(3) By substituting "fiscal year 2002 (after the transfer date described in subsection (d)(5))" for "the fiscal year beginning on such October 1".

(4) By substituting "under subsection (d)" for "as of October 1 of such fiscal year".

(5) By substituting "(as of the close of fiscal year 2002)" for "(as of the close of such fiscal year)".

(d) TECHNICAL AMENDMENTS.—* * *

(2) Section 303(a)(5) of the Social Security Act is amended in the second proviso by inserting "or 903(d)(4)" after "903(c)(2)".

(e) REGULATIONS.—The Secretary of Labor may prescribe any operating instructions or regulations necessary to carry out this section and the amendments made by this section.

* * *

[CCH Explanation at ¶ 205. Committee Reports at ¶ 10,060.]

TITLE IV—MISCELLANEOUS AND TECHNICAL PROVISIONS

Subtitle A—General Miscellaneous Provisions

[¶ 7055] ACT SEC. 401. ALLOWANCE OF ELECTRONIC 1099's.

Any person required to furnish a statement under any section of subpart B of part III of subchapter A of chapter 61 of the Internal Revenue Code of 1986 for any taxable year ending after the date of the enactment of this Act, may electronically furnish such statement (without regard to any first class mailing requirement) to any recipient who has consented to the electronic provision of the statement in a manner similar to the one permitted under regulations issued under section 6051 of such Code or in such other manner as provided by the Secretary.

* * *

[CCH Explanation at ¶ 350. Committee Reports at ¶ 10,200.]

[¶ 7060] ACT SEC. 405. INTEREST RATE RANGE FOR ADDITIONAL FUNDING REQUIREMENTS.

* * *

(b) AMENDMENTS TO THE EMPLOYEE RETIREMENT INCOME SECURITY ACT OF 1974.—

(1) SPECIAL RULE.—Clause (i) of section 302(d)(7)(C) of such Act (29 U.S.C. 1082(d)(7)(C)) is amended by adding at the end the following new subclause:

"(III) SPECIAL RULE FOR 2002 AND 2003.—For a plan year beginning in 2002 or 2003, notwithstanding subclause (I), in the case that the rate of interest used under subsection (b)(5) exceeds the highest rate permitted under subclause (I), the rate of interest used to determine current liability under this subsection may exceed the rate of interest otherwise permitted under subclause (I); except that such rate of interest shall not exceed 120 percent of the weighted average referred to in subsection (b)(5)(B)(ii).".

(2) QUARTERLY CONTRIBUTIONS.—Subsection (e) of section 302 of such Act (29 U.S.C. 1082) is amended by adding at the end the following new paragraph:

"(7) SPECIAL RULES FOR 2002 AND 2004.—In any case in which the interest rate used to determine current liability is determined under subsection (d)(7)(C)(i)(III)—

"(A) 2002.—For purposes of applying paragraphs (1) and (4)(B)(ii) for plan years beginning in 2002, the current liability for the preceding plan year shall be redetermined using 120 percent as the specified percentage determined under subsection (d)(7)(C)(i)(II).

"(B) 2004.—For purposes of applying paragraphs (1) and (4)(B)(ii) for plan years beginning in 2004, the current liability for the preceding plan year shall be redetermined using 105 percent as the specified percentage determined under subsection (d)(7)(C)(i)(II).".

(c) PBGC.—Clause (iii) of section 4006(a)(3)(E) of the Employee Retirement Income Security Act of 1974 (29 U.S.C. 1306(a)(3)(E)) is amended by adding at the end the following new subclause:

"(IV) In the case of plan years beginning after December 31, 2001, and before January 1, 2004, subclause (II) shall be applied by substituting '100 percent' for '85 percent'. Subclause (III) shall be applied for such years without regard to the preceding sentence. Any reference to this clause by any other sections or subsections shall be treated as a reference to this clause without regard to this subclause.".

* * *

[CCH Explanation at ¶ 505. Committee Reports at ¶ 10,240.]

Subtitle B—Technical Corrections

[¶ 7065] ACT SEC. 411. AMENDMENTS RELATED TO ECONOMIC GROWTH AND TAX RELIEF RECONCILIATION ACT OF 2001.

* * *

(i) Amendments Relating to Section 602 of the Act.—

* * *

(2) Section 4(c) of [the] Employee Retirement Income Security Act of 1974 is amended—

(A) by inserting "and part 5 (relating to administration and enforcement)" before the period at the end, and

(B) by adding at the end the following new sentence: "Such provisions shall apply to such accounts and annuities in a manner similar to their application to a simplified employee pension under section 408(k) of the Internal Revenue Code of 1986.".

(j) Amendments Relating to Section 611 of the Act.—

* * *

(3) Section 611(i) of the Economic Growth and Tax Relief Reconciliation Act of 2001 is amended by adding at the end the following new paragraph:

"(3) Special Rule.—In the case of [a] plan that, on June 7, 2001, incorporated by reference the limitation of section 415(b)(1)(A) of the Internal Revenue Code of 1986, section 411(d)(6) of such Code and section 204(g)(1) of the Employee Retirement Income Security Act of 1974 do not apply to a plan amendment that—

"(A) is adopted on or before June 30, 2002,

"(B) reduces benefits to the level that would have applied without regard to the amendments made by subsection (a) of this section, and

"(C) is effective no earlier than the years described in paragraph (2).".

● ● *EGTRRA OF 2001 ACT SEC. 611(i) BEFORE AMENDMENT*————————————

ACT SEC. 611. INCREASE IN BENEFIT AND CONTRIBUTION LIMITS.

* * *

(i) Effective Dates.—

(1) In General.—The amendments made by this section shall apply to years beginning after December 31, 2001.

(2) Defined benefit plans.—The amendments made by subsection (a) shall apply to years ending after December 31, 2001.

---

* * *

(n) Amendments Relating to Section 619 of the Act.—

* * *

(2) Section 619(d) of the Economic Growth and Tax Relief Reconciliation Act of 2001 is amended by striking "established" and inserting "first effective".

● ● *EGTRRA OF 2001 ACT SEC. 619(d) AS AMENDED* ————————————

ACT SEC. 619. CREDIT FOR PENSION PLAN STARTUP COSTS OF SMALL EMPLOYERS.

* * *

(d) EFFECTIVE DATE.—The amendments made by this section shall apply to costs paid or incurred in taxable years beginning after December 31, 2001, with respect to qualified employer plans *first effective* after such date.

* * *

(r) AMENDMENTS RELATING TO SECTION 648 OF THE ACT.—

* * *

(2) Section 205(g) of the Employee Retirement Income Security Act of 1974 is amended—

(A) in paragraph (1) by striking "exceed the dollar limit under section 203(e)(1)" and inserting "exceed the amount that can be distributed without the participant's consent under section 203(e)", and

(B) in paragraph (2)(A) by striking "exceeds the dollar limit under section 203(e)(1)" and inserting "exceeds the amount that can be distributed without the participant's consent under section 203(e)".

* * *

(t) AMENDMENTS RELATING TO SECTION 657 OF THE ACT.—Section 404(c)(3) of the Employee Retirement Income Security Act of 1974 is amended—

(1) by striking "the earlier of" in subparagraph (A) the second place it appears, and

(2) by striking "if the transfer" and inserting "a transfer that".

(u) AMENDMENTS RELATING TO SECTION 659 OF THE ACT.—

* * *

(2) Section 204(h)(9) of the Employee Retirement Income Security Act of 1974 is amended by striking "significantly" both places it appears.

(3) Section 659(c)(3)(B) of the Economic Growth and Tax Relief Reconciliation Act of 2001 is amended by striking "(or" and inserting "(and".

● ● *EGTRRA OF 2001 ACT SEC. 659(c)(3)(B) AS AMENDED* ————————————

ACT SEC. 659. EXCISE TAX ON FAILURE TO PROVIDE NOTICE BY DEFINED BENEFIT PLANS SIGNIFICANTLY REDUCING FUTURE BENEFIT ACCRUALS.

* * *

(c) EFFECTIVE DATES.—

* * *

(3) SPECIAL NOTICE RULE.—

* * *

(B) REASONABLE NOTICE.—The amendments made by this section shall not apply to any plan amendment taking effect on or after the date of the enactment of this Act if, before April 25, 2001, notice was provided to participants and beneficiaries adversely affected by the plan amendment *(and* their representatives) which was reasonably expected to notify them of the nature and effective date of the plan amendment.

(v) AMENDMENTS RELATING TO SECTION 661 OF THE ACT.—

* * *

(2) Section 302(c)(9)(B) of the Employee Retirement Income Security Act of 1974 is amended—

(A) in clause (ii) by striking "125 percent" and inserting "100 percent", and

(B) by adding at the end the following new clause:

"(iv) A change in funding method to use a prior year valuation, as provided in clause (ii), may not be made unless as of the valuation date within the prior plan year, the value of the assets of the plan are not less than 125 percent of the plan's current liability (as defined in paragraph (7)(B)).".

* * *

(x) EFFECTIVE DATE.—Except as provided in subsection (c), the amendments made by this section shall take effect as if included in the provisions of the Economic Growth and Tax Relief Reconciliation Act of 2001 to which they relate.

* * *

[CCH Explanation at ¶ 530, ¶ 540, ¶ 545, ¶ 555, ¶ 560 and ¶ 610. Committee Reports at ¶ 10,270.]

[¶ 7070] ACT SEC. 414. AMENDMENTS RELATED TO THE TAXPAYER RELIEF ACT OF 1997.

(a) AMENDMENTS RELATED TO SECTION 311 OF THE ACT.—Section 311(e) of the Taxpayer Relief Act of 1997 (Public Law 105-34; 111 Stat. 836) is amended—

(1) in paragraph (2)(A), by striking "recognized" and inserting "included in gross income", and

(2) by adding at the end the following new paragraph:

"(5) DISPOSITION OF INTEREST IN PASSIVE ACTIVITY.—Section 469(g)(1)(A) of the Internal Revenue Code of 1986 shall not apply by reason of an election made under paragraph (1).".

● ● *TAXPAYER RELIEF ACT OF 1997 ACT SEC. 311(e) AS AMENDED———————*

ACT SEC. 311. MAXIMUM CAPITAL GAINS RATES FOR INDIVIDUALS.

* * *

(e) ELECTION TO RECOGNIZE GAIN ON ASSETS HELD ON JANUARY 1, 2001.—For purposes of the Internal Revenue Code of 1986—

* * *

(2) TREATMENT OF GAIN OR LOSS.—

(A) Any gain resulting from an election under paragraph (1) shall be treated as received or accrued on the date the asset is treated as sold under paragraph (1) and shall be *included in gross income* notwithstanding any provision of the Internal Revenue Code of 1986.

(B) Any loss resulting from an election under paragraph (1) shall not be allowed for any taxable year.

* * *

(5) *DISPOSITION OF INTEREST IN PASSIVE ACTIVITY.—Section 469(g)(1)(A) of the Internal Revenue Code of 1986 shall not apply by reason of an election made under paragraph (1).*

(b) EFFECTIVE DATE.—The amendments made by this section shall take effect as if included in section 311 of the Taxpayer Relief Act of 1997.

* * *

[CCH Explanation at ¶ 320. Committee Reports at ¶ 10,300.]

[¶ 7075] ACT SEC. 417. CLERICAL AMENDMENTS.

* * *

(21) Section 159 of the Community Renewal Tax Relief Act of 2000 (114 Stat. 2763A-624) is amended by striking "fuctions" and inserting "functions".

● ● *COMMUNITY RENEWAL ACT OF 2000 ACT SEC. 159 AS AMENDED ——————*

ACT SEC. 159. RESOURCES.

The Secretary shall provide to the Advisory Council appropriate resources so that the Advisory Council may carry out its duties and *functions* under this part.

(22) The amendment to section 170(e)(6)(B)(iv) made by section 165(b)(1) of the Community Renewal Tax Relief Act of 2000 (114 Stat. 2763A-626) shall be applied as if it struck "in any of the grades K-12".

(23) Section 618(b)(2) of the Economic Growth and Tax Relief Reconciliation Act of 2001 (Public Law 107-16; 115 Stat. 108) is amended—

(A) in subparagraph (A) by striking "203(d)" and inserting "202(f)", and

(B) in subparagraphs (C), (D), and (E) by striking "203" and inserting "202(f)".

● ● *EGTRRA OF 2001 ACT SEC. 618(b)(2) AS AMENDED* ————————————

ACT SEC. 618. NONREFUNDABLE CREDIT TO CERTAIN INDIVIDUALS FOR ELECTIVE DEFERRALS AND IRA CONTRIBUTIONS.

* * *

(b) CREDIT ALLOWED AGAINST REGULAR TAX AND ALTERNATIVE MINIMUM TAX.—

* * *

(2) CONFORMING AMENDMENTS.—

(A) Section 24(b)(3)(B), as amended by sections 201(b) and *202(f)*, is amended by striking "section 23" and inserting "sections 23 and 25B".

(B) Section 25(e)(1)(C), as amended by section 201(b), is amended by inserting "25B," after "24,".

(C) Section 26(a)(1), as amended by sections 201(b) and *202(f)*, is amended by striking "and 24" and inserting ", 24, and 25B".

(D) Section 904(h), as amended by sections 201(b) and *202(f)*, is amended by striking "and 24" and inserting ", 24, and 25B".

(E) Section 1400C(d), as amended by sections 201(b) and *202(f)*, is amended by striking "and 24" and inserting ", 24 and 25B."

---

(24)(A) Section 525 of the Ticket to Work and Work Incentives Improvement Act of 1999 (Public Law 106-170; 113 Stat. 1928) is amended by striking "7200" and inserting "7201".

● ● *TICKET TO WORK ACT OF 1999 ACT SEC. 525 AS AMENDED* ————————————

ACT SEC. 525. PRODUCTION FLEXIBILITY CONTRACT PAYMENTS.

Any option to accelerate the receipt of any payment under a production flexibility contract which is payable under the Federal Agriculture Improvement and Reform Act of 1996 (7 U.S.C. *7201* et seq.), as in effect on the date of the enactment of this Act, shall be disregarded in determining the taxable year for which such payment is properly includible in gross income for purposes of the Internal Revenue Code of 1986.

(B) Section 532(c)(2) of such Act (113 Stat. 1930) is amended—

(i) in subparagraph (D), by striking "341(d)(3)" and inserting "341(d)", and

(ii) in subparagraph (Q), by striking "954(c)(1)(B)(iii)["] and inserting "954(c)(1)(B)".

● ● *TICKET TO WORK ACT OF 1999 ACT SEC. 532(c)(2) AS AMENDED* ─────

ACT SEC. 532. CLARIFICATION OF TAX TREATMENT OF INCOME AND LOSS ON DERIVATIVES.

* * *

(c) CONFORMING AMENDMENTS.—

* * *

(2) Each of the following sections of such Code are amended by striking "section 1221(1)" and inserting "section 1221(a)(1)":

* * *

(D) Section *341(d)*.

* * *

(Q) Section *954(c)(1)(B)*.

* * *

───

* * *

[CCH Explanation at ¶ 30,050. Committee Reports at ¶ 10,320.]

TITLE V—SOCIAL SECURITY HELD HARMLESS; BUDGETARY TREATMENT OF ACT

[¶ 7080] ACT SEC. 501. NO IMPACT ON SOCIAL SECURITY TRUST FUNDS.

(a) IN GENERAL.—Nothing in this Act (or an amendment made by this Act) shall be construed to alter or amend title II of the Social Security Act (or any regulation promulgated under that Act).

(b) TRANSFERS.—

(1) ESTIMATE OF SECRETARY.—The Secretary of the Treasury shall annually estimate the impact that the enactment of this Act has on the income and balances of the trust funds established under section 201 of the Social Security Act (42 U.S.C. 401).

(2) TRANSFER OF FUNDS.—If, under paragraph (1), the Secretary of the Treasury estimates that the enactment of this Act has a negative impact on the income and balances of the trust funds established under section 201 of the Social Security Act (42 U.S.C. 401), the Secretary shall transfer, not less frequently than quarterly, from the general revenues of the Federal Government an amount sufficient so as to ensure that the income and balances of such trust funds are not reduced as a result of the enactment of this Act.

[Committee Reports at ¶ 10,350.]

[¶ 7085] ACT SEC. 502. EMERGENCY DESIGNATION.

Congress designates as emergency requirements pursuant to section 252(e) of the Balanced Budget and Emergency Deficit Control Act of 1985 the following amounts:

(1) An amount equal to the amount by which revenues are reduced by this Act below the recommended levels of Federal revenues for fiscal year 2002, the total of fiscal years 2002 through 2006, and the total of fiscal years 2002 through 2011, provided in the conference report accompanying H. Con. Res. 83, the concurrent resolution on the budget for fiscal year 2002.

(2) Amounts equal to the amounts of new budget authority and outlays provided in this Act in excess of the allocations under section 302(a) of the Congressional Budget Act of 1974 to the Committee on Finance of the Senate for fiscal year 2002, the total of fiscal years 2002 through 2006, and the total of fiscal years 2002 through 2011.

[Committee Reports at ¶ 10,360.]

TITLE VI—EXTENSIONS OF CERTAIN EXPIRING PROVISIONS

[¶ 7090] ACT SEC. 601. ALLOWANCE OF NONREFUNDABLE PERSONAL CREDITS AGAINST REGULAR AND MINIMUM TAX LIABILITY.

* * *

(b) CONFORMING AMENDMENTS.—

* * *

(2) The amendments made by sections 201(b), 202(f), and 618(b) of the Economic Growth and Tax Relief Reconciliation Act of 2001 shall not apply to taxable years beginning during 2002 and 2003.

(c) EFFECTIVE DATE.—The amendments made by this section shall apply to taxable years beginning after December 31, 2001.

[CCH Explanation at ¶ 270. Committee Reports at ¶ 10,400.]

[¶ 7095] ACT SEC. 602. CREDIT FOR QUALIFIED ELECTRIC VEHICLES.

* * *

(b) CONFORMING AMENDMENTS.—

* * *

(2) Subsection (b) of section 971 of the Taxpayer Relief Act of 1997 is amended by striking "and before January 1, 2005".

● ● *TAXPAYER RELIEF ACT OF 1997 ACT SEC. 971(b) AS AMENDED———————*

ACT SEC. 971. EXEMPTION OF THE INCREMENTAL COST OF A CLEAN FUEL VEHICLE FROM THE LIMITS ON DEPRECIATION FOR VEHICLES.

* * *

(b) EFFECTIVE DATE.—The amendments made by this section shall apply to property placed in service after the date of the enactment of this Act [August 5, 1997].

(c) EFFECTIVE DATE.—The amendments made by this section shall apply to property placed in service after December 31, 2001.

* * *

[CCH Explanation at ¶ 370. Committee Reports at ¶ 10,410.]

[¶ 7100] ACT SEC. 616. REAUTHORIZATION OF TANF SUPPLEMENTAL GRANTS FOR POPULATION INCREASES FOR FISCAL YEAR 2002.

Section 403(a)(3) of the Social Security Act (42 U.S.C. 603(a)(3)) is amended by adding at the end the following:

"(H) REAUTHORIZATION OF GRANTS FOR FISCAL YEAR 2002.—Notwithstanding any other provision of this paragraph—

"(i) any State that was a qualifying State under this paragraph for fiscal year 2001 or any prior fiscal year shall be entitled to receive from the Secretary for fiscal year 2002 a grant in an amount equal to the amount required to be paid to the State under this paragraph for the most recent fiscal year in which the State was a qualifying State;

"(ii) subparagraph (G) shall be applied as if '2002' were substituted for '2001'; and

"(iii) out of any money in the Treasury of the United States not otherwise appropriated, there are appropriated for fiscal year 2002 such sums as are necessary for grants under this subparagraph.".

[Committee Reports at ¶ 10,580.]

[¶ 7105] ACT SEC. 617. 1-YEAR EXTENSION OF CONTINGENCY FUND UNDER THE TANF PROGRAM.

Section 403(b) of the Social Security Act (42 U.S.C. 603(b)) is amended—

(1) in paragraph (2), by striking "and 2001" and inserting "2001, and 2002"; and

(2) in paragraph (3)(C)(ii), by striking "2001" and inserting "2002".

[Committee Reports at ¶ 10,590.]

Committee Reports

Job Creation and Worker Assistance Act of 2002

Introduction

[¶ 10,001]

The Job Creation and Worker Assistance Act of 2002 (P.L. 107-147) was introduced in the House as "Economic Security and Recovery Act of 2001," on October 11, 2001, as H.R. 3090. The House Ways and Means Committee favorably reported on the bill on October 17, 2001 (H.R. REP. NO. 107-251). The bill passed the House on October 24, 2001.

The Senate Finance Committee (SFC) favorably reported an amendment in the nature of a substitute to H.R. 3090 on November 8, 2001, but the SFC did not publish a written report. The Senate did not pass the substitute legislation.

The House Ways and Means Committee favorably reported on an amendment in the nature of a substitute to H.R. 3090, which retitled the act "The Job Creation and Worker Assistance Act of 2002," on March 7, 2002. A written report was not published. The House passed the substitute legislation on the same day and the measure was sent to the Senate. The Senate passed the substitute legislation without amendment on March 8, 2002, and the President signed it on March 9, 2002.

This section includes the pertinent texts of the committee reports that explain the changes enacted in the Job Creation and Worker Assistance Act of 2002. The following material is the official wording of the relevant House Report and Joint Committee on Taxation Explanation. The Joint Committee on Taxation's Technical Explanation of the "Job Creation and Worker Assistance Act of 2002," as released on March 6, 2002, is included in this section to aid in the reader's understanding of the relevant provisions, but may not be cited as the official Conference Committee Report accompanying the 2002 Act. Likewise, portions of H.R. REP. NO. 107-251 are included to aid in the reader's understanding of the relevant provisions, but may not be cited as the controlling Committee Report accompanying the 2002 Act. Headings have been added for convenience in locating the committee reports. Any omission of text is indicated by asterisks (* * *). References are to the following reports:

● The Joint Committee on Taxation, *Technical Explanation of the "Job Creation and Worker Assistance Act of 2002"* (JCX-12-02) (H.R. 3090, March 6, 2002) is referred to as **Joint Committee on Taxation** (J.C.T. REP. NO. JCX-12-02).

● The Economic Security and Recovery Act of 2001 (H.R. 3090), House Ways and Means Committee Report, reported on October 17, 2001, is referred to as **House Committee Report** (H.R. REP. NO. 107-251). Only selected portions of this report are included.

[¶ 10,010]   Act Sec. 101. Special depreciation allowance for certain property

Joint Committee on Taxation (J.C.T. REP. NO. JCX-12-02)

[Caution: The Technical Explanation of the "Job Creation and Worker Assistance Act of 2002" (JCX-12-02), below, is included to assist the reader's understanding but may not be cited as the official Conference Committee Report to P.L. 107-147.—CCH]

[Code Sec. 168(k)]

Present Law

Depreciation deductions

A taxpayer is allowed to recover, through annual depreciation deductions, the cost of certain property used in a trade or business or for the production of income. The amount of the depreciation deduction allowed with respect to tangible property for a taxable year is determined under the modified accelerated cost recovery system ("MACRS"). Under MACRS, different types of property generally are assigned applicable recovery periods and depreciation methods. The recovery periods applicable to most tangible personal property (generally tangible property other than residential rental property and nonresidential real property) range from 3 to 25 years. The depreciation methods generally applicable to tangible personal property are the 200-percent and 150-percent declining balance methods, switching to the straight-line method for the taxable year in which the depreciation deduction would be maximized.

Section 280F limits the annual depreciation deductions with respect to passenger automobiles to specified dollar amounts, indexed for inflation.

Section 167(f)(1) provides that capitalized computer software costs, other than computer software to which section 197 applies, are recovered ratably over 36 months.

In lieu of depreciation, a taxpayer with a sufficiently small amount of annual investment generally may elect to deduct up to $24,000 (for taxable years beginning in 2001 or 2002) of the cost of qualifying property placed in service for the taxable year (sec. 179). This amount is increased to $25,000 for taxable years beginning in 2003 and thereafter. In general, qualifying property is defined as depreciable tangible personal property that is purchased for use in the active conduct of a trade or business.

Explanation of Provision

The provision allows an additional first-year depreciation deduction equal to 30 percent of the adjusted basis of qualified property. The additional first-year depreciation deduction is allowed for both regular tax and alternative minimum tax purposes for the taxable year in which the property is placed in service.[2] The basis of the property and the depreciation allowances in the year of purchase and later years are appropriately adjusted to reflect the additional first-year depreciation deduction. In addition, the provision provides that there would be no adjustment to the allowable amount of depreciation for purposes of computing a taxpayer's alternative minimum taxable income with respect to property to which the provision applies. A taxpayer is allowed to elect out of the additional first-year depreciation for any class of property for any taxable year.

In order for property to qualify for the additional first-year depreciation deduction it must meet all of the following requirements. First, the property must be property to which the general rules of MACRS[3] apply with (1) an applicable recovery period of 20 years or less, (2) water utility property (as defined in section 168(e)(5)), (3) computer software other than computer software covered by section 197, or (4) qualified leasehold improvement property[4]. Second, the original use[5] of the property must commence with

---

[2] The additional first-year depreciation deduction is subject to the general rules regarding whether an item is deductible under section 162 or subject to capitalization under section 263 or section 263A.

[3] A special rule precludes the additional first-year depreciation deduction for property that is required to be depreciated under the alternative depreciation system of MACRS.

[4] Qualified leasehold improvement property is any improvement to an interior portion of a building that is nonresidential real property, provided certain requirements are met. The improvement must be made under or pursuant to a lease either by the lessee (or sublessee) of that portion of the building, or by the lessor of that portion of the building. That portion of the building is to be occupied exclusively by the lessee (or any sublessee). The improvement must be placed in service more than three years after the date the building was first placed in service.

Qualified leasehold improvement property does not include any improvement for which the expenditure is attributable to the enlargement of the building, any elevator or escalator, any structural component benefiting a common area, or the internal structural framework of the building.

For purposes of the provision, a binding commitment to enter into a lease would be treated as a lease, and the parties to the commitment would be treated as lessor and lessee. A lease between related persons would not be considered a lease for this purpose.

Finally, New York Liberty Zone qualified leasehold improvement property is not eligible for the additional first year depreciation deduction.

[5] The term "original use" means the first use to which the property is put, whether or not such use corresponds to the use of such property by the taxpayer. It is intended that, when evaluating whether property qualifies as "original use," the factors used to determine whether property qualified as "new section 38 property" for purposes of the investment tax credit would apply. See Treasury Regulation 1.48-2. Thus, it is intended that additional capital expenditures incurred to recondition or rebuild acquired property (or owned property) would satisfy the "original use" re-

the taxpayer on or after September 11, 2001.[6] Third, the taxpayer must purchase the property within the applicable time period. Finally, the property must be placed in service before January 1, 2005. An extension of the place in service date of one year (i.e., January 1, 2006) is provided for certain property with a recovery period of ten years or longer and certain transportation property.[7] Transportation property is defined as tangible personal property used in the trade or business of transporting persons or property.

The applicable time period for acquired property is (1) after September 10, 2001 and before September 11, 2004, and no binding written contract for the acquisition is in effect before September 11, 2001 or (2) pursuant to a binding written contract which was entered into after September 10, 2001, and before September 11, 2004. With respect to property that is manufactured, constructed, or produced by the taxpayer for use by the taxpayer, the taxpayer must begin the manufacture, construction, or production of the property after September 10, 2001, and before September 11, 2004. Property that is manufactured, constructed, or produced for the taxpayer by another person under a contract that is entered into prior to the manufacture, construction, or production of the property is considered to be manufactured, constructed, or produced by the taxpayer. For property eligible for the extended placed in service date, a special rule limits the amount of costs eligible for the additional first year depreciation. With respect to such property, only the portion of the basis that is properly attributable to the costs incurred before September 11, 2004 ("progress expenditures") shall be eligible for the additional first year depreciation.[8]

The limitation on the amount of depreciation deductions allowed with respect to certain passenger automobiles (sec. 280F of the Code) is increased in the first year by $4,600 for automobiles that qualify (and do not elect out of the increased first year deduction). The $4,600 increase is not indexed for inflation.

The following examples illustrate the operation of the provision.

EXAMPLE 1.—Assume that on March 1, 2002, a calendar year taxpayer acquires and places in service qualified property that costs $1 million. Under the provision, the taxpayer is allowed an additional first-year depreciation deduction of $300,000. The remaining $700,000 of adjusted basis is recovered in 2002 and subsequent years pursuant to the depreciation rules of present law.

EXAMPLE 2.—Assume that on March 1, 2002, a calendar year taxpayer acquires and places in service qualified property that costs $50,000. In addition, assume that the property qualifies for the expensing election under section 179. Under the provision, the taxpayer is first allowed a $24,000 deduction under section 179. The taxpayer then is allowed an additional first-year depreciation deduction of $7,800 based on $26,000 ($50,000 original cost less the section 179 deduction of $24,000) of adjusted basis. Finally, the remaining adjusted basis of $18,200 ($26,000 adjusted basis less $7,800 additional first-year depreciation) is to be recovered in 2002 and subsequent years pursuant to the depreciation rules of present law.

Effective Date

The provision applies to property placed in service after September 10, 2001.

(Footnote Continued)

quirement. However, the cost of reconditioned or rebuilt property acquired by the taxpayer would not satisfy the "original use" requirement. For example, if on February 1, 2002, a taxpayer buys from X for $20,000 a machine that has been previously used by X. Prior to September 11, 2004, the taxpayer makes an expenditure on the property of $5,000 of the type that must be capitalized. Regardless of whether the $5,000 is added to the basis of such property or is capitalized as a separate asset, such amount would be treated as satisfying the "original use" requirement and would be qualified property (assuming all other conditions are met). No part of the $20,000 purchase price would qualify for the additional first year depreciation.

[6] A special rule applies in the case of certain leased property. In the case of any property that is originally placed in service by a person and that is sold to the taxpayer and leased back to such person by the taxpayer within three months after the date that the property was placed in service, the property would be treated as originally placed in service by the taxpayer not earlier than the date that the property is used under the leaseback.

[7] In order for property to qualify for the extended placed in service date, the property is required to have a production period exceeding two years or an estimated production period exceeding one year and a cost exceeding $1 million.

[8] For purposes of determining the amount of eligible progress expenditures, it is intended that rules similar to sec. 46(d)(3) as in effect prior to the Tax Reform Act of 1986 shall apply.

House Committee Report (H.R. REP. NO. 107-251)

[Caution: The House Committee Report on the "Economic Security and Recovery Act of 2001," as passed by the House (H.R. Rep. No. 107-251), below, is included to assist the reader's understanding but may not be cited as the controlling Committee Report to P.L. 107-147.—CCH]

Present Law

Depreciation deductions

A taxpayer is allowed to recover, through annual depreciation deductions, the cost of certain property used in a trade or business or for the production of income. The amount of the depreciation deduction allowed with respect to tangible property for a taxable year is determined under the modified accelerated cost recovery system ("MACRS"). Under MACRS, different types of property generally are assigned applicable recovery periods and depreciation methods. The recovery periods applicable to most tangible personal property (generally tangible property other than residential rental property and nonresidential real property) range from 3 to 25 years. The depreciation methods generally applicable to tangible personal property are the 200-percent and 150-percent declining balance methods, switching to the straight-line method for the taxable year in which the depreciation deduction would be maximized.

Section 280F limits the annual depreciation deductions with respect to passenger automobiles to specified dollar amounts, indexed for inflation.

Section 167(f)(1) provides that capitalized computer software costs, other than computer software to which section 197 applies, are recovered ratably over 36 months.

Expensing election

In lieu of depreciation, a taxpayer with a sufficiently small amount of annual investment may elect to deduct up to $24,000 (for taxable years beginning in 2001 or 2002) of the cost of qualifying property placed in service for the taxable year (sec. 179). This amount is increased to $25,000 for taxable years beginning in 2003 and thereafter. In general, qualifying property is defined as depreciable tangible personal property that is purchased for use in the active conduct of a trade or business. The $24,000 ($25,000 for taxable years beginning in 2003 and thereafter) amount is reduced (but not below zero) by the amount by which the cost of qualifying property placed in

service during the taxable year exceeds $200,000. In addition, the amount eligible to be expensed for a taxable year may not exceed the taxable income for a taxable year that is derived from the active conduct of a trade or business (determined without regard to this provision). Any amount that is not allowed as a deduction because of the taxable income limitation may be carried forward to succeeding taxable years (subject to similar limitations). No general business credit under section 38 shall be allowed with respect to any amount for which a deduction is allowed under section 179.

Reasons for Change

The Committee believes that allowing additional first-year depreciation will accelerate purchases of equipment, promote capital investment, modernization, and growth, and will help to spur an economic recovery.

Explanation of Provision

The provision allows an additional first-year depreciation deduction equal to 30 percent of the adjusted basis of certain qualified property that is placed in service before January 1, 2005. The additional depreciation deduction is allowed for both regular tax and alternative minimum tax purposes for the taxable year in which the property is placed in service.[1] The basis of the property and the depreciation allowances in the year of purchase and later years is appropriately adjusted to reflect the additional first-year depreciation deduction. A taxpayer is allowed to elect out of the additional first-year depreciation for any class of property for any taxable year.

Property qualifies for the additional first-year depreciation deduction if the property is (1) property to which MACRS applies with a recovery period of 20 years or less other than leasehold improvements, (2) water utility property as defined in section 168(e)(5), or (3) computer software other than computer software covered by section 197. In order to be qualified property, the original use[2] of the property must commence with the taxpayer on or after September 11, 2001.[3] A special rule precludes the additional first-year depreciation deduction for property that is required to be depreciated under the alternative depreciation system of MACRS.

In addition, property qualifies only if acquired by the taxpayer (1) after September 10, 2001 and before September 11, 2004, and no binding written contract for the acquisition is in effect before

---

[1] The additional depreciation deduction is subject to the general rules regarding whether an item is deductible under section 162 or subject to capitalization under section 263 or section 263A.

[2] The term "original use" means the first use to which the property is put, whether or not such use corresponds to the use of such property by the taxpayer. Except as otherwise provided in Treasury Regulations, repaired or reconstructed property is not qualified property.

[3] A special rule applies in the case of certain leased property. In the case of any property that is originally placed in service by a person and that is sold to the taxpayer and leased back to such person by the taxpayer within three months after the date that the property was placed in service, the property is treated as originally placed in service by the taxpayer not earlier than the date that the property is used under the leaseback.

September 11, 2001 or (2) pursuant to a binding written contract which was entered into after September 10, 2001, and before September 11, 2004. Finally, property that is manufactured, constructed, or produced by the taxpayer for use by the taxpayer qualifies if the taxpayer begins the manufacture, construction, or production of the property after September 10, 2001, and before September 11, 2004 (and all other requirements are met). Property that is manufactured, constructed, or produced for the taxpayer by another person under a contract that is entered into prior to the manufacture, construction, or production of the property is considered to be manufactured, constructed, or produced by the taxpayer.

The limitation on the amount of depreciation deductions allowed with respect to certain passenger automobiles (sec. 280F of the Code) is increased in the first year by $4,600 for automobiles that qualify (and do not elect out of the increased first year deduction).

The following examples illustrate the operation of the provision.

EXAMPLE 1.—Assume that on March 1, 2002, a calendar year taxpayer acquires and places in service qualified property that costs $1 million. Under the provision, the taxpayer is al-lowed an additional first-year depreciation deduction of $300,000. The remaining $700,000 of adjusted basis is to be recovered in 2002 and subsequent years pursuant to the depreciation rules of present law.

EXAMPLE 2.—Assume that on March 1, 2002, a calendar year taxpayer acquires and places in service qualified property that costs $50,000. In addition, assume that the property qualifies for the expensing election under section 179. Under the provision, the taxpayer is first allowed a $35,000 deduction under section 179.[4] The taxpayer then is allowed an additional first-year depreciation deduction of $4,500 based on $15,000 ($50,000 original cost less the section 179 deduction of $35,000) of adjusted basis. Finally, the remaining adjusted basis of $11,500 ($15,000 adjusted basis less $4,500 additional first-year depreciation) is to be recovered in 2002 and subsequent years pursuant to the depreciation rules of present law.

Effective Date

The provision applies to property placed in service after September 10, 2001.

[Law at ¶ 5095. CCH Explanation at ¶ 305.]

[¶ 10,020]   Act Sec. 102. Five-year carryback of net operating losses

Joint Committee on Taxation (J.C.T. REP. NO. JCX-12-02)

[Caution: The Technical Explanation of the "Job Creation and Worker Assistance Act of 2002" (JCX-12-02), below, is included to assist the reader's understanding but may not be cited as the official Conference Committee Report to P.L. 107-147.—CCH]

[Code Sec. 56(d) and Code Sec. 172]

Present Law

A net operating loss ("NOL") is, generally, the amount by which a taxpayer's allowable deductions exceed the taxpayer's gross income. A carryback of an NOL generally results in the refund of Federal income tax for the carryback year. A carryforward of an NOL reduces Federal income tax for the carryforward year.

In general, an NOL may be carried back two years and carried forward 20 years to offset taxable income in such years. Different rules apply with respect to NOLs arising in certain circumstances. For example, a three-year carryback applies with respect to NOLs (1) arising from casualty or theft losses of individuals, or (2) attributable to Presidentially declared disasters for taxpayers engaged in a farming business or a small business. A five-year carryback period applies to NOLs from a farming loss (regardless of whether the loss was incurred in a Presidentially declared disaster area). Special rules also apply to real estate investment trusts (no carryback), specified liability losses (10-year carryback), and excess interest losses (no carryback to any year preceding a corporate equity reduction transaction).

The alternative minimum tax rules provide that a taxpayer's NOL deduction cannot reduce the taxpayer's alternative minimum taxable income ("AMTI") by more than 90 percent of the AMTI.

Explanation of Provision

The provision temporarily extends the general NOL carryback period to five years (from two years) for NOLs arising in taxable years ending in 2001 and 2002.[9] In addition, the five-year car-

---

[4] A subsequent provision in the bill temporarily increases the amount deductible under section 179 to $35,000. [This provision was not included in the final version of H.R. 3090 that was enacted as P.L. 107-147.—CCH]

[9] The provision does not affect the terms and conditions that the Internal Revenue Service may impose on a taxpayer seeking approval for a change in its annual accounting period. *See e.g.*, Rev. Proc. 2000-11, 2000-1 C.B. 309, sec. 5.06 ("If the corporation (or consolidated group) has a

NOL (or consolidated NOL) in the short period required to effect the change, the NOL may not be carried back but must be carried over in accordance with the provisions of sec. 172 beginning with the first taxable year after the short period. However, the short period NOL (or consolidated NOL) is carried back or carried over in accordance with sec. 172 if it is either: (a) $50,000 or less, or (b) results from a short period of 9 months or longer and is less than the NOL

ryback period applies to NOLs from these years that qualify under present law for a three-year carryback period (i.e., NOLs arising from casualty or theft losses of individuals or attributable to certain Presidentially declared disaster areas).

A taxpayer can elect to forgo the five-year carryback period. The election to forgo the five-year carryback period is made in the manner prescribed by the Secretary of the Treasury and must be made by the due date of the return (including extensions) for the year of the loss. The election is irrevocable. If a taxpayer elects to forgo the five-year carryback period, then the losses are subject to the rules that otherwise would apply under section 172 absent the provision.

The provision also allows an NOL deduction attributable to NOL carrybacks arising in taxable years ending in 2001 and 2002, as well as NOL carryforwards to these taxable years, to offset 100 percent of a taxpayer's AMTI.[10]

Effective Date

The 5-year carryback provision is effective for net operating losses generated in taxable years ending after December 31, 2000.

The provision allowing the use of NOL carrybacks and carryforwards to offset 100 percent of AMTI is effective for taxable years ending before January 1, 2003.

House Committee Report (H.R. Rep. No. 107-251)

[Caution: The House Committee Report on the "Economic Security and Recovery Act of 2001," as passed by the House (H.R. Rep. No. 107-251), below, is included to assist the reader's understanding but may not be cited as the controlling Committee Report to P.L. 107-147.—CCH]

Present Law

A net operating loss ("NOL") is, generally, the amount by which a taxpayer's allowable deductions exceed the taxpayer's gross income. An NOL that is carried back may be deducted from gross income in the carryback year, thereby resulting in a refund of Federal income tax for the carryback year. Similarly, an NOL that is carried forward may be deducted from gross income in a carryforward year, thus reducing the Federal income tax liability for the carryforward year.

In general, an NOL may be carried back two years and carried forward 20 years to offset taxable income in such years. Different rules apply with respect to NOLs arising in certain circumstances. For example, a three-year carryback applies with respect to NOLs (1) arising from casualty or theft losses of individuals, or (2) attributable to Presidentially declared disasters for taxpayers engaged in a farming business or a small business. A five-year carryback period applies to NOLs from a farming loss (regardless of whether the loss was incurred in a Presidentially declared disaster area). Special rules also apply to real estate investment trusts (no carryback), specified liability losses (10-year carryback), and excess interest losses (no carryback).

The alternative minimum tax rules provide that a taxpayer's NOL deduction cannot reduce the taxpayer's alternative minimum taxable income ("AMTI") by more than 90 percent of the AMTI.

Reasons for Change

The NOL carryback and carryforward rules allow taxpayers to smooth out swings in business income (and Federal income taxes thereon) that result from business cycle fluctuations and unexpected financial losses. The current uncertain economic conditions have resulted in many taxpayers incurring unexpected financial losses. A temporary extension of the NOL carryback period will provide taxpayers in all sectors of the economy who experience such losses the ability to increase their cash flow through the refund of income taxes paid in prior years. The provision will free up funds that can be used for capital investment or other expenses that will provide stimulus to the economy.

Explanation of Provision

The provision temporarily extends the general NOL carryback period to five years (from two years) for NOLs arising in taxable years ending on or after September 11, 2001, and ending before September 11, 2004. In addition, the five-year carryback period applies to NOLs from these years that qualify under present law for a three-year carryback period (i.e., NOLs arising from casualty or theft losses of individuals or attributable to certain Presidentially declared disaster areas).

The provision also allows an NOL deduction attributable to these taxable years to offset 100 percent of a taxpayer's AMTI in a carryback year.[7]

A taxpayer can elect to forgo the five-year carryback period. The election to forgo the five-year carryback period is made in the manner prescribed by the Secretary of the Treasury and must be made by the due date of the return (including extensions) for the year of the loss. The election is irrevocable. If a taxpayer elects to

---

(Footnote Continued)

(or the consolidated NOL) for a full 12-month period beginning with the first day of the short period.")

[10] Section 172(b)(2) should be appropriately applied in computing AMTI to take proper account of the order that the NOL carryovers and carrybacks are used as a result of this provision. *See* section 56(d)(1)(B)(ii).

[7] Section 172(b)(2) should be appropriately applied in computing AMTI to take proper account of the order that the NOL carryovers and carrybacks are used as a result of this provision. *See* section 56(d)(1)(B)(ii).

forgo the five-year carryback period, then the losses are subject to the rules that otherwise would apply under section 172 absent the provision.

Effective Date
* * *

[Law at ¶ 5060 and ¶ 5105. CCH Explanation at ¶ 310.]

[¶ 10,050]   Act Sec. 201, Act Sec. 202, Act Sec. 203, Act Sec. 204, Act Sec. 205, Act Sec. 206, Act Sec. 207 and Act Sec. 208. Unemployment assistance

Joint Committee on Taxation (J.C.T. REP. NO. JCX-12-02)

[Caution: The Technical Explanation of the "Job Creation and Worker Assistance Act of 2002" (JCX-12-02), below, is included to assist the reader's understanding but may not be cited as the official Conference Committee Report to P.L. 107-147.—CCH]

[Act Sec. 201, Act Sec. 202, Act Sec. 203, Act Sec. 204, Act Sec. 205, Act Sec. 206, Act Sec. 207 and Act Sec. 208]

Present Law

States set unemployment benefit rules within a broad federal framework. The maximum length of benefits is 26 weeks in all but two states. The average duration on unemployment was 14 weeks in 2001. During fiscal year 2001, 28 percent of recipients used all of their eligibility or "exhausted eligibility."

Under the regular Federal-State Extended Benefits Program, up to an additional 13 weeks of benefits are available in states suffering severe economic distress. These benefits become available when a state's "insured" unemployment rate is 5 percent and 120 percent of the average over the last two years or, at state option, if the "insured" rate is 6 percent. States also may adopt another trigger, a total unemployment rate of 6.5 percent and 110 percent of the average over the past two years. The benefits are 50 percent federally-funded. (Regular unemployment benefits are funded by state taxes levied on employers.)

Explanation of Provision

The bill provides for up to 13 weeks of temporary extended unemployment benefits for eligible displaced workers. These benefits would be available following enactment in any state entering into an agreement with the Secretary of Labor to provide such extended benefits. Benefits would be available to workers who filed an initial claim for unemployment benefits on or after March 15, 2001 (that is, approximately when the recent recession began) and who remain unable to find work after having exhausted their regular unemployment benefits.

The provision follows current law regarding certain eligibility rules for receipt of extended benefits, for example providing that individuals qualify for the lesser of 13 weeks of extended benefits or 50 percent of the length of time they qualified for regular unemployment benefits under the laws of their state; to ensure that workers with a strong attachment to the workforce qualify, individuals must have worked 20 weeks of full-time insured employment or earned the equivalent in insured wages to be eligible for these extended benefits.

In states continuing to experience a high rate of unemployment (those with an insured unemployment rate of at least 4%) displaced workers who exhaust their up to 13 weeks of temporary extended unemployment benefits provided nationwide, as described above, would be eligible for up to an additional 13 weeks of temporary extended unemployment benefits.

The benefits would be 100 percent federally funded and would be available through December 31, 2002, or until a state terminates its agreement, if sooner.

Effective Date

The temporary extended unemployment provision would be effective upon enactment.

[Law at ¶ 7010, ¶ 7015, ¶ 7020, ¶ 7025, ¶ 7030, ¶ 7035, ¶ 7040 and ¶ 7045. CCH Explanation at ¶ 205.]

[¶ 10,060]   Act Sec. 209. Special Reed Act transfer in fiscal year 2002

Joint Committee on Taxation (J.C.T. REP. NO. JCX-12-02)

[Caution: The Technical Explanation of the "Job Creation and Worker Assistance Act of 2002" (JCX-12-02), below, is included to assist the reader's understanding but may not be cited as the official Conference Committee Report to P.L. 107-147.—CCH]

[Act Sec. 209]

Present Law

When three federal accounts in the Unemployment Trust Fund (UTF) reach their statutory limits at the end of a federal fiscal year, any excess funds are transferred to the individual state accounts in the UTF. These transfers are called "Reed Act" distributions. States can use this funding for payment of cash benefits and administrating their unemployment compensation and employment services programs. The Balanced Budget Act of 1997 limited Reed Act transfers to states to $100 million after each of fiscal years 1999, 2000, and 2001 and limited these funds' use to paying administrative expenses of unemployment compensation laws.

If the Secretary finds that a state is not eligible to receive Reed Act transfers at the beginning of a fiscal year, the amount available for transfer to the state instead is transferred to the federal unemployment account. If the state becomes eligible during the following one year period, the amount which was available for transfer will be transferred from the federal unemployment account to the state's account. If the state does not become eligible within one year, the amount remains in the federal unemployment account for other uses. If any state has borrowed from the federal unemployment account, any amount that would be transferred is retained and credited against any balance due to the state.

Explanation of Provision

The $100 million limit on distributions from excess federal funds available at the end of fiscal year 2001 is repealed. The provision also repeals the limitation on the use of funds applied to the $100 million special distribution under the Balanced Budget Act of 1997. This limitation applied only to special distributions at the end of fiscal years 1999, 2000, and 2001, and with the repeal of the underlying special distribution provision is no longer relevant.

The Secretary of the Treasury will transfer excess federal UTF balances as of the close of fiscal year 2001 into the account of each state in the UTF. Total transfers will be capped at no more than $8 billion.

At the option of the state, amounts transferred to state accounts may be used for the payment of cash benefits to individuals with respect to unemployment, including regular unemployment compensation or additions to regular benefits. States also may use these funds to support payment of benefits to individuals not otherwise eligible for regular unemployment compensation benefits under the laws of the state, such as individuals seeking only part-time work or those eligible only under an alternative base period.

Other than for cash benefits, states may use amounts transferred to their accounts in the administration of their public employment laws and public employment offices, including for the provision of employment services needed to help individuals return to work.

Effective Date

Transfers under this provision shall be made within 10 days following enactment.

[Law at ¶ 5320, ¶ 5325 and ¶ 7050. CCH Explanation at ¶ 205.]

[¶ 10,100]   Act Sec. 301(a) and Act Sec. 301(b). Expansion of work opportunity tax credit targeted categories to include certain employees in New York City

Joint Committee on Taxation (J.C.T. Rep. No. JCX-12-02)

[Caution: The Technical Explanation of the "Job Creation and Worker Assistance Act of 2002" (JCX-12-02), below, is included to assist the reader's understanding but may not be cited as the official Conference Committee Report to P.L. 107-147.—CCH]

[Code Sec. 38(c) and Code Sec.1400L(a)]

Present Law

In general

The work opportunity tax credit ("WOTC") is available on an elective basis for employers hiring individuals from one or more of eight targeted groups. The credit equals 40 percent (25 percent for employment of less than 400 hours) of qualified wages. Generally, qualified wages are wages attributable to service rendered by a member of a targeted group during the one-year period beginning with the day the individual began work for the employer.

The maximum credit per employee is $2,400 (40 percent of the first $6,000 of qualified first-year wages). With respect to qualified summer youth employees, the maximum credit is $1,200 (40 percent of the first $3,000 of qualified first-year wages).

For purposes of the credit, wages are generally defined as under the Federal Unemployment Tax Act, without regard to the dollar cap.

Targeted groups eligible for the credit

The eight targeted groups are: (1) families eligible to receive benefits under the Temporary Assistance for Needy Families ("TANF") Program; (2) high-risk youth; (3) qualified ex-felons; (4) vocational rehabilitation referrals; (5) qualified summer youth employees; (6) qualified veterans; (7) families receiving food stamps; and (8) persons receiving certain Supplemental Security Income ("SSI") benefits.

¶ 10,100   Act Sec. 301(a)

The employer's deduction for wages is reduced by the amount of the credit.

Expiration date

The credit is effective for wages paid or incurred to a qualified individual who began work for an employer before January 1, 2002.

Explanation of Provision

The bill creates a new targeted group for the WOTC and extends WOTC only for this purpose.[11] Generally, the new targeted group is individuals who perform substantially all their services in the recovery zone for a business located on or south of Canal street, East Broadway (east of its intersection with Canal Street), or Grand Street (east of its intersection with East Broadway) in the Borough of Manhattan, New York, New York (the "New York Liberty Zone"). The new targeted group also includes individuals who perform substantially all their services in New York City for a business that relocated from the New York Liberty Zone elsewhere within New York City due to the physical destruction or damage of their workplaces within the New York Liberty Zone by the September 11, 2001 terrorist attack. It is anticipated that only otherwise qualified businesses that relocate due to significant physical damage will be eligible for the credit.

Generally qualified wages for purposes of this targeted group are wages paid or incurred for work performed in the New York Liberty Zone after December 31, 2001 and before January 1, 2004 by such qualified individuals. Also, in the case of otherwise qualified businesses that relocated due to the destruction or damage of their workplaces by the September 11, 2001 terrorist attack, the credit can be claimed for work performed outside of the zone but within New York City subject to the dates specified above. Other rules like the minimum employment periods (sec. 51(i)(3)) of the WOTC apply.

Unlike the other targeted categories, the credit for the new targeted group is available for wages paid to both new hires and existing employees. For each qualified business that relocated from the New York Liberty Zone elsewhere within New York City due to the physical destruction or damage of their workplaces within the New York Liberty Zone, the number of that employer's employees whose wages are eligible under the new targeted category may not exceed the number of its employees in the New York Liberty Zone on September 11, 2001. Other qualified businesses (e.g., businesses that operate in the New York Liberty Zone both on and after Sept. 11, 2001 and businesses that move into the New York Liberty Zone after September 11, 2001) would not be subject to that limitation.

No credit for this new category of workers is allowed if the otherwise qualifying employer on average employed more than 200 employees during the taxable year in question.

Unlike the other targeted categories, members of this targeted group will not require certification for their wages to qualify for the credit.

For the new category, the maximum credit is $2,400 (40 percent of $6,000 of qualified wages) per qualified employee in each taxable year.

The portion of each employer's WOTC credit attributable to the new targeted group is allowed against the alternative minimum tax.

Effective Date

The provision is effective in taxable years ending after December 31, 2001 (for wages paid or incurred to qualified individuals for work after December 31, 2001 and before January 1, 2004).

[Law at ¶ 5040 and ¶ 5300. CCH Explanation at ¶ 405 and ¶ 410.]

[¶ 10,110]   Act Sec. 301(a). Special depreciation allowance for certain property

Joint Committee on Taxation (J.C.T. Rep. No. JCX-12-02)

[Caution: The Technical Explanation of the "Job Creation and Worker Assistance Act of 2002" (JCX-12-02), below, is included to assist the reader's understanding but may not be cited as the official Conference Committee Report to P.L. 107-147.—CCH]

[Code Sec. 1400L(b) and Code Sec. 1400L(h)]

Present Law

Depreciation deductions

A taxpayer is allowed to recover, through annual depreciation deductions, the cost of certain

property used in a trade or business or for the production of income. The amount of the depreciation deduction allowed with respect to tangible property for a taxable year is determined under the modified accelerated cost recovery system ("MACRS"). Under MACRS, different types of property generally are assigned applicable recovery periods and depreciation methods. The recovery periods applicable to most tangible personal property (generally tangible property other than residential rental property and nonresidential real property) range from 3 to 25 years. The deprecia-

---

[11] A separate provision of this bill includes a general 2-year extension of WOTC.

tion methods generally applicable to tangible personal property are the 200-percent and 150-percent declining balance methods, switching to the straight-line method for the taxable year in which the depreciation deduction would be maximized. In lieu of depreciation, a taxpayer with a sufficiently small amount of annual investment generally may elect to deduct up to $24,000 (for taxable years beginning in 2001 or 2002) of the cost of qualifying property placed in service for the taxable year (sec. 179). For taxable years beginning in 2003 and thereafter, the amount deductible under section 179 is increased to $25,000.

Section 167(f)(1) provides that capitalized computer software costs, other than computer software to which section 197 applies, are recovered ratably over 36 months.

Explanation of Provision

The provision allows an additional first-year depreciation deduction equal to 30 percent of the adjusted basis of qualified New York Liberty Zone ("Liberty Zone") property. The additional first-year depreciation deduction is allowed for both regular tax and alternative minimum tax purposes for the taxable year in which the property is placed in service.[12] The basis of the property and the depreciation allowances in the year of purchase and later years are appropriately adjusted to reflect the additional first-year depreciation deduction. In addition, the provision provides that there would be no adjustment to the allowable amount of depreciation for purposes of computing a taxpayer's alternative minimum taxable income with respect to property to which the provision applies. A taxpayer is allowed to elect out of the additional first-year depreciation for any class of property for any taxable year.

In order for property to qualify for the additional first-year depreciation deduction it must meet all of the following requirements. First, the property must be property to which the general rules of MACRS[13] apply with (1) an applicable recovery period of 20 years or less, (2) water utility property (as defined in section 168(e)(5)), (3) certain nonresidential real property and residential rental property, or (4) computer software other than computer software covered by section

197. A special rule precludes the additional first year depreciation under this provision for (1) qualified New York Liberty Zone leasehold improvement property[14] and, (2) property eligible for the additional first year depreciation under section 168(k) (i.e., property is eligible for only one 30% additional first year depreciation). Second, substantially all of the use of such property must be in the Liberty Zone. Third, the original use[15] of the property in the Liberty Zone must commence with the taxpayer on or after September 11, 2001.[16] Finally, the property must be acquired by purchase[17] by the taxpayer (1) after September 10, 2001 and placed in service on or before December 31, 2006. For qualifying nonresidential real property and residential rental property the property must be placed in service on or before December 31, 2009 in lieu of December 31, 2006. Property will not qualify if a binding written contract for the acquisition of such property is in effect before September 11, 2001.

Nonresidential real property and residential rental property is eligible for the additional first-year depreciation only to the extent such property rehabilitates real property damaged, or replaces real property destroyed or condemned as a result of the terrorist attacks of September 11, 2001. Property shall be treated as replacing destroyed property, if as part of an integrated plan, such property replaces real property which is included in a continuous area which includes real property destroyed or condemned. For purposes of this provision, it is intended that real property destroyed (or condemned) only include circumstances in which an entire building or structure was destroyed (or condemned) as a result of the terrorist attacks. Otherwise, such property is considered damaged real property. For example, if certain structural components (e.g., walls, floors, or plumbing fixtures) of a building are damaged or destroyed as a result of the terrorist attacks but the building is not destroyed (or condemned), then only costs related to replacing the damaged or destroyed components qualifies for the provision.

Property that is manufactured, constructed, or produced by the taxpayer for use by the taxpayer qualifies if the taxpayer begins the manufacture, construction, or production of the property after

---

[12] The additional first-year depreciation deduction is subject to the general rules regarding whether an item is deductible under section 162 or subject to capitalization under section 263 or section 263A.

[13] A special rule precludes the additional first-year depreciation deduction for property that is required to be depreciated under the alternative depreciation system of MACRS.

[14] Qualified New York Liberty Zone leasehold improvement property is defined in another provision of the bill. Leasehold improvements that do not satisfy the requirements to be treated as "qualified New York Liberty Zone leasehold improvement property" are eligible for the 30 percent additional first-year depreciation deduction (assuming all other conditions are met).

[15] Thus, used property may constitute qualified property so long as it has not previously been used within the Liberty

Zone. In addition, it is intended that additional capital expenditures incurred to recondition or rebuild property the original use of which in the Liberty Zone began with the taxpayer would satisfy the "original use" requirement. See Treasury Regulation 1.48-2 Example 5.

[16] A special rule applies in the case of certain leased property. In the case of any property that is originally placed in service by a person and that is sold to the taxpayer and leased back to such person by the taxpayer within three months after the date that the property was placed in service, the property would be treated as originally placed in service by the taxpayer not earlier than the date that the property is used under the leaseback.

[17] For purposes of this provision, purchase is defined under section 179(d).

September 10, 2001, and the property is placed in service on or before December 31, 2006[18] (and all other requirements are met). Property that is manufactured, constructed, or produced for the taxpayer by another person under a contract that is entered into prior to the manufacture, construction, or production of the property is considered to be manufactured, constructed, or produced by the taxpayer.

The Liberty Zone means the area located on or south of Canal Street, East Broadway (east of its intersection with Canal Street), or Grand Street (east of its intersection with East Broadway) in the Borough of Manhattan in the City of New York, New York.

The following examples illustrate the operation of the provision.

EXAMPLE 1.—Assume that on March 1, 2002, a calendar year taxpayer acquires and places in service qualified property in the Liberty Zone that costs $1 million. Under the provision, the taxpayer is allowed an additional first-year depreciation deduction of $300,000. The remaining $700,000 of adjusted basis is recovered in 2002 and subsequent years pursuant to the depreciation rules of present law.

EXAMPLE 2.—Assume that on March 1, 2002, a calendar year taxpayer acquires and places in service qualified property in the Liberty Zone that costs $100,000. In addition, assume that the property qualifies for the expensing election under section 179. Under the provision, the taxpayer is first allowed a $59,000 deduction under section 179.[19] The taxpayer then is allowed an additional first-year depreciation deduction of $12,300 based on $41,000 ($100,000 original cost less the section 179 deduction of $59,000) of adjusted basis. Finally, the remaining adjusted basis of $28,700 ($41,000 adjusted basis less $12,300 additional first-year depreciation) is to be recovered in 2002 and subsequent years pursuant to the depreciation rules of present law.

[Law at ¶ 5300. CCH Explanation at ¶ 405, ¶ 410, ¶ 415, ¶ 420, ¶ 425, ¶ 430 and ¶ 435.]

[¶ 10,120] Act Sec. 301(a). Authorize issuance of tax-exempt private activity bonds for rebuilding the portion of New York City damaged in the September 11, 2001, terrorist attack

Joint Committee on Taxation (J.C.T. REP. NO. JCX-12-02)

[Caution: The Technical Explanation of the "Job Creation and Worker Assistance Act of 2002" (JCX-12-02), below, is included to assist the reader's understanding but may not be cited as the official Conference Committee Report to P.L. 107-147.—CCH]

[Code Sec. 1400L(d), Code Sec. 1400L(h) and Code Sec. 1400L(i)]

Present Law

Rules governing issuance of tax-exempt bonds

In general

Interest on debt incurred by States or local governments is excluded from income if the proceeds of the borrowing are used to carry out governmental functions of those entities or the debt is repaid with governmental funds (sec. 103). Interest on bonds that nominally are issued by States or local governments, but the proceeds of which are used (directly or indirectly) by a private person and payment of which is derived from funds of such a private person is taxable unless the purpose of the borrowing is approved specifically in the Code or in a non-Code provision of a revenue Act. These bonds are called "private activity bonds."[20] The term "private person" includes the Federal Government and all other individuals and entities other than States or local governments.

Private activities eligible for financing with tax-exempt private activity bonds

Present law includes several exceptions permitting States or local governments to act as conduits providing tax-exempt financing for private activities. Both capital expenditures and limited working capital expenditures of charitable organizations described in section 501(c)(3) of the Code ("qualified 501(c)(3) bonds") may be financed with tax-exempt bonds.

States or local governments may issue tax-exempt "exempt-facility bonds" to finance property for certain private businesses. Business facilities eligible for this financing include transportation (airports, ports, local mass commuting, and high

---

[18] December 31, 2009 with respect to nonresidential real property and residential rental property.

[19] Section 301 provides that property in the Liberty Zone is eligible for an additional $35,000 of expensing under section 179.

[20] Interest on private activity bonds (other than qualified 501(c)(3) bonds) is a preference item in calculating the alternative minimum tax.

speed intercity rail facilities); privately owned and/or privately operated public works facilities (sewage, solid waste disposal, local district heating or cooling, and hazardous waste disposal facilities); privately owned and/or operated low-income rental housing;[21] and certain private facilities for the local furnishing of electricity or gas. A further provision allows tax-exempt financing for "environmental enhancements of hydro-electric generating facilities." Tax-exempt financing also is authorized for capital expenditures for small manufacturing facilities and land and equipment for first-time farmers ("qualified small-issue bonds"), local redevelopment activities ("qualified redevelopment bonds"), and eligible empowerment zone and enterprise community businesses.

Tax-exempt private activity bonds also may be issued to finance limited non-business purposes: certain student loans and mortgage loans for owner-occupied housing ("qualified mortgage bonds" and "qualified veterans' mortgage bonds"). Purchasers of houses financed with qualified mortgage bonds must be first-time homebuyers satisfying prescribed income limits, the purchase prices of the houses is limited, the amount by which interest rates charged to homebuyers may exceed the interest paid by issuers is restricted, and a recapture provision applies to target the benefit to purchasers having longer-term need for the subsidy provided by the bonds. Qualified veterans' mortgage bonds are not subject to these limitations, but these bonds may only be issued by five States and may only be used to finance mortgage loans to veterans who served on active duty before January 1, 1977.

With the exception of qualified 501(c)(3) bonds, private activity bonds may not be issued to finance working capital requirements of private businesses.

In most cases, the aggregate volume of tax-exempt private activity bonds that may be issued in a State is restricted by annual volume limits. These annual volume limits are equal to $62.50 per resident of the State, or $187.5 million if greater. The volume limits are scheduled to increase to the greater of $75 per resident of the State or $225 million in calendar year 2002. After 2002, the volume limits will be indexed annually for inflation.

Arbitrage restrictions on tax-exempt bonds

The Federal income tax does not apply to the income of States and local governments that is derived from the exercise of an essential governmental function. To prevent these tax-exempt entities from issuing more Federally subsidized tax-exempt bonds than is necessary for the activity

being financed or from issuing such bonds earlier than needed for the purpose of the borrowing, the Code includes arbitrage restrictions limiting the ability to profit from investment of tax-exempt bond proceeds. In general, arbitrage profits may be earned only during specified periods (e.g., defined "temporary periods" before funds are needed for the purpose of the borrowing) or on specified types of investments (e.g., "reasonably required reserve or replacement funds"). Subject to limited exceptions, profits that are earned during these periods or on such investments must be rebated to the Federal Government. Governmental bonds are subject to less restrictive arbitrage rules that most private activity bonds.

Miscellaneous additional restrictions on tax-exempt bonds

Several additional restrictions apply to the issuance of tax-exempt bonds. First, private activity bonds (other than qualified 501(c)(3) bonds) may not be advance refunded. Governmental bonds and qualified 501(c)(3) bonds may be advance refunded one time. An advance refunding occurs when the refunded bonds are not retired within 90 days of issuance of the refunding bonds.

Issuance of private activity bonds is subject to restrictions on use of proceeds for the acquisition of land and existing property, use of proceeds to finance certain specified facilities, (e.g., airplanes, skyboxes, other luxury boxes, health club facilities, gambling facilities, and liquor stores) and use of proceeds to pay costs of issuance (e.g., bond counsel and underwriter fees). Additionally, the term of the bonds generally may not exceed 120 percent of the economic life of the property being financed and certain public approval requirements (similar to requirements that typically apply under State law to issuance of governmental debt) apply under Federal law to issuance of private activity bonds. Present law precludes substantial users of property financed with private activity bonds from owning the bonds to prevent their deducting tax-exempt interest paid to themselves. Finally, owners of most private-activity-bond-financed property are subject to special "change-in-use" penalties if the use of the bond-financed property changes to a use that is not eligible for tax-exempt financing while the bonds are outstanding.

Explanation of Provision

In general

The provision authorizes issuance during calendar years 2002, 2003, and 2004 of an aggregate amount of $8 billion of tax-exempt private activity bonds to finance the construction and rehabilitation of nonresidential real property[22] and

---

[21] Residential rental projects must satisfy low-income tenant occupancy requirements for a minimum period of 15 years.

[22] No more than $800 million of the authorized bond amount may be used to finance property used for retail sales of tangible property (e.g., department stores, restaurants,

residential rental real property[23] in a newly designated "Liberty Zone" (the "Zone") of New York City.[24] Property eligible for financing with these bonds includes buildings and their structural components, fixed tenant improvements,[25] and public utility property (e.g., gas, water, electric and telecommunication lines). All business addresses located on or south of Canal Street, East Broadway (east of its intersection with Canal Street), or Grand Street (east of its intersection with East Broadway) in the Borough of Manhattan are considered to be located within the New York Recovery Zone. Issuance of bonds authorized under the provision is limited to projects approved by the Mayor of New York City or the Governor of New York State, each of whom may designate up to $4 billion of the bonds authorized under the bill.

If the Mayor or the Governor determines that it is not feasible to use all of the authorized bond proceeds which he is authorized to designate for property located in the Zone, up to $1 billion of bond proceeds may designated by each to be used for the acquisition, construction, and rehabilitation of commercial real property (including fixed tenant improvements) located outside the Zone and within New York City.[26] Bond-financed property located outside the Zone must meet the additional requirements that the project have at least 100,000 square feet of usable office or other commercial space in a single building or multiple adjacent buildings.

Subject to the following exceptions and modifications, issuance of these tax-exempt bonds is subject to the general rules applicable to issuance of exempt-facility private activity bonds:

(1) Issuance of the bonds is not subject to the aggregate annual State private activity bond volume limits (sec. 146);

(2) The restriction on acquisition of existing property is applied using a minimum requirement of 50 percent of the cost of acquiring the building being devoted to rehabilitation (sec. 147(d));

(3) The special arbitrage expenditure rules for certain construction bond proceeds apply to available construction proceeds of the bonds (sec. 148(f)(4)(C));

(4) The tenant targeting rules applicable to exempt-facility bonds for residential rental property (and the corresponding change in use penalties for violation of those rules) do not apply to such property financed with the bonds (secs. 142(d) and 150(b)(2));

(5) Repayments of bond-financed loans may not be used to make additional loans, but rather must be used to retire outstanding bonds (with the first such retirement occurring 10 years after issuance of the bonds);[27] and

(6) Interest on the bonds is not a preference item for purposes of the alternative minimum tax preference for private activity bond interest (sec. 57(a)(5)); and

[Sic.—CCH]

Effective Date

The provision is effective for bonds issued after the date of enactment and before January 1, 2005.

[Law at ¶ 5300. CCH Explanation at ¶ 405, ¶ 410, ¶ 415, ¶ 420, ¶ 425, ¶ 430 and ¶ 435.]

[¶ 10,130]   Act Sec. 301(a). Allow one additional advance refunding for certain previously refunded bonds for facilities located in New York City

Joint Committee on Taxation (J.C.T. Rep. No. JCX-12-02)

[Caution: The Technical Explanation of the "Job Creation and Worker Assistance Act of 2002" (JCX-12-02), below, is included to assist the reader's understanding but may not be cited as the official Conference Committee Report to P.L. 107-147.—CCH]

[Code Sec. 1400L(e), Code Sec. 1400L(h) and Code Sec. 1400L(i)]

Present Law

Interest on bonds issued by States or local governments is excluded from income if the proceeds of the borrowing are used to carry out governmen-

---

(Footnote Continued)

etc.) and functionally related and subordinate property. The term nonresidential real property includes structural components of such property if the taxpayer treats such components as part of the real property structure for all Federal income tax purposes (e.g., cost recovery). The $800 million limit is divided equally between the Mayor and the Governor.

[23] No more than $1.6 billion of the authorized bond amount may be used to finance residential rental property. The $1.6 billion limit is divided equally between the Mayor and the Governor.

[24] Current refundings of outstanding bonds issued under the provision do not count against the $8 billion volume

limit to the extent that the principal amount of the refunding bonds does not exceed the outstanding principal amount of the bonds being refunded. The bonds may not be advance refunded.

[25] Fixtures and equipment that could be removed from the designated zone for use elsewhere are not eligible for financing with these bonds.

[26] Public utility property and residential property located outside the Zone cannot be financed with the bonds.

[27] It is intended that redemptions will occur at least semiannually beginning at the end of 10 years after the bonds are issued; however, amounts of less than $250,000 are not to be required to be used to redeem bonds at such intervals.

tal functions of those entities or the debt is repaid with governmental funds (sec. 103). Interest on bonds that nominally are issued by States or local governments, but the proceeds of which are used (directly or indirectly) by a private person and payment of which is derived from funds of such a private person is taxable unless the purpose of the borrowing is approved specifically in the Code or in a non-Code provision of a revenue Act. These bonds are called private activity bonds. Present law includes several exceptions permitting States or local governments to act as conduits providing tax-exempt financing for private activities. One such exception is the provision of financing for activities of charitable organizations described in section 501(c)(3) of the Code ("qualified 501(c)(3) bonds").

A refunding bond is used to redeem a prior bond issuance. The Code contains different rules for "current" as opposed to "advance" refunding bonds. Tax-exempt bonds may be refunded currently an indefinite number of times. A current refunding occurs when the refunded debt is redeemed within 90 days of issuance of the refunding bonds. Governmental bonds and qualified 501(c)(3) bonds also may be advance refunded one time (sec. 149(d)).[28] An advance refunding occurs when the refunded debt is not redeemed within 90 days after the refunding bonds are issued. Rather, proceeds of the refunding bonds are invested in an escrow account and held until a future date when the refunded debt may be redeemed until the terms of the refunded bonds.

Explanation of Provision

The bill permits certain bonds for facilities located in New York City to be advance refunded one additional time. These bonds include only bonds for which all present-law advance refunding

authority was exhausted before September 12, 2001, and with respect to which the advance refunding bonds authorized under present law were outstanding on September 11, 2001.[29] Further, to be eligible for the additional advance refunding, at least 90 percent of the refunded bonds must have been used to finance facilities located in New York City,[30][31] and the bonds must be—

(1) Governmental general obligation bonds of New York City;

(2) Governmental bonds issued by the Metropolitan Transportation Authority of the State of New York;

(3) Governmental bonds issued by the New York Municipal Water Finance Authority; or

(4) Qualified 501(c)(3) bonds issued by or on behalf of New York State or New York City to finance hospital facilities (as defined in section 145(c).

The maximum amount of advance refunding bonds that may be issued pursuant to this provision is $9 billion. Eligible advance refunding bonds must be designated as such by the Mayor of New York City or the Governor of New York State. Up to $4.5 billion of bonds may be designated by each of these officials. Advance refunding bonds issued under the provision must satisfy all requirements of section 148 and 149(d) except for the limit on the number of advance refundings allowed under section 149(d).

Effective Date

The provision is effective on the date of enactment and before January 1, 2005.

[Law at ¶ 5300. CCH Explanation at ¶ 405, ¶ 410, ¶ 415, ¶ 420, ¶ 425, ¶ 430 and ¶ 435.]

[¶ 10,140]   Act Sec. 301(a). Increase in expensing treatment for business property used in the New York Liberty Zone

Joint Committee on Taxation (J.C.T. Rep. No. JCX-12-02)

[Caution: The Technical Explanation of the "Job Creation and Worker Assistance Act of 2002" (JCX-12-02), below, is included to assist the reader's understanding but may not be cited as the official Conference Committee Report to P.L. 107-147.—CCH]

[Code Sec. 1400L(f) and Code Sec. 1400L(h)]

Present Law

Present law provides that, in lieu of depreciation, a taxpayer with a sufficiently small amount

of annual investment may elect to deduct up to $24,000 (for taxable years beginning in 2001 or 2002) of the cost of qualifying property placed in service for the taxable year (sec. 179). This amount is increased to $25,000 of the cost of qualified property placed in service for taxable years beginning in 2003 and thereafter. The $24,000 ($25,000 for taxable years beginning in 2003 and thereafter) amount is phased-out (but not below zero) by the amount by which the cost

---

[28] Bonds issued before 1986 and pursuant to certain transition rules contained in the Tax Reform Act of 1986 may be advance refunded more than one time in certain cases.

[29] Thus, at no time after the advance refunding authorized under the provision occurs may there be more than two sets of bonds outstanding.

[30] This requirement is 95 percent in the case of eligible qualified 501(c)(3) bonds.

[31] In the case of bonds for water facilities issued by the New York Municipal Water Finance Authority, property located outside New York City that is functionally related and subordinate to property located in the city is deemed to be located in the city.

of qualifying property placed in service during the taxable year exceeds $200,000.

Additional section 179 incentives are provided with respect to a qualified zone property used by a business in an empowerment zone (sec. 1397A). Such a business may elect to deduct an additional $20,000 of the cost of qualified zone property placed in service in year 2001. The $20,000 amount is increased to $35,000 for taxable years beginning in 2002 and thereafter. In addition, the phase-out range is applied by taking into account only 50 percent of the cost of qualified zone property that is section 179 property.

The amount eligible to be expensed for a taxable year may not exceed the taxable income for a taxable year that is derived from the active conduct of a trade or business (determined without regard to this provision). Any amount that is not allowed as a deduction because of the taxable income limitation may be carried forward to succeeding taxable years (subject to similar limitations). No general business credit under section 38 is allowed with respect to any amount for which a deduction is allowed under section 179.

Explanation of Provision

The provision increases the amount a taxpayer can deduct under section 179 for qualifying property used in the New York Liberty Zone.[32] Specifically, the provision increases the maximum dollar amount that may be deducted under section 179

by the lesser of (1) $35,000 or (2) the cost of qualifying property placed in service during the taxable year. This amount is in addition to the amount otherwise deductible under section 179.

Qualifying property means section 179 property[33] purchased and placed in service by the taxpayer after September 10, 2001 and before January 1, 2007, where (1) substantially all of its use is in the New York Liberty Zone in the active conduct of a trade or business by the taxpayer in the zone, and (2) the original use of which in the New York Liberty Zone commences with the taxpayer after September 10, 2001.

As under present law with respect to empowerment zones, the phase-out range for the section 179 deduction attributable to New York Liberty Zone property is applied by taking into account only 50 percent of the cost of New York Liberty Zone property that is section 179 property. Also, no general business credit under section 38 is allowed with respect to any amount for which a deduction is allowed under section 179.

Effective Date

The provision is effective for taxable years beginning on December 31, 2001 and before January 1, 2007.

[Law at ¶ 5300. CCH Explanation at ¶ 405, ¶ 410, ¶ 415, ¶ 420, ¶ 425, ¶ 430 and ¶ 435.]

[¶ 10,150] Act Sec. 301(a). Extension of replacement period for certain property involuntarily converted in the New York Liberty Zone

Joint Committee on Taxation (J.C.T. REP. NO. JCX-12-02)

[Caution: The Technical Explanation of the "Job Creation and Worker Assistance Act of 2002" (JCX-12-02), below, is included to assist the reader's understanding but may not be cited as the official Conference Committee Report to P.L. 107-147.—CCH]

[Code Sec. 1400L(g) and Code Sec. 1400L(h)]

Present Law

A taxpayer may elect not to recognize gain with respect to property that is involuntarily converted if the taxpayer acquires within an applicable period (the "replacement period") property similar or related in service or use (sec. 1033). If the taxpayer does not replace the converted property with property similar or related in service or use, then gain generally is recognized. If the taxpayer elects to apply the rules of section 1033, gain on the converted property is recognized only to the extent that the amount realized on the

conversion exceeds the cost of the replacement property. In general, the replacement period begins with the date of the disposition of the converted property and ends two years after the close of the first taxable year in which any part of the gain upon conversion is realized.[34] The replacement period is extended to three years if the converted property is real property held for the productive use in a trade or business or for investment.[35]

Special rules apply for property converted in a Presidentially declared disaster.[36] With respect to a principal residence that is converted in a Presidentially declared disaster, no gain is recognized by reason of the receipt of insurance proceeds for unscheduled personal property that was part of the contents of such residence. In addition, the replacement period for the replacement of such a principal residence is extended to four years after

---

[32] The "New York Liberty Zone" means the area located on or south of Canal Street, East Broadway (east of its intersection with Canal Street), or Grand Street (east of its intersection with East Broadway) in the Borough of Manhattan in the City of New York, New York.

[33] As defined in section 179(d)(1).

[34] Section 1033(a)(2)(B).

[35] Section 1033(g)(4).

[36] Section 1033(h). For this purpose, a "Presidentially declared disaster" means any disaster which, with respect to the area in which the property is located, resulted in a subsequent determination by the President that such area warrants assistance by the Federal Government under the Disaster Relief and Emergency Assistance Act.

the close of the first taxable year in which any part of the gain upon conversion is realized. With respect to investment or business property that is converted in a Presidentially declared disaster, any tangible property acquired and held for productive use in a business is treated as similar or related in service or use to the converted property.

Explanation of Provision

The provision extends the replacement period to five years for a taxpayer to purchase property to replace property that was involuntarily converted within the New York Liberty Zone[37] as a result of the terrorist attacks that occurred on September 11, 2001. However, the five-year period is available only if substantially all of the use of the replacement property is in New York City. In all other cases, the present-law replacement period rules continue to apply.

Effective Date

The provision is effective for involuntary conversions in the New York Liberty Zone occurring on or after September 11, 2001, as a consequence of the terrorist attacks on such date.

[Law at ¶ 5300. CCH Explanation at ¶ 405, ¶ 410, ¶ 415, ¶ 420, ¶ 425, ¶ 430 and ¶ 435.]

[¶ 10,160]   Act Sec. 301(a). Treatment of qualified leasehold improvement property

Joint Committee on Taxation (J.C.T. REP. No. JCX-12-02)

[Caution: The Technical Explanation of the "Job Creation and Worker Assistance Act of 2002" (JCX-12-02), below, is included to assist the reader's understanding but may not be cited as the official Conference Committee Report to P.L. 107-147.—CCH]

[Code Sec. 1400L(c) and Code Sec. 1400L(h)]

Present Law

Depreciation of leasehold improvements

Depreciation allowances for property used in a trade or business generally are determined under the modified Accelerated Cost Recovery System ("MACRS") of section 168. Depreciation allowances for improvements made on leased property are determined under MACRS, even if the MACRS recovery period assigned to the property is longer than the term of the lease (sec. 168(i)(8)).[38] This rule applies regardless whether the lessor or lessee places the leasehold improvements in service.[39] If a leasehold improvement constitutes an addition or improvement to non-residential real property already placed in service, the improvement is depreciated using the straight-line method over a 39-year recovery period, beginning in the month the addition or improvement was placed in service (secs. 168(b)(3), (c)(1), (d)(2), and (i)(6)).[40]

Treatment of dispositions of leasehold improvements

A lessor of leased property that disposes of a leasehold improvement which was made by the lessor for the lessee of the property may take the adjusted basis of the improvement into account for purposes of determining gain or loss if the improvement is irrevocably disposed of or abandoned by the lessor at the termination of the lease.[41] This rule conforms the treatment of lessors and lessees with respect to leasehold improvements disposed of at the end of a term of lease. For purposes of applying this rule, it is expected that a lessor must be able to separately account for the adjusted basis of the leasehold improvement that is irrevocably disposed of or abandoned. This rule does not apply to the extent section 280B applies to the demolition of a structure, a portion of which may include leasehold improvements.[42]

Explanation of Provision

The provision provides that 5-year property for purposes of the depreciation rules of section 168 includes qualified New York Liberty Zone lease-

---

[37] The "New York Liberty Zone" has the same definition throughout this bill.

[38] The Tax Reform Act of 1986 modified the Accelerated Cost Recovery System ("ACRS") to institute MACRS. Prior to the adoption of ACRS by the Economic Recovery Act of 1981, taxpayers were allowed to depreciate the various components of a building as separate assets with separate useful lives. The use of component depreciation was repealed upon the adoption of ACRS. The Tax Reform Act of 1986 also denied the use of component depreciation under MACRS.

[39] Former Code sections 168(f)(6) and 178 provided that in certain circumstances, a lessee could recover the cost of leasehold improvements made over the remaining term of the lease. These provisions were repealed by the Tax Reform Act of 1986.

[40] If the improvement is characterized as tangible personal property, ACRS or MACRS depreciation is calculated using the shorter recovery periods and accelerated methods applicable to such property. The determination of whether certain improvements are characterized as tangible personal property or as nonresidential real property often depends on whether or not the improvements constitute a "structural component" of a building (as defined by Treas. Reg. sec. 1.48-1(e)(1)). See, for example, *Metro National Corp.*, 52 TCM 1440 (1987); *King Radio Corp.*, 486 F.2d 1091 (10th Cir., 1973); *Mallinckrodt, Inc.*, 778 F.2d 402 (8th Cir., 1985) (with respect various leasehold improvements).

[41] The conference report describing this provision mistakenly states that the provision applies to improvements that are irrevocably disposed of or abandoned by the *lessee* (rather than the *lessor*) at the termination of the lease.

[42] Under present law, section 280B denies a deduction for any loss sustained on the demolition of any structure.

hold improvement property ("qualified NYLZ leasehold improvement property"). The term qualified NYLZ leasehold improvement property means property defined in section 168(e)(6)[43] that is placed in service after September 10, 2001 and before January 1, 2007 (and not subject to a binding contract on September 10, 2001) in the New York Liberty Zone. The straight-line method is required to be used with respect to qualified NYLZ leasehold improvement property. A 9-year period is specified as the class life of qualified NYLZ leasehold improvement property for purposes of the alternative depreciation system.

[Law at ¶ 5300. CCH Explanation at ¶ 405, ¶ 410, ¶ 415, ¶ 420, ¶ 425, ¶ 430 and ¶ 435.]

[¶ 10,200]   Act Sec. 401. Allowance of electronic Forms 1099

Joint Committee on Taxation (J.C.T. REP. NO. JCX-12-02)

[Caution: The Technical Explanation of the "Job Creation and Worker Assistance Act of 2002" (JCX-12-02), below, is included to assist the reader's understanding but may not be cited as the official Conference Committee Report to P.L. 107-147.—CCH]

[Act Sec. 401]

Present Law

Many provisions in the Code require entities to file information returns with the IRS and to provide copies to taxpayers. For example, employers are required to provide information with respect to wages paid to employees, and entities (such as banks and credit unions) that pay interest to individuals are also required to provide information with respect to those payments. In general, the copies of the information returns that are provided to taxpayers are provided on paper via the U.S. mail.

Temporary regulations allow Form W-2 to be furnished electronically on a voluntary basis. Under Temp. Treas. Reg. § 31.6051-1T(j), a recipient must have affirmatively consented to receive the statement electronically and must not have withdrawn that consent before the statement is furnished. A similar rule cannot be implemented administratively with respect to some information returns, because the Code requires that the copies furnished to individuals must be furnished either in person or in a statement sent by first-class mail in a specified format.[44]

IRS Form 5498 is used to report contributions to an Archer MSA, an Individual Retirement Account, or a Coverdell education savings accounts. In addition, distributions from these accounts are reported on IRS Form 1099. Under present law, the Secretary has the authority to issue rules under which Forms 5498 and 1099 related to these accounts may be provided electronically.

Explanation of Provision

The provision removes the statutory impediment to providing copies of specified information returns to taxpayers electronically. Accordingly, these copies may be furnished electronically to a recipient who has consented to this; the copies may be furnished in a manner similar to the one permitted with respect to Form W-2 or in another manner provided by the Secretary.

Effective Date

The provision is effective on date of enactment.

[Law at ¶ 7055. CCH Explanation at ¶ 350.]

[¶ 10,210]   Act Sec. 402. Discharge of indebtedness of an S Corporation

Joint Committee on Taxation (J.C.T. REP. NO. JCX-12-02)

[Caution: The Technical Explanation of the "Job Creation and Worker Assistance Act of 2002" (JCX-12-02), below, is included to assist the reader's understanding but may not be cited as the official Conference Committee Report to P.L. 107-147.—CCH]

[Code Sec. 108(d)(7)]

Present Law

In general, an S corporation is not subject to the corporate income tax on its items of income and loss. Instead, an S corporation passes through its items of income and loss to its shareholders. Each shareholder takes into account separately his or her pro rata share of these items on their individual income tax returns. To prevent double taxation of these items, each shareholder's basis in the stock of the S corporation is increased by the amount included in income (including tax-exempt income) and is decreased by the amount of any losses (including nondeductible losses) taken into account. A shareholder may deduct losses only to the extent of a shareholder's basis in his or her stock in the S corporation plus the shareholder's adjusted basis in any indebtedness of the corporation to the shareholder. Any loss that is disallowed by reason of lack of basis is "suspended" at the corporate level and is carried forward and allowed

---

[43] Section 168(e)(6) regarding qualified leasehold improvement property is added by section 205 of the bill.

[44] See 6042(c), 6044(e), and 6049(c)(2).

in any subsequent year in which the shareholder has adequate basis in the stock or debt.

In general, gross income includes income from the discharge of indebtedness. However, income from the discharge of indebtedness of a taxpayer in a bankruptcy case or when the taxpayer is insolvent (to the extent of the insolvency) is excluded from income.[45] The taxpayer is required to reduce tax attributes, such as net operating losses, certain carryovers, and basis in assets, to the extent of the excluded income.

In the case of an S corporation, the eligibility for the exclusion and the attribute reduction are applied at the corporate level. For this purpose, a shareholder's suspended loss is treated as a tax attribute that is reduced. Thus, if the S corporation is in bankruptcy or is insolvent, any income from the discharge of indebtedness by a creditor of the S corporation is excluded from the corporation's income, and the S corporation reduces its tax attributes (including any suspended losses).

To illustrate these rules, assume that a sole shareholder of an S corporation has zero basis in its stock of the corporation. The S corporation borrows $100 from a third party and loses the entire $100. Because the shareholder has no basis in its stock, the $100 loss is "suspended" at the corporate level. If the $100 debt is forgiven when the corporation is in bankruptcy or is insolvent, the $100 income from the discharge of indebtedness is excluded from income, and the $100 "suspended" loss should be eliminated in order to achieve a tax result that is consistent with the economics of the transactions in that the shareholder has no economic gain or loss from these transactions.

Notwithstanding the economics of the overall transaction, the United States Supreme Court ruled in the case of *Gitlitz v. Commissioner*[46] that, under present law, income from the discharge of indebtedness of an S corporation that is excluded from income is treated as an item of income which increases the basis of a shareholder's stock in the S corporation and allows the suspended corporate loss to pass thru to a shareholder. Thus, under the decision, an S corporation shareholder is allowed to deduct a loss for tax purposes that it did not economically incur.

Explanation of Provision

The provision provides that income from the discharge of indebtedness of an S corporation that is excluded from the S corporation's income is not taken into account as an item of income by any shareholder and thus does not increase the basis of any shareholder's stock in the corporation.

Effective Date

The provision generally applies to discharges of indebtedness after October 11, 2001. The provision does not apply to any discharge of indebtedness before March 1, 2002, pursuant to a plan of reorganization filed with a bankruptcy court on or before October 11, 2001.

House Committee Report (H.R. Rep. No. 107-251)

[Caution: The House Committee Report on the "Economic Security and Recovery Act of 2001," as passed by the House (H.R. Rep. No. 107-251), below, is included to assist the reader's understanding but may not be cited as the controlling Committee Report to P.L. 107-147.—CCH]

Present Law

In general, an S corporation is not subject to the corporate income tax on its items of income and loss. Instead, an S corporation passes through its items of income and loss to its shareholders. Each shareholder takes into account separately his or her pro rata share of these items on their individual income tax returns. To prevent double taxation of these items, each shareholder's basis in the stock of the S corporation is increased by the amount included in income (including tax-exempt income) and is decreased by the amount of any losses (including nondeductible losses) taken into account. A shareholder may deduct losses only to the extent of a shareholder's basis in his or her stock in the S corporation plus the shareholder's adjusted basis in any indebtedness of the corporation to the shareholder. Any loss that is disallowed by reason of lack of basis is "suspended" at the corporate level and is carried forward and allowed in any subsequent year in which the shareholder has adequate basis in the stock or debt.

In general, gross income includes income from the discharge of indebtedness. However, income from the discharge of indebtedness of a taxpayer in a bankruptcy case or when the taxpayer is insolvent (to the extent of the insolvency) is excluded from income.[31] The taxpayer is required to reduce tax attributes, such as net operating losses, certain carryovers, and basis in assets, to the extent of the excluded income.

In the case of an S corporation, the eligibility for the exclusion and the attribute reduction are applied at the corporate level. For this purpose, a shareholder's suspended loss is treated as a tax attribute that is reduced. Thus, if the S corporation is in bankruptcy or is insolvent, any income

---

[45] Special rules also apply to certain real estate debt and farm debt.

[46] 531 U.S. 206 (2001). [2001-1 USTC ¶ 50,147—CCH]

[31] Special rules also apply to certain real estate debt and farm debt.

from the discharge of indebtedness by a creditor of the S corporation is excluded from the corporation's income, and the S corporation reduces its tax attributes (including any suspended losses).

To illustrate these rules, assume that a sole shareholder of an S corporation has zero basis in its stock of the corporation. The S corporation borrows $100 from a third party and loses the entire $100. Because the shareholder has no basis in its stock, the $100 loss is "suspended" at the corporate level. If the $100 debt is forgiven when the corporation is in bankruptcy or is insolvent, the $100 income from the discharge of indebtedness is excluded from income, and the $100 "suspended" loss should be eliminated in order to achieve a tax result that is consistent with the economics of the transactions in that the shareholder has no economic gain or loss from these transactions.

Notwithstanding the economics of the overall transaction, the United States Supreme Court ruled in the case of *Gitlitz v. Commissioner*[32] that, under present law, income from the discharge of indebtedness of an S corporation that is excluded from income is treated as an item of income which increases the basis of a shareholder's stock in the S corporation and allows the suspended corporate loss to pass thru to a shareholder. Thus, under the decision, an S corporation shareholder is allowed to deduct a loss for tax purposes that it did not economically incur.

Reasons for Change

The Committee believes that it is inappropriate for a shareholder of an insolvent or bankrupt S corporation to take into account excluded income from the discharge of the S corporation's indebtedness and thereby increase the shareholder's adjusted basis in the stock. Under the provisions of the Code, an increase in the stock basis allows the shareholder a deduction for an amount of loss that is not economically borne by the shareholder.

As a general matter, the Committee believes that where, in the case of the present statute under section 108, the plain text of a provision of the Internal Revenue Code produces an ambiguity, the provision should be read as closing, not maintaining, a loophole that would result in an inappropriate reduction of tax liability.

Explanation of Provision

The provision provides that income from the discharge of indebtedness of an S corporation that is excluded from the S corporation's income is not taken into account as an item of income by any shareholder and thus does not increase the basis of any shareholder's stock in the corporation.

Effective Date

The provision applies to discharges of indebtedness after October 11, 2001.

[Law at ¶ 5075. CCH Explanation at ¶ 315.]

[¶ 10,220] Act Sec. 403. Limitation on use of non-accrual experience method of accounting

Joint Committee on Taxation (J.C.T. Rep. No. JCX-12-02)

[Caution: The Technical Explanation of the "Job Creation and Worker Assistance Act of 2002" (JCX-12-02), below, is included to assist the reader's understanding but may not be cited as the official Conference Committee Report to P.L. 107-147.—CCH]

[Code Sec. 448(d)(5)]

Present Law

An accrual method taxpayer generally must recognize income when all the events have occurred that fix the right to receive the income and the amount of the income can be determined with reasonable accuracy. An accrual method taxpayer may deduct the amount of any receivable that was previously included in income that becomes worthless during the year.

Accrual method taxpayers are not required to include in income amounts to be received for the performance of services which, on the basis of experience, will not be collected (the "non-accrual experience method"). The availability of this

method is conditioned on the taxpayer not charging interest or a penalty for failure to timely pay the amount charged.

Generally, a cash method taxpayer is not required to include an amount in income until received. A taxpayer generally may not use the cash method if purchase, production, or sale of merchandise is an income producing factor. Such taxpayers generally are required to keep inventories and use an accrual method of accounting. In addition, corporations (and partnerships with corporate partners) generally may not use the cash method of accounting if their average annual gross receipts years exceed $5 million. An exception to this $5 million rule is provided for qualified personal service corporations. A qualified personal service corporation is a corporation (1) substantially all of whose activities involve the performance of services in the fields of health, law, engineering, architecture, accounting, actuarial science, performing arts or consulting and (2) substantially all of the stock of which is owned by

---

[32] 531 U.S. 206 (2001). [2001-1 ustc ¶ 50,147—CCH]

current or former employees performing such services, their estates or heirs. Qualified personal service corporations are allowed to use the cash method without regard to whether their average annual gross receipts exceed $5 million.

Explanation of Provision

Under the provision, the non-accrual experience method of accounting is available only for amounts to be received for the performance of qualified services and for services provided by certain small businesses. Amounts to be received for all other services are subject to the general rule regarding inclusion in income. Qualified services are services in the fields of health, law, engineering, architecture, accounting, actuarial science, performing arts or consulting. As under present law, the availability of this method is conditioned on the taxpayer not charging interest or a penalty for failure to timely pay the amount charged.

Under a special rule, the non-accrual experience method of accounting continues to be available for the performance of non-qualified services if the average annual gross receipts (as defined in sec. 448(c)) of the taxpayer (or any predecessor) does not exceed $5 million. The rules of paragraph (2) and (3) of section 448(c) (i.e., the rules regarding the aggregation of related taxpayers, taxpayers not in existence for the entire three year period, short taxable years, definition of gross receipts, and treatment of predecessors) apply for purposes of determining the average annual gross receipts test.

The provision requires that the Secretary of the Treasury prescribe regulations to permit a taxpayer to use alternative computations or formulas if such alternative computations or formulas accurately reflect, based on experience, the amount of its year-end receivables that will not be collected. It is anticipated that the Secretary of the Treasury will consider providing safe harbors in such regulations that may be relied upon by taxpayers. In addition, the provision also provides that the Secretary of the Treasury permit taxpayers to adopt, or request consent of the Secretary of the Treasury to change to, an alternative computation or formula that clearly reflects the taxpayer's experience. The provision requires the Secretary of Treasury to approve a request provided that the alternative computation or formula clearly reflects the taxpayer's experience.

Effective Date

The provision is effective for taxable years ending after date of enactment. Any change in the taxpayer's method of accounting required as a result of the limitation on the use of the non-accrual experience method is treated as a voluntary change initiated by the taxpayer with the consent of the Secretary of the Treasury. Any resultant section 481(a) adjustment is to be taken into account over a period not to exceed the lesser of the number of years the taxpayer has used the non-accrual experience method of accounting or four years under principles consistent with those in Rev. Proc. 99-49.[47]

House Committee Report (H.R. Rep. No. 107-251)

[Caution: The House Committee Report on the "Economic Security and Recovery Act of 2001," as passed by the House (H.R. Rep. No. 107-251), below, is included to assist the reader's understanding but may not be cited as the controlling Committee Report to P.L. 107-147.—CCH]

Present Law

An accrual method taxpayer generally must recognize income when all the events have occurred that fix the right to receive the income and the amount of the income can be determined with reasonable accuracy. An accrual method taxpayer may deduct the amount of any receivable that was previously included in income that becomes worthless during the year.

Accrual method taxpayers are not required to include in income amounts to be received for the performance of services which, on the basis of experience, will not be collected (the "non-accrual experience method"). The availability of this method is conditioned on the taxpayer not charg-

ing interest or a penalty for failure to timely pay the amount charged.

Generally, a cash method taxpayer is not required to include an amount in income until received. A taxpayer generally may not use the cash method if purchase, production, or sale of merchandise is an income producing factor. Such taxpayers generally are required to keep inventories and use an accrual method of accounting. In addition, corporations (and partnerships with corporate partners) generally may not use the cash method of accounting if their average annual gross receipts years exceed $5 million. An exception to this $5 million rule is provided for qualified personal service corporations. A qualified personal service corporation is a corporation (1) substantially all of whose activities involve the performance of services in the fields of health, law, engineering, architecture, accounting, actuarial science, performing arts or consulting and (2) substantially all of the stock of which is owned by current or former employees performing such services, their estates or heirs. Qualified personal

---

[47] 1999-2 C.B. 725

service corporations are allowed to use the cash method without regard to whether their average annual gross receipts exceed $5 million.

Reasons for Change

The Committee understands that the use of the non-accrual experience method provides the equivalent of a bad debt reserve, which generally is not available to taxpayers using an accrual method of accounting. The Committee believes that accrual method taxpayers should be treated similarly, unless there is a strong indication that different treatment is necessary to clearly reflect income or to address a particular competitive situation.

The Committee understands that accrual basis providers of qualified services (services in the fields of health, law, engineering, architecture, accounting, actuarial science, performing arts or consulting) compete on a regular basis with competitors using the cash method of accounting. The Committee believes that this competitive situation justifies the continued availability of the non-accrual experience method with respect to amounts due to be received for the performance of qualified services. The Committee believes that it is important to avoid the disparity of treatment between competing cash and accrual method providers of qualified services that could result if the non-accrual experience method were eliminated with regard to amounts to be received for such services.

The Committee also recognizes the burdens placed on small businesses to comply with the complexity of the federal income tax code and, in this time of economic uncertainty, the importance of cash flow to small businesses. As such, the Committee believes that small business service providers using an accrual method of accounting should be permitted to continue to use the non-accrual experience method.

In addition, the Committee believes that the formula contained in Temp. Reg. section 1.448-2T may not clearly reflect the amount of income that, based on experience, will not be collected for many qualified services providers, especially for those where significant time elapses between the rendering of the service and a final determination that the account will not be collected. Providers of qualified services should not be subject to a formula that requires the payments of taxes on receivables that will not be collected.

Explanation of Provision

Under the provision, the non-accrual experience method of accounting is available only for amounts to be received for the performance of qualified services and for services provided by certain small businesses. Amounts to be received for all other services are subject to the general rule regarding inclusion in income. Qualified services are services in the fields of health, law, engineering, architecture, accounting, actuarial science, performing arts or consulting. As under present law, the availability of this method is conditioned on the taxpayer not charging interest or a penalty for failure to timely pay the amount charged.

Under a special rule, the non-accrual experience method of accounting continues to be available for the performance of non-qualified services if the average annual gross receipts (as defined in sec. 448(c)) of the taxpayer (or any predecessor) does not exceed $5 million. The rules of paragraph (2) and (3) of section 448(c) (i.e., the rules regarding the aggregation of related taxpayers, taxpayers not in existence for the entire three year period, short taxable years, definition of gross receipts, and treatment of predecessors) apply for purposes of determining the average annual gross receipts test.

The provision requires that the Secretary of the Treasury prescribe regulations to permit a taxpayer to use alternative computations or formulas if such alternative computations or formulas accurately reflect, based on experience, the amount of its year-end receivables that will not be collected. It is anticipated that the Secretary of the Treasury will consider providing safe harbors in such regulations that may be relied upon by taxpayers. In addition, the provision also provides that the Secretary of the Treasury permit taxpayers to adopt, or request consent of the Secretary of the Treasury to change to, an alternative computation or formula that clearly reflects the taxpayer's experience. The provision requires the Secretary of Treasury to approve a request provided that the alternative computation or formula clearly reflects the taxpayer's experience.

Effective Date

The provision is effective for taxable years ending after date of enactment. Any change in the taxpayer's method of accounting required as a result of the limitation on the use of the non-accrual experience method is treated as a voluntary change initiated by the taxpayer with the consent of the Secretary of the Treasury. Any resultant section 481(a) adjustment is to be taken into account over a period not to exceed the lesser of the number of years the taxpayer has used the non-accrual experience method of accounting or four years under principles consistent with those in Rev. Proc. 99-49.[33]

[Law at ¶ 5190. CCH Explanation at ¶ 345.]

---

[33] 1999-2 C.B. 725

[¶ 10,230]   Act Sec. 404. Expansion of the exclusion from income for qualified foster care payments

Joint Committee on Taxation (J.C.T. REP. NO. JCX-12-02)

[Code Sec. 131(b)]

Present Law

If certain requirements are satisfied, an exclusion from gross income is provided for qualified foster care payments paid to a foster care provider by either (1) a State or local government; or (2) a tax-exempt placement agency. Qualified foster care payments are amounts paid for caring for a qualified foster care individual in the foster care provider's home and difficulty of care payments.[48] A qualified foster care individual is an individual living in a foster care family home in which the individual was placed by: (1) an agency of the State or local government (regardless of the individual's age at the time of placement); or (2) a tax-exempt placement agency licensed by the State or local government (if such individual was under the age of 19 at the time of placement).

Explanation of Provision

The bill makes two modifications to the present-law exclusion for qualified foster care payments. First, the bill expands the definition of qualified foster care payments to include payments by any placement agency that is licensed or certified by a State or local government, or an entity designated by a State or local government to make payments to providers of foster care. Second, the bill expands the definition of a qualified foster care individual by including foster care individuals placed by a qualified foster care placement agency (regardless of the individual's age at the time of placement).

Effective Date

The provision is effective for taxable years beginning after December 31, 2001.

[Law at ¶ 5080. CCH Explanation at ¶ 210.]

[¶ 10,240]   Act Sec. 405. Interest rate used in determining additional required contributions to defined benefit plans and PBGC variable rate premiums

Joint Committee on Taxation (J.C.T. REP. NO. JCX-12-02)

[Code Sec. 412(l) and Code Sec. 412(m)]

Present Law

In general

ERISA and the Code impose both minimum and maximum[49] funding requirements with respect to defined benefit pension plans. The minimum funding requirements are designed to provide at least a certain level of benefit security

by requiring the employer to make certain minimum contributions to the plan. The amount of contributions required for a plan year is generally the amount needed to fund benefits earned during that year plus that year's portion of other liabilities that are amortized over a period of years, such as benefits resulting from a grant of past service credit.

Additional contributions for underfunded plans

Additional contributions are required under a special funding rule if a single-employer defined benefit pension plan is underfunded.[50] Under the special rule, a plan is considered underfunded for

---

[48] A difficulty of care payment is a payment designated by the person making such payment as compensation for providing the additional care of a qualified foster care individual in the home of the foster care provider which is required by reason of a physical, mental, or emotional handicap of such individual and with respect to which the State has determined that there is a need for additional compensation.

[49] The maximum funding requirement for a defined benefit plan is referred to as the full funding limitation. Additional contributions are not required if a plan has reached the full funding limitation.

[50] Plans with no more than 100 participants on any day in the preceding plan year are not subject to the special funding rule. Plans with more than 100 but not more than 150 participants are generally subject to lower contribution requirements under the special funding rule.

a plan year if the value of the plan assets is less than 90 percent of the plan's current liability.[51] The value of plan assets as a percentage of current liability is the plan's "funded current liability percentage."

If a plan is underfunded, the amount of additional required contributions is based on certain elements, including whether the plan has an unfunded liability related to benefits accrued before 1988 or 1995 or to changes in the mortality table used to determine contributions, and whether the plan provides for unpredictable contingent event benefits (that is, benefits that depend on contingencies that are not reliably and reasonably predictable, such as facility shutdowns or reductions in workforce). However, the amount of additional contributions cannot exceed the amount needed to increase the plan's funded current liability percentage to 100 percent.

Required interest rate

In general, a plan's current liability means all liabilities to employees and their beneficiaries under the plan. The interest rate used to determine a plan's current liability must be within a permissible range of the weighted average of the interest rates on 30-year Treasury securities for the four-year period ending on the last day before the plan year begins.[52] The permissible range is from 90 percent to 105 percent. As a result of debt reduction, the Department of the Treasury does not currently issue 30-year Treasury securities.

Timing of plan contributions

In general, plan contributions required to satisfy the funding rules must be made within 8-1/2 months after the end of the plan year. If the contribution is made by such due date, the contribution is treated as if it were made on the last day of the plan year.

In the case of a plan with a funded current liability percentage of less than 100 percent for the preceding plan year, estimated contributions for the current plan year must be made in quarterly installments during the current plan year. The amount of each required installment is 25 percent of the lesser of (1) 90 percent of the amount required to be contributed for the current plan year or (2) 100 percent of the amount required to be contributed for the preceding plan year.[53]

PBGC premiums

Because benefits under a defined benefit pension plan may be funded over a period of years,

plan assets may not be sufficient to provide the benefits owed under the plan to employees and their beneficiaries if the plan terminates before all benefits are paid. In order to protect employees and their beneficiaries, the Pension Benefit Guaranty Corporation ("PBGC") generally insures the benefits owed under defined benefit pension plans. Employers pay premiums to the PBGC for this insurance coverage.

In the case of an underfunded plan, additional PBGC premiums are required based on the amount of unfunded vested benefits. These premiums are referred to as "variable rate premiums." In determining the amount of unfunded vested benefits, the interest rate used is 85 percent of the interest rate on 30-year Treasury securities for the month preceding the month in which the plan year begins.

Explanation of Provision

Additional contributions

The provision expands the permissible range of the statutory interest rate used in calculating a plan's current liability for purposes of applying the additional contribution requirements for plan years beginning after December 31, 2001, and before January 1, 2004. Under the provision, the permissible range is from 90 percent to 120 percent for these years. Use of a higher interest rate under the expanded range will affect the plan's current liability, which may in turn affect the need to make additional contributions and the amount of any additional contributions.

Because the quarterly contributions requirements are based on current liability for the preceding plan year, the provision also provides special rules for applying these requirements for plans years beginning in 2002 (when the expanded range first applies) and 2004 (when the expanded range no longer applies). In each of those years ("present year"), current liability for the preceding year is redetermined, using the permissible range applicable to the present year. This redetermined current liability will be used for purposes of the plan's funded current liability percentage for the preceding year, which may affect the need to make quarterly contributions and for purposes of determining the amount of any quarterly contributions in the present year, which is based in part on the preceding year.

PBGC variable rate premiums

Under the provision, the interest rate used in determining the amount of unfunded vested benefits for variable rate premium purposes is in-

---

[51] Under an alternative test, a plan is not considered underfunded if (1) the value of the plan assets is at least 80 percent of current liability and (2) the value of the plan assets was at least 90 percent of current liability for each of the two immediately preceding years or each of the second and third immediately preceding years.

[52] The interest rate used under the plan must be consistent with the assumptions which reflect the purchase rates

which would be used by insurance companies to satisfy the liabilities under the plan (section 412(b)(5)(B)(iii)(II)).

[53] No additional quarterly contributions are due once the plan's funded current liability percentage for the plan year reaches 100 percent.

creased to 100 percent of the interest rate on 30-year Treasury securities for the month preceding the month in which the plan year begins.

Effective Date

The provision is effective with respect to plan contributions and PBGC variable rate premiums for plan years beginning after December 31, 2001, and before January 1, 2004.

[**Law at ¶ 5165 and ¶ 7060. CCH Explanation at ¶ 505.**]

[¶ 10,250]   Act Sec. 406. Deduction for classroom materials

Joint Committee on Taxation (J.C.T. REP. No. JCX-12-02)

[Caution: The Technical Explanation of the "Job Creation and Worker Assistance Act of 2002" (JCX-12-02), below, is included to assist the reader's understanding but may not be cited as the official Conference Committee Report to P.L. 107-147.—CCH]

[Code Sec. 62(a) and Code Sec. 62(d)]

Present Law

In general, ordinary and necessary business expenses are deductible (sec. 162). However, unreimbursed employee business expenses are deductible only as an itemized deduction and only to the extent that the individual's total miscellaneous deductions (including employee business expenses) exceed two percent of adjusted gross income.

An individual's otherwise allowable itemized deductions may be further limited by the overall limitation on itemized deductions, which reduces itemized deductions for taxpayers with adjusted gross income in excess of $137,300 (for 2002).[54] In addition, miscellaneous itemized deductions are not allowable under the alternative minimum tax.

Explanation of Provision

The bill provides an above-the-line deduction for up to $250 annually of expenses paid or incurred by an eligible educator for books, supplies (other than nonathletic supplies for courses of instruction in health or physical education), computer equipment (including related software and services) and other equipment, and supplementary materials used by the eligible educator in the classroom. To be eligible for this deduction, the expenses must be otherwise deductible under 162 as a trade or business expense.

An eligible educator is a kindergarten through grade 12 teacher, instructor, counselor, or principal in a school for at least 900 hours during a school year. A school means any school which provides elementary education or secondary education, as determined under State law.

Effective Date

The provision is effective for taxable years beginning after December 31, 2001, and before January 1, 2004.

[**Law at ¶ 5065. CCH Explanation at ¶ 215.**]

[¶ 10,260]   Act Sec. 411(a)-(h). Tax technical corrections [EGTRRA 2001]

Joint Committee on Taxation (J.C.T. REP. No. JCX-12-02)

[Caution: The Technical Explanation of the "Job Creation and Worker Assistance Act of 2002" (JCX-12-02), below, is included to assist the reader's understanding but may not be cited as the official Conference Committee Report to P.L. 107-147.—CCH]

[Code Sec. 23, Code Sec. 24, Code Sec. 38, Code Sec. 45F, Code Sec. 63, Code Sec. 137, Code Sec. 530, Code Sec. 2016, Code Sec. 2101, Code Sec. 2511 and Code Sec. 6428]

Except as otherwise provided, the technical corrections contained in the bill generally are effective as if included in the originally enacted related legislation.

Amendments to the Economic Growth and Tax Relief Reconciliation Act of 2001

Section 6428 credit interaction with refundable child tax credit.—The provision treats the section 6428 credit (rate reduction) like a nonrefundable personal credit, thus allowing it prior to determining the refundable child credit.

Child tax credit.—The provision clarifies that for taxable years beginning in 2001, the portion of the child credit that is refundable is determined by referring in Code section 24(d)(1)(B) to "the

---

[54] The effect of this overall limitation is phased down beginning in 2006, and is repealed for 2010.

aggregate amount of credits allowed by this sub-part." This would retain prior law that was inadvertently changed by the Act.

Transition rule for adoption tax credit.— Under prior law, the maximum amount of adoption expenses which could be taken into account in computing the adoption tax credit for any child was $5,000 ($6,000 in the case of special needs adoptions). Under prior and present law, the credit generally is allowed in the taxable year following the taxable year the expenses are paid or incurred where expenses are paid or incurred before the taxable year the adoption becomes final. The Act increased the maximum amount of expenses to $10,000 for taxable years beginning after 2001, but did not include a provision describing the dollar limit for amounts paid or incurred during taxable years beginning before January 1, 2002, for adoptions that do not become final in those years. The provision clarifies that amount of expenses paid or incurred during taxable years beginning before January 1, 2002, which are taken into account in determining a credit allowed in a taxable year beginning after December 31, 2001, are subject to the $5,000 (or $6,000) dollar cap in effect immediately prior to the enactment of the Act.

Dollar amount of credit for special needs adoptions.—The provision clarifies that, for special needs adoptions that become final in taxable years beginning after 2002, the adoption expenses taken into account shall be increased by the excess (if any) of $10,000 over the aggregate adoption expenses for the taxable year the adoption becomes final and all prior taxable years.

Employer-provided adoption assistance exclusion with respect to special needs adoptions.—The provision clarifies that, for taxable years beginning after 2002, the amount of adoption expenses taken into account in determining the exclusion for employer-provided adoption assistance in the case of a special needs adoption is increased by the excess (if any) of $10,000 over the aggregate qualified adoption expenses with respect to the adoption for the taxable year the adoption becomes final and all prior taxable years.

Credit for employer expenses for child care assistance.—The provision clarifies that recapture tax with respect to this credit is treated like recapture taxes with respect to other credits under chapter 1 of the Code. Thus, it would not be treated as a tax for purposes of determining the amounts of other credits or determining the amount of alternative minimum tax.

Elimination of marriage penalty in standard deduction.—The provision provides rules that were inadvertently omitted providing for separate returns and rounding rules for the standard deduction for the transition period years.

Education IRAs; non-application of 10-percent additional tax with respect to amounts for which HOPE credit is claimed.—Under the law prior to the Act, taxpayers could not claim the HOPE (or Lifetime learning) credit in the same year that they claimed an exclusion from income from an education IRA. Taxpayers were permitted to waive the exclusion in order to claim the HOPE (or Lifetime learning) credit. For taxpayers electing the waiver, earnings from amounts withdrawn from education IRAs and attributable to education expenses for which a HOPE (or Lifetime learning) credit was claimed were includable in income, but the additional ten percent tax was not applied. Under the Act, taxpayers are permitted to claim the education IRA exclusion and claim a HOPE (or Lifetime learning) credit in the same year, provided they do not claim both with respect to the same educational expenses. The election to waive the education IRA exclusion was thus unnecessary, and was dropped. However, a reference to the election was retained (sec. 530(d)(4)(b)(iv)). The reference to the election was intended to preserve the rule relating to the non-application of the 10-percent additional tax for education IRA earnings that are includable in income solely because the HOPE (or Lifetime learning) credit is claimed for those expenses. The provision clarifies the present-law rules to reflect this result.

The provision prevents the 10-percent additional tax from applying to a distribution from an education IRA (or qualified tuition program) that is used to pay qualified higher education expenses, but the taxpayer elects to claim a HOPE or Lifetime Learning credit in lieu of the exclusion under section 530 or 529. Thus, the income distributed from the education IRA (or qualified tuition program) would be subject to income tax, but not to the 10-percent additional tax.

Transfers in trust.—The provision clarifies that the effect of section 511(e) of the Act (effective for gifts made after 2009) is to treat certain transfers in trust as transfers of property by gift. The result of the clarification is that the gift tax annual exclusion and the marital and charitable deductions may apply to such transfers. Under the provision as clarified, certain amounts transferred in trust will be treated as transfers of property by gift, despite the fact that such transfers would be regarded as incomplete gifts or would not be treated as transferred under the law applicable to gifts made prior to 2010. For example, if in 2010 an individual transfers property in trust to pay the income to one person for life, remainder to such persons and in such portions as the settlor may decide, then the entire value of the property will be treated as being transferred by gift under the provision, even though the transfer of the remainder interest in the trust would not be treated as a completed gift under current Treas. Reg. sec. 25.2511-2(c). Similarly, if in 2010 an individual transfers property in trust to pay the income to one person for life, and makes no transfer of a remainder interest, the entire value of the property will be treated as being transferred by gift under the provision.

Recovery of taxes claimed as credit (State death tax credit).—The provision eliminates as deadwood a reference to the State death tax credit.

* * *

[¶ 10,270]   Act Sec. 411(i)-(w). Tax technical corrections [EGTRRA 2001, Pension Related Provisons]

Joint Committee on Taxation (J.C.T. Rep. No. JCX-12-02)

[*Caution: The Technical Explanation of the "Job Creation and Worker Assistance Act of 2002" (JCX-12-02), below, is included to assist the reader's understanding but may not be cited as the official Conference Committee Report to P.L. 107-147.—CCH*]

[Code Sec. 25B, Code Sec. 45E, Code Sec. 401, Code Sec. 402, Code Sec. 403, Code Sec. 404, Code Sec. 408, Code Sec. 409, Code Sec. 412, Code Sec. 414, Code Sec. 415, Code Sec. 416, Code Sec. 417, Code Sec. 457 and Code Sec. 4980F]

Except as otherwise provided, the technical corrections contained in the bill generally are effective as if included in the originally enacted related legislation.

* * *

Pension-Related Amendments to the Economic Growth and Tax Relief Reconciliation Act of 2001

Individual Retirement Arrangements ("IRAs").—Under the Act, a qualified employer plan may provide for voluntary employee contributions to a separate account that is deemed to be an IRA. The provision clarifies that, for purposes of deemed IRAs, the term "qualified employer plan" includes the following types of plans maintained by a governmental employer: a qualified retirement plan under section 401(a), a qualified annuity plan under section 403(a), a tax-sheltered annuity plan under section 403(b), and an eligible deferred compensation plan under section 457(b). The provision also clarifies that the Employee Retirement Income Security Act ("ERISA") is intended to apply to a deemed IRA in a manner similar to a simplified employee pension ("SEP").

Increase in benefit and contribution limits.—Under the Act, the benefit and contribution limits that apply to qualified retirement plans are increased. These increases are generally effective for years beginning after December 31, 2001, but the increase in the limit on benefits under a defined benefit plan is effective for years ending

after December 31, 2001. In the case of some plans that incorporate the benefit limits by reference and that use a plan year other than the calendar year, the increased benefit limits became effective under the plan automatically, causing unintended benefit increases. The provision permits an employer to amend such a plan by June 30, 2002, to reduce benefits to the level that applied before enactment of the Act without violating the anticutback rules that generally apply to plan amendments.

In connection with the increases in the benefit and contribution limits under the Act, a new base period applies in indexing the 2002 dollar amounts for future cost-of-living adjustments. The same indexing method applies to the dollar amounts used to determine eligibility to participate in a SEP and to determine the proper period for distributions from an employee stock ownership plan ("ESOP"). The provision changes these dollar amounts to the 2002 indexed amounts so that future indexing will operate properly.

Modification of top-heavy rules.—Under the Act, in determining whether a plan is top-heavy, distributions made because of separation from service, death, or disability are taken into account for one year after distribution. Other distributions are taken into account for five years. The Act also permits distributions from a section 401(k) plan, a tax-sheltered annuity plan, or an eligible deferred compensation plan to be made when the participant has a severance from employment (rather than separation from service). The provision clarifies that distributions made after severance from employment (rather than separation from service) are taken into account for only one year in determining top-heavy status.

Elective deferrals not taken into account for deduction limits.—The provision clarifies that elective deferrals to a SEP are not subject to the deduction limits and are not taken into account in applying the limits to other SEP contributions. The provision also clarifies that the combined deduction limit of 25 percent of compensation for qualified defined benefit and defined contribution plans does not apply if the only amounts contributed to the defined contribution plan are elective deferrals.

Deduction limits.—Under present law, contributions to a SEP are included in an employee's income to the extent they exceed the lesser of 15 percent of compensation or $40,000 (for 2002), subject to a reduction in some cases. Under prior law, the annual limitation on the amount of deductible contributions to a SEP was 15 percent of compensation. Under the Act, the annual limitation on the amount of deductible contributions that can be made to a SEP is increased from 15 percent of compensation to 25 percent of compensation. The provision makes a conforming change to the rule that limits the amount of SEP contributions that may be made for a particular employee. Under the provision, contributions are included in an employee's income to the extent they exceed the lesser of 25 percent of compensation or $40,000 (for 2002), subject to a reduction in some cases.

Under present law, the Secretary of the Treasury has the authority to require an employer who makes contributions to a SEP to provide simplified reports with respect to such contributions. Consistent with present law and the provision, such reports could appropriately include information as to compliance with the requirements that apply to SEPs, including the contribution limits.

Nonrefundable credit for certain individuals for elective deferrals and IRA contributions.—The provision clarifies that the amount of contributions taken into account in determining the credit for elective deferrals and IRA contributions is reduced by the amount of a distribution from a qualified retirement plan, an eligible deferred compensation plan, or a traditional IRA that is includible in income or that consists of after-tax contributions. The provision retains the rule that distributions that are rolled over to another retirement plan do not affect the credit.

Small business tax credit for new retirement plan expenses.—The provision clarifies that the small business tax credit for new retirement plan expenses applies in the case of a plan first effective after December 31, 2001, even if adopted on or before that date.

Additional salary reduction catch-up contributions.—Under the Act, an individual aged 50 or over may make additional elective deferrals ("catch-up contributions") to certain retirement plans, up to a specified limit. A plan may not permit catch-up deferrals in excess of this limit. The provision clarifies that, for this purpose, the limit applies to all qualified retirement plans, tax-sheltered annuity plans, SEPs and SIMPLE plans maintained by the same employer on an aggregated basis, as if all plans were a single plan. The limit applies also to all eligible deferred compensation plans of a government employer on an aggregated basis.

Under the Act, catch-up contributions up to the specified limit are excluded from an individual's income. The provision also clarifies that the total amount that an individual may exclude from income as catch-up contributions for a year cannot exceed the catch-up contribution limit for that year (and for that type of plan), without regard to whether the individual made catch-up contributions under plans maintained by the more than one employer.

The provision clarifies that an individual who will attain age 50 by the end of the taxable year is an eligible participant as of the beginning of the taxable year rather than only at the attainment of age 50. The provision also clarifies that a participant in an eligible deferred compensation plan of a government employer may make catch-up contributions in an amount equal to the greater of the amount permitted under the new catch-up rule and the amount permitted under the special catch-up rule for eligible deferred compensation plans.

The provision revises the lists of requirements that do not apply to catch-up contributions to reflect other statutory amendments made by the Act and to reflect the fact that catch-up contributions can be made only to a qualified defined contribution plan, not to a qualified defined benefit plan. The provision also clarifies that the special nondiscrimination rule for mergers and acquisitions applies for purposes of the nondiscrimination requirement applicable to catch-up contributions.

Equitable treatment for contributions of employees to defined contribution plans.—Under prior law, the limits on contributions to a tax-sheltered annuity plan applied at the time contributions became vested. Under the Act, tax-sheltered annuity plans are generally subject to the same contribution limits as qualified defined contribution plans, but certain special rules were retained.

The provision clarifies that the limits apply to contributions to a tax-sheltered annuity plan in the year the contributions are made without regard to when the contributions become vested. The provision also clarifies that contributions may be made for an employee for up to five years after retirement, based on includible compensation for the last year of service before retirement. The provision also restores special rules for ministers and lay employees of churches and for foreign missionaries that were inadvertently eliminated.

Under the Act, amounts deferred under an eligible deferred compensation plan are generally subject to the same contribution limits as qualified defined contribution plans. The provision conforms the definition of compensation used in applying the limits to an eligible deferred com-

Act Sec. 411(i)-(w) ¶ 10,270

pensation plan to the definition used for defined contribution plans.

Rollovers of retirement plan and IRA distributions.—Under prior law and under the Act, a qualified retirement plan must provide for the rollover of certain distributions directly to a qualified defined contribution plan, a qualified annuity plan, a tax-sheltered annuity plan, a governmental eligible deferred compensation plan, or a traditional IRA, if the participant elects a direct rollover. The provision clarifies that a qualified retirement plan must provide for the direct rollover of after-tax contributions only to a qualified defined contribution plan or a traditional IRA. The provision also clarifies that, if a distribution includes both pretax and after-tax amounts, the portion of the distribution that is rolled over is treated as consisting first of pretax amounts.

Employers may disregard rollovers for purposes of cash-out amounts.—Under prior and present law, if a participant in a qualified retirement plan ceases to be employed with the employer maintaining the plan, the plan may distribute the participant's nonforfeitable accrued benefit without the consent of the participant and, if applicable, the participant's spouse, if the present value of the benefit does not exceed $5,000. Under the Act, a plan may provide that the present value of the benefit is determined without regard to the portion of the benefit that is attributable to rollover contributions (and any earnings allocable thereto) for purposes of determining whether the participant must consent to the cash-out of the benefit. The provision clarifies that rollover amounts may be disregarded also in determining whether a spouse must consent to the cash-out of the benefit.

Notice of significant reduction in plan benefit accruals.—Under the Act, notice must be provided to participants if a defined benefit plan is amended to provide for a significant reduction in the future rate of benefit accrual, including any elimination or reduction of an early retirement benefit or retirement-type subsidy. The provision clarifies that the notice requirement applies to a defined benefit plan only if the plan is qualified. The provision further clarifies that, in the case of an amendment that eliminates an early retirement benefit or retirement-type subsidy, notice is required only if the early retirement benefit or retirement-type subsidy is significant. The provision also eliminates inconsistencies in the statutory language.

Modification of timing of plan valuations.—Under the Act, a plan valuation may be made as of any date in the immediately preceding plan year if, as of such date, plan assets are not less than 100 percent of the plan's current liability. Under the Act, a change in funding method to use a valuation date in the prior year generally may not be made unless, as of such date, plan assets are not less than 125 percent of the plan's current liability. The provision conforms the statutory language to Congressional intent as reflected in the Statement of Managers.

ESOP dividends may be reinvested without loss of dividend deduction.—Under prior and present law, a deduction is permitted for a dividend paid with respect to employer stock held in an ESOP if the dividend is (1) paid in cash directly to participants or (2) paid to the plan and subsequently distributed to the participants in cash no later than 90 days after the close of the plan year in which the dividend is paid to the plan. The deduction is allowable for the taxable year of the corporation in which the dividend is paid or distributed to the participants.

Under the Act, in addition to the deductions permitted under present law, a deduction is permitted for a dividend paid with respect to employer stock that, at the election of the participants, is payable in cash directly to participants or paid to the plan and subsequently distributed to the participants in cash no later than 90 days after the close of the plan year in which the dividend is paid to the plan, or paid to the plan and reinvested in qualifying employer securities. Under the provision, the deduction for dividends that are reinvested in qualifying employer securities at the election of participants is allowable for the taxable year in which the later of the reinvestment or the election occurs. The provision also clarifies that a dividend that is reinvested in qualifying employer securities at the participant's election must be nonforfeitable.

* * *

[Effective Date]

[Except as otherwise provided, the technical corrections contained in the bill generally are effective as if included in the originally enacted related legislation.—CCH]

[Law at ¶ 5020, ¶ 5052, ¶ 5135, ¶ 5140, ¶ 5145, ¶ 5150, ¶ 5155, ¶ 5160, ¶ 5165, ¶ 5170, ¶ 5175, ¶ 5180, ¶ 5185, ¶ 5195, ¶ 5338 and ¶ 7065. CCH Explanation at ¶ 510, ¶ 515, ¶ 520, ¶ 525, ¶ 530, ¶ 535, ¶ 540, ¶ 545, ¶ 550, ¶ 555, ¶ 560, ¶ 565, ¶ 570, ¶ 575, ¶ 580, ¶ 585, ¶ 590, ¶ 595, ¶ 605 and ¶ 610.]

[¶ 10,280]   Act Sec. 412. Tax technical corrections [CRTRA of 2000]

Joint Committee on Taxation (J.C.T. REP. NO. JCX-12-02)

[Caution: The Technical Explanation of the "Job Creation and Worker Assistance Act of 2002" (JCX-12-02), below, is included to assist the reader's understanding but may not be cited as the official Conference Committee Report to P.L. 107-147.—CCH]

[Code Sec. 151, Code Sec. 358, Code Sec. 469, Code Sec. 1091, Code Sec. 1233, Code Sec. 1234A and Code Sec. 1234B]

Except as otherwise provided, the technical corrections contained in the bill generally are effective as if included in the originally enacted related legislation.

* * *

Amendments to the Community Renewal Tax Relief Act of 2000

Phaseout of $25,000 amount for certain rental real estate under passive loss rules.— Present law provides for a phaseout of the $25,000 amount allowed in the case of certain deductions and certain credits with respect to rental real estate activities, for taxpayers with adjusted gross income exceeding $100,000. The phaseout rule does not apply, or applies separately, in the case of the rehabilitation credit, the low-income housing credit, and the commercial revitalization deduction. The provision clarifies the operation of the ordering rules to reflect the exceptions and separate phaseout rules for these items.

Treatment of missing children.—Present law provides that in the case of a dependent child of the taxpayer that is kidnapped, the taxpayer may continue to treat the child as a dependent for purposes of the dependency exemption, child credit, surviving spouse filing status, and head of household filing status. A similar rule applies under the earned income credit. The provision clarifies that, if a taxpayer met the household maintenance requirement of the surviving spouse filing status or the head of household filing status, respectively, with respect to his or her dependent child immediately before the kidnapping, then the taxpayer would be deemed to continue to meet that requirement for purposes of the filing status rule of section 2 of the Code until the child would have reached age 18 or is determined to be dead.

Basis of property in an exchange by a corporation involving assumption of liabilities.— The provision clarifies that the basis reduction rule of section 358(h) of the Code gives rise to a basis reduction in the amount of any liability that is assumed by another party as part of the exchange in which the property (whose basis exceeds its fair market value) is received, so long as the other requirements under section 358(h) apply.

Tax treatment of securities futures contracts.—The provision clarifies that the termination of a securities contract is treated in a manner similar to a sale or exchange of a securities futures contract for purposes of determining the character of any gain or loss from a termination of a securities futures contract. Under the provision, any gain or loss from the termination of a securities futures contract (other than a dealer securities futures contract) is treated as gain or loss from the sale or exchange of property that has the same character as the property to which the contract relates has (or would have) in the hands of the taxpayer.

The provision also clarifies that losses from the sale, exchange, or termination of a securities futures contract (other than a dealer securities futures contract) to sell generally are treated in the same manner as losses from the closing of a short sale for purposes of applying the wash sale rules. Thus, the wash sale rules apply to any loss from the sale, exchange, or termination of a securities futures contract (other than dealer securities futures contract) if, within a period beginning 30 days before the date of such sale, exchange, or termination and ending 30 days after such date: (1) stock that is substantially identical to the stock to which the contract relates is sold; (2) a short sale of substantially identical stock is entered into; or (3) another securities futures contract to sell substantially identical stock is entered into.

The provision clarifies that a securities futures contract to sell generally is treated in a manner similar to a short sale for purposes of the special holding period rules in section 1233. Thus, subsections (b) and (d) of section 1233 may apply to characterize certain capital gains as short-term capital gain and certain capital losses as long-term capital loss, and to determine holding periods where certain securities futures contracts to sell are entered into while holding the substantially identical stock.

* * *

[Effective Date]

[Except as otherwise provided, the technical corrections contained in the bill generally are effective as if included in the originally enacted related legislation.—CCH]

[Law at ¶ 5090, ¶ 5130, ¶ 5200, ¶ 5265, ¶ 5275, ¶ 5280 and ¶ 5282. CCH Explanation at ¶ 225, ¶ 245, ¶ 325 and ¶ 335.]

[¶ 10,290]   Act Sec. 413. Tax technical corrections [TREA 1999]

Joint Committee on Taxation (J.C.T. REP. NO. JCX-12-02)

[Caution: The Technical Explanation of the "Job Creation and Worker Assistance Act of 2002" (JCX-12-02), below, is included to assist the reader's understanding but may not be cited as the official Conference Committee Report to P.L. 107-147.—CCH]

[Code Sec. 857(b)(7)]

Except as otherwise provided, the technical corrections contained in the bill generally are effective as if included in the originally enacted related legislation.

* * *

Amendment to the Tax Relief Extension Act of 1999

Taxable REIT subsidiaries—100 percent tax on improperly allocated amounts.—The provision clarifies that redetermined rents, to which the excise tax applies, are the excess of the amount treated by the REIT as rents from real property under Code section 856(d) over the amount that would be so treated after reduction under Code section 482 to clearly reflect income as a result of services furnished or rendered by a taxable REIT subsidiary of the REIT to a tenant of the REIT. Similarly, redetermined deductions are the excess of the amount treated by the taxable REIT subsidiary as other deductions over the amount that would be so treated after reduction under Code section 482.

* * *

[*Effective Date*]

[Except as otherwise provided, the technical corrections contained in the bill generally are effective as if included in the originally enacted related legislation.—CCH]

[Law at ¶ 5235. CCH Explanation at ¶ 360.]

[¶ 10,300]   Act Sec. 414. Tax technical corrections [TRA 1997]

Joint Committee on Taxation (J.C.T. REP. NO. JCX-12-02)

[Caution: The Technical Explanation of the "Job Creation and Worker Assistance Act of 2002" (JCX-12-02), below, is included to assist the reader's understanding but may not be cited as the official Conference Committee Report to P.L. 107-147.—CCH]

[Act Sec. 414]

Except as otherwise provided, the technical corrections contained in the bill generally are effective as if included in the originally enacted related legislation.

* * *

Amendments to the Taxpayer Relief Act of 1997

Election to recognize gain on assets held on January 1, 2001; treatment of gain on sale of principal residence.—The provision clarifies that the gain to which the mark-to-market election applies is included in gross income. Thus, the exclusion of gain on the sale of a principal residence under Code section 121 would not apply with respect to an asset for which the election to mark to market is made. The provision is consistent with the holding of Rev. Rul. 2001-57.

Election to recognize gain on assets held on January 1, 2001; treatment of disposition of interest in passive activity.—The provision clarifies that the election to mark to market an interest in a passive activity does not result in the deduction of suspended losses by reason of section 469(g)(1)(A). Any gain taken into account by reason of an election with respect to any interest in a passive activity is taken into account in determining the passive activity loss for the taxable year (as defined in section 469(d)(1)). Section 469(g)(1)(A) may apply to a subsequent disposition of the interest in the activity by the taxpayer.

* * *

[*Effective Date*]

[Except as otherwise provided, the technical corrections contained in the bill generally are effective as if included in the originally enacted related legislation.—CCH]

[Law at ¶ 7070. CCH Explanation at ¶ 320.]

[¶ 10,310]   Act Sec. 415. Tax technical corrections [Balanaced Budget Act of 1997]

Joint Committee on Taxation (J.C.T. REP. NO. JCX-12-02)

[Caution: The Technical Explanation of the "Job Creation and Worker Assistance Act of 2002" (JCX-12-02), below, is included to assist the reader's understanding but may not be cited as the official Conference Committee Report to P.L. 107-147.—CCH]

[Code Sec. 26(b)(2)]

Except as otherwise provided, the technical corrections contained in the bill generally are effective as if included in the originally enacted related legislation.

* * *

Amendment to the Balanced Budget Act of 1997

Medicare+Choice MSA.—The provision conforms the treatment of the additional tax on Medicare+Choice MSAs distributions not used for qualified medical expenses if a minimum balance is not maintained to the treatment of the additional tax on Archer MSA distributions not used for qualified medical expenses, for purposes of determining whether certain taxes are included within regular tax liability under Code section 26(b).

* * *

[Effective Date]

[Except as otherwise provided, the technical corrections contained in the bill generally are effective as if included in the originally enacted related legislation.—CCH]

[Law at ¶ 5025. CCH Explanation at ¶ 242.]

[¶ 10,320]   Act Sec. 416, Act Sec. 417 and Act Sec. 418. Tax technical corrections

Joint Committee on Taxation (J.C.T. REP. NO. JCX-12-02)

[Caution: The Technical Explanation of the "Job Creation and Worker Assistance Act of 2002" (JCX-12-02), below, is included to assist the reader's understanding but may not be cited as the official Conference Committee Report to P.L. 107-147.—CCH]

[Code Sec. 21, Code Sec. 23, Code Sec. 25B, Code Sec. 32, Code Sec. 42, Code Sec. 51A, Code Sec. 56, Code Sec. 137, Code Sec. 151, Code Sec. 170, Code Sec. 172, Code Sec. 351, Code Sec. 475, Code Sec. 529, Code Sec. 741, Code Sec. 857, Code Sec. 943, Code Sec. 995, Code Sec. 1221, Code Sec. 1256, Code Sec. 1394, Code Sec. 4980E, Code Sec. 6103, Code Sec. 6105, Code Sec. 6224, Code Sec. 6227, Code Sec. 6228, Code Sec. 6229, Code Sec. 6231, Code Sec. 6234, Code Sec. 6331 and Code Sec. 7702A]

Except as otherwise provided, the technical corrections contained in the bill generally are effective as if included in the originally enacted related legislation.

* * *

Amendment to other Acts

Advance payments of earned income credit.—The provision corrects a reference in section 32(g)(2) to refer to credits allowable under this part (i.e., all tax credits) rather than under this subpart (i.e., the refundable credits). The provision is effective as if included in section 474 of the Tax Reform Act of 1984.

Coordination of wash sale rules and section 1256 contracts.—The bill clarifies that the wash sale rules do not apply to any loss arising from a section 1256 contract. This rule is similar to the rule in present-law section 475 applicable to securities that are marked to market under that section. The provision is effective as if included in section 5075 of the Technical and Miscellaneous Revenue Act of 1988.

Disclosure by the Social Security Administration to Federal child support enforcement agencies.—Section 6103(1)(8) permits the Social Security Administration (SSA) to disclose certain tax information in its possession to State child support enforcement agencies. The Office of Child Support Enforcement (OCSE), a Federal agency, oversees child support enforcement at the Federal level and acts as a coordinator for most programs involved with child support enforcement. OCSE acts as a conduit for the disclosure of tax information from the Internal Revenue Service to the various State and local child support enforcement agencies. The change to section 6103(1)(8) permits SSA to make disclosures directly to OCSE, which in turn would make the disclosures to the State and local child support enforcement agencies. The provision is effective on the date of enactment.

Treatment of settlements under partnership audit rules.—The provision clarifies that the partnership audit procedures that apply to settlement agreements entered into by the Secretary also apply to settlement agreements entered into by the Attorney General. Under present law, when the Secretary enters into a settlement agreement with a partner with respect to partnership items, those items convert to nonpartnership items, and the other partners in the partnership have a right to request consistent settlement terms. The conversion of the settling partner's partnership items to nonpartnership items is the mechanism by which the settling partner is removed from the ongoing partnership proceeding. If these rules did not apply to settlement agreements entered into by the Attorney General (or his delegate), it is possible that a settling partner would inadvertently be bound by the outcome of the partnership proceeding rather than the settlement agreement entered into with the Attorney General (or his delegate) (sec. 6224(c)(2)). Similar changes are made to related provisions with respect to settlement agreements. The provision is effective for settlement agreements entered into after the date of enactment.

Clarification of permissible extension of limitations period for installment agreements.—Uncertainty existed as to whether the permissible extension of the period of limitations in the context of installment agreements is governed by reference to an agreement of the parties pursuant to section 6502 or by reference to the period of time during which the installment agreement is in effect pursuant to sections 6331(k)(3) and (i)(5). A 2000 technical correction clarified that the permissible extension of the period of limitations in the context of installment agreements is governed by the pertinent provisions of section 6502. The provision further clarifies that the elimination of the application of the section 6331(i)(5) rules applies only to section 6331(k)(2)(C). The provision modifies section 313(b)(3) of H.R. 5662, the Community Renewal Tax Relief Act of 2000 (Pub. Law No. 106-554). This is the further technical correction referred to in footnote 185a, Joint Committee on Taxation, *General Explanation of Tax Legislation Enacted in the 106th Congress* (JCS-2-01), April 19, 2001, page 162. The provision is effective on the date of enactment.

Determination of whether a life insurance contract is a modified endowment contract.—The provision clarifies that, for purposes of determining whether a life insurance contract is a modified endowment contract, if there is a material change to the contract, appropriate adjustments are made in determining whether the contract meets the 7-pay test to take into account the cash surrender value under the contract. No reference is needed to the cash surrender under the "old contract" (as was provided under section 318(a)(2) of H.R. 5662, the Community Renewal

Tax Relief Act of 2000 (Pub. Law No. 106-554)) because prior and present law provide a definition of cash surrender value for this purpose (by cross reference to section 7702(f)(2)(A)). It is reiterated that Code section 7702A(c)(3)(ii) is not intended to permit a policyholder to engage in a series of "material changes" to circumvent the premium limitations in section 7702A. Thus, if there is a material change to a life insurance contract, it is intended that the fair market value of the contract be used as the cash surrender value under the provision, if the amount of the putative cash surrender value of the contract is artificially depressed. For example, if there is a material change because of an increase in the face amount of the contract, any artificial or temporary reduction in the cash surrender value of the contract is not to be taken into account, but rather, it is intended that the fair market value of the contract be used as cash surrender value, so that the substance rather than the form of the transaction is reflected. Further, as stated in the 1988 Act legislative history to section 7702A,[55] in applying the 7-pay test to any premiums paid under a contract that has been materially changed, the 7-pay premium for each of the first 7 contract years after the change is to be reduced by the product of (1) the cash surrender value of the contract as of the date that the material change takes effect (determined without regard to any increase in the cash surrender value that is attributable to the amount of the premium payment that is not necessary), and (2) a fraction the numerator of which equals the 7-pay premium for the future benefits under the contract, and the denominator of which equals the net single premium for such benefits computed using the same assumptions used in determining the 7-pay premium. The provision is effective as if section 318(a) of the Community Renewal Tax Relief Act of 2000 (114. Stat. 2763A-645) had not been enacted.

Clerical amendments

The bill makes a number of clerical and typographical amendments to the Code.

Additional Corrections

Adoption credit and employer-provided adoption assistance exclusion rounding rules.—The provision provides uniform rounding rules (to the nearest multiple of $10) for the inflation-adjusted dollar limits and income limitations in the adoption credit and the employer-provided adoption assistance exclusion. The provision is effective as if included in the provision of the Economic Growth and Tax Reform Reconciliation Act of 2001 to which it relates.

Dependent care credit.—The provision conforms the dollar limit on deemed earned income of

---

[55] Conference Report to accompany H.R. 4333, the "Technical and Miscellaneous Revenue Act of 1988" (H. Rep. No. 100-1104), Oct. 21, 1988, vol. II, p. 105.

a taxpayer's spouse who is either (1) a full-time student, or (2) physically or mentally incapable of caring for himself, to the dollar limit on employment-related expenses applicable in determining the maximum credit amount. The 2001 Act increased the dollar limit on employer-related expenses to $3,000 for one qualifying individual or $6,000 for two or more qualifying individuals annually but did not conform the dollar limit on deemed earned income of a spouse. The provision is effective as if included in the provision of the Economic Growth and Tax Reform Reconciliation Act of 2001 to which it relates.

[Effective Date]

[Except as otherwise provided, the technical corrections contained in the bill generally are effective as if included in the originally enacted related legislation.—CCH]

[Law at ¶ 5005, ¶ 5010, ¶ 5020, ¶ 5035, ¶ 5045, ¶ 5057, ¶ 5060, ¶ 5085, ¶ 5090, ¶ 5100, ¶ 5105, ¶ 5125, ¶ 5205, ¶ 5210, ¶ 5225, ¶ 5235, ¶ 5245, ¶ 5260, ¶ 5270, ¶ 5285, ¶ 5290, ¶ 5335, ¶ 5340, ¶ 5345, ¶ 5350, ¶ 5355, ¶ 5360, ¶ 5365, ¶ 5370, ¶ 5375, ¶ 5380, ¶ 5395 and ¶ 7075. CCH Explanation at ¶ 234, ¶ 238, ¶ 240, ¶ 255, ¶ 260, ¶ 330, ¶ 355, ¶ 363, ¶ 365 and ¶ 30,050.]

[¶ 10,350]   Act Sec. 501. No impact on social security trust funds

Joint Committee on Taxation (J.C.T. REP. NO. JCX-12-02)

[Caution: The Technical Explanation of the "Job Creation and Worker Assistance Act of 2002" (JCX-12-02), below, is included to assist the reader's understanding but may not be cited as the official Conference Committee Report to P.L. 107-147.—CCH]

[Act Sec. 501]

Present Law

Present law provides for the transfer of Social Security taxes and certain self-employment taxes to the Social Security trust fund. In addition, the income tax collected with respect to a portion of Social Security benefits included in gross income is transferred to the Social Security trust fund.

Explanation of Provision

The bill provides that the Secretary is to annually estimate the impact of the bill on the income and balances of the Social Security trust fund. If the Secretary determines that the bill has a negative impact on the income and balances of the fund, then the Secretary is to transfer from the general revenues of the Federal government an amount sufficient so as to ensure that the income and balances of the Social Security trust funds are not reduced as a result of the bill. Such transfers are to be made not less frequently than quarterly.

The bill provides that the provisions of the bill are not to be construed as an amendment of title II of the Social Security Act.

Effective Date

The provision is effective on the date of enactment.

[Law at ¶ 7080.]

[¶ 10,360]   Act Sec. 502. Emergency designation

Joint Committee on Taxation (J.C.T. REP. NO. JCX-12-02)

[Caution: The Technical Explanation of the "Job Creation and Worker Assistance Act of 2002" (JCX-12-02), below, is included to assist the reader's understanding but may not be cited as the official Conference Committee Report to P.L. 107-147.—CCH]

[Act Sec. 502]

Present Law

Under the Balanced Budget and Emergency Deficit Control Act of 1985, as amended, any legislation that reduces revenues or increases outlays is subject to a pay-as-you-go ("PAYGO") requirement. The PAYGO system tracks legislation that may increase budget deficits using a "scorecard" estimated by the Office of Management and Budget. Under PAYGO requirements, in order to avoid sequestration, any revenue loss or increase in outlays would need to be offset by revenue increases or reductions in direct spending.

If a provision of direct spending or receipts legislation is enacted that the President designates as an emergency requirement and that the Congress so designates in statute, the amounts of new budget authority, outlays, and receipts in all fiscal years resulting from that provision are not taken into account in determining the PAYGO scorecard.

Explanation of Provision

The provision designates any revenue loss, new budget authority, and new outlays under the bill in excess of those allowed under the FY 2002 budget resolution as emergency requirements pursuant to section 252(e) of the Balanced Budget and Emergency Deficit Control Act of 1985.

Effective Date

The provision is effective on the date of enactment.

[Law at ¶ 7085.]

Act Sec. 502   ¶ 10,360

[¶ 10,400]   Act Sec. 601. Extend alternative minimum tax relief for individuals

Joint Committee on Taxation (J.C.T. Rep. No. JCX-12-02)

[Caution: The Technical Explanation of the "Job Creation and Worker Assistance Act of 2002" (JCX-12-02), below, is included to assist the reader's understanding but may not be cited as the official Conference Committee Report to P.L. 107-147.—CCH]

[Code Sec. 26(a) and 904(h)]

Present Law

Present law provides for certain nonrefundable personal tax credits (i.e., the dependent care credit, the credit for the elderly and disabled, the adoption credit, the child tax credit[56], the credit for interest on certain home mortgages, the HOPE Scholarship and Lifetime Learning credits, the IRA credit, and the D.C. homebuyer's credit). For taxable years beginning after 2001, these credits (other than the adoption credit, child credit and IRA credit) are allowed only to the extent that the individual's regular income tax liability exceeds the individual's tentative minimum tax, determined without regard to the minimum tax foreign tax credit. The adoption credit, child credit, and IRA credit are allowed to the full extent of the individual's regular tax and alternative minimum tax.

For taxable years beginning in 2001, all the nonrefundable personal credits are allowed to the extent of the full amount of the individual's regular tax and alternative minimum tax.

The alternative minimum tax is the amount by which the tentative minimum tax exceeds the regular income tax. An individual's tentative minimum tax is an amount equal to (1) 26 percent of the first $175,000 ($87,500 in the case of a married individual filing a separate return) of alterna-tive minimum taxable income ("AMTI") in excess of a phased-out exemption amount and (2) 28 percent of the remaining AMTI. The maximum tax rates on net capital gain used in computing the tentative minimum tax are the same as under the regular tax. AMTI is the individual's taxable income adjusted to take account of specified pref-erences and adjustments. The exemption amounts are: (1) $45,000 ($49,000 in taxable years begin-ning before 2005) in the case of married individu-als filing a joint return and surviving spouses; (2) $33,750 ($35,750 in taxable years beginning before 2005) in the case of other unmarried indi-viduals; (3) $22,500 ($24,500 in taxable years beginning before 2005) in the case of married individuals filing a separate return; and (4) $22,500 in the case of an estate or trust. The exemption amounts are phased out by an amount equal to 25 percent of the amount by which the individual's AMTI exceeds (1) $150,000 in the case of married individuals filing a joint return and surviving spouses, (2) $112,500 in the case of other unmarried individuals, and (3) $75,000 in the case of married individuals filing separate returns or an estate or a trust. These amounts are not indexed for inflation.

Explanation of Provision

The provision allows an individual to offset the entire regular tax liability and alternative mini-mum tax liability by the personal nonrefundable credits in 2002 and 2003.

Effective Date

The provision is effective for taxable years be-ginning in 2002 and 2003.

House Committee Report (H.R. Rep. No. 107-251)

[Caution: The House Committee Report on the "Economic Security and Recovery Act of 2001," as passed by the House (H.R. Rep. No. 107-251), below, is included to assist the reader's understanding but may not be cited as the controlling Committee Report to P.L. 107-147.—CCH]

Present Law

Present law provides for certain nonrefundable personal tax credits (i.e., the dependent care credit, the credit for the elderly and disabled, the adoption credit, the child tax credit[15], the credit for interest on certain home mortgages, the HOPE Scholarship and Lifetime Learning credits, the IRA credit, and the D.C. homebuyer's credit). For taxable years beginning after 2001, these credits (other than the adoption credit, child credit and IRA credit) are allowed only to the extent that the individual's regular income tax liability ex-ceeds the individual's tentative minimum tax, determined without regard to the minimum tax foreign tax credit. The adoption credit, child credit, and IRA credit are allowed to the full extent of the individual's regular tax and alterna-tive minimum tax.

For taxable years beginning in 2001, all the nonrefundable personal credits are allowed to the extent of the full amount of the individual's regu-lar tax and alternative minimum tax.

---

[56] A portion of the child credit may be refundable.

[15] A portion of the child credit may be refundable.

The alternative minimum tax is the amount by which the tentative minimum tax exceeds the regular income tax. An individual's tentative minimum tax is an amount equal to (1) 26 percent of the first $175,000 ($87,500 in the case of a married individual filing a separate return) of alternative minimum taxable income ("AMTI") in excess of a phased-out exemption amount and (2) 28 percent of the remaining AMTI. The maximum tax rates on net capital gain used in computing the tentative minimum tax are the same as under the regular tax. AMTI is the individual's taxable income adjusted to take account of specified preferences and adjustments. The exemption amounts are: (1) $45,000 ($49,000 in taxable years beginning before 2005) in the case of married individuals filing a joint return and surviving spouses; (2) $33,750 ($35,750 in taxable years beginning before 2005) in the case of other unmarried individuals; (3) $22,500 ($24,500 in taxable years beginning before 2005) in the case of married individuals filing a separate return; and (4) $22,500 in the case of an estate or trust.[16] The exemption amounts are phased out by an amount equal to 25 percent of the amount by which the individual's AMTI exceeds (1) $150,000 in the case of married individuals filing a joint return and surviving spouses, (2) $112,500 in the case of other unmarried individuals, and (3) $75,000 in the case of married individuals filing separate returns or an estate or a trust. These amounts are not indexed for inflation.

Reasons for Change

The Committee believes that the nonrefundable personal credits should be useable without limitation by reason of the alternative minimum tax. This will result in significant simplification.

Explanation of Provision

The provision allows an individual to offset the entire regular tax liability and alternative minimum tax liability by the personal nonrefundable credits in 2002 and 2003.

Effective Date

The provision is effective for taxable years beginning in 2002 and 2003.

[Law at ¶ 5025, ¶ 5240 and ¶ 7090. CCH Explanation at ¶ 270.]

[¶ 10,410]　Act Sec. 602. Extend credit for purchase of electric vehicles

Joint Committee on Taxation (J.C.T. REP. NO. JCX-12-02)

[Caution: The Technical Explanation of the "Job Creation and Worker Assistance Act of 2002" (JCX-12-02), below, is included to assist the reader's understanding but may not be cited as the official Conference Committee Report to P.L. 107-147.—CCH]

[Code Sec. 30 and Code Sec. 280F]

Present Law

A 10-percent tax credit is provided for the cost of a qualified electric vehicle, up to a maximum credit of $4,000 (sec. 30). A qualified electric vehicle is a motor vehicle that is powered primarily by an electric motor drawing current from rechargeable batteries, fuel cells, or other portable sources of electrical current, the original use of which commences with the taxpayer, and that is acquired for the use by the taxpayer and not for resale. The full amount of the credit is available for purchases prior to 2002. The credit phases down in the years 2002 through 2004, and is unavailable for purchases after December 31, 2004.[57]

Explanation of Provision

The bill defers the phase down of the credit for two years. Taxpayers may claim the full amount of the credit for qualified purchases made in 2002 and 2003. Under the bill, the phase down of the credit value commences in 2004 and the credit is unavailable for purchases after December 31, 2006. A conforming modification is made to section 280F.

Effective Date

The provision is effective for property placed in service after December 31, 2001.

House Committee Report (H.R. REP. NO. 107-251)

[Caution: The House Committee Report on the "Economic Security and Recovery Act of 2001," as passed by the House (H.R. Rep. No. 107-251), below, is included to assist the reader's understanding but may not be cited as the controlling Committee Report to P.L. 107-147.—CCH]

[Present Law]

A 10-percent tax credit is provided for the cost of a qualified electric vehicle, up to a maximum

---

[16] Section 202(b) of the bill increases certain of the exemption amounts.

[57] The amount the taxpayer may claim as a depreciation deduction for any passenger automobile is limited (sec. 280F). In the case of a passenger vehicle designed to be propelled primarily by electricity and built by an original equipment manufacturer, the otherwise applicable limitation amounts are tripled. These exceptions from sec. 280F apply to vehicles placed in service prior to January 1, 2005.

credit of $4,000 (sec. 30). A qualified electric vehicle is a motor vehicle that is powered primarily by an electric motor drawing current from rechargeable batteries, fuel cells, or other portable sources of electrical current, the original use of which commences with the taxpayer, and that is acquired for the use by the taxpayer and not for resale. The full amount of the credit is available for purchases prior to 2002. The credit phases down in the years 2002 through 2004, and is unavailable for purchases after December 31, 2004.[17]

Reasons for Change

The Committee believes that continued economic incentive is warranted to increase the presence of electric vehicles on the nation's roadways.

Explanation of Provision

The bill defers the phase down of the credit by two years. Taxpayers may claim the full amount of the credit for qualified purchases made in 2002 and 2003. Under the bill, the phase down of the credit value commences in 2004 and the credit is unavailable for purchases after December 31, 2006. A conforming modification is made to section 280F.

Effective Date

* * *

[Law at ¶ 5030, ¶ 5120 and ¶ 7095. CCH Explanation at ¶ 370.]

[¶ 10,420]   Act Sec. 603. Extend Section 45 credit for production of electricity from wind, closed loop biomass and poultry litter

Joint Committee on Taxation (J.C.T. Rep. No. JCX-12-02)

[Caution: The Technical Explanation of the "Job Creation and Worker Assistance Act of 2002" (JCX-12-02), below, is included to assist the reader's understanding but may not be cited as the official Conference Committee Report to P.L. 107-147.—CCH]

[Code Sec. 45(c)(3)]

Present Law

An income tax credit is allowed for the production of electricity from either qualified wind energy, qualified "closed-loop" biomass, or qualified poultry waste facilities (sec. 45).

The credit applies to electricity produced by a wind energy facility placed in service after December 31, 1993, and before January 1, 2002, to electricity produced by a closed-loop biomass facility placed in service after December 31, 1992, and before January 1, 2002, and to a poultry waste facility placed in service after December 31, 1999, and before January 1, 2002. The credit is allowable for production during the 10-year period after a facility is originally placed in service. In order to claim the credit, a taxpayer must own the facility and sell the electricity produced by the facility to an unrelated party. In the case of a poultry waste facility, the taxpayer may claim the credit as a lessee/operator of a facility owned by a governmental unit.

Closed-loop biomass is plant matter, where the plants are grown for the sole purpose of being used to generate electricity. It does not include waste materials (including, but not limited to, scrap wood, manure, and municipal or agricultural waste). The credit also is not available to taxpay-

ers who use standing timber to produce electricity. Poultry waste means poultry manure and litter, including wood shavings, straw, rice hulls, and other bedding material for the disposition of manure.

The credit for electricity produced from wind, closed-loop biomass, or poultry waste is a component of the general business credit (sec. 38(b)(8)). The credit, when combined with all other components of the general business credit, generally may not exceed for any taxable year the excess of the taxpayer's net income tax over the greater of (1) 25 percent of net regular tax liability above $25,000, or (2) the tentative minimum tax. For credits arising in taxable years beginning after December 31, 1997, an unused general business credit generally may be carried back one year and carried forward 20 years (sec. 39). To coordinate the carryback with the period of application for this credit, the credit for electricity produced from closed-loop biomass facilities may not be carried back to a tax year ending before 1993 and the credit for electricity produced from wind energy may not be carried back to a tax year ending before 1994 (sec. 39).

Explanation of Provision

The bill extends the placed in service date for qualified facilities by two years to include those facilities placed in service prior to January 1, 2004.

Effective Date

The provision is effective for facilities placed in service after December 31, 2001.

---

[17] The amount the taxpayer may claim as a depreciation deduction for any passenger automobile is limited (sec. 280F). In the case of a passenger vehicle designed to be propelled primarily by electricity and built by an original equipment manufacturer, the otherwise applicable limitation amounts are tripled. These exceptions from sec. 280F apply to vehicles placed in service prior to January 1, 2005.

House Committee Report (H.R. Rep. No. 107-251)

[Caution: The House Committee Report on the "Economic Security and Recovery Act of 2001," as passed by the House (H.R. Rep. No. 107-251), below, is included to assist the reader's understanding but may not be cited as the controlling Committee Report to P.L. 107-147.—CCH]

Present Law

An income tax credit is allowed for the production of electricity from either qualified wind energy, qualified "closed-loop" biomass, or qualified poultry waste facilities (sec. 45).

The credit applies to electricity produced by a wind energy facility placed in service after December 31, 1993, and before January 1, 2002, to electricity produced by a closed-loop biomass facility placed in service after December 31, 1992, and before January 1, 2002, and to a poultry waste facility placed in service after December 31, 1999, and before January 1, 2002. The credit is allowable for production during the 10-year period after a facility is originally placed in service. In order to claim the credit, a taxpayer must own the facility and sell the electricity produced by the facility to an unrelated party. In the case of a poultry waste facility, the taxpayer may claim the credit as a lessee/operator of a facility owned by a governmental unit.

Closed-loop biomass is plant matter, where the plants are grown for the sole purpose of being used to generate electricity. It does not include waste materials (including, but not limited to, scrap wood, manure, and municipal or agricultural waste). The credit also is not available to taxpayers who use standing timber to produce electricity. Poultry waste means poultry manure and litter, including wood shavings, straw, rice hulls, and other bedding material for the disposition of manure.

The credit for electricity produced from wind, closed-loop biomass, or poultry waste is a component of the general business credit (sec. 38(b)(8)). The credit, when combined with all other components of the general business credit, generally may not exceed for any taxable year the excess of the taxpayer's net income tax over the greater of (1) 25 percent of net regular tax liability above $25,000, or (2) the tentative minimum tax. For credits arising in taxable years beginning after December 31, 1997, an unused general business credit generally may be carried back one year and carried forward 20 years (sec. 39). To coordinate the carryback with the period of application for this credit, the credit for electricity produced from closed-loop biomass facilities may not be carried back to a tax year ending before 1993 and the credit for electricity produced from wind energy may not be carried back to a tax year ending before 1994 (sec. 39).

Reasons for Change

The Committee believes that continued economic incentive is warranted to increase the presence of these more environmentally friendly generation sources in the nation's electricity grid.

Explanation of Provision

The bill extends the placed in service date for qualified facilities by two years to include those facilities placed in service prior to January 1, 2004.

Effective Date

* * *

[Law at ¶ 5050. CCH Explanation at ¶ 372.]

[¶ 10,430]   Act Sec. 604. Extend the work opportunity tax credit

Joint Committee on Taxation (J.C.T. Rep. No. JCX-12-02)

[Caution: The Technical Explanation of the "Job Creation and Worker Assistance Act of 2002" (JCX-12-02), below, is included to assist the reader's understanding but may not be cited as the official Conference Committee Report to P.L. 107-147.—CCH]

[Code Sec. 51]

Present Law

In general

The work opportunity tax credit ("WOTC") is available on an elective basis for employers hiring individuals from one or more of eight targeted groups. The credit equals 40 percent (25 percent for employment of less than 400 hours) of qualified wages. Generally, qualified wages are wages attributable to service rendered by member of a targeted group during the one-year period beginning with the day the individual began work for the employer.

The maximum credit per employee is $2,400 (40 percent of the first $6,000 of qualified first-year wages). With respect to qualified summer youth employees, the maximum credit is $1,200 (40 percent of the first $3,000 of qualified first-year wages).

For purposes of the credit, wages are generally defined as under the Federal Unemployment Tax Act, without regard to the dollar cap.

Targeted groups eligible for the credit

The eight targeted groups are: (1) families eligible to receive benefits under the Temporary Assistance for Needy Families ("TANF") Program; (2) high-risk youth; (3) qualified ex-felons; (4) vocational rehabilitation referrals; (5) qualified summer youth employees; (6) qualified veterans; (7) families receiving food stamps; and (8) persons receiving certain Supplemental Security Income ("SSI") benefits.

The employer's deduction for wages is reduced by the amount of the credit.

Expiration date

The credit is effective for wages paid or incurred to a qualified individual who began work for an employer before January 1, 2002.

Explanation of Provision

The bill extends the work opportunity tax credit for two years (through December 31, 2003).

Effective Date

The provision is effective for wages paid or incurred to a qualified individual who begins work for an employer on or after January 1, 2002, and before January 1, 2004.

House Committee Report (H.R. REP. NO. 107-251)

[Caution: The House Committee Report on the "Economic Security and Recovery Act of 2001," as passed by the House (H.R. Rep. No. 107-251), below, is included to assist the reader's understanding but may not be cited as the controlling Committee Report to P.L. 107-147.—CCH]

Present Law

In general

The work opportunity tax credit ("WOTC") is available on an elective basis for employers hiring individuals from one or more of eight targeted groups. The credit equals 40 percent (25 percent for employment of less than 400 hours) of qualified wages. Generally, qualified wages are wages attributable to service rendered by a member of a targeted group during the one-year period beginning with the day the individual began work for the employer.

The maximum credit per employee is $2,400 (40 percent of the first $6,000 of qualified first-year wages). With respect to qualified summer youth employees, the maximum credit is $1,200 (40 percent of the first $3,000 of qualified first-year wages).

For purposes of the credit, wages are generally defined as under the Federal Unemployment Tax Act, without regard to the dollar cap.

Targeted groups eligible for the credit

The eight targeted groups are: (1) families eligible to receive benefits under the Temporary Assistance for Needy Families ("TANF") Program; (2) high-risk youth; (3) qualified ex-felons; (4) vocational rehabilitation referrals; (5) qualified summer youth employees; (6) qualified veterans; (7) families receiving food stamps; and (8) persons receiving certain Supplemental Security Income ("SSI") benefits.

The employer's deduction for wages is reduced by the amount of the credit.

Expiration date

The credit is effective for wages paid or incurred to a qualified individual who begins work for an employer before January 1, 2002.

Reasons for Change

The Committee believes that a temporary extension of this credit will allow the Congress and the Treasury and Labor Departments to continue to monitor the effectiveness of the credit.

Explanation of Provision

The bill extends the work opportunity tax credit for two years (through December 31, 2003).

Effective Date

The provision is effective for wages paid or incurred to a qualified individual who begins work for an employer on or after January 1, 2002, and before January 1, 2004.

[Law at ¶ 5055. CCH Explanation at ¶ 374.]

[¶ 10,440] Act Sec. 605. Extend the Welfare-To-Work Tax Credit

Joint Committee on Taxation (J.C.T. REP. NO. JCX-12-02)

[Caution: The Technical Explanation of the "Job Creation and Worker Assistance Act of 2002" (JCX-12-02), below, is included to assist the reader's understanding but may not be cited as the official Conference Committee Report to P.L. 107-147.—CCH]

[Code Sec. 51A]

Present Law

In general

The welfare-to-work tax credit is available on an elective basis for employers for the first $20,000 of eligible wages paid to qualified long-term family assistance recipients during the first two years of employment. The credit is 35 percent of the first $10,000 of eligible wages in the first year of employment and 50 percent of the first $10,000 of eligible wages in the second year of employment. The maximum credit is $8,500 per qualified employee.

Qualified long-term family assistance recipients are: (1) members of a family that has received family assistance for at least 18 consecutive months ending on the hiring date; (2) members of a family that has received family assistance for a total of at least 18 months (whether or not consecutive) after the date of enactment of this credit if they are hired within 2 years after the date that the 18-month total is reached; and (3) members of a family that is no longer eligible for family assistance because of either Federal or State time limits, if they are hired within two years after the

Federal or State time limits made the family ineligible for family assistance. Family assistance means benefits under the Temporary Assistance to Needy Families ("TANF") program.

For purposes of the credit, wages are generally defined under the Federal Unemployment Tax Act, without regard to the dollar amount. In addition, wages include the following: (1) educational assistance excludable under a section 127 program; (2) the value of excludable health plan coverage but not more than the applicable premium defined under section 4980B(f)(4); and (3) dependent care assistance excludable under section 129.

The employer's deduction for wages is reduced by the amount of the credit.

Expiration date

The welfare to work credit is effective for wages paid or incurred to a qualified individual who began work for an employer before January 1, 2002.

Explanation of Provision

The bill extends the welfare to work credit for two years (through December 31, 2003).

Effective Date

The provision is effective for wages paid or incurred to a qualified individual who begins work for an employer on or after January 1, 2002, and before January 1, 2004.

House Committee Report (H.R. REP. NO. 107-251)

[Caution: The House Committee Report on the "Economic Security and Recovery Act of 2001," as passed by the House (H.R. Rep. No. 107-147), below, is included to assist the reader's understanding but may not be cited as the controlling Committee Report to P.L. 107-147.—CCH]

Present Law

In general

The welfare-to-work tax credit is available on an elective basis for employers for the first $20,000 of eligible wages paid to qualified long-term family assistance recipients during the first two years of employment. The credit is 35 percent of the first $10,000 of eligible wages in the first year of employment and 50 percent of the first $10,000 of eligible wages in the second year of employment. The maximum credit is $8,500 per qualified employee.

Qualified long-term family assistance recipients are: (1) members of a family that has received family assistance for at least 18 consecutive months ending on the hiring date; (2) members of

a family that has received family assistance for a total of at least 18 months (whether or not consecutive) after the date of enactment of this credit if they are hired within 2 years after the date that the 18-month total is reached; and (3) members of a family that is no longer eligible for family assistance because of either Federal or State time limits, if they are hired within two years after the Federal or State time limits made the family ineligible for family assistance. Family assistance means benefits under the Temporary Assistance to Needy Families ("TANF") program.

For purposes of the credit, wages are generally defined under the Federal Unemployment Tax Act, without regard to the dollar amount. In addition, wages include the following: (1) educational assistance excludable under a section 127 program; (2) the value of excludable health plan coverage but not more than the applicable premium defined under section 4980B(f)(4); and (3) dependent care assistance excludable under section 129.

The employer's deduction for wages is reduced by the amount of the credit.

Act Sec. 605 ¶ 10,440

Expiration date

The welfare to work credit is effective for wages paid or incurred to a qualified individual who begins work for an employer before January 1, 2002.

Reasons for Change

The Committee believes that the welfare-to-work credit should be temporarily extended to provide the Congress and Treasury and Labor Departments a better opportunity to assess the operation and effectiveness of the credit in meeting its goals. These goals are: (1) to provide an incentive to hire long-term welfare recipients; (2) to promote the transition from welfare to work by increasing access to employment for these individ-uals; and (3) to encourage employers to provide these individuals with training, health coverage, dependent care and ultimately better job attachment.

Explanation of Provision

The bill extends the welfare to work credit for two years (through December 31, 2003).

Effective Date

The provision is effective for wages paid or incurred to a qualified individual who begins work for an employer on or after January 1, 2002, and before January 1, 2004.

[Law at ¶ 5057. CCH Explanation at ¶ 376.]

[¶ 10,450]   Act Sec. 606. Extend deduction for qualified clean-fuel vehicle property and qualified clean-fuel vehicle refueling property

Joint Committee on Taxation (J.C.T. Rep. No. JCX-12-02)

[Caution: The Technical Explanation of the "Job Creation and Worker Assistance Act of 2002" (JCX-12-02), below, is included to assist the reader's understanding but may not be cited as the official Conference Committee Report to P.L. 107-147.—CCH]

[Code Sec. 179A]

Present Law

Certain costs of qualified clean-fuel vehicle property and clean-fuel vehicle refueling property may be expensed and deducted when such property is placed in service (sec. 179A).[58] Qualified clean-fuel vehicle property includes motor vehicles that use certain clean-burning fuels (natural gas, liquefied natural gas, liquefied petroleum gas, hydrogen, electricity and any other fuel at least 85 percent of which is methanol, ethanol, any other alcohol or ether). The maximum amount of the deduction is $50,000 for a truck or van with a gross vehicle weight over 26,000 pounds or a bus with seating capacities of at least 20 adults; $5,000 in the case of a truck or van with a gross vehicle weight between 10,000 and 26,000 pounds; and $2,000 in the case of any other motor vehicle. Qualified electric vehicles do not qualify for the clean-fuel vehicle deduction.

Clean-fuel vehicle refueling property comprises property for the storage or dispensing of a clean-burning fuel, if the storage or dispensing is the point at which the fuel is delivered into the fuel tank of a motor vehicle. Clean-fuel vehicle refuel-ing property also includes property for the recharging of electric vehicles, but only if the property is located at a point where the electric vehicle is recharged. Up to $100,000 of such property at each location owned by the taxpayer may be expensed with respect to that location.

The deduction for clean-fuel vehicle property phases down in the years 2002 through 2004, and is unavailable for purchases after December 31, 2004. The deduction for clean-fuel vehicle refueling property is unavailable for property placed in service after December 31, 2004.

Explanation of Provision

The bill defers the phase down of the deduction for clean-fuel vehicle property by two years. Taxpayers may claim the full amount of the deduction for qualified vehicles placed in service in 2002 and 2003. Under the bill, the phase down of the deduction for clean-fuel vehicles commences in 2004 and the deduction is unavailable for purchases after December 31, 2006. A conforming modification is made to section 280F.

The provision extends the placed in service date for clean-fuel vehicle refueling property by two years. The deduction for clean-fuel vehicle refueling property is available for property placed in service prior to January 1, 2007.

Effective Date

The provision is effective for property placed in service after December 31, 2001.

---

[58] The amount the taxpayer may claim as a depreciation deduction for any passenger automobile is limited (sec. 280F). In the case of a qualified clean-burning fuel vehicle, the limitation of sec. 280F applies only to that portion of the vehicle's cost not represented by the installed qualified clean-burning fuel property. The taxpayer may claim an amount otherwise allowable as a depreciation deduction on the installed qualified clean-burning fuel property, without regard to the limitation. These exceptions from sec. 280F apply to vehicles placed in service prioe rto January 1, 2005.

House Committee Report (H.R. Rep. No. 107-251)

[Present Law]

Certain costs of qualified clean-fuel vehicle property and clean-fuel vehicle refueling property may be expensed and deducted when such property is placed in service (sec. 179A).[18] Qualified clean-fuel vehicle property includes motor vehicles that use certain clean-burning fuels (natural gas, liquefied natural gas, liquefied petroleum gas, hydrogen, electricity and any other fuel at least 85 percent of which is methanol, ethanol, any other alcohol or ether). The maximum amount of the deduction is $50,000 for a truck or van with a gross vehicle weight over 26,000 pounds or a bus with seating capacities of at least 20 adults; $5,000 in the case of a truck or van with a gross vehicle weight between 10,000 and 26,000 pounds; and $2,000 in the case of any other motor vehicle. Qualified electric vehicles do not qualify for the clean-fuel vehicle deduction.

Clean-fuel vehicle refueling property comprises property for the storage or dispensing of a clean-burning fuel, if the storage or dispensing is the point at which the fuel is delivered into the fuel tank of a motor vehicle. Clean-fuel vehicle refueling property also includes property for the recharging of electric vehicles, but only if the property is located at a point where the electric vehicle is recharged. Up to $100,000 of such property at each location owned by the taxpayer may be expensed with respect to that location.

The deduction for clean-fuel vehicle property phases down in the years 2002 through 2004, and is unavailable for purchases after December 31, 2004. The deduction for clean-fuel vehicle refueling property is unavailable for property placed in service after December 31, 2004.

Reasons for Change

The Committee believes that continued economic incentive is warranted to increase the presence of alternative fuel vehicles in the market.

Explanation of Provision

The bill defers the phase down of the deduction for clean-fuel vehicle property by two years. Taxpayers may claim the full amount of the deduction for qualified vehicles placed in service in 2002 and 2003. Under the bill, the phase down of the deduction for clean-fuel vehicles commences in 2004 and the deduction is unavailable for purchases after December 31, 2006. A conforming modification is made to section 280F.

The provision extends the placed in service date for clean-fuel vehicle refueling property by one year. The deduction for clean-fuel vehicle refueling property is available for property placed in service prior to January 1, 2007.

Effective Date
* * *

[Law at ¶ 5110. CCH Explanation at ¶ 378.]

[¶ 10,470]   Act Sec. 607. Taxable income limit on percentage depletion for marginal production

Joint Committee on Taxation (J.C.T. Rep. No. JCX-12-02)

[Code Sec. 613A]

Present Law

In general

Depletion, like depreciation, is a form of capital cost recovery. In both cases, the taxpayer is allowed a deduction in recognition of the fact that an asset—in the case of depletion for oil or gas interests, the mineral reserve itself—is being expended in order to produce income. Certain costs incurred prior to drilling an oil or gas property are recovered through the depletion deduction. These include costs of acquiring the lease or other interest in the property and geological and geophysical costs (in advance of actual drilling). Depletion is available to any person having an economic interest in a producing property.

Two methods of depletion are allowable under the Code: (1) the cost depletion method, and (2) the percentage depletion method (secs. 611-613).

---

[18] The amount the taxpayer may claim as a depreciation deduction for any passenger automobile is limited (sec. 280F). In the case of a qualified clean-burning fuel vehicle, the limitation of sec. 280F applies only to that portion of the vehicle's cost not represented by the installed qualified clean-burning fuel property. The taxpayer may claim an amount otherwise allowable as a depreciation deduction on the installed qualified clean-burning fuel property, without regard to the limitation. These exceptions from sec. 280F apply to vehicles placed in service prior to January 1, 2005.

Under the cost depletion method, the taxpayer deducts that portion of the adjusted basis of the depletable property which is equal to the ratio of units sold from that property during the taxable year to the number of units remaining as of the end of taxable year plus the number of units sold during the taxable year. Thus, the amount recovered under cost depletion may never exceed the taxpayer's basis in the property.

Under the percentage depletion method, generally, 15 percent of the taxpayer's gross income from an oil- or gas-producing property is allowed as a deduction in each taxable year (sec. 613A(c)). The amount deducted generally may not exceed 100 percent of the net income from that property in any year (the "net-income limitation") (sec. 613(a)). The Taxpayer Relief Act of 1997 suspended the 100-percent-of-net-income limitation for production from marginal wells for taxable years beginning after December 31, 1997, and before January 1, 2000. The limitation subsequently was extended to include taxable years beginning before January 1, 2002. Additionally, the percentage depletion deduction for all oil and gas properties may not exceed 65 percent of the taxpayer's overall taxable income (determined before such deduction and adjusted for certain loss carrybacks and trust distributions) (sec. 613A(d)(1)).[59] Because percentage depletion, unlike cost depletion, is computed without regard to the taxpayer's basis in the depletable property, cumulative depletion deductions may be greater than the amount expended by the taxpayer to acquire or develop the property.

A taxpayer is required to determine the depletion deduction for each oil or gas property under both the percentage depletion method (if the taxpayer is entitled to use this method) and the cost depletion method. If the cost depletion deduction is larger, the taxpayer must utilize that method for the taxable year in question (sec. 613(a)).

Limitation of oil and gas percentage depletion to independent producers and royalty owners

Generally, only independent producers and royalty owners (as contrasted to integrated oil companies) are allowed to claim percentage depletion. Percentage depletion for eligible taxpayers is allowed only with respect to up to 1,000 barrels of average daily production of domestic crude oil or an equivalent amount of domestic natural gas (sec. 613A(c)). For producers of both oil and natural gas, this limitation applies on a combined basis.

In addition to the independent producer and royalty owner exception, certain sales of natural gas under a fixed contract in effect on February 1, 1975, and certain natural gas from geopressured brine, are eligible for percentage depletion, at rates of 22 percent and 10 percent, respectively. These exceptions apply without regard to the 1,000-barrel-per-day limitation and regardless of whether the producer is an independent producer or an integrated oil company.

Explanation of Provision

The provision extends the period when the 100-percent net-income limit is suspended to include taxable years beginning in 2002 and 2003.

Effective Date

The provision is effective for taxable years beginning after December 31, 2001 and before January 1, 2004.

House Committee Report (H.R. REP. NO. 107-251)

[Caution: The House Committee Report on the "Economic Security and Recovery Act of 2001," as passed by the House (H.R. Rep. No. 107-251), below, is included to assist the reader's understanding but may not be cited as the controlling Committee Report to P.L. 107-147.—CCH]

Present Law

In general

Depletion, like depreciation, is a form of capital cost recovery. In both cases, the taxpayer is allowed a deduction in recognition of the fact that an asset—in the case of depletion for oil or gas interests, the mineral reserve itself—is being expended in order to produce income. Certain costs incurred prior to drilling an oil or gas property are recovered through the depletion deduction. These include costs of acquiring the lease or other interest in the property and geological and geophysical costs (in advance of actual drilling). Depletion is available to any person having an economic interest in a producing property.

Two methods of depletion are allowable under the Code: (1) the cost depletion method, and (2) the percentage depletion method (secs. 611-613). Under the cost depletion method, the taxpayer deducts that portion of the adjusted basis of the depletable property which is equal to the ratio of units sold from that property during the taxable year to the number of units remaining as of the end of taxable year plus the number of units sold during the taxable year. Thus, the amount recovered under cost depletion may never exceed the taxpayer's basis in the property.

Under the percentage depletion method, generally, 15 percent of the taxpayer's gross income

---

[59] Amounts disallowed as a result of this rule may be carried forward and deducted in subsequent taxable years, subject to the 65-percent taxable income limitation for those years.

from an oil- or gas-producing property is allowed as a deduction in each taxable year (sec. 613A(c)). The amount deducted generally may not exceed 100 percent of the net income from that property in any year (the "net-income limitation") (sec. 613(a)). The Taxpayer Relief Act of 1997 suspended the 100-percent-of-net-income limitation for production from marginal wells for taxable years beginning after December 31, 1997, and before January 1, 2000. The limitation subsequently was extended to include taxable years beginning before January 1, 2002. Additionally, the percentage depletion deduction for all oil and gas properties may not exceed 65 percent of the taxpayer's overall taxable income (determined before such deduction and adjusted for certain loss carrybacks and trust distributions) (sec. 613A(d)(1)).[19] Because percentage depletion, unlike cost depletion, is computed without regard to the taxpayer's basis in the depletable property, cumulative depletion deductions may be greater than the amount expended by the taxpayer to acquire or develop the property.

A taxpayer is required to determine the depletion deduction for each oil or gas property under both the percentage depletion method (if the taxpayer is entitled to use this method) and the cost depletion method. If the cost depletion deduction is larger, the taxpayer must utilize that method for the taxable year in question (sec. 613(a)).

Limitation of oil and gas percentage depletion to independent producers and royalty owners

Generally, only independent producers and royalty owners (as contrasted to integrated oil companies) are allowed to claim percentage depletion. Percentage depletion for eligible taxpayers is allowed only with respect to up to 1,000 barrels of average daily production of domestic crude oil or an equivalent amount of domestic natural gas (sec. 613A(c)). For producers of both oil and natural gas, this limitation applies on a combined basis.

In addition to the independent producer and royalty owner exception, certain sales of natural gas under a fixed contract in effect on February 1, 1975, and certain natural gas from geopressured brine, are eligible for percentage depletion, at rates of 22 percent and 10 percent, respectively. These exceptions apply without regard to the 1,000-barrel-per-day limitation and regardless of whether the producer is an independent producer or an integrated oil company.

Reasons for Change

The Committee notes that oil is, and will continue to be, vital to the American economy. The Committee believes that extension of the current waiver of the 100-percent-of-income-limit will contribute to investment in domestic oil and gas production.

Explanation of Provision

The provision extends the period when the 100-percent net-income limit is suspended to include taxable years beginning after December 31, 2001 and before January 1, 2004.

Effective Date
* * *

[Law at ¶ 5220. CCH Explanation at ¶ 380.]

[¶ 10,480]   Act Sec. 608. Extension of authority to issue qualified zone academy bonds

Joint Committee on Taxation (J.C.T. Rep. No. JCX-12-02)

[Caution: The Technical Explanation of the "Job Creation and Worker Assistance Act of 2002" (JCX-12-02), below, is included to assist the reader's understanding but may not be cited as the official Conference Committee Report to P.L. 107-147.—CCH]

[Code Sec. 1397E]

Present Law

Tax-exempt bonds

Interest on State and local governmental bonds generally is excluded from gross income for Federal income tax purposes if the proceeds of the bonds are used to finance direct activities of these governmental units or if the bonds are repaid with revenues of the governmental units. Activities that can be financed with these tax-exempt bonds include the financing of public schools (sec. 103).

Qualified zone academy bonds

As an alternative to traditional tax-exempt bonds, States and local governments are given the authority to issue "qualified zone academy bonds" ("QZABs") (sec. 1397E). A total of $400 million of qualified zone academy bonds may be issued annually in calendar years 1998 through 2001. The $400 million aggregate bond cap is allocated each year to the States according to their respective populations of individuals below the poverty line. Each State, in turn, allocates the credit authority to qualified zone academies within such State.

Financial institutions that hold qualified zone academy bonds are entitled to a nonrefundable tax credit in an amount equal to a credit rate multiplied by the face amount of the bond. A taxpayer holding a qualified zone academy bond

---

[19] Amounts disallowed as a result of this rule may be carried forward and deducted in subsequent taxable years, subject to the 65-percent taxable income limitation for those years.

on the credit allowance date is entitled to a credit. The credit is includable in gross income (as if it were a taxable interest payment on the bond), and may be claimed against regular income tax and AMT liability.

The Treasury Department sets the credit rate at a rate estimated to allow issuance of qualified zone academy bonds without discount and without interest cost to the issuer. The maximum term of the bond is determined by the Treasury Department, so that the present value of the obligation to repay the bond is 50 percent of the face value of the bond.

"Qualified zone academy bonds" are defined as any bond issued by a State or local government, provided that (1) at least 95 percent of the proceeds are used for the purpose of renovating, providing equipment to, developing course materials for use at, or training teachers and other school personnel in a "qualified zone academy" and (2) private entities have promised to contribute to the qualified zone academy certain equipment, technical assistance or training, employee services, or other property or services with a value equal to at least 10 percent of the bond proceeds.

A school is a "qualified zone academy" if (1) the school is a public school that provides education and training below the college level, (2) the school operates a special academic program in cooperation with businesses to enhance the academic curriculum and increase graduation and employment rates, and (3) either (a) the school is located in an empowerment zones enterprise community designated under the Code, or (b) it is reasonably expected that at least 35 percent of the students at the school will be eligible for free or reduced-cost lunches under the school lunch program established under the National School Lunch Act.

Explanation of Provision

The provision authorizes issuance of up to $400 million of qualified zone academy bonds annually in calendar years 2002 and 2003.

Effective Date

The provision is effective for obligations issued after the date of enactment.

House Committee Report (H.R. Rep. No. 107-251)

[Caution: The House Committee Report on the "Economic Security and Recovery Act of 2001," as passed by the House (H.R. Rep. No. 107-251), below, is included to assist the reader's understanding but may not be cited as the controlling Committee Report to P.L. 107-147.—CCH]

Present Law

Tax-exempt bonds

Interest on State and local governmental bonds generally is excluded from gross income for Federal income tax purposes if the proceeds of the bonds are used to finance direct activities of these governmental units or if the bonds are repaid with revenues of the governmental units. Activities that can be financed with these tax-exempt bonds include the financing of public schools (sec. 103).

Qualified zone academy bonds

As an alternative to traditional tax-exempt bonds, States and local governments are given the authority to issue "qualified zone academy bonds" ("QZABs") (sec. 1397E). A total of $400 million of qualified zone academy bonds may be issued annually in calendar years 1998 through 2001. The $400 million aggregate bond cap is allocated each year to the States according to their respective populations of individuals below the poverty line. Each State, in turn, allocates the credit authority to qualified zone academies within such State.

Financial institutions that hold qualified zone academy bonds are entitled to a nonrefundable

tax credit in an amount equal to a credit rate multiplied by the face amount of the bond. A taxpayer holding a qualified zone academy bond on the credit allowance date is entitled to a credit. The credit is includable in gross income (as if it were a taxable interest payment on the bond), and may be claimed against regular income tax and AMT liability.

The Treasury Department sets the credit rate at a rate estimated to allow issuance of qualified zone academy bonds without discount and without interest cost to the issuer. The maximum term of the bond is determined by the Treasury Department, so that the present value of the obligation to repay the bond is 50 percent of the face value of the bond.

"Qualified zone academy bonds" are defined as any bond issued by a State or local government, provided that (1) at least 95 percent of the proceeds are used for the purpose of renovating, providing equipment to, developing course materials for use at, or training teachers and other school personnel in a "qualified zone academy" and (2) private entities have promised to contribute to the qualified zone academy certain equipment, technical assistance or training, employee services, or other property or services with a value equal to at least 10 percent of the bond proceeds.

A school is a "qualified zone academy" if (1) the school is a public school that provides education and training below the college level, (2) the school operates a special academic program in cooperation with businesses to enhance the academic curriculum and increase graduation and employment rates, and (3) either (a) the school is located in an empowerment zones enterprise community designated under the Code, or (b) it is reasonably expected that at least 35 percent of the students at the school will be eligible for free or reduced-cost lunches under the school lunch program established under the National School Lunch Act.

Reasons for Change

The Committee believes that extension of authority to issue qualified zone academy bonds is appropriate in light of the educational needs that exist today.

Explanation of Provision

The provision authorizes issuance of up to $400 million of qualified zone academy bonds annually in calendar years 2002 and 2003.

Effective Date

* * *

[Law at ¶ 5295. CCH Explanation at ¶ 382.]

[¶ 10,490]   Act Sec. 609. Extension of increased coverover payments to Puerto Rico and the Virgin Islands

Joint Committee on Taxation (J.C.T. Rep. No. JCX-12-02)

[Caution: The Technical Explanation of the "Job Creation and Worker Assistance Act of 2002" (JCX-12-02), below, is included to assist the reader's understanding but may not be cited as the official Conference Committee Report to P.L. 107-147.—CCH]

[Code Sec. 7652]

Present Law

A $13.50 per proof gallon[60] excise tax is imposed on distilled spirits produced in, or imported or brought into, the United States. The excise tax does not apply to distilled spirits that are exported from the United States or to distilled spirits that are consumed in U.S. possessions (e.g., Puerto Rico and the Virgin Islands).

The Code provides for coverover (payment) of $13.25 per proof gallon of the excise tax imposed on rum imported (or brought) into the United States (without regard to the country of origin) to Puerto Rico and the Virgin Islands during the period July 1, 1999 through December 31, 2001. Effective on January 1, 2002, the coverover rate is scheduled to return to its permanent level of $10.50 per proof gallon.

Amounts covered over to Puerto Rico and the Virgin Islands are deposited into the treasuries of the two possessions for use as those possessions determine.

Explanation of Provision

The provision extends the $13.25-per-proof-gallon coverover rate for two additional years, through December 31, 2003.

Effective Date

The provision is effective for articles brought into the United States after December 31, 2001.

House Committee Report (H.R. Rep. No. 107-251)

[Caution: The House Committee Report on the "Economic Security and Recovery Act of 2001," as passed by the House (H.R. Rep. No. 107-251), below, is included to assist the reader's understanding but may not be cited as the controlling Committee Report to P.L. 107-147.—CCH]

Present Law

A $13.50 per proof gallon[20] excise tax is imposed on distilled spirits produced in, or imported or brought into, the United States. The excise tax does not apply to distilled spirits that are exported from the United States or to distilled spirits that are consumed in U.S. possessions (e.g., Puerto Rico and the Virgin Islands).

The Code provides for coverover (payment) of $13.25 per proof gallon of the excise tax imposed on rum imported (or brought) into the United States (without regard to the country of origin) to Puerto Rico and the Virgin Islands during the period July 1, 1999 through December 31, 2001. Effective on January 1, 2002, the coverover rate is scheduled to return to its permanent level of $10.50 per proof gallon.

Amounts covered over to Puerto Rico and the Virgin Islands are deposited into the treasuries of the two possessions for use as those possessions determine.

Reasons for Change

The Committee believes that extension of the increased coverover rate to Puerto Rico and the Virgin Islands will contribute to economic stability in those possessions.

---

[60] A proof gallon is a liquid gallon consisting of 50 percent alcohol.

[20] A proof gallon is a liquid gallon consisting of 50 percent alcohol.

Explanation of Provision

The provision extends the $13.25-per-proof-gallon coverover rate for two additional years, through December 31, 2003.

The Committee is aware that Puerto Rico currently allocates a portion of the coverover payments it receives to the Puerto Rico Conservation Trust. The Committee believes it is appropriate that this allocation continue through the period when the $13.25-per-proof-gallon rate is extended.

Effective Date
* * *

[Law at ¶ 5390. CCH Explanation at ¶ 390.]

[¶ 10,500]   Act Sec. 610. Tax on failure to comply with Mental Health Parity requirements

Joint Committee on Taxation (J.C.T. Rep. No. JCX-12-02)

[Caution: The Technical Explanation of the "Job Creation and Worker Assistance Act of 2002" (JCX-12-02), below, is included to assist the reader's understanding but may not be cited as the official Conference Committee Report to P.L. 107-147.—CCH]

[Code Sec. 9812]

Prior Law

The Mental Health Parity Act of 1996 amended ERISA and the Public Health Service Act to provide that group health plans that provide both medical and surgical benefits and mental health benefits cannot impose aggregate lifetime or annual dollar limits on mental health benefits that are not imposed on substantially all medical and surgical benefits. The provisions of the Mental Health Parity Act are effective with respect to plan years beginning on or after January 1, 1998, but do not apply to benefits for services furnished on or after September 30, 2001.

The Taxpayer Relief Act of 1997 added to the Internal Revenue Code the requirements imposed under the Mental Health Parity Act, and imposed an excise tax on group health plans that fail to meet the requirements. The excise tax is equal to $100 per day during the period of noncompliance and is imposed on the employer sponsoring the plan if the plan fails to meet the requirements. The maximum tax that can be imposed during a taxable year cannot exceed the lesser of 10 percent of the employer's group health plan expenses for the prior year or $500,000. No tax is imposed if the Secretary determines that the employer did not know, and exercising reasonable diligence would not have known, that the failure existed.

The excise tax is applicable with respect to plan years beginning on or after January 1, 1998, and expired with respect to benefits for services provided on or after September 30, 2001.

Section 701 of Public Law 107-116 (providing appropriations for the Departments of Labor, Health and Human Services, and Education for fiscal year 2002), which was enacted January 10, 2002, restored the excise tax retroactively to September 30, 2001. The excise tax will expire with respect to benefits provided for services on or after December 31, 2002.

Explanation of Provision

With respect to services provided on or after September 30, 2001, the excise tax on failures to comply with mental health parity requirements is amended to apply to benefits for such services provided on or after January 10, 2002, and before January 1, 2004.

Effective Date

The provision is effective with respect to plan years beginning after December 31, 2000.

House Committee Report (H.R. Rep. No. 107-251)

[Caution: The House Committee Report on the "Economic Security and Recovery Act of 2001," as passed by the House (H.R. Rep. No. 107-251), below, is included to assist the reader's understanding but may not be cited as the controlling Committee Report to P.L. 107-147.—CCH]

Prior Law

The Mental Health Parity Act of 1996 amended ERISA and the Public Health Service Act to provide that group health plans that provide both medical and surgical benefits and mental health benefits cannot impose aggregate lifetime or annual dollar limits on mental health benefits that are not imposed on substantially all medical and surgical benefits. The provisions of the Mental Health Parity Act are effective with respect to plan years beginning on or after January 1, 1998, but do not apply to benefits for services furnished on or after September 30, 2001.

The Taxpayer Relief Act of 1997 added to the Internal Revenue Code the requirements imposed under the Mental Health Parity Act, and imposed an excise tax on group health plans that fail to meet the requirements. The excise tax is equal to $100 per day during the period of noncompliance and is imposed on the employer sponsoring the plan if the plan fails to meet the requirements. The maximum tax that can be imposed during a taxable year cannot exceed the lesser of 10 percent of the employer's group health plan expenses for the prior year or $500,000. No tax is imposed if the Secretary determines that the employer did not know, and exercising reasonable diligence would not have known, that the failure existed.

The excise tax is applicable with respect to plan years beginning on or after January 1, 1998, and expired with respect to benefits for services provided on or after September 30, 2001.

Reasons for Change

The Committee believes it appropriate to provide an extension of the mental health parity provisions.

Explanation of Provision

* * *

Effective Date

* * *

[Law at ¶ 5400. CCH Explanation at ¶ 615.]

[¶ 10,520]   Act Sec. 611. Suspension of reduction of deductions for mutual life insurance companies

Joint Committee on Taxation (J.C.T. REP. NO. JCX-12-02)

[Caution: The Technical Explanation of the "Job Creation and Worker Assistance Act of 2002" (JCX-12-02), below, is included to assist the reader's understanding but may not be cited as the official Conference Committee Report to P.L. 107-147.—CCH]

[Code Sec. 809]

Prior and Present Law

In general, a corporation may not deduct amounts distributed to shareholders with respect to the corporation's stock. The Deficit Reduction Act of 1984 added a provision to the rules governing insurance companies that was intended to remedy the failure of prior law to distinguish between amounts returned by mutual life insurance companies to policyholders as customers, and amounts distributed to them as owners of the mutual company.

Under the provision, section 809, a mutual life insurance company is required to reduce its deduction for policyholder dividends by the company's differential earnings amount. If the company's differential earnings amount exceeds the amount of its deductible policyholder dividends, the company is required to reduce its deduction for changes in its reserves by the excess of its differential earnings amount over the amount of its deductible policyholder dividends. The differential earnings amount is the product of the differential earnings rate and the average equity base of a mutual life insurance company.

The differential earnings rate is based on the difference between the average earnings rate of the 50 largest stock life insurance companies and the earnings rate of all mutual life insurance companies. The mutual earnings rate applied under the provision is the rate for the second calendar year preceding the calendar year in which the taxable year begins. Under present law, the differential earnings rate cannot be a negative number.

A company's equity base equals the sum of: (1) its surplus and capital increased by 50 percent of the amount of any provision for policyholder dividends payable in the following taxable year; (2) the amount of its nonadmitted financial assets; (3) the excess of its statutory reserves over its tax reserves; and (4) the amount of any mandatory security valuation reserves, deficiency reserves, and voluntary reserves. A company's average equity base is the average of the company's equity base at the end of the taxable year and its equity base at the end of the preceding taxable year.

A recomputation or "true-up" in the succeeding year is required if the differential earnings amount for the taxable year either exceeds, or is less than, the recomputed differential earnings amount. The recomputed differential earnings amount is calculated taking into account the average mutual earnings rate for the calendar year (rather than the second preceding calendar year, as above). The amount of the true-up for any taxable year is added to, or deducted from, the mutual company's income for the succeeding taxable year.

Explanation of Provision

The provision provides a zero rate for both the differential earnings rate and recomputed differential earnings rate ("true-up") for a life insurance company's taxable years beginning in 2001, 2002, or 2003, under the rules requiring reduction in certain deductions of mutual life insurance companies (sec. 809).

Effective Date

The provision is effective for taxable years beginning after December 31, 2000.

[Law at ¶ 5230. CCH Explanation at ¶ 384.]

[¶ 10,530]   Act Sec. 612. Extension of Archer Medical Savings Accounts ("MSAs")

Joint Committee on Taxation (J.C.T. Rep. No. JCX-12-02)

[Caution: The Technical Explanation of the "Job Creation and Worker Assistance Act of 2002" (JCX-12-02), below, is included to assist the reader's understanding but may not be cited as the official Conference Committee Report to P.L. 107-147.—CCH]

[Code Sec. 220]

Present Law

In general

Within limits, contributions to a an Archer medical savings account ("MSA") are deductible in determining adjusted gross income if made by an eligible individual and are excludable from gross income and wages for employment tax purposes if made by the employer of an eligible individual. Earnings on amounts in an Archer MSA are not currently taxable. Distributions from an Archer MSA for medical expenses are not taxable. Distributions not used for medical expenses are taxable. In addition, distributions not used for medical expenses are subject to an additional 15-percent tax unless the distribution is made after age 65, death, or disability.

Eligible individuals

Archer MSAs are available to employees covered under an employer-sponsored high deductible plan of a small employer and self-employed individuals covered under a high deductible health plan.[61] An employer is a small employer if it employed, on average, no more than 50 employees on business days during either the preceding or the second preceding year. An individual is not eligible for an Archer MSA if they are covered under any other health plan in addition to the high deductible plan.

Tax treatment of and limits on contributions

Individual contributions to an Archer MSA are deductible (within limits) in determining adjusted gross income (i.e., "above the line"). In addition, employer contributions are excludable from gross income and wages for employment tax purposes (within the same limits), except that this exclusion does not apply to contributions made through a cafeteria plan. In the case of an employee, contributions can be made to an Archer MSA either by the individual or by the individual's employer.

The maximum annual contribution that can be made to an Archer MSA for a year is 65 percent of the deductible under the high deductible plan in the case of individual coverage and 75 percent of the deductible in the case of family coverage.

Definition of high deductible plan

A high deductible plan is a health plan with an annual deductible of at least $1,600 and no more than $2,400 in the case of individual coverage and at least $3,200 and no more than $4,800 in the case of family coverage. In addition, the maximum out-of-pocket expenses with respect to allowed costs (including the deductible) must be no more than $3,200 in the case of individual coverage and no more than $5,850 in the case of family coverage.[62] A plan does not fail to qualify as a high deductible plan merely because it does not have a deductible for preventive care as required by State law. A plan does not qualify as a high deductible health plan if substantially all of the coverage under the plan is for permitted coverage (as described above). In the case of a self-insured plan, the plan must in fact be insurance (e.g., there must be appropriate risk shifting) and not merely a reimbursement arrangement.

Taxation of distributions

Distributions from an Archer MSA for the medical expenses of the individual and his or her spouse or dependents generally are excludable from income.[63] However, in any year for which a contribution is made to an Archer MSA, withdrawals from an Archer MSA maintained by that individual generally are excludable from income only if the individual for whom the expenses were incurred was covered under a high deductible plan for the month in which the expenses were incurred.[64] For this purpose, medical expenses are defined as under the itemized deduction for medical expenses, except that medical expenses do not include expenses for insurance other than long-term care insurance, premiums for health care continuation coverage, and premiums for health care coverage while an individual is receiving unemployment compensation under Federal or State law.

Distributions that are not used for medical expenses are includible in income. Such distributions

---

[61] Self-employed individuals include more than 2-percent shareholders of S corporations who are treated as partners for purposes of fringe benefit rules pursuant to section 1372.

[62] These dollar amounts are for 2001. These amounts are indexed for inflation in $50 increments.

[63] This exclusion does not apply to expenses that are reimbursed by insurance or otherwise.

[64] The exclusion still applies to expenses for continuation coverage or coverage while the individual is receiving unemployment compensation, even for an individual who is not an eligible individual.

are also subject to an additional 15-percent tax unless made after age 65, death, or disability.

Cap on taxpayers utilizing Archer MSAs

The number of taxpayers benefiting annually from an Archer MSA contribution is limited to a threshold level (generally 750,000 taxpayers). If it is determined in a year that the threshold level has been exceeded (called a "cut-off" year) then, in general, for succeeding years during the pilot period 1997-2002, only those individuals who (1) made an Archer MSA contribution or had an employer Archer MSA contribution for the year or a preceding year (i.e., are active Archer MSA participants) or (2) are employed by a participating employer, those individuals are eligible for an Archer MSA contribution. In determining whether the threshold for any year has been exceeded, Archer MSAs of individuals who were not covered under a health insurance plan for the six month period ending on the date on which coverage under a high deductible plan commences would not be taken into account.[65] However, if the threshold level is exceeded in a year, previously uninsured individuals are subject to the same restriction on contributions in succeeding years as other individuals. That is, they would not be eligible for an Archer MSA contribution for a year following a cut-off year unless they are an active Archer MSA participant (i.e., had an Archer MSA contribution for the year or a preceding year) or are employed by a participating employer.

The number of Archer MSAs established has not exceeded the threshold level.

End of Archer MSA pilot program

After 2002, no new contributions may be made to Archer MSAs except by or on behalf of individuals who previously had Archer MSA contributions and employees who are employed by a participating employer. An employer is a participating employer if (1) the employer made any Archer MSA contributions for any year to an Archer MSA on behalf of employees or (2) at least 20 percent of the employees covered under a high deductible plan made Archer MSA contributions of at least $100 in the year 2001.

Self-employed individuals who made contributions to an Archer MSA during the period 1997-2002 also may continue to make contributions after 2002.

Explanation of Provision

The provision extends the Archer MSA program for another year, through December 31, 2003.

Effective Date

The provision is effective on the January 1, 2002.

House Committee Report (H.R. REP. NO. 107-251)

[Caution: The House Committee Report on the "Economic Security and Recovery Act of 2001," as passed by the House (H.R. Rep. No. 107-251), below, is included to assist the reader's understanding but may not be cited as the controlling Committee Report to P.L. 107-147.—CCH]

Present Law

In general

Within limits, contributions to an Archer medical savings account ("MSA") are deductible in determining adjusted gross income if made by an eligible individual and are excludable from gross income and wages for employment tax purposes if made by the employer of an eligible individual. Earnings on amounts in an Archer MSA are not currently taxable. Distributions from an Archer MSA for medical expenses are not taxable. Distributions not used for medical expenses are taxable. In addition, distributions not used for medical expenses are subject to an additional 15-percent tax unless the distribution is made after age 65, death, or disability.

Eligible individuals

Archer MSAs are available to employees covered under an employer-sponsored high deductible plan of a small employer and self-employed individuals covered under a high deductible health plan.[22] An employer is a small employer if it employed, on average, no more than 50 employees on business days during either the preceding or the second preceding year. An individual is not eligible for an Archer MSA if they are covered under any other health plan in addition to the high deductible plan.

Tax treatment of and limits on contributions

Individual contributions to an Archer MSA are deductible (within limits) in determining adjusted gross income (i.e., "above the line"). In addition, employer contributions are excludable from gross income and wages for employment tax purposes (within the same limits), except that this exclusion does not apply to contributions made through a cafeteria plan. In the case of an employee, contributions can be made to an Archer MSA either by the individual or by the individual's employer.

---

[65] Permitted coverage, as described above, does not constitute coverage under a health insurance plan for this purpose.

[22] Self-employed individuals include more than 2-percent shareholders of S corporations who are treated as partners for purposes of fringe benefit rules pursuant to section 1372.

The maximum annual contribution that can be made to an Archer MSA for a year is 65 percent of the deductible under the high deductible plan in the case of individual coverage and 75 percent of the deductible in the case of family coverage.

Definition of high deductible plan

A high deductible plan is a health plan with an annual deductible of at least $1,600 and no more than $2,400 in the case of individual coverage and at least $3,200 and no more than $4,800 in the case of family coverage. In addition, the maximum out-of-pocket expenses with respect to allowed costs (including the deductible) must be no more than $3,200 in the case of individual coverage and no more than $5,850 in the case of family coverage.[23] A plan does not fail to qualify as a high deductible plan merely because it does not have a deductible for preventive care as required by State law. A plan does not qualify as a high deductible health plan if substantially all of the coverage under the plan is for permitted coverage (as described above). In the case of a self-insured plan, the plan must in fact be insurance (e.g., there must be appropriate risk shifting) and not merely a reimbursement arrangement.

Taxation of distributions

Distributions from an Archer MSA for the medical expenses of the individual and his or her spouse or dependents generally are excludable from income.[24] However, in any year for which a contribution is made to an Archer MSA, withdrawals from an Archer MSA maintained by that individual generally are excludable from income only if the individual for whom the expenses were incurred was covered under a high deductible plan for the month in which the expenses were incurred.[25] For this purpose, medical expenses are defined as under the itemized deduction for medical expenses, except that medical expenses do not include expenses for insurance other than long-term care insurance, premiums for health care continuation coverage, and premiums for health care coverage while an individual is receiving unemployment compensation under Federal or State law.

Distributions that are not used for medical expenses are includible in income. Such distributions are also subject to an additional 15-percent tax unless made after age 65, death, or disability.

Cap on taxpayers utilizing Archer MSAs

The number of taxpayers benefiting annually from an Archer MSA contribution is limited to a threshold level (generally 750,000 taxpayers). If it is determined in a year that the threshold level has been exceeded (called a "cut-off" year) then, in general, for succeeding years during the pilot period 1997-2002, only those individuals who (1) made an Archer MSA contribution or had an employer Archer MSA contribution for the year or a preceding year (i.e., are active Archer MSA participants) or (2) are employed by a participating employer, those individuals are eligible for an Archer MSA contribution. In determining whether the threshold for any year has been exceeded, Archer MSAs of individuals who were not covered under a health insurance plan for the six month period ending on the date on which coverage under a high deductible plan commences would not be taken into account.[26] However, if the threshold level is exceeded in a year, previously uninsured individuals are subject to the same restriction on contributions in succeeding years as other individuals. That is, they would not be eligible for an Archer MSA contribution for a year following a cut-off year unless they are an active Archer MSA participant (i.e., had an Archer MSA contribution for the year or a preceding year) or are employed by a participating employer.

The number of Archer MSAs established has not exceeded the threshold level.

End of Archer MSA pilot program

After 2002, no new contributions may be made to Archer MSAs except by or on behalf of individuals who previously had Archer MSA contributions and employees who are employed by a participating employer. An employer is a participating employer if (1) the employer made any Archer MSA contributions for any year to an Archer MSA on behalf of employees or (2) at least 20 percent of the employees covered under a high deductible plan made Archer MSA contributions of at least $100 in the year 2001.

Self-employed individuals who made contributions to an Archer MSA during the period 1997-2002 also may continue to make contributions after 2002.

Reasons for Change

Archer MSAs were enacted to provide additional health insurance options and to give individuals more control over their health care dollars by providing incentives for individuals to be more cost conscious consumers of health care. The Committee believes that an extension of the Archer MSA program is appropriate in order to continue to pursue such objectives.

Explanation of Provision

The provision extends the Archer MSA program for another year, through December 31, 2003.

Effective Date
* * *

[Law at ¶ 5115. CCH Explanation at ¶ 275.]

---

[23] These dollar amounts are for 2001. These amounts are indexed for inflation in $50 increments.

[24] This exclusion does not apply to expenses that are reimbursed by insurance or otherwise.

[25] The exclusion still applies to expenses for continuation coverage or coverage while the individual is receiving unem-ployment compensation, even for an individual who is not an eligible individual.

[26] Permitted coverage, as described above, does not constitute coverage under a health insurance plan for this purpose.

[¶ 10,540] Act Sec. 613. Extension of tax incentives for investment on Indian reservations

Joint Committee on Taxation (J.C.T. REP. NO. JCX-12-02)

[Caution: The Technical Explanation of the "Job Creation and Worker Assistance Act of 2002" (JCX-12-02), below, is included to assist the reader's understanding but may not be cited as the official Conference Committee Report to P.L. 107-147.—CCH]

[Code Sec. 45A and Code Sec. 168(j)]

Present Law

Present law provides the following tax incentives in order to encourage investment on Indian reservations.

Indian employment credit

A general business credit is available for an employer of qualified employees that work on an Indian reservation.[66] The credit is equal to 20 percent of the excess of qualified wages and health insurance costs paid to qualified employees in the current year over the amount paid in 1993, up to a maximum of $20,000. Wages for which the work opportunity credit is available are not qualified wages and are not eligible for the credit.

Employees generally are qualified employees if they (or their spouse) are enrolled in an Indian tribe and live on or near the Indian reservation where they work, perform services that are all or substantially all within an Indian reservation, and do not receive wages greater than $30,000 (adjusted for inflation after 1994) for the taxable year. The credit is not available for employees involved in certain gaming activities or who work in a building that houses certain gaming activities.

The Indian employment credit is not available after December 31, 2003.

Accelerated depreciation of property on Indian reservations

A special depreciation recovery period is available to qualified Indian reservation property.[67] In general, qualified Indian reservation property is property used predominantly in the active conduct of a trade or business within an Indian reservation, which is not used outside the reservation on a regular basis and was not acquired from a related person. Property used to conduct or house certain gaming activities is not qualified Indian reservation property.

The applicable recovery period for qualified Indian reservation property is as follows:

In the case of:	The applicable recovery period is:
3 year property	2 years
5 year property	3 years
7 year property	4 years
10 year property	6 years
15 year property	9 years
20 year property	12 years
Nonresidential real property	22 years

Accelerated depreciation of property on Indian reservations is not available for property placed in service after December 31, 2003.

Explanation of Provision

The provision extends for one year (i.e., through December 31, 2004) the Indian employment credit and the accelerated depreciation rules for property on Indian reservations.

Effective Date

The provision is effective on the date of enactment.

[Law at ¶ 5051 and ¶ 5095. CCH Explanation at ¶ 386.]

[¶ 10,550] Act Sec. 614. Extension and modification of exceptions under Subpart F for active financing income

Joint Committee on Taxation (J.C.T. REP. NO. JCX-12-02)

[Caution: The Technical Explanation of the "Job Creation and Worker Assistance Act of 2002" (JCX-12-02), below, is included to assist the reader's understanding but may not be cited as the official Conference Committee Report to P.L. 107-147.—CCH]

[Code Sec. 953 and Code Sec. 954]

Present Law

Under the subpart F rules, 10-percent U.S. shareholders of a controlled foreign corporation ("CFC") are subject to U.S. tax currently on certain income earned by the CFC, whether or not such income is distributed to the shareholders. The income subject to current inclusion under the

---

[66] Section 45A.

[67] Section 168(j).

subpart F rules includes, among other things, foreign personal holding company income and insurance income. In addition, 10-percent U.S. shareholders of a CFC are subject to current inclusion with respect to their shares of the CFC's foreign base company services income (i.e., income derived from services performed for a related person outside the country in which the CFC is organized).

Foreign personal holding company income generally consists of the following: (1) dividends, interest, royalties, rents, and annuities; (2) net gains from the sale or exchange of (a) property that gives rise to the preceding types of income, (b) property that does not give rise to income, and (c) interests in trusts, partnerships, and REMICs; (3) net gains from commodities transactions; (4) net gains from foreign currency transactions; (5) income that is equivalent to interest; (6) income from notional principal contracts; and (7) payments in lieu of dividends.

Insurance income subject to current inclusion under the subpart F rules includes any income of a CFC attributable to the issuing or reinsuring of any insurance or annuity contract in connection with risks located in a country other than the CFC's country of organization. Subpart F insurance income also includes income attributable to an insurance contract in connection with risks located within the CFC's country of organization, as the result of an arrangement under which another corporation receives a substantially equal amount of consideration for insurance of other country risks. Investment income of a CFC that is allocable to any insurance or annuity contract related to risks located outside the CFC's country of organization is taxable as subpart F insurance income (Prop. Treas. Reg. sec. 1.953-1(a)).

Temporary exceptions from foreign personal holding company income, foreign base company services income, and insurance income apply for subpart F purposes for certain income that is derived in the active conduct of a banking, financing, or similar business, or in the conduct of an insurance business (so-called "active financing income").[68]

With respect to income derived in the active conduct of a banking, financing, or similar business, a CFC is required to be predominantly engaged in such business and to conduct substantial activity with respect to such business in order to qualify for the exceptions. In addition, certain nexus requirements apply, which provide that income derived by a CFC or a qualified business unit ("QBU") of a CFC from transactions with customers is eligible for the exceptions if, among other things, substantially all of the activities in

connection with such transactions are conducted directly by the CFC or QBU in its home country, and such income is treated as earned by the CFC or QBU in its home country for purposes of such country's tax laws. Moreover, the exceptions apply to income derived from certain cross border transactions, provided that certain requirements are met. Additional exceptions from foreign personal holding company income apply for certain income derived by a securities dealer within the meaning of section 475 and for gain from the sale of active financing assets.

In the case of insurance, in addition to a temporary exception from foreign personal holding company income for certain income of a qualifying insurance company with respect to risks located within the CFC's country of creation or organization, certain temporary exceptions from insurance income and from foreign personal holding company income apply for certain income of a qualifying branch of a qualifying insurance company with respect to risks located within the home country of the branch, provided certain requirements are met under each of the exceptions. Further, additional temporary exceptions from insurance income and from foreign personal holding company income apply for certain income of certain CFCs or branches with respect to risks located in a country other than the United States, provided that the requirements for these exceptions are met.

In the case of a life insurance or annuity contract, reserves for such contracts are determined as follows for purposes of these provisions. The reserves equal the greater of: (1) the net surrender value of the contract (as defined in sec. 807(e)(1)(A)), including in the case of pension plan contracts; or (2) the amount determined by applying the tax reserve method that would apply if the qualifying life insurance company were subject to tax under Subchapter L of the Code, with the following modifications. First, there is substituted for the applicable Federal interest rate an interest rate determined for the functional currency of the qualifying insurance company's home country, calculated (except as provided by the Treasury Secretary in order to address insufficient data and similar problems) in the same manner as the mid-term applicable Federal interest rate (within the meaning of sec. 1274(d)). Second, there is substituted for the prevailing State assumed rate the highest assumed interest rate permitted to be used for purposes of determining statement reserves in the foreign country for the contract. Third, in lieu of U.S. mortality and morbidity tables, mortality and morbidity tables are applied that reasonably reflect the cur-

---

[68] Temporary exceptions from the subpart F provisions for certain active financing income applied only for taxable years beginning in 1998. Those exceptions were modified and extended for one year, applicable only for taxable years

beginning in 1999. The Tax Relief Extension Act of 1999 (P.L. No. 106-170) clarified and extended the temporary exceptions for two years, applicable only for taxable years beginning after 1999 and before 2002.

rent mortality and morbidity risks in the foreign country. Fourth, the Treasury Secretary may provide that the interest rate and mortality and morbidity tables of a qualifying insurance company may be used for one or more of its branches when appropriate. In no event may the reserve for any contract at any time exceed the foreign statement reserve for the contract, reduced by any catastrophe, equalization, or deficiency reserve or any similar reserve.

Present law also provides a temporary exception from foreign personal holding company income for income from investment of assets equal to 10 percent of reserves (determined for purposes of the provision) for contracts regulated in the country in which sold as life insurance or annuity contracts. This exception does not apply to investment income with respect to excess surplus.

Explanation of Provision

The provision extends for five years the present-law temporary exceptions from subpart F foreign personal holding company income, foreign base company services income, and insurance income for certain income that is derived in the active conduct of a banking, financing, or similar business, or in the conduct of an insurance business.

The provision generally retains present law with respect to the determination of an insurance company's reserve for a life insurance or annuity contract under these exceptions. The provision does, however, permit a taxpayer in certain circumstances, subject to approval by the IRS through the ruling process or in published guidance, to establish that the reserve for such contracts is the amount taken into account in

determining the foreign statement reserve for such contract (reduced by catastrophe, equalization, or deficiency reserve or any similar reserve). IRS approval is to be based on whether the method, the interest rate, the mortality and morbidity assumptions, and any other factors taken into account in determining foreign statement reserves (taken together or separately) provide an appropriate means of measuring income for Federal income tax purposes. In seeking a ruling, the taxpayer is required to provide the IRS with necessary and appropriate information as to the method, interest rate, mortality and morbidity assumptions and other assumptions under the foreign reserve rules so that a comparison can be made to the reserve amount determined by applying the tax reserve method that would apply if the qualifying insurance company were subject to tax under Subchapter L of the Code (with the modifications provided under present law for purposes of these exceptions). The IRS also may issue published guidance indicating its approval. Present law continues to apply with respect to reserves for any life insurance or annuity contract for which the IRS has not approved the use of the foreign statement reserve. An IRS ruling request under this provision is subject to the present-law provisions relating to IRS user fees.

Effective Date

The provision is effective for taxable years of foreign corporations beginning after December 31, 2001, and before January 1, 2007, and for taxable years of U.S. shareholders with or within which such taxable years of such foreign corporations end.

House Committee Report (H.R. REP. NO. 107-251)

[Caution: The House Committee Report on the "Economic Security and Recovery Act of 2001," as passed by the House (H.R. Rep. No. 107-251), below, is included to assist the reader's understanding but may not be cited as the controlling Committee Report to P.L. 107-147.—CCH]

Present Law

Under the subpart F rules, 10-percent U.S. shareholders of a controlled foreign corporation ("CFC") are subject to U.S. tax currently on certain income earned by the CFC, whether or not such income is distributed to the shareholders. The income subject to current inclusion under the subpart F rules includes, among other things, foreign personal holding company income and insurance income. In addition, 10-percent U.S. shareholders of a CFC are subject to current inclusion with respect to their shares of the CFC's foreign base company services income (i.e., income derived from services performed for a re-

lated person outside the country in which the CFC is organized).

Foreign personal holding company income generally consists of the following: (1) dividends, interest, royalties, rents, and annuities; (2) net gains from the sale or exchange of (a) property that gives rise to the preceding types of income, (b) property that does not give rise to income, and (c) interests in trusts, partnerships, and REMICs; (3) net gains from commodities transactions; (4) net gains from foreign currency transactions; (5) income that is equivalent to interest; (6) income from notional principal contracts; and (7) payments in lieu of dividends.

Insurance income subject to current inclusion under the subpart F rules includes any income of a CFC attributable to the issuing or reinsuring of any insurance or annuity contract in connection with risks located in a country other than the CFC's country of organization. Subpart F insurance income also includes income attributable to an insurance contract in connection with risks located within the CFC's country of organization, as the result of an arrangement under which another corporation receives a substantially equal amount of consideration for insurance of other country risks. Investment income of a CFC that is allocable to any insurance or annuity contract related to risks located outside the CFC's country of organization is taxable as subpart F insurance income (Prop. Treas. Reg. sec. 1.953-1(a)).

Temporary exceptions from foreign personal holding company income, foreign base company services income, and insurance income apply for subpart F purposes for certain income that is derived in the active conduct of a banking, financing, or similar business, or in the conduct of an insurance business (so-called "active financing income").[27]

With respect to income derived in the active conduct of a banking, financing, or similar business, a CFC is required to be predominantly engaged in such business and to conduct substantial activity with respect to such business in order to qualify for the exceptions. In addition, certain nexus requirements apply, which provide that income derived by a CFC or a qualified business unit ("QBU") of a CFC from transactions with customers is eligible for the exceptions if, among other things, substantially all of the activities in connection with such transactions are conducted directly by the CFC or QBU in its home country, and such income is treated as earned by the CFC or QBU in its home country for purposes of such country's tax laws. Moreover, the exceptions apply to income derived from certain cross border transactions, provided that certain requirements are met. Additional exceptions from foreign personal holding company income apply for certain income derived by a securities dealer within the meaning of section 475 and for gain from the sale of active financing assets.

In the case of insurance, in addition to a temporary exception from foreign personal holding company income for certain income of a qualifying insurance company with respect to risks located within the CFC's country of creation or organization, certain temporary exceptions from insurance income and from foreign personal holding company income apply for certain income of a qualifying branch of a qualifying insurance company with respect to risks located within the home country of the branch, provided certain requirements are met under each of the exceptions. Further, additional temporary exceptions from insurance income and from foreign personal holding company income apply for certain income of certain CFCs or branches with respect to risks

located in a country other than the United States, provided that the requirements for these exceptions are met.

In the case of a life insurance or annuity contract, reserves for such contracts are determined as follows for purposes of these provisions. The reserves equal the greater of: (1) the net surrender value of the contract (as defined in sec. 807(e)(1)(A)), including in the case of pension plan contracts; or (2) the amount determined by applying the tax reserve method that would apply if the qualifying life insurance company were subject to tax under Subchapter L of the Code, with the following modifications. First, there is substituted for the applicable Federal interest rate an interest rate determined for the functional currency of the qualifying insurance company's home country, calculated (except as provided by the Treasury Secretary in order to address insufficient data and similar problems) in the same manner as the mid-term applicable Federal interest rate (within the meaning of sec. 1274(d)). Second, there is substituted for the prevailing State assumed rate the highest assumed interest rate permitted to be used for purposes of determining statement reserves in the foreign country for the contract. Third, in lieu of U.S. mortality and morbidity tables, mortality and morbidity tables are applied that reasonably reflect the current mortality and morbidity risks in the foreign country. Fourth, the Treasury Secretary may provide that the interest rate and mortality and morbidity tables of a qualifying insurance company may be used for one or more of its branches when appropriate. In no event may the reserve for any contract at any time exceed the foreign statement reserve for the contract, reduced by any catastrophe, equalization, or deficiency reserve or any similar reserve.

Present law also provides a temporary exception from foreign personal holding company income for income from investment of assets equal to 10 percent of reserves (determined for purposes of the provision) for contracts regulated in the country in which sold as life insurance or annuity contracts. This exception does not apply to investment income with respect to excess surplus.

Reasons for Change

In the Taxpayer Relief Act of 1997, one-year temporary exceptions from foreign personal holding company income were enacted for income from the active conduct of an insurance, banking, financing, or similar business.[28] In the Tax and Trade Relief Extension Act of 1998, the Congress

---

[27] Temporary exceptions from the subpart F provisions for certain active financing income applied only for taxable years beginning in 1998. Those exceptions were modified and extended for one year, applicable only for taxable years beginning in 1999. The Tax Relief Extension Act of 1999

(P.L. No. 106-170) clarified and extended the temporary exceptions for two years, applicable only for taxable years beginning after 1999 and before 2002.

[28] The President canceled this provision in 1997 pursuant to the Line Item Veto Act. On June 25, 1998, the U.S.

extended the temporary exceptions for an additional year, with certain modifications designed to treat various types of businesses with active financing income more similarly to each other than did the 1997 provision.[29] In the Tax Relief Extension Act of 1999, Congress extended the temporary extensions for an additional two years, as modified by the 1998 Act, and with a clarification relating to the application of prior law in the event of future non-application of the temporary provisions.[30] The Committee believes that it is appropriate to permanently extend the temporary provisions, as modified by the previous legislation, with an additional modification relating to the determination of certain reserves for life insurance and annuity contracts. The Committee believes that the use of foreign statement reserves for exempt life insurance and annuity contracts may be appropriate under these exceptions in certain circumstances, provided IRS approval is obtained, based on whether such use with respect to those foreign contracts provides an appropriate means of measuring income for Federal income tax purposes.

Explanation of Provision

* * *

The provision generally retains present law with respect to the determination of an insurance company's reserve for a life insurance or annuity contract under these exceptions. The provision does, however, permit a taxpayer in certain circumstances, subject to approval by the IRS through the ruling process, to establish that the reserve for such contracts is the amount taken into account in determining the foreign statement reserve for the contract (reduced by catastrophe, equalization, or deficiency reserve or any similar reserve). IRS approval is to be based on whether the method, the interest rate, the mortality and morbidity assumptions, and any other factors taken into account in determining foreign statement reserves (taken together or separately) provide an appropriate means of measuring income for Federal income tax purposes. In seeking a ruling, the taxpayer is required to provide the IRS with necessary and appropriate information as to the method, interest rate, mortality and morbidity assumptions and other assumptions under the foreign reserve rules so that a comparison can be made to the reserve amount determined by applying the tax reserve method that would apply if the qualifying insurance company were subject to tax under Subchapter L of the Code (with the modifications provided under present law for purposes of these exceptions). Present law continues to apply with respect to reserves for any life insurance or annuity contract for which the IRS has not approved the use of the foreign statement reserve. An IRS ruling request under this provision is subject to the present-law provisions relating to IRS user fees.

Effective Date

* * *

[Law at ¶ 5250 and ¶ 5255. CCH Explanation at ¶ 388.]

[¶ 10,560]   Act Sec. 615. Repeal of dyed-fuel requirement for registered diesel or kerosene terminals

Joint Committee on Taxation (J.C.T. Rep. No. JCX-12-02)

[Caution: The Technical Explanation of the "Job Creation and Worker Assistance Act of 2002" (JCX-12-02), below, is included to assist the reader's understanding but may not be cited as the official Conference Committee Report to P.L. 107-147.—CCH]

[Code Sec. 4101]

Present Law

Excise taxes are imposed on highway motor fuels, including gasoline, diesel fuel, and kerosene, to finance the Highway Trust Fund programs. Subject to limited exceptions, these taxes are imposed on all such fuels when they are removed from registered pipeline or barge terminal facilities, with any tax-exemptions being accomplished by means of refunds to consumers of the fuel.[69] One such exception allows removal of diesel fuel or kerosene without payment of tax if the fuel is destined for a nontaxable use (e.g., use as heating oil) and is indelibly dyed.

Terminal facilities are not permitted to receive and store non-tax-paid motor fuels unless they are registered with the Internal Revenue Service. Under present law, a prerequisite to registration is that if the terminal offers for sale diesel fuel, it must offer both dyed and undyed diesel fuel. Similarly, if the terminal offers for sale kerosene, it

---

(Footnote Continued)

Supreme Court held that the cancellation procedures set forth in the Line Item Veto Act are unconstitutional. *Clinton v. City of New York*, 524 U.S. 417 (1998).

[29] The Tax and Trade Relief Extension Act of 1998, Division J, Making Omnibus Consolidated and Emergency Supplemental Appropriations for Fiscal Year 1999, P. L. No. 105-277, sec. 1005 (1998).

[30] The Tax Relief Extension Act of 1999, P.L. No. 106-170, sec. 503 (1999).

[69] Tax is imposed before that point if the motor fuel is transferred (other than in bulk) from a refinery or if the fuel is sold to an unregistered party while still held in the refinery or bulk distribution system (e.g., in a pipeline or terminal facility).

must offer both dyed and undyed kerosene. This "dyed-fuel mandate" was enacted in 1997, to be effective on July 1, 1998. Subsequently, the effective date was delayed until July 1, 2000, and later until January 1, 2002.

Explanation of Provision

The diesel fuel and kerosene dyeing mandate is repealed.

Effective Date

The provision is effective on January 1, 2002.

House Committee Report (H.R. REP. NO. 107-251)

[Caution: The House Commitee Report on the "Economic Security and Recovery Act of 2001," as passed by the House (H.R. Rep. No. 107-251), below, is included to assist the reader's understanding but may not be cited as the controlling Committee Report to P.L. 107-147.—CCH]

Present Law

Excise taxes are imposed on highway motor fuels, including gasoline, diesel fuel, and kerosene, to finance the Highway Trust Fund programs. Subject to limited exceptions, these taxes are imposed on all such fuels when they are removed from registered pipeline or barge terminal facilities, with any tax-exemptions being accomplished by means of refunds to consumers of the fuel.[21] One such exception allows removal of diesel fuel or kerosene without payment of tax if the fuel is destined for a nontaxable use (e.g., use as heating oil) and is indelibly dyed.

Terminal facilities are not permitted to receive and store non-tax-paid motor fuels unless they are registered with the Internal Revenue Service. Under present law, a prerequisite to registration is that if the terminal offers for sale diesel fuel, it must offer both dyed and undyed diesel fuel. Similarly, if the terminal offers for sale kerosene, it must offer both dyed and undyed kerosene. This "dyed-fuel mandate" was enacted in 1997, to be effective on July 1, 1998. Subsequently, the effec-

tive date was delayed until July 1, 2000, and later until January 1, 2002.

Reasons for Change

When the rules governing taxation of kerosene used as a highway motor fuel were enacted [i]n 1997, the Congress was concerned that dyed kerosene and diesel fuel (destined for nontaxable uses) might be unavailable in markets where those fuels were commonly used (e.g., as heating oil). To ensure availability of untaxed, dyed fuels for those uses, the Congress included a requirement that terminals offer both dyed and undyed kerosene and diesel fuel (if they offered the fuels for sale at all) as a condition of receiving untaxed fuels. Since that time, markets have provided dyed kerosene and diesel fuel for nontaxable uses where there is a demand for them. The Committee believes a further delay in this registration requirement is appropriate to allow a more complete evaluation of whether the requirement should be repealed or implemented.

Explanation of Provision

The effective date of the diesel fuel and kerosene dyeing mandate is delayed for two additional years, until January 1, 2004.

Effective Date
* * *

[Law at ¶ 5330. CCH Explanation at ¶ 392.]

[¶ 10,580]   Act Sec. 616. Reauthorization of TANF Supplemental Grants for population increases for fiscal year 2002

Joint Committee on Taxation (J.C.T. REP. NO. JCX-12-02)

[Caution: The Technical Explanation of the "Job Creation and Worker Assistance Act of 2002" (JCX-12-02), below, is included to assist the reader's understanding but may not be cited as the official Conference Committee Report to P.L. 107-147.—CCH]

[Act Sec. 616]

Present Law

The Personal Responsibility and Work Opportunity Reconciliation Act of 1996 (P.L. 104-193) established a separate grant authority for certain states with high population growth and/or low

federal expenditures per poor person under the preceding welfare program Aid to Families with Dependent Children (AFDC). A total of $800 million was appropriated for fiscal years 1998 through 2001 to states that qualified under a formula that considered state population growth and historical federal AFDC expenditures relative to the number of poor persons in the state. Grant amounts per state were determined by a formula, and grew each year a state met the qualifying criteria. Authorization and appropriations for the Supplemental Grant program expired on September 30, 2001.

---

[21] Tax is imposed before that point if the motor fuel is transferred (other than in bulk) from a refinery or if the fuel is sold to an unregistered party while still held in the

refinery or bulk distribution system (e.g., in a pipeline or terminal facility).

A total of 17 states received Supplemental Grants in 2001, totaling $319 million. The states were: Alabama, Alaska, Arizona, Arkansas, Colorado, Florida, Georgia, Idaho, Louisiana, Mississippi, Montana, Nevada, New Mexico, North Carolina, Tennessee, Texas, and Utah.

Explanation of Provision

The Temporary Assistance for Needy Families (TANF) Supplemental Grant program is reauthorized and appropriations are provided for one year (fiscal year 2002) with individual state grant amounts frozen at the exact amount received by the state in fiscal year 2001.

Effective Date

The provision is effective upon enactment.

[Law at ¶ 7100.]

[¶ 10,590]   Act Sec. 617. 1-Year extension of contingency fund under the TANF program

Joint Committee on Taxation (J.C.T. REP. NO. JCX-12-02)

[Caution: The Technical Explanation of the "Job Creation and Worker Assistance Act of 2002" (JCX-12-02), below, is included to assist the reader's understanding but may not be cited as the official Conference Committee Report to P.L. 107-147.—CCH]

[Act Sec. 617]

Present Law

P.L. 104-193 established a contingency fund, a capped matching grant program for states that experience high and increasing unemployment rates or increased food stamp caseloads. A total of $1.960 billion was appropriated to the contingency fund for fiscal years 1997 through 2001. To qualify for contingency funds, a state had to meet one of two criteria of "need": an unemployment rate of at least 6.5 percent during the most recent 3-month period and at least 10 percent higher than the rate in the corresponding 3-month period in either of the previous 2 years; or a food stamp caseload at least 10 percent higher in the most recent 3-month period than in the corresponding 3-month period in fiscal year 1994 or 1995. (The fiscal year 1994 and 1995 food stamp participation numbers were adjusted by subtracting those made ineligible for food stamp benefits by the 1996 welfare reform law.) A state also had to meet a special maintenance of effort requirement—100 percent of the fiscal year 1994 level of state spending for AFDC and related emergency assistance and job training programs—and match any contingency funds it receives with state funds.

Explanation of Provision

The TANF contingency fund is reauthorized for one year.

Effective Date

The provision is effective upon enactment.

[Law at ¶ 7105.]

Effective Dates

Job Creation and Worker Assistance Act of 2002

¶ 20,001

This CCH-prepared table presents the general effective dates for major law provisions added, amended or repealed by the Job Creation and Worker Assistance Act of 2002, enacted March 9, 2002. Entries are listed in Code Section order.

Special note regarding sunset provision for technical corrections to EGTRRA. The Economic Growth and Tax Relief Reconciliation Act of 2001 (P.L. 107-16) provided that all provisions of, and amendments by, the 2001 Act shall not apply to taxable, plan or limitation years beginning after December 31, 2010 (Act Sec. 901(a) of P.L. 107-16). The IRC and ERISA will thereafter be applied and administered as if these provisions and amendments had not been enacted (Act Sec. 901(b) of P.L. 107-16.)

Code Sec.	Act Sec.	Act Provision Subject	Effective Date
21(d)(2)(A)	418(b)(1)	Additional corrections—dependent care credit	Tax years beginning after December 31, 2002
21(d)(2)(B)	418(b)(2)	Additional corrections—dependent care credit	Tax years beginning after December 31, 2002
23(a)(1)	411(c)(1)(A)	Amendments related to Economic Growth and Tax Relief Reconciliation Act of 2001—expansion of adoption credit and adoption assistance programs—corrections to credit for adoption expenses—technical correction	Tax years beginning after December 31, 2002
23(a)(2)	411(c)(1)(C)	Amendments related to Economic Growth and Tax Relief Reconciliation Act of 2001—expansion of adoption credit and adoption assistance programs—corrections to credit for adoption expenses—technical correction	Tax years beginning after December 31, 2001
23(a)(3)	411(c)(1)(B)	Amendments related to Economic Growth and Tax Relief Reconciliation Act of 2001—expansion of adoption credit and adoption assistance programs—corrections to credit for adoption expenses—technical correction	Tax years beginning after December 31, 2002
23(b)(1)	411(c)(1)(D)	Amendments related to Economic Growth and Tax Relief Reconciliation Act of 2001—expansion of adoption credit and adoption assistance programs—corrections to credit for adoption expenses—technical correction	Tax years beginning after December 31, 2001

Code Sec.	Act Sec.	Act Provision Subject	Effective Date
23(h)	418(a)(1)	Additional corrections—expansion of adoption credit and adoption assistance programs	Tax years beginning after December 31, 2001
23(i)	411(c)(1)(E)	Amendments related to Economic Growth and Tax Relief Reconcilation Act of 2001—expansion of adoption credit and adoption assistance programs—corrections to credit for adoption expenses—technical correction	Tax years beginning after December 31, 2002
24(d)(1)(B)	411(b)	Amendments related to Economic Growth and Tax Relief Reconcilation Act of 2001—modifications to child tax credit—technical correction	Tax years beginning after December 31, 2000
25B(d)(2)(A)	411(m)	Amendments related to Economic Growth and Tax Relief Reconcilation Act of 2001—nonrefundable credit to certain individuals for elective deferrals and IRA contributions—technical correction	Tax years beginning after December 31, 2001
25B(g)-(h)	417(1)	Clerical amendment	March 9, 2002
26(a)(2)	601(a)	Allowance of nonrefundable personal credits against regular and minimum tax liability	Tax years beginning after December 31, 2001
26(b)(2)(P)-(R)	415(a)	Amendments related to the Balanced Budget Act of 1997—Medicare+Choice MSA—technical correction	Tax years beginning after December 31, 1998
30(b)(2)(A)-(C)	602(a)(1)(B)	Credit for qualified electric vehicles	Property placed in service after December 31, 2001
30(b)(2)	602(a)(1)(A)	Credit for qualified electric vehicles	Property placed in service after December 31, 2001
30(e)	602(a)(2)	Credit for qualified electric vehicles	Property placed in service after December 31, 2001
32(g)(2)	416(a)(1)	Other technical corrections—coordination of advanced payments of earned income credit	Tax years beginning after December 31, 1983, generally
38(b)(15)	411(d)(2)	Amendments related to Economic Growth and Tax Relief Reconcilation Act of 2001—allowance of credit for employer expenses for child care assistance—technical correction	Tax years beginning after December 31, 2001 SM05 00 wrap is set at 60

Code Sec.	Act Sec.	Act Provision Subject	Effective Date
38(c)(2)(A)	301(b)(2)	Tax benefits for area of New York City damaged in terrorist attacks on September 11, 2001—credit allowed against regular and minimum tax—conforming amendment	Tax years ending after December 31, 2001
38(c)(3)-(4)	301(b)(1)	Tax benefits for area of New York City damaged in terrorist attacks on September 11, 2001—credit allowed against regular and minimum tax	Tax years ending after December 31, 2001
42(h)(3)(C)	417(2)	Clerical amendment	March 9, 2002
42(m)(1)(B)	417(3)	Clerical amendment	March 9, 2002
45(c)(3)(A)-(C)	603(a)	Credit for electricity produced from certain renewable resources	Facilities placed in service after December 31, 2001
45A(f)	613(a)	Incentives for Indian employment and property on Indian reservations—employment	March 9, 2002
45E(e)(1)	411(n)(1)	Amendments related to Economic Growth and Tax Relief Reconciliation Act of 2001—credit for pension plan startup costs of small employers—technical correction	Costs paid or incurred in tax years beginning after December 31, 2001, with respect to qualified employer plans first effective after such date
45F(d)(4)(B)	411(d)(1)	Amendments related to Economic Growth and Tax Relief Reconciliation Act of 2001—allowance of credit for employer expenses for child care assistance—technical correction	Tax years beginning after December 31, 2001
51(c)(4)(B)	604(a)	Work opportunity credit	Individuals who begin work for the employer after December 31, 2001
51A(c)(1)	417(4)	Clerical amendment	March 9, 2002
51A(f)	605(a)	Welfare-to-work credit	Individuals who begin work for the employer after December 31, 2001
56(a)(1)(A)	417(5)	Clerical amendment	March 9, 2002
56(d)(1)(A)	102(c)(1)	Carryback of certain net operating losses allowed for 5 years; temporary suspension of 90 percent AMT limit—temporary suspension of 90 percent limit on certain NOL carryovers	Tax years ending before January 1, 2003

Code Sec.	Act Sec.	Act Provision Subject	Effective Date
62(a)(2)(D)	406(a)	Adjusted gross income determined by taking into account certain expenses of elementary and secondary school teachers	Tax years beginning after December 31, 2001
62(d)	406(b)	Adjusted gross income determined by taking into account certain expenses of elementary and secondary school teachers—eligible educator	Tax years beginning after December 31, 2001
63(c)(2)	411(e)(1)	Amendments related to Economic Growth and Tax Relief Reconciliation Act of 2001—elimination of marriage penalty in standard deduction—technical correction	Tax years beginning after December 31, 2004
63(c)(4)	411(e)(2)	Amendments related to Economic Growth and Tax Relief Reconciliation Act of 2001—elimination of marriage penalty in standard deduction—technical correction	Tax years beginning after December 31, 2004
108(d)(7)(A)	402(a)	Excluded cancellation of indebtedness income of S corporation not to result in adjustment to basis of stock of shareholders	Discharges of indebtedness after October 11, 2001, in tax years ending after such date, generally
131(b)(1)	404(a)	Exclusion for foster care payments to apply to payments by qualified placement agencies	Tax years beginning after December 31, 2001
131(b)(2)(B)	404(b)	Exclusion for foster care payments to apply to payments by qualified placement agencies—qualified foster individuals to include individuals placed by qualified placement agencies	Tax years beginning after December 31, 2001
131(b)(3)-(4)	404(c)	Exclusion for foster care payments to apply to payments by qualified placement agencies—qualified foster care placement agency defined	Tax years beginning after December 31, 2001
137(a)	411(c)(2)(A)	Amendments related to Economic Growth and Tax Relief Reconciliation Act of 2001—expansion of adoption credit and adoption assistance programs—corrections to exclusion for employer-provided adoption assistance—technical correction	Tax years beginning after December 31, 2002
137(b)(2)	411(c)(2)(B)	Amendments related to Economic Growth and Tax Relief Reconciliation Act of 2001—expansion of adoption credit and adoption assistance programs—corrections to	Tax years beginning after December 31, 2001

Code Sec.	Act Sec.	Act Provision Subject	Effective Date
		exclusion for employer-provided adoption assistance—technical correction	
137(f)	418(a)(2)	Additional corrections—expansion of adoption credit and adoption assistance programs	Tax years beginning after December 31, 2001
151(c)(6)(B)	417(6)	Clerical amendment	March 9, 2002
151(c)(6)(C)	412(b)	Amendments related to Community Renewal Tax Relief Act of 2000—treatment of missing children with respect to certain tax benefits—technical correction	Tax years ending after December 21, 2000
168(j)(8)	613(b)	Incentives for Indian employment and property on Indian reservations—property	March 9, 2002
168(k)	101(a)	Special depreciation allowance for certain property acquired after September 10, 2001, and before September 11, 2004	Property placed in service after September 10, 2001, in tax years ending after such date
170(e)(6)(B)	417(22)	Clerical amendment	March 9, 2002
170(e)(6)(B)	417(7)	Clerical amendment	March 9, 2002
172(b)(1)(F)	417(8)	Clerical amendment	March 9, 2002
172(b)(1)(H)	102(a)	Carryback of certain net operating losses allowed for 5 years; temporary suspension of 90 percent AMT limit	Net operating losses for tax years ending after December 31, 2000
172(j)-(k)	102(b)	Carryback of certain net operating losses allowed for 5 years; temporary suspension of 90 percent AMT limit—election to disregard 5-year carryback	Net operating losses for tax years ending after December 31, 2000
179A(b)(1)(B)	606(a)(1)	Deduction for clean-fuel vehicles and certain refueling property	Property placed in service after December 31, 2001
179A(f)	606(a)(2)	Deduction for clean-fuel vehicles and certain refueling property	Property placed in service after December 31, 2001
220(i)(2)	612(a)	Availability of medical savings accounts	January 1, 2002
220(i)(3)(B)	612(a)	Availability of medical savings accounts	January 1, 2002
220(j)(2)	612(b)(1)	Availability of medical savings accounts—conforming amendment	January 1, 2002
220(j)(4)(A)	612(b)(2)	Availability of medical savings accounts—conforming amendment	January 1, 2002
280F(a)(1)(C)	602(b)(1)	Credit for qualified electric vehicles—conforming amendment	Property placed in service after December 31, 2001

Code Sec.	Act Sec.	Act Provision Subject	Effective Date
351(h)(1)	417(9)	Clerical amendment	March 9, 2002
358(h)(1)(A)	412(c)	Amendments related to Community Renewal Tax Relief Act of 2000—prevention of duplication of loss through assumption of liabilities giving rise to a deduction—technical correction	Assumptions of liabilities after October 18, 1999
401(a)(30)	411(o)(2)	Amendments related to Economic Growth and Tax Relief Reconciliation Act of 2001—catch-up contributions for individuals age 50 or over—technical correction	Tax years beginning after December 31, 2001
401(a)(31)(C)	411(q)(1)	Amendments related to Economic Growth and Tax Relief Reconciliation Act of 2001—rollovers of after-tax contributions—technical correction	Distributions made after December 31, 2001
402(c)(2)	411(q)(2)	Amendments related to Economic Growth and Tax Relief Reconciliation Act of 2001—rollovers of after-tax contributions—technical correction	Distributions made after December 31, 2001
402(g)(1)	411(o)(1)	Amendments related to Economic Growth and Tax Relief Reconciliation Act of 2001—catch-up contributions for individuals age 50 or over—technical correction	Tax years beginning after December 31, 2001
402(g)(7)(B)	411(p)(6)	Amendments related to Economic Growth and Tax Relief Reconciliation Act of 2001—equitable treatment for contributions of employees to defined contribution plans—technical correction	Tax years beginning after December 31, 2001
402(h)(2)(A)	411(l)(3)	Amendments related to Economic Growth and Tax Relief Reconciliation Act of 2001—deduction limits (simplified employee pensions)—technical correction	Years beginning after December 31, 2001
403(b)(1)	411(p)(1)	Amendments related to Economic Growth and Tax Relief Reconciliation Act of 2001—equitable treatment for contributions of employees to defined contribution plans—technical correction	Years beginning after December 31, 2001, generally
403(b)(3)	411(p)(3)	Amendments related to Economic Growth and Tax Relief Reconciliation Act of 2001—equitable treatment for contributions of employees to defined contribution plans—technical correction	Years beginning after December 31, 2001, generally

Code Sec.	Act Sec.	Act Provision Subject	Effective Date
403(b)(6)	411(p)(2)	Amendments related to Economic Growth and Tax Relief Reconcilation Act of 2001—equitable treatment for contributions of employees to defined contribution plans—technical correction	Years beginning after December 31, 2001, generally
404(a)(1)(D)	411(s)	Amendments related to Economic Growth and Tax Relief Reconcilation Act of 2001—maximum contribution deduction rules modified and applied to all defined benefit plans—technical correction	Plan years beginning after December 31, 2001
404(a)(7)(C)	411(l)(4)	Amendments related to Economic Growth and Tax Relief Reconcilation Act of 2001—deduction limits—technical correction	Years beginning after December 31, 2001
404(a)(12)	411(l)(1)	Amendments related to Economic Growth and Tax Relief Reconcilation Act of 2001—deduction limits—technical correction	Years beginning after December 31, 2001
404(k)(1)	411(w)(1)(A)	Amendments related to Economic Growth and Tax Relief Reconcilation Act of 2001—ESOP dividends may be reinvested without loss of dividend deduction—technical correction	Tax years beginning after December 31, 2001
404(k)(2)(B)	411(w)(1)(B)	Amendments related to Economic Growth and Tax Relief Reconcilation Act of 2001—ESOP dividends may be reinvested without loss of dividend deduction—technical correction	Tax years beginning after December 31, 2001
404(k)(4)(B)-(C)	411(w)(1)(D)	Amendments related to Economic Growth and Tax Relief Reconcilation Act of 2001—ESOP dividends may be reinvested without loss of dividend deduction—technical correction	Tax years beginning after December 31, 2001
404(k)(4)(B)	411(w)(1)(C)	Amendments related to Economic Growth and Tax Relief Reconcilation Act of 2001—ESOP dividends may be reinvested without loss of dividend deduction—technical correction	Tax years beginning after December 31, 2001
404(k)(7)	411(w)(2)	Amendments related to Economic Growth and Tax Relief Reconcilation Act of 2001—ESOP dividends may be reinvested without loss of dividend deduction—technical correction	Tax years beginning after December 31, 2001

Code Sec.	Act Sec.	Act Provision Subject	Effective Date
404(n)	411(l)(2)	Amendments related to Economic Growth and Tax Relief Reconciliation Act of 2001—elective deferrals not taken into account for purposes of deduction limits—technical correction	Years beginning after December 31, 2001
408(k)(2)(C)	411(j)(1)(A)	Amendments related to Economic Growth and Tax Relief Reconciliation Act of 2001—increase in benefit and contribution limits—technical correction	Years beginning after December 31, 2001
408(k)(8)	411(j)(1)(B)	Amendments related to Economic Growth and Tax Relief Reconciliation Act of 2001—increase in benefit and contribution limits—technical correction	Years beginning after December 31, 2001
408(q)(3)(A)	411(i)(1)	Amendments related to Economic Growth and Tax Relief Reconciliation Act of 2001—deemed IRAs under employer plans—technical correction	Plan years beginning after December 31, 2002
409(o)(1)(C)	411(j)(2)	Amendments related to Economic Growth and Tax Relief Reconciliation Act of 2001—increase in benefit and contribution limits—technical correction	Years beginning after December 31, 2001, generally
412(c)(9)(B)	411(v)(1)	Amendments related to Economic Growth and Tax Relief Reconciliation Act of 2001—modification of timing of plan valuations—technical correction	Plan years beginning after December 31, 2001
412(l)(7)(C)	405(a)(1)	Interest rate range for additional funding requirements—special rule	March 9, 2002
412(m)(7)	405(a)(2)	Interest rate range for additional funding requirements—quarterly contributions	March 9, 2002
414(v)(2)(D)	411(o)(3)	Amendments related to Economic Growth and Tax Relief Reconciliation Act of 2001—catch-up contributions for individuals age 50 or over—technical correction	Tax years beginning after December 31, 2001
414(v)(3)(A)	411(o)(4)	Amendments related to Economic Growth and Tax Relief Reconciliation Act of 2001—catch-up contributions for individuals age 50 or over—technical correction	Tax years beginning after December 31, 2001
414(v)(3)(B)	411(o)(5)	Amendments related to Economic Growth and Tax Relief Reconciliation Act of 2001—catch-up contributions for individuals age 50 or over—technical correction	Tax years beginning after December 31, 2001

¶ 20,001

Code Sec.	Act Sec.	Act Provision Subject	Effective Date
414(v)(4)(B)	411(o)(6)	Amendments related to Economic Growth and Tax Relief Reconciliation Act of 2001—catch-up contributions for individuals age 50 or over—technical correction	Tax years beginning after December 31, 2001
414(v)(5)(A)	411(o)(7)(B)	Amendments related to Economic Growth and Tax Relief Reconciliation Act of 2001—catch-up contributions for individuals age 50 or over—technical correction	Tax years beginning after December 31, 2001
414(v)(5)(B)	411(o)(7)(C)	Amendments related to Economic Growth and Tax Relief Reconciliation Act of 2001—catch-up contributions for individuals age 50 or over—technical correction	Tax years beginning after December 31, 2001
414(v)(5)	411(o)(7)(A)	Amendments related to Economic Growth and Tax Relief Reconciliation Act of 2001—catch-up contributions for individuals age 50 or over—technical correction	Tax years beginning after December 31, 2001
414(v)(6)(C)	411(o)(8)	Amendments related to Economic Growth and Tax Relief Reconciliation Act of 2001—catch-up contributions for individuals age 50 or over—technical correction	Tax years beginning after December 31, 2001
415(c)(7)	411(p)(4)	Amendments related to Economic Growth and Tax Relief Reconciliation Act of 2001—equitable treatment for contributions of employees to defined contribution plans—technical correction	Years beginning after December 31, 2001, generally
416(c)(1)(C)	411(k)(1)	Amendments related to Economic Growth and Tax Relief Reconciliation Act of 2001—modification of top-heavy rules—technical correction	Years beginning after December 31, 2001
416(g)(3)(B)	411(k)(2)	Amendments related to Economic Growth and Tax Relief Reconciliation Act of 2001—modification of top-heavy rules—technical correction	Years beginning after December 31, 2001
417(e)(1)	411(r)(1)(A)	Amendments related to Economic Growth and Tax Relief Reconciliation Act of 2001—employers may disregard rollovers for purposes of cash-out amounts—technical correction	Distributions after December 31, 2001

¶ 20,001

Code Sec.	Act Sec.	Act Provision Subject	Effective Date
417(e)(2)(A)	411(r)(1)(B)	Amendments related to Economic Growth and Tax Relief Reconciliation Act of 2001—employers may disregard rollovers for purposes of cash-out amounts—technical correction	Distributions after December 31, 2001
448(d)(5)	403(a)	Limitation on use of nonaccrual experience method of accounting	Tax years ending after March 9, 2002, generally
457(e)(5)	411(p)(5)	Amendments related to Economic Growth and Tax Relief Reconciliation Act of 2001—equitable treatment for contributions of employees to defined contribution plans—technical correction	Years beginning after December 31, 2001, generally
457(e)(18)	411(o)(9)	Amendments related to Economic Growth and Tax Relief Reconciliation Act of 2001—catch-up contributions for individuals age 50 or over—technical correction	Tax years beginning after December 31, 2001
469(i)(3)(E)	412(a)	Amendments related to Community Renewal Tax Relief Act of 2000—designation of and tax incentives for renewal communities—technical correction	December 21, 2000
475(g)(3)	417(10)	Clerical amendment	March 9, 2002
529(e)(3)(B)	417(11)	Clerical amendment	March 9, 2002
530(d)(4)(B)	411(f)	Amendments related to Economic Growth and Tax Relief Reconciliation Act of 2001—modifications to education individual retirement accounts—technical correction	Tax years beginning after December 31, 2001
613A(c)(6)(H)	607(a)	Taxable income limit on percentage depletion for oil and natural gas produced from marginal properties	Tax years beginning after December 31, 2001
741	417(12)	Clerical amendment	March 9, 2002
809(j)	611(a)	Temporary special rules for taxation of life insurance companies—reduction in mutual life insurance company deductions not to apply in certain years	Tax years beginning after December 31, 2000
857(b)(7)(B)	413(a)(1)	Amendments related to the Tax Relief Extension Act of 1999—taxation of REITs and their subsidiaries—technical correction	Tax years beginning after December 31, 2000
857(b)(7)(B)	417(13)	Clerical amendment	March 9, 2002
857(b)(7)(C)	413(a)(2)	Amendments related to the Tax Relief Extension Act of 1999—taxation of REITs and their subsidiaries—technical correction	Tax years beginning after December 31, 2000

Code Sec.	Act Sec.	Act Provision Subject	Effective Date
904(h)	601(b)(1)	Allowance of nonrefundable personal credits against regular and minimum tax liability—conforming amendment	Tax years beginning after December 31, 2001
943(e)(4)(B)	417(14)	Clerical amendment	March 9, 2002
953(e)(10)	614(a)(1)	Subpart F exemption for active financing	Tax years beginning after December 31, 2001
954(h)(9)	614(a)(2)	Subpart F exemption for active financing	Tax years beginning after December 31, 2001
954(i)(4)(B)	614(b)	Subpart F exemption for active financing—life insurance and annuity contracts	Tax years beginning after December 31, 2001
995(b)(3)(B)	417(15)	Clerical amendment	March 9, 2002
1091(e)(2)	412(d)(2)(C)	Amendments related to Community Renewal Tax Relief Act of 2000—tax treatment of securities futures contracts—technical correction	December 21, 2000
1091(e)	412(d)(2)(A)-(B)	Amendments related to Community Renewal Tax Relief Act of 2000—tax treatment of securities futures contracts—technical correction	December 21, 2000
1091(e)	412(d)(2)(D)	Amendments related to Community Renewal Tax Relief Act of 2000—tax treatment of securities futures contracts—technical correction	December 21, 2000
1221(b)(1)(B)	417(20)	Clerical amendment	March 9, 2002
1233(e)(2)(C)-(E)	412(d)(3)(A)	Amendments related to Community Renewal Tax Relief Act of 2000—tax treatment of securities futures contracts—technical correction	December 21, 2000
1234A	412(d)(1)(A)	Amendments related to Community Renewal Tax Relief Act of 2000—tax treatment of securities futures contracts—technical correction	December 21, 2000
1234B(a)(1)	412(d)(1)(B)	Amendments related to Community Renewal Tax Relief Act of 2000—tax treatment of securities futures contracts—technical correction	December 21, 2000
1234B(b)	412(d)(1)(B)	Amendments related to Community Renewal Tax Relief Act of 2000—tax treatment of securities futures contracts—technical correction	December 21, 2000
1234B(b)	412(d)(3)(B)	Amendments related to Community Renewal Tax Relief Act of 2000—tax treatment of securities futures contracts—technical correction	December 21, 2000

Code Sec.	Act Sec.	Act Provision Subject	Effective Date
1234B(f)	412(d)(1)(B)	Amendments related to Community Renewal Tax Relief Act of 2000—tax treatment of securities futures contracts—technical correction	December 21, 2000
1256(f)(5)	416(b)(1)	Other technical corrections—special rule related to wash sale losses	Sales made after November 10, 1988 in tax years ending after such date
1394(c)(2)	417(16)	Clerical amendment	March 9, 2002
1397E(e)(1)	608(a)	Qualified zone academy bonds	Obligations issued after March 9, 2002
1400L	301(a)	Tax benefits for area of New York City damaged in terrorist attacks on September 11, 2001—tax benefits for New York liberty zone	March 9, 2002
2016	411(h)	Amendments related to Economic Growth and Tax Relief Reconciliation Act of 2001—credit for State death taxes replaced with deduction for such taxes—technical correction	Estates of decedents dying and generation-skipping transfers after December 31, 2004
2101(b)	411(g)(2)	Amendments related to Economic Growth and Tax Relief Reconciliation Act of 2001—additional reductions of estate and gift tax rates—technical correction	Estates of decedents dying and gifts made after December 31, 2001
2511(c)	411(g)(1)	Amendments related to Economic Growth and Tax Relief Reconciliation Act of 2001—additional reductions of estate and gift tax rates—technical correction	Gifts made after December 31, 2009
3304(a)(4)(B)	209(d)(1)	Special Reed Act transfer in fiscal year 2002—technical correction	March 9, 2002
3306(f)(2)	209(d)(1)	Special Reed Act transfer in fiscal year 2002—technical correction	March 9, 2002
4101(e)	615(a)	Repeal of requirement for approved diesel or kerosene terminals	January 1, 2002
4980E	417(17)(A)	Clerical amendment	March 9, 2002
4980F(e)(1)	411(u)(1)(A)	Amendments related to Economic Growth and Tax Relief Reconciliation Act of 2001—excise tax on failure to provide notice by defined benefit plans significantly reducing future benefit accruals—technical correction	Plan amendments taking effect on or after June 7, 2001, generally
4980F(f)(2)(A)	411(u)(1)(B)	Amendments related to Economic Growth and Tax Relief Reconciliation Act of 2001—excise tax on failure to provide notice by defined benefit plans significantly reducing future benefit accruals—technical correction	Plan amendments taking effect on or after June 7, 2001, generally

¶ 20,001

Code Sec.	Act Sec.	Act Provision Subject	Effective Date
4980F(f)(3)	411(u)(1)(C)	Amendments related to Economic Growth and Tax Relief Reconciliation Act of 2001—excise tax on failure to provide notice by defined benefit plans significantly reducing future benefit accruals—technical correction	Plan amendments taking effect on or after June 7, 2001, generally
6103(l)(8)(A)	416(c)(1)(B)	Other technical corrections—disclosure by Social Security Administration to Federal child support agencies	March 9, 2002
6103(l)(8)	416(c)(1)(A)	Other technical corrections—disclosure by Social Security Administration to Federal child support agencies	March 9, 2002
6105(c)(1)(C)	417(18)	Clerical amendment	March 9, 2002
6105(c)(1)(E)	417(18)	Clerical amendment	March 9, 2002
6224(c)(1)-(2)	416(d)(1)(A)	Other technical corrections—treatment of settlements under partnership audit rules	Settlement agreements entered into after March 9, 2002
6227(d)	417(19)(A)	Clerical amendment	March 9, 2002
6228(a)(1)	417(19)(B)	Clerical amendment	March 9, 2002
6228(a)(3)(A)	417(19)(B)	Clerical amendment	March 9, 2002
6228(b)(1)	417(19)(B)	Clerical amendment	March 9, 2002
6228(b)(2)(A)	417(19)(B)	Clerical amendment	March 9, 2002
6229(f)(2)	416(d)(1)(B)	Other technical corrections—treatment of settlements under partnership audit rules	Settlement agreements entered into after March 9, 2002
6231(b)(1)(C)	416(d)(1)(C)	Other technical corrections—treatment of settlements under partnership audit rules	Settlement agreements entered into after March 9, 2002
6231(b)(2)(B)	417(19)(C)	Clerical amendment	March 9, 2002
6234(g)(4)(A)	416(d)(1)(D)	Other technical corrections—treatment of settlements under partnership audit rules	Settlement agreements entered into after March 9, 2002
6331(k)(3)	416(e)(1)	Other technical corrections—amendment related to procedure and administration	March 9, 2002
6428(b)	411(a)(1)	Amendments related to Economic Growth and Tax Relief Reconciliation Act of 2001—reduction in income tax rates for individuals—technical correction	Tax years beginning after December 31, 2000
6428(d)	411(a)(2)(A)	Amendments related to Economic Growth and Tax Relief Reconciliation Act of 2001—reduction in income tax rates for individuals—conforming amendment—technical correction	Tax years beginning after December 31, 2000

Code Sec.	Act Sec.	Act Provision Subject	Effective Date
6428(e)(2)	411(a)(2)(B)	Amendments related to Economic Growth and Tax Relief Reconcilation Act of 2001—reduction in income tax rates for individuals—conforming amendment—technical correction	Tax years beginning after December 31, 2000
7652(f)(1)	609(a)	Cover over of tax on distilled spirits	Articles brought into the United States after December 31, 2001
7702A(c)(3)(A)	416(f)	Other technical corrections—modified endowment contracts	March 9, 2002
9812(f)	610(a)	Parity in the application of certain limits to mental health benefits	Plan years beginning after December 31, 2000
.....	201	Temporary Extended Unemployment Compensation Act of 2002	March 9, 2002
.....	202(a)	Federal-State agreements	March 9, 2002
.....	202(b)	Federal-State agreements—provisions of agreement	March 9, 2002
.....	202(c)	Federal-State agreements—exhaustion of benefits	March 9, 2002
.....	202(d)	Federal-State agreements—weekly benefit amount, etc.	March 9, 2002
.....	202(e)	Federal-State agreements—election by States	March 9, 2002
.....	203(a)	Temporary extended unemployment compensation account	March 9, 2002
.....	203(b)(1)	Temporary extended unemployment compensation account—amount in account	March 9, 2002
.....	203(b)(2)	Temporary extended unemployment compensation account—amount in account—weekly benefit amount	March 9, 2002
.....	203(c)(1)	Temporary extended unemployment compensation account—special rule	March 9, 2002
.....	203(c)(2)	Temporary extended unemployment compensation account—special rule—extended benefit period	March 9, 2002
.....	204(a)	Payments to States having agreements for the payment of temporary extended unemployment compensation	March 9, 2002
.....	204(b)	Payments to States having agreements for the payment of temporary extended unemployment compensation—treatment of reimbursable compensation	March 9, 2002

Code Sec.	Act Sec.	Act Provision Subject	Effective Date
. . . . .	204(c)	Payments to States having agreements for the payment of temporary extended unemployment compensation—determination of amount	March 9, 2002
. . . . .	205(a)	Financing provisions	March 9, 2002
. . . . .	205(b)	Financing provisions—certification	March 9, 2002
. . . . .	205(c)	Financing provisions—assistance to States	March 9, 2002
. . . . .	205(d)	Financing provisions—appropriations for certain payments	March 9, 2002
. . . . .	206(a)	Fraud and overpayments	March 9, 2002
. . . . .	206(b)	Fraud and overpayments—repayment	March 9, 2002
. . . . .	206(c)(1)	Fraud and overpayments—recovery by State agency	March 9, 2002
. . . . .	206(c)(2)	Fraud and overpayments—recovery by State agency—opportunity for hearing	March 9, 2002
. . . . .	206(d)	Fraud and overpayments—review	March 9, 2002
. . . . .	207	Definitions	March 9, 2002
. . . . .	208	Applicability	March 9, 2002
. . . . .	209(a)(1)	Special Reed Act transfer in fiscal year 2002—repeal of certain provisions added by the Balanced Budget Act of 1997 (relating to the Social Security Act)	March 9, 2002
. . . . .	209(a)(2)	Special Reed Act transfer in fiscal year 2002—repeal of certain provisions added by the Balanced Budget Act of 1997 (relating to the Social Security Act)—savings provision	March 9, 2002
. . . . .	209(b)	Special Reed Act transfer in fiscal year 2002—special transfer in fiscal year 2002	March 9, 2002
. . . . .	209(c)	Special Reed Act transfer in fiscal year 2002—limitations on transfers	March 9, 2002
. . . . .	209(d)(2)	Special Reed Act transfer in fiscal year 2002—technical correction	March 9, 2002
. . . . .	209(e)	Special Reed Act transfer in fiscal year 2002—regulations (Secretary of Labor)	March 9, 2002
. . . . .	301(c)	Tax benefits for area of New York City damaged in terrorist attacks on September 11, 2001—clerical amendment	March 9, 2002
. . . . .	401	Allowance of electronic 1099's	March 9, 2002

Code Sec.	Act Sec.	Act Provision Subject	Effective Date
. . . . .	405(b)(1)	Interest rate range for additional funding requirements—amendments to ERISA—special rule	March 9, 2002
. . . . .	405(b)(2)	Interest rate range for additional funding requirements—amendments to ERISA—quarterly contributions	March 9, 2002
. . . . .	405(c)	Interest rate range for additional funding requirements—PBGC	March 9, 2002
. . . . .	411(c)(1)(F)	Amendments related to Economic Growth and Tax Relief Reconciliation Act of 2001—expansion of adoption credit and adoption assistance programs—corrections to credit for adoption expenses—technical correction	Tax years beginning after December 31, 2002
. . . . .	411(i)(2)	Amendments related to Economic Growth and Tax Relief Reconciliation Act of 2001—deemed IRAs under employer plans—technical correction	Plan years beginning after December 31, 2002
. . . . .	411(j)(3)	Amendments related to Economic Growth and Tax Relief Reconciliation Act of 2001—special rule—technical correction	June 7, 2001
. . . . .	411(n)(2)	Amendments related to Economic Growth and Tax Relief Reconciliation Act of 2001—credit for pension plan startup costs of small employers—technical correction	Costs paid or incurred in tax years beginning after December 31, 2001, with respect to qualified employer plans established after such date
. . . . .	411(r)(2)	Amendments related to Economic Growth and Tax Relief Reconciliation Act of 2001—employers may disregard rollovers for purposes of cash-out amounts—technical correction	Distributions after December 31, 2001
. . . . .	411(t)	Amendments related to Economic Growth and Tax Relief Reconciliation Act of 2001—automatic rollovers of certain mandatory distributions—technical correction	Distributions made after final regulations implementing Section 647(c)(2)(A) of the EGTRRA are prescribed
. . . . .	411(u)(2)	Amendments related to Economic Growth and Tax Relief Reconciliation Act of 2001—excise tax on failure to provide notice by defined benefit plans significantly reducing future benefit accruals—technical correction	Plan amendments taking effect on or after June 7, 2001, generally

Code Sec.	Act Sec.	Act Provision Subject	Effective Date
.....	411(u)(3)	Amendments related to Economic Growth and Tax Relief Reconcilation Act of 2001—excise tax on failure to provide notice by defined benefit plans significantly reducing future benefit accruals—technical correction	Plan amendments taking effect on or after June 7, 2001, generally
.....	411(v)(2)	Amendments related to Economic Growth and Tax Relief Reconcilation Act of 2001—modification of timing of plan valuations—technical correction	Plan years beginning after December 31, 2001
.....	414(a)	Amendments related to the Taxpayer Relief Act of 1997—maximum capital gains rate for individuals—technical correction	Tax years ending after May 6, 1997
.....	417(17)(B)	Clerical amendment	March 9, 2002
.....	417(21)	Clerical amendment (Community Renewal Tax Relief Act of 2000)	March 9, 2002
.....	417(23)	Clerical amendments (Economic Growth and Tax Relief Reconciliation Act of 2001)	March 9, 2002
.....	417(24)	Clerical amendments (Ticket to Work and Work Incentives Improvement Act of 1999)	March 9, 2002
....	501(a)	No impact on Social Security trust funds	March 9, 2002
.....	501(b)(1)	No impact on Social Security trust funds—transfers—estimate of Secretary	March 9, 2002
.....	501(b)(2)	No impact on Social Security trust funds—transfers—transfer of funds	March 9, 2002
.....	502	Emergency designation	March 9, 2002
.....	601(b)(2)	Allowance of nonrefundable personal credits against regular and minimum tax liability—conforming amendment	Tax years beginning after December 31, 2001
.....	602(b)(2)	Credit for qualified electric vehicles—conforming amendment	Property placed in service after December 31, 2001
.....	616	Reauthorization of TANF supplemental grants for population increases for fiscal year 2002	March 9, 2002
.....	617	One-year extension of contingency fund under the TANF program	March 9, 2002

Code Section to Explanation Table

¶ 25,001

Code Sections Added, Amended or Repealed

The list below notes all the Code Sections or subsections of the Internal Revenue Code that were added, amended or repealed by the Job Creation and Worker Assistance Act of 2002 (H.R. 3090). The first column indicates the Code Section added, amended or repealed and the second column indicates the Act Section.

¶ 25,005

Code Sec.	Act Sec.	Code Sec.	Act Sec.
21(d)(2)(A)-(B)	418(b)(1)-(2)	172(j)-(k)	102(b)
23(a)(1)	411(c)(1)(A)	179A(b)(1)(B)	606(a)(1)(A)
23(a)(2)	411(c)(1)(C)	179A(b)(1)(B)(i)-(iii)	606(a)(1)(B)
23(a)(3)	411(c)(1)(B)	179A(f)	606(a)(2)
23(b)(1)	411(c)(1)(D)	220(i)(2)	612(a)
23(h)	418(a)(1)(A)-(B)	220(i)(3)(B)	612(a)
23(i)	411(c)(1)(E)	220(j)(2)	612(b)(1)
24(d)(1)(B)	411(b)	220(j)(4)(A)	612(b)(2)
25B(d)(2)(A)	411(m)	280F(a)(1)(C)(iii)	602(b)(1)
25B(g)-(h)	417(1)	351(h)(1)	417(9)
26(a)(2)	601(a)(1)-(2)	358(h)(1)(A)	412(c)
26(b)(2)(P)-(R)	415(a)	401(a)(30)	411(o)(2)
30(b)(2)	602(a)(1)(A)	401(a)(31)(C)(i)	411(q)(1)
30(b)(2)(A)-(C)	602(a)(1)(B)	402(c)(2)	411(q)(2)
30(e)	602(a)(2)	402(g)(1)(C)	411(o)(1)
32(g)(2)	416(a)(1)	402(g)(7)(B)	411(p)(6)
38(b)(15)	411(d)(2)	402(h)(2)(A)	411(l)(3)
38(c)(2)(A)(ii)(II)	301(b)(2)	403(b)(1)	411(p)(1)
38(c)(3)-(4)	301(b)(1)	403(b)(3)	411(p)(3)(A)-(B)
42(h)(3)(C)	417(2)	403(b)(6)	411(p)(2)
42(m)(1)(B)(ii)	417(3)	404(a)(1)(D)(iv)	411(s)
45(c)(3)(A)-(C)	603(a)	404(a)(7)(C)	411(l)(4)
45A(f)	613(a)	404(a)(12)	411(l)(1)
45E(e)(1)	411(n)(1)	404(k)(1)	411(w)(1)(A)
45F(d)(4)(B)	411(d)(1)	404(k)(2)(B)	411(w)(1)(B)
51(c)(4)(B)	604(a)	404(k)(4)(B)	411(w)(1)(C)
51A(c)(1)	417(4)	404(k)(4)(B)-(C)	411(w)(1)(D)
51A(f)	605(a)	404(k)(7)	411(w)(2)
56(a)(1)(A)(ii)	417(5)	404(n)	411(l)(2)
56(d)(1)(A)	102(c)(1)	408(k)(2)(C)	411(j)(1)(A)
62(a)(2)(D)	406(a)	408(k)(8)	411(j)(1)(B)
62(d)	406(b)	408(q)(3)(A)	411(i)(1)
63(c)(2)	411(e)(1)(E)	409(o)(1)(C)(ii)	411(j)(2)(A)-(B)
63(c)(2)(A)-(D)	411(e)(1)(A)-(D)	412(c)(9)(B)(ii)	411(v)(1)(A)
63(c)(4)	411(e)(2)(A)	412(c)(9)(B)(iv)	411(v)(1)(B)
63(c)(4)	411(e)(2)(C)	412(l)(7)(C)(i)(III)	405(a)(1)
63(c)(4)(B)(i)	411(e)(2)(B)	412(m)(7)	405(a)(2)
108(d)(7)(A)	402(a)	414(v)(2)(D)	411(o)(3)
131(b)(1)	404(a)	414(v)(3)(A)(i)	411(o)(4)
131(b)(2)(B)	404(b)	414(v)(3)(B)	411(o)(5)
131(b)(3)-(4)	404(c)	414(v)(4)(B)	411(o)(6)
137(a)	411(c)(2)(A)	414(v)(5)	411(o)(7)(A)-(C)
137(b)(2)	411(c)(2)(B)	414(v)(6)(C)	411(o)(8)
137(f)	418(a)(2)	415(c)(7)	411(p)(4)
151(c)(6)(B)(iii)	417(6)	416(c)(1)(C)(iii)	411(k)(1)
151(c)(6)(C)	412(b)(1)-(2)	416(g)(3)(B)	411(k)(2)
168(j)(8)	613(b)	417(e)(1)	411(r)(1)(A)
168(k)	101(a)	417(e)(2)(A)	411(r)(1)(B)
170(e)(6)(B)(i)(III)	417(7)	448(d)(5)	403(a)
172(b)(1)(F)(i)	417(8)(A)-(B)	457(e)(5)	411(p)(5)
172(b)(1)(H)	102(a)	457(e)(18)	411(o)(9)

Code Sec.	Act Sec.	Code Sec.	Act Sec.
469(i)(3)(E)(ii)-(iv)	412(a)	2511(c)	411(g)(1)
475(g)(3)	417(10)	3304(a)(4)(B)	209(d)(1)
529(e)(3)(B)(i)	417(11)	3306(f)(2)	209(d)(1)
530(d)(4)(B)(iv)	411(f)	4101(e)	615(a)
613A(c)(6)(H)	607(a)	4980E	417(17)(A)
741	417(12)	4980F(e)(1)	411(u)(1)(A)
809(j)	611(a)	4980F(f)(2)(A)	411(u)(1)(B)
857(b)(7)(B)(i)	413(a)(1)	4980F(f)(3)	411(u)(1)(C)
857(b)(7)(B)(i)	417(13)	6103(l)(8)	416(c)(1)(A)
857(b)(7)(C)	413(a)(2)	6103(l)(8)(A)	416(c)(1)(B)
904(h)	601(b)(1)	6105(c)(1)(C)	417(18)
943(e)(4)(B)	417(14)	6105(c)(1)(E)	417(18)
953(e)(10)	614(a)(1)(A)-(B)	6224(c)(1)-(2)	416(d)(1)(A)
954(h)(9)	614(a)(2)	6227(d)	417(19)(A)
954(i)(4)(B)	614(b)(1)	6228(a)(1)	417(19)(B)(i)
995(b)(3)(B)	417(15)	6228(a)(3)(A)	417(19)(B)(ii)
1091(e)	412(d)(2)(A)-(D)	6228(b)(1)	417(19)(B)(iii)
1221(b)(1)(B)(i)	417(20)	6228(b)(2)(A)	417(19)(B)(iii)
1233(e)(2)(C)-(E)	412(d)(3)(A)	6229(f)(2)	416(d)(1)(B)
1234A(1)-(3)	412(d)(1)(A)	6231(b)(1)(C)	416(d)(1)(C)
1234B(a)(1)	412(d)(1)(B)(i)	6231(b)(2)(B)(i)	417(19)(C)
1234B(b)	412(d)(1)(B)(i)	6234(g)(4)(A)	416(d)(1)(D)
1234B(b)	412(d)(3)(B)	6331(k)(3)	416(e)(1)
1234B(f)	412(d)(1)(B)(ii)	6428(b)	411(a)(1)
1256(f)(5)	416(b)(1)	6428(d)	411(a)(2)(A)
1394(c)(2)	417(16)	6428(e)(2)	411(a)(2)(B)
1397E(e)(1)	608(a)	7652(f)(1)	609(a)
1400L	301(a)	7702A(c)(3)(A)(ii)	416(f)
2016	411(h)	9812(f)	610(a)
2101(b)	411(g)(2)		

Table of Amendments to Other Acts

¶ 25,010

Job Creation and Worker Assistance Act of 2002

Amended Act Sec.	H.R. 3090 Sec.	Par. (¶)	Amended Act Sec.	H.R. 3090 Sec.	Par. (¶)
TAXPAYER RELIEF ACT OF 1997			**SOCIAL SECURITY ACT**		
311(e)(2)(A)	414(a)(1)	7070	303(a)(5)	209(d)(2)	7050
311(e)(5)	414(a)(2)	7070	403(a)(3)(H)	616	7100
971(b)	602(b)(2)	7095	403(b)(2)	617	7105
TICKET TO WORK AND WORK INCENTIVES IMPROVEMENT ACT OF 1999			403(b)(3)(C)(ii)	617	7105
			903(a)(3)	209(a)(1)(A)	7050
			903(b)	209(c)(1)-(5)	7050
525	417(24)(A)	7075	903(c)(2)	209(a)(1)(B)	7050
532(c)(2)(D)	417(24)(B)(i)	7075	903(d)	209(b)	7050
532(c)(2)(Q)	417(24)(B)(ii)	7075	**EMPLOYEE RETIREMENT INCOME SECURITY ACT OF 1974**		
COMMUNITY RENEWAL TAX RELIEF ACT OF 2000			4(c)	411(i)(2)(A)-(B)	7065
159	417(21)	7075	204(h)(9)	411(u)(2)	7065
165(b)(1)	417(22)	7075	205(g)(1)	411(r)(2)(A)	7065
ECONOMIC GROWTH AND TAX RELIEF RECONCILIATION ACT OF 2001			205(g)(2)(A)	411(r)(2)(B)	7065
			302(c)(9)(B)(ii)	411(v)(2)(A)	7065
			302(c)(9)(B)(iv)	411(v)(2)(B)	7065
611(i)(3)	411(j)(3)	7065	302(d)(7)(C)(i)(III)	405(b)(1)	7060
618(b)(2)(A)	417(23)(A)	7075	302(e)(7)	405(b)(2)	7060
618(b)(2)(C)-(E)	417(23)(B)	7075	404(c)(3)	411(t)(2)	7065
619(d)	411(n)(2)	7065	404(c)(3)(A)	411(t)(1)	7065
659(c)(3)(B)	411(u)(3)	7065	4006(a)(3)(E)(iii)(IV)	405(c)	7060

Table of Act Sections Not Amending Internal Revenue Code Sections

¶ 25,015

Job Creation and Worker Assistance Act of 2002

Act Sections Amending Code Sections

Act Sec.	Code Sec.	Act Sec.	Code Sec.
101(a)	168(k)	411(o)(5)	414(v)(3)(B)
102(a)	172(b)(1)(H)	411(o)(6)	414(v)(4)(B)
102(b)	172(j)-(k)	411(o)(7)(A)-(C)	414(v)(5)
102(c)(1)	56(d)(1)(A)	411(o)(8)	414(v)(6)(C)
209(d)(1)	3304(a)(4)(B)	411(o)(9)	457(e)(18)
209(d)(1)	3306(f)(2)	411(p)(1)	403(b)(1)
301(a)	1400L	411(p)(2)	403(b)(6)
301(b)(1)	38(c)(3)-(4)	411(p)(3)(A)-(B)	403(b)(3)
301(b)(2)	38(c)(2)(A)(ii)(II)	411(p)(4)	415(c)(7)
402(a)	108(d)(7)(A)	411(p)(5)	457(e)(5)
403(a)	448(d)(5)	411(p)(6)	402(g)(7)(B)
404(a)	131(b)(1)	411(q)(1)	401(a)(31)(C)(i)
404(b)	131(b)(2)(B)	411(q)(2)	402(c)(2)
404(c)	131(b)(3)-(4)	411(r)(1)(A)	417(e)(1)
405(a)(1)	412(l)(7)(C)(i)(III)	411(r)(1)(B)	417(e)(2)(A)
405(a)(2)	412(m)(7)	411(s)	404(a)(1)(D)(iv)
406(a)	62(a)(2)(D)	411(u)(1)(A)	4980F(e)(1)
406(b)	62(d)	411(u)(1)(B)	4980F(f)(2)(A)
411(a)(1)	6428(b)	411(u)(1)(C)	4980F(f)(3)
411(a)(2)(A)	6428(d)	411(v)(1)(A)	412(c)(9)(B)(ii)
411(a)(2)(B)	6428(e)(2)	411(v)(1)(B)	412(c)(9)(B)(iv)
411(b)	24(d)(1)(B)	411(w)(1)(A)	404(k)(1)
411(c)(1)(A)	23(a)(1)	411(w)(1)(B)	404(k)(2)(B)
411(c)(1)(B)	23(a)(3)	411(w)(1)(C)	404(k)(4)(B)
411(c)(1)(C)	23(a)(2)	411(w)(1)(D)	404(k)(4)(B)-(C)
411(c)(1)(D)	23(b)(1)	411(w)(2)	404(k)(7)
411(c)(1)(E)	23(i)	412(a)	469(i)(3)(E)(ii)-(iv)
411(c)(2)(A)	137(a)	412(b)(1)-(2)	151(c)(6)(C)
411(c)(2)(B)	137(b)(2)	412(c)	358(h)(1)(A)
411(d)(1)	45F(d)(4)(B)	412(d)(1)(A)	1234A(1)-(3)
411(d)(2)	38(b)(15)	412(d)(1)(B)(i)	1234B(a)(1)
411(e)(1)(A)-(D)	63(c)(2)(A)-(D)	412(d)(1)(B)(i)	1234B(b)
411(e)(1)(E)	63(c)(2)	412(d)(1)(B)(ii)	1234B(f)
411(e)(2)(A)	63(c)(4)	412(d)(2)(A)-(D)	1091(e)
411(e)(2)(B)	63(c)(4)(B)(i)	412(d)(3)(A)	1233(e)(2)(C)-(E)
411(e)(2)(C)	63(c)(4)	412(d)(3)(B)	1234B(b)
411(f)	530(d)(4)(B)(iv)	413(a)(1)	857(b)(7)(B)(i)
411(g)(1)	2511(c)	413(a)(2)	857(b)(7)(C)
411(g)(2)	2101(b)	415(a)	26(b)(2)(P)-(R)
411(h)	2016	416(a)(1)	32(g)(2)
411(i)(1)	408(q)(3)(A)	416(b)(1)	1256(f)(5)
411(j)(1)(A)	408(k)(2)(C)	416(c)(1)(A)	6103(l)(8)
411(j)(1)(B)	408(k)(8)	416(c)(1)(B)	6103(l)(8)(A)
411(j)(2)(A)-(B)	409(o)(1)(C)(ii)	416(d)(1)(A)	6224(c)(1)-(2)
411(k)(1)	416(c)(1)(C)(iii)	416(d)(1)(B)	6229(f)(2)
411(k)(2)	416(g)(3)(B)	416(d)(1)(C)	6231(b)(1)(C)
411(l)(1)	404(a)(12)	416(d)(1)(D)	6234(g)(4)(A)
411(l)(2)	404(n)	416(e)(1)	6331(k)(3)
411(l)(3)	402(h)(2)(A)	416(f)	7702A(c)(3)(A)(ii)
411(l)(4)	404(a)(7)(C)	417(1)	25B(g)-(h)
411(m)	25B(d)(2)(A)	417(2)	42(h)(3)(C)
411(n)(1)	45E(e)(1)	417(3)	42(m)(1)(B)(ii)
411(o)(1)	402(g)(1)(C)	417(4)	51A(c)(1)
411(o)(2)	401(a)(30)	417(5)	56(a)(1)(A)(ii)
411(o)(3)	414(v)(2)(D)	417(6)	151(c)(6)(B)(iii)
411(o)(4)	414(v)(3)(A)(i)	417(7)	170(e)(6)(B)(i)(III)

Act Sec.	Code Sec.	Act Sec.	Code Sec.
417(8)(A)-(B)	172(b)(1)(F)(i)	602(a)(1)(B)	30(b)(2)(A)-(C)
417(9)	351(h)(1)	602(a)(2)	30(e)
417(10)	475(g)(3)	602(b)(1)	280F(a)(1)(C)(iii)
417(11)	529(e)(3)(B)(i)	603(a)	45(c)(3)(A)-(C)
417(12)	741	604(a)	51(c)(4)(B)
417(13)	857(b)(7)(B)(i)	605(a)	51A(f)
417(14)	943(e)(4)(B)	606(a)(1)(A)	179A(b)(1)(B)
417(15)	995(b)(3)(B)	606(a)(1)(B)	179A(b)(1)(B)(i)-(iii)
417(16)	1394(c)(2)	606(a)(2)	179A(f)
417(17)(A)	4980E	607(a)	613A(c)(6)(H)
417(18)	6105(c)(1)(C)	608(a)	1397E(e)(1)
417(18)	6105(c)(1)(E)	609(a)	7652(f)(1)
417(19)(A)	6227(d)	610(a)	9812(f)
417(19)(B)(i)	6228(a)(1)	611(a)	809(j)
417(19)(B)(ii)	6228(a)(3)(A)	612(a)	220(i)(2)
417(19)(B)(iii)	6228(b)(1)	612(a)	220(i)(3)(B)
417(19)(B)(iii)	6228(b)(2)(A)	612(b)(1)	220(j)(2)
417(19)(C)	6231(b)(2)(B)(i)	612(b)(2)	220(j)(4)(A)
417(20)	1221(b)(1)(B)(i)	613(a)	45A(f)
418(a)(1)(A)-(B)	23(h)	613(b)	168(j)(8)
418(a)(2)	137(f)	614(a)(1)(A)-(B)	953(e)(10)
418(b)(1)-(2)	21(d)(2)(A)-(B)	614(a)(2)	954(h)(9)
601(a)(1)-(2)	26(a)(2)	614(b)(1)	954(i)(4)(B)
601(b)(1)	904(h)	615(a)	4101(e)
602(a)(1)(A)	30(b)(2)		

Clerical Amendments

¶ 30,050

The Job Creation and Worker Assistance Act of 2002 (P.L. 107-147) makes numerous clerical amendments to the Internal Revenue Code and various non-Code provisions of previous Acts (Act Sec. 417 of the 2002 Act).

The following Code Sections are amended to reflect these changes:

(1) Code Sec. 25B(g)-(h) relating to elective deferrals and IRA contributions by certain individuals;

(2) Code Sec. 42(h)(3)(C) relating to state housing credit ceilings;

(3) Code Sec. 42(m)(1)(B)(ii) relating to plans for allocation of the low-income housing credit among projects;

(4) Code Sec. 51A(c)(1) relating to the work opportunity credit and long-term family assistance recipients;

(5) Code Sec. 56(a)(1)(A)(ii) relating to adjustments in computing alternative minimum taxable income that apply to all taxpayers;

(6) Code Sec. 151(c)(6)(B)(iii) relating to exemptions for missing children;

(7) Code Sec. 170(e)(6)(B)(i)(III) relating to charitable contributions of computer technology and equipment;

(8) Code Sec. 172(b)(1)(F)(i) relating to net operating loss carrybacks and carryovers;

(9) Code Sec. 351(h)(1) relating to transfers to controlled corporations;

(10) Code Sec. 475(g)(3) relating to regulatory authority for mark-to-market accounting method for securities dealers;

(11) Code Sec. 529(e)(3)(B)(i) relating to the eligibility of room and board under qualified tuition programs;

(12) Code Sec. 741 relating to gain or loss on the sale or exchange of a partnership interest;

(13) Code Sec. 857(b)(7)(B)(i) relating to the tax on redetermined rents for real estate investment trusts;

(14) Code Sec. 943(e)(4)(B) relating to elections by a foreign corporation to be treated as a domestic corporation;

(15) Code Sec. 995(b)(3)(B) relating to taxable income attributable to military property for a DISC;

(16) Code Sec. 1221(b)(1)(B)(i) relating to the definition of capital asset;

(17) Code Sec. 1394(c)(2) relating to enterprise zone facility bonds;

(18) Code Sec. 4980E relating to Archer MSA employer contributions;

(19) Code Sec. 6105(c)(1) relating to confidentiality of information arising under treaty obligations;

(20) Code Sec. 6227(d) relating to partnership administrative adjustment requests;

(21) Code Sec. 6228 relating to judicial review where a partnership administrative adjustment request is not allowed in full; and

(22) Code Sec. 6231(b)(2)(B)(i) relating to items that cease to be partnership items in certain cases.

Clerical amendments were also made to the following non-Code provisions contained in prior legislation by Act Sec. 417 of the 2002 Act:

(1) Act Sec. 159 of the Community Renewal Tax Relief Act of 2002 (P.L. 106-554), dealing with the Advisory Council on Community Renewal;

(2) Act Sec. 165(b) of the Community Renewal Tax Relief Act of 2002 (P.L. 106-554) dealing with contributions of computer technology and equipment for educational purposes (Code Sec. 170(e)(6));

(3) Act Sec. 618(b)(2) of the Economic Growth and Tax Relief Reconciliation Act of 2002 (P.L. 107-16), relating to conforming amendments made with respect to the nonrefundable credit to certain individuals for elective deferrals and IRA contributions;

(4) Act Sec. 525 of the Ticket to Work and Work Incentives Improvement Act of 1999 (P.L. 106-170), relating to production flexibility contract payments payable under the Federal Agricultural Improvement and Reform Act of 1996; and

(5) Act Sec. 532(c)(2) of the Ticket to Work and Work Incentives Improvement Act of 1999 (P.L. 106-170), relating to conforming amendments with respect to tax treatment of income and loss on derivatives under Code Sec. 1221.

★ *Effective date.* No specific effective date is provided by the 2002 Act. These provisions are, therefore, considered effective on March 9, 2002, the date of enactment.

INDEX

References are to explanation paragraph (¶) numbers.

DEC